Record Makers and Breakers

Music in American Life

A list of books in the series appears
at the end of this book.

Record Makers and Breakers

Voices of the Independent
Rock 'n' Roll Pioneers

John Broven

UNIVERSITY OF ILLINOIS PRESS

URBANA AND CHICAGO

Labels and illustrations: Courtesy John Broven,
pages 1, 9, 53, 93, 116, 149, 166, 187, 208 (lower),
231, 254 (upper), 277, 297 (1), 319, 358, 379,
415, 454; Freddy Elzinga, 73; Leon Rene Family
Partnership, 33 (upper); Gordon Skadberg, Early
Bird Records, 245 (lower); Richard Tapp, Juke
Blues, 208 (upper).

The necessary permissions have been applied for
and received. If there are any inadvertent omissions,
please advise the author for due acknowledgment in
future editions.

Library of Congress Cataloging-in-Publication Data
Broven, John.
Record makers and breakers : voices of the
independent rock 'n' roll pioneers / John Broven.
p.   cm. — (Music in American life)
Includes bibliographical references and index.
ISBN 978-0-252-03290-5 (cloth : alk. paper)
1. Sound recording executives and producers—
United States—Biography. 2. Sound recording
industry—United States—History. I. Title.
ML405.B76   2008
781.64092'273—dc22 [B]   2008027204

To my dear wife, Shelley
(the daughter of a record maker);
to my parents,
Jack and Joyce;
and to the late Mike Leadbitter,
who was there from school on up—
and still is.
Then, of course, to the pioneering
record men and women
who have given us so much
great music and pleasure,
forever.

These are the men [and women] who know.
Their importance cannot be overestimated
and all attempts should be made to interview.

—Mike Leadbitter, *Blues Unlimited*, 1970

Contents

Preface   ix

Acknowledgments   xiii

Introduction   1

PART 1: The Independent Revolution

    1. We're Rolling—Take One!   9

    2. The Super Indies   21

    3. California Booming   33

    4. New York: Big City and Little Tiffany   53

    5. The Battle of the Speeds and Golden Records' Seeds   73

PART 2: Regional Sounds

    6. Riding the Nashville Airwaves   93

    7. The Chess Game   116

    8. King of Them All   131

    9. Behind the Southern Sun   149

    10. Louisiana Gumbo   166

PART 3: The Hustle Is On

    11. *Billboard* and *Cash Box:* Stars and Bullets   187

    12. A-Hustle and A-Scuffle at Old Town   208

    13. Mercury Rising and the Roulette Wheel   231

    14. Tin Pan Alley and Beyond   254

15. Hillbilly Boogie   277

16. West Coast Rockin' and Rollin'   297

17. From Motown to Manhattan: In Almost Perfect Harmony   319

18. Harlem Hotshots and the Black Experience   341

19. On and Off Broadway   358

20. Gold Coast Platters and Stock Matters   379

PART 4: Rock 'n' Roll Is Here to Stay

21. The London American Group: Rockin' around the World   397

22. Teen Scene   415

23. Corporate Takeover and Talent Makeover   439

24. The Payola Scandal and Changing Times   454

25. End of Session: Art Rupe's New Rules at Specialty Records   472

PART 5: Appendixes

Appendix A: U.S. Record Sales, 1921–69   483

Appendix B: Independent Record Distributors' Network:
1946–48, 1954, 1960   487

Appendix C: Pressing Plants, 1946   491

Appendix D: Original Postwar Record Labels:
Locations, Launch Dates, and Current Owners   493

Appendix E: Rock and Roll Hall of Fame: Record Men Inductees,
1986–2008   496

Appendix F: Record Makers: Biographical Data (Selective)   498

Appendix G: Oral History   504

Notes   509

Bibliography   545

Index   557

Illustrations follow pages 52, 148, 296, and 438

Preface

This book is first and foremost an attempt to capture the record makers' truly fascinating stories, in turn biographical, analytical, funny, and occasionally tall. Also, I want to highlight the historical importance of the independent record men and women within a vanishing world before it is too late. The general thrust is more a series of case studies than an encyclopedic account of the independent record business. If there appears to be an excess of insider detail at times, I make no apologies. I contend, simply, that the subject deserves this sort of approach. Besides, I have been ever mindful of the strict and wise counsel of Art Rupe, of Specialty Records: "You will realize that taking on a writing project, particularly one requiring considerable research and scholarship for historical accuracy, will be extremely challenging."[1] Along the way, my interviewees, who I think represent a broad spectrum of the pioneering participants, lend their voices by weaving in and out of integral events such as the birth of the post–World War II independent record industry; the battles between the performance rights organizations BMI and ASCAP; musicians' union strikes; the introduction of the LP and 45 single records; the eruption of rock 'n' roll; the payola scandal; and the inevitable decline of the first-wave independent era. Yet the original recordings still have impact.

The prime period covered is 1944 to 1966, with intentional overlaps on either side of the calendar. There may be some repetition of certain events from different viewpoints, but each reference has relevance.

With the independent record business boasting a closely integrated working model, I touch on the important ancillary aspects of the industry: music publishing, recording studios, record manufacturing and pressing plants, distribution (including one-stops and rack jobbing), record shops, the jukebox industry, radio/television/movies, trade magazines, record promotion, international licensing, conventions, booking agencies and artist management, photographic studios, and even the oft-forgotten children's market. Except for the broadcasting and movie elements, much of this infrastructure (the engine room of the record industry) has been explored only fragmentarily in the past. As record men/distributors Joe Bihari and Henry Stone told me, there is not much information on the important distribution side in rock 'n' roll history books. Even the intriguing jukebox business has been confined mainly to glossy pictorial coffee table books. By the same token, where are the books on music publishers? In the course of trying to present a rounded picture of the indie record business, I found many surprising overlaps and secret liaisons along the way. Naturally, I hope this book will inspire further research.

No academic qualifications were required to become a record company owner, not even a rigid apprenticeship. Indeed, labels were sprung by a weird and wonderful assortment of entrepreneurs, including record retailers, disc jockeys (known also as disk jockeys), even lawyers and record collectors. Then there were investors (in turn, shrewd and foolhardy), outright speculators, and the rest. Generally, it was necessary to have an abundance of creative ideas, a vibrant personality, a facility to spot talent, a hard work ethic, an awareness of the latest trends, a need to move quickly (in thought and deed), and an ability to sell. A slick record company name, distinctive label design, and a stash of capital did no harm, either.

Although my focus is on the independent record makers, it is impossible to ignore the work and influence of the major labels and their personalities. And I have not. Supposedly fringe figures are given attention, too, because they had definite roles to play in the record food chain, from the studio and pressing plant to the phonograph player at home. For example, everybody in the industry at various times knew record executives Berle Adams and Mimi Trepel, promo man Howard Bedno, branch manager Colonel Jim Wilson, and distributor's salesman Harold Ladell (who moonlighted in his disc jockey alias of Mr. Blues), but few outsiders did. It is time for the less visible to have their turn in the spotlight.

The interviewees, therefore, range from the internationally known to the undeservedly unknown. Most of the conversations were taped in person, a few were recorded over the telephone, and letters and e-mails were also exchanged. When discussing fast-moving events from several decades ago, it is inevitable that some recollections have become hazy, disjointed, or on occasion factually mistaken. Even the articulate Art Rupe, again, was moved to say, "What you're getting from me is filtered [through] many, many years of memory, and I haven't been in the industry for well over forty-five years. So I don't know how much use this will be to you, but whatever it is, good luck."

To overcome possible missteps in conversation, I have checked and corrected quoted facts where possible, especially fuzzy dates and uncertain chart positions. Even if, in time, some stories have been magnified or perhaps diminished, the message that comes through to me is one of strong and original enterprise when there was no game plan at all for an independent record industry. A special opportunity arose, and it was taken with splendid relish.

I have concentrated on chart records, even those of variable musical merit, simply because these were the golden goals for the record makers—and they do give useful contemporaneous benchmarks. Besides, history is littered with labels that withered on the hitless, profitless vine. As for chart placings, I have resorted to Joel Whitburn's exemplary publications based on the *Billboard* lists (but see chapter 11 for the lowdown on "intuitive" chart rankings). While on the subject of numbers, allowance should be made for the impact of inflation on the dollar sums quoted.[2]

Haven't we lost so much with the demise of the 45–rpm single? There, artists had all of two minutes, thirty seconds (or so) in which to squeeze out their creative juices and musical hooks. The time restriction was a first-class disciplinary measure against overblown excess. Maybe there was room for an uplifting eight-bar tenor sax solo underpinned by the rich ambience of a baritone saxophone or an electrifying guitar break; maybe fiddle and steel guitar trading licks or the surreal sound of the amplified harmonica; even a cooing chorus or ethereal doo-wops. Perhaps there were percussive handclaps, finger clicks, or foot stomps that are so rarely heard these days. Occasionally, orchestral strings or brass were added for perceived touches of class and as means to get white airplay. Then there were those ever-popular piano triplets. And how about the joys of the judicious fade-out? The sum total was enveloped warmly in echo and compression for listening pleasure on the home phonograph or for hot airplay on the radio and jukebox. Best of all, from the 1940s until the early 1960s, most recordings were captured live in the studio in glorious mono.

Song titles on record are a veritable minefield, but I have adhered as far as possible to the registered titles or, failing that, to the designations on the original releases. As for reproduction of copyrighted song lyrics, regrettably but practically, I have had to restrict myself to the "fair use" requirement of "first lines only." Likewise, historically valuable book, magazine, and newspaper extracts have been made under the general understanding of the "fair use" stipulations. For extra-long quotes, the relevant permissions have been obtained: thank you, Berle Adams, Art Rupe, and Jerry Wexler.

What about those juicy "kiss-and-tell" stories? Since the beginning of time, twisted relationships, romantic indiscretions, and sexual favors have been ever present. Then there are the long tentacles of organized crime. Record man Roquel "Billy" Davis once told a third party, "Why does everybody keep asking me about the Mafia? If I knew, I wouldn't tell anyway!" Certainly, the wise guys had their armory of corruption, loan sharking, extortions, grafts, and shakedowns, along with the occasional rub out. The mob's general policy, though, was not to kill the fatted calf but rather to make a quick buck out of hit records by whatever means it took. In an ironic way, the Mafia often provided desperately needed working capital for a grossly underfunded young industry when there were few venture capitalists in sight, let alone traditional bankers. From a record maker's perspective, if you valued your assets (and your ass), you didn't get involved, period. And so while sex and the mob in rock 'n' roll are not ignored, these aspects are kept within bounds. For a take on the murkier side of the business from the 1960s on, read Fredric Dannen's *Hit Men*.

At this point, I should acknowledge the research work of many other authors and researchers, notably Charlie Gillett with *The Sound of the City: The Rise of Rock and Roll* and Arnold Shaw with *Honkers and Shouters: The Golden Years of Rhythm and Blues*. Both books supremely convey the independent spirit. Also worthy of special mention are *American Popular Music Business in the 20th Century* (the title says it all) by Russell Sanjek, updated by son David, and Galen Gart's documentation of the trade magazines in his *First Pressings* series. For an evocation of the first stages of the record men era, look no further than Martin Hawkins's *A Shot in the Dark: Making Records in Nashville, 1945–1955*. And for a contrarian view of rock 'n' roll but with a unique insider's take on the music industry (1963 version), I recommend *Anything Goes: The World of Popular Music* by David Dachs. Perhaps my most well-thumbed reference book, along with the Whitburn chart compendiums, is the Bill Daniels–inspired tour de force by Galen Gart, *ARLD: The American Record Label Directory and Dating Guide, 1940–1959*. For full details of books, magazines, and newspapers consulted in this work, please refer to the bibliography.

I have revisited old stomping grounds to interview again several record men chronicled in my two books on New Orleans R&B and South Louisiana music, but none of the interview material from those tomes is repeated here. Similarly, I have not accorded in-depth treatment to several important record men who were featured previously. In particular, I am thinking of Joe Banashak (Minit-Instant), Dave Bartholomew (Imperial), Allen Toussaint (Sansu), and Johnny Vincent (Ace). Indeed, the majority of the interview extracts are published here for the first time.

I think it should be remembered that for all the successful record makers, there were many thousands who failed (sometimes valiantly, sometimes not). That makes the winners even more impressive. Dreams and schemes notwithstanding, it was a cutthroat business full of roller-coaster excitement and epoch-making history. These record men and women, in the main, survived the Depression as children and World War II as young adults. As a collective, daring and bold, they are the "greatest generation" of the record industry representing the adventurous spirit that fueled America's growth. To my mind, these pioneers are the frequently overlooked activists in the lexicon of rock 'n' roll. Read on and rock on!

Acknowledgments

First, I must say a big "thank you" to all the pioneering record makers, artists, and others who contributed so willingly and graciously to this project. Please see chapter headings and appendix G for detailed lists of interviewees. Great names, great people!

At this stage, I wish to acknowledge the powerful mentorship of *Blues Unlimited* cofounder Mike Leadbitter, who died so tragically in 1974 at thirty-two, an absurdly young age for a true visionary who had much more to offer the record research community; and the wisdom and business sense of Mike's partner, Simon Napier, who also died too early.

Special thanks, especially, to my stoic friends who critiqued drafts at different stages and made many constructive comments: Stuart Colman and Colin Escott, fellow Brit expatriates and such erudite music historians, both living in Tennessee; the late (very sadly) Tad Jones of New Orleans; and Dave Sanjek, formerly of BMI, New York. Peter Guralnick has been a consistent vocal supporter, and so has Richard Tapp. As well, I am indebted to Eric LeBlanc for much valuable biographical data. Naturally, the final outcome must be my responsibility.

Many researchers and colleagues have been generous in their help and inspiration. For being on hand through the years with choice nuggets of information and any assistance whenever needed, I am very happy to acknowledge Gladys Adams, Danny Adler, Johnnie Allan, Roger Armstrong, Mike Atherton, Ace Atkins, Bruce Bastin, John Beecher, Chris Bentley, Bo Berglind, Shane Bernard, Nichola Bienstock, Flip Black, Helene Blue, Dave Booth, Rob Bowman, Jay Bruder, Dave Burke, Tony Burke, Trevor Cajiao, Emily Campbell, Ted Carroll, Frances Chantly, Trevor Churchill, Jim Cole, Rick Coleman, Tony Collins, Dan Cooper, Jorge Cortes, Bill Dahl, Larry Dale, Rich Dangel, Jim Dawson, Walter DeVenne, Rex Doane, Frank Driggs, Bob Eagle, Bebe Evans (Hoss Allen's daughter), Carol Fawcett, Rob Finnis, Bob Fisher, Vicki Fox, Peter Gibbon, Marv Goldberg, Ferdie Gonzalez, Robin Gosden, Michael Gray, Bill Greensmith, Charlie Gillet, Peter Grendysa, Jay Halsey, Jeff Hannusch, Paul Harris, Martin Hawkins, Stephen Hawkins, Norbert Hess, Kenneth Higney, Jaap Hindriks, Steve Hoffman, Paul Hotchkiss, Cilla Huggins, Rob Hughes, John Inglis, Jack Jackson (Sony-Tree), Ted Jarrett, Tony Jones, David Kearns, Dan Kochakian, Teri Landi, Connie and James LaRocca, Joe Leonard, Floyd Lieberman, Miriam Lina, Frank Lipsius, Michael Lydon, Moe Lytle, Rose Marie McCoy, Seamus McGarvey, David McGee, Rollee McGill, Bill Millar, Billy

Miller, Jeff Miller, Kent Morrill, Tom Moulton, Gloria Mullen, Opal Louis Nations, Paul Oliver, Jim O'Neal, Ed Osborne, Alec Palao, Victor Pearlin, Jacques Perin, Gilles Petard, Madeleine Pfister, Bruce Pollock, Tracy Powell, Elizabeth Power, Steve Propes, Mike Randolph, Fred Reif, John Ridley, Guido van Rijn, Andrea Rotondo, Tony Russell, Wayne Russell, Joe Saccone, Rob Santos, Dave Sax, Neil Scaplehorn, Nick Shaffran, Elsie and Johnny Shuler, Dick Shurman, Roy Simonds, Gordon Skadberg, Wes Smith, Chris Soileau, Joe Specht, John Stainze, Sam Szczepanski, Steve Tracy, Vicky Vento, Mike Vernon, Brian Walsh, Russ Wapensky, Alan Warner, Tony Watson (Australia), Tony Watson (England), Barry Weiss, Diana Weller, Cliff White, David Whiteis, Sally Wilbourn, Dave Williams, and Chuck Young. I would also like to thank the staff of the New York Public Library, Rodgers and Hammerstein Division, an excellent research facility, and photo specialists Finishing Touch, East Setauket, Long Island. And thanks go, of course, to the professionals at the University of Illinois Press.

Record Makers and Breakers

Introduction

"Hymie, my goombah, you are a survivor. A connoisseur of the street, the jobbers, the hustlers, the syndicators and backbiters, the unknown stockroom, the chargeback, the freebie, the cut-rate studio; platonic ideal of the indomitable underfinanced indie, rising Phoenix-like from the ashes of insolvency time and again."

That tribute came from Jerry Wexler, of Atlantic Records, on the fiftieth anniversary of Hy Weiss's Old Town Records in 2003.[1] It would be hard to find a more whimsical yet affectionate description of a hustling old-time record man. Hy Weiss and Jerry Wexler were contemporaries in one sense, but in many other ways, they were not. Intellectually polar opposites, they ran their record companies with totally different philosophies and with vastly different levels of success. What both record men did, however, was to mine and preserve American music when it was overflowing with rich creativity. Vive la différence!

I have been privileged to meet and interview many record men and women through the years: the original record makers and breakers. Let me say here that I slip occasionally into the vernacular term "record men" to cover "record women," even if "record makers" is technically more correct. With the pioneers starting out at the dawn of the independent record era in the 1940s, it does not take a mathematical genius to calculate that most of the survivors are now septuagenarians and octogenarians, even older. Mindful of the passage of time, I stepped up my interview schedule in 2004 to archive as many of their stories as possible.

When these independent record makers were in their prime, until the turn of the 1960s, there was little of substance written about them or their work. Almost all contemporaneous references of value were in the form of news stories and press releases in those dedicated trade papers, *Billboard* and *Cash Box*. From the 1970s on, music history research developed apace, and so did the number of books, magazine articles, TV documentary films, and, in recent times, Web sites and blogs. Even now a major problem is that precious few record company files are open to public scrutiny, while much paperwork has been lost, dumped, or shredded along the way.

In general, there has been a tendency for publications to be centered on the artists, with their higher profiles, and not the manufacturers who gave their signings seemingly unlimited opportunities to record and so gain vital exposure from these releases. I hope, therefore, that this work will help to redress the balance by featuring the record men and women with their irresistible seizure of the moment, the regional music they championed, and the rough-and-tumble brave new world in which they operated.

The record makers were, in a sense, business majors, bankers, and social activists (and gamblers) wrapped up as one. There are many lessons arising from their often untutored modus operandi, which takes in the fundamentals of every entrepreneurial venture: a superior product or service, an efficient supply chain, good marketing and promotion, and motivated people. Renowned management guru Peter Drucker was a firm adherent of the principle that the business enterprise, built around the basic functions of marketing and innovation, has only one valid purpose: to create a customer.[2] In the record world, a million of them, or thereabouts, were required to earn that coveted gold disc.

The label owners were the ultimate risk takers and, in a free enterprise, capitalist society, deserved the bulk of any rewards. That said, many of them were no angels, and much conniving went along with the creativity. Very often it was a case of resorting to baser instincts for survival to cover the next meal ticket, the next rent payment, the overdue bills (from pressing plants to union locals), the dreaded tax notices, or, God forbid, the royalty demands (from artists and publishers alike). Here were the harsh realities of cash flow control, or the lack thereof. And what on earth was that weird document called a business plan?

Then there was the greed factor, pure and simple. To this day, without any apparent selectivity, blanket accusations of manipulation, corruption, and treachery by "record men" against innocent recording artists (and songwriters) continue to endure. In public relations terms, it is a near disaster. For me, the reasons for the record maker phenomenon and its justification are as complex as they are fascinating: hence this book.

While many record makers have told their stories, many more have not. For some, it is too late. Think of what was lost: the factual insights, the business education, the unknown intrigues, the history.[3]

Nonetheless, I am honored to have captured the input of many pioneering participants, especially Joe Bihari (Modern Records and teenage jukebox operator), who was always there; Bobby Robinson (Fire-Fury), who provided me with regular lunchtime discourses; and Art Rupe (Specialty) and Jerry Wexler (Atlantic), who offered their spirited support. At this point I wish to pause and acknowledge the contributions of those record men (and lady) who are no longer with us. There is particular sadness with Don Pierce (4 Star and Starday), who specifically said, "Make sure I'm still alive when the book is published," and with Mimi Trepel (London), who so much wanted to see the results of my endeavors.[4] Last but never least, onetime neighbor Hy Weiss gave priceless glimpses of a traditional record man going about his daily business in a strange new world while holding on to past glories.

This book, then, is based on my own interviews and conversations with the original players, whose overriding sense of entrepreneurialism combined with business logic has continued to impress me. Here are their stories as they lived them and as they saw them. Only a handful of potential candidates refused to be interviewed, but they had every right to decline for whatever different reasons.

Many of the gramophone records I have been collecting since January 1, 1957, have an extra dimension after meeting this terrific body of people. Without wishing to sound too grand or pompous, their recordings are vital snapshots of a time and a place that is long gone and that represent now an invaluable part of America's cultural heritage. Surely here is a definition of "classical" music. That is the independent record makers' real legacy.

My introduction to the wonderful world of records began in England when my father, Jack, hauled a Bush radiogram into our Polegate, Sussex, home in 1956. The first 78–rpm records that he placed on the Garrard auto-changer were "Rock Around the Clock" by Bill Haley and his Comets (U.K. Brunswick), "Blueberry Hill" by Fats Domino, and "Only You (and You Alone)" by the Hilltoppers (both London American). Soon I understood that London Records was a repository for the output of many independent companies that were mushrooming wildly in the distant U.S.A. This magical country was already serenading us with its movie and TV exports, from cowboys and Indians to Sergeant Bilko and Marilyn Monroe.

The beguiling musical sounds apart, credits on London's classy black-and-silver labels began to take on an unreal fascination for me. For example, on "Searchin'" by the Coasters (HLE 8450, I readily recall), there was the stark legend: "Recorded by ATLANTIC, New York." Strictly speaking, the designation should have been to Atco instead of its Atlantic parent. Regardless of that faux pas, who were the label owners? Who was the recording engineer, and what was the studio? Who were "Leiber, Stoller" (the writers), and what was "M.C.P.S." (the U.K. music publishing collection agency)? Who contributed to "Instrumental Accompaniment"? Indeed, who were "The Coasters—Vocal"? Time would answer many such riddles, usually through the work of an army of obsessive and amateur but, in practice, very professional music researchers.[5] As a footnote, I realized in the course of finishing this book that "Young Blood" (the flip side) featured the great Plas Johnson on saxophone. It had taken a full half century for that factoid to permeate my subconscious, useful or not. I guess I am still searchin'.

My personal voyage of discovery into the record makers' universe had begun. The mystical independent record scene slowly unraveled itself as my (mainly) London American record collection increased in number, wrapped in those inviting dark blue bags with white stripes. Along with Atlantic, label accreditations began to appear with increasing frequency for companies such as Chess, Imperial, Specialty, and Sun—and what great records they invariably were! In February 1958, Mike Leadbitter, my charismatic classmate at Bexhill Grammar School and later cofounder of *Blues Unlimited*, approached me before the General Certificate of Education Ordinary Level mock examinations to advise me that Fats Domino's Imperial recordings were actually made at the Cosimo studios in New Orleans. Somehow the test papers dimmed into insignificance upon this startling revelation.

Events took an upward swing when I acquired copies of *Cash Box* and *Billboard Music Week* in the early 1960s. The advertisement displays from many independent labels caught my imagination. And so Leadbitter and I began writing to these record companies for information on their artists and labels and, by the way, "Would you mind sending records for review in *Blues Unlimited*?" Lo and behold, we started to receive from the United States letters, catalogs, publicity photographs, and sometimes boxes of promo records. Soon, lists and catalogs began arriving from far-off Tennessee courtesy of Ernie's Record Mart in Nashville and Randy's Record Shop in Gallatin. And before long, packets of 45s and, slowly, LPs were being airmailed wondrously to England.

The 1960s idealism was overwhelming. For a while, it seemed, everybody was listening to their postwar blues—and soul—records, armed with James Baldwin's novel *The Fire Next Time*.

By bizarre coincidence, I contributed to the first issue in 1963 of *Blues Unlimited* with an article on a record man: J. D. Miller of Crowley, Louisiana.[6] During my inaugural U.S. trip in 1970, with Leadbitter and friend Robin Gosden, I met Miller, Joe Banashak (Minit-Instant), Floyd Soileau (Jin-Swallow), and Lee Lavergne (Lanor), all in Louisiana; Johnny Vincent and Lillian McMurry briefly in Jackson, Mississippi; and Bob Koester (Delmark) in Chicago.

It was by pure chance that we stayed at the New Orleans home of *Blues Unlimited* subscriber James LaRocca, whose mother, Connie, had run the Frisco label a decade earlier with disc jockey Hal Atkins. I was mystified when James told me that his mother had lost many thousands of dollars with Frisco, wondering how that was possible. Stacks of forlorn-looking tape boxes and 45-rpm singles in a closet were the sole visible relics of that brave yet unfortunate venture (the music publishing side was unknown to me then). I did not know, either, that Connie's brother-in-law was Nick LaRocca, the leader of the Original Dixieland Jazz Band, which made the first popular jazz recordings in 1917 for Victor.

In time, I learned about the record makers' ways of doing business—good, bad, and indifferent. I was spellbound by their stories of triumph and failure, artistry and artlessness, humor and pathos, inspiration and duplicity. This interest in music history through my record collecting habit resulted in the authorship of *Walking to New Orleans* in 1974 (republished in the United States as *Rhythm and Blues in New Orleans*) and then *South to Louisiana: The Music of the Cajun Bayous* in 1983. Some two years later, I helped launch *Juke Blues* magazine with Cilla Huggins and Bez Turner after *Blues Unlimited* had ground to a halt.

In 1991, having left behind a satisfying career in branch-banking management with Midland Bank, it was almost predestined that I would join a record company: Ace of England (not Jackson, Mississippi!). I always saw Ace as a kind of latter-day London American. The company seemed to be a perfect fit for my taste and knowledge in music, and for almost fourteen years it was. In the interim, I married Shelley, the daughter of record man Clark Galehouse of Golden Crest Records, in 1995 and made the move from the cricket-loving village of Newick, Sussex, to the North Shore of Long Island, New York. Shelley has been my love and inspiration. Looking back over it all, I suppose this book was meant to be.

The Independent Revolution

1

CHAPTER

We're Rolling—Take One!

CAST OF CHARACTERS
Seymour Stein, Sire Records
Irv Lichtman, *Cash Box* and *Billboard*
Shelby Singleton, Mercury and SSS International–Sun Records
Jerry Wexler, Atlantic Records
Ahmet Ertegun, Atlantic Records
Cosimo Matassa, jukebox operator's field service engineer
Art Rupe, Specialty Records

"The first ballot of the Rock and Roll Hall of Fame was back in 1985," said industry leader Seymour Stein.

To qualify for induction, you had to have had a record released twenty-five years before. That meant we backtracked to activity before 1960. The final ballot had forty-one names on it, and thirty-nine of them started their careers on an independent label.

There were two exceptions: Gene Vincent on Capitol . . . didn't get in the first year, but he was on the ballot. Then there was Buddy Holly, who was inducted and whose first solo effort was on Coral, a subsidiary of Decca. Buddy's records were produced independently by Norman Petty in Clovis, New Mexico. His recordings, and those by the Crickets as well, were either licensed or sold to Decca. So technically speaking, he was on a major label.

The other nine artists inducted the first year all started on independent labels: Elvis Presley and Jerry Lee Lewis on Sun, Chuck Berry on Chess, James Brown on King, Fats Domino on Imperial, Sam Cooke on Specialty and Keen, Little Richard also on Specialty, Ray Charles on Swing Time and Atlantic, and the Everly Brothers on Cadence. Most of the influential indies were represented in this list.[1]

Stein, who was president of the Rock and Roll Hall of Fame in 2007, could not have put into better perspective the dramatic and colossal impact of the pioneering record makers and their labels (or indeed the abundant pool of talent on hand). Yet the stereotype of an "independent record man" is of a seedy, hustling, low-life character from a Damon Runyon story or, in a more modern time frame, *The Sopranos.* There were the "Tonys," hanging out after hours with guys in smoky New York bars, puffing giant cigars with glasses of bourbon whiskey in hand, chatting up and bedding dolls after cheating artists out of their royalties. The music was the money in the bank, not the music in the grooves.

Such a sweeping caricature, while true in part (particularly during the fighting 1940s and the fabulous 1950s), ignores the genuine entrepreneur, the educated and cerebral, the inventive, the music-minded, and the *honest* record men and women. So were the record makers, as a group, saints or sinners?

This was a diverse breed, certainly, that scouted, recorded, manufactured, published, promoted, sold, and (they hoped) collected at the same time. The record makers worked all hours because they had to, mostly on shoestring budgets with a barrage of external factors to overcome. Yet they gave hitherto unimagined opportunities to artists and musicians of every persuasion, talented and untalented. The record manufacturers, as they were also known, did it all.

Many record men were first- or second-generation Americans from Jewish immigrant families who had escaped the atrocities that erupted following a wave of anti-Semitic pogroms in the Russian Empire; other factors were the discrimination that barred Jews from key Russian cities and the coming of the Russian Revolution. These desperate people were the "new" Russian Jews in contrast to the established, "elitist" German Jews.

"The German Jews, who preceded the Russian Jews by many decades, did tend to look down on the Russian Jews," said Irv Lichtman, editor of *Cash Box* and later deputy editor at *Billboard.* "But they set up many charitable endeavors to help their poorer brethren. One of the reasons so many Jews entered the music business, as well as the motion-picture business, was partly the result of discrimination against both groups [of Jews] in the United States. Because it was difficult to break into various established businesses and professions, it was easier to join newly created businesses. The movie and music industries were born just as immigration of the Jews and Italians into the United States boomed."

The Jewish populace, with its ancient peddler tradition, in particular seemed to revel in the freedom and independence that America, the "land of milk and honey," offered. "Of course, you find Jewish people involved in every kind of business," said Nashville record man Shelby Singleton,

> but it may be more predominant in the music business. They are very clannish in the fact [that] they will help each other; they may be competing in some ways, but a brother will help a brother, or a father will help a son, or a son will help a cousin. I

think the music industry . . . lends itself to the fact that they had that nose for making money. It was a fast way to make money if you had a hit record, and they were willing to put their dollars into it to make it happen. That's basically it: they were gamblers; that's what they were.

But *all* the record men are real characters, real strong, real different people. Some of them go broke, some of them come back, some of them go broke again, come back again. But, you know, we're all gamblers. That's where I'm going tomorrow, to the casinos in Mississippi—that's what life's about!

The record man was further analyzed, in stylistic terms, by Atlantic's Jerry Wexler, one of the most important of the fraternity. "You see, in the beginning nobody knew anything, but there were three styles involved. One was the documentary style; that was what Leonard [Chess] did. If you heard Muddy Waters perform something in a bar on the South Side [of Chicago] on a Tuesday night, he'd say in the studio, 'You play what you played in the bar yesterday.' Then there was the songwriter/producer like a Buck Ram. And then there were guys like me and Ahmet. We worked as fans; we had fans' knowledge of jazz and blues music which people like Leonard didn't have. He had a gut instinct."[2]

Ahmet Ertegun was the last working first-generation record man. Until October 2006, when he was critically injured in a fall at a Rolling Stones concert, of all places, he was still making the daily commute to the Atlantic Records office at 1290 Avenue of the Americas, New York. To the end, which came six weeks later, he was instantly recognizable from those dusty photographs with his trademark spectacles, shiny pate, and dapper appearance. Two years earlier, he was in feisty form when asked about his fellow record men. "One of the very first meetings that I went to of independent record companies was in a hotel somewhere on Times Square around 1948," he said.

It was a big meeting room that had a huge table, around which were sitting some of these sixty or seventy owners of independent record labels. And most of those people were ex–jukebox operators or people who somehow had nightclubs, either in the hillbilly areas or rhythm and blues–type areas. Anyway, it was a rough bunch.

I was sitting there, and there was a very elegant gentleman sitting on my right who was Italian. He didn't speak English that well. So he and I were speaking in French, and there was a very rough and tough–looking guy on my left. He said, "What are you all talking about?" I said, "Well, I'm speaking French." So he looks at this Italian gentleman and says, "Are you new to the record business? What kind of records do you make?" He said, "Why? I just do opera recordings." So he says, "Opera recordings? Does that shit sell?" [*hearty laugh*]. So the man asks me, "What did he say?" And I hesitated to tell him in French what he had called the kind of music he made.

Of the early indie men, whom did Ertegun admire most? "I admired none of them!" he retorted.

As a matter of fact, the reason I went into the record business is because I met a lot of people who owned independent record labels in the '40s, during the war, which is when most of these labels came into being because of the shortage of shellac. There was a demand for certain kinds of records that the majors had stopped producing. So a lot of labels came into being in the early '40s.

I met a lot of these people; they were mostly crooks! And they didn't know a trumpet from a saxophone, and they knew nothing about music. They cared less; they just made records by accident. That's why I thought that I should be able to make a living making records. There were no admirable people in either the majors or the independents. I should reconsider that. There were a few gentlemen in the majors, but mostly they were just trash. They were crap.

A person like Alfred Lion [of Blue Note, the esteemed jazz label], you had a great deal of respect for. Herman Lubinsky [of Savoy Records] ran a record shop in New Jersey somewhere. . . . You know, the independent record people of those times unfortunately gave the independent record business the kind of reputation from which we at Atlantic suffered. We did not do any of the kind of things that they did. I never drove a truck in my life, but they all had trucks; they drove around the country and sold records for cash [at a discount to the prices of the appointed territorial distributors].

We came from basically a different background from most of these people. These people came from . . . well, they grew up poor, and they never developed a respect for the artists until the artists became so big that then the artists had no respect for them. We had something bigger than that; we had bookkeepers, and we were people who went to universities. I'm talking about the partners in my company: Herb Abramson, Miriam Bienstock, who was then his wife, Jerry Wexler, and my brother Nesuhi. We all came from families where we were taught ethical values and morals, and we acted in the same way.

On October 4, 2006—just three and a half weeks before his cruel accident—Ahmet Ertegun was charm personified. This lifelong socialite, lover of fine arts, and keen soccer fan had mellowed somewhat in his views of the original record men, citing more favorably in dispatches the names of Leonard and Phil Chess (Chess), Lew Chudd (Imperial), the Bihari brothers (Modern), Bobby Robinson (Fire-Fury), and the Messners (Aladdin), "who were very good, I thought; they had a jazz feel." But Ertegun couldn't resist another jab: "Most of these guys did it for just a quick buck; that's why they were in it."

As the most successful of all record men in terms of prestige and longevity and an early record collector, Ertegun displayed the expected keen awareness of stylistic trends through the decades. "Music was diffused around the world starting with the advent of radio and the phonograph," he said. "Aside [from] the first popular music and classical recordings, the music that transcended in all countries was black American music, or the imitations thereof. Now in 1917, the Original Dixieland Jazz Band made a recording ["Livery Stable Blues," Victor] that took over the whole world, and the world became jazz crazy. Everyone danced in the '20s; it was called the Jazz Age, and the Jazz Age was people dancing to black music. That continued into the swing era in the '30s and the '40s; into the R&B era of the late '40s, '50s, and '60s; to rock 'n' roll of the late '50s, '60s, and '70s. And rap, which is now everywhere. It's a continuation of the black tradition."

The Perfect Storm

In the early 1940s, the record industry was dominated by RCA Victor, Decca, and a reemergent Columbia. These organizations, known as major labels, were vertical in structure and necessarily bureaucratic in nature. They controlled every facet of the business, from a record's inception to manufacturing, distribution, and points of sale. Big numbers were sought from the homogenous popular market just as the modern consumer society was taking root. It is often overlooked that the parent company of RCA Victor was NBC and that of Columbia was CBS, the powerful national radio (and then TV) networks that were headed respectively by those combative titans General David Sarnoff and William Paley.

The postwar independent record era was kick-started by a serendipitous confluence of events that may be described, without understatement or originality, as the perfect storm. There was the launch of BMI (Broadcast Music, Inc.) in 1940, America's dramatic entry into World War II in 1941, and the union strike by the American Federation of Musicians (AFM) in 1942.

With the formation of BMI, the monopoly of the New York–based elitist Tin Pan Alley popular music publishers and writers would be broken. From the teeming cities to the rural outposts, doors were opened to independent publishing companies and a classless society of songwriters throughout the United States. The ugly battle between BMI and ASCAP (American Society of Composers, Authors and Publishers) had erupted when the broadcasters (the investors in BMI) felt it was necessary to compete in the performing rights song royalty collection business. With apparently unlimited resources, BMI was able to massage its growth with generous advances and guarantees to its members, old and new. The internecine BMI/ASCAP rivalry, involving constant legal sparring and government lobbying, was to persist throughout the rock 'n' roll era. But, hallelujah, American music was emancipated.[3]

"BMI is really a great story for what would eventually turn into rock 'n' roll," said music journalist and song publisher Irv Lichtman.

> Now, ASCAP was this 1914–formed, somewhat staid organization of the Broadway writers and the great Tin Pan Alley writers that was in dispute with broadcasting. The broadcasters formed BMI, and to this day it's a broadcast-owned entity. Now what do you do when you're a new licensing organization and your old competitor has got everything locked up? Well, you turn to other kinds of music. I would say the fact that BMI established itself and had to dig into blues and R&B and country was one way in which it began to help expose all that music to a more general public. It was a very significant move. Of course, ASCAP eventually caught on, but it was late in the game. In fact, stories are replete of how ASCAP writers and executives would say, "Garbage music, terrible music, how can you foist this on us?" Well, later on it was rock 'n' roll. Then, of course, ASCAP today competes easily with BMI in all areas, while BMI has built up a major catalog of Broadway, movie, and classical works. But BMI's formation really, I think, gets deserved credit for, through necessity, . . . forcing

itself to sign country artists, to sign blues artists, and [to] create what would eventually be a major, major part of the business.

Meanwhile, the record industry had to overcome a grievous double whammy: shellac rationing and the AFM recording ban. Shellac was the crucial binding agent for the compounds in the manufacture of 78–rpm records and was imported primarily from the forests of India and Siam (now Thailand). Following the United States' entry into the war, the supply line was endangered to such an extent by Japanese action that the shellac stocks were placed under the control of the War Production Board from April 1942. The country's diminishing shellac mountain was diverted from the manufacture of records (and other products) to wartime munitions, leading to the evocative term "from ballads to bullets." The major labels had no option but to prioritize their releases and to prune their artist rosters in order of popularity. Ethnic regional music, including "old familiar tunes" and "race records," was a poor also-ran.

The musicians' union strike, involving some 140,000 members, began on August 1, 1942. A run-up news story in *Billboard* noted that "ever since the broadcasters gave ASCAP such a thumping in their now historic battle, it has been known that some radio factions have been looking forward to a showdown with the AFM. Some observers think this is it, and that when the full force of the radio station plus mounting anti-AFM newspaper opinion is brought to bear against the AFM, [union president James C.] Petrillo will have a face-saving job on his hands that will make Hirohito's explanations of the Midway battle look like child's play."[4]

It didn't quite work out that way, and for a while the astonishingly brazen Petrillo was the empowered dictator of American music. The 1942 recording ban had at its heart the desire for the protection of live music for union members (many of whom were on radio station payrolls) at the expense of cancerous "canned" music. There were visions not only of better job security and improved conditions for the musicians but also of increased revenue for the union's coffers. Petrillo's sights, therefore, were set firmly at the rapidly evolving "sound carriers," that is, the phonograph record and electrical transcription companies, the radio stations, and the jukebox industry.

Memories of the flare-up have been dimmed by the passage of time, but Arthur Shimkin, of Golden Records, had a strong recall of AFM's president, a Chicago-born son of an Italian sewer digger: "Petrillo was crazy, a total absolute egomaniac; he thought he was a czar. He would never shake hands with you, afraid of germs. . . . He was bombastic, declaratory, and he chewed out a lot of people. That was his technique. He was irascible; that's the best term I can think of."

Without surprise, Petrillo profited personally from his presidency. On August 8, 1942, *Billboard,* not in his corner by any means, gleefully reprinted a report from the *Chicago Sun* that indicated Petrillo was "paid $26,000 a year as president of the Chicago local and $20,000 as head of the international." Then there were the fat-cat fringe benefits: "In 1937, the Chicago local gave him . . . $5,000 for expenses, $25,000 for an armored car and bodyguards, a $25,000 house, $12,000 worth of furnishings,

$1,700 for garden maintenance and $16,000 for income taxes." He was said to have three homes, including "an apartment at the Waldorf-Astoria in New York, where the international's headquarters are located."[5]

At first, the major record companies prospered at the expense of the musicians' union, thanks to an ongoing flow of big-selling discs. In time, the pendulum swung the way of the dogged Petrillo. Out of necessity, a troubled Decca arrived at a "complete understanding" with the union and settled in September 1943, followed closely by recently formed Capitol and a rising number of small independents. As a result, these companies had head starts over stubborn holdouts RCA Victor and Columbia. In a shrewd public relations move, the union authorized the production of V-discs for the U.S. Armed Services on a nonprofit basis. Eventually, the two renegade major labels were unable to wait any longer for the expected help from their friends in government. Fearful of an exodus of their top artists to Decca and Capitol, in particular, the industry leaders were forced to bow ignominiously to Petrillo's demands for the establishment of a musicians' compensation fund by way of a small royalty percentage on each record sold. The strike had lasted for two years and three months.

During the recording ban, a pent-up demand for music of all stylistic denominations had built up because of a lack of new sounds. Not only that, but new markets were being created by the migrants from the southern states to the major urban centers of Los Angeles, Chicago-Detroit, and New York. When normal service was resumed, the combined vision of the three major labels did not extend much beyond the cozy, profitable pop and classical sectors. And so from the end of World War II in 1945 until the disc jockey payola scandal emerged in 1959, the independent record companies led the way in showing the major labels how to mine and exploit the rich, deep resources of American music. It was a case of tapping the many profitable and diverse seams while the gold remained. Big economic assists came by way of a postwar spending boom, a housing boom, an automobile boom, and, of course, a baby boom.

Seymour Stein of Sire Records and onetime apprentice at both King Records and *Billboard* gave a personal overview of the historical scenario involving the major and independent labels that ushered in the rock 'n' roll era: "With few exceptions, the major labels stuck to mainstream pop and jazz [and classical]. I'm talking about going back to the earliest days of the music business, right up through the Second World War. The majors were also quite active in the country field [known as hillbilly], and in fact one of Victor's earliest gold records was 'The Prisoner's Song' by Vernon Dalhart in 1925." Victor and Columbia were recording race (later known as rhythm and blues) and other roots music, too.

Continued Stein:

Decca, which was launched by Sir Edward Lewis from England in 1934 [and run by Jack Kapp with brother Dave], signed a lot of country and black artists, aided in part by two exceptional A&R [artists and repertoire] men: Milt Gabler, who they brought over from the indie Commodore, and Paul Cohen.

Before Capitol, formed in 1942, there wasn't much of a record business going on in California. There was however, a strong contingent of Tin Pan Alley songwriters lured there to write for musical films instead of the Broadway stage. In the late 1940s, some pioneering R&B and jazz labels sprung up in South Central, Los Angeles, including Aladdin, Specialty, Exclusive, Modern, and Swing Time.

Most R&B artists, ignored by the majors, were not getting the attention they deserved. They were making some of the best music around and gave rise to independent record companies like Apollo, Savoy, King, Chess, Atlantic, Imperial, Duke-Peacock, Herald-Ember, Vee-Jay, Specialty, Rama-Tico, and Old Town. With the exception of King, which was a full-service indie, these companies started as one- or two-person operations run by people from the seat of their pants.

But what men and women they were, legends all! There was Bess and Ike Berman, Herman Lubinsky, Leonard and Phil Chess, Lew Chudd, Don Robey, Al Silver, Vivian Carter and Jimmy Bracken with Ewart Abner, Art Rupe, Hy Weiss, and four of my great mentors: Syd Nathan, George Goldner, Jerry Wexler, and Ahmet Ertegun. These guys were spread all around the country in New York, Chicago, Cincinnati, Houston, Philadelphia, and Los Angeles. That was a good thing, because the artists were all over the country. So you had regional sounds, and there was a whole new business.[6]

In the slipstream of these revered labels came the pop-rock companies that have been unfairly treated by history because, as Stein said, "their music wasn't as sexy." Yet who can argue that such imprints did not wave the independent banner with fierce spirit? In the final analysis, these labels and their record men were all part of the colorful indie mosaic.[7]

Jukebox Jury

A pivotal contributor in sparking liftoff for the independent record companies in the 1940s was the ornate, shimmering jukebox. Following the repeal of Prohibition in 1933, thousands of taverns and cocktail lounges opened up, and most of the locations took in jukeboxes to provide cheap entertainment for a public wearied by the Great Depression. New major label Decca was the first to service the jukebox sector in a big way—Bing Crosby's records were bonanzas for all concerned—and was to remain the market leader for many years, to be joined by emergent Capitol.[8]

Initially, the business centered on the jukebox distributors, who supplied (and often funded) phonograph machines, title strips, needles, and parts to the jukebox operators; records were a natural adjunct. The operators placed their phonographs in various locations, which were known collectively as "routes." In several cases, the jukebox distributors were also jukebox operators.

Cosimo Matassa, son of a New Orleans jukebox operator and himself a field service engineer, witnessed the rocket-like ascendancy of the jukebox culture. As well, he saw firsthand the birth of the mom-and-pop record store and was responsible for launching one of the first regional recording studios. "The jukebox sales were a huge part of the market then," he said.

I mean, we made short records because jukebox operators wanted short records. That proves how influential they were. If you'd listen to the jocks, if they wanted to end a record quickly, they'd do some foolish kind of talk-over and skid the needle over. With the jukebox, they were stuck [laughs]. And the records wore out so fast. With a hit record, you had to put a new one on every week.

That's what really got us into the record business, because we started selling the records we took off [the jukeboxes] as long as the record was still playable. We'd put a new record on, and we'd take those back to the office and sell them as used records. People kept coming in buying the used records and started asking for new records; the used records were probably around half price, fifty cents. It sort of grew.

The independents had the best records. Not all the time; Louis Jordan was on Decca. But the independents just ate their lunch [with black music] almost every time they turned around. The companies I was to do recordings for, as soon as they started up they had impact: De Luxe, King, the guys on the West Coast. All of them did real good because the guys who for the most part did it liked the music; . . . [it was more than] a business or a job. They put more action into it.

Here was an alternative view to that of Ahmet Ertegun's on the record men faction. "There were the three major jukebox manufacturers," continued Matassa,

Wurlitzer, Seeburg, and Rock-Ola. It was a toss-up which was best. I would say design-wise, Wurlitzer was always on top, just for appearances. That Model 1015 is what everybody these days thinks . . . a jukebox looks like, the one with the curved top and the columns down the [sides] with the flashing lights. . . . That's what they expect as a picture of a jukebox—they were so popular.

The jukeboxes were fairly simple mechanisms, so wear is the primary problem you had; there were not a lot of technical problems. These were all mechanical devices, so the things that would wear out would be drive cams, roller arms, things that were moving a lot. The first pickup arms were very heavy; that was one reason the damn records wore out. But the Seeburg came in after Wurlitzer, and through aggressive promotion, they were cutting deals right and left with jukebox operators to sell them cheap; they were buying ten and getting one free, that kind of thing. Then Rock-Ola was very well entrenched with certain operators: the old guard, large-scale guys. A lot of them were exclusive Rock-Ola guys; I don't know why.[9]

In a front page story dated April 22, 1950, *Billboard* confirmed the strategic value of the jukebox industry: "With some 400,000 boxes on location owned and operated by some 5,550 operators who buy in the neighborhood of 46,000,000 records annually, the diskers are finding that the jukebox business is building to its most prominent position since the end of the war."

The jukebox business, however, was at once abrasive and foreboding. Its checkered history was outlined in an April 1960 *Billboard* story based on a Senate report:

1. The music, amusement and cigarette vending segments of the coin industry, particularly, have been victimized by an astounding number of racketeers. Almost

"every infamous criminal in America has held interest in some segment" of the coin industry during the past 20 years. They have posed both as owners and union leaders.

2. Early experience with gambling machines "derived by the underworld through infiltration in this field" has made it possible for criminals to extend their operations into non-gambling amusement games, jukeboxes and to a minor extent, vending machines. Such holdings have been obtained by investing money received from "illicit enterprises; and by force, terror, and the corruption of management, union and public officials." They have attained a great measure of success in urban centers of New York, New Jersey, Illinois, Louisiana, Ohio, Michigan, Florida and Indiana.[10]

On the positive side, the jukebox trade did provide vital stability to the independent labels by way of volume sales, and there was the "free audition" promotional element whenever a jukebox record was played. As Matassa implied, the jukebox manufacturers, distributors, and operators didn't stand for any nonsense. They demanded and got a reliable end product (musically and technically) to maximize profits. Accordingly, they instilled important quality-control standards into the nascent independent record business.[11]

Such stipulations included the need for consistent "coin-grabbing" artists (such as a Chuck Berry, a Fats Domino, or a George Jones), better disc-making compounds for improved reproduction, uniform volume levels, pressings with assured lead-in and lead-out grooves, those shorter times, and even attractive flip sides for extra revenue. Most important, the jukebox manufacturers would embrace the lightweight 45–rpm single over the clumsy 78. Through the cajoling of the jukebox industry, the *loud* trademark sound of American rock 'n' roll would evolve.

The jukebox brotherhood, with its ready-made outlets, was the catalyst for an intricate nationwide network of independent record distributors with closely defined label-franchised territories (in best syndicated tradition, it might be said). Here were the crucially important "middle men" whose job it was to get the records from the individual manufacturers to the retailers—and to the public—with all haste in the pre-interstate, pre–mass airline era. Apart from being precocious entrants into a market loaded with growth potential, they would benefit by getting records for their routes at wholesale prices (or less for high volume purchases).

Nevertheless, the jukebox men did not have an exclusive on record distribution. Explained Atlantic's Ahmet Ertegun, "A lot of these distributors were distributors of refrigerators; they were distributors of radios or phonographs or televisions when it started—they distributed other things as well as records. For this period of time, it was a very good business for the distributors, and it was a good business for the independent record companies. It was set up in a very good way. Every area had more than one distributor, so if you had good product which sold, they wanted it. That has not changed. If you don't make product that somebody wants to buy, you are not in business."

The close record man/distributor relationship gave rise to a simple definition of an indie record label, as offered by Dave Burgess of Challenge Records: "An independent record company distributes through independent distributors; that's why they call [it] an independent record company. Each major city had independent distributors not controlled by a major label, and these independent distributors distributed those small little labels in the beginning like Dot, Liberty, Challenge, Roulette, and A&M. Those were independent record companies as opposed to a major record company, which had its own distributors in every major city."

Whereas a regular distributor would handle certain allotted record lines, a one-stop merchant catered for all labels. In effect, one-stops were subdistributors that were set up initially for the purpose of servicing jukebox operators from a single location. "I think, in writing history, the role of the one-stop, again like the jukebox operators, tends to be overlooked," said Shelby Singleton. "The one-stop was really a major player in the retail sale of records, because it was just exactly what the word means. Instead of a guy having to go to the Columbia, RCA, Decca, and Capitol distributors and to the independents in town, he could pay five cents more for a record and go to one place for all of his records. So he didn't have to spend the whole day going around town. The one-stop fulfilled the need of being able to go to one place."

Frontier World

From the mid-1940s on, the stranglehold of the network radio stations (the familiar NBC and CBS, new ABC, and now-forgotten MBS—Mutual Radio) was being loosened by the emergence of small independent radio stations everywhere. With record shows becoming an important part of the new order, the disc jockeys began taking on added importance when it was realized that constant play of a record in a specific regional outpost could spark off (or "break") a hit nationwide. In essence, the dee-jay present-ers were selling music over the radio while providing entertainment at minimal cost to the stations and at no cost to the listeners. Even with accelerating station numbers, competition for radio play would become frighteningly intense. It would be impossible to avoid the celebrity disc jockey.

Payola was as old as the hills, but the age of the independents would bring a new dimension to the greased-palm syndrome. As early as 1947, Joe Carlton, of *Billboard* and future record man, saw the looming problem in a piece where the headline said it all: "Disk Jock Payola Bugaboo: Platter Spinners as Next Breeding Ground for Payoff?" Carlton concluded that "unless the issues are exposed now the evil that may develop later will be to the great detriment of all broadcast record programs in America."[12]

With great rapidity, a critical union had developed between the independent record companies, distributors (and soon one-stops), jukebox operators, disc jockeys, and re-tailers in literally transmitting records to the ears of the general public. "We were very symbiotic; we needed each other badly," said Atlantic's Jerry Wexler.

These distributors were part of the community. The manager for [RCA] Victor or Columbia, he'd go to his suburban villa for the weekend. But these guys stayed around all weekend long; they'd be barbecuing ribs in the backyard and have the jockeys over to the swimming pool. They also had a certain financial advantage. Let's say the bookkeeping wasn't closely supervised; they were their own bosses [*laughs*]. So independent distributors were very important to us because they homed in on the local scene, and in a sense they had a better feel for the business.

We appointed distributors by guess or by God! Usually there were two or three distributors in town, and the reason you went with any given distributor was that the other two hadn't paid you. So by elimination, *faux de guerre,* we'd wind up with the fellow that paid us . . . experimental. If you'd stayed hot, then you'd get the money at the end of the month, but as soon as you went cold, all you could see was these records coming back. It was a very grim prospect to see these trucks unloading all these unwanted records. Today a collector might pay seventy-five dollars for a record, but by the thousands in those days they were only worth three cents apiece.

We went any place where we thought we could sell records, and we always used to sell to one-stops. There was a fellow in Pittsburgh; he had a hardware store, and he was the best distributor in Pittsburgh. I mean, you went in there, and it was frightening because you saw this hardware store, and then in one room in the corner, portioned off, there was one table with a few boxes of records on it. And that was the operation! But this was the guy that was getting the disc jockeys to play the records, and then the operators [would buy them]. He used to sell our records in shoeshine parlors; they'd have a little stand of the latest Fats Domino, the latest Drifters record, and so on.

A jukebox operator would come into a one-stop, or distributor for that matter, and he'd ask for a certain record. The operator would know it in many cases before the jobber because he had demands for it [at] certain locations, and then that filtered back to us. If it was one of our records, fine; if not, we could cut it and provide them with a new version. We didn't sell to the jukebox operators direct; we didn't have the mechanism.

Those record men who survived and thrived had to come to grips, quickly, with the new business environment. A swift succession of revolutionary innovations, such as magnetic recording tape from Germany, unbreakable LP and 45–rpm records, and the introduction of solid-body electric guitars and overdubbing techniques (both popularized by Les Paul), served only to keep everyone alert. Specialty Records' Art Rupe, one of the more articulate of the record men, wrote up his own instruction manual for employees in the mid-1950s. "I periodically gave these instructions to the recording and promotion men I trained," he said. "No one taught me, so I figured these instructions would spare them the hit-or-miss experiences I went through."[13]

This was the feverish, frontier-like world that thrusting young record men and a few women throughout the nation were discovering and mapping out. Artists could have a hit whether they were based in New York, Chicago, Nashville, or Los Angeles—or even in Clovis, New Mexico, or Phoenix, Arizona, for that matter. Entry level was easy, or so it seemed. Our session is about to begin: "We're rolling—take one!"

2

CHAPTER

The Super Indies

CENTRAL CHARACTER
Berle Adams, Mercury Records
also featuring the Capitol Records' founders; Irving Green,
Mercury Records; Jack Kapp, Decca Records; and Louis
Jordan, Decca and Mercury artist

Capitol Records' Know-How

A gradual buildup in the independent record business had been under way during the early 1940s despite the desperate circumstances affecting the music industry. The shining beacon was Capitol Records, yet the label had to overcome the worst possible timing of its launch. In April 1942, a mere fifteen days after Capitol had pressed its first discs, the War Production Board ordered a draconian 70 percent reduction in the available shellac stock. The recording strike by the American Federation of Musicians, just three months later, seemed to be the final nail in the coffin.

As it happened, the Capitol founders were men of talent, grit, and financial substance, attributes that enabled the label to survive and prosper, eventually. President Buddy DeSylva, Vice President Johnny Mercer, and General Manager Glenn Wallichs were a dream team. *Billboard* agreed as much, noting in 1944 that the "answer to Capitol's progress is fairly simple. The gents running it have the know-how."[1]

Songwriter Buddy DeSylva was an executive producer at Paramount Pictures and contributed the total start-up capital of $25,000. Johnny Mercer is acknowledged as one of the finest tunesmiths ever, with "Blues in the Night," "Come Rain or Come Shine," "Fools Rush In," "Goody Goody," "Moon River," and "That Old Black Magic" standing out in an astonishing portfolio. The third indispensable partner, Glenn Wallichs, was founder of Music City, located at the corner of Sunset and Vine in Los Angeles. His futuristic superstore was stocked with records, radios, and sheet music and offered custom-recording facilities. The clientele included Hollywood stars attracted by the latest in fashionable fads.

Wallichs knew the distribution business intimately. He was particularly annoyed and frustrated that major labels RCA Victor, Columbia, and Decca would service only their own outlets in Los Angeles, and certainly not his Music City emporium. Thus was Capitol Records conceived. Wallichs's visionary innovations included the establishment of a nationwide network of branches to bypass much of the infant independent distributors' network and the launching of a transcription service for radio stations. Most important, he ensured that disc jockeys were supplied with regular free records, and in doing so he gave early recognition to the industry's future power brokers. This pro-airplay model was contrary to the common belief that radio broadcasts would harm record sales rather than stimulate them. It was a critical philosophical breakthrough for the industry at large.

Another key element in Capitol's growth was a record-pressing agreement, in 1944, with the Scranton Record Co. (then the world's largest pressing plant based in Scranton, Pennsylvania) that was followed by outright purchase for $2 million within two years. The recruitment of James B. Conkling, also in 1944, was another big plus. Here was the man who managed the label's A&R strategy of producing impeccable-sounding records and who developed an expert marketing and promotion machine.

Indeed, the entire Capitol organization was embossed with the seal of quality, epitomized by an enviable roster that would range from Nat "King" Cole, Peggy Lee, and Frank Sinatra to Gene Vincent, the Beatles, and the Beach Boys. Capitol's quest for excellence was also signified by the "domed" logo with its four stars as well as by the magnificent album artwork that was introduced for the early 78–rpm collections and that later set the standard for vinyl LP jackets.

If it seemed that Capitol Records was preordained to become an establishment-biased major label, it is easy to forget that it had sprung from true indie roots. Even so, Capitol suffered the fate of most successful, fast-growing independent companies in any business: it was taken over by a larger, cash-rich corporation. The buyer was London-based Electric and Musical Industries Limited (EMI), which paid $8.5 million for a 95 percent controlling interest in January 1955.

The background to EMI's acquisition of Capitol was that EMI had lost the American Columbia international licensing rights from 1953 to Dutch Philips and would lose RCA Victor in 1957 to U.K. Decca. Together, Columbia and RCA accounted for a large chunk of EMI's business, which had given rise to monopoly concerns. As well, Columbia's New York management was unhappy at EMI's slow adoption of their LP invention, according to Columbia's George Avakian.[2] Sensing danger ahead and needing to spread the load, EMI had already concluded a licensing agreement with MGM (known also as M-G-M) in 1948. The Capitol discussions were opened when it became clear that the Columbia void had to be filled, and RCA would not be renewing its longstanding agreement. An American repertoire was seen, quite correctly, as all-important.

Wallichs stayed on as Capitol's president and became a director of EMI, whose main labels at the time were His Master's Voice (HMV, with the "Nipper dog" trademark that was shared with RCA), Columbia (with the "magic notes" trademark that belonged to EMI), and Parlophone. Capitol was still a division of EMI into the twenty-first century. But back in the 1940s, an eternity away, the imprint was an inspiration to all budding record makers.

Berle Adams and Mercury Records

The name of Mercury Records also survived into the new millennium, under the parasol of French corporate behemoth Vivendi-Universal. Mercury's intriguing launch in Chicago in October 1945 was made just one month after the Japanese surrender signaled the end of World War II.

A *Billboard* report noted that "another boost toward putting Chi. on the map as a record-producing center came this week with the opening of the Mercury Record plant here. New independent label, which is already pressing plenty platters a week, intends to hike production to 700,000 disks weekly within the next year with 72 presses in St. Louis and 48 in their Chi. outlet."[3] Joining "local plastics expert" Irving Green at the Mercury Radio and Television Corporation were Berle Adams, a talent agent–manager in the Chicago cocktail lounge business, and Green's friend, Ray Greenberg, another manufacturer.

Irving Green, whose father, Al, ran the National label out of New York, was to be the face of Mercury until 1969, even after it was taken over by Philips of Holland in 1961. "A nice man, a good man," Jerry Wexler observed of Irving Green. But with Mercury being based in old Chicago—with its gangland control of the jukebox operations and the involvement of the "crooked nose boys" in entertainment generally—there was more than a whiff of laundered mob money in the background.

Mercury Records' opening artist roster was a reflection of the vibrant Windy City club scene of the time and of the important involvement of Berle Adams, the first president. Some sixty years later, this most genial of men had keen memories of how Mercury established itself quickly, effectively, and professionally. Our conversations were interspersed with periodic chuckles as his still-lively mind recaptured the excitement of a newborn era. "It was virgin territory for anybody," Adams said, "because in the war years, big companies weren't signing new talent. It was a good opportunity for all of us who wanted to go into the business. That's how Capitol got started and how we got started. There were a dozen or so labels that came in at the same time." Like Capitol, Mercury soon outgrew its status as an indie start-up label and within a decade had become a quasi-major record company.

While his Russian-born father did the milk rounds for Capitol Dairy, Beryl Adasky was consumed by the entertainment business in his formative years in Prohibition-era Chicago. The Toddlin' Town environment proved to be an ideal launchpad for young Berle's career. "When I was growing up, everything was stage shows," he said.

All the big comics, all the big bands, they all played on the stage. Every city had its own stage show with a movie; the movies were the big production. Later on they became concerts and all these other ways of entertainment.

I was a big fan of . . . Benny Goodman when he was playing at the Congress Hotel, Chicago. I was too young to attend; I was hearing him on the radio every night [broadcast by NBC]. Radio had all the big bands in Chicago, always. In those days, a band would go into a hotel and stay there for months in order to get the airtime to make them more popular. The radio was the big thing—that was the contact with the outside world. Then the bands would have records, and when they became popular they'd go and play one-nighters where they made most of their money. That's the way it all worked.

Adams entered the booking agency business with General Amusement Corporation (GAC) after working first as a record salesman for Targ and Diner, distributors of the thirty-five-cent Varsity label.[4] The Varsity owner was the towering, six-foot-plus Eli Oberstein, who dominated as an executive at RCA Victor and in the industry at large. Said Adams:

Eli Oberstein had started a new record company [in 1939], and I sent him a letter every day that [said] I wanted to work for the distributor. He never answered my letters. I read a book called *Sell with a Sizzle* [by Earle Wheeler]: be original! So I went to my doctor, and I had his secretary write a [reference] letter to Mr. Oberstein telling him that "You've got to give Berle a job; he's got music in his blood."

And so I got my first job. Eli Oberstein was a clever record man; he understood the business. He knew how to pick tunes, he knew how to pick talent, and he knew how to pick orchestras, too. Don't forget he had Glenn Miller, Benny Goodman, and Artie Shaw, all at Victor Records. That's the magic of the record business, to be able to find good talent and find the right material for them to record.

Some of the orchestras who recorded for Eli were managed by the General Amusement Corporation, who represented big bands. That was their big business, selling them on one-nighters and in hotels. GAC allowed me to build a small band department. I came along with this idea of selling small groups in cocktail lounges, which to them was small business. They didn't think it had any value; that's why they let a kid like me get started in that business. The clubs were downtown and in the commercial areas where people could get to very easily. Before television, their big entertainment was the jukeboxes and the talent in the cocktail lounges.

By working in Chicago's glitzy club land and as a record distributor's salesman, Berle Adams had acquired many important contacts. And so Adams was recommended to Irving Green, who was setting up a pressing plant facility but had no customers. "Well, Irving Green manufactured vats for beer," said Adams,

and he decided that was a bad business. So he converted his factory into a pressing plant for records.[5] He didn't know how to get any business, so he went to a fellow by the name of Ben Orloff, who owned the cocktail lounges which I put bands in. Ben knew that I had a relationship with Decca Records, because I represented an attraction called Louis Jordan. We were very successful on records.

So Orloff told Irv Green, "I'll have you meet Berle Adams." The big companies [RCA Victor, Columbia, and Decca] weren't pressing records for independents. They had a larger business and shellac was hard to get, they were making small runs, and they didn't want to take on independent work. You have to pay, and the independents usually are bad payers. So the big companies didn't want that business at all. I did a deal with Irving that I would work on a commission basis for everything that I brought in, any of the new pressing jobs. Well, I knew everybody, so I went to the guys and said, "You're making records; we'll press them for you." So we started our business that way.

Berle Adams's sales pitch was that the records would be delivered on time and at a keen price.

Irving Green, an imposing man physically and in personality, was raised on Chicago's impoverished West Side. His father, Al, a union official, founded National Records in Manhattan in 1944. Was Al Green involved with Mercury? "Not at all," said Berle Adams, emphatically. "He had his own company; we had our own company. Irving worked with us; he didn't work for his father—totally separate."

After an early spell in his father's paint contracting business, Irving Green had gone into the sheet metal trade before becoming interested in building hydraulic presses. An engineering genius with vision, he started manufacturing sixteen-inch lacquer transcription discs for radio programming in the war years. But to make his pressing plant profitable, he needed to ensure regular supplies of shellac for the production of ten-inch 78–rpm discs. Ever the go-getter, what did he do? He went to the source, of course, traveling to the EMI plant in the squalid Dum Dum suburb of Calcutta, India, and arranging for the factory manager, J. W. George, to ship shellac supplies direct to Chicago.[6]

The first 78–rpm records pressed by Irving Green in the summer of 1945 were subcontracted by Boris Morros's ARA label of Hollywood and involved the Hoagy Carmichael hit "Hong Kong Blues." Green also did work for Decca. On November 3, in a *Billboard* advertisement, the "Mercury Record Plant" proclaimed itself "the largest independent record manufacturers in the world now pressing over 1,000,000 records per month." The ad also incorporated a mock invitation for "Dealers and Operators" to inspect the plant.

Even so, Berle Adams could see problems ahead: "Originally there was a shortage of pressing plants, but other people got in the business. Everybody has competition. Pretty soon the war was over, and the Columbia and RCA pressing plants became available [to the indie labels], too. We were fortunate; we started our company during the time when they weren't available. So I called Irving, and I told him it's not going to work: 'This is all going to evaporate because the big companies are going to take on all of these little people eventually and we're going to be without any business. I think we should form our own record company.' He agreed, and we formed a company called Mercury Radio and Television Company."

Already the smartest of negotiators, the twenty-eight-year-old Adams secured a 40 percent share in the new organization, with Irving Green and Ray Greenberg each having a 30 percent stake. As president, Adams was responsible for the selection and recording of talent, sales, and other administrative duties. Green was chairman of the board, responsible for production.[7]

The inspiration for the company's name apparently came when Green's eye caught a billboard for a 1946 Mercury automobile while driving to work at 215 South Peoria. This particular Mercury was destined to become a messenger of new sounds, but there was an immediate hitch. "We were in business for a week or so," said Adams,

> and a transcription company sued us because they had the name Mercury, which we had no knowledge of. So we went to court, and I testified before the judge that we were a commercial record company and they were a transcription company. We weren't competitive at all because their customers wouldn't be our customers. But the judge said, "Is there a needle on the machine you use?" and I said, "Yes, sir." "You put that on a record, there's a sound you make?" I said, "Yes, sir." He said, "You're in the same business!" So I bought the name for $5,000.
>
> That's how we got started. And I decided that we should be a specialized company, only R&B, country, and polkas. So having been in the black business for years, I started with the African American artists that worked the clubs in Chicago for me. One of the big stars was Albert Ammons; he and Pete Johnson were terrific—the Boogie Woogie Boys. Then we used Bill Samuels and his Cats 'N' Jammers, who were working for Ben Orloff, and they were very successful for us. We weren't that successful in hillbilly as we were with R&B and popular music. We just didn't pick the right [hillbilly] artists; we didn't have any talent there. When you know R&B, you don't know country; there's a lot of difference [laughs].
>
> From the beginning, we had quite a big organization because we covered all the areas. We had to appoint distributors and make sure they'd get the right stores to service. I hired people to look after the distributors. If you don't have control of the people who are selling, you are out of business. We had a guy working on sales [Morrie Price], we had a guy on advertising [Art Talmadge], we had lawyers who signed the contracts. They all had secretaries and everything else [including future royalty department manager Lucille Press]. We had a pretty big organization for a new company. Irving Green and I were very close friends.

Berle Adams's busy desk was surrounded by no less than three telephones. One was specifically for communicating with the pressing plant (and Green), another for sales, and a third for general use (including calls from the stars and song-pitching publishers). "You had to make yourself available," said Adams.

A second Mercury pressing plant had been acquired cheaply in St. Louis after Lee Turner developed a spanking-new modern facility but had overrun his budget, according to Adams. There was one commodity missing—the actual pressing machines. That was an easy task for the inventive Irving Green to remedy, and so Green-Lee Plastics was formed. Within a few months, the cash-strapped Turner was unable to meet an Internal Revenue Service tax bill. Thus, the Green-Lee Plastics pressing plant was brought into the Mercury fold.

With a large weekly production capacity to fill at its two pressing plants and with not enough outside business, Mercury Records couldn't justify such a grand setup by targeting only the segmented markets for race music, polka, and hillbilly. Indeed, the company was having severe problems in collecting some $80,000 from its network of distributors. Mercury was being kept alive by an impromptu advance of $50,000 from the Berle Adams Agency. A crisis collection campaign netted $60,000 from the tardy distributors to pay off Adams's agency business and provide extra working capital, but other measures had to be taken.[8]

"After we were successful [early on]," said Adams, "we had to bring in other people with money to help us to get started. Our stockholders were a little disappointed that we didn't have any familiar names on the label. They wanted people they could talk about when they went to their country clubs."

In his self-published book, *A Sucker for Talent*, Berle Adams stated there were six other investors ("all close friends of Irving") who took up 40 percent of the stock. As a result, Adams's holding was diluted to 20 percent, as were the stakes of Irving Green and Ray Greenberg. Berle told how the vice president of American National Bank warned him that some of the new partners had "shadowy reputations" and that the bank would finance his own ventures, but "no money is available for Mercury Records."[9]

Nevertheless, with this new blood, Mercury entered the pop music arena. Crooner Tony Martin was signed through the investor connection and gave Mercury its first big hit with "To Each His Own" in the summer of 1946, before he absconded into the long arms of Eli Oberstein at RCA Victor. Adams, displaying his flair in the talent field, engineered the signings of Vic Damone and Frankie Laine, who had Mercury's first million-seller with "That's My Desire" in 1947. On the race record front, there were Top 10 hits by Albert Ammons with "Swanee River Boogie," Eddie Vinson with the coupling of "Old Maid Boogie" and "Kidney Stew Blues," and Gene "Jug" Ammons (Albert's son) with "Red Top." Then Dinah Washington, the queen of the blues and the jukeboxes, commenced a belated but extensive run of chart hits from 1948.

"Irving Green had nothing to do with talent," emphasized Adams. "That was my area. We had two different responsibilities. He made sure the records were manufactured, and I made sure we got people to make the records. The big thing was to sell the records to the jukebox operators; they were the big outlet. If you had a good record, they bought it, and they put it all over. They promoted your records because people heard it on the jukebox, and they went out to buy it after that. The gentlemen that ran the jukebox business in Chicago were all former hoodlums. They divided the city up into areas; each had their own areas, but they didn't fight with each other. Chicago's a big city, a lot of apartment buildings, a lot of places where people didn't have music in their homes. They'd like to go to places where they had jukeboxes. It was a very good business to be in, and a cash business."

With the movers and shakers of the jukebox industry being headquartered in the same locale, the Mercury management had little difficulty in obtaining entry into their twilight world. Moreover, the Mercury team understood that the jukebox operators, with their ready-made routes and no-nonsense tactics, were naturals for the fledgling independent record distribution network. Among Mercury's jukebox operator distributors were Amos and Dan Heilicher, who landed the account for Minnesota and distant North and South Dakota.[10]

By the end of 1947, under the auspices of its own Record Distributors, Inc. facility, Mercury had built up a nationwide network of twenty-eight independent distributors and another in Toronto, Canada, augmented by seven branch offices. Expansion was helped by an earlier decision to grant a 5 percent return program, which placed Mercury in the same bracket as RCA Victor, Decca, Columbia, and Capitol as well as long-lost Musicraft and Majestic (soon to be swallowed up by Mercury).[11]

Mercury targeted the rapidly growing independent radio stations and again hit the bull's-eye. "Disc jockeys are very important, too," said Adams.

> We had all the links with disc jockeys. I decided to be different, [to] do it differently [from] everybody else. So I hired girls as my contacts with the disc jockeys, and they were very successful. It worked out very well for us.
>
> I hired people to record: Mitch Miller came over [promoted to music director in December 1947 with John Hammond, who was appointed as vice president and head of the firm's classical department].[12] I brought Norman Granz in for *Jazz at the Philharmonic*; the first records [in the series] were made on Mercury. He always was a difficult man to work with; I loved him. Mitch Miller was not an easy man to work with, either, a talented man. Talented people are always difficult. I always appreciated they were so different, so talented; that's why I made all the exceptions for them.

As evidence that Mercury was becoming a significant force in the industry, the hitherto four separate corporations—Mercury Radio and Television Company, Olsen and Tilgner Manufacturing (of Chicago), Green-Lee Plastics (of St. Louis), and Record Distributors, Inc.—had already been brought under the umbrella of the Mercury Record Corporation as of March 1, 1947. The covering news story in *Billboard* carried an April 12 dateline: "Shuffle in execs had Berle Adams, ex-prexy, moving in as chairman of the board, in which capacity he will supervise the whole Mercury operation. Previously he was primarily working on talent inking and recording. Irv Green was named prexy and will handle production and distribution, with Art Talmadge being made a v.-p. in charge of advertising and promotion, and Jimmy Hilliard a v.-p. in charge of recording."[13] Irwin H. Steinberg was to become a big influence in the post of chief accountant and was appointed president of Mercury Records in 1969.

Jack Kapp and Louis Jordan

During his tenure at Mercury, Berle Adams doubled as an enterprising personal manager through his own agency with a book headed by Louis Jordan. "I knew everybody in the R&B field," he said, casually. "With Louis Jordan, you had an entrée to everybody."

Under Adams's careful guidance, Louis Jordan was transformed into the hottest act on the Negro circuit in the 1940s and helped to popularize the saxophone solo in R&B and then in rock 'n' roll. In a sense, Jordan was the daddy of rhythm and blues and king of the jukebox whose exploits inspired independent record men everywhere, even if he was signed to Decca Records.

Through Jordan, Adams had a direct line to Decca's Jack Kapp. Adams was in awe of the way Kapp steered Decca to major label status. "Jack Kapp *is* Decca," he said.

> Jack Kapp started it, Jack Kapp picked all the talent, Jack Kapp was the leader of the band, as we say. He was my mentor; he wanted me to read the best books and to learn a lot about business. He was a fabulous man. He had a record shop in Chicago; he was a Chicago man. The head of Decca of England, Sir Edward Lewis, convinced him to start U.S. Decca. Mr. Lewis told them how to sell records at thirty-five cents in the dime stores, three for a dollar.[14]

> Jack Kapp [was integral in] building the record business. His talents were his business senses, and as a record man he was ahead of the field. He recorded the spoken word, [he was] the first man to do a Broadway show [*Oklahoma!* with original cast, 1943], he was first in everything.[15] [Brother] Dave Kapp was a marvelous man; he did a lot of the records with the black [and hillbilly] artists and newcomers. But Jack was the master who took all the big people and made them bigger. He brought Bing Crosby to Decca, the Andrews Sisters, Ella Fitzgerald . . . that was all Jack Kapp [supported by GAC's Tom Rockwell]. They asked Bing Crosby why he was so successful, [and] he said, "I'd do whatever Jack would tell me to do."

Kapp died far too early in the game in 1949, at age forty-seven, and was succeeded as Decca's president by company treasurer Milton Rackmil.

Berle Adams revived Louis Jordan's stalled solo career in late 1941 with the help of Chicago music entrepreneur J. Mayo Williams, who supervised black talent for Decca.[16] The first Jordan record from this new deal, negotiated with Jack Kapp, was a double-sided seller: "I'm Gonna Move to the Outskirts of Town" and "Knock Me a Kiss." At a July 1942 session, stocking up material in anticipation of the imminent Petrillo recording ban, the exuberant alto saxophonist cut nine songs, including his first No. 1 race record, "What's the Use of Getting Sober," and "Five Guys Named Moe," a No. 3 race hit that would lend its title to the 1992 Broadway musical success. "Louis Jordan's big sale was black," said Adams, "and some of them carried over to white. The original 'Is You Is or Is You Ain't (Ma' Baby)' was a big white seller, 'Choo Choo Ch'Boogie' was a big white seller, 'Ain't Nobody Here but Us Chickens' was a big white seller, and a number of others. He was the biggest GI popular star; the soldiers were crazy about him. He did 'G.I. Jive' written by Capitol's Johnny Mercer." "Caldonia," published by Adams's Preview Music in 1945, was another monster No. 1 race record that, like "G.I. Jive," spilled over into the white pop charts.

"We did four full-length Louis Jordan pictures in big black theaters for Astor Film Corporation," added Adams. "Also, we were one of the first . . . to do the jukebox shorts. When you make records, nobody sees you, so the shorts that we made for the Soundies helped a lot. It showed what he looked like on the screen." You could almost say that these three-minute Soundies, at a dollar a view, were the "visual jukeboxes" where Dick Clark's *American Bandstand* and MTV, with its music videos, were rooted.[17]

Louis Jordan's annual tours, which started in Houston every Labor Day, were raging triumphs. The promoter for the Texas leg was Don Robey, the future Duke-Peacock record man and head of Buffalo Booking Agency. Contrary to popular opinion, Adams stated that Robey "was terrific; he was a great guy. I worked with him every year; I sold to him. He was a promoter [then]. He was not a booking agency. We only played in the big ballrooms and the [Houston] Auditorium. . . . He was very good to do business with, he was honest, he promoted well, and we made money with him. That's why we came back every year."

To put Louis Jordan's dominance into perspective, between 1942 and 1950 he had eighteen No. 1 hits on the race charts, seven No. 2 hits, and ten No. 3 hits. His records, which forever raise a smile, overloaded every jukebox in black areas. While this income (including publishing) was very welcome, Berle Adams saw Jordan's records primarily as promotional tools to bolster his artist's prestige in the entertainment business at large—and to enhance his booking fees and guarantees.

Jordan's amazing streak of smash releases would not have gone unnoticed by Adams's colleagues at Mercury, yet Berle insisted that his breezy hit-maker should remain at Decca. If Jack Kapp had not treated Jordan so well, said Adams, "I would have grabbed him for Mercury. In 1950, Louis's career went downhill; the business changed, too. It was rock 'n' roll, and all that other stuff came in."

It was no accident when, in 1955, Jordan's A&R man at Decca, Milt Gabler, scored worldwide by producing the breakthrough rock 'n' roll record, "Rock Around the Clock" by Bill Haley and his Comets.[18] Haley, a refugee from Dave Miller's indie Essex Records of Philadelphia, indulged in a shuffle rhythm that owed much stylistically to those jukebox giants western-swing king Bob Wills and of course Louis Jordan.

On the R&B front, perhaps the most influential of all future artists was Louis Jordan fan Chuck Berry. Sinuous in movement like Jordan, Berry displayed a similar whimsical dexterity in his song lyrics, while he was a clear disciple of T-Bone Walker and the early school of amplified jazz guitarists. In 1956, Mercury Records managed to sign Jordan. Although he was marketed as "the original rock and roller," it was too late. The good times had stopped rolling for him and, indeed, for other rhythm and blues pioneers.

Toward the end of 1947, just prior to the second Petrillo AFM ban, Berle Adams quit Mercury in a flash, or so it seemed. "We got very hot, and I left because I had an illness," he said. "I had a bad back [caused by a serious gym injury the previous May]. On doctor's orders, I departed Chicago for sunny California and spent a year in bed recuperating. When I left, I sold my stock to the other stockholders. You can't be interested in something when you're not around, especially a new company. Big companies, you can own stock in, but with a little company when you're starting something, you can't do that."

Under medication and with a steel cast on his back, Adams had tired of the continual round of meetings, pressures, and responsibilities, and so he resisted Irving Green's offer of a well-paid five-year consultancy. There was a twist to the last. Under the company's bylaws, Adams's partners had thirty days in which to match the pr. tag on his stock but were dithering. While on a recording assignment in New York, Adams was invited by Jack Mitnick to dinner at Patsy's, the fancy Italian restaurant off Broadway. Adams was confined to the studio, so his beloved wife, Lucy, was dined instead by Mitnick with a stand-in mutual friend, Salvatore "Tutti" Camarata (the musical director at newly formed London Records). After dinner, Mitnick graciously escorted Lucy to her seat at the theater for the new Irving Berlin hit musical *Annie Get Your Gun*. It did not take long for the word to get out among New York's chattering classes.

In his book *A Sucker for Talent*, Adams finished the story: "He [Jack Mitnick] turned out to be one of the owners of Runyon Sales, which controlled jukeboxes and record shops in New Jersey. He had been a first lieutenant to Louis 'Lepke' Buchalter, a notorious gangster who was executed in prison at Sing Sing [in the Hudson Valley] in 1944. Mitnick and his associates wanted my Mercury Records stock so that they could have a strong position in the company. When I reported his interest to my partners at Mercury, they suddenly became cooperative and agreed to pay the price I had asked. Lee Eastman [Linda McCartney's attorney father] prepared the papers, they signed and handed me the check. No problems."[19]

Did the smooth charmer Jack Mitnick, who plied Lucy with orchids at the outset, try to convince her that Berle should sell his Mercury stock to Mitnick's partners? "He knew he would not do well with her," said Adams, laughing. "She was smarter than I was! He had to do business with me. Lucy stood her ground; he didn't have a chance with her."[20]

Adams was not sidelined for long. By October 1949, *Billboard* was noting that he had entered into a "special arrangement" with RCA Victor, where he "gets the artists and records them at his own expense, but gets the use of RCA's Coast studios." Here was an early example of a postwar independent production deal with a major label. It was also reported that Adams "holds the post of blues and rhythm a.&r. chief at London Records, co-owns Pic and Preview Music pubberies, and manages Decca artist Louis Jordan."[21]

Soon Adams, now in Hollywood, was on his way to a second glittering career as a talent executive to the stars at MCA under the dynamic leadership of Lew Wasserman.[22] Adams even took up the reins of a deflated Decca Records in the 1960s. "When MCA bought Universal Pictures [in 1962], Decca was one of the assets," he said. "We weren't buying it for the record company; we were buying it for the motion picture company and the studio, and we bought the real estate too.[23] We started our own record label, MCA Records. At the time Decca Records was doing badly, I used to call them 'Decadent' Records. They asked me to try to help, so I said, 'Okay, I'll do it for awhile.'" At MCA, Adams rose to the post of executive vice president and was a major stockholder before retiring in early 1971.[24]

"Entertainment comes in many forms: records, stage, radio, motion pictures, and television," Adams noted in reflection. "I was lucky to taste of them all." In particular, he relished his time as a pioneering record man at Mercury, even if Irving Green has tended to hog the plaudits. "With a new company like Mercury, you never think it's going to be as big as it turns out to be," said Adams, "but you always hope it's going to be big. When you're running something, you have great confidence that it's going to be big because you pick the talent; you have confidence in them. But it is a business product first, not artistic. You can't hold yourself to a higher standard than other businessmen. We became a major company."

Within a year or so of Adams's exit from Mercury, he had a "vicarious kick" when the label scored No. 1 pop hits by two of his signings: Vic Damone with "You're Breaking My Heart" and Frankie Laine with "That Lucky Old Sun." Mercury ensured further growth by acquiring the master catalogs of Keynote and Majestic and by embracing the brand-new LP album and 45-rpm singles markets. In late 1950, following a tip from Jerry Wexler at *Billboard*, Mercury had one of the biggest pop hits ever with the hillbilly song "The Tennessee Waltz" by Patti Page that sold by the millions. Mercury's fleet-footed progress to near–major label status was assured.

3
CHAPTER

California Booming

CAST OF CHARACTERS
    Johnny Otis, Excelsior Records artist
    Rafael "Googie" Rene, Exclusive Records assistant
    Joe Bihari, jukebox operator's assistant and Modern Music
       (Modern) Records
    Art Rupe, Juke Box and Specialty Records
    Don Pierce, 4 Star Records
    Henry Stone, early record distributor
    also featuring Leon Rene, Exclusive Records; Otis Rene,
    Excelsior Records; and Jules and Saul Bihari, Modern Music
    (Modern) Records

By 1945, California was booming due to a confluence of factors. The United States was patently winning World War II, and the defense, film, and agricultural industries were prospering in the triumphant economy. To offset the wartime manpower shortages, the state was attracting migrant workers of different races from all over, especially from Mexico, Texas, and Oklahoma. Many of these new arrivals wanted their own music from "down home." There was a genuine feel-good atmosphere in the Golden State, first under President Franklin D. Roosevelt and then President Harry S. Truman. In this intoxicating environment, California was a critical base for the early independent record companies (or "off brands," as they were known at the time). The gold rush was on for the gold records.

Johnny Otis: Excelsior Records Artist

Johnny Otis was caught up in the crusading spirit of those heady, zoot-suited times. In late 1945, he started his career with a regional hit, "Harlem Nocturne," on Excelsior Records of Los Angeles. Born of Greek heritage and a natural leader of men, Otis had a pronounced African American empathy and great business savvy. By avoiding the many industry pitfalls, he became an enterprising R&B bandleader, songwriter, music publisher, and record man. If that wasn't enough, he was a club owner, A&R man, disc jockey, broadcaster, author, painter, raconteur, and more recently a marketer of his own organic apple juice. His curriculum vitae could not be more impressive.

"I started my own thing after I had formed the Otis-Love Band with Preston Love in Omaha," Otis said when touring England in 1972.[1]

I made my first record for Otis Rene, who owned the pioneering Excelsior Records. On that date [September 13, 1945] Count Basie loaned Jimmy Rushing as a singer, also two sidemen. I had a nice big band of my own at the time and we were well rehearsed. We did an instrumental with Preston Love and two sides by Jimmy Rushing. I said "Great! We finished early." "What do you mean we finished early?" came Rene's reply. "Three records in four hours" [I said]. Then Rene said, "No, *four* records in *three* hours." "Oh shit!" I said. So we hurriedly looked in my music book and found Ray Noble's "Harlem Nocturne" [composed by Earle Hagen], which was really Mickey Mouse music. We did our own arrangement, and although it was done as an afterthought[,] that was the one that made it.

The main West Coast labels were Modern [the Bihari brothers], Specialty [Art Rupe], Swing Time [Jack Lauderdale], Aladdin [Leo and Eddie Mesner], Imperial [Lew Chudd], Exclusive [Leon Rene], and Excelsior [Otis Rene]. I am sure that people like the Rene brothers or Art Rupe never dreamt their records would smack and crash their way across the country when they first started. "Drifting Blues" by Charles Brown was the black national anthem for two years; it was all you heard.[2] Hits lasted longer in those days. Things like "I Wonder" by Private Cecil Gant [Gilt-Edge] and "The Honeydripper" by Joe Liggins [Exclusive] were on the jukeboxes all over Central Avenue [Los Angeles].

At the time, to hear a record you either had to buy it, listen on a jukebox, or maybe see an artist in person. There was not much air exposure. The pressures and competition which cause a record to die quickly were not the same. The record owners used to work out deals with the jukebox men; the jukebox was a vital outlet.

Radio became all important in promoting records, but first it was limited to a few hours a day. The main disc jockeys on the West Coast were Joe Adams and Hunter Hancock. Adams hardly played any blues at first, mainly big band swing. But Hancock was more into "folk," and his first R&B show was *Harlematinee*, followed by *Huntin' with Hunter*. Al Jarvis, the first big white dee-jay in L.A. who died in 1970, said there was an unwritten law about playing black records; they just were not played.

Joe Adams, a young black from Watts, was Jarvis'[s] assistant and I learned a lot from him. He later had his own show on KDAY and acted as announcer when my shows were broadcast from the Club Alabam; he became Ray Charles'[s] manager. Hunter was on for one hour every Sunday and was the first black program in South California. At first it was mainly big band jazz by Duke Ellington and Count Basie. Hunter took "Harlem Nocturne" and made it into a hit. Then at last he got music on the air every day and hit a wider audience. Little by little rock 'n' roll was born. Way back east the song pluggers used to operate, and they spread to the West Coast when Hunter got going. That's the magic of airplay, and then payola. That's how civilization develops [*laughs*].

At first there was so much overlapping of musical styles. There was more emphasis on rhythm; more animation, less bluesy. Historians point to "Gee" by the Crows and "Sh-Boom" by the Chords as the beginning of rock 'n' roll. Admittedly they were the first [R&B] records that went pop but there was a white audience before that. In 1948 the whites used to turn up at the Barrelhouse every Friday night; they ranged from the young up to forty [years old]. The accent was far more on rhythm on Fridays. Big Jay McNeely was my tenor man, and the crowd went wild when he played on his knees, then on his back shaking his legs.

Becoming a shrewd manipulator on the indie record scene, Johnny Otis label-hopped among Savoy, Mercury, Federal, and Duke-Peacock (for whom he produced two landmark R&B records, Willie Mae Thornton's "Hound Dog" and Johnny Ace's "Pledging My Love," as well as a struggling young Little Richard). Then he proceeded to form the Dig, Eldo, and other imprints. As an artist, Otis starred with "Willie and the Hand Jive" (Capitol), which, with its wicked Bo Diddley beat, was a big No. 9 hit in 1958. "We had a nice relationship[,] but they [Capitol] weren't geared for R&B," Otis stated. "They said themselves that if Atlantic had had 'Willie and the Hand Jive,' it would have sold twice as many copies." In the early 1970s, Otis was one of the first people to apply the term "national treasure" to then-forgotten R&B heroes such as Louis Jordan, Big Joe Turner, Ivory Joe Hunter, Joe Liggins, and Roy Milton. Although vastly overused since then, that accolade has been earned by Johnny Otis, too.

Leon Rene and Otis Rene: Exclusive and Excelsior Records

In the fall of 1943, following the first round of settlements with James Petrillo's AFM, led by Decca and Capitol, and with the ink hardly dry on the pacts, Leon and Otis Rene went into action by ramping up their respective Exclusive and Excelsior labels. The Rene brothers' activities were closely entwined at the outset by way of the RGR partnership, formed with jukebox distributor Jack Gutshall, who became their national record distributor. Leon, always the more progressive record man of the brothers, later made it big in the rock 'n' roll era with Class Records.

In 1931, Leon and Otis Rene, born of Creole heritage, established themselves by writing "When It's Sleepy Time Down South" with Clarence Muse for a Hollywood stage play, *Under a Virginia Moon.* The song was recorded by Louis Armstrong for OKeh after it was pitched to him during a traditional New Orleans gumbo dinner at the Rene family home in Los Angeles, with Otis singing and Leon playing piano. Featuring an early incarnation of Armstrong's scat vocals, "Sleepy Time" became Satchmo's beguiling theme song (although the original hit was by Paul Whiteman's Orchestra with Mildred Bailey for Victor). Leon Rene consolidated this success by writing another standard, "When the Swallows Come Back to Capistrano," which soared up the hit parade through sheet music sales and recordings by the Ink Spots and Glenn Miller. The result was an ASCAP award for Outstanding Song of the Year in 1940.

Being located on the West Coast, even with the movie studios at hand, the Rene brothers were having difficulty in getting the New York–based major labels to record their material. It was not easy to pitch songs to the big bands, either. As a result, the brothers, in addition to being immersed in the first wave of independent record men, were among the first black record men. Their initial target, however, was the white pop market, not the world of race music, because that was where the action was and where their musical background lay.[3]

During the 1940–41 period, Leon Rene recorded the popular jazz-based (Nat) King Cole Trio for Decca and Cole's Quartet for Jack Gutshall's Ammor label. One Cole single for Ammor would also show up on Varsity and Savoy. Leon had essayed a brief association in 1941 with pioneering personality disc jockey Al Jarvis on Make Believe Ballroom Records, named after Jarvis's KFWB radio show. The theme song, "Your Make Believe Ballroom," was written by Leon Rene and Capitol's Johnny Mercer, with Jarvis being cut in for a one-third share.[4]

Next, Otis Rene entered the frame when he released on his Excelsior marque three singles by the Cole Trio. Soon Capitol, already showing its muscle, swooped to acquire the Excelsior master of "All for You." With the resources of Glenn Wallichs and company behind it, the new release shot to No. 1 in the race charts in late 1943 (just after Capitol had settled with Petrillo). Then Leon Rene opened his account for Exclusive with former Duke Ellington vocalist Ivy Anderson's "Mexico Joe (The Jumpin' Jivin' Caballero)," a No. 16 pop hit, in the spring of 1944. Another Cole single on Excelsior, "I'm Lost," scored well regionally before he was lost forever to Capitol. Still, the associations with Al Jarvis, Johnny Mercer, and the talented, inspirational young Nat "King" Cole vividly illustrated the standing of the Rene brothers in the Los Angeles music community.[5]

Besides Nat Cole and the Johnny Otis Orchestra, the Excelsior catalog also included future jazz great Charles Mingus's first recordings as a leader with his Sextette and Orchestra (featuring vocalist Claude Trenier) and the debut by the Five Blind Boys of Mississippi (as the Jackson Harmoneers). Before long, however, Leon Rene's Exclusive Records was outpacing Otis's label with a string of race hits. Soon, the brothers would go their separate ways. The more talented Leon, a very opinionated man, was sometimes hard to get along with. By contrast, Otis was easier going, and he continued Excelsior with the support of wife Marge but without living up to earlier expectations. The brothers never wrote songs together again.[6]

Leon Rene had hit the big time in the late summer of 1945 with bandleader Joe Liggins's "The Honeydripper," a race chart topper, reputedly a million-seller, and a shining rhythmic symbol of the bright era ahead. Luminaries such as Jimmie Lunceford (with the Delta Rhythm Boys), Roosevelt Sykes (after taking "I Wonder" to the No. 1 spot), and Cab Calloway, somewhat late in the day, leapt in with cover versions that all made Top 3 in the race markets. The marauding "Honeydripper" was everywhere. Liggins and his Honeydrippers (what else?) followed up impressively with "Got a Right to Cry" (No. 2) and "Tanya" (No. 3).

Other big Exclusive records in 1945 were "I Left a Good Deal in Mobile" by Herb Jeffries (with the Honeydrippers) and "Blues at Sunrise" by Ivory Joe Hunter. In 1947,

Jeffries scored again with "When I Write My Song," followed by Johnny Moore's Three Blazers' "Merry Christmas Baby" with Charles Brown vocalizing. A later Exclusive release by Big Jay McNeely with its vanity title would hint at the growing influence of Hunter Hancock and disc jockeys generally: "Hoppin' with Hunter."

Leon's son Rafael "Googie" Rene recorded prolifically for his father's Class label during the 1950s and into the mid-1960s. When I met him in October 2004, he was living in a nursing home in Woodland Hills outside of Los Angeles, located with great serendipity on Capistrano Avenue. Recovering from a series of debilitating ailments, Googie had not lost his sunny disposition and bravely recalled the enlightened careers of his father and uncle.[7]

"Leon lived down near Baton Rouge, in Covington, Louisiana," said Googie Rene; "he was born there. Otis T. Rene was his dad. He and Mama Lee didn't have any money. Papa was a contractor—he worked on bridges—and he taught Leon how to do bricklaying. Leon was very good at it. He wore gloves to protect his hands because he played piano at night. It was terrible on his hands, mortar and all that stuff. In New Orleans, Leon played with Buddy Petit [in 1920], one of the early jazz bands, and they all played Dixieland.[8] Then Leon and Otis moved out to, like, Pennsylvania, to one of those places that were covered with steel mines." After that, the West Coast beckoned.

When Exclusive and Excelsior started up in earnest in 1944, Allied Records was the only independent pressing plant of consequence in Los Angeles. At the time, each customer was limited to the manufacture of just two hundred records a week. Nobody was allowed to enter the plant because Allied wanted to keep secret its record-pressing methods, although the technology was well established and comparatively simple. In effect, the general principle behind the record-making process was nothing more than the duplication of a surface. It was a method established in leather embossing, for example, sometimes with rollers but often by compression.[9]

In a bid to overcome the small allocations, Leon and Otis coerced Allied's employee Jimmy Beard, a black man, into building their first record press at a cost of $1,000. Thus, the Rene brothers started the RGR partnership with Jack Gutshall. Googie Rene gave a colorful description of the primitive manufacturing plant, which illustrated the do-it-yourself spirit of the times:

Now what Leon did, he bought a Packard engine and put a pulley on it like a conveyor belt, and they hired Jimmy Beard. The government wouldn't allow you to buy much shellac. I remember taking my '36 Ford coupe, a little bit of a hot rod, and putting in the trunk every record that I could buy from all the people around my area. And I got so damned many, I broke four springs carrying the heavy loads of records! They had a whole bunch: Columbia records, Decca records, Victor, and there were so many classical records.

So I would collect the records and Jimmy would melt them up [as part of the "filler," known in the business as "regrind," to augment the rationed supplies of virgin shellac]. He would use them as little briquettes, what we call biscuits. They'd take out the centers, throw them away, melted them, and made a square bar. You'd put them on the conveyor belt, you'd take them off, put them in the machine, pull it down. In three minutes you'd cut this thing, put a razor around the edge, and you made 78s! I remember the guy who made the records was Al Levine. Next door was the place that made the "silver" records. They put the mothers on this hot plate, masters to mothers—they made copies of those for the stampers. That's how they made records.[10]

Then Jack Gutshall got the distributors all over the country, and so we had distributors we'd send the record to.[11] What happened was that Joe Liggins had this hit, "The Honeydripper." Phew! We had people lined up around the block to hit the stores to buy that record. It was that big at that time, in California anyhow.

Actually, "The Honeydripper" stayed at No. 1 in the national race charts for an unprecedented eighteen weeks beginning September 8, 1945, and even crept into the pop lists at No. 13 in October. A less sophisticated version had been cut by Liggins for the Bronze label, but owner Leroy Hurte became distracted and could not promote his recording before the Exclusive hit was unleashed. Just as intriguingly, Hurte, a classically trained black musician, recorded the first rendition of "I Wonder" by Cecil Gant on Bronze in late 1944. Then Richard Nelson at Gilt-Edge stepped in to rerecord what would be the hit version using the exact arrangement. Here were two of the independent era's important breakthrough discs coming from the same source, and yet the gentlemanly Leroy Hurte managed to lose them both to hungrier competitors.[12]

Exclusive Records, basking in the success of "The Honeydripper" and way ahead of its time, self-published a promotional booklet to tie in with the National Association of Music Merchants convention in Chicago in 1946. In the introduction, it was noted that as "president of Exclusive Records, Mr. Rene stands for sure-fire hit compositions, outstanding recording artists and *new* ideas. It can truly be said that the Exclusive trademark is the crest of the distinctive wave." In a personal note, Rene added, "From symphonies to jazz, the war-weary people all over the world are music-hungry. It is up to the entire industry to serve these peoples with the best in recorded entertainment."

This was literally a mission statement, not only for Exclusive Records but for the burgeoning independent record industry as well. The promo booklet, which included artwork from the multitalented Leon Rene, hinted at Exclusive's growing ambitions, if not grand illusions:

Exclusive Records, located at Sunset and Vine, is but a stones-throw away from the pulse-beat of the entertainment world. Exclusive is surrounded by such famous Hollywood landmarks as National Broadcasting Company, Music City, Columbia Broadcasting System, Capitol Records, Vine Street—Hollywood's "Tin Pan Alley"—and all important motion picture studios.

Unique features of Exclusive's luxurious new offices designed by noted Hollywood decorator Ralph Vaughan are impressionistic murals depicting jazz trends, custom-built furniture, indirect lighting, and mirrored walls duplicating the beauty of modernistic suites.

The booklet gave welcome recognition to the "office girls": Miss Allen, Miss Kort, Miss Moseley, and Mrs. Curtice (there were no first names or initials quoted in accordance with standard practice for working women at the time). And there was no mention of brother Otis or his Excelsior label, not even in Leon's biographical write-up.

By 1948, Leon Rene, ever resourceful and adventurous but prompted by a need to combat a bootlegging epidemic through local representation, had opened a New York distribution center under the management of loyal Parker Prescott. This branch was located on Tenth Avenue in the area known in the trade as Jukebox Row, the busy East Coast hub of the aggressive jukebox distributors and operators and record distributors. There were major problems for Exclusive: trends had moved on from the sophisticated cool of the West Coast club acts, and the hits had dried up.

On December 31, 1949, *Billboard* ran a story declaring solemnly that "Exclusive Records, once one of the strongest of the Coast's indie labels, has suspended operations and placed all its masters on the sales block for the benefit of creditors. . . . Exclusive bowed in the early '40s and was one of the first in a string of locally born indie labels to reap wartime profits. During the postwar years, when other indies folded, Exclusive continued to remain strong in the indie ranks until mounting production costs caused Rene to slowly curtail costs during the past year."[13] It was like a death notice: Exclusive Records had liabilities of some $40,000.[14]

Specialty's Art Rupe attempted to purchase the Joe Liggins masters to meet distributor demand for the bandleader's old hits but was unable to come to terms with the creditors' committee. Instead, he signed Liggins direct to his label and rerecorded the Exclusive songs as catalog items. In the summer of 1950, Rupe was rewarded for his adventurous spirit when Liggins enjoyed a thirteen-week stay at No. 1 R&B with the joyous "Pink Champagne."[15] Meanwhile, Leon's brother Otis had wound down Excelsior Records earlier in 1949 to take up a more reliable vocation as a qualified pharmacist.

Leon Rene bounced back immediately from his serious setback by improbable chance: his song "Boogie Woogie Santa Claus" found itself coupled with Patti Page's mammoth Mercury hit of 1950–51, "The Tennessee Waltz." Although Mercury dropped Leon's flip side after the record continued to sell past the Christmas season, he ended up with a huge windfall as writer and publisher of "Boogie Woogie Santa Claus."

Hesitantly, Rene started up Class Records in 1953 but soon took refuge as an independent producer under the wing of Modern Records. "Leon had been a friend of the Bihari brothers since 1945 when he had the Exclusive label," explained Modern's Joe Bihari. "He felt we were the best company and had the best record promotion to do justice to [his lounge act] Oscar McLollie." In August 1956, Leon Rene relaunched Class and would reinvent himself as a forward-looking record man in the rock 'n' roll era.

The Bihari Brothers: Modern Music (Modern) Records

In 2004, Joe Bihari celebrated his seventy-ninth birthday. Relaxed and trim, he had aged well from his early adulthood, when he had the swarthy good looks of a Hollywood movie star and an energetic panache to match. In meeting and conversing with him in his latter years, it was hard to believe that this gentle, polite man was at the fulcrum of American music history. Joe Bihari was justifiably proud of his family's achievements, and his own, with Modern Records.

With brothers Jules and Saul, Joe recorded blues and R&B heroes such as Jesse Belvin, Richard Berry, Hadda Brooks, Charles Brown, the Cadets/the Jacks, Lowell Fulson, Smokey Hogg, John Lee Hooker, Elmore James, Etta James, Saunders King, Little Richard, Little Willie Littlefield, Jimmy McCracklin, Ike Turner, Johnny "Guitar" Watson, Jimmy Witherspoon, and many more. The outstanding star was B. B. King.

The three Bihari brothers started Modern Records as a tiny backstreet affair to fill their own jukeboxes within a few days of the death of President Roosevelt on April 12, 1945. Within a decade, the label was transformed into a major independent company rivaling revered labels such as Atlantic, Chess, Imperial, King, and Specialty. Jules, the senior brother of the trio, was an abrasive music man who as company president was the patriarch of the organization. The personable Saul, secretary/treasurer and front man, was always on the road in the early years, meeting and greeting and wining and dining with legendary largesse. Youngest brother Joe was vice president with responsibilities for sales and recording and was much closer to Saul than to Jules.[16]

The new label was called Modern Music, inspired by the name of a Galveston, Texas, jukebox operator where eldest Bihari brother Lester worked as a money collector in the pre–World War II days. Lester would play only a peripheral role in the growing organization before being dispatched to Memphis, where he founded the Meteor label in 1952. Modern Records was a real family business ("out of necessity," said Joe succinctly), with sisters Florette, Rosalind, and Maxine (but not Serene) working for the company in administration roles. There were a lot of mouths to feed.

This generation of Biharis (a name that has Asian and Indian origins) was the offspring of Esther Taub and Edward Bihari, who married in Philadelphia in 1911. Grandfather Joseph was a university professor in Budapest, Hungary, before joining the Jewish mass migration from Eastern Europe. Joseph is believed to have landed at Ellis Island in 1893 but was not accepted into the American university system even though he could speak seven languages. He started out in the Promised Land selling apples from a pushcart on the bustling streets of New York.

Joseph's son Edward, the Biharis' father, was employed by the Kraft Cheese Company as a salesman and became southern district manager of Myles Salt Company before starting a wholesale grain and seed business in Tulsa, Oklahoma. In 1930, he had a fatal heart attack while attempting to lift a hundred-pound bag of flour, leaving wife Esti to raise a large family of eight children in the Depression years. To ease the burden, young Joe and sister Maxine were dispatched to the Jewish Children's Home on St. Charles Avenue in uptown New Orleans and attended nearby Isidore Newman School (caustically known as "The Jewman" by pupils from other schools). Joe loved his stay in the Crescent City, soaking up the jazz and blues and the parades. By the late 1930s, he was listening to the big bands on a crystal radio set while brother Lester was sending him used jukebox records from Galveston. This is where Joe's formal education in music began.

Second brother Jules had started working for a pinball machine and jukebox operator in Oklahoma around 1935, just as the Depression was ending. Although money was in short supply, business was helped to some degree by minimal licensing requirements, low taxes, and sparse competition. What helped the sector to take off was the repeal of the Prohibition laws at the end of 1933. With his jukebox routes being located in black areas, Jules built up a useful knowledge of blues records. How Jules, or Lester, stumbled upon the emergent but ruthless coin machine sector was not exactly known to young Joe: "Jules didn't talk much about Oklahoma. He was a good jukebox operator; he knew how to handle customers. That was one of the keys: to get your jukebox in a good location, because quite often an operator [rival] would get the other jukeboxes turned around and put his own in. But Jules was smart; he knew when to give a bigger percentage to the location. That's why he kept good locations."

After the family had melded together again on the West Coast, attracted by work in the defense industries, Jules introduced Joe to the nether world of the jukebox operator. The experience was invaluable for the future record men. "Jules was operating jukeboxes in the South Central area in Los Angeles," said Joe Bihari.

He was working with Jay Bullock, an older man, an ex-miner from Nevada who was crippled—probably from gold mining [*laughs*]. I used to go down after high school and help [Jules] change records in black locations, move the machines, and collect monies. There were many jukebox operators; some would have twenty-five jukeboxes, maybe ten. We had a hundred that we operated at times.

They didn't work all the time; there was a lot of repair on jukeboxes in those days. Of course, if you'd seen some of the places that you had jukeboxes! They'd get all banged up in those little juke joints; there'd be fights, and they'd break them. So you'd get a call next day; they'd say, "Hey, jukebox not working." So you'd go out, and there it is all banged up, so you'd have to take it back and give them another one, if it's a good location. If it wasn't a good location, you'd say, "Oh, the hell with it! You don't get another one." And the more money it made, the better jukebox you gave them—a newer jukebox, one that looked better. Because there was nothing being manufactured; these were all old jukeboxes. During the war they didn't make any more jukeboxes.[17]

We operated two brands, Wurlitzer and Seeburg, and they were constantly in repair. The tubes would go out—they weren't transistorized or anything [*laughs*]—or else the record would skip and it wouldn't change. Oh man, we were constantly repairing them. You had one play for a nickel, but you got two plays for ten cents and five plays for a quarter.[18] You split the proceeds fifty-fifty, but if it was a real good location, you'd give them sixty and you'd take forty.

Another thing we'd do, we'd put fingernail polish on so many quarters and give them to the owners. It stimulated other people to play. So if nobody was playing any music, all of a sudden the owner or the bartender would go and put a quarter in. We knew how many quarters that had fingernail polish on. If there were more than that number, then we knew they were fooling around [with the cash box].

Good records are the whole secret. The better the location, the more often you changed the records. You didn't put in many new records in those days, because there weren't that many. You know, the records didn't last long because the material was so bad, and they played them 'til they were almost white from the needle going round and round and wearing them out. But it was very difficult to buy any blues records. It was 1944, '45, and the major record companies put out very few blues records. What RCA, Columbia, and Decca did, like for Los Angeles, they would send out twenty-five records for the whole city. So one day Jules said, "If we can't buy them, let's start making them." Saul got out of the army and he had the money; he saved eight hundred dollars. We stopped operating jukeboxes once we got into the record business.

The disc that inspired the Biharis to take the plunge into the record manufacturing morass was "I Wonder" by Private Cecil Gant, the No. 1 race hit for Gilt-Edge that entered the charts in October 1944. "That was on Bronze Records, the original one; it was [produced by] Leroy Hurte," said Joe Bihari.

He had a little pressing plant with two presses, and he worked for Allied Records, which was a record-pressing company that did work for Capitol.

We had a little storefront record store on First and San Pedro [four blocks from Central Avenue]; it's where we operated jukeboxes out of too. "I Wonder" came out, and we started buying it. The black train porters would come down and buy as many as they could buy from us. Then they'd take them back on the trains and sell them on their stops. And man, there was such a demand for that record; that was when we really noticed [the potential], because we were using them on the jukeboxes as well as in the record store.

It was during the war: "I wonder, my little darling, where can you be again tonight? / While the moon is shining bright, I wonder . . ." It was just a sentimental song with the GIs abroad . . . with Private Cecil Gant playing piano and singing. And Leroy had a little recording studio; he did it in his garage. What happened was he lost the record to Dick Nelson at Gilt-Edge after going to court, but I don't know how. In fact, our first test record, "Swingin' the Boogie" by Hadda Brooks, had a "Bronze" label on it.

The colossal impact of Cecil Gant's "I Wonder" far exceeded its chart status.[19] "'I Wonder' just gave me the goose bumps," recalled Don Pierce, a minority partner in the associated 4 Star Records—primarily a hillbilly imprint. "It was just something. And then I met Cecil Gant. Cliff McDonald [also of 4 Star] told me quite a lot about him: how he could never play the same song the same way twice; everything was improvised at all times. Indeed, it was very interesting to me. It was on Gilt-Edge and it started that label. I don't know how many that sold, but I do know this: I was told that one of the ways that it spread was from the Pullman porters on the railroads. They would take it to Chicago, and it would get played on the air. Then whenever they were on the run to Chicago, they would take two hundred to three hundred records with them because they could sell them for three dollars or four dollars a copy."[20] In effect, the train porters were early record distributors and promo men.

The Biharis went ahead with the formation of Modern Music Records despite the wartime shellac shortage. On April 28, 1945, *Billboard* ran a story with an April 21 dateline headed "New Recording Company Starts in Los Angeles," stating: "Heading the firm is Jules BiHari [*sic*], who for a number of years was associated in the jukebox business with Jay Bullock. Bullock is still in the music box business and he and BiHari are still associated in other activities."[21]

Catching the piano boogie-woogie fervor of the time, the elegant debut artist Hadda Brooks sold well with "Swingin' the Boogie" and "Rockin' the Boogie." Often employing classical music figures in her piano work and vocalizing like a female Nat "King" Cole, she was described by Joe Bihari as "really accomplished." He gave her credit for helping to establish Modern by selling to both white and black markets. "What I did [at the start]," said Bihari, "I'd load records into my car and go to the stores to sell them. The stores didn't have the inventories, either; they always needed new records. So I'd go around the city [and] sell them: ten to this store, twenty-five to that, or fifty. It was all cash, and we needed the cash to get the next day's production."

The grosses from the early Hadda Brooks releases led the Bihari brothers to set up their own pressing plant facility with a daily capacity of some five hundred shellac records (after rejects) over two or three shifts. There was also a 1920s hand-fed printing press. The next step was to devise a nationwide distribution system, aided by Jack Gutshall, before establishing Modern Music Distributing Company by early 1946.

"Let me tell you what happened," said Joe Bihari.

There was another company that came out with a jukebox, and Jules was very clever with jukeboxes. We went down to the distributor, who was Jack Gutshall Distributing Company, and I think the jukebox was called AMI. Jules looked at me and said, "Joe, there is gonna be nothing but trouble with this jukebox." It was a new one; there was Wurlitzer and Seeburg, and this one came out. And he knew! It didn't last very long.

The good thing was that Jack Gutshall said to Jules and myself, "I understand you got a hit record. Why don't you ship me five thousand of them?" Wow, we thought, five thousand! So we shipped him five thousand, and he sold them in California, and he reordered. And that was the time that we said, "What the hell. If he can buy that many, let's really get these jukebox operators and make them distributors."

Jack Gutshall is a forgotten father of independent record distribution. He instigated a national network by soliciting record orders from his jukebox friends in other cities. In January 1946, *Billboard* noted that "Gutshall's selling techniques and aggressiveness have proved the value of coinmen entering the record distribution." Although Gutshall did not appear to retain his initial drive, he was still listed in the grandly named 1954 *Cash Box* "Annual Encyclopedia and Directory of the Coin-Machine Industry" as a member of the elitist "20 Year Club."[22] Continued Joe Bihari:

There were three early distributors: Jack Gutshall here in Los Angeles, Julius Bard in Chicago, and Paul Reiner in Cleveland.[23] Then Saul and I got an idea, and we both took a trip around the country. See, our biggest promotion in those days was jukeboxes.

If you got a record on a jukebox, you're gonna sell records in the record store. So we sold a lot to jukebox operators directly around the country and found out who were the big buyers. Saul took a certain territory, and I took a certain territory. We went to the jukebox operators and said, "You're buying our records for your jukeboxes; you're buying Exclusive and Excelsior records. It's time for you to put on a salesman and go to the record stores. Now that you are a record distributor, you have a certain territory." That's what started the independent record distributors.

At the Modern distributors Los Angeles headquarters, Lester Sill, who had been hawking religious statuettes, was brought in as salesman. Without prompting, Joe Bihari recalled several other early Modern distributors who were "big jukebox operators": Bill Davis in Denver (Davis Sales); Jake Friedman in Atlanta (Southland Distributing Company); Buster Williams in Memphis and New Orleans (Music Sales Co.); Milt Salstone in Chicago (M. S. Distributing Co.), the "best promoter who had radio locked up"; and Sam Taran in Florida (Taran Distributing Co.), who came down from Minneapolis "with a long rap sheet . . . was as tough as he looked" but "was very friendly with Saul."

"So we started them doing the distribution of phonograph records," said Joe Bihari.[24] "Our sales to jukeboxes were probably 50 percent right at the beginning." The Modern Music distribution network was soon fully integrated on a national scale and was especially strong in Texas. By 1948, a new Houston-based distributor had been added in the form of Macy's Record Distributing Co., run by Macy Henry and young Steve Poncio. Joe remembered when brother Saul tried to convince Mrs. Henry to stock back-catalog items for the first time. Here was a lady who apparently had "her fair share of female vanity."[25] "I started checking the inventory," said Joe, "and she exploded: 'I paid for those records, they're mine, get your ass out of here!' Next day she placed a large order for back catalog." Saul Bihari had realized there was extra income to be squeezed from the popular releases of yesteryear in addition to current product.

"But we were in the right place at the right time," acknowledged Joe. "It was all timing then; I mean, the war was still going on in '45. I guess a lot of it was luck; it just happened. Oh, you had to work, oh surely; you had to have something. And, not only that, we had a lot of fun, too; it was a fun business. We also had a record store on Vermont Avenue; my sisters ran that. Then eventually they came into the office as secretaries."

According to a *Billboard* retrospective, the Bihari brothers "watched their disk manufacturing expand to hit gross sales of over $118,000 for the [first] year." Meanwhile, the Mesner brothers, near neighbors and competitors over at Aladdin, were faring well, too: "Sales of 1,500,000, reported for 1945, were contracted thru disk jockeys, juke boxes and special radio programs." On the other hand, Lew Chudd's future rhythm and blues behemoth, Imperial, was "specializing in all types of foreign folk music" and "has gained its biggest recognition in the Latin-American market."[26]

In November 1946, Modern Music had its first race chart hit with "So Long" by Johnny Moore's Three Blazers (No. 4). Six months later, the label scored with Hadda Brooks's "That's My Desire" (No. 4), a brazen competitor of the Frankie Laine smash for Mercury. Joe Bihari reckoned that a hit in those days constituted sales of at least 50,000. By now, most of the recordings were being produced at the Radio Recorders studio in Hollywood, still by cutting direct to disc, with Austin McCoy as A&R man. The introduction of wire recording was a non-event. "It didn't work very well," agreed Joe, "so from the wire then Ampex came out with their tape machine, and Magnecord came out with theirs."

Modern was doing well enough to announce in March 1947 "the opening of our new offices and plant" at 686 North Robertson Boulevard, Hollywood. These premises were acquired from defunct ARA Records. Interestingly, the ARA bankruptcy along with the faltering of other labels led to the widespread belief at the time that the days of the independent sector were limited. There was loose trade talk of "muddled finances," label mergers, formation of "distribution combines," and the "pooling" of pressing facilities.[27] The Bihari brothers clearly had more confidence in the future. Now outside business was being sought to keep the presses at full tilt, with the machinery being operated mainly by the downtrodden, recently liberated Japanese exiles living in California. This facility lasted until 1950, when the Biharis sold out to expansion-minded Mercury Records.

Modern Records (minus the "Music" tag) was incorporated formally on January 28, 1948, just as the second Petrillo recording ban was taking effect. The slicker-named organization had its first race chart topper in November 1948 with "Blues after Hours" by guitarist Pee Wee Crayton, who followed up with "Texas Hop," a No. 5 success.

Joe Bihari loved the action surrounding hit records.

You were constantly on the telephone; you couldn't relax. A hit made you feel good because you'd call a disc jockey, [and] they'd say, "We're on that, man; it's moved up to No. 3 [locally]." Then you'd get on the phone with the distributor, he'd maybe have five hundred still in stock, and I'd say, "I've just talked to this guy, he said it's No. 3 and it's going up to No. 1." "You'd better send me another thousand." You got on the phone to sell. It was an exciting business in those days.[28]

We had some distributors that were slow paying, but we went along with it. You didn't cut them off. A lot of companies would say, "You can't get anymore until I get paid," but we wouldn't. We knew that in time we'd get paid. They might be short with money right now, but they had your inventory: the "accounts receivable" in the books. We knew what being a distributor was like. If we felt things were going bad, we'd say, "Have you anything you want to return to reduce your bill?" You are like a banker.

Aware of the strength of down-home music, the Biharis picked up masters from the Texas labels of Gold Star, run by Houston studio owner Bill Quinn (Harry Choates and Lightnin' Hopkins), and Blue Bonnet, run by Dallas distributor Herb Rippa (Smokey Hogg). In the San Francisco–Oakland area, acetates were acquired from David Rosenbaum's Rhythm label (Saunders King) and from Bob Geddins's Down Town (Lowell Fulson, Roy Hawkins, and Jimmy McCracklin). By buying in this finished product, the Biharis were easing the pressures on their own creative endeavors in the recording studios while facilitating the growth of their label. It was a strategy that was implemented by other larger independents.

The Pee Wee Crayton hits for Modern were followed swiftly by John Lee Hooker's "Boogie Chillen," a bought-in master purchase that became a No. 1 race hit in February 1949. Hooker's vocal and Stella guitar rang out, literally, from every jukebox in black locations in the South. The record was broken over Radio WLAC, Nashville, after Saul Bihari had negotiated a deal for the brand new acetate with Bernie Besman and John Kaplan of Pan American Record Distributors (Modern's Detroit outlet). "I went to Nashville," said Joe Bihari. "[Disc jockey] Gene Nobles heard it, [and] he said, 'Oh, let me have that!' It's not even out yet, it's that new. He put it on twelve straight times, just over and over and over again, and, of course, it's a 50,000–watt clear-channel station. Next day I talked to Jules, and he said, 'What's this "Boogie Chillen"?' I said, 'Oh, you haven't heard it yet?' He said, 'We're having calls from every distributor in the country.' It was just an overnight smash." This success with "Boogie Chillen" would encourage the Biharis (and other indie record men) to venture deeper into the down-home blues idiom and to recognize the selling power of Radio WLAC.

Earlier in January 1948, Saul Bihari set up an eastern distribution headquarters for Modern along the lines of the Exclusive Records initiative.[29] From July until the following February, younger brother Joe was placed in charge of this facility in New York. There, he was able to convince Bob Shad, who was struggling with his Sittin' In With label, that there was a much better market for blues recordings than for jazz. Recalled Joe:

> I took Bobby out on a trip, and he had his jazz, and he couldn't sell very much of it. Jazz was okay for New York, Boston, Chicago, but not for the South; he didn't even have distribution [there]. I introduced him to our distributors. They would take ten of this, twenty-five of that, whereas I was selling five thousand at each distributor. He saw the difference; now he woke up. 'I know what I'm doing wrong,' he said. He realized he couldn't stay in business by just making jazz records.
>
> Then we were travelling from New York, [and] we got outside New Orleans. It was a Friday, and I was driving. Bobby said, "What's your hurry?" I said, "I wanna get in and go to temple tonight." He didn't know I was Jewish [*laughs*].

While on the road in 1949, possibly on the same trip, Joe Bihari recorded for Modern's new Colonial subsidiary the street blues guitarist Pine Top Slim in Atlanta and Cajun swing artists Chuck Guillory and Papa Cairo at a radio station in Crowley, Louisiana (probably KSIG). "The old French Cajuns, we knew we could sell the records there, purely to sell in Texas and Louisiana, some in Mississippi, too," said Bihari, "because Ed Roberson, our distributor at Music Sales in New Orleans, told us so." Here was a striking example of local distributor knowledge adding value to regional markets.[30]

As a sure sign of Modern's rapid growth and increasing stature, the Bihari brothers formed in 1950 another subsidiary label, RPM. The thinking behind this decision, which was repeated by most indie companies, was conveyed in a press release in *Bill-*

board dated October 7, 1950: "Modern Records is launching its subsid label, RPM Records, thru a new web of 25 distribs, thereby permitting the firm to have two outlets in a single territory. Coast-based indie found many of its distribs unwilling to absorb too many releases of the Modern line. Hence to avoid existing distribs carrying heavy inventory, it is funneling its subsid label to the new distribs. RPM's talent roster will differ from artists on the Modern label, but label's policy will adhere to the rhythm-blues line held by Modern."[31]

By widening the distributor network, Modern-RPM was spreading the load and avoiding the risk of any delinquent accounts disproportionately upsetting cash flow. Just as significantly, these subsidiary labels were welcomed by the dee-jays in order to give the outward impression, at least, that certain labels were not being favored excessively.[32]

Much of the Biharis' mastery in making Modern Records a strong indie force could be attributed to their integrated teamwork and hard work. "Recording, traveling," said Joe with a sigh. "I worked my eight to ten hours in the office; I was always the first one there, and I did all my recording at night. When I was traveling, it was recording, visiting distributors, and promotion. Stay up all night with disc jockeys that had a show from midnight to 1 A.M., or 11 P.M. to 1 A.M. You were up with them; it became routine. Like in Houston, I had to see my distributor the next day, [so] I didn't go to bed. After him I just slept, then drive all night long." Atlanta distributor Jake Friedman called Joe a "little macher"—a hustling young operator.

Already the Biharis were showing a keen understanding of the developing rhythm and blues market through their excellent relations with the jukebox industry and the ever-rising number of disc jockeys, aided by a first-class nationwide distribution system and releases that had commercial appeal. Moreover, the publishing adjunct Modern Music (the old record company name) was to be a veritable cash cow. By the advent of the 1950s, Modern Records was much more than a local California label.

Art Rupe: Juke Box and Specialty Records

Art Rupe, among the smartest of independent record men, guided Specialty Records into making the transition from niche R&B and gospel music to international rock 'n' roll with a most impressive artist lineup, including Roy Milton, the Soul Stirrers, Lloyd Price, Guitar Slim, Sam Cooke, Larry Williams, and Little Richard.

In 2006, the tireless eighty-nine-year-old Art Rupe was engrossed in administering his educational foundation. Over a three-year period, this perpetually reluctant interviewee reflected graciously, by tape and e-mail, on the industry factors that enabled Specialty Records and its competitors to thrive. I had first met him at his Sunset Boulevard office in 1975 when visiting Los Angeles to dig into the Specialty vaults to compile vinyl albums for Sonet Records of London and Sweden. At the time nearly sixty years old, Rupe had long retired as a full-time record man but was still full of nervous energy. Regrettably, those Sonet releases were ruined by the ghastly use of the electronic/pseudo-"stereo" mechanism of the time.

The cerebral Arthur Goldborough had set out for the West Coast in 1939 from his home state of Pennsylvania, intent on making a career in the movies. After studying at UCLA, he discovered the film industry was too much of a closed shop. The infant record business, on the other hand, offered better opportunities to the bright if raw novice (who by now had taken on a new identity, Rupe).[33] Art's learning curve moved sharply upward in early 1944 when he invested a few hundred dollars in Robert Scherman's Premier Records, soon changed to Atlas, and lost it all.

Seeing that the "sepia" record market (an alternative term to "race") was wide open, an unshaken Art Rupe made a detailed analysis of what it took to produce a hit record. He noted that many popular records had the word "boogie" in the title and that the jukebox operators were the main customers. And so his first release was "Boogie #1" on the new Juke Box label by the Sepia Tones. Recorded in August 1944, it sold some 70,000 copies to replenish his depleted bank account and provide him with vital working capital.

In a quick-fix attempt to achieve national status for his new label, Rupe merged the Juke Box operation with Sterling Records of New York and promptly found himself with a No. 2 national race hit, "R. M. Blues" by Roy Milton and his Solid Senders. The train of events was related by Rupe:

> Shortly after my ill-fated investment in Premier-Atlas Records, which was really the precursor to my entry into the recording industry, I started Juke Box Records. Since I had only limited exposure to the industry (about three months), needed more know-how, and had virtually no capital, I made Ben Siegert, who was recently laid off by Premier, a one-third partner rather than have to pay him much salary.
>
> After a while, it became apparent to me that Ben really had neither the distribution savvy nor record experience I had hoped for. Despite our limited distribution, our early Juke Box Records, particularly "R. M. Blues," were making some industry noise, and about that time Ben had phoned Al Middleman for information. Ben mentioned that Al Middleman (whom I believe he knew from Pittsburgh) had just sold Hit Records, really knew distribution, and was based in New York City.
>
> Before I knew it, being in my twenties and naive, Juke Box had some additional partners. Shortly thereafter, I discovered that Al Middleman (and us) had a silent partner, Eli Oberstein, Al's silent partner in Hit Records. Of interest, Eli Oberstein was the A&R man at RCA Records, arguably the largest record company in the country. My idea was to get both national distribution and business guidance, since my goal was to just be a creative and effective record producer. The sales and distribution part of the business didn't appeal to me.

Running a pressing plant did not appeal to Rupe, either, but it was a necessity, as he recalled: "In the early days of shellac composition 78–rpm records, pressing plants were few, and supply couldn't keep pace with demand. When I partnered with Middleman and Oberstein, we decided to build our own plant in Los Angeles. Not being mechanically inclined, I did research on hydraulics and materials in the library, and with consulting help from other record plant employees, I cobbled together a pressing plant.

Needless to say, running a factory wasn't my cup of tea, and as soon as more capacity from competing plants became available, we shut down our plant. The period of this experience was all of 1945 and early 1946."

At Juke Box Records, a monetary wrangle blew up during the course of Roy Milton's twenty-five-week chart run from spring to fall 1946. "The dispute and breakup occurred because I felt we weren't getting meaningful and proper accounting," related Art Rupe, "along with the fact that I didn't feel comfortable with the limited communication between us in Los Angeles and them in New York. At the partnership dissolution, I became independent and alone because Ben Siegert decided his future would best be served by remaining with them, and he did." From then on, Rupe was always in control of his various businesses. It was another valuable lesson.

As a postscript to the failed partnership, Sterling cut the debut recordings by Hank Williams soon after Rupe's abrupt departure. The first record, "Calling You" (with the Country Boys), introduced "a new Hillbilly series" and was advertised in *Billboard:* "For singing real country songs Hank Williams is tops. He's a big favorite wherever he's heard, and this record will sell like hot cakes."[34] The promising hillbilly artist was signed to Sterling on a short-term, flat-fee, no royalty contract through the highly respected Fred Rose (of the rapidly expanding Nashville music publishers Acuff-Rose). Before long, Williams was placed with the quasi-major MGM label under Frank Walker's direction and would change country music forever.[35]

Plainly disillusioned, Rupe credited Modern's Jules Bihari with giving him the necessary moral support to start up another label with those Juke Box masters. "Yes, I was despondent and nervous after the split," he said.

> I had now failed in my first two partnerships in the record industry. I knew Jules Bihari of Modern Records and approached him for a job as a record producer. With all the brothers and sisters in his family already in the business, he really didn't need me. Instead, he encouraged me to go it alone. I did, and Specialty Records was born.
>
> The original Juke Box masters which I had recorded were returned to me in the dissolution. However, my former partners continued to sell my recordings by claiming they were just selling old inventory, which I always suspected otherwise. So, I had unintended competition from my own records.

Somewhat uncertainly, Specialty Records was launched in August 1946 from 2719 West Seventh Street, Los Angeles. Included in the retrieved catalog was the compulsively swinging, tightly arranged "R. M. Blues" by Roy Milton and his Solid Senders. Milton, who left Rupe temporarily to help form the Roy Milton label (with its irreverent cartoon labels), was to rack up seventeen race and R&B hits on Specialty between 1947 and 1953. He was the linchpin of the label's early roster, along with his torch singing/boogie-woogie pianist Camille Howard, orchestra leader brothers Jimmy and Joe Liggins, and songsmith supreme Percy Mayfield. There was a solid gospel line headed by the Pilgrim Travelers and the Soul Stirrers.

Just like Leon Rene and the Bihari brothers, Art Rupe quickly understood the need for a national distribution setup. "I realized that the key to getting efficient record distribution was to establish our own independent network of record distributors," he said.

> I started a pilot program called Specialty Record Sales Co. when we were at 311 Venice Boulevard in Los Angeles [from February 1947] and distributed Specialty, Savoy, and Downbeat Records.
>
> After about six months, based on this limited distribution experience, I convinced Aladdin, Miracle, and several other of my peers to join together to create our own distribution outlets. That's the way our first joint venture—Central Record Sales in Los Angeles—was born with Jim Warren as manager. Before long, the partners began to feel that other members of the group were getting more emphasis on their labels than they did, and there was internecine grumbling. So much for that venture, and we dissolved.

Billboard alluded to this dissolution in a short story dated November 26, 1949: "The Portem distribbery will take over the New York distribution of Specialty, Aladdin and Aladdin's subsidiary, Score. The three lines were formerly handled by the AMS branch office here. . . . The AMS tag originally stood for Aladdin, Miracle and Specialty, and was conceived as a co-op branch distribbery. Miracle, however, withdrew from the arrangement here, but the AMS name persisted."[36]

"So I decided to go it alone," said Art Rupe, "and set up distribution outlets. In order to get other labels, because Specialty Records was really not large enough to support a well-functioning staff, the individual record sales people I partnered with landed additional label lines for distribution. It wasn't revealed that Specialty Records was really the funder and a very silent partner. After a few years, I sold my interests to each of the managers. The independent record industry grew and profited by having these additional distribution points in key cities."

In addition to Jim Warren at Central Sales in Los Angeles, Rupe remembered his network of record salesmen partners as including Dick Sturgell at A-1 Distribution Co., New Orleans (followed by Joe Banashak); Steve Poncio at United Record Distributors, Houston; Paul Glass at Allstate Distributing Co., Chicago; and Henry Stone "and then someone else" in Miami. There was also the forgotten head of Central Record Sales, New York.

In those past interviews, Art Rupe rarely, if ever, acknowledged that his brother Manny Goldberg headed the influential firm of Mangold Distributors in Baltimore, Maryland, while another brother, Phil, ran distributorships in Charlotte, North Carolina. "I helped set up my two brothers, both younger than I and now deceased, in Baltimore and Charlotte," Rupe confirmed in 2006. "They were fairly good distributors and did well for Specialty and the other labels they handled."

What did Specialty's distributors expect from Art Rupe, apart from potential hit records? "This is an easy one," he said.

> They wanted freebies, favorable terms, and expanded territories, little of which we gave them. The distributor was very important, if he was efficient—that is, getting

out sample records to the key jockeys, getting them publicized, and getting the record heard. If the record began to be in demand, then the efficient distributor had good inventory control and . . . was able to keep on top of the demand by ordering in sufficient quantities.

I had sales representatives; each one handled a territory consisting of several distributors. Like the eastern rep would handle the whole East Coast and part of the Midwest, then the southern rep would handle part of the Midwest and the South. And then I had one here on the West Coast. I concentrated on product creation and advertising ideas with minimal distribution contact on my own.

As for record pressing, the other part of the equation in the quest for self-sufficiency, Art Rupe devised a national network of yet more silent partnerships that endured from "late 1946 through the 1960s."[37] Specialty Records, therefore, was extremely well positioned to take advantage of the upcoming rock 'n' roll revolution.

Henry Stone: Early Record Distributor

Henry Stone's interest in record distribution and label ownership was nurtured in the industry's infancy in the Golden State, before he moved to Florida in late 1947. He had found himself in California around 1946 with his mother and sister after a spell in the army. Born in the Bronx, he had played trumpet as a teenager in his band, Rocky Stone and his Little Pebbles, in the popular Jewish resorts in the Catskill Mountains. He was to make his name first as a pivotal distributor in Miami and then as an integral cog of the 1970s disco boom through his TK label.

In 2004, the eighty-three-year-old Stone still had his trademark Colonel Sanders–type beard. He had slowed down following a failed eye operation that had left him legally blind. However, he was intent on using the Internet to sell his old (and new) product and, just as important, to proclaim his place in history. If he had held on to his masters and publishing, he would be worth $25 million, he reckoned. Nevertheless, he was living comfortably with his wife, Inez, in a penthouse suite in opulent grounds overlooking the water at Grove Isle, Florida. This was wealthy Old Miami. He recalled, breezily, his Californian beginnings.

Of course, being interested in the music business I got involved with Ben Pollack. He was from Jewel Records . . . not Stan Lewis's Jewel [of Shreveport, Louisiana]. Ben Pollack was an old band leader for Benny Goodman, etc., and I ended up sort of working for Ben Pollack as an all-duty man. He had Kay Starr, the "Wheel of Fortune" girl, [and] also Boyd Raeburn. No hits but just good, great music.

I was real young and energetic, making a sort of a living there a little bit. I ended sort of working for Modern Records, for Jules and Saul Bihari. I needed to make extra money, so I picked up records at the end of the day. They had one of the first pressing plants after the war. Of course, the biggest demand was from jukeboxes; the operators needed material for their routes to make money. There were no record players—maybe some old Victrolas, but there were no 45s, LPs, all that stuff. People would say, "What business are you in?" or, "What's a record?" because there was no demand [for records] at all. Whatever music they heard was on the radio. It was the old transcriptions, steel things with a little vinyl on top, sixteen-inch discs. That's the way the music basically came from, all live bands, because there were no records.

But they started a pressing plant, Jules, Saul, and young Joe. And what I did while I was working for Ben Pollack, I used to go to Modern, Exclusive, Excelsior, and Cadet Records [owned by Jack Riley]. They had started to make records, and there were no outlets basically other than in Central Avenue. There were a few shoeshine parlors, furniture stores; I mean, there were hardly any record stores. So I took these records to the jukebox operators out of my car.

While I was bringing all these little independents' records around, nobody knew what they were. The little stores, whatever, they didn't know what a Modern record was or who was on it. I came up with an idea, and I put out a thing called the *Indie Index*. My brother-in-law was a printer, [and] he put a magazine together. I used to go down and put the type together, cross-listed the artists and the titles; I did all this. Modern Records had a printing press, and I took it over to Modern and I printed up the *Indie Index*, which I circulated all through California. Then I started sending it out to whatever stores were out there in the rest of the country.

"He didn't know where to go to have them printed," confirmed Joe Bihari, "so we printed the first ones for him. Didn't make any money, either; I think we just did it as a favor."

Could Henry Stone see the potential in the record business? "No, no! If I'd have thought about it, I would have opened up a distributing company in California. I was only selling records out of the back of my car." That was in true pioneering record man style, of course. But with enterprising people in control such as Leon Rene, the Bihari brothers, and Art Rupe, the independent labels were taking off in California— and elsewhere.

Early independent record pressing plant, 78–rpm metal-stamper era: King Records, Cincinnati, Ohio, c. 1947. Courtesy Gusto Records, Inc., Nashville.

Berle Adams, first president of Mercury Records, at his desk, c. 1946. Courtesy Berle Adams.

Mercury Records' Irving Green with label pop artists Frankie Laine *(left)* and Vic Damone *(right)*, c. 1947. Courtesy Showtime Music Productions.

Berle Adams *(right)*, Louis Jordan's personal manager, with Jordan, 1948. Courtesy Berle Adams.

The Bihari family dining at Max Rosenbloom's nightclub, Slapsie Maxie's, in Los Angeles just after the launch of Modern Music Records, 1946. Jules Bihari *(bottom left)*, Saul Bihari *(to his left)*, and Joe Bihari *(bottom right)*. Courtesy Joe Bihari.

"THE JOINT'S JUMPIN'" says juke box king Barney "Sugie" Sugerman of Runyon Sales, Exclusive's N. Y. Distributors, as he discusses the sensational success of Joe Liggins' Exclusive recording of the "Honeydripper." (left to right) Sugerman, Leon Rene, Distributor Jack Gutshall and Liggins.

Bernard Sugarman (Runyon Sales), Leon Rene (Exclusive Records), Joe Liggins, and Jack Gutshall (distributor), 1946 (top). Exclusive's executive secretary "Miss" Gloria Kort, with brother Bob Hayward (bottom). Courtesy Rafael "Googie" Rene and Tony Jones, Leon Rene Family Partnership.

Exclusive Records trade display, 1946, showing 78–rpm releases headed by Joe Liggins's "The Honeydripper"; photographs of musical director Buddy Baker *(left)* and label head Leon Rene; and a section highlighting the label's distributors. Courtesy Rafael "Googie" Rene and Tony Jones, Leon Rene Family Partnership.

Art Rupe at Specialty office, 311 Venice Boulevard, Los Angeles, c. 1947. Courtesy Showtime Music Productions.

Henry Stone on the bandstand before a career as a distributor and record man, Camp Kilmer, New Brunswick, New Jersey, 1942. Courtesy Dan Kochakian and *Blues & Rhythm*, with acknowledgment to Henry Stone.

Advertisement for Taran Distributing, the major early Florida jukebox and record distributor, 1954. Courtesy John Broven.

Herman Lubinsky, Savoy
Records, with obligatory cigar,
1940s. Courtesy Showtime
Music Productions.

Bess Berman, Apollo Records,
with the "5" Royales, 1954.
Courtesy John Broven.

Jerry Wexler, Ahmet Ertegun, and Miriam Abramson at Atlantic Records office with a *Cash Box* award, 1954. Background artist photographs *(clockwise from top):* the Clovers, Joe Turner, Clyde McPhatter and the Drifters, and Ruth Brown. By PoPsie, courtesy Michael Randolph.

Arthur Shimkin, Golden Records *(second right),* listening to playback with Jimmy Dorsey, Tommy Dorsey, and A&R man Morty Palitz *(standing)* at Fine Studios, New York, 1953. Courtesy John Broven, with acknowledgment to Arthur Shimkin.

Golden Records' Arthur Shimkin *(left)* and Columbia A&R man Mitch Miller in studio editing room, New York, 1954. Courtesy John Broven, with acknowledgment to Arthur Shimkin.

Johnny Otis outside Capitol Tower, Hollywood, c. 1958. Courtesy Showtime Music Productions.

JOHNNY OTIS

4

CHAPTER

New York: Big City and Little Tiffany

CAST OF CHARACTERS
Doc Pomus, Apollo Records artist and songwriter
Lee Magid, National and Savoy Records
Jerry Wexler, Atlantic Records
Miriam Bienstock, Atlantic Records
Ahmet Ertegun, Atlantic Records
also featuring Bess Berman, Apollo Records;
Al Green, National Records; and Herman Lubinsky,
Savoy Records

Jerome Felder, known professionally as Doc Pomus, was an ardent admirer and advocate of the effervescent New York music scene throughout his lifetime. A unique man who overcame the terrible affliction of polio, he started out as a Jewish blues shouter in the 1940s and emerged as a noted writer of teen songs in the rock 'n' roll age. In 1958, he had the briefest of flirtations with label ownership when he formed R n B Records with Fred Huckman, resulting in the release of "Kiss and Make Up" by the Crowns. The nucleus of this group, including Ben E. King and Charlie Thomas, was promptly embedded into a new set of Drifters who cut "Save the Last Dance for Me," Pomus's all-time classic collaboration with Mort Shuman for Atlantic Records.

Long confined to a wheelchair, Doc Pomus was in exuberant form over Sunday brunch in 1986 as he set the scene for those electric times in 1940s New York. "There were clubs all over the place—and excitement," he enthused.

> You felt great energy, great vibes all over the place. I guess the band got "sent" by the crowd, and the crowd got "sent" by the band. In those days, when people went out they would always get dressed up.

Not only that, but they got along well with each other. There was no racial problem—at least I wasn't aware of that; there was no such thing as a club that was all black or all white.

The music was jazz and rhythm and blues. Fifty-second Street was a long row of jazz clubs, between Fifth Avenue and Eighth Avenue. Among the clubs were the Three Deuces and Jimmy Ryan's. They all had the best jazz musicians—but it was fascinating! In one club, Kelly's Stable, they put on a show where instead of a singer, you would have a saxophone player like Coleman Hawkins or Pete Brown. They would get up and do three songs, backed by an orchestra, and then they would get down. Now you could go from club to club. You'd see Art Tatum, [in] the next club you'd see Billie Holiday, and [in] the next club you'd see Milt Jackson working.

In Brooklyn there was at least forty clubs that had a black kind of entertainment. And then you had Harlem with an enormous amount of clubs. The Baby Grand on 125th Street was the main club in Harlem which featured always a great blues singer, like Joe Turner. Then they would have a shake dancer, like a stripper, and very often a popular singer of songs. The master of ceremonies for many, many years was Nipsey Russell. I was discouraged from spending time at the Savoy Ballroom because there was a long flight of steps to get up there. But it had a phenomenal reputation. Buddy Johnson had the house band, and Arthur Prysock used to sing with Ella Johnson. There was a group from there called the Lindy-Hoppers, which was a great troupe of dancers featuring Rosetta Davis. She was an absolutely gorgeous girl, breathtakingly beautiful!

Music man Lee Magid had good memories of the Big Apple, too. "New York was the place," he said. "You had Fifty-second Street with all the jazz clubs. And you had the big nightclub revues: you had the Latin Quarter, you had Leon and Eddie's, the Copacabana, a lot of stuff. There were a lot of ballrooms and dance halls in Manhattan at the time, and they had a lot of Latin bands. Everybody had a different night for different dances. Up in the Bronx . . . every borough had their own thing."

Hand in hand with this bright nightlife, a strong independent record scene was taking root. Doc Pomus remembered some of the early record characters, their labels, and his own sessions:

I used to know Joe Davis as a guy who made rhythm and blues records [on Beacon] very early in the 1940s. He probably had some records that were popular with a small segment of the population, but it was not as popular, say, as an Apollo or Savoy. They were more popular in terms of building that kind of music, which at that time was called race music.

Apollo Records was owned by a woman, Bess Berman. She was a very tough kind of lady, and everybody was terrified of being in a room with her because she seemed a very strong, aggressive woman. I think Apollo was a very influential label. I was very fortunate recording for them, but they were influential because they had people like Wynonie Harris and Mahalia Jackson. There was no such thing as an A&R man then. I remember when we were recording, there was a guy at Apollo who was in charge of the sessions, a saxophone player, Jerry Jerome. He'd come in at the beginning of a session and say, "Well, you guys, everybody's showed up." They all signed the [union] slip. And then he'd say, "Well, you guys know what you are doing." And we did. There was us and the engineer; it was always like that [*laughs*].

Bess Berman was a formidable lady indeed. A May 29, 1948, news story in *Billboard*, "Apollo Names Mrs. Berman to Head Firm," indicated that there had been a palace revolution at Apollo: "Mrs. Bess Berman was elected prexy of Apollo Records at a board of directors' meeting Thursday [May 27]. . . . This followed her outright purchase of the holdings of former-Prexy Hy Siegal and partner Sam Schneider last week. Mrs. Berman is well known in the trade for activity in the juke box field and with the diskery. Contrary to earlier reports, her husband, Isaac (Ike) Berman, who operates a pressing plant, did not acquire any portion and will not be directly connected with the Apollo organization. But his plant will continue to press for the diskery." Under Queen Bee's new rule, a hive full (literally) of directors was named by *Billboard* confirming that Apollo was an indie label of some substance.[1]

Apollo Records had emerged from Rainbow Music Shop on 125th Street in Harlem way back in 1944. The changing of the guard came just after Mahalia Jackson had hit the national charts with "Move On Up a Little Higher" in January 1948, and she continued to be Apollo's best-seller in the gospel and pop fields. In 1953, the "5" Royales had No. 1 R&B hits with "Baby, Don't Do It" and "Help Me Somebody." After Mahalia absconded to Columbia a year later, by "mutual agreement," Bess Berman fell ill, and her label was never a real force again.[2] But *Cash Box* was right when it described her in 1954 as "the only woman ever able to break through with outstanding success in the male-dominated recording industry."[3]

Continuing his personal trawl of the early New York labels, Doc Pomus said:

Derby was owned by Larry Newton. He had a partner who owned Rainbow Records, Eddie Heller. Now Derby was a bad payer. I really had to threaten Larry Newton to pay me my money he owed me. On the record I did for them, the saxophone was played by Freddie Mitchell, who later played on a big hit record called "Easter Parade" [No. 7 R&B, April 1950]. Larry Newton became the head of ABC-Paramount Records.[4]

Then I used to see a label called Gotham [founded by maverick retail discounter Sam Goody and acquired in 1948 by Philadelphia record presser Ivin Ballen]. There were lots of little jazz labels that come into existence to record people like Charlie Parker and Dizzy Gillespie [such as Guild and Manor]. I only know these labels as a collector because I always considered myself in those days to be more of a collector who, incidentally, made records for himself.

The Big Apple jazz labels also numbered Commodore (Milt Gabler), Blue Note (Alfred Lion and Francis Wolff), and, in 1950, Prestige (Bob Weinstock).

"National Records was the company that recorded the first song of mine," stated Pomus. "It was Gatemouth Moore with 'Love Doctor Blues' [in 1946]. But what was interesting about it, I met Herb Abramson, producer at National Records, and Tommy Dowd, the engineer. They were extraordinary. They were really kings of blues and rhythm and blues, producers and engineers. Then they brought their expertise into Atlantic Records. I'm sure that everything that Ahmet Ertegun and Jerry Wexler learned, they learned from Herb Abramson and Tommy Dowd."

Lee Magid: National and Savoy Records

Lee Magid joined National Records in July 1948 to handle the music publishing and to carry out studio duties. Although it was the middle of the second Petrillo recording ban, National's hard-drinking boss Al Green needed to replace A&R man Herb Abramson, who had jumped ship earlier to cofound Atlantic Records.

Ever the hustler with the staccato speech to match, Magid was intrigued by the big bands as a youngster. "I was always looking to connect," he said,

> to be with somebody where I could play my horn. And we took the big orchestrations from Glenn Miller, all stock arrangements, that's what we did. So I was a little different to most of the kids; most everybody else lived in the poolroom [*laughs*]. I was shipping [sheet] music over at Warner Brothers, at Harms; I was a high-class errand boy. I became the youngest song plugger; they put me in the union [about 1945].
>
> You know, everybody cared. Tin Pin Alley was part of the community, and everybody knew each other. There was always a special place for everyone to hang out: the comics had their place, the musicians had the others, the singers had theirs, the booking agents had theirs, the managers . . . I played around with all of it. It was a different era. Everybody thought they were another Irving Berlin or Cole Porter. The young black artists, the writers who weren't making it then, they were still in the service.
>
> I was at 1650 Broadway; that's where all the action was, there and at 1619 Broadway. So I went between both buildings [and] made a lot of contacts, including Jerry Blaine at Cosnat distributors, who liked what I was doing. So I came to work for Jerry. I said, "I'll promote your records; I know some disc jockeys and promoters." So I wound up with three or four accounts: National Records was one of our accounts, and we had Billy Eckstine, Joe Turner, the Ravens, Dusty Fletcher. At the time I was busted out, but I got something like fifteen dollars apiece for each account, and I had these record companies, and I had cash now. I never had that kind of money.

And so Lee Magid, "working wherever I could make a buck," became a record promotion man for Cosnat, trying to break race artists on white radio stations. It was an almost impossible task unless his satchel contained the smooth sounds of Billy Eckstine and the Ravens. To put the era into perspective, the breakthrough black ballplayer Jackie Robinson did not start playing for the Brooklyn Dodgers until 1947.

The Cosnat name, incidentally, was an amalgam of two record labels: Cosmo and National. Jerry Blaine himself was a bandleader who had three hits on Bluebird in 1938 and was destined to assume an important if rather understated historical role in developing the independent record business. He was the East Coast pioneer distributor equivalent of California's Jack Gutshall.

"Jerry Blaine? I loved him," said Lee Magid.

He was a jolly kind of a guy. He used to be a trombone player, but he was a business-man; he had two brothers, Elliot and Ben, and they helped him. He was great: I could call him on the phone any time. He screwed a lot of people and things like that, they say, but I don't think so.

Al Green was the president of National. He was an old union organizer from Chi-cago: the Painters Union.[5] We had the biggest independent company because we had our own pressing plant [National Record Pressing]. Al Green used to press the records on "sand and pebble" [inferior material for making records] so that the people would break their needles and [had to] go out and buy new needles and records [laughs]. He was the father of Irving Green, who came into Mercury Records.

So I got to learn everything. . . . I stayed with National for about two years until they went down. If you can believe it, "If I Knew You Were Comin' I'd've Baked a Cake" with Eileen Barton . . . was a smash [No. 1 pop, spring 1950]. Anyway, it killed us because we had already lost Billy Eckstine to MGM, [and] we lost the Ravens and they were breaking up; Ben Bart [the talent agent] took them. The record distributors wouldn't do nothing for us anymore; we couldn't make enough money to pay the bills. He [Al Green] had to close up his pressing plants. And we had it all because everyone would come to us for pressings when they couldn't get shellac. That's how we stayed in business until they closed up.

Thus, Lee Magid began working as an A&R man for the Savoy label in November 1950 following an introduction from Irving Siders, a top agent with Shaw Artists Cor-poration.

Founded eight years earlier, Savoy Records was based at 58 Market Street, Newark, New Jersey, and soon rose to prominence as a heavyweight independent label on the eastern seaboard. Savoy's owner, Herman Lubinsky, was already a rich man but was an arrogant bully with his wealth. Here was the quintessential loudmouth, overweight, cigar-smoking record man with little apparent charm or saving graces. Of his many quirks, he would insist upon letters being written (for the record) instead of taking telephone calls. And if he made a call, even to a distributor, he would call collect. With his ruthless, self-serving business practices, he did his industry few public rela-tions favors. Yet he always had a firm handle on the ever-evolving independent record industry. In short, for all his personal failings, he was a brilliant record man.

On paper, Savoy Records was an excellent operation with a stellar roster that would include Charlie Parker, Lester Young, Erroll Garner, Paul Williams, Little Jimmy Scott, and Johnny Otis with Little Esther. A firm devotee of the blues and jazz markets, Lu-binsky never came to grips with rock 'n' roll music and quietly wound down the R&B division after the 1959 payola scandal. However, Savoy was able to create an enviable niche in the relatively payola-free gospel field, first through Clara Ward and the Ward Singers and then with the various choirs of Reverend James Cleveland. Savoy was an assiduous gatherer of defunct indie labels through the years, including Otis Rene's Ex-celsior Records, Ben Pollack's Jewel Records, Fred Mendelsohn's Regent Records—and Al Green's National Records.

Lubinsky had become a radio pioneer in 1923 when he founded New Jersey station WRAZ. Within two years he had changed the call letters to WNJ (Wireless New Jersey) that became known as the Voice of Newark and New Jersey's Friendly Station. Aware of the indigenous immigrant populations, he broadcast programs in Italian, Polish, and Lithuanian. By 1928, he had set up the Radio Investment Co. and built a studio in Hotel St. Francis, Newark. A freewheeler even then, he was unable to get his license renewed in 1932 by the Federal Radio Commission due to his refusal to confine the width of his station's frequency to prescribed limits.[6] And so he started the United Radio Company, selling radios and parts, undertaking repairs, and retailing a few gramophone records.

Savoy Records was actually launched on November 7, 1942, from Lubinsky's new Radio Record Shop. The customers, including keen young members of the Hot Club of Newark, were able to hear the latest sounds in listening booths. There were also nineteen-cent bins where "steals" for earnest collectors could be found. Although the Petrillo AFM strike had been in force for three months, Lubinsky managed to circumvent the ban legally. He did this by acquiring a batch of jazz masters from his record-man mentor, Eli Oberstein, augmented by his own 1939 recordings of the Savoy Dictators. Even so, Lubinsky was not averse to recording acts under pseudonyms to avoid union detection. Savoy Records was able to establish itself (and the King Solomon gospel subsidiary) simply by supplying recordings new to a marketplace that was aching for fresh sounds. There was another Newark label start-up, in 1945, that has long since been overshadowed by Savoy but had a similar musical policy: Irving Berman's Manor Records, which had success with Savannah Churchill in particular.

At Savoy, with talented A&R men Buck Ram and Teddy Reig at the controls, Herman Lubinsky was able to tap into the rich New York jazz talent base, including upcoming young turks such as Charlie Parker and Dexter Gordon and older hands Coleman Hawkins and Ben Webster. All these artists received their chance on Lubinsky's notoriously tight dollar. Savoy didn't take off chartwise until the fall of 1948 with the No. 1 hit "Corn Bread" by Hal Singer, followed immediately by Brownie McGhee's "My Fault" (No. 2). Within six months, Paul Williams had notched up what would be the biggest R&B record of 1949 with "The Huckle-Buck" in the wake of another Savoy No. 1, Big Jay McNeely's "The Deacon's Hop." Aside from the melodic McGhee hit, these records were honking, bar-walking, saxophone-led instrumentals. It was R&B but with distinct jazz roots.

Recalling his time at Savoy after taking the label in a more commercial direction, Lee Magid said, "When I met with Herman, I had all the experience he liked; I'd got around, and I got the job right away. He gave me twenty-five dollars a week and fifteen dollars expenses. Shit, I was sitting on the moon! I worked out of my office in New York, and I went there to Newark almost every day, but I didn't like the trip. So I worked out of that little desk I had at 1650 Broadway as an independent producer. And I learned to get screwed for years [laughs]. Lubinsky was all right for me, though, in a way because I knew I was going to have to take a beating. But I didn't beef, I was just happy to have a job."

Diligent young songwriter Clyde Otis, up from Mississippi, remembered pitching his first songs to Savoy: "Herman recorded a couple of my songs, one of which was by the Four Buddies. Well, that was a grand time for me. . . . [For] any song that I gave him [Lubinsky], all I would get is the twenty-five dollars up front. That was it; I never got any royalties from him, not ever. I thought that was how it was supposed to be. He took the copyright, everything, oh yeah [*laughs*]." At least Otis had a toehold in the business and, like Magid, had no regrets at his rude initiation with Lubinsky.

The Lee Magid R&B production hits for Savoy included "Stacked Deck" by Billy Wright (Little Richard's role model), recorded on location in Atlanta in 1950, and "Mercy, Mr. Percy" by Varetta Dillard in 1953. In the summer of 1953, Magid went on a southern trek and cut the first recordings by future New Orleans R&B stars Earl King and Huey "Piano" Smith. "I used to collect monies from the distributors to pay for the sessions," Magid said. "Lubinsky sent me down there to collect the money he was owed, and I became very tight with everybody. They all liked me, so they gave me money [*laughs*]; nobody liked Lubinsky."

The key person uniting the Savoy family was the well-respected A&R man Fred Mendelsohn, who directed artists such as Big Maybelle, Little Jimmy Scott, and Nappy Brown. Other important A&R men in Savoy's annals were Ralph Bass and Ozzie Cadena.

Magid quit Savoy in October 1953 to become a record man at Central Records with Derby's Larry Newton. Central had a New York regional hit with "The Beating of My Heart" by the Charmers, but within a year Newton had bought out his partner. "Then I took Al Hibbler over to Decca," said Magid; "Took me six months to sell him. We hit with 'Unchained Melody' [No. 3 pop, summer 1955]. That's a whole story in itself." Later, Magid mapped out with great dexterity the careers of Della Reese (whom he introduced to his ex-boss Jerry Blaine at Jubilee Records) and Lou Rawls.

"Everything was jumping, and if it wasn't jumping I'd make it jump," concluded Magid. "All you needed was one hit and they came around . . . like bees to honey. . . . I was inside, but I was a perimeter cat: I liked being around Milton Berle and all the guys at NBC and ABC. I was glad to mix it up with the big bands and rhythm and blues and all."

Miriam Bienstock, Ahmet Ertegun, and Jerry Wexler: Atlantic Records

The Derby and Central headquarters were housed near "Jukebox Row" on Tenth Avenue. Bob Rolontz, a *Billboard* reporter, vividly caught the atmosphere of this bustling record alley in 1953:

There is a street in New York that is rarely visited by dealers, publishers, a.&r. men, and other distinguished members of the music fraternity. It has no plush restaurants, no uniformed elevator operators, and few Cadillacs. Pushcart peddlers still sell hot dogs and pop from their carts, and on hot summer days no male wears a coat or tie. Yet it is, in a competitive sense, one of the most vital and stimulating avenues of the music business. The street is Tenth Avenue, and, in the area bounded on the north by 56th Street and the south by 42nd Street, are poured daily the hard work and the boundless optimism of a score of indie labels, indie distributors, one-stops and juke-box operators.[7]

This street of "hopes and dreams," located not inappropriately in the Hell's Kitchen neighborhood, was home to the more aggressive drivers of the independent record business. And on the northeastern borders of this throbbing milieu were based the various headquarters of Atlantic Records.

As Ahmet Ertegun had indicated to me, forcibly, Atlantic Records saw itself as a superior independent label. Jerry Wexler, who came on board in 1953, also distanced himself from the competition, calling Atlantic a "Little Tiffany" in an allusion to the high-quality artistic products of Tiffany & Co. "We were college graduates, readers, thinkers," he said. "We were not part of the riffraff like [Herman] Lubinsky and [Syd] Nathan, who were gross and self-reverential. They were the operators and manipulators, the pond scum."

Elitist that Ertegun and Wexler may have been, there is always an aura of admiration whenever Atlantic's name crops up in conversation. It goes well beyond the longevity of the label, albeit as part of the Warner Music Group. "The independent labels were like the ancient Judean tribes in the desert; there were literally dozens of them," added Wexler. "They're all gone now except for Atlantic: they're the Israelites of the indies."

Harold "Mr. Blues" Ladell, disc jockey of WNJR, Newark, and head salesman for Essex Record Distributors (which had the Atlantic line for New Jersey), spoke for many of his contemporaries when he said, "Ahmet! I didn't call him Ahmet when I met him, I assure you. It was always 'Mr. Ertegun.' There was blue blood there, and I felt it and I treated it as such. Jerry certainly was down to earth; he could mingle, talk about recording sessions: who did the A&R, 'Man, what a fabulous tenor player playing those licks in the background,' who it was. You'd get into that with Jerry. Ahmet was different. He was blue blood, he was a little high, he was a little bit aloof. I'll never forget the shock I felt reading about Ahmet Ertegun in the newspapers rubbing elbows with pretty much the society of the United States. He was not of the New York cut; Atlantic was never of the New York cut. They were royalty; they were different."

The Atlantic story has been told often, well and eruditely, by Ahmet Ertegun and Jerry Wexler.[8] Nevertheless, the sheer weight of personality and accomplishments of this pair has tended to obscure the contributions of Herb Abramson and his then-wife, Miriam. In June 2004, I approached with some hesitation the plush Upper East Side, New York, apartment of Miriam Bienstock, long married to successful music publisher Freddy Bienstock. With her tough reputation ("tough" is the favored adjective, it seems, to describe any record woman), would she look back with pleasure on her Atlantic years, or would she be awkwardly dismissive?

As Mrs. Bienstock opened the door, my mind flashed back to those 1950s photographs in *Cash Box*. Her hair was still bouffant-styled, but she was smaller than I had imagined—and graciously welcoming. Miriam talked about the past with good recall in the expected direct manner but laced with an unexpected droll humor.

Women label owners were hard to find in the intensely macho 1940s independent record environment (or in any other business). Along with Miriam Abramson and Bess Berman, there were, in different pockets of the country, Evelyn Aron (Aristocrat), Lillian Claiborne (DC), Idessa Malone (Staff), Devora Brown (Fortune), and Macy Henry (Macy's). Soon other brave ladies came along, such as Lillian McMurry (Trumpet), Vivian Carter (Vee-Jay), Mimi Trepel (London), Blanche "Bea" Kaslin (Hull-Mascot), Zell Sanders (J & S), Lee Rupe (Ebb), Mira Smith (Ram), Connie LaRocca (Frisco), Florence Greenberg (Scepter-Wand), and Estelle Axton (Stax). It was a slow awakening.

The story of record woman Miriam Bienstock takes in the pre-launch years of Atlantic Records in the 1940s and continues into the soul era of the 1960s. "I personally became interested in the music business because of my interest in jazz," she said.

There was a disc jockey that was on WNYC when I was sixteen or seventeen, Ralph Berton; I used to listen to him on the radio and became interested in jazz. I was playing classical music myself, but the idea of that whole ad lib aspect of jazz was very interesting. At that time it was fascinating to be a jazz fan because there were some very interesting people, and we all knew each other. It was not like you're a Madonna fan and there were zillions of people; I mean, it was like being in a fan club, but it was all jazz-oriented.

There were small periodicals that wrote about jazz; there were journals about jazz collecting. We could exchange records or buy records. The records became obsolete or very rare. It was a different time. At the beginning it was New Orleans [jazz], and we graduated to bebop. The swing bands were in my youth part of a different culture, the dance culture, so I never collected swing records.

I had met my first husband [Herb] through my interest in jazz, and he became a producer of records for a company called National Records. We were newly married and we were very close, so I was really involved in a lot of the records he made at that time. So from very early on, I was involved in the record business through that association.

National Records was very interesting. The man who owned the company . . . was Al Green (not the singer); he had a plastics plant in Phillipsburg, New Jersey. During the war, he thought instead of making toilet seat covers, which he had been making, he could make records. At that time, records were pressed on shellac.[9]

So he [Green] decided to start a record company but had no idea about anything; he knew nothing about music at all. And so he hired a woman [possibly future wife Sylvia Langler] who was a music educator and had no idea of the record business at all. She was a friend of Herb's, so she brought him into the business, and that's how that got started. Herb was responsible for hits like "Open the Door, Richard!" [by Dusty Fletcher] and the Billy Eckstine band with all those jazz musicians like Fats Navarro.

Then shortly after that, we decided to start our own record company [with the financial backing of Max "Waxie Maxie" Silverman of Quality Music Store]. One of our friends in Washington was Ahmet Ertegun, who had just graduated from university. He thought we would go into it together, so we decided on two labels. One label would be a sort of a gospel label, which was called Jubilee Records, and the other label would be a pop/jazz label [Quality Records, named after Silverman's store].

As noted by Harold Ladell and countless others, Ahmet Ertegun's background was poles apart, literally, from that of the Abramsons or any other record person. "We did not come to America as refugees," Ertegun said, emphatically. "My father was ambassador at the Turkish Embassy. The house that my father bought, which is now the Turkish Embassy, is probably one of the grandest houses in Washington. We had sixteen servants, and we lived in a grand manner. My family was not rich people, but being in the position my father was . . . it's like if you become president and you live in the White House."

With elder brother Nesuhi, Ahmet was an obsessive teenage jazz record collector. After arriving at Washington in 1935, he discovered Max Silverman's store in the black part of town, and "that's where I got a lot of the records which built my company." As well, the brothers would knock on doors in the black parts of the city to buy "Bessie Smiths and Louis Armstrong Hot Fives, Fletcher Hendersons, all those records—and a lot of blues records." The Erteguns were rare Caucasian visitors to the Howard Theater where they saw the "big black bands," many being territorial outfits long forgotten. Inspired by John Hammond's *Spirituals to Swing* epic of 1938, the brothers began promoting racially mixed jazz concerts in Washington. Ahmet branched out into cutting discs for his own pleasure before entering the commercial world with a "no name" label and then with Jubilee Records and Quality with Herb and Miriam Abramson.

"The Jubilee label didn't go very far," said Miriam. "There was no real activity. And that's why we sold. We had certain masters that were comedy; I don't how we got that. The little repertoire that we had was interesting to our New York distributor, Jerry Blaine [of Cosnat], and he bought the labels and put different kinds of records out at that time without any success.[10] He wasn't involved in any musical way; he was our distributor, and we would talk to him all the time because he was our customer. He had been a bandleader at one time, so he was sort of interesting in a way. I think we were very pleased to get rid of the labels. We decided to do something bigger. Ahmet got a loan [$10,000] from his family dentist, Dr. Vahdi Sabit, and we invested some [$2,500]. And we started Atlantic Records."

The debut Atlantic sessions were conducted by Herb Abramson in late 1947. Seemingly there was no time to lose as the second Petrillo ban was fast approaching. A formal announcement of the label's launch "with pre-deadline masters of the race and hot jazz variety" was made in a *Billboard* story datelined January 10, 1948, under the innocuous headline "Atlantic Diskery Makes Its Debut."[11]

Even with some two hundred masters in the can, it was an inopportune launch. "Yes, we made a big mistake," admitted Ahmet Ertegun. "We knew there was going to be a recording ban in 1948 [beginning January 1], and we thought, 'My gosh, we'd better just record a lot of stuff.' So we recorded whatever we could find, which was a big mistake because a lot of it we never released. It wasn't really [good enough], or if we released it, it went out and flopped right away. Also we didn't realize, even though there was a recording ban, the majors could record in Europe. We couldn't record in Europe, but we did realize that 'Europe' started [with illicit non-union sessions] in New Jersey! All the musicians were very happy to make a buck and make a great record anywhere you wanted. So all that rushing was for naught. Some of it was successful: Tiny Grimes, Joe Morris, and the pianist Erroll Garner's records; he became quite popular in this area. Those were the first real jazz records that we made."

"The Petrillo ban did affect us," agreed Miriam Bienstock. "We recorded surreptitiously, shall we say, during the ban. We made quite a few records at that time in the studio at night. I would assume other labels were doing the same—not the big labels . . ., because they were too obvious. But the small labels, yes. We never did record a cappella because we supported the musicians in the strike."

Unlike the circumstances surrounding the 1942 ban, AFM president James C. Petrillo now had many more record labels to contend with. With less leverage at his disposal, it was only a matter of time before the strike was settled in December 1948.

"At the start, Ahmet didn't have very much experience," said Miriam. "Herb had quite a bit because he was doing all this stuff for National. So Ahmet sat with him and learned and eventually contributed. At that time he was really very creative because not only was he helping in producing records but he could actually write songs soon afterward. Anyway, Ahmet was recording big bands like Boyd Raeburn's."

Ertegun again:

> I was very fond of Herb; he was a terrific guy, but he had ideas . . . what I call his crazy ideas. I would try this and that. In the beginning, I wasn't sure of myself, but a year or two after, I began to put my foot down about making records that had soul, that would appeal to a black audience. And I had very much of an understanding of what it was that brought about the kind of satisfaction in a listener that would make them buy a record. [That was a result of] my spending years of hanging around with people like Waxie Maxie in the shop, seeing who comes in and buys what, and listening to R&B music continuously. . . . I listened to R&B music as I listened to jazz. R&B music always had a lot of blues in it, and I loved the blues. The blues to me was the key to jazz and R&B and everything. Blues was then the expression of black Americans.
>
> We couldn't find material; that's why I started to write songs to get into the funky thing because there were no blues players in New York. There were no blues singers, no musicians. The only blues people in New York were Sonny Terry and Brownie McGhee. Our first big hit was with Brownie McGhee's brother, Stick McGhee, "Drinkin' Wine, Spo-Dee-O-Dee" [No. 2 R&B in a chart stay lasting almost half a year, even making No. 26 pop in August 1949]. But we had good sellers from the beginning. We recorded a very good band with Johnny Griffin and Joe Morris, who were alumni of the Lionel Hampton Orchestra. And we recorded several saxophone players, honking saxes, like Frank "Floor Show" Culley, and [guitarist] Tiny Grimes.

When we first started to have some success, a couple of people came from Columbia Records, and they wanted to work out a deal with us. They said they would take over our label and we would continue to record; they would place our records through their own distribution channels, and they would give us a royalty. So I said, "What kind of a royalty would you give us?" They said, "Oh, 4 or 5 percent." I said, "That's what we pay the artists." And this man, Mr. Wallerstein, who was a vice president, said, "You're gonna spoil the business for everybody." And then they walked out. I wasn't seriously considering going with them; I just wanted to hear what their offer was. I thought they would offer us 50 percent of profits or something, give us a big advance. They wanted to give us no advance and a small royalty.

Distribution? It took time, but we got it done. It wasn't easy to get distributors everywhere right away; . . . our music was too sophisticated for the Deep South. That's why I kept trying to make soulful records that would sell. And [in time] we accidentally made records that sold to white southerners because the records we made were easily understood by them because they were not quite authentic as black records. Jerry Blaine was the main distributor; he bought our Jubilee label. Yes, he was a very good distributor.

Added Jerry Wexler: "In the beginning, we had very few distributors. We used to sell to some stores direct, like Waxie Maxie's in Washington. By the time I came to Atlantic in 1953, they had a solid little network of distributors. But before that it was very experimental. One New York distributor [Cosnat] would distribute as far north as Maine, Connecticut, west Pennsylvania. The idea that distributors would spring up in small localities didn't occur."[12]

"We had trouble getting paid by some of them," said Ertegun, "but we managed eventually to get paid. You know, we had Miriam Bienstock. She is a person of the utmost rigidity and honesty. She was our office manager, and she *ran* our office. It was very important. She saw to it that we paid our bills in time and we discounted our bills. And we paid our royalties. When we didn't have enough money to pay our royalties, we went to our own [personal] bank accounts and got the money and paid the royalties on time."

"Oh yes, it was a struggle," admitted Miriam.

It was a struggle because we were undercapitalized and we were too naive to know what to do about it in the sense that we never realized that we could take a loan. The first time that we took a loan was when we had our first hit, "Drinkin' Wine, Spo-Dee-O-Dee." The pressing plant was afraid to give us the kind of production that we needed because of our history with them, which was very, very little production. And so they asked us to take a loan, which we did; we all signed it personally. We gave the money to the pressing plant and produced the records, which really put us over the top.

It was a surprise hit; it was a cover. The distributors were saying they couldn't get the original record. Herb had recorded Brownie McGhee, and he realized that Stick McGhee was his brother, so we just went into the studio. We recorded exactly the same thing, and we were able to produce for the people who wanted it. They couldn't get it on the original label.[13]

Ruth Brown came in also on a fluke after we had spare time at a session with Eddie Condon's band, which was a Dixieland band. . . . She had just had this terrible automobile accident in Philadelphia, [but] she came into the studio and we recorded two sides with her. For a while I was acting as Ruth Brown's manager, so I would be in Harlem all the time. And I'd be sitting in the Apollo Theatre—I knew all the stagehands; it was quite a different atmosphere [then]. We were there all the time.

Ruth Brown's "So Long," with the surrealistically named Eddie Condon NBC Television Orchestra, was the second Atlantic hit (No. 4 R&B). According to a Herb Abramson press release, the record had clocked up sales of 65,000 copies in the first three months to December 1949.[14]

"In the late '40s, there was just the three of us," said Bienstock. "Then we got a bookkeeper; she was the first employee: Fran Wakschal. I see her quite often. At that time, I was really doing everything. You have to understand that records were delivered by truck . . . to the sidewalk. So I would go down and I'd carry the big boxes up [the stairs], then I'd pack them again and send to disc jockeys and to distributors as samples. I'd do all of that. When I look at it now it was ridiculous, but, of course, I was very young. These were the 78s; they were heavy."

Miriam's main task was to keep the office glued together, which she did with strong authority. The first settled location was in the Jefferson Hotel on Broadway and West Fifty-sixth Street. "It was really a kind of a theatrical hotel," she remembered,

[a] lot of actors and so forth. We had a two-room suite, and the living room was the office. The bedroom was used by Ahmet, who had come from Washington at that time, and he didn't have a permanent address until he got an apartment. He lived in the back with a cousin of his. Ahmet used to go out to talk to disc jockeys. Eventually, we had a staff to do that across the country.

I think we felt we were establishing ourselves when we moved to Fifty-seventh Street [in 1956]. Those offices began to look like offices; they didn't look like they were compromised. At that time we began to sell a lot of records; we had a respectable business. A lot of artists who are still alive are very angry or very vituperative about me because I was supposed to be very, very difficult to do business with. But most of the problems that we had with artists were that they wanted [royalty] advances, and that was very difficult for us. . . . It was just that we were undercapitalized for a long time.

We learned about publishing early on, oh yes! But we eventually sold our publishing company to Freddy [Bienstock]'s cousins the Aberbachs [of Hill & Range, in 1962]. It was called Progressive Music.[15] I was in charge of the publishing company; I was the president, whatever that matters. It was a very small operation. Most of the things that I did I was able to do because there was no great activity. It was a very small company. And I got to know all the musicians because I was signing their checks for the sessions and I would be calling them to sessions. I mean, I had nothing to do with the music.

Ruth Brown proved to be the early keeper of the Atlantic flame. She was on fire with a streak of No. 1 R&B hits that lasted from 1950 through 1954: "Teardrops from My Eyes," "5-10-15 Hours," "(Mama) He Treats Your Daughter Mean," "Oh, What a

Dream," and "Mambo Baby." During this run, Big Joe Turner broke through as well. "Herb had recorded Joe Turner for National Records," said Miriam, "and when he became available, he just picked him up again. And of course Ahmet was fascinated with him, and he wrote a lot of songs for him, including 'Chains of Love' [No. 2 R&B, 1951], before he hit big with 'Shake, Rattle and Roll' [No. 1 R&B, No. 22 pop, 1954]." Turner also scored No. 1 R&B with "Honey Hush," a huge jukebox record in 1953.

The Clovers, under Buddy Bailey's lead, was another act that fostered Atlantic's growth with no less than 20 R&B hits over a six-year period from 1951, including three No. 1s: "Don't You Know I Love You," "Fool, Fool, Fool," and "Ting-a-Ling." The group prospered under the management of colorful Lou Krefetz, a former Washington, D.C., distribution man. Miriam preferred the Drifters to the Clovers, though. With Clyde McPhatter as the immaculate lead, the Drifters scored important hits with "Money Honey" (No. 1 R&B for eleven weeks at the turn of 1954) and "Honey Love" (No. 1 R&B and No. 21 pop in the summer of 1954). The Drifters also had a high-profile manager in George Treadwell.

Atlantic was building up steam nicely when Herb Abramson was drafted as a first lieutenant in the U.S. Army's Dental Corps and, on February 4, 1953, headed for Germany (where he was to rise to the rank of captain). Said Miriam, "That's when Jerry Wexler came in to fill the void [in June 1953]. He had been working with *Billboard* [and music publishers Robbins, Feist, and Miller], and he was interested in our music. Jerry was into what Ahmet was doing, so he learned to do it on his own. He took much more of an interest in the business side, and he got to deal with disc jockeys, in a very extraordinary way actually."

Apart from being a music fan with an outsized street personality, Jerry Wexler brought to the Atlantic table his hip music knowledge, trade magazine connections, and music publishing experience. In turn, Wexler wanted to be a record producer. Settling in very quickly, he must have been gratified to see Atlantic quoted by *Billboard* in March 1954 as the top "money-making" R&B label, ahead of King-Federal, RPM-Modern, and Imperial (and, for the record, OKeh and RCA Victor).[16] From then on, Wexler and Ertegun ensured that Atlantic was at the forefront of the crossover revolution as the segregated R&B, gospel, and hillbilly musical styles were integrated into rock 'n' roll. This seismic transition was anticipated by Wexler and Ertegun in a farsighted article in *Cash Box*, in July 1954, devoted to what they called "cat music" (an early incarnation of rock 'n' roll). The headline read "The Latest Trend: R&B Disks Are Going Pop."[17] In the same month, Atlantic broke through with "Sh-Boom" by the Chords (No. 5 pop, No. 2 R&B) on a new subsidiary: Cat Records.

Miriam Abramson took rock 'n' roll in her stride. "There was a whole change in the industry to satisfy that," she said. "The introduction of the 45 was not a big deal. The point is [that] when there was a demand for that type of record, we produced it, no question. The distributors would ask for it because customers were asking the shops for it." In April 1956, Miriam was quoted by *Billboard* as saying that Atlantic was selling 75 percent of its singles on 45s, whereas the year before "78's were outselling

45's by two to one." In the same story, reporter Is Horowitz noted that "in the r. & b. field, traditionally considered the 78 holdout, the advances of the newer speed are on the sensational side." Leonard Chess "of the Chess and Checker empire" confirmed, obliquely, that "single sales are favoring 45's by seven to three."[18]

Atlantic Records was continually evolving. The recordings were symbols of an increasing refinement in the company, being superbly engineered by Tom Dowd with a hallmark clean-cut rhythmic sound that was full of enthusiastic bravado. "Tom Dowd used to mix our records for many, many years," said Jerry Wexler. "He used to sit at my left hand for so long it was unbelievable, because I counted upon his skill so much. I never put my hands on the board unless someone wanted hands for extra sliders, you know. And Tom as an engineer was very contributory to the actual realization of the sessions and making musical contributions from the board."

Although the R&B sector was still important, the partners were trying to break out into other markets by seeking the critical white radio airplay. In this regard, they were assisted exemplarily by a coterie of talented arrangers, black and white, such as Howard Biggs, Budd Johnson, Jesse Stone, Teacho Wiltshire, Ray Ellis, and Stan Applebaum. The high-caliber session men would include Sam "The Man" Taylor (tenor sax), Mickey Baker (guitar), and Panama Francis (drums). Said Miriam, "Although I was not involved in the producing, we changed in different ways. We had Nesuhi Ertegun come in to the big business, and there was a big change in the fact that we had more jazz. We began to do a lot of nightclub performers like Mabel Mercer [and] Bobby Short and a lot of very, very sophisticated nightclub music. We really progressed into trying to have a varied label; we didn't do any classical but had all kinds of pop."

Nesuhi Ertegun was brought into the Atlantic fold hurriedly in 1955 while he was considering an offer from Lew Chudd to head up Imperial's proposed jazz division on the West Coast. Under Nesuhi's leadership, Atlantic built up a quality jazz-album catalog led by the consistent-selling Modern Jazz Quartet.[19]

By the mid-1950s, Atlantic product was starting to find its way across the ocean through localized licensing agreements. "We became aware of the overseas market I think originally because of our friendship with people in France," said Miriam.

We knew Eddie Barclay who had the Barclay label. At that time, what we used to do was exchange masters, because we never bought anything. If they wanted something that we had, we would exchange for something that they had, which was jazz usually. I think the English people [first Columbia (EMI), then London American (Decca)] approached us in a way to represent us in England, and we only did single records at that time. It was not a whole label [deal] to begin with. They were more or less doing us a favor. When we were more established and had more hits, we were able to make more demands. Then we had a permanent deal with Decca.

We were surprised by the overseas sales—and by the sales we got in the United States, too [laughs]. We were surprised to see people in the record shops buying our records. I was the one who came to England at the beginning to negotiate all those deals [in the fall of 1955]. I would deal with people there who were not really comfortable with women in business, so . . . we would do business very quickly and get it over with. But they were charming. Sir Edward Lewis was wonderful; we became great friends. We kept in touch after I left Atlantic.[20]

Without any fanfare, Herb Abramson had returned to the office from army duty in April 1955. At the time, Ahmet Ertegun and Jerry Wexler were as hot as could be with Joe Turner's "Flip Flop and Fly," a No. 2 R&B hit. Even better, Ray Charles was heading for No. 1 R&B with "I've Got a Woman," an important record that saw rhythm and blues go to church, with soul music as the eventual outcome. Proven singers who could write songs were signed: Ivory Joe Hunter and Chuck Willis. On the distaff side, Ruth Brown had just cooled with "Mambo Baby," but LaVern Baker announced her arrival into the big time with "Tweedlee Dee." In such a fast-moving scene, it was almost as if Abramson was adrift on the open sea after his enforced hiatus.

"Atco Records was given to him as his own sort of project," remarked a circumspect Miriam, "because [during] the time he was gone, he had lost the impetus of where he was before. Ahmet and Jerry were working together, and they'd thought the three of them could work together. So they gave him his own little empire. We were all in the same place; it was just a different room. There were no hits at the beginning [on Atco], but nobody had hits right at the beginning. Bobby Darin and the Coasters were the turning points." Atco Records had been launched as a subsidiary label in August 1955 with the exemplary publicity line "A New Label with the Old Know How!"

The problem was that Abramson had returned with a German girlfriend. The atmosphere in the Atlantic office must have been poisonous. It couldn't last, and it didn't. Miriam and Herb summarily divorced, and she married music publisher Freddy Bienstock. Herb bowed to the inevitable when he sold his interest in Atlantic to the other stockholders in December 1958. The new management lineup was Ahmet Ertegun (president), Jerry Wexler (executive vice president and general manager), Nesuhi Ertegun (executive vice president, LP department), and Miriam Bienstock (vice president, publishing). Atlantic was now a fully formed record company on a roll. In fact, the company was doing so well that scheduled releases were being held back. Gushed Ahmet Ertegun to *Cash Box* in February 1959: "All our labels had records due to come out, but we couldn't expect any more from the disk jockeys than they are doing right now. They are giving us a king-size portion of their programming time now and we appreciate that."[21]

It must have been galling for Herb Abramson to see, as early as the summer of 1959, that Atlantic grossed in excess of $1 million for two consecutive months thanks to big hits by the Drifters, Ray Charles, Bobby Darin, the Coasters, LaVern Baker, and Clyde McPhatter. Abramson looked on, helplessly, as Atlantic grew and grew while the stockholders' wealth appreciated in tandem. He opened up the A-1 Recording Studios at 242 West Seventy-sixth Street in May 1962 and landed one more significant national hit with "Hi-Heel Sneakers" by Tommy Tucker (Checker) in 1964. But Abramson's final years in impecunious circumstances out west were sad to behold.

Miriam's allegiance in the office was more to original partner Ahmet Ertegun than to latecomer Jerry Wexler. "Ahmet was always an executive," she said. "He had great presence, great charm. He was always very popular with all the artists." As well, she was another admirer of Tom Dowd's technological prowess: "He influenced us to buy one of the first stereo tape machines [in 1958]. For us, that was very expensive: an 8–track. He really wanted that and thought it would really add to what they were doing. It took a long time to set up, but that's child's play when you think about it now."

Miriam was keen to correct one part of Atlantic mythology at the 234 West Fifty-sixth Street office-cum-studio. "That was where we had this famous studio where the desk had to be moved," she said, before adding, "Please understand that there were not *two* desks like Tommy Dowd says! It was one desk, which was called a partners desk. There are seats on both sides; one person sits on one side, and the other opposite. So when it was pushed aside it was *one* desk, not two!"

Always aware of the need to conserve expenditure, Miriam was not in favor of hiring Jerry Leiber and Mike Stoller as independent producers. She stated (sotto voce):

I was very much against using them because we had to pay them as producers. Whereas if it was Ahmet or Jerry doing it, there were no producer's royalties to pay! So I checked against using them at the beginning. [But] the hits changed things, and they became a very active part of our organization until they went into business with George Goldner. It wasn't a blow to Atlantic.

Oh yes, I attended that famous [disc jockey] convention in Miami [in 1959]. It had a terrible reputation for sexual misbehavior, which I didn't actually see or participate in, either [*laughs*]. I kept saying if my mother knew I had gone, she would never have let me go. But I was not a kid at the time; it was a joke. That was a terrific convention, actually. The only thing I remember about it has nothing to do with music interests; it was just incredibly hot. But you saw a lot of people; it was fun in that sense. That was the only one I went to. There is a very famous picture of me, by the way: there's Max Silverman, Ahmet Ertegun, Jerry Wexler, and I'm sitting in a big planter's chair. That was at that convention.

The payola scandal came hard on the heels of that Miami convention. Assertive as ever, Miriam stated:

But payola was an everyday fact of life at the time; it went on. I was cited by the federal government; we all were. You know that story about Louis Armstrong recording outside his label? When they played the record for him and asked, "Who's that trumpet player?" he said, "I don't know . . . but I'll never do it again." Well, that's what we had to do. We said to the federal government, "We didn't do it . . . but we'll never do it again." I think it was more bewildering than [us] being nervous. I mean, when you're very young, you have the sense of immortality. I don't think we really were terribly worried about it, and I don't think payola really died down, ever. Maybe it wasn't as flagrant as it was to begin with, but you always had to find a way to interest people in your interests.

As we employed more and more people, of course, my need for staying in the office became less important. We had a lot of people: we had sales managers, we had promotion people, we had controllers. All of the production stuff was done by hand; eventually computers came in, but most of the time everything was done by spit and polish, really. We had to calculate all the penny royalties, absolutely. I can't remember what the turnover was; it would be laughable if I told you. But we did well; we really thrived.

In alluding to the mold-breaking Ruth Brown royalty settlement that was thrust upon Atlantic (and led to the formation of the Rhythm & Blues Foundation), Miriam was quite forthright:

I think the artists always complained. There were a couple of very famous searches by accountants for various artists, but they were not very serious. Generally, we didn't try to cheat people. We were too much starstruck to do that. When . . . somebody comes out in the '80s and says, "I didn't get enough royalties . . ." Well, royalties of the '80s were not what royalties were in the '50s.

If you try to ameliorate the situation retroactively, I think it's terrible. Because we didn't try to cheat anybody, and we did what was the normal practice at the time. If I could tell you what people used to get to record and you see what people get to record today, you can't equate them. It's ridiculous. As for Cadillac cars, that may have been true of some artists, but I don't remember anybody demanding anything like that. We paid the royalties, and if they had problems, we'd give them money.[22]

Added a still-vexed Ahmet Ertegun, "We're the ones today who suffered [from the royalty criticism] since we're the only surviving independent. All those other companies, the people you talk about, all went under. They revel in the wonderful old days when, whatever they were doing, they didn't deny they didn't pay royalties. You know what, all we were trying to do was to stay alive. We were trying to make hits, and we were interested in the music. We were music fans: Jerry Wexler and Miriam and I and Nesuhi, my brother, we were into music, and we listened to *everything*. So we knew what the hit sound of the day was."

"There were periods without hits," said Miriam. "That happened all the time, but you weren't desperate. That happens in every business, not only the record business; it happens in book publishing and everything, movies. There's a period when you're hot and there's a period when you're cold, and you just have to ride through it. Some people survive, and some people don't. What you must have is a backlog of stuff that keeps you more or less above drowning. LPs came in, and we did a lot of repackaging. A lot of the Ray Charles things we repackaged, like *Do the Twist* and stuff like that."

The Atlantic partners were rocked to the core when two of their star artists were poached at the turn of the 1960s. This was part of the major labels' strategy of picking off established hit acts from indie labels and bypassing the painful, expensive procedure of developing new acts. "I think the biggest blows of [artists] leaving Atlantic were Ray Charles and then Bobby Darin," admitted Miriam. "Those were surprising departures. I don't think it was possible to retain them because Ray Charles was doing another kind of deal, and Bobby Darin was offered something which involved his participation in films. They were terrific deals, and I don't think we could have matched them at the time. But considering where they came from and what our relationship was, I think we were hurt by those two." Another unfortunate decampment was that of Clyde McPhatter for MGM a little earlier, in 1959.

Miriam Bienstock was bought out as a minority stockholder in September 1964 and was greeted with a stark *Billboard* front-page story headed "Mrs. Bienstock Exits Atlantic." The report noted that "her duties, to be absorbed by Atlantic's executives, included serving as president of its publishing firms (Walden and Cotillion Music), supervising manufacturing, and handling relations with foreign affiliates." It was also stated that "she will enter the fashion field."[23]

"I was not in favor of selling the company," said Miriam, with fierce aplomb, "and they had to get rid of me in order to sell the company. I was at Atlantic when they had Solomon Burke and acquired the Stax masters [originally owned by Jim Stewart and Estelle Axton out of Memphis]. Jerry was real interested [in selling Atlantic] because he felt the company could not last forever. And they bought my interest and the dentist's [Dr. Sabit] at the same time." Ahmet Ertegun was not happy about selling, either, but was outvoted by the "older" Jerry Wexler and Nesuhi Ertegun. In fairness, Wexler, in particular, was concerned at what he saw as the rapid disintegration of the old indie-label order at the time. Thus, the sale of Atlantic to Warner–Seven Arts for $17.5 million was completed in October 1967. Soon, Atlantic transformed itself under Ahmet Ertegun's inspired leadership into a leading rock label as part of the WEA (Warner-Elektra-Atlantic) group.

So what was it like being a woman in the record business in the classic independent era? "I didn't feel like a pioneer," explained Miriam modestly.

I felt I was doing my job. At that particular time, there were very few women in the record business who were in an executive position. But you have to understand that at that time, I was really involved in administration. If somebody would call, for example, on the telephone, they'd say, "I'd like to talk to the boss," and I'd reply, "Yes, well, what is it you want to say?" They didn't understand it was a woman who could actually be involved in an executive capacity in that industry. At that time, you know, they used to give discounts for traveling, but not for women. The record industry organizations would have meetings in the New York Athletic Club, which didn't allow women to come in. I mean, it was just really remarkable the change that has occurred.

It seems glamorous, but when I look back at it, I think it's really amazing how *hard* we worked. And we didn't think anything about it, when you think of what came out of it. I mean, it was sort of a wonderful adventure, yes. It gives me a lot of pride, oh yes, it does. We had an aura that belonged all to ourselves; we were not like the other record companies. I don't want to use the word "class," but that's really what it was. And you can hear the records are like that, too.

That element of quality explained why the good ship Atlantic Records sailed into the twenty-first century with Ahmet Ertegun still at the helm and with Miriam Bienstock and Jerry Wexler below deck in well-earned retirement. At the end of our interview in October 2006, Ertegun logged these wise, reflective words:

The worst thing you can do in the record business is to start off with a hit, because you think it is easy. If you want to build a good record company, you have to start off with a few years of flops, and you learn how to live under tough conditions. So when the hits start to come, you learn how to conserve what you make and not throw it out. It's very hard to do, because what happens is that you press your records and you get a discount by paying on time, so you pay on time. Now you send a bunch of records out. The distributors are supposed to pay you a month after they get the stuff, but they really pay you two or three months later. And there's a lag. So you're waiting for three months. In the meantime, if you have a hit, they keep ordering records, so if you don't supply them, you are going to lose the sales. You have to supply them, you have to keep buying the material to make the records, and you're not getting paid. This lag occurs, and you need financing. And that's where a lot of people lose their company. Either they can't finance it, or the banks won't help them. Anyway, we survived that.[24]

The biggest thrill is when you hear a hit in the studio. Maybe not everybody does have that, but I think I know the music well enough. Like when I first heard the band run down the chords of "Mack the Knife" that I was making with Bobby Darin, I knew that was going to be a million-seller. Same thing with "What'd I Say" with Ray Charles, the same thing when you first heard Aretha Franklin singing "Respect," or when she was first singing gospel-style instead of her "Columbia" style. We thought "Shake, Rattle and Roll" by Joe Turner was special, yes. Look, the greatest enjoyment we got is from the music. We were not businessmen—and we became businessmen.

Within three months of our second interview, made at his request, Ahmet Ertegun was dead at the age of eighty-three. He had lived the life of a record man just like one of his rock stars. It was a magnificent innings that drew worldwide applause, especially in his native Turkey. Atlantic Records, always a shining gem, was the epitome of what an independent record company could and should be.

5

CHAPTER

The Battle of the Speeds and Golden Records' Seeds

CAST OF CHARACTERS
  George Avakian, Columbia Records
  Arthur Shimkin, Golden and Bell Records
  Cy Leslie, Cricket and Pickwick Records
  Mitch Miller, A&R man, Golden and Columbia Records
  *also featuring William Paley, Columbia Records; and
  General David Sarnoff, RCA Victor Records*

In the late 1930s, New York was attracting an army of talented musicians by way of job opportunities in radio, theater, nightclubs, and recording. The city's reputation as an enlightened music capital was endorsed by a host of liberal, highly articulate young jazz fans including Herb and Miriam Abramson, George Avakian, Milt Gabler, John Hammond, Orrin Keepnews, Alfred Lion, Bob Thiele, Jerry Wexler, and Ahmet and Nesuhi Ertegun, whenever up from Washington. These aficionados' favorite hangouts were the Commodore Music Shop, owned by Milt Gabler's father on East Forty-second Street, and Steve Smith's Hot Record Society record store on Seventh Avenue.

The members of this elitist club may have been rebellious and subversive in their musical (and political) tastes, but these were exactly the right qualifications for the influential record people that they would all become. With this clientele of jazz cognoscenti, the Commodore Music Shop in particular, and almost blasphemously, in view of jazz's cerebral status, can lay claim to being one of the birthplaces of the rock 'n' roll revolution. Moreover, Milt Gabler's Commodore Records and Hot Record Society's H.R.S. imprint, both founded in

1938, were years ahead of their time by licensing jazz masters from the majors for reissue as well as by making new recordings. Gabler's prowess led to his important appointment as an A&R man at Decca.

George Avakian: Columbia Records

In 2005, Armenian-born Yale graduate George Avakian looked and sounded exactly like the veteran jazz man he was. Goatee-bearded, of lively mind and generous in deed, he was living a very comfortable existence with his musician wife Anahid at their Riverdale home overlooking the magical Hudson River. George joined Columbia Records in 1940 and worked his way up the corporate ladder to become director of popular albums and director of the international department. Avakian's major signings for Columbia were Miles Davis and Johnny Mathis, while he recorded star artists such as Louis Armstrong, Dave Brubeck, and Erroll Garner. *Billboard* noted in 1958 that sales of Avakian's "jazz albums on Columbia are estimated to be among the highest of any jazz label."[1]

Avakian saw firsthand two crucial innovations in the record industry, both delivering better-sounding, unbreakable gramophone records: the 33⅓-rpm long-playing album (the "LP") from Columbia, and the 45–rpm single (the "45") from RCA Victor. Patently, the 78–rpm shellac disc with its weight, clumsiness, fragility, noisy surface, and poor wear (not to mention heavy transportation costs and storage space requirements) was living on borrowed time. At first, there was no indication that the two new-speed formats would be able to coexist. The intense battle between Columbia and RCA Victor for the supremacy of the speeds, with the ultimate winner intending to take all, would have a big impact on the independent labels of the time. George Avakian unraveled the story with historical relish:

> In the 1940s, Columbia definitely was in third place. We didn't really get going until the LP cue came along. Ted Wallerstein had been in charge of RCA; he was an austere and serious gentleman. Wallerstein had conceived the idea because he was a great classical music fan, and he felt that there had to be a better way than just a 78–rpm disc for classical music. Because of the use of the 33–rpm turntables by radio stations, he knew that the technology was there, if the public would change over and buy 33–rpm turntables.
>
> There was an attempt at RCA in the early 1930s to produce long-playing records, but [it] had failed for a number of reasons. First of all, the public was not going to buy new turntables, because money was short during the Depression. The number of people buying records was relatively small, because radio came along in the mid-1920s, and all of a sudden you could get free entertainment, without having to buy either music on records or spoken-word comedy. As a result, the money wasn't there to get into it as deeply as was necessary in terms of research. Also, as the slow-playing record had to bear more weight from the passage of the pickup and needle, the material that the record was made out of wore out faster. And so in some cases they found the record would wear out after very few plays. So that was a terrible series of handicaps.

However, when Mr. Wallerstein was asked by Bill Paley, the president of CBS, if he would be interested in starting a record company, he told Paley, "Yes, I certainly would be, but forget about starting a record company from scratch." By the way, the impulse that drove Paley was his enormous rivalry with General Sarnoff at NBC-RCA; they hated each other. So Wallerstein said, "What you should do is buy the American Record Corporation, which has all these masters and contracts with artists. You can start right away, but classical records, forget it; you can never overtake RCA. Red Seal is absolutely 'it' in the United States. But this idea of trying to develop whatever works out, you will steal a march on the Red Seal catalog because there is a real need in the future for a long-playing record on which you can get a whole symphony on two sides or maybe four sides."

Paley agreed, and so on January 1, 1939, the company was launched as Columbia. One other thing Mr. Wallerstein said was that when you buy American Record Corporation, you acquire the rights of the Columbia label, which was perfect for the Columbia Broadcasting name and which RCA didn't have [with NBC]. It was an accident, absolutely. RCA, I should say, was not the term used to describe the record company until many, many years after. It was always Victor Records, because Victor was the established record name. The public didn't care that RCA had become the owner of the Victor phonograph company. Bluebird [the budget subsidiary] was really the bulk of RCA's business.

Before Columbia became the main name, Brunswick was the operating name. It was supported by Vocalion, [which] was later changed to OKeh, because the name Vocalion was lost as well as Brunswick to Decca. The Brunswick-Balke-Collender Company, which built pool tables and billiard tables and bowling alley equipment, acquired the rights to a lot of masters; that's how the Brunswick name came about. Vocalion was an invention. The company in 1931 contracted with American Record Corporation to have the Brunswick and Vocalion names used.[2]

Columbia Records, newly constituted, deliberately killed off the Brunswick and Vocalion names because they wanted to concentrate on Columbia as the main label at fifty cents instead of seventy-five cents for Brunswick. Jack Kapp, who had been deeply involved in Brunswick in the old days, acquired the name of Brunswick for Decca Records. Then Columbia Records adopted OKeh as the thirty-five-cent label.[3]

OKeh gradually became the label on which rhythm and blues was steered to for two reasons: first of all, the thirty-five-cent price was attractive to that market, and second, on the Columbia side, Mitch Miller had come in 1950 and . . . had little use for the new trend of black music and so on. So it was very convenient to steer it off to a separate label. There was a distribution split so that in many cases around the country, different distributors handled the OKeh label [under Danny Kessler], followed by Epic [launched in late 1953], than those who handled the Columbia label. Hal Cook, with his role in distribution, was very important.[4]

Here we get into the origin of the successful long-playing record, which has never been properly studied and reported on, if I may say so. What happened was that when Wallerstein proposed the idea to Paley, he did the natural thing and turned it over to his CBS research department. And the man who ran the research for radio and eventually television was Peter G. Goldmark. Godfrey Goldmark, who always insisted on being called Godfrey, was a very unpleasant Hungarian Jew—you know, the bloke who goes through the revolving door behind and always comes out ahead. That comment was repeated many times by Columbia's engineers because he was roundly disliked.

Goldmark got together with Wallerstein, who brought in Jim Hunter. He was the man in charge of the manufacturing at the RCA pressing plant who came and supervised the Columbia manufacturing plant at Bridgeport, Connecticut. In fact, he was head of the Wallerstein program to develop the long-playing record at RCA. So the project stumbled along unsuccessfully until 1946. Early in that same period, Goldmark was working on the development of television for the future market in terms of color television. RCA was doing the same thing, but they had two very different systems between the two companies. The CBS system was a little bit superior in terms of reproduction on the screens at home; [it was] a large three-foot color wheel. The showdown came in '46 when both companies presented systems to the industry. Overwhelmingly the RCA system was chosen, essentially what we have now [in 2005].

This was a terrible blow to Paley, and knowing that the LP thing was going nowhere, he said, "Let's forget about the LP; we don't need two failures in the same year." RCA was not doing anything as far as any of us knew. The way it played out was that Wallerstein still believed in the LP as the only sound medium of the future for classical music and scores for pop albums. He persuaded Paley to let his own engineers, that is, the Columbia Records engineering department, which had been working closely with Goldmark and his people, to take over the project. Paley said, "Go to it!"

The hiring by Wallerstein of William Bachman, who was a young engineer out of Cornell University who had developed a lightweight cartridge, was very important to Mr. Wallerstein. Under Bachman, the elements that were salvageable from the CBS [research] effort were preserved as a foundation. But the results ended up being that in less than two years, Bachman produced a workable long-playing record that could be put on the market, in 1948. There is very little literature about him. I'd tried for years to get credit for him and nobody was interested, but when the fiftieth anniversary of the LP came along, I decided to do it.

The true story was suppressed by Bill Paley. He was so anxious to have not a word come out about the failure to develop a long-playing record for seven years, then along comes this new guy. In less than two years there are a hundred pop LPs and a hundred classical LPs on the market. He said, "No interviews are to be given out, or anything to be written or said by CBS–Columbia Records personnel, about this without verifying with my office." He didn't want anything negative said about Goldmark following the television debacle.

Mr. Wallerstein made the announcement to the assembled people representing major record companies, and he said, "We're about now to copyright the long-playing record. We want it to be used by everybody freely, because the more of you who do so the better it will grow and become the norm. And that's what we must all do." The problem of the record player was solved by having Philco develop a small tabletop unit which you could plug into your radio or [that could] work independently. This was eventually reduced from $19.99 to $9.99, and for $9.99 you'd also get maybe half a dozen free LPs to get you started. The whole thing was the hook to get you going.

RCA immediately said, "No, we're not interested!" I found out what really happened later when I went to RCA to take over their pop department [in 1960]. At one of the meetings with all the principal executives, I said in passing, "At Columbia we all had this thing going about how you developed the 45 and it was not the greatest speed and all that, but it was just a case of 78 minus 33 equals 45." Everybody laughed and said, "No, no, it's not true." Then I'm walking down the hall with the controller, [and] he said, "George, don't tell anybody, but that's absolutely what happened." So I had it from the highest echelon, but it's never been admitted publicly. On the other hand, RCA said they had been working on this for years and years, and I don't believe they were at all.[5]

I'm sure from what I gathered also, when I worked briefly for two years at RCA, that it was developed right after the 33 was announced. I have a copy of a letter from someone high up in the RCA organization dated 1948 which is the most horrible, chastising letter addressed to a whole group of executives on the order of "You guys were asleep at the wheel and for Christ's sake get off your butts!"

For a long time we kept the 78 going because of the market; jukeboxes had not yet converted to 33. When RCA finally came out with the 45 in 1949, the announcement was that the seven-inch size was perfect for being compact and the 45 speed is the ideal speed. The seven-inch 45 was chosen because the biggest volume of sales in the Red Seal department was in arias and overtures and other short pieces, which fitted perfectly because the timing was something like under nine minutes. All that turned out of course to be really bullshit, but it made a good story. And they got away with it for quite a while.

The power of RCA and Columbia in the market was still such that everybody had to end up going 45 and 33, and the 78 dropped finally. RCA had their own [record] players and everything, it was very cleverly done, and they had more money than anybody else in the business put together. So they shoved it down the public's throat. Finally [by the 1970s], the public rejected the 45 and everything became 33.

Importantly for Columbia in the LP stakes, Bill Paley had headhunted Jim Conkling as president from Capitol. It was under Conkling's inspired leadership that Columbia was able to fully capitalize on its invention of the LP through the formation of the Columbia Record Club in 1955. The background research work was conducted in great secrecy for fear of alerting the competition and upsetting the regular retailers and was masterminded by mail-order expert Lester Wunderman in conjunction with Columbia's enlightened executive vice president Goddard Lieberson and Conkling. Sales volumes were huge as the mailmen delivered middle-of-the-road LPs into the homes of grateful record fans living in every corner of the heartland, from Alabama to Wisconsin, where few record shops (or distributors) existed.

The industry at large was taken aback at the way the LP market was being siphoned off and manipulated. RCA Victor and Capitol were completely wrong-footed, giving Columbia a virtual monopoly in the club sector for the first two years. Moreover, these below-the-wire sales eluded the published album charts, which were based on representative samplings of retailers' sales. The LP charts of the day, therefore, were hardly models of accuracy.

In a sense, the runaway success of the record club was one of the reasons (along with A&R man Mitch Miller's ambivalence toward the new "teenage" music) why the Columbia executives missed out on exploiting first-wave rock 'n' roll. "There was a fair amount of concern at that," said Avakian. "But not as much as you might expect, because the company had become oriented so solidly in terms of the quality and enormous success of the LP, which brought in more money than anybody realized at the time."

RCA Victor's first batch of 45–rpm seven-inch vinyl records was released on March 31, 1949, supported by a mass-marketing campaign under the heading "'45' is sweeping the country." As Avakian indicated, RCA manufactured a special record player (the RCA Victor 45J), which was an attachment that "plays thru any set" and was sold at a knock-down price of "only $12.95."[6] Nevertheless, in the ensuing months there were real concerns whether or not this new singles format would be accepted by the record-buying public. A report in *Cash Box*, dated November 5, 1949, highlighted the general unease with a buried page-20 story headed "RCA Victor Denies Reports That 45 rpm Will Fold."

The critical early support for RCA came from Seeburg, by then the leading jukebox manufacturer, which readily saw the advantages of the new lightweight disc. Within a year, Seeburg had introduced the 100–selection M100B Select-O-Matic 45–rpm-only jukebox. Soon, the sharper jukebox-oriented independent practitioners were embracing the 45 single, which was dubbed the "doughnut disk" due to the large 1½-inch center hole. These alert record men included Irving Green (Mercury), Herman Lubinsky (Savoy), Jerry Blaine (Jubilee), and the Bihari brothers (Modern). In effect, these visionaries were taking advantage of the excessive promotional publicity that RCA was expending in establishing the 45.

Showing how quickly the landscape was changing, the Biharis inaugurated in the fall of 1950 their initial line of seven 33⅓-rpm ten-inch LPs at a price of $2.85 each (compared to seventy-nine cents for 45s). The enterprise was living up to its advertising slogan: "Be Modern, Buy Modern." Once pressing costs became more economic by the mid-1950s, the twelve-inch album (with its greater time allowance) would prevail over the ten-inch album. In many cases, the bottom line was aided by secret deals with music publishers for reduced rates (at 1.5 cents per song, for example, against the statutory rate of 2 cents).[7] The term "album," incidentally, was purloined by Columbia from the original 78–rpm record portfolios with handsome artwork.

It would be several years before long-playing albums would become profitable for the independent companies, which could not possibly compete with the majors in the adult markets for classical music and sound tracks from movies and shows, nor in the actual volume of releases. Often in the rock 'n' roll era, indie LP compilations would consist of the latest hit single and "B" side with ten "fillers" that would be rush-recorded. Then the session and other associated production costs would be debited to the artists' royalty accounts, thereby wiping out the immediate financial rewards of a chart record.

The mini-album EP (the 45–rpm extended play with picture sleeves, consisting usually of four songs) was widely introduced in 1952. Although it was a well-loved format for a decade or so for impecunious teenagers who could not afford LPs, it never took off in volume/profit terms.

There was no doubt about it: the 45 single was the facilitator of rock 'n' roll music. "That's what kept the 45 going longer than it would otherwise," agreed George Avakian. "The 45 became the unit of choice for the jukeboxes, which was a key to what was going on with the independents and the marketable rhythm and blues business. The jukebox sales promoted the records to the public that was listening on the jukeboxes as well as the radio, and they went out and bought the records for home use. The 45 was the heart of that aspect of the business."

From 1956 on, teenagers fully embraced the 45–rpm single that was at once unbreakable and easy to carry and contained the hippest of rock 'n' roll music. The "speed" makeup and dollar value of record sales in retail stores was analyzed by *Billboard* for the week ending February 1, 1958, just as rock 'n' roll was peaking. In dollar terms, if not in volume, the LP was already well ahead on points. The Battle of the Speeds would be won as the teens, maturing into young adults, would gravitate with ease to rock music and to albums.

Table 5.1

	Share of Unit Sales	Share of Dollar Market
45 rpm	65.7%	33.9%
33⅓ rpm	24.0%	58.1%
45-rpm EP	5.5%	4.3%
78 rpm	4.6%	2.7%
Other	0.2%	1.0%

Arthur Shimkin: Golden and Bell Records

The full impact and importance of children's records in the 1940s and into the 1950s is lost in the mist of history. Yet here was a big market, with few published popularity charts, that was almost underground in nature even though it was dominated by the major labels. Inclusive of educational and entertainment values, the medium would serve to introduce baby-boomer toddlers to the wonders of the record player and to the phonograph record.

In the summer of 1948, Arthur Shimkin, only twenty-five years old, presented himself bravely to fearsome AFM president James C. Petrillo to negotiate terms on behalf of a new children's label, Golden Records. The autocratic union head had recently called out America's professional musicians on strike for the second time in six years. A catalyst for the latest recording ban was the broadcasters' decision to dispense with staff musicians to provide live music. As for Shimkin, he was seeking a modification in the standard union terms for cutting children's records. In arguing his case, he explained the virtues of the genre to "Jimmy" Petrillo. "We engaged in the first negotiations for a new contract," said Shimkin. "I had already seen the elite Mr. Petrillo, a chubby yet imposing man, because I had a problem. The normal time of a pop record was three minutes, and I was making children's records that were half that length: one and a half minutes. I wanted the right to do eight children's sides in a three-hour session. Normally, the AFM allowed only four regular sides in a three-hour session. So I had to go up and present my case to Mr. Petrillo, which I did . . . eloquently," Shimkin recalled with a smile.

"I told him that for the future success and employment of American Federation of Musicians, he would have to encourage a record industry that would only grow if children were enticed to use and buy records. If the children bought records, they would buy records as adults. The industry would grow, and more musicians would get employed. That's why he had to give us what we wanted. He thought I was nuts! Then as I was leaving, he laughed and he said to his assistant, 'Give this young fellow what he wants.' And I got a contract."

In 2004, some three years before he died, diminutive New Yorker Shimkin belied his eighty-one years. He was living in a plum midtown location near the East River with his Broadway singer/songwriter wife, Bonnie Lee Sanders. Known in his prime as "the live wire," "the little guy packed with energy," and even a "swinger," he had an excellent recall of his time as a successful record pioneer. Just as remarkably, he was a throat cancer survivor. After being stricken at age fifty-nine, he had to learn to talk all over again and adjust to a new way of life, which he did with stylish élan. By the way, Arthur abhorred the term "kiddies' records." "Children are young persons and should be treated with dignity, even at an early age," he insisted.

Golden Records was launched under the wing of book publishers Simon and Schuster, which itself was then owned by Chicago store magnate Marshall Field. By taking advantage of the extremely efficient marketing and distribution systems of the well-capitalized publishing house, Golden was able to grow quickly and securely. Compared to the other scuffling independent companies of the time, Golden Records was operating in a rarified atmosphere of privilege. Interestingly, this distribution/finished-goods model would be used to excellent effect a full decade later by ABC-Paramount, the London American Group, and others.[8] Even so, competition for the parents' dollar was intense for Golden, particularly from Columbia, those shooting stars Capitol and Mercury, and a veritable flock of smaller indies.

Arthur Shimkin's story reverberated with the sparkle of New York's music scene that emerged exuberantly from the war years. A graduate of Columbia University and a forgotten nephew of Leo Shimkin of Simon and Schuster, Arthur obtained a permanent job with the book publishers after war service through the good offices of Dick Simon, a senior partner in the firm (and father of singers Carly and Lucy Simon). Shimkin's salary was $250 a week, "which in 1947 was a lot of money." He was dispatched to the Madison Avenue office to work in a research department independent of the corporation. One year and some 140 failed project ideas later, the department was disbanded as "frivolous." However, with a commendable sense of staff relations, the company gave him a chance to come up with a money-making project based on his research work. "Well, as hard as I tried," he said, "I couldn't find *one* project that I thought would make a dime. So I invented one in my capacity as research director."

Simon and Schuster had "information please" postcards that were inserted into every book for building up their "fabulous" mailing list. This was an early form of direct marketing. Shimkin discovered with the fast-growing Little Golden Books juvenile line that many parents would respond in the allotted space on the reply cards: "The book was fine, we loved it, but if I have to read this book to my child one more time, I'll *scream!*"

Arthur continued:

> So a lightbulb lit in my brain and I wrote a very fateful memo to MLS (Max Schuster), RLS (Richard L. Simon), and LS (Leon Shimkin). Every internal communication was done by initials, not full names! I proposed that the project that would make money was to be called Little Golden Records [registered as Golden Records]. And they should be made to sell for the same twenty-five cents each that the new Little Golden books were selling for and mass marketed in the same way to racks, food stores, supermarkets, drugstores, etc.
>
> Both partners, Max and Dick, felt that they would have to look into it a little more. Records were not their cup of tea; they were book people. Besides, they found out from their various attorneys that you couldn't copyright recordings, and they didn't believe that anything that was not copyrightable was worth publishing. Anybody could steal it. I explained that there was common law copyright, but [my explanation] didn't seem to bother them too much.

With little apparent progress being made, Shimkin was invited by Dick Simon to lunch at the Rockefeller Luncheon Club with none other than General David Sarnoff, the imposing head of NBC-RCA Victor and Simon's friend. "He was a general (honorary) in World War II," said Shimkin.

> He sat at the luncheon table and they talked up until coffee. At the coffee break, Dick finally addressed the fact that young Arthur was sitting at the table, and David said hello to me. "Young Arthur has an idea; he wants to do a little children's record line." David said, "Of course, Dick." I said, "Well, we wanted to do Little Golden Records to go with the Little Golden Books." "What do you think?" asked Dick. David said, "Well, Dick, if one of my young people came to me and suggested that RCA published books, I wouldn't do it. I would come to my friend Dick Simon and say, 'Dick, we have an idea; we'd like to put out some books. Will you publish them for us?' RCA Records would be glad to do it for you."
>
> Two days later, Mr. Schuster had lunch with Jack Kapp, who was the head of Decca. Jack Kapp told him the same kind of story if in tougher terms, not as suave as David Sarnoff. And I said to my newly acquired wife at the time, "I think another good

idea has been shot down." But I was surprised about a week later to be called up to the twenty-eighth floor where the Simon and Schuster executive offices were. "You know, Arthur, we're gonna do it." I said, "Really?" "Yes, we've got two of the most successful record company heads in the country who think it's such a good idea for us to come to RCA or Decca to do it. There must be something to it. But we want to keep it away from the company." That was because Simon and Schuster was one of the foremost publishers of music books written by Cole Porter, Rodgers and Hart, Rodgers and Hammerstein, all the top writers. They thought they would be capitalizing on their association with these stellar names, and therefore they wanted it to be independent.

So they said, "Arthur, you'll head up Little Golden Records. We will have an exclusive contract with you for the manufacture and the distribution of the records, and you create them and make them subject, of course, to our approval. And we will finance you as needed."

I was thrilled. I didn't know too many professionals in the business at that time. I had been a clarinet player, not a good one, but I admired woodwind players a great deal. And one of the finest was a fellow by the name of Mitchell Miller, who was an oboe player and played with Toscanini and the NBC Symphony. I found that he was also the adviser on classical music to Irving Green, president of Mercury Records. So I got a hold of Mitch's number.

I called Mitch Miller and asked him if we could meet to discuss his being the music director of my new company, which was [now] going to be called Golden Records. He sounded a little puzzled, but he agreed. I still remember the day I met with Mitch. He was a thoroughly delightful fellow! I mean, anybody that walked around all day long with tuxedo pants, a white shirt capable of being tied with a formal black tie, a tuxedo jacket folded into his oboe case, wearing a tweed sports jacket, had my admiration.

He was playing concerts in the evening and advising Mercury Records during the day, building up a reputation [as] a creative A&R record man. So he was very busy as a result of that. He introduced me to an older man by the name of Alec Wilder, one of the great American popular and classical composers. Alec had a fabulous facility. He was one of the few arrangers I ever knew that could stand at a piano (not the keyboard but the other end) during a recording session while everybody was playing, pull out music paper, and write sixteen-part arrangements for a *different* piece of music. He was our arranger.

The first Golden [releases] were recorded at the WOR radio studio on Broadway, and they had a record cutter up there that we recorded directly to. So God forbid if you made a mistake in one minute, thirty seconds; you had to start all over again. There was no splicing or editing. The records were timed to a minute and a half because we only had six-inch discs, and the number of lines per inch you could cut a children's record with were eighty or ninety played at 78 rpm. All of the sides were in that dimension so the six-inch record could fit inside the size of a Little Golden book jacket and sales rack.

The ones that were done at the beginning were very short: *The Poky Little Puppy, Scuffy the Tugboat, Saggy Baggy Elephant, Tootle the Train, The Five Little Firemen.* These were the little popular stories. The words were written by the finest authors in children's books [published by Simon and Schuster or in the public domain], and they were all musicalized and dramatized. *The Night before Christmas* was a perfect example; it was one of the best-sellers year in and year out. The unbreakable records were great for children. They'd take them and fling them around the room!

The Golden discs were pressed by Bestway Products Inc. of Rahway, New Jersey. This company was a pioneer in injection molding, a rapid, low-cost disc producing method. Co-owner Al Massler was to intrude on Arthur Shimkin's story in an ominous way through their subsequent partnership in Bell Records. "Al Massler had a very, very lovely partner by the name of Jim Wilson," said Shimkin,

a straightforward, honest guy. He was the technical man behind the injection molding of these little records. But Al Massler was the business end of it. He was the guy that was always overcharging us, and Jim was the guy that was always correcting all the mistakes.

Massler had a company called Glassy-Finish Process Company, and he made things like rosary bead boxes through injection molding. He and his partner made a deal with a big company, Watson-Stillman, which manufactured machinery, and they created the automatic injection molder. Bestway had a shed in Rahway, and they made a deal with this company to put their machines in their shed one or two at a time. They would run them as test prototypes.

Finally Simon and Schuster put up the money to buy the machines necessary to turn out the records in volume.

"As a result of pressing Golden Records," continued Shimkin,

Massler managed to get to replicate London and a bunch of very minor labels. So he got a tremendous business going for a while. The pressing plant controls everything. I know Golden Records were sold out of the back of a truck in Newark in 1948 through unaccounted press overruns.

We used to record at night, since most everyone worked all day. We'd go in there about eight o'clock at night and work until about midnight or 1 A.M. and pay everybody exorbitantly well, much more than union scale. So they all came running. Well, one night we were locked in Reeves Sound Studios on Forty-fourth Street and Third Avenue where the engineer was Bob Fine. He invented margin control; a wonderful, wonderful engineer.[9] So we called all the men that we needed. There were usually no more than eight to ten at a time; it was a small chamber group.

We were working away, and we come upon *Old King Cole*. And I turned round to Mitch Miller and said, "Mitch, we don't have a fiddle player!" He said, "Call this guy and tell him to get his ass over here. It's a hundred dollars, and it will only take him fifteen minutes." He scribbled a telephone number on my take sheet. So I called the number, it was ringing four or five times, [and] a voice comes on the phone and said, "Don't bother me; I'm fucking!" I go back to Mitch and I told him, [and] he said, "That's all right; call him back in ten minutes and we'll get him." So I called him back in ten minutes, and sure enough, twenty minutes later he showed up.

He was the first violin with the Budapest String Quartet.

Arthur Shimkin remembered signing a waiver to Miller's contract with Golden Records that enabled Miller to take up the prestigious post of A&R director at Columbia in 1950. The name of the "Mitchell Miller Orchestra" was still appearing on Golden releases as late as 1957. "We put his name on the record even if he didn't produce it," said Shimkin, with a smile. "Mitch didn't mind because he was getting a royalty anyway!"

Shimkin had a sneaking respect for the omnipotent James Petrillo and his dominance of the music industry. "The union was very powerful because it was very well guided," he said. Young Arthur attended a series of negotiating meetings between the record labels and the AFM, indicating that Golden Records was becoming a positive force in the industry at large. "So here we were, about twelve of us at the headquarters of the AFM on Lexington Avenue in Mr. Petrillo's conference room with a table that was about forty-eight feet long. He sat at head of the table, and on the sides of the table sat the members of the AFM executive board. At the *foot* of the table sat the ten or twelve record company presidents on *folding* chairs. That was the introduction to the negotiations," stated Shimkin.

> Then at one of the meetings, Petrillo said, "If any of you guys want to record without a contract, you'll have to go to China." I think it was Sarnoff's right-hand man Emanuel "Manie" Sacks [who] said, "Mr. Petrillo, there are a lot of Chinese joints in New York and L.A." Petrillo didn't like that at all; he was very angry about it. But there were a lot of scab sessions going on. Petrillo did all right for his union. He won the royalty, and he won the no-tracking [that is, no overdubs] and many other things.
>
> The second strike was the reason for the [belated] formation of the Recording Industry Association of America [RIAA]. The representatives of the record companies were called together for a meeting. They were Goddard Lieberson (Columbia), Manie Sacks (RCA), Dave Kapp (Decca), Irv Green (Mercury), Frank Walker (MGM), somebody from Capitol [Glenn Wallichs], and young struggling people Ahmet Ertegun or Herb Abramson from little Atlantic that was just starting. London would send somebody once in a while.

Based on size of turnover with commensurate annual dues, five alphabetical categories were set up. "There was a group C that they had in there," said Shimkin, "and somebody did $2 million. There was only one company in that group: Golden Records! So I automatically became a founding member of the RIAA."[10]

The RIAA trade association was established in February 1952 after months of preparation and swung into action immediately by sponsoring a New York State anti-piracy bill.[11] A lasting RIAA triumph was to certify gold records for million-selling discs, a system that has seemed to be in operation forever but in fact was not introduced formally until 1958. Said Shimkin, "I always liked the idea of 'gold' records being [the name of] the awards. It seemed to verify the standard of our own 'Golden' record label."

Golden Records itself had a fantastic breakthrough at the American Booksellers Association convention in Chicago in 1948. "Our sales manager showed the rack to the American book publishing wholesalers," recalled Shimkin, "and made the famous phone call back to Simon and Schuster. We had made twelve titles, and the phone call was: 'We'll need 50,000 each!' That was 600,000 records." On the back of this success, a valuable licensing deal was landed in negotiation with Walt Disney himself, leading to the release of such children's classics as *Alice in Wonderland, Snow White, Pinocchio, Three Little Pigs,* and *Lady and the Tramp.* Simon and Schuster was already publishing the Disney books.

Between 1948 and 1958, the Disney-related recordings would account for some 50 percent of the Golden turnover. With a low retail price—initially twenty-five cents—it was necessary to trim every possible cost to the bone. Artist royalties and recording expenses were juggled, while it was necessary to get a break in the publishing royalties. Shimkin remembered negotiating a difficult deal with Disney's music publisher, Bourne Music. The owner was the lordly Saul "Sol" Bourne, who would introduce himself by saying, "My middle name is Oscar; my initials are S.O.B.!"

"So Simon and Schuster undertook the distribution through their book distributing network," said Arthur Shimkin. "Since they had the exclusive right to manufacture and sell, all I had was the masters and the ownership and the right to create new titles. Other labels came in: Peter Pan, Cricket, Young People's Records, etc. They all tried, but they didn't have the distribution. I feel the key to [our] success was the rack distribution and, I think, the selection of product. We had the first racks for records. Pocket Books [a division of Simon and Schuster] invented racks for paperback books, and Golden Records adapted from this experience."

Golden Records' biggest seller was "The Ballad of Davy Crockett" by the Sandpipers in 1955. "Little Golden [releases] outsold in numbers any pop record that was out," said Shimkin, bristling with an air of frustration. "But the trade magazines never put them on the national charts; they had a separate list of children's best-sellers. Ridiculous, a record is a record! 'Davy Crockett' made the lists because it was put out on a pop label [Columbia], so the Fess Parker picture version made the charts. The Golden record of 'Davy Crockett' outsold Fess Parker by three to one [Bill Hayes's version hit No. 1 on Cadence]. We sold 6 million copies of that record, including our twenty-five-cent release and a premium record. We even signed Bing Crosby, Danny Kaye, and Roy Rogers. And Golden Records did great."[12]

A constant bugbear for Arthur Shimkin (as indeed it was for the entire recording industry) was the 10 percent excise tax, which led him to resign from RIAA because he felt the trade group was not lobbying hard enough for its reduction or removal. In 1958, an internal solution was conceived by Simon and Schuster's accountants, who set up as a legitimate "intermediary" tax-shelter company A. A. Records: Arthur (Shimkin) and Al (Massler). Shimkin, therefore, was forced into an unwanted, unfortunate partnership with Massler.[13]

In 1952, Arthur Shimkin dreamed up the idea of targeting the new teenage audience (the original young children) by releasing cover versions of pop hits on a budget-priced label. He was also looking toward the lucrative jukebox market, which was denied to Golden Records. Inspiration had come while he was watching the *Your Hit Parade* TV broadcasts sponsored by Lucky Strike cigarettes. This show, dating back to 1935 on the radio, introduced the public at large to the concept of popular hits of the week.[14]

After choosing the name Bell and conducting a test marketing exercise in twelve cities, Shimkin discovered that a Brooklyn manufacturer of Yiddish records, one Benny Bell, had a label using his own last name. "I asked him what's the best seller he's ever had," recalled Shimkin.

> "Well," Benny said, "I had a record a couple of years ago I sold 12,000 copies." I said, "12,000 copies, how many did you get paid for?" So he started to break up. I said, "Look, I'm prepared to give you a check for $2,500 *now.* I want to use the name, and you've got to give it up. Your name you can use any time you want, Benny Bell, but Bell Records belongs to us." He shook his head and said, "I don't like it, I don't like it . . . I'll take it!"
>
> Pocket Books–Simon and Schuster thought it was a wonderful idea to sell Golden Records to teenagers. It didn't work out that way, but they backed it. Pocket Books at that point was the distributing division. Al Massler pressed the records, and I hired all the artists and musicians. We had everybody; we had the works. We released eight to twelve singles a month; they were always covers of hit records. And I tracked the sales of all the pop records that were on the pop charts. We did not imitate the original pop hits; we interpreted them.[15]

A major marketing innovation for indie pop singles was Bell's eye-catching picture sleeves, similar to those on the Golden children's releases. One of the models was Jayne Mansfield just before she costarred with Tom Ewell in rock 'n' roll's best movie in 1956, *The Girl Can't Help It* (which, incidentally, heavily satirized the "Sign here, son; I'm gonna make you a star" syndrome and signaled, perceptively, the role of organized crime in the music industry).

Even though Arthur Shimkin offered only a marginal royalty rate, he was able to attract star names to Golden and Bell with the bait of big unit sales (just as Decca had done in the 1930s). Simon and Schuster dropped out of the picture in early 1965, and Shimkin, increasingly unhappy with Al Massler's business methods, soon headed for the exit door, leaving Massler in control of Bell and Golden. This is the same Bell Records that would reinvent itself as a prominent indie pop and soul label under the capable direction of Larry Uttal, previously owner of Madison Records. "So Larry took over, and he didn't get along with Massler any more than I did," said Shimkin. "All Massler wanted was to become a big mogul in the record business . . . but he didn't." Shimkin himself was not finished with the children's record business. "In 1967, I was invited to join Columbia Records," he recalled, "which had got a new young president for its pop label, Clive Davis, who I knew from years before through Goddard Lieberson and Mitch Miller. Clive said, 'Come up, we'll give you a suite of offices, we'll give you all the money you need, let's do what you did for Golden for Columbia.' I brought him Sesame Street Records in 1969."

Shimkin was not finished with Al Massler, either. In the same year, Shimkin started protracted legal proceedings against his ex-partner for "breach of contract" for non-payment of Golden royalties. A multimillion-dollar judgment was made in Shimkin's favor, but he was never able to collect against Massler or the estate. "He went broke. . . . He took the money to Spain, France, Switzerland, wherever," said a disdainful Shimkin. Somehow, the world of children's records was not quite as innocent as it had seemed.[16]

Cy Leslie: Cricket and Pickwick Records

Back in the late 1940s, Cy Leslie had set up Cricket Records as a friendly rival to Golden. "We showed together at all the trade shows," he said. "We had booths next to each other. Golden was probably No. 1 as a children's label, [but] we ran it pretty close at Cricket."

Easily grasping the rack-selling principles, Leslie would transform Pickwick Records into an internationally renowned economy-priced record merchandiser, according to *Record World* magazine. A self-made multimillionaire and a marketing and promotion genius, Leslie attended the same Bronx high school (DeWitt Clinton) as Hy Weiss of Old Town Records, but their careers and fortunes would take radically different paths. After branching out from children's records, Leslie took advantage of the new LP invention, albeit in the budget sector. At a stroke, Cy Leslie had set himself apart from the singles orientation of the traditional record men.

In effect, Leslie was following in the footsteps of larger-than-life Eli Oberstein, who was flooding the market in the early 1950s with bottom-feeding pop and classical product on ridiculously priced ten-inch LPs (a Varsity line was retailed at sixty-nine cents). Oberstein had finally quit RCA Victor in 1948, where he was "manager, popular artists and repertoire." Typically, he cocked a snook at his former employers by naming his new indie group Record Corporation of America: RCA. "Eli was very important," said Leslie. "He was quite an operator."

In 2005, the urbane Leslie traced his personal path to success via the mass marketing route. "I was released from the army in January 1946," he said.

> I was intrigued by the voice, and I made very basic square picture records called Voco greeting cards that were parodies of public domain tunes, plus originals. A buyer of the Kresge Company said, "Why don't you try to make some children's records with pictures on them? Show me some sketches, give me a little recording, [but] don't spend a lot of money." I gave him ten sketches, and he told me if he did like them, he would put them in 699 toy departments. I was absolutely nonplussed. Here [I was] a kid at that time . . . [and] thought that was the entire world; 699 covered everything, didn't it? That's the way we started children's records. We did very well with Cricket Records. We had a pretty good entrée now into *all* the mass market outlets.
>
> That gave us the opportunity to expand into those albums with Pickwick in 1952. We got hold of a lot of interesting markets that we thought might make it on low-priced LPs because LPs had just started up. But . . . the record stores . . . wouldn't touch us;

they had the high-priced stuff, which they didn't want cut into. We had LPs for $1.49, and we were doing very, very nicely: Korvette stores, Woolworth's, supermarkets, discount stores. You name them.

Then we decided [in the early 1960s] we'd better go beyond this into better material.[17] I went to my friends over at Capitol Records. I made the first very important deal, I think, with Alan Livingston and Stanley Gortikov, and I licensed the noncurrent catalog of Capitol Records. They wouldn't put out the catalog at low prices; they didn't want it to interfere with their basic product line. Eventually I got Sinatra, Nat "King" Cole, Peggy Lee—a whole bunch of stuff, even classical. We were then very successful at that. So here's the opportunity going around to our other friends in the business; everybody knew everybody at that time. We licensed Mercury Records, a whole host of them, including ultimately RCA, which included Elvis Presley. When he passed away [in 1977], absolutely sure-shot they wanted him back. Columbia was the only one of any major importance I couldn't license from. My best friends over at Columbia had a line of their own, Harmony, in addition to the record club.

Pickwick was looking beyond the reissue market for a while and employed as songwriters Lou Reed and John Cale, who were the founding members of the Velvet Underground (managed by Andy Warhol from 1965 to 1967). Along the way, Pickwick had acquired a Long Island pressing plant, the successful rack jobbing operations of the Heilicher brothers and Dan Gittleman (among others), and the Musicland retail chain. Thus, Pickwick controlled content, manufacturing, distribution, and points of sale.

The Pickwick Group achieved further growth by operating professionally on an international level, especially in Great Britain under Monty Lewis's leadership. "Now we're all over the map," said Cy Leslie. "Other people did the same, but not quite to the extent we did. We had lots of staff, but the object is to keep overhead as tight as you can—and keep a good reputation; that's important."

Pickwick thrived through the 1960s and well into the 1970s before the group was sold to the American Can Company, just as the LP era was fizzling out. The sale was timed to perfection. Although Leslie's budget volume business was shunned by serious record collectors, their narrow niche was not his concern. In a way, this mass-marketing concept contributed to the demise of the traditional independent record industry by creating excess product and impossible price pressures. "I was once called 'King of the Cheapies' by the *Financial Times* of London," he said with self-deprecating authority. No matter; he saw and realized the full range of opportunities that the independent record business offered. "People thrive now on reissues," he added. "They're everywhere."

The Mitch Miller Legacy

Columbia Records' Mitch Miller (and a Golden Records surrogate) alluded to this recycling process when I sought an interview in 2004. The grandee of popular music declined the invitation robustly, saying, "I was a giant, but I'm ninety-two years old and I'm tired." With a flickering flame in his belly, he opined, "I can't understand the fascination with rock 'n' roll. Everything only lasts twenty-five years." Then he noted that standard songs were making a comeback (at the time).

Miller's antipathy toward rock 'n' roll has been painted in such antagonistic terms that his own important legacy as a record man has been impaired. It must be said that those dated *Sing Along* albums (but huge-selling in their day) have done nothing to shore up his reputation. Yet in his prime at Columbia, he personified the role of the autocratic A&R man: he was involved in the selection and canvassing of songs, in choosing arrangers, and in nominating contractors to hire the studio musicians. Apart from reintroducing country music into the pop mainstream after the initial wartime flurry, he enhanced studio production values to such an extent that it can be argued he paved the way for Phil Spector's "Wall of Sound," the Beach Boys' good vibrations, and the Beatles' magical mystery tours. Most important, he helped Columbia to reassert itself as a genuine major label with hit single after hit single in the 1950s by career artists such as Rosemary Clooney, Doris Day, Frankie Laine, and Johnny Mathis. On the other hand, Frank Sinatra (Columbia's fading bobby-sox star) fought endlessly with Mitch and couldn't wait to leave for Capitol.

The Miller regime, full of drama, led to the Clive Davis era at Columbia with Bob Dylan, the Byrds, and Simon & Garfunkel. Davis himself was part of the new breed of major label businessmen/record men sophisticates, along with Irving Azoff, David Geffen, Doug Morris, Mo Ostin, Steve Ross, and Walter Yetnikoff.

Atlantic's Jerry Wexler was always ready to laud the pioneering A&R man's virtues. "Mitch Miller was very, very inventive and very clever, and a brilliant record man," Wexler said. He remembered that "I gave Mitch a little independent record called 'Cry,' which he gave to Johnnie Ray. But most important, I brought him Hank Williams's record of 'Cold Cold Heart' [recorded by Tony Bennett]. That opened up the whole thing. And that started all the covers of country and western that became popular in that period. Later on I met Hank Williams in Mitch's office with Fred Rose, the publisher. So I was sort of a tune pimp [*laughs*]." *Billboard*, for whom Wexler was a reporter at the time writing mainly on publishing stories, came up with a memorable headline: "Golden Oatunes: H. Williams Clefs 22 Hillbilly Toppers."[18]

A little-known fact is that Mitch Miller did attempt to introduce rhythm and blues to Columbia upon his arrival there in 1950 when he made a deal with booking agency head Ben Bart of Universal Attractions to sign the Ravens, Arnett Cobb, Wini Brown, and Herb Lance. The idea was to lure away Bart's top artist, Dinah Washington, from Mercury (Miller's previous employer), but the scheme faltered.[19] Even more intriguingly, according to publisher Julian Aberbach, Miller was in the race to buy Elvis Presley's contract from Sun in 1956 but felt the asking price was too high for "a local artist."[20] Then in 1959, Mitch was involved in aborted negotiations for the production services of then-kingpins Jerry Leiber and Mike Stoller. It was a sure sign of Columbia's concern, and that of Miller's, at missing the rock 'n' roll train. But as Columbia colleague George Avakian said, succinctly, "Mitch Miller resented the rock 'n' roll and R&B

movement. And he was so *successful* that it stayed that way until he departed the company in the '60s."

While attending an Alec Wilder memorial concert in New York in 1998, I ran into Mitch Miller, still a commanding figure although well into his eighties. Locked in an elevator with him, I asked if it was true that he had criticized rock 'n' roll in the late 1950s as being "no more than 'three chords.'" "Too right," the great man retorted, "and that was being fucking generous!" He was correct in that any given trend usually had a limited life cycle. But the fact that rock 'n' roll was still around after fifty years and was still being absorbed, analyzed, and enjoyed was a tribute to the indie record makers—and to the regional sounds they fostered.

PART

2

Regional
Sounds

6

Riding the Nashville Airwaves

CAST OF CHARACTERS
Jerry Wexler, Atlantic Records
Bill "Hoss" Allen, disc jockey, Radio WLAC, Nashville
Shannon Williams, Ernie's Record Mart and Excello-
  Nashboro Records
Fred Foster, Monument–Sound Stage 7 Records
*also featuring Gene Nobles and John Richbourg, disc
jockeys, WLAC; Randy Wood, Randy's Record Shop and
Dot Records; and Ernie Young, Ernie's Record Mart and
Excello-Nashboro Records*

Radio was a key element in the growth of independent labels from regional to national entities and was eagerly targeted by the more enterprising record men and their distributors. Without radio spins, a record had little chance; it was as simple as that. This led seamlessly to the rise of the personality disc jockey and to payola—the "pay for play" scam.

Enter Alan Freed: After arriving from Cleveland, Ohio, as the Moondog in 1954, he felt well at home in the New York music community (especially with his fellow Russian Jews). Having popularized the term "rock 'n' roll," he conspired to develop profitable business enterprises for himself and other cronies. As his Radio WINS show implied, he was unleashing a wild "rock 'n' roll party."

Freed was part of a breed of disc jockeys that was as colorful and influential as the records that were spun in regional pockets throughout the nation. For a mad spell, these men and other jive talkers were the self-anointed kings of radio.[1]

"A dee-jay, back then, became a personality," remembered soul singer Maxine Brown, "and he helped to make the artist by breaking

the record. Like Jocko [Henderson] who can say, 'Ooh-poo-pah-doo, how do you do? I'm
on the scene with the record machine saying ooh-poo-pah-doo, how do you do!' They
had this rap that they would do, 'Oh it sounds so nice, I think I'm gonna play it twice!'
And they'd drop the needle again; a dee-jay could do that. Now you have to have computer skills, you have to have a college education, and they are b-o-r-i-n-g [laughs]."

Back in the 1940s, the mighty but staid NBC and CBS radio networks still controlled the home entertainment market, just as their major label offshoots, RCA Victor
and Columbia, dominated the popular record business (with Decca). Television, with
NBC and CBS leading the charge, was looming large as a potent force to ensnare the
mass national audience and with it the heavy-duty advertising money.[2] Meanwhile,
with the encouragement of the Federal Communications Commission (FCC), tiny
small-town radio stations independent of network affiliation were providing alternative news, weather forecasts, and other local programming backed by sponsorship and
advertising. Often there was live music by neighborhood acts. In time, however, record
shows would prove to be practical, cheap, and popular ways of filling the schedules of
these minnow stations. A similar programming strategy was employed by the emerging small chains and network affiliates. This reliance on gramophone records, at the
expense of live productions, was to change the radio and music landscapes forever.

CBS-affiliate WLAC of Nashville, Tennessee, was one of the most influential regional
radio stations of the era, along with neighboring WSM, host of the *Grand Ole Opry*.
Thanks to a gargantuan 50,000–watt signal, Radio WLAC became a magnet for radio
play for the thrusting indie record men. With its radio waves bouncing readily over the
Jim Crow barriers of segregation, the station became a major factor in exposing R&B and
gospel records to new audiences in the South and beyond. It was this listener crossover
movement, from the southern black communities to (mainly) white teenagers over a
large swathe of the country, that would help to stoke the rock 'n' roll revolution.

At Atlantic Records, Ahmet Ertegun and Jerry Wexler were ahead of the curve in
spotting this trend after an early tip from music publisher friend Howie Richmond.
"Then we got our first feedback from the distributors in the South," said Wexler.

> They began to tell us, much to our amazement, that rhythm and blues records were
> being sold in white locations. We ran down this trail, and what we found out . . . es-
> sentially it was that powerful radio station in Nashville, WLAC. So it was just an
> amazing confluence of happenings.
>
> First of all, the spots were ridiculously cheap, so the people that realized this were
> the mail-order companies like Randy's [Record Shop] and Ernie's Record Mart. This
> music was going clear-channel to about twenty-two states. People would automati-
> cally hear this music, and white people would start to hear by mistake. Again, it was
> a very odd confluence, because the disc jockeys were white, the entrepreneurs were
> white, while the intended audience and music were all black. The intended audience
> was black because, besides the records, they were selling black cosmetic products:
> hair straighteners, complexion lighteners. They also sold items that the FCC wouldn't

approve of, such as tonic water to help ladies in distress at "that time of the month"—selling all these disreputable products, so-called.

Then the first white group that cottoned on to this music was high school [and] college kids in the South. So our distributors in the Carolinas, Virginia, Georgia, were telling us that white people were starting to buy these records, including jukebox operators in white locations.[3] This was before integration.

Along with this, a little later on was the phenomenon of the beach party scene in the Carolinas. So the white kids took their first transistor radios to the beach, and they started to hear LaVern Baker and Fats Domino, especially out of Nashville with Gene Nobles. And what happened was these kids began listening to the [R&B] records, and some of them even ventured to try to play the music. Next thing, rock 'n' roll!

But our relationship with the disc jockeys was one of total and shameless corruption [*laughs*]. The idea of the little pittances that we used to give them was just absurd; it was establishing a relationship. These guys would make like sixty dollars a week and [were] sweeping the transmitter [floor] for the same price, you know. So if we bought them a bottle of booze or Orlon sports shirts, it was a big thing. We'd also try to get some of our artists to appear on their record hops.

I have to tell you about Okey Dokey—remember James W. Smith in New Orleans? "Okey Dokey Stomp" [by Clarence "Gatemouth" Brown, Peacock] was written for him. He and I became very good pals. I hit New Orleans one time and was about to make his acquaintance. I said, "Oke, I want to get some of that good Chess Records treatment." He said, "If you want some of that good Chess Records treatment, you got to lay some of that good Atlantic bread on me!"

Bill "Hoss" Allen: The Early Years

From 1949 on, William Allen (known affectionately as "Hoss," or sometimes "The Hossman") was a member of the illustrious WLAC on-air disc jockey team, along with Gene Nobles and John Richbourg, in the station's heyday. Allen was a record man himself in the 1960s, heading Rogana Productions, which incorporated the Athens and Hermitage labels.

At the time of our interview in 1992, at the relocated WLAC radio station near Nashville's Music Row, Hoss was in frail health following a triple heart bypass operation, and he died not quite five years later. Yet his mind was sharp, and with impeccable detail he related his story, which took in the growth of radio and the associated expansion of the independent record business. Without any surprise, he was a natural interviewee at the microphone of a tape recorder. It was almost as if he was addressing his far-flung WLAC audience of old.

Young Bill Allen's childhood was spent happily just thirty miles north of Nashville in Depression-era Gallatin, Tennessee. This sleepy country town, like most in the South, was centered on the courthouse in the square but achieved unsuspected fame when it became the home of Randy's Record Shop and then Dot Records. The Hossman's music education was enhanced by playing swing-era 78-rpm records on a front-porch Victrola and beating out 4/4 time rhythms on a rudimentary set of drums, a gift from his grandmother.

Following army duty in special services at Fort McPherson, near Atlanta, Georgia, with "a lot of actors and dancers and stuff," Allen had thoughts of studying drama through the enlightened GI Bill scheme. After re-enrolling for college at Vanderbilt in late 1946, he discovered there was a new station going on air, Radio WKDA, which would have the first all-music format in Nashville.

"So I went over there," he said.

Of course, I had absolutely no experience in spinning records or anything, but they gave me a job answering the phones at night and on the weekends. Now WKDA is at the corner of Fourth Avenue and Union Street, atop the First American Bank building. One block down the street at Fourth and Church, atop the Third National Bank building, is WLAC with Gene Nobles and John R. playing all of this blues and stuff. Randy's Record Shop had sprung up in Gallatin and was sponsoring these shows. I knew nothing about that—I only knew WLAC because of the sports; they carried baseball games. Herman Grizzard, who later did Buckley's Record Shop's *After Hours* show on the air, was the "Old Colonel": he was the sports announcer.

But people were asking me in Nashville, . . ."You're from Gallatin, right, Hoss? Well, tell me about the Randy's Record Shop." I said, "They've got just a few records in the five-and-dime store there." "Whoa," they said, "I hear this program on WLAC and it's sponsored by the Randy's Record Shop and"—it was in the vernacular that they said it—"they're playing nigger music." I said, "What do you mean, they're playing nigger music?" And they said, "You know, like blues and stuff."

After graduating from college, Hoss Allen learned that two Gallatin businessmen—Mr. Henry, the Buick dealer, and Mr. Perkins, a pharmacist—were joining the independent radio station gold rush. "They were simply putting a radio up because they understood that small town radio stations were good investments," said Allen.

You could make some money out of them. They opened up all of these places on the dial like 1240 and 1010. This particular spot was a 1,000–watt daytime station at 1010 AM on the dial. It was WHIN, in a field with cows on Highway 109.

So I went out and I introduced myself to Wes Britt, the station manager, and he gave me a little piece of copy to read. He said, "Oh, I think you'll do great." I think the voice caught his attention; I had a much deeper and much more resonant voice than I do now. And so he said, "We pay forty bucks a week. You can come to work immediately, and you can help me set up the music library." Well, as I remember, we used tracks off the old Capitol [Records] transcriptions. That was the big sixteen-inch[-disc] library that had Alvino Rey and the King Sisters, Stan Kenton and June Christy, Paul Weston and Jo Stafford, and a lot of individual things. There were fifteen-minute shows that they put together so you could play a complete show on one side of these big sixteen-inch [transcription] discs, you know. We went on the air Labor Day, September 1, 1948, and we had two announcers.

So I start this show at HIN called *The Harlem Hop*, and I'm playing my big band music. I'm on from 3:30 (we're a daytime station) until we close; it was around 4:45

[in the] summer, and it would be as late as 6:30 during the winter. But after about two weeks, we had a coverage that was middle Tennessee, southern Kentucky, and north Alabama. This is a 1,000–watt station, daytime. I started getting mail, but not for what I was playing. They wanted Private Cecil Gant, they wanted Roy Brown, they wanted Wynonie Harris, they wanted Bull Moose Jackson, they wanted T-Bone Walker. And I said, "Who the hell are these people?" I'd never heard of them except for Cecil Gant, because he was a Nashville guy. Bullet Records had cut him, and I was familiar with that.

Gene Nobles: Disc Jockey, Radio WLAC, Nashville

After awhile, Bill Allen met his Gallatin neighbor Randy Wood, who enthused about the prospects for this brand of race music (which would soon be called rhythm and blues). In fact, Wood confided to Allen that Gene Nobles had been playing such records for him over WLAC since February 1947. "So Randy brought me down and introduced me to Gene," said Allen.

He was this little short guy who'd had polio, infantile paralysis, and he was crippled with it. He had this big bottle of Seagram's Seven Crowns sitting on the table with a Coke and a mic, and he had this guy, "Cohort," who sat in and played the records. At the time, Cohort was an integral part of the show, a young guy whose name was George Karsch. Gene was in another little studio with just a mic; he'd say something, then he'd say, "Ain't that right, Cohort?" So Cohort would play the Johnny Weissmuller Tarzan yell: *Ahhh-ahhh-ahhh-ahhhaawoo*, you know that thing. That's all you ever heard outta Cohort; he never said a word, except he'd play this yell. Well, that became a great part of the show. Gene had a very successful show before Randy [came along].

WLAC was CBS-affiliated, and we weren't doing anything different than any other CBS affiliate. We were riding the network until 10 P.M., and we had local news from 10 until 10:15. Then you had a local disc jockey like Gene Nobles who happened to be on that particular shift and who played music until midnight, then we signed off. So 10:15 until 11 was just music, but 11 until 12 he called it *The Dance Hour*.

Now Gene was an old carnie man, he was a clowner, and he talked in carnie a lot. Carnie is sort of a pig-Latin type. At that time, there were hundreds of carnivals roaming all over the country. *Billboard* magazine, about half of it was personal ads from carnival workers to other carnival workers: "Join me in El Paso . . .," all sending messages back and forth via *Billboard*. So the carnies picked up on him. They were calling him, and they were writing him to send messages, which he would do in carnie talk. People were talking about him from that.

After Gene Nobles began playing boogie and blues records, the listeners' mail started flowing in from all over the country. The potential audience was far larger and more widely dispersed than the WLAC management had anticipated. Explained Hoss:

We had 50,000 watts, but we were directional. Now by "directional" I mean we protected two other stations on 1510, our place on the dial, one in Boston and one in Seattle. So we had what we called a sky wave. For our transmitters, we had five towers rather than one tower. We'd pull our signal back from the northeast and the northwest after six o'clock at night, and [it was] almost like throwing 100,000 watts southeast and southwest, and directly north and south.

I mean, we used to send from Canal Street to the Loop, from New Orleans to Chicago, just like a local station; everything up through Indiana, Illinois, and Ohio, in a straight line like that. We'd go up to about Richmond [Virginia] without any interference. You can get it in St. Louis, then it goes south of Missouri into Oklahoma, and down into Texas. It's just like a giant saucer. Then it goes out into the Bahamas, Jamaica, and places like that.

By pure circumstance, therefore, the Randy Wood–sponsored Gene Nobles record show was the impromptu catalyst behind Radio WLAC's growth and that of rhythm and blues music. The simple beginnings of the remarkable Wood, who was born into a family of educators and became one of the most successful indie record men ever— and in quick time, too—were recalled by Hoss Allen:

He'd just come back from the army. He was from McMinnville, Tennessee. He met a guy from Gallatin in the army, and they wanted to get into the electrical appliance business. His partner [William Kirkpatrick] was gonna rewire lamps, waffle irons, and things like that. Randy, who was an electrical engineer, was gonna build custom hi-fi sets. That was the new thing, hi-fi. So they get this little shop [Kirk and Randy's] on the corner of West Franklin and South Water Avenue, Gallatin, and Randy starts to build the hi-fi sets. So he figures, well, I should sell records with my hi-fi sets.

He's selling sets 'bout as fast as he can build them, but he's not selling any records particularly, and so he's got this oversupply. Well, there was a guy named Bob Holmes who worked for Capitol Records; he was a promotion man, and he sold Randy records. He'd come to Gallatin; that was his area. He'd sell him some Alvino Rey, he would sell him some Jo Stafford, or he'd sell him some Johnny Mercer or Nat Cole, any of those people that were on Capitol at the time. But Bob also called on Gene Nobles as a promotion man to get him to play these records on this *Dance Hour* show, 11 til 12. And so Randy said, "God, I just can't buy any more records; I'm overloaded." So Bob Holmes says, "You should meet this disc jockey Gene Nobles down at WLAC in Nashville. People listen to him all over, maybe four or five states." He had no idea we reached thirty states. Anyhow, he said, "Maybe he could sell some more for you."

So Bob takes Randy down to WLAC one night, introduces him to Gene, and they talk. Gene says, "Well, maybe we could sell some [records] . . . [the station is] selling some chickens." By this time we're selling chickens by mail and baby chicks: "$2.98 a hundred; at this low price no sex or breed guaranteed." So you know you're gonna get cockerels and they're gonna grow up and attack your dog!

Anyhow, Bob Holmes brings the two people together, and history is made: Randy Wood meets Gene Nobles. So Randy decides to buy a spot, one spot a night, at 11:30 each night, Monday through Saturday, at the then-exorbitant price of six dollars a spot . . . something like that.

The first c.o.d. sales pitch was for four records by Johnny Mercer, Nat "King" Cole, Ella Mae Morse (all Capitol artists), and Eddy Arnold (RCA Victor) at $1.05 each. And nothing happened.

"But all the time Gene is playing this black music," continued Hoss.

He's gone out and gotten some other records on his own, and he's playing some records. People are listening, and they're writing in. All of a sudden, they hear this name, Randy's Record Shop, [and] that they can order records by mail. He was not offering any black records, but he was offering *records*. So Randy told WLAC after two weeks to cancel [his advertising spot]; he couldn't afford it. By this time he'd spent nearly sixty [or] seventy bucks on this; forget it. But on the third Monday morning, he got an armload of mail after he'd canceled the spot. Ninety percent was for these black records Gene was playing.

Randy had never offered these for sale, but "Can you send me Wynonie Harris, 'Who Threw the Whiskey in the Well'?" So Randy calls Gene and says, "I'm getting these orders, but what are they . . . race music, race records?" Then Randy sees the light, and he buys fifteen minutes, and he starts looking everywhere for black product, and he makes up a couple of black [music] packages. So they offer five records for $2.98 plus c.o.d. and handling. Now, the records, he's buying wholesale from the distributor. Where you make your money is on the c.o.d. and handling. Well, they just took off like wildfire. Within probably another three or four months, he's up to forty-five minutes, and he's on from 10:15 every night until 11 P.M.

But Wood's partner, William Kirkpatrick, was not happy at this escalating expenditure, and their partnership was dissolved.

"We had this guy nobody ever mentions," added Allen.

His name was E. G. Blackman, and he was the [WLAC] sales manager. He saw the great commercial potential in this black music and in this black audience that no one had ever tapped. The powers that be at this radio station weren't too happy about having a "nigger" radio station. Business people around town were beginning to hear about it, and they were kidding them on the golf course, at the country clubs. The station had been owned by Life and Casualty Insurance Company, which was LAC, but now it was owned by Mr. Truman Ward, who had been manager of it when Life and Casualty let it go.

So ol' man Ernie Young, Ernest Young, had a record shop down on Third Avenue here in Nashville, and he came to Blackman and wanted to buy some time. He sold him 9 in the evening to 9:45, and Gene would do that [show] too. So then here comes [Louis] Buckley, who's the old jukebox operator who's got all these records out there [at Buckley's Record Shop], and he wants to get on. They've already got Sterling Beer sponsoring 11 to midnight [*The Dance Hour*], and there's nothing open. So Buckley takes midnight to 1 A.M., and Gene's doing all three of these record shops. Now in the summer of '47, Gene wanted to go on vacation, so John Richbourg, who was the newsman, takes over.

John Richbourg: Disc Jockey, Radio WLAC, Nashville

"John R." would go on air employing his trademark introductory patter: "Well, have a little mercy there, honey. John R. Yeah, I'm here, way down South in the middle of Dixie." A natural entrepreneur, John Richbourg would have a fruitful extracurricular spell as a record man with Sound Stage 7 Records (through J. R. Enterprises) and be-come involved with Southern Record Distributors and Cape Ann Music publishing company. If there were any conflicts of interest with his disc jockey duties, he didn't seem too concerned, nor did the management of Radio WLAC at the time.[4]

Full of admiration and respect for his station colleague, Hoss Allen said:

John had this enormous, wonderful, beautiful voice—and a vocabulary from here to Brisbane, Australia. He never used a word with two syllables when he could get by with five! John was the most unlikely man to become such a great black disc jockey; everybody used to think he was black. He'd actually been a Shakespearean actor in New York, tried to make the stage, drove a cab up there for a long time. Then he came back to his hometown, Charleston, South Carolina, to play on the radio when he couldn't make it on the stage. Eventually he came over here as the newsman in about '42, then went in the navy for a while and came back in '45.

They didn't have anybody to sit in for Gene, so they got John. Well, John had heard Gene sell these chickens by mail, and by this time he was selling some other things, and he was, of course, selling records. But no one could follow Gene Nobles; no one could be Gene. I mean, he had no format that you could come in and [follow and] fill his shoes; he was just such a complete different thing.

John Richbourg started taking note of mail-order announcers from other stations that were playing mainly hillbilly music and developed his own homespun style that echoed their "genuine" sincerity. "These were big hard-pitch men," said the Hossman:

"Hello neighbor, this is Irving Victor, send no money." So this was what John knew. But he thought that as he was playing black music, he would try to turn it a little bit, and he used a little colloquialism, "Yo' understand." He'd be telling them, "We got this great thing, yo' understand . . ." because he'd heard somebody talk that way. So he works for Ernie for two weeks, he works for Buckley for two weeks, he works for Randy.

Well now, ol' man Ernie Young always thought Gene worked harder for Randy than he did for him. So when John did the show, his mail picked up appreciably the two weeks that John was on, 'cause John did everybody equally. Maybe Ernie had some good offers on that week, I don't know, but the mail picked up—or at least Mr. Young thought so. So when Gene came back, ol' man Ernie Young came up to "Blackie" Blackman, the WLAC sales manager, and said, "I want John Richbourg to do my show from now on." So this is how John got into it; he always did *Ernie's Record Parade.* Gene continued to do Randy's and Buckley's, and Gene was happy for John to do Er-nie's. Gene didn't give a shit; I mean, the less work he could do, the better he cared. 'Course, he was close to Randy.

Now, John Richbourg, everybody called him "Richberg." It had a Jewish connota-tion, but it was "bourg." He was [French] Huguenot; he was very, very proud of his Huguenot ancestors. There were some racial slurs about Richbourg, kidding around the station and from guys in town. Businessmen [and] newspaper guys were kidding the general manager about how it was Jews were doing nigger music. That's why he changed his name to John R., but I always called him John *Awrra,* 'cause blacks say *awrr.* That made him mad, too.

But most people thought John was black. I never worked at it; John did. When he'd get off the air, he'd go right back to his gentlemanly character. John went home at night, he didn't drink, he didn't party. We used to have a place right behind where we were located downtown called "The Alley," Printers Alley. It was a bunch of little clubs. The record guys would come to town, and we would party all night long. It was a little hard on families.

Hoss Allen: Disc Jockey, Radio WLAC, Nashville

While still at WHIN in Gallatin, twenty-six-year-old Bill Allen met WLAC's Blackie Blackman at a Christmas party in 1948. "Then Randy [Wood] got into the thing," said Allen. "He said, 'I want him to sit in for Gene Nobles on my show whenever Gene leaves on vacation.' Well, Gene was crazy about the horses, and if there was a track open anywhere near, Gene was gone. He might be gone for two days, or if he was lucky he might be gone for two weeks, and nobody was gonna fire him. I mean, he was responsible for this explosion at night, you see."

Starting at WLAC in April 1949 and using his real name, Bill Allen first deputized for Gene Nobles as the voice of Randy's record show around June. By this time, Randy's Record Shop was promoting itself as "The Nation's Largest Mail Order House" to "Juke Box Ops" (and "Dealers and Disk Jocks!!"), showing that Wood was well aware of the important movers and shakers in the record industry.[5] Consider, too, that Wood had appended his first name to a business that was selling *black* rhythm and blues and gospel records in the heart of the segregated South.

Shortly after Allen's radio debut, Randy Wood became a serious player as a record manufacturer. The personable and highly motivated Wood chose the name of Dot Records because it was intentionally short, sharp, and thus memorable; a slick early slogan was "Hot on Dot."[6] Wood's inspiration and helper was battle-scarred Jim Bulleit of Bullet Records in Nashville. The initial Dot releases, consisting of blues, hillbilly, and gospel, were used to fill Randy's mail-order packages, but before long, the indie imprint would have far-reaching ramifications in the annals of pop and rock 'n' roll.

As a "thank you" gesture for Gene Nobles's radio support, Wood gave him a 10 percent stake in the label, according to Hoss Allen. It was a great deal for both parties. All the while, the shop and mail-order division continued to expand rapidly under Gilbert Brown, another 10 percent stockholder in Dot.

Randy Wood sold Dot Records to Paramount Pictures in April 1957 and in doing so became the first indie record man to sell out at this level. At the time, the label was racking up an astonishing run of pop hits by Pat Boone, the Fontane Sisters, the Hilltoppers, Jim Lowe, and Gale Storm under musical director/ex-Hilltopper Billy Vaughn, a Fletcher Henderson devotee. Driving the organization was the unbeatable team of Wood, sales manager Al Bennett (also with a 10 percent stake that would enable him to invest in Liberty Records), and veteran plugger Mickey Addey, known imperiously as "the baron." In the cold light of day, Randy Wood had made the unbelievable, triumphant leap from rural Tennessee to Tinseltown a mere seven years after starting his label. It is fair to say that he is an underappreciated, even maligned figure in the independent record makers story, especially among the hardcore rock 'n' roll–collecting fraternity who hate with a passion those Dot cover versions of R&B hits. But these detractors conveniently ignore Wood's impact on the emergent rhythm and blues market as an innovative record mail-order retailer and the quality of bought-in Dot classics such as Sanford Clark's "The Fool" and the Dell-Vikings' "Come Go with Me" and "Whispering Bells."

Wood's dismal reputation did not deter wide-eyed young English researcher Rob Finnis from interviewing him in Beverly Hills in 1970. After stalking through the record man's front garden and stumbling into a garbage can, the intrepid Brit was greeted by the startled record man. Deciding not to call the cops and offering coffee instead, Wood gave Finnis the impression that he was modest, even ambivalent about his remarkable contribution to music history. He seemed just as anxious to convey a "prim and proper" image, said Finnis. Nevertheless, Randy Wood did remember with affection his early R&B hits by the Griffin Brothers in 1950 and his first big pop hit, "Trying" by the Hilltoppers, in 1952.[7]

"Randy was enormously successful," said Hoss Allen. "Well, Pat Boone would cover everything that Fats Domino or Little Richard put out; like on 'Tutti Frutti,' Richard did about 650,000 and Pat did 1,500,000! And, of course, this was the start of whites covering black [R&B] music."

So Bill Allen, after learning his craft as an all-round radio man and honing his skills as a dee-jay for some eight years, would finally take over a WLAC slot full-time now that Gene Nobles had hit the jackpot with his Dot Records stock and retired.[8]

Randy Wood was not alone in reaping the benefits of the Nashville station's strong signal and the potent selling power of its disc jockeys. "By '50, the record guys were beginning to hear about WLAC," said Hoss. "I mean, [Leonard and Phil] Chess were in business in Chicago and they were making their way down, and the Biharis out on the coast with Modern Records were coming in. The word got around: You get to this station in Nashville and get your records on there, things can happen. Or: You get to Randy's Record Shop, make a deal with Randy and get on his show, you can sell some records, and then other jocks will pick it up and start playing it. It was a whole movement that started right here." When various record men began showing up at the record shop in Gallatin, with their "big cigars and big cars," the surprised local folks were convinced the gangsters were rolling into town.

"So I took over the show," Allen continued. "I took over *Randy's Record Hi-Lights* and *The Dance Hour.* I didn't use the nickname 'Hoss' on the air until I took over the show for Gene. But Gene was such a character that there was no following him. I had a natural southern accent; I used so many black colloquialisms from my growing up on the street. I wanted to be so different from Gene that I really started trying to just fall back into a very deep southern accent. And they'd think this guy has *gotta* be black.

When I came on, I'd always say, 'It's git-down time with the Hossman!' And 'git-down time,' that's . . . for the pimps. That's when the whores gotta hit the street: git-down time. [I used] all of these little colloquialisms that blacks use and that probably the whites did not know."

Wisely, Allen ditched Gene Nobles's long-running introductory theme ("Swanee River Boogie" by Albert Ammons, Mercury) in favor of a Count Basie tune written by Frank Foster, "Blues in Frankie's Flat." With commendable alacrity, the song was retitled "Blues in Hoss' Flat" through the good offices of Morris Levy and Teddy Reig at Roulette Records. Hoss Allen had truly arrived.

"I'd come on, I'd say: 'Awright! It's the Hossman, and I am down once again. Look out here for the Randy Record Shop: R-A-N-D-Y in Gallatin G-A-L-L-A-T-I-N, Gallatin, Tennessee. Honey, we got records! We'll ship 'em to you anywhere, and let's start right now.' And then for Royal Crown I would say: 'Look, I am down for Royal Crown, America's favorite hairdressing. Let me tell you somethin' honey, just a touch means so much. Awright!'"

Every disc jockey had favorite tales of creating hit records, and the Hossman was no exception. "John and I both think we broke 'Please, Please, Please' by James Brown," Allen said.

I was working for Gene in '56, and I found this old 78 record on the Federal label in a discard box, which was rare then because they had probably gone to 45. I put it on back in the record room, and it blew me away. So I took it and started playing it [on air]. By the time Gene had got back two weeks later, it was a hit. Now John says he was playing it at the same time. He could have been; I'm sure he was. I wasn't listening to John, and he wasn't listening to me. But James Brown says he put the record in John's hands, so as far as I am concerned, we both broke it.

There were other records. "So Fine" by the Fiestas on Old Town, I worked on that hard. I was supposed to have the publishing on that, Hy-Hoss Music: Hy Weiss and Hoss Allen. Then I found out Hy didn't own the goddamn tune in the first place; it was Johnny Otis. Hy set up this Hy-Hoss Music; he went as far as putting it on his door. He said, "Look, I'm putting you in the business, look at it, Hy-Hoss Music!" I felt bad; it was on the label and everything.[9] But we broke so many records here at the station. Of course, John was probably single-handedly responsible for Otis Redding. Now Ernie would tell John what to play every night and Randy would tell me what to play because they knew what was selling. Other than that, we played what we wanted.

Another hit broken by Hoss Allen was "Sea Cruise" by Frankie Ford on Ace in the late spring of 1959. According to the artist, the record was treading water as a regional disc in the New Orleans area until Hoss began promoting it, whereupon Bob Green in Miami and Bill Randle in Cleveland stepped in to widen the net. Then Dick Clark, who monitored the WLAC shows for *American Bandstand,* picked up on "Sea Cruise," and "that was the end!" said Ford, as the record sailed to No. 14 nationally. Later that same year, the payola bombshell would explode to upset this tried-and-tested if cozy system of breaking indie label hits.

"The payola thing happened," admitted Hoss. "I guess we didn't know enough to ask for more than we got, but it certainly played a part in [our income]. I was on the payroll of about eight or nine companies who sent me a check every month. They sent me a tax withholding statement at the end of the year, where they had paid me *x* dollars and had not taken out any withholding. I always paid tax on it and always deposited checks so there were records at the bank. They got John and myself, but they didn't do anything. We had turned it in as far as taxes were concerned, and there was no law against payola per se at the time, 1959. But after the law, they made us sign this disclosure thing that we would not accept any money and all this sort of stuff. Then it turned to other things."

Shannon Williams: Ernie's Record Mart and Excello-Nashboro Records

Shannon Williams still presented a bright-minded and youthful figure in 1995. He was an employee of Nashboro Records and its Excello subsidiary for twenty-one years, from 1960, and advanced to the post of vice president, A&R. Working with founder Ernie Young for the first six years before Young sold out, Williams witnessed the brilliant way that his boss meshed the labels with his Ernie's Record Mart mail-order business. As a result, the Nashboro group record sales were well above the norm for mainstream blues and gospel product that was aimed essentially at the segmented black southern market. Quite properly, Nashboro's letterhead declared the company was "Located in the Record Center of The South."

Ernie's Record Mart and Randy's Record Shop were serious competitors, but there was more than enough business flooding in from the WLAC listeners for them to coexist comfortably. Both operations were targeting a vast rural audience that was attuned to shopping for worldly goods through the venerable Montgomery Ward and Sears, Roebuck mail-order houses. Said Shannon Williams:

> Randy's claimed in their advertising, of course, to be "The World's Largest . . .," but in reality I think we pulled probably almost twice as much mail. Ernie was getting a demand in the mail order for this type of music, . . . black music, which was not available at every little country town. Black people wanted records by black artists, [and] it just fell naturally: "Well, maybe I'll record some for them myself." This is how it started.
>
> Now Ernest Young in Nashville, prior to being in the label situation or mail-order records, operated a string of jukeboxes about town. The jukeboxes were the thing in those days as far as entertainment in most cafés, restaurants, and what have you. It's my understanding that Ernest Young had one of the biggest, if not the biggest, jukebox route in the city. I believe I have heard that he had about 148 or so locations about the Nashville area, which seems to me to be a really large route. Of course, as owner of those boxes, he had to keep up and change the records to the newest releases. Apparently he set up a store in the beginning to dispose of all the used records that were taken off of the jukeboxes, and that put him into the retail business. This was the [early] 1940s, and it was the 78s, of course, on the jukeboxes.

Naturally, if it's a black location, they certainly wouldn't want any hillbilly on their box, whereas across town it was probably strictly a country operation. Ernie's business covered both divides, absolutely. There were no black jukebox operators operating at the time. Even when I joined Ernie in '60, he was still doing business with many jukebox operators who bought their records at Ernie's.

An industry latecomer, Ernie Young was already in his fifties by the time he was retailing surplus jukebox records at the Record Mart in the mid-1940s. After moving to a choice central location at 179 Third Avenue North, he personalized the business as Ernie's Record Mart before launching Nashboro Records in June 1951. Excello Records was introduced in August 1952 after an early Nashboro hillbilly series was aborted.[10] The Nashboro label, therefore, was transformed into a dedicated gospel line with Excello earmarked mainly for blues and R&B. The stripped-down early sessions were engineered by Ernie Young himself and featured artists mainly from across the tracks in segregated Nashville.

"So Ernie started recording in Ernie's Record Mart after closing hours," said Williams.

He had this little recording equipment which he would set up in the front. Then later on, many of the early Nashboro gospel releases were cut at the WLAC radio station studio. Once Ernie saw what he was on to, that this thing was going to be popular, then he invested into constructing his own studio there on the top floor of the building.

This was a three-level building. The bottom level was Ernie's Record Mart, which faced Third Avenue, but it was like almost on a hillside. So the top level exited out into what's called Printers Alley, a well-known striptease area of joints and bars. The Excello studio was really among all these places. The second level . . . had no windows or exits, [and this] was where all the packing was done. The records, of course, were on the first level, and all the orders were pulled there; also on the first level was an office area where three or four women billed these orders and prepared them for packing. Then they were loaded in all the way to the post office.

When I first saw it in 1960, I didn't know much about studios, so I guess I was fascinated by it. But by today's standards, it was quite a dingy place; people have better equipment in their homes nowadays. He had these great old big Telefunken mics, huge things; he'd have one for the lead vocalist and one of those for a background group. Occasionally he might have another mic if the artist used drums, but he hated to entertain the thought of recording drums because he couldn't control the sound in that room. And the drums just got into everything. So he wouldn't permit hardly anything but maybe just a snare, and you can hear that on some of the early gospel recordings; he also used a stand-up bass. He was the engineer; it was all done on single-track mono—he never recorded a stereo in his life! But he did it all. If he didn't like the take, he'd do it again.[11]

One of Excello's best Nashville R&B artists, Roscoe Shelton, remembered Ernie Young supervising sessions: "He would chew on his cigar, and he would sit up there. I never did see him light one, but you could tell he'd been smoking. And he would yell all over the speaker, 'Let's run that down again; something wasn't right there. Drummer, you let off a little; piano, you come up a little; Roscoe, you back up a little . . . step in a little closer.' That's one thing about Ernie, he had full control of everything that he did in that studio." Shelton always regretted leaving the small Excello family and getting lost among John Richbourg's bigger stable of artists.

Shannon Williams grew up fifty-five miles northeast of Nashville near the Smith County seat of Carthage, Tennessee. "It's where Vice President Al Gore is from," he said.

It was very much out in the country. I never went to school with a black person in my life. As a child, we had all the little country radio stations; they call them "sunup to sundown" stations here. They are required by the federal law to go off the air in the evening. So that means that if you're listening to radio later in the day, you have to tune in to the more powerful stations in Nashville or somewhere else. This was before the days that we ever owned a television, so for me it was WLAC. For some reason, I was fascinated by a man that came on WLAC at seven o'clock every night by the name of Herbert W. Armstrong with *The World Tomorrow*. And being brought up in a Pentecostal religious environment, I felt this man knew how to explain the Bible more than anybody I'd ever heard in my life.

By the time I went to work for Nashboro, I knew all about Brother Joe May, Madame Edna Gallmon Cooke, and the Swanee Quintet. When I was living way back in the country, I never dreamed that I'd ever have anything to do with any of that. It all came by such accident. I answered a blind ad in the newspaper once we had moved to Nashville for me to go to school at the University of Tennessee branch here. I needed the work to earn money to help pay for education.

A few days later I get a call from Dorothy Keaton, who was Ernie's secretary, wanting to know if I would come down for Mr. Young to interview me. I went down to Third Avenue North. When I got there and discovered what kind of [down-home] operation this was, it was a real shock, because here it was. This was the place?

But Mr. Young was the perfect southern gentleman, like a Colonel Sanders without the beard. He had snow-white hair, perfectly groomed, [and] always dressed in fine clothes; he shopped at an exclusive men's store in Nashville by the name of Joseph Frank & Sons. He bought a new Cadillac every year, although the current model never had more than a few thousand miles on the clock. His wife, Elizabeth, had a new car almost every year, but she had to settle for a Pontiac, not a Cadillac. They lived in a very exclusive part of town known as Oak Hill, where many country stars came to live.

So he hired me that very day. My first duties were to fill mail orders. I have seen days where cash would exceed $5,000 a day, plus all the c.o.d. money orders, plus all of the new orders. It took the women several hours in the morning to just open the mail. Monday was the heaviest day because you'd have the buildup from Saturday and Sunday, when you didn't get deliveries. I've seen Mondays where there were 5- to 6,000 orders to process. Monday mail probably took sometimes till Wednesday to complete. But with the staff that we had, I've seen them put out 1,500 to near[ly] 2,000 packages a day.

The WLAC listeners would simply sit down with their pen and paper: "Dear Ernie's, Send me so-and-so." And we would package it up [and] send it to them. On the outside of the package there would be a little card that listed what we were due for the record, what the post office was due for the c.o.d. fee, and the total. So the postman delivers this package to their door and collects the money, then the post office issues Ernie's . . . a money order. That's why we got such stacks of money orders and not many refusals, because the service was so quick. By the volume we sent out, we got tremendous amounts of records back, but I'm persuaded to believe it was maybe 5 percent or less [as] refusals. Our philosophy was to get it out immediately before they changed their minds, because the quicker you can get it to their door, the more apt you are to get paid.

The southern states were the main market, of course. That's not to say there wasn't a big pool from northern areas, but certainly your North and South Carolinas, Georgia, Florida, Alabama, Mississippi, Arkansas—those Deep South areas. It was totally the black market [at one time]. It did increase. I'm not patting myself on the back, but it hit its peak when I took over the mail-order business in '63.

I started doing offers that they hadn't done before. One of the most successful packages that I ever ran was a Chess package. Now I have to tell you I didn't get any payola from Chess [*laughs*]. But I put on albums by [black comedians] Moms Mabley and Pigmeat Markham, and we called it Ernie's "Party Special." And John R. would run a little of Moms Mabley up to the punch line where she was about to get a little dirty, and then he would stop it and say, "Well, I can't go no farther with that; you'll just have to order it to see what is happening next." People were ordering that thing like mad. We probably sold 25- to 30,000 packages of this combination through the mail; it was two albums for $4.98. John R. played one of them one night and the other one the next night. The people had never been offered this kind of record before. So to build the business, I thought, "Hey, they like that."

Ernie's specials were always six 45–rpm records for somewhere between the prices of $3.19 or $3.29. I tried to edge that up to maybe $3.59, $3.79. We tried to keep it to where maybe they would always be paying in the sixty-cent range per record. Most of these were hits. You couldn't expect to sell a lot of packages if you had a lot of what we'd call "dogs" in the package. The choice was ours. There were times when there might be three Excellos in the package, and the volume would suffer tremendously because of too much blues.

During my best period, we had all the great Motown Sound people: the Supremes, the Marvelettes, Mary Wells. I remember our biggest-selling record was "Baby Workout" by Jackie Wilson [Brunswick]; we sold about 80,000 copies of that. So we'd load 'em up with five good hits and then put us a Lazy Lester [Excello] in there; the listeners didn't mind taking the Lazy Lester to get the five hits. We just picked the names of the packages at random. There was Ernie's "Rainbow Special," we had one called Ernie's "Pink Lizard Special," and Ernie's "Big Boss Special." I just continued the program that they had been doing, and I guess Ted Adams had done this before me [while working at Ernie's in the 1950s].

The fun of filling the mail orders was reading the letters from the people. Although WLAC is a 50,000–watt station, if you've ever heard it in other cities it sometimes fades in and fades out. I recall one time we had a record by Professor Harold Boggs. I picked up a letter from a dear lady one day who was ordering her some gospel records, and she said, "Send me that new release by Professor *Harybox*." And you had to know what they meant because if not you'd miss a sale. The listeners wouldn't order by title; they'd order by a line in the song or a phrase or whatever the catch line was. It was a challenge.[12]

The 45s were basically around eighty-nine cents, but we offered what was called Ernie's discount sheet, which was a green sheet. It was a page that had on one side spirituals and on the other side . . . blues, and you could order anything off this page for sixty-nine cents. Chess records, for example, cost us thirty-two cents per 45, while others were usually thirty-five to thirty-seven cents. As far as albums, Chess was selling us for $1.10, and we were selling for $2.98 [in 1963]. Chess was always a little bit better deal than everybody else on both the gospel and the blues. I think the powers that be at Chess recognized the power of WLAC, and in order to get their product played, they gave Ernie a better price.

As an aside, here was an example of Leonard Chess's masterly business tactics. Shannon Williams said,

It was my choice what went on the air, every selection, what went in the package, what didn't. Ernie gave me a totally free hand. He just insisted on a track list of the daily program, and that was no more to see that his Excellos and Nashboros were being played on the air [*laughs*]. They would all have their spots, because he didn't put out that many new releases. He'd only have one or two Excellos at a time, and they'd all get airplay. Oh sure, he believed in advertising in *Cash Box* every week; he got some sort of special rate.

The WLAC spots were in place when I came aboard in 1960. We were on two hours on Saturday night, and I would feature every new release we had on Excello and Nashboro because [we had] so much time. The way it would run was this: we would open up with a single or two, and then we'd offer a package, and that was repeated throughout the whole program. They were the hits of the day, but we'd mix the Excellos in, so you might have "Green Onions" by Booker T. & the MGs followed by "Bed Bug Blues" by Lightnin' Slim. That's just the way it worked.

John [R.] would name every record in the package and usually play two. Normally the record before the package announcement would be in the package, and then he'd say: "Now, I'm gonna tell you about Ernie's 'Whiz Bang Blues Special.' You gonna get six 45–rpm records, all of them hits, at the amazing low price of three dollars and twenty-nine cents. Now, you can't beat that with a stick, can you?" He'd come on and name every record, both sides, tell them how much it was, and "Send in your order to Ernie's Record Mart, 179 Third Avenue North, Nashville. And nowhere else but Nashville." He'd always say "nowhere else but Nashville" because Randy's was out in Gallatin!

Some of the idiots would get mixed up all the time and send the order for the "Whiz Bang" out to Gallatin. But we got Randy's orders, too, so we had this sort of working agreement between Randy's and Ernie's where we always kept each other posted of what we had in our specials. So if somebody writes to Gallatin to Randy's and says send me the "Whiz Bang Blues Special," well, Randy's would send it to them. They'd carry the Excello records, of course; they were a good dealer for us. Randy's sold a lot of Nashboro and Excello, and we serviced them just like a regular distributor.

We also did a bit of what was called one-stopping for little mom-and-pop record stores down in the South that had no access to other distributors. We would sell to them on a c.o.d. basis at a special price of fifty-five cents for 45s.

All the bigwigs from all the labels were constantly calling, visiting Nashville, knocking on your door, and trying to get you to promote their products. But when it got away from Chess, Motown, Vee-Jay, and our own stuff [Excello-Nashboro], Sue, Fire-Fury, a handful of labels like that, we didn't have time for anything else. Atlantic, of course, that was my big thing, and occasionally I would speak with the Erteguns or Wexler. Wexler would spend his time producing people, but in the office this fellow Bob Kornheiser was the contact. Through him I had access to Atlantic and everything Atlantic distributed: Volt and Otis Redding, Stax out of Memphis.

Ernie despised Leonard Chess because it was his impression Chess was infiltrating Ernie's programs on WLAC [through payola]. Mr. Young, being "the religious man that he was," was totally opposed to any such idea, and it worried him greatly that these kinds of things would be going on in his business. He was concerned about the legal ramifications of it, too. One thing that he told me, when he decided that he would pluck me to be in charge of Ernie's, is that if he ever caught me taking payola [for radio programming or for including certain records in packages], I would be fired immediately. I had heard Hoss Allen talk about it, and of course he admits openly that he was on Chess's payroll. And so Chess seemed to get to the people at WLAC.

Despite Shannon Williams's negative Chess comments, Leonard Chess clearly had an excellent business tie-in with Ernie Young. Paul Gayten, Chess promo man and artist, held a different view from Williams of the relationship when he told me, "Little Ernie Young of Excello and Leonard used to run together all the time; they were good friends. So were Randy Wood and Stan Lewis from Shreveport."[13]

On the other hand, with King Records' Syd Nathan, there was no doubt about Ernie Young's stance. "He always felt like Nathan was just an outright crook," said Williams. "I remember when James Brown just takes [contracted Nashboro gospel act] the Swanee Quintet [to record], and Nathan releases them on his Federal label. Immediately Ernie just turns three shades of red! He is just not going to take it and calls his lawyer immediately: Jordan Stokes."[14]

Excello Records had a handful of national hits headed by the Crescendos' "Oh Julie" (No. 5, early 1958) on the Nasco pop subsidiary. Earlier, in the spring of 1957, "Little Darlin'" by the Gladiolas had peaked at No. 41 before being knocked into oblivion by the Diamonds' expert cover version on Mercury. This was a rare example of an original recording being outclassed by an imitator. The Slim Harpo swamp blues successes, "Rainin' in My Heart" (No. 34 pop, No. 17 R&B, 1961) and "Baby Scratch My Back" (No. 16 pop, No. 1 R&B, 1966), were produced independently by Jay Miller in Crowley, Louisiana. Miller's recordings were the sound of Excello, being far more impressive than the rinky-dink productions of Ernie Young in Nashville. But with the thriving mail-order business, Young had no desperate need for hits. The order of the day was a constant flow of new product for the WLAC postal packages, whether for specific purchases or for inclusion as "dogs."

Ernie Young benefited considerably from the publishing income generated by Excellorec Music, especially through the covers of Arthur Gunter's "Baby Let's Play House" by Elvis Presley and, of course, "Little Darlin'" by the Diamonds. Shannon Williams believed the publishing venture started out as "a convenience business" to avoid paying mechanical royalties to other publishers on "*all* those songs that were recorded." He continued, "You'll notice that practically every song on the early Nashboro albums is either something claimed to be Excellorec Music or it was P.D. [public domain]. But you never found them straying over into Savoy's or Peacock's catalogs, cutting something that they had to pay for. He [Young] just wouldn't do that, and his contracts called for that: 'When you enter into an artist contract with Nashboro, you also will enter into a publishing agreement.'"

The Nashboro gospel artists enjoyed Radio WLAC airtime on Ernie's Sunday evening spiritual show, the theme song of which was the Nashboro version of "Touch Me Lord Jesus" by the Angelic Gospel Singers (originally a No. 13 R&B hit in 1949 for Gotham). "These artists at that point were interested in two things," said Williams,

having records to sell at their public appearances across the country *and* to get themselves heard and exposed on WLAC radio. That was it. It was a promotion vehicle for them, but as far as realizing a lot of royalties from those records, few of them ever did because the advances that he would give them would always outweigh what they were due.

The people that really made money, gospel-wise, on Nashboro, I can think of one group: The Consolers. They had hits, for one thing. The Consolers' biggest seller was "Waiting for My Child." This was a husband-and-wife team from Miami, Florida. Mr. [Sullivan] Pugh wrote all the songs and Excellorec published them all; they never went into anybody else's catalog. Many of these songs were picked up and recorded by other artists. Ernie was fair; he paid them. I mean, he never did cheat them.

I must say Madame Edna Gallmon Cooke was one of the most devoted, religious artists I ever encountered. Very few that I ever found were really true, and as the gospel song says, "I'm Gonna Live the Life I Sing About." Edna would go into the studio, and while the musicians were rehearsing or there was time out, she would be reading the Bible and praying. She was the only one I ever knew that did that. But the only others that seemed really true were the Consolers. Mrs. [Iola] Pugh, she'd get happy and shout in the studio over a song that they were doing. It would just fill her so full that she would just burst into shouting. Sometimes we'd have to take it again because that disrupted the whole thing.

Ernie Young sold the Nashboro group of companies in 1966, soon after Slim Harpo's "Baby Scratch My Back" had hit the Top 20. In the Motown-dominated era of the time, the record turned out to be one of the biggest R&B sellers of the year. Young had retired on a high. Recalling that final hit, Shannon Williams said with laughter:

It was just madness with Mr. Young and Dorothy Keaton trying to handle this hit, just the two of them. He finally would get to where he would allow the pressing plant to drop ship [direct to the distributors]. This was something that was far into his thinking, though. He thought everything should come to his back door and we should ship it away. When Harpo's "Scratch My Back" got so big, he discovered he couldn't do that, and the majority of it would have to be shipped from the plant. But he tried.

Ernie sold the business for $250,000, the whole thing: Ernie's Record Mart, Excellorec Music, and Nashboro-Excello, the building, lock, stock, and barrel—$250,000 cash! He thought it was fair. There was a counterbid that came through at almost the same time that the Crescent Company [a billion-dollar conglomerate] had reached a decision to buy. It came from a group of folks headed by John R., the disc jockey, and Ted Adams. We felt at that point that Leonard Chess was the moneyman behind that deal, because neither Ted Adams nor John R. had that amount of money.

The building was torn down. In fact, the Crescent Company, the ones who bought the business from Ernie, sold the property to Life and Casualty Insurance Company [the owners of Radio WLAC], which scraped away the whole thing and built a multilevel parking garage.

Randy's Record Shop in Gallatin was razed to the ground, too.

Hoss Allen: Promo Man and Record Man

In the uncertain aftermath of the payola scandal, Hoss Allen left WLAC at the end of 1960 to become a member of the Chess-Checker-Argo organization handling "promotion, sales and A&R in the south."[15] It was a good excuse for Allen to continue to party his life away. The Hossman's seat at the WLAC microphone was kept warm for three years by "Big Hugh Baby" Jarrett from Elvis Presley's vocal group, the Jordanaires. During this period, the hottest disc jockey in town was Noel Ball on rival station WSIX (radio and TV). The flamboyant, clever Ball was the man behind the Crescendos' 1958 Nasco hit "Oh Julie" and Dot's R&B/soul star, Arthur Alexander.

Explaining the background to his promo job, Hoss said:

I sorta took over the friendship that Gene [Nobles] had with Leonard Chess, which was very close. Then Leonard and I became pretty close friends. He said, "Why don't you come to work for me? I need a disc jockey." This was just the beginning of the format radio system, the Top 40 format business, where all stations were playing their short lists. Disc jockeys no longer could play what they wanted. A program director or a music director was telling them what to play, and it was a very tight list. So Leonard said, "I need somebody to get my records on these new format stations. I don't want you to call the black stations in particular. I want WNOE in New Orleans, I want WQXI and WAKE in Atlanta, I want this station in Charlotte, I want this station in Dallas and Houston," and so on.

Leonard made me a good deal—well, I think it was. I'd had a few years of playing the records now, and this sounded awfully glamorous to me, to break into record promotion. Because, I mean, payola was still around, and instead of taking it, I'd be passing it out. I liked to tip the bottle pretty well, and I'd be taking guys out and entertaining them and all that shit. I stayed with him through '61, '62, and up to September '63.

On a piece of good advice handed out by Leonard Chess, the Hossman was told to hang around record distributors where there were no sizable labels in town to flush out local regional hits. Leonard's wise words could have landed Chess with a big record in the summer of 1961, but the chance went begging. "There were no record manufacturers at the time in Atlanta," recalled Hoss.

One day I'm standing at Southland Distributors [owned by Jake Friedman], which was a big distributor in the South. In comes this black lady, fourteen or fifteen years old; she was pretty and she's got a record. So we asked the young lady to play it, and I said, "Can I have that dub?" I scooted it to Leonard; two days later he comes on the phone, "Why did you send me a fucking *Lois Music*?" [The song was from] Lois Music, Syd Nathan's goddamn publishing company!

The song had been on King [recorded by the Royals on the Federal subsidiary in 1952]. I said, "I didn't know about the publishing, [but] it's a hell of a record." It was Gladys Knight and the Pips, "Every Beat of My Heart." I had it first.[16] It was the same thing with "You Can't Sit Down" by Phil Upchurch [No. 29, Boyd (distributed by United Artists), also summer 1961]. But Leonard wanted it all, especially the publishing. Of course, Syd Nathan would have done the same thing. He would have been mad if somebody had brought him a tune that was Arc Music, which was Leonard.

During the 1960s, Hoss Allen with Gene Kennedy operated Rogana Productions, with soul men Earl Gaines and Sam Baker as the principal artists. These recordings would appear on Hoss's Hermitage and Athens imprints and on labels such as Chess, Excello, Hollywood, and Old Town. Always, there was the implied promise of exposure on Radio WLAC.

John Richbourg: Sound Stage 7 Records

John R.'s involvement as a record man was on a much grander scale than Hoss Allen's through Sound Stage 7 Records, in conjunction with Fred Foster of Monument. Foster had nothing but good words to say of their partnership, which produced slabs of superior southern soul. "There are only two kinds of music, good and bad," explained Foster. "Monument had become such a pet of the dee-jays, and they would play a Monument record without auditioning it first. I had letters that told me that over and over again: 'You're the only label we'll put on the air without listening first.' Then I did an R&B record, put it on Monument, shipped it out, and I got a barrage of phone calls, telegrams. 'What are you doing? We put on this record, my God, it's not like what you've been releasing. It's rhythm and blues!'"

Foster had trouble, too, from Nashville's country music hierarchy, who objected to him recording "this awful nigger music." He received support from studio owner Owen Bradley, who told him over lunch, "I hear you've heard from the old guard. Don't pay any attention to those people; they don't know what they're doing anyway. You're making great music; keep doing it. I just want to tell you my studio is available to you anytime you need it. Whether you have money to pay for it or not doesn't matter; I want you to get going." Foster said he never forgot that unsolicited support from Bradley.

But Fred Foster had to "have a label for R&B" so they wouldn't "confuse our records" with the Monument output: "And the name just came to me; I thought I'd call it 'Sound Stage.' Then I thought there may be a 'Sound Stage' somewhere, so I'll just call it 'Sound Stage 7,' three S's. Then John Richbourg comes to me, John R., the legendary John R. He wanted to know what he could do to help me 'cause he was real excited we were a rhythm and blues label. And I said, 'Well, you can run it.' So he took it over and he brought in Joe Simon, Roscoe Shelton, Lattimore Brown, Ella Washington, and all these traditionally great artists. So it was wonderful. We were very successful."[17]

The first Sound Stage 7 hit was "(Down at) Papa Joe's" by the Dixiebelles, which crept into the Top 10 in the fall of 1963. The idea was brought to Foster by Bill Justis, the original hit recorder of "Raunchy" on Phillips International, the Sun subsidiary. "This is a hilarious story," said Foster.

Bill had a song called "(Down at) Papa Joe's," which he wanted to do as a black record with a girl group, but we didn't have a black girl group. He said, "I can handle that." So he gets Margie Singleton, Priscilla Hubbard, and some other girl I think was black in the studio, and they did this song. It's a very fun thing, handclapping and all that. It sounded like a real great black group, and it was a huge record. Dick Clark called and wants to do it [on *American Bandstand*], and I had named the group the Dixiebelles. He wanted to book the Dixiebelles, and there weren't any Dixiebelles.

I said, "Bill, you gotta come up with the Dixiebelles." So he goes to Memphis and auditions black girl singers. I don't know how he did this, but he put together the most ragamuffin group you ever saw. They didn't look like they'd ever seen each other, let alone ever been working together. But he teaches them all their parts, rehearsing them until they can do it, and they go out on tour. Then they came back from the tour, [and] they all wanted big advances and everything. I said, "Bill, you can't do this, because once you start that, it's like trying to feed a dragon. You can't ever satisfy them." I just told them they'd have to get by. They're not going to starve; they're making money.

Then this one of the group comes in. She said, "Mr. Bill, I need an advance; I have to have an operation." He said, "Oh, gosh, I'm sorry, what kind of operation?" "I can't tell you." Bill said, "If you can't tell me, I sure can't let you have any money." This goes on for an hour or more. Finally she said, "I have to have my vagina moved. . . ." Bill thought that's too far out to be made up; it has to be true, but he's never heard of such a thing. He said, "Why do you have to have your vagina moved?" She said, "Because the way it is I can't have no fun with men." Okay, so we'll give her an advance. She gets her operation done and then they go out on another tour. And we start getting calls, "The Dixiebelles, there's only two of them showing up." There's one of them that won't show up half the time. She's laying around with some guy! So that was just about the end of the Dixiebelles.

With Sound Stage 7, it was success all the way, from day one. Then it was a time when traditional R&B was just really cold [from 1970 on]. It was funky and disco music, which was not John R.'s bag. We sat down one day and talked it over. He said, "I don't like this new style. Joe Simon is a timeless artist; that's different. All this crazy stuff, I don't know anything about that. I just want to stick with my own thing." I said, "John R., we need to keep up with the marketplace if we can." He said, "I don't think I'm the man for it. I want to start my own little thing." I said "Okay, God bless you," and he did. We stayed great friends.[18]

Hoss Allen: The Closing Years

The Hossman was back again at Radio WLAC in 1963 and was told, "You can work 11 until 1; you do Royal Crown and Buckley." Allen found the 1960s to be as invigorating as the past decade, even if the music and the ways of doing business were changing drastically. "You had Stax that came on," he said, "you had the Motown Sound, you had the Philly Sound. You had all these great black sounds that came in at the same time as rock music. So we had plenty of product. Excello was still very important as a blues label, but to me Nashboro was more important because it gave so many great gospel artists a start."

Allen conceptualized and hosted in 1966 The!!!!Beat TV show that lasted for twenty-six weekly half-hour episodes. The surviving film reveals a historically valuable extravaganza of national soul stars mingling with local Nashville R&B acts, with the adornment of glamorous go-go dancers. There was no difficulty in signing up acts, since the Hossman reckoned the artists owed him favors for those many WLAC spins.

With WLAC under new ownership and switching program formats from R&B to Top 40, Hoss stopped playing blues in 1971. A big competitive factor in this decision was the rapid advance of FM radio, which broadcast in clear-channel stereo (to which the record companies responded by ditching mono LPs for stereo, real or pseudo). Shannon Williams remembered that these upheavals at WLAC prompted the demise of the sponsored shows by the mail-order houses, much to the detriment of the indie record labels. When Hoss's buddy John R. went off the air on August 1, 1973, it signified the end of a sensational era.

In difficult personal circumstances, Hoss Allen was able to launch the long-lived *Early Morning Gospel Time* on WLAC. "I had become a confirmed alcoholic," he admitted, candidly. "I haven't had a drink since 1972, but I'm still an alcoholic. But I had really bottomed out. I had been to a couple of hospitals to dry out a couple of times. I retired in '88, but I'm still staying on. I still do national commercials, but primarily local and regional."

Hoss Allen, in 1992, reflected wistfully on the enormous cultural and social changes brought about by Radio WLAC, his colleagues, and himself:

Here I am; I'm the last one left: Gene has gone, John has gone, and it's the end of an era. But we, without knowing it, made black music what it is today, due to the radio station with its coverage and with a lot of lucky things happening. All right, LAC, because of the power of the station, put black music into so many homes, particularly [with] white kids. This was the subterranean audience that we never knew we were playing for. Randy [Wood] realized it from mail orders because of the [hand]writing; so many blacks in the South just could not write. We were playing for blacks; we weren't playing for whites.

The white audience was ordering the records to be sent to their grandmothers, to their aunts, because their folks wouldn't allow them to have black music in their home. Elvis came along and made it a lot better about '54 because he was white and sounded black. But in the South, it just wasn't cool to have a black record in the house if you were white. The parents thought this horrible music, this wild jungle African music, was going to ruin our children's minds. The preachers got up in the pulpit and preached about it, especially the fundamentalists, the Pentecostalists. . . .

I feel awfully fortunate that I was able to be a part of it. I sort of came along as a kid behind Gene and John. You just can't believe how lucky you are. I find it hard to believe that all this is so important now when it was just so much fun for me when I was doing it.

We were on a commission for mail order. Of course, if we broke a record, we got money from a record company, but you got paid 5 to 10 percent of how much you sold on the ad. So we were working like hell to sell the chicken, we sold records, we sold pain medicine, sold medicine for nature problems. John R. would sell weight-on tablets for six months, then he'd turn around and sell weight-off tablets for the next six months!

We weren't making much money as a base salary. Everyone suspected we were getting all this stuff on the side, but we weren't getting that much. John did very well with publishing and things like that, and Gene, of course, got this money from Randy. But most of the dee-jays died practically penniless. So really, I've been very lucky to hold on as a freelance. I guess it was a piece of history, and we were only selling products.

Hoss concluded our interview by stating, surprisingly, "I'm doing a documentary now. I've got about twenty-six hours on tape from the standpoint of an old record man. I've talked to Art Rupe's daughter Beverly, Joe Bihari, Stan Lewis, Shelby Singleton, Fred Mendelsohn of Savoy, Hy Weiss, Phil Chess . . . Phil can't tell me anything much. If only I could have gotten to Leonard; he was like a daddy to me." Hoss Allen's project, which was never finished in his lifetime, may just have been the subconscious spark I needed to seriously start this book.

7

CHAPTER

The Chess Game

<small>Cast of Characters</small>
   Marshall Chess, Chess-Checker-Argo Records
   Howard Bedno, Cobra Records, Allstate Record Distributing
      Co., and independent promo man
   Paul Gayten, promo man, Chess Records
   also featuring Leonard and Phil Chess, Chess Records;
   and Eli Toscano, Cobra Records

Leonard Chess was the dynamo behind Chess Records, the label that, along with Atlantic and Sun, has come to epitomize the independent record business. His legacy is seen in the enduring, diverse work of his main artists Chuck Berry, Bo Diddley, Etta James, Muddy Waters, Little Walter, Howlin' Wolf, the Moonglows, Ahmad Jamal, and Ramsey Lewis. Leonard Chess set new standards for the industry in artist development, deal making, networking, and marketing and promotion and in his surreal sharpness. Hardly a surprise, then, that he burned himself out at the unbelievably young age of fifty-two in 1969. Just as tragically, like so many other record makers, he never told his own story.

Marshall Chess: Chess-Checker-Argo Records

Leonard's son Marshall has kept the Chess flame burning as CEO of Arc Music, the family publishing company run in conjunction with his uncle Phil Chess and longtime partner Gene Goodman.[1] Based in New York, Arc has become one of the largest independent publishers anywhere. The enviable group catalog includes the Chess/Arc copyrights and those of fellow Chicago indie label Vee-Jay by way of Conrad Music. However, the Chess masters fell out of family control long ago, having been sold in 1969 just prior to Leonard's death. Current owner Universal Music Group (a division of Vivendi, the French conglomerate) has done a good job in making available many of the wonderful recordings under the aegis of Andy McKaie, but such is the depth of the catalog that many tracks have stayed marooned in the vaults.

As with the chronicles of Atlantic and Sun, the Chess story has been recounted many times.[2] Nevertheless, in 2004, Marshall Chess was more than happy to relate the family saga in record-men terms as he sat comfortably in his New York office filled with record company photographs (many depicting his father and uncle) and an impressive display of label shots from the Chess heyday.

"A record man is a very unique person in the entertainment business," said Marshall.

They don't really exist [as an entity] much anymore. A record man comes from the independent record business; a record man did everything. He found the artist, he produced the record, he promoted it, he sold it with the distributors, he was involved in every aspect of manufacturing, printing . . . the whole kit [and] caboodle from top to bottom. You had to know how to order your records, pressing, and printing labels. When albums came in, it was printing the fronts in the right place, [then] the backs, and gluing them together. Collecting the money . . . it was all part of your job.

My father and uncle were part of the original record men. . . . They were the first wave of real record men. There was stagnancy with the major labels, and racial prejudice existed on radio and with the major labels. The crucial element of the birth of the independent record men was payola. It wasn't illegal then, so I have no shame in saying it, but it was the vehicle that evolved that allowed the independents to establish themselves. I knew payola went on because I was with my father when I was very young when he gave a red Lincoln convertible to Al Benson, who was the main radio personality of Chicago, black radio. Those were the days before commercial black radio; most of the small radio outlets were foreign language stations. What they would do, they would sell so many hours a day to the disc jockey . . . , and then he would sell the advertising. So he would play whatever he wants. It was his time.

But my father and Phil Chess knew really what elements they wanted to put into the record that they thought would make it sell. They were very powerful in getting the artists to do what they wanted; they had the feel of the street: totally. I mean, they got that from owning the nightclub and businesses in the ghetto before they went into the record business. That was why my father wanted to go in the record business. He saw this market beginning to build, people came in to record live, he started to question. Then he worked with this Aristocrat Records [founded by Charles and Evelyn Aron in 1947] before he bought it; he worked there. Phil wasn't even around at that time; Phil was in the army.

Marshall Chess has always been keen to give equal credit for Chess's international brand reputation to Uncle Phil, of the trademark porkpie hat and fat cigar. When Leonard was inducted posthumously into the Rock and Roll Hall of Fame, Marshall stressed that he was accepting the award on behalf of his surviving uncle, too.

In my eyes, my father was the alpha, the main character. But I always say Phil gets way too little attention, because my father couldn't have done what he did without Phil being there. There was a very clever way of delegation, even though we all had our own little segments, and we would cross over jobs. Both of them were tight with all the artists, but there were certain people that liked my father in the studio, and certain ones [liked] Phil.

Phil had a sensibility to the doo-wop, and my father more with the blues. This is my personal observation. Chuck Berry and Muddy were my father's guys; so was Etta. But Phil was there, and they loved Phil. When they came into the Chess family, they had the whole fucking salmon here. For instance, when Chuck Berry came out of prison after his St. Louis Mann Act conviction [in 1960], he came straight to Chicago. I took him to buy his new clothes down to State Street; he recorded "Nadine" right after [November 15, 1963]. My dad gave me three hundred dollars to buy him a new wardrobe when he went on tour afterward. I was his first road manager, but he was my father's guy.

My father was a total workaholic, and I really began going by the company very young. I loved the atmosphere of Chess Records; it was just a lot of fun. There was a lot of laughter, a lot of music. I felt very comfortable there, and I was very much accepted. Because my father and uncle were immigrants, they [had worked] in the junkyard for their father. So there was no problem in giving me *work* to do. When you're thirteen, fourteen, fifteen, you don't care about record catalog numbers or contracts, those kinds of things. I was getting coffee, I was loading trucks, I was even learning how to produce at that time.

We always wanted to have a Chess in the business, so they taught me very young not so much to be a producer in the creative sense but a producer in keeping the session moving. My father used to say, "These guys are from the South. If you don't push 'em, the second you turn your back they're sitting around bullshitting about women." All of a sudden it stops. You have to keep pushing and pushing. I sort of emulated my father and uncle on those early sessions, "Keep it rolling, take 2," you know, that kind of stuff. There was no formula. You could make anything you wanted; you could become as creative as you wanted without fear. The only fear was that a record didn't sell.

Basically my father wanted me to learn these different aspects. I worked in the pressing plant; I worked the press—I was like a junior. I used to go in at five or six in the morning. It was 45s and the beginning of the LP era. One of my first jobs was stuffing albums into the covers and then shrink-wrapping them. When we had a hit with the Ahmad Jamal jazz album, Argo 628 [popularly known as *At the Pershing*], the distributor would take the truck from Cleveland, . . . drive in just to get it, get the records, and drive straight back. It sold in the 10,000s and not the 100,000s. A big hit was 40– to 50,000.[3]

The Chess albums had distinctive cover artwork featuring photographs taken by Don Bronstein (with others including black lensman Chuck Stewart). "Don Bronstein at that time was the original photo editor of *Playboy* magazine when it was started," said Marshall Chess. "He was Jewish. We weren't a racist company, but he fitted in fine; it was like an old pair of shoes. And he was a great photographer, he had his own studio, and *Playboy* was just beginning, so he wasn't that busy. He became basically our company photographer, but he was also a music lover and not prejudiced; [he had]

no fear of black people. It was founded in Chicago, *Playboy*." From airbrushed nude models to Muddy Waters it might have been, but this background explained why Bronstein's photographic portraits had such a majestic quality.

"As far as the record men I'd met, I knew them all," said Marshall.

Everyone had friendships. There were certain people that didn't like each other—of course, that's life. But what we had was a real camaraderie amongst all the independents. There was Hymie Weiss from Old Town, the Erteguns and Jerry Wexler from Atlantic. I'd meet the Biharis—I used to go to their houses on the West Coast—and George Goldner, [who] I used to see all the time in Chicago. They'd come by Chess, all of the New York and Detroit guys.

We were all sharing information and disc jockeys. If my dad was tight with a disc jockey and Atlantic needed a record played, they could call and exchange information. It wasn't going to hurt us if they played an Atlantic record. When we got the station in Chicago, WVON, it became so powerful. We helped Morris Levy, Ahmet Ertegun, Hymie, there wasn't even a question. One phone call, and the record was on the list. When we had our pressing plant, we would press records for Old Town and for Atlantic when they had a hit and they couldn't get enough records quick enough.

Hymie was a typical Brill Building–Tin Pan Alley–Damon Runyon character kind of record guy. I'm not sure, because I never worked with Hymie in the studio, how artistically involved he was with his productions, but he was a tough guy. He knew how to get records played. I think he genuinely loved some of his records, loved the music. I always got along well with Hymie, even when Phil and him used to gas me with their fucking cigars. They always had those giant cigars in their mouths. I didn't even smoke cigars. The two of them together, it was like you needed a gas mask.

I used to take regular trips three or four times a year to New York with Phil. I remember staying right here on Times Square at one of these hotels. We would go to see Gene Goodman at the Brill Building, where the original Arc Music offices were. Our distributor in New York was Sam Weiss, Hymie's brother; he was over by the river at Tenth Avenue there [at Superior distributors]. So we'd go there.

At that time, Hymie and Sam were close, but they had their sibling rivalries. I was shocked at Hymie's office. It was on [1697] Broadway, right by the Brill Building. The part I still find funny is that most of the furniture was made of 45–rpm singles boxes, stacked like a table; there were two stacks with a piece of wood across the top. Hymie's whole office was like a stockroom that you worked out of. I found it very amusing, but again, it was a warm relationship. We'd go up to Jack Dempsey's restaurant, and I would order cheesecake for all of them.

Hy's own take was that he painted only three of the four walls, otherwise his artists and songwriters would think he was making too much money.

"It was a lot different [from] the Chess offices," added Marshall.

We were much more, I felt, a *business*, run like a business. Old Town wasn't like the kind of structure of Chess. We had a bookkeeper, we had girls doing the billing, we had our own studios, we had record business offices. Always from the beginning at Forty-seventh Street [and South Cottage Grove], they were offices for business.

The studio at 2120 South Michigan was built by Jack Weiner. That's the famous studio where the Rolling Stones came to record [in 1964]; that's where we had so many of the great hits. Yeah, he was important as far as being part of the team. Then of course Malcolm Chisholm, the other great engineer at Chess, also had his own sound. They were a part of it. Even early at 2120, we'd do our own mastering with a Neumann German lathe. I remember we knew that [if it] sounded good in that mastering room, it would sound great on the radio. That was how you sold the records. We didn't care a fuck; nobody was interested if it was in stereo. It had to sound great on the radio; that's what made people buy it. And on the jukeboxes, it was the same idea.[4]

A key element to the success of the independents was getting exposure on radio and on television. The majors were sort of asleep and very stagnant, and they allowed this whole thing to develop. Jim Lounsbury in Chicago was like a copy of Dick Clark's *American Bandstand*; all cities had their local versions of those kind of hop shows. I used to go dance on Jim Lounsbury's *Record Hop*.

My father was constantly going on trips, mostly by car—this was before using airline transportation—and they always wanted to carry the records. You could actually put a thousand records in your trunk and take care of the disc jockeys in one of these cities and go right to the distributor and sell them records based on the fact that it was being played on the radio. I remember with my dad, one of the early road trips was to the South where you would give some new records to the disc jockey [and] give him some money to play it. Then we'd tell the guy we're just leaving, and we'd go to a motel on the outskirts of town. This was to make sure he lived up to it [the payola]! I also traveled with Max Cooperstein, to whom I owe a lot.

The disc jockeys were like part of the family: give them a record, and they played it. Those guys liked the music, such as Porky Chedwick in Pittsburgh. The West Coast really didn't develop [for us] until we had Paul Gayten. We hired him in New Orleans . . . very shortly after we opened our little two-room West Coast office. There were three disc jockeys: Huggy Boy in the window [at John Dolphin's record store], Hunter Hancock at two strong L.A. stations, and that little guy who invented "burnin'," Magnificent Montague: "Burn baby burn!" They were all my old friends. I went to college in L.A., so I really got to know that scene well. Paul Gayten was my mentor there. He became very important because he got the records played.

We would test the market locally, definitely, definitely. We would do it in many localities, depending on the moment—what disc jockeys you could get to do it, who you could trust. We had close friends like the WLAC guys. Gene Nobles was a friend of the family, and so was Hoss Allen. You'd send them a record, you could tell 'em to run a record, and you would check to see if the distributors got calls. Yeah, that was done often. I'd say WLAC was very important, WILD in Boston, Zenas Sears at WAOK in Atlanta; they were part of the extended family. Hoss Allen working for Chess was more of a payback [for] all the great things he did for Chess when he was on the radio: "I'm fired; I need work." "You do what you can, find us an artist, do this." What really was the impetus was our love for those people who helped us [and] made us a lot of money. We had this kind of symbiotic relationship. They were playing our records; we were sending them cash.

With Stan Lewis [in Shreveport] it was a close, very close relationship. He was very important in the South. If you needed a record [broken], he knew how to get it on the air and get it in the shops in that area: Louisiana, New Orleans, all the way up to Arkansas. He brought us people like Dale Hawkins [with "Susie-Q"]; that all came from Stan. Buster Williams [in Memphis] was a very important person; he's the one who inspired my father, I think, to start Chess Records with his own name [in place of Aristocrat]. Buster used to fly up in his own plane to Chicago. He'd sleep in my bedroom, and I had to sleep on the couch. He was a businessman, he was a factory owner, he definitely had a business instinct. Likewise, Sam Phillips was important to Chess. We got Howlin' Wolf from him and "Rocket 88" by Jackie Brenston.[5]

Occasionally we had good-natured battles, like the signing of James Brown: . . . we were rushing to sign James Brown, and King-Federal through Ralph Bass got him first by a few hours. The one I remember the most was Lee Andrews and the Hearts, "Long Lonely Nights," where Atlantic and us both wanted to buy the master. We got it, they were pissed, so they covered it with Clyde McPhatter. That was a battle, "Those motherfuckers . . ." and that kind of shit.[6] By the same token, Ahmet and Nesuhi [Ertegun] were at my bar mitzvah. Not so much Ahmet with me but Nesuhi, I always had a very close feeling for him. It was like a big, extended family, and everyone gained from it.

By that time, the independents like Chess and Atlantic had grown to real record companies. The guys like Hy Weiss and George Goldner were floundering; they were like seat-of-the-pants operators with no infrastructure. We were a real record company, man: we had three studios, songwriters grinding out music. We just didn't have a few R&B hits. Out of all the labels we had a gospel line, we had a jazz line, we had the biggest black comedy line (Moms Mabley), we had all the fabulous sermons of Reverend C. L. Franklin. Of course, I took it into that rock/psychedelic thing. We were really a full-scale record company.

My family went into the radio business in the early 1960s just observing that this was a market ready to be mined. My father actually had one of the first commercial black radio stations, really commercial. He had major sponsors, Budweiser beer, Chevrolet . . . and it was a big success: WVON became No. 1 in Chicago, with low power, even. It definitely distracted my father, without a doubt. My father definitely was bored, I think, a little with the record business and was very interested in keeping in radio and black television. Before he died, he was planning to go into black television way ahead of its time, still in Chicago. It would have been a monster.

The first Chess overseas licensing deal was made with London American and lasted from 1956 until 1960 before being taken over by Pye International. Marshall Chess handled the renewal in 1964. He admitted, "It turned out I miscalculated and there was no profit; we were going to break even. Louis Benjamin [of Pye] knew it and said, 'Marshall, you fucked up; I'm going to let you off the hook.' I said, 'No! I'll never forget it, no way, I'll have to bite the bullet.' Again, I was emulating my father."

"It became a very successful thing," Marshall Chess continued, "and we made a tremendous amount of money over the years. I started with Pye, and we came up with the whole idea of putting out all the blues with Chuck Berry and Bo Diddley on March Arch, their discount label. That was part of my deal because we wanted to spread it and we knew that money [pricing] was a part of it. Of course, I was very enamored with England because I was treated for the first time like a music celebrity. I was going to see Mike Raven [an original pirate radio disc jockey]. [And] I was going to all these BBC [and ITV] shows because the English were just very aware of this Chess—Chuck Berry, Bo Diddley, Muddy Waters, Sonny Boy [Williamson]—they were very aware. I'd go to all these clubs, [and] I met the Rolling Stones and the Beatles, all of them. They were, like, 'Wow, Chess!'"

Despite its relative strength, Chess Records could not avoid being swallowed up in 1969 by GRT for $6.5 million cash (including a *reverse* loan of $1.79 million from Leonard Chess) plus (declining) GRT stock.[7] The takeover was a replay of the relentless capitalist corporate cycle. "I was devastated," said Marshall.

It was quite a rough time for me because I'd been raised to take it over. I had no contracts on anything I'd ever done. To this day, I don't make royalties on any of my records that I produced. Why would I make the contract with myself? My dad used to say at the time, just tell the guy whatever you need to live, and at the end of the week we'll get it. It was not getting a salary; it was family.

Yeah, I was devastated. Number one: that they sold it. Number two: that my dad died when they did sell it. I was going to get $1 million down the line on the deal and get to start my own label. It just was fine; I had no problem with that. But my dad didn't have a will, [and] taxation hit that: 77 percent. I never got my money to start my own label. That's why I went with the Rolling Stones' label. I was like in a pretty deep depression when I did the Stones thing. It took a long time to overcome that pain. It was like I had trained for an athletic event for twenty years, then they canceled that event a month before the Olympics.

Looking back, I feel it was stupid that we ever sold it. Number one: there was a fabulously high offer for the time because GRT was booming from the tape. It was the beginning of the cassette and 8-track [cartridge] days. Everyone, Columbia, all the big labels, had to go to either Ampex or GRT, the manufacturers. Their stock was shooting. So it was a very high price for the time, although a big part of the price was in stock. Number two: it was a difficult time for white people to own a black business. We were getting a lot of pressure from [Reverend] Jesse Jackson, you know: "How come you don't have enough black executives? You sell your product to the black people . . ."

Marshall was referring to Operation Breadbasket, a second phase of the civil rights movement. He added that Leonard and Phil thought it was a great business deal with GRT.

Marshall Chess has long put those gray days behind him. He recognized that he was in a position of privilege as part of the Chess family *and* the record men community. "My early experience with those guys," he recalled,

was my pot smoking at sixteen—that was in 1958 before kids smoked—and hookers. It was fun, these guys had fun, they had a lot of fun. The thing about the independent business that I remember is that I've been in everyone's company offices—Old Town, Atlantic—and there was always laughter and cursing, music playing. Now if you go into record companies, you don't even hear music.

The excitement of a hit was the closest thing I've seen to looking at those old movies where they get the oil gushers. That's how it used to be when you got a hit. It was just amazing; it would be going like a wave going across the country. Records would break, and the phones would start ringing. We'd yell up and down the hall, like "Detroit 13,000!" I mean, you'd be running and running trying to get the pressings, and it would just roll across the country. Those were exciting days, and I am still associated. I mean, the Chess name is bigger now than ever historically.

Howard Bedno: Cobra Records and Chicago Promo Man

While Chess and black-owned Vee-Jay ruled the roost in the 1950s Windy City, there were many smaller labels that came and went throughout the decade, including Chance-Sabre (owned by respected record presser and distributor Art Sheridan with assistance from ambitious young Ewart Abner), Parrot-Blue Lake (disc jockey Al Benson and then, in 1956, John "Lawyer" Burton), and United-States (Leonard Allen, a tailor, with A&R man Lew Simpkins, who was previously with Miracle and Premium). The sounds purveyed represented the wide range of Chicago music from doo-wop to jazz, even pop. It wasn't all tough electric blues, by any means.

One of the more important second-division labels was Cobra Records, which was set up by Eli Toscano in 1956 in company with Howard Bedno, Leonard Chess's friend and Marshall's mentor. Marshall said, "I worked with Howard for over a year and a half [at Chess]. He was really a top-level record promotion man, intuitively and [knowing] the psychology [of it]. So I was his sidekick, like his driver; he never drove a car. We used to go to all the radio stations. Howard worked for our distributors in Chicago: Paul Glass, Allstate. He could ask favors and get them. People liked him."

Howard Bedno, two years prior to his death in 2006 and well into his eighties, was still active in independent record promotion. He was worried about a pending federal investigation into his segment of the music business and was willing to talk only about the "great days." With his long friendships with record men, distributors, and disc jockeys, he was fully conversant with the underbelly of the independent record scene, but even with the passage of time, he remained circumspect in his statements. Here was a professional man revered within the industry but hardly known outside of it, mainly through his own choosing. Still, he was proud to relate his involvement in Cobra's opening strike.

"Cobra Records was ABC TV and Repair Shop run by Eli Toscano, who was of Mexican descent," said Bedno.

He had an ear for the blues coming from Texas. Eli was a great TV mechanic, and he opened up a record store in front. I lived in the neighborhood and started to hang around there and get involved with him. We were on the West Side, 2854 West Roosevelt Road; it's a real ghetto today. It was getting stronger and stronger with the movement of black people into that area; it was turning from white to black. The West Side was a haven for blues. Most all of the artists lived on the West Side, and there were a lot of clubs.

The first record we ever cut was Otis Rush's "I Can't Quit You Baby" at Boulevard studio. That was a big record [No. 6 R&B, fall 1956]. It broke in Chicago and then Nashville radio. When it hit WLAC, it happened all over the South; everybody in them days listened to WLAC: "Well, I can't quit you baby, but I got to put you down for a while."[8] It's a great line! Each artist was married, [but] they had what they call an "old lady"; the girlfriend would be the old lady. Most of the lyrics on blues were about their struggles, their love life. Willie Dixon wrote the other side of the record, "Sit Down Baby," but he gave it to me [the writer's credit]. Me and Willie were very close. He was an enormous man [in physical size and stature].

As well as the Cobra label, Eli Toscano ran A.B.'s One-Stop operation, managed by wife Archie. With a makeshift demo/rehearsal recording studio in the rear, the shop was the focal point for Chicago's eager West Side blues community. "One of the first people I met going into the record business, Joe Brown, he helped us start in the R&B business," said Howard Bedno.

He had J. B. Lenoir on JOB Records. Cobra had Joe Brown's stuff, too; it was on another label, ABCO. He was a small little guy, just [a] fantastic kind of a person. I'm glad people know what Joe Brown did in the business. Joe used to hang around our shop all the time. He brought Arbee Stidham and a few more artists.

In those days when we were first selling records, part of it was 78s, and 78s were very breakable. Sometimes a person would buy the same record two or three times over. We'd say, "What the hell happened to the one you just bought?" He had leaned on it at the bar and broke it and bought another one. And they'd question a 45 because they'd say the 45 did not have all the music on it because a 78 was twice as big!

Everybody was in the record retail business at that time. There was the barber's shop, the beauty shop, the grocery shop; people would come to the one-stop and pick up the hits for cash and sell them.

With a few stacks of 78s lined up on the back counters, these ad hoc storefronts were known in the trade as "floating record shops" and were despised by the regular record dealers. "Our one-stop also supplied the jukeboxes," added Bedno. "It was good business. We got the records from the distributors. The jukebox chains were run by the hoodlums."

The 1960 Senate rackets report made it clear that the $300 million jukebox industry nationwide was subject to "collusive ventures by racketeers in operator associations and union locals."[9] The murky Chicago jukebox and bootlegging operations were specifically highlighted, as reported by *Billboard* on April 4, 1960:

In 1956, according to the probers, "major hoodlums" made further inroads in the jukebox industry by forcing operators to buy records from the Lormar Distributing Company. Lormar was owned by Charles (Chuck) English, close associate of "notorious gangsters" such as Sam (Mooney) Giancana and Paul (The Waiter) Ricca. To force operators to buy their records from Lormar, pressure was put on by "Jukebox" Smith and his union, and by Teamster official Joey Glimco. As a result, a legitimate one-stop business, Singer One-Stop Record Company, lost about $800,000 per year in business.

Still not satisfied with their ill-gotten gains, the syndicate made further profits by the counterfeiting and sale of large numbers of phonograph records.[10]

In effect, Lormar was undercutting other distributors and then fulfilling many orders with bootleg records, stated to be pressed by Rite Records in Cincinnati. Despite its hard-hitting nature, the *Billboard* feature languished deep on page 81. Yet when the magazine first broke the story in February 1958, it had hit the front page. Among the bootlegged labels listed then were Brunswick, Cadence, Cameo, Chancellor, Chess-Checker, Dot, Herald-Ember, Keen, Roulette, Swan, and Vee-Jay. For its handling of this unsavory black-market merchandise, Lormar Distributing was fined the grand sum of $100. It has to be said that the judge's edict was of the distinct feather-duster variety.[11] And without any surprise, none of the manufacturers took any legal action against Lormar.

As an aside, how on earth did Leonard and Phil Chess escape the clutches of the Chicago mob? In answer to that question, another Chess promo man (and recording artist), Paul Gayten, told me succinctly, "The gangsters were not involved. They wanted to get in, but Leonard was too smart for them."

Then Gayten added an interesting postscript regarding the Chess relationship with Vee-Jay and the indies generally: "There was a little friction between Chess and Vee-Jay because of Jimmy Bracken. He and Leonard had had some kind of misunderstanding a few years back. But as far as promoting records, I helped Vee-Jay because Leonard told me to: 'You help all small record companies!' When I'd go on the road, I'd have Vee-Jay records in my bag, too. Every small company that came to Chicago, first place they'd hang out was with Leonard. And Leonard got so big he couldn't do this [anymore] and he felt bad because there was a lot of people he couldn't see."[12]

Continued Howard Bedno:

Of course, people would hear a record on a jukebox, and they'd run into the record shop. Our store was four houses away from a big tavern on a corner, where everybody celebrated Friday night and Saturday night. They'd go in the tavern and hear a record, [and] they'd want it. For example, we used to buy two hundred [copies of] Little Walter, "My Babe" [No. 1 R&B, spring 1955]. We restocked as fast as we could get them; sometimes we sold out on Saturday afternoon, but Chess was closed already. So we were out of a record until Monday. Our business was Friday night, Saturday night.

The popular records were by the blues artists, a lot of Chess Records by Little Walter, Howlin' Wolf, and Sonny Boy Williamson. We used to buy the records for the one-stop; we'd go out to South Cottage Grove for Checker, Chess, also Argo. The records sold for seventy-nine cents, and we paid Chess about fifty cents, if I remember right. Handling 78s, if you picked up fifty 78s, it's like picking up a hundred pounds. Chess had its own pressing plant, too, where his [Leonard's] first office was. He had a sort of a minor partner, Russ Fratto, who was a printer and owned the building.

The publicity-shy Fratto was accorded, infamously, one-third of the songwriter credits on Chuck Berry's first hit, "Maybellene," along with disc jockey Alan Freed. Later, an aggrieved Berry ensured that this iniquitous "double favor" by Leonard Chess would not endure.

"But record sales were all down the line," said Howard Bedno,

> because there was B. B. King at that time, Bobby "Blue" Bland, Elmore James, Lightnin' Hopkins. Muddy Waters was one of the best sellers out there because Muddy was exposed on the radio [and in the South Side clubs].
>
> We had great R&B radio at that time with Sam Evans, Al Benson, "Ric" Ricardo (known as "Little Richard"), Larry Wynn, and Big Bill Hill. *Jam with Sam*, Sam Evans would go down the basement every night from ten o'clock to eleven o'clock; he'd say, "Let's go down the basement and play some blues!" And then he'd play the hard blues. Big Bill Hill would do a remote from his dry cleaning shop with a shotgun in his lap; it was a bad neighborhood where he had it. Big Bill Hill was one the fathers of the blues here.
>
> If there was a brand-new record, they'd play it a couple of times, and the next day everybody in the world wanted the record. We had to make sure it was in stock.

Bedno added that if Al Benson, "The Swingmaster," didn't play your record on Radio WGES, you couldn't sell anything in volume.

"I don't know what Leonard Chess did, but I liked payola," said Bedno, paradoxically.

> You got [in return] what you gave. The guys that didn't declare it as income got into trouble. The scandal affected business maybe temporarily, but it rebounded; it came back quickly. People didn't give a damn. A couple of guys got hurt reputation-wise, but that's all. Later in Chicago, in black radio, when Leonard owned the WVON station, I dealt with Rodney Jones and with Herb Kent, a lot of new black jockeys. Leonard bought the radio station to play his own records, then he's required by the FCC to only play a percentage of the records on his playlist. So he was limited. FCC controls radio; it's a federal body.
>
> I started with jazz originally. All the jazz artists would hang out at the Blue Note on North Clark Street, and after a main gig they would come by there and have a jam session. I hung around the club where the owner [Frank Holzfeind] would bring in Billie Holiday, early Miles Davis and stuff, Anita O'Day, all the early jazz artists, the good ones. I remember when Miles [Davis] got out of Lexington, Kentucky, where he was in there for drug rehab, and came by the club.
>
> Then I went into the blues. I just waltzed into the music business; what else was there to do? When I first went in it, I didn't know what the hell I was doing. I took a grasp very quickly because Eli was fixing television sets. He recorded in the back; we had a lot of blues artists hanging around the store. There was a young man, Mel London; he wrote some hit songs including "Messing with the Kid" for Junior Wells [Chief], and he died at an early age. He was brilliant because his lyrics would describe the life he was leading. He was the first hanger-around at the store.[13]

Interestingly, the Cobra publishing company Armel Music seemed to be an amalgamation of the first names of Mrs. Archie Toscano and Mel London.

Emboldened by Otis Rush's debut hit, the Toscanos moved premises to 3346 West Roosevelt Road, again with a record shop in the front and a small studio out the back. Cobra Records developed an impressive lineup of emerging young blues and R&B talent. The music man behind Cobra, which was more of an artistic than a commercial success, was independent producer, songwriter, and upright bass player Willie Dixon. For his Cobra productions, he was fortunate to be able to take advantage of Bill Putnam's cavernous-sounding Universal studios, with jazz-slanted tenor saxophonists Harold Ashby and Red Holloway on call. Although Dixon was freelancing primarily for Chess with Chuck Berry and Muddy Waters at the time, he saw in Cobra an opportunity to work with Chicago's brightest new artists. Even better, this outlet afforded further exposure to his songs.

"Willie Dixon's best place to write was the toilet," said Bedno. "We used to say,'When are you going to take a crap so you can write us a new song?' Whenever you looked for Willie, Willie was in the toilet. He liked us; that's why he was working for us *and* Chess. Maybe we took care of Willie better than Leonard would take care of him, probably more money. There was always difficulty with Willie and the publishing company, Arc Music. He had a lot of great songs."[14]

Cobra Records collapsed in a heap late in the summer of 1959. It was widely thought by early collectors that owner Eli Toscano was the victim of a mob rubout around this time, being drowned in Lake Michigan. Many years later, Ace Atkins turned up evidence that Toscano did indeed drown, but not until 1967. Moreover, the coroner was satisfied that Toscano died accidentally while drunk on a fishing trip (on the Fox River) very late one evening. The death certificate revealed the cause of death as "asphyxiation by drowning" and that he "fell overboard from boat while trying to start outboard motor."[15] What did Bedno think of the drowning incident? "He went fishing one night, I don't know . . . ," he said cautiously, "and he drowned. And that was suspicious to me."

In real life, Eli Toscano was yet another record man who was a compulsive gambler and would be bailed out by Leonard Chess. After Cobra's fall, Leonard added Otis Rush (fleetingly) and Buddy Guy (profitably) to his label roster but made a rare misstep by not snapping up the contracts of Magic Sam and Betty Everett. Together with Harold Burrage (recently departed to Vee-Jay), this was a team ready-made for the decade ahead in terms of new-age Chicago blues and soul.

Bedno had already departed Cobra Records for the superior prospects at Chess. "I traveled with Phil or with Leonard," he said. "I was a sort of assistant. Leonard Chess was a fabulous, fabulous record guy, died too early. Oh, Leonard was the whiz! Any time a crisis came up, Phil had to go to the toilet to take a piss. Everybody around there knew it. Leonard was the whole driver of Chess Records. He loved R&B music, picking up Little Walter, picking up Howlin' Wolf. Mind you, he was also one of the first [independents] to have pop records, with Dale Hawkins and Chuck Berry. Leonard had a reputation. When you're cold and you put records out that are not selling, they don't want anything to do with you. But he had a hot label."

Bedno recalled the circumstances involved in recording jazz pianist Ahmad Jamal's *At the Pershing,* the No. 3 top-selling LP for Chess's Argo subsidiary that was on the pop charts for more than two years from September 1958: "One time Phil Chess says to me, 'Ahmad Jamal is cutting at the Pershing Hotel; I want you to go down there and supervise the session with Max Cooperstein.' So I go down there, and I got drunk. I didn't know what the hell was going on. From that became one of the biggest albums Chess ever had, by Ahmad Jamal; he had a song [on it] called 'Poinciana.' The music was at the right time and the right place. Sometimes you wonder what's in a record. Since then I've claimed to be a great genius [*laughs*], and we did not have a damned thing to do with the whole session." Actually, the album sleeve credited Dave Usher as producer with Malcolm Chisholm as engineer. It's still a good story.

Bedno, a tireless worker, left Chess Records in September 1960 to replace Earl Glicken as sales manager at Paul Glass's Allstate Record Distributing Co., located on Chicago's "record row" at 1450 South Michigan. "Leonard was smart," said Bedno. "He made a deal for Paul to pay me, and I represented Leonard in promotion. We had Atlantic in those days, we had Imperial Records, Specialty Records. Paul came from Dallas, Texas, a white southern boy who grew up on that R&B music in the South. He was a good, nice person, and he liked the music. He knew what he was doing."

By the time Paul Glass arrived in the Windy City, he was already an experienced distributor, having been with Big State in Dallas and an Allstate branch in Atlanta. In effect, with Howard Bedno on hand as promo man, Allstate in Chicago became a part of Leonard Chess's business web. This backdoor Chess involvement in Allstate was unknown to silent partner Art Rupe of Specialty Records, who said almost a half century later, "Yes, Allstate [Record] Distributing Co. was our Chicago distribution outlet. I partnered with Paul Glass. We bought a building on South Michigan Avenue, which would be worth a fortune today. Leonard Chess had no connection to us, so I'm not certain how Leonard handled Chicago."

Howard Bedno remembered important Chicago distributors Ernie and George Leaner of United Record Distributors (and owners of the Mar-V-Lus, One-derful! and M-Pac! labels in the 1960s). "They got into it, they were black, they were on the street," Bedno said. "They were very good at what they did. There was M. S. Distributors [founded in 1945 and run by Milt Salstone, who first employed the Leaners], King Records, MGM . . . all down Michigan Avenue. There'd be feuds going on: 'You stepped on my territory!' or whatever."

What were the duties of distributors' promo men? "First of all, they go to radio," said Bedno. "They make sure radio gets the record exposed, and they make sure the records are in the stores to follow up the airplay. So you had a double duty. The big thing was to get airplay; once you got airplay, you sold records. If you didn't get airplay, you didn't sell any records. Sometimes you had a lot of records in your hand [and] you didn't know which one to [push]. Leonard and Paul Glass had a deal with Al Benson to play sixteen records a day. It was my job to go there and change the records when I thought something had stopped selling. So one day Benson gives me the records for me to change. He counts the records and says, 'You're trying to screw me on one record. I only made a deal for sixteen; you're giving me seventeen!'"

Just like Paul Gayten, Howard Bedno did promo jobs for Leonard Chess's main Chicago rival, Vee-Jay Records. The label scored its first No. 1 with Gene Chandler's doo-wop inspired "Duke of Earl" in 1962, followed closely by three No. 1s by the 4 Seasons, independently produced by Bob Crewe in New York. Incredibly, Vee-Jay was a temporary beneficiary of Capitol's unfortunate myopia by licensing the Beatles' first U.S. release, "Please Please Me," from U.K. EMI in the summer of 1963. Although the record stalled after selling around 5,500 copies, it became a No. 3 hit when rereleased by Vee-Jay a little later at the height of Beatlemania.[16] But the company's inherent strength was derived from the consistent sales of Jimmy Reed (who had more national hits than any other Chicago blues artist), Jerry Butler, John Lee Hooker, the Dells, the Spaniels, and the Staple Singers.

"[Ewart] Abner was a dear friend of mine at Vee-Jay," said Howard Bedno,

Jimmy Bracken and Vivian Carter, too. She was a dee-jay playing a lot of spiritual music in Gary; she was on the air. That's how they got the Staple Singers: Pop Staples and Mavis.

Every Friday night there was a crap game, a card game. Whatever Jimmy Bracken gave them, he would take it back, and this would go on all night long. Hy Weiss comes into town on a Friday, and Vee-Jay sets up a game of poker. There's Calvin Carter, Vivian's brother who was the A&R man, and Bunky Sheppard. I'm sitting next to Hy, and we're losing every fucking hand. So I say to Hy, "I think this fucking game is fixed!"

It was Ewart Abner's well-reported gambling debts allied to a foolish management expansion program that helped to bring down Vee-Jay with a resounding crash in 1966.

Notable among the hits that Howard Bedno broke with Paul Glass out of Chicago was "Kind of a Drag" by the Buckinghams, a rock act, which became an improbable No. 1 in early 1967 on Glass's USA label. Disappointed with his personal reward, Bedno dabbled again in label ownership when he partnered with artist manager Peter Wright in the small soul imprint Twinight Records.[17]

In the early 1970s, Howard Bedno became a fully fledged independent promo man at a time when anyone with his promotional expertise was in great demand. "I called Jerry Wexler at Atlantic Records," said Bedno. "'If I go independent, will you hire me?' And he says, 'In a minute!' Morris Levy, Roulette Records, all of them encouraged me, and that's when I went on my own." In a glowing testimony, Stan Lewis of Jewel Records considered Howard Bedno to be "one of the best promotion people in the country at that time."

Bringing his story up to date in 2004, Bedno said, "I've been doing it ever since. But it's very strange out there; it's not the way I broke independents in. Later on, black radio became very hard to handle . . . racist, yeah. Currently, I think the best in the business is Doug Morris [head of Universal Records]; they got into the hip-hop business, and that's where they're doing the big business. But it's far different today. The big trouble in the record business is there are too many kinds of formats around. This station is playing hard AC [adult contemporary], that one soft AC, Top 40, alternative—and alternative music is not selling. There's nobody to play blues music on the radio right now; nobody will play it. And the mom-and-pop stores have all gone. The music business is terrible out there now; there is no creativity. The trouble is there are no record people running the labels any more."

In a familiar refrain, you could almost hear Howard Bedno crying for the return of the master, Leonard Chess, and his contemporaries from those "fabulous days." Nonetheless, with bulging Rolodex near at hand, he was still carrying on the independent promo man tradition until felled by a heart attack in May 2006. He was almost eighty-eight years of age, and he had seen it all.

8
CHAPTER

King of Them All

CAST OF CHARACTERS
Colonel Jim Wilson, King Records branch manager
Billy Butler, guitarist on "Honky Tonk"
Henry Stone, De Luxe Records
Seymour Stein, King Records apprentice
Julius Dixson, King Records songwriter
Don Pierce, Starday-King Records
Freddy Bienstock, Tennessee Recording and Publishing Co.
also featuring Syd Nathan, King-Federal Records

For any record collector visiting Cincinnati, Ohio, there was always one essential pilgrimage to make: to the site of the old King Records factory complex in the Evanston neighborhood. I could almost smell the history as I walked around the exterior of the 9,000–square foot edifice, once an ice plant. The section where the recording studio was housed was still visible into the twenty-first century, while by the parking lot ran a small creek where guitarist Jimmy Nolen used to smoke joints in between James Brown sessions.

Here was where blues and R&B stars such as Wynonie Harris, Little Willie John, and Freddy King recorded their big hits; where Cowboy Copas, the Delmore Brothers, Hank Penny, and Hawkshaw Hawkins ruled the country roost; where Bill Doggett and Earl Bostic cut album after instrumental album; and where top vocal groups the Dominoes and Hank Ballard and the Midnighters got their start. Yes, 1540 Brewster Avenue was Syd Nathan's royal palace, and spiritually it impressed, still.

King Records became a driving force in the independent record business because Nathan recognized the huge potential in the regional sounds of hillbilly and then race music. In Cincinnati, a railroad hub city straddling the North and South divides, he was perfectly located for the music and for setting up his distribution system. Myopic, but only in the physical sense, the bespectacled Nathan was in the same rough, tough, bombastic mold as his perennial adversary, Herman Lubinsky of Savoy Records. In his mind, the supremely confident Nathan played out the early label slogan: The "King" of Them All!

Syd Nathan was a scheming wheeler-dealer, one of the smartest, in fact. For all his bumptiousness, he was aware of the need to have good people around him, including family. He could not have wished for a better lawyer than the loathsome Jack Pearl, while another trusted adviser was Howard Kessell, president of Royal Plastics Co. (the pressing plant division). On the creative front, Henry Glover and Ralph Bass were a formidable A&R team.

During the 1930s, Nathan tried his hand at several ventures, from wrestling promotion to photo finishing. His ascendancy began in 1942 when he opened Syd's Record Shop at 1351 Central Avenue in Cincinnati, offering used 78–rpm records that he would buy cheap from jukebox operators. The turning point came when he acquired the record stock, mostly hillbilly, of his former radio shop boss, Max Frank. What impressed Nathan most of all was that he was drumming up good business in record sales in what was supposed to be a retail and cultural desert. Quite by accident, he had uncovered the blue-collar workforce of largely rural Kentuckians and Tennesseans employed at the Cincy factories. Among Nathan's customers were future King hillbilly stars Alton and Rabon Delmore (the Delmore Brothers), Grandpa Jones, and Merle Travis, who would record collectively as country-gospel act Brown's Ferry Four. Kentucky-born Travis would prove to be an immense guitar-picker influence in a commanding line through Scotty Moore, Chet Atkins, Joe Maphis, James Burton, and Reggie Young.

King Records was launched innocuously in November 1943 with crudely manufactured 78s by the same Grandpa Jones and Merle Travis, who were recorded in a makeshift studio in Dayton, Ohio. The next August, Syd Nathan raised $25,000 from family members to give his label the necessary capital for expansion, including the acquisition of a five-year lease on 1540 Brewster and the construction of a small pressing plant. Displaying precocious ingenuity, he would secure pre-orders for his early releases from sixty-nine jukebox operator accounts spread throughout the South, right down to Big Spring, Texas.[1]

A constant source of hillbilly talent was provided by the popular *Boone County Jamboree* show (renamed *Midwestern Hayride* in 1945) that was being broadcast over 50,000–watt Radio WLW, Cincinnati. The show was a good promotional outlet, too. Sensing that he couldn't survive on hillbilly music alone and seeing the opportunities in the race market on his travels, Syd Nathan ushered in Queen Records in September 1945. This operation would be merged with the King label in 1947.

Colonel Jim Wilson: King Records Branch Manager, Detroit

The early stirrings, inner workings, and strategies of the King Records business model were explained to me in 1992 by Colonel Jim Wilson, master record salesman and promo man. At the time, he was vice president of sales and marketing for Shelby Singleton's Sun Entertainment Corporation of Nashville. Colonel Jim, a genuine southern gentleman from Kentucky but with no formal military ranking, joined King Records in 1949 as the Detroit branch manager. In time-honored tradition, he was even accorded a vanity record on the Federal subsidiary: "Jim Wilson Boogie" by Little Willie Littlefield. Usually, this was a favorite device for record men to sweeten the egos of popular disc jockeys, thereby encouraging more spins for their product. Wilson was thrilled at the accolade some forty years after the event.

Colonel Jim reflected on the emergence of King Records out of the humble beginnings of Syd's Record Shop: "I'm sure Syd thought, 'Well, golly, if the people are this hungry for records and music, then there must be a place out there for a little record company.' Early on, if it was an R&B record, only black people would buy it. Or if it was a country record, then only the white southerners would be buying it, the hillbillies so to speak. All of that would change."

A crucial aspect of King Records' game plan was Syd Nathan's decision to develop a self-administered distribution system through branch offices in key market areas throughout the United States. "Now this was an unheard of thing for a small independent record company," said Wilson.

> King was a self-contained company. It had its own recording studio; it had its own mastering, pressing, plating, distribution, and promotion. I think that Syd's theory was that we could control our own destiny to some degree by selling our own product, and if we got working to develop other labels' product, then we were taking away from the development of our own artists. For the most part, we controlled the artist and we controlled the publishing. The profit thing was much greater on an artist that belonged to us, an in-house artist.
>
> Theoretically, you could walk into King Records in the morning, record, then walk out of there with a dee-jay copy in your hand to take to the radio stations. So that in itself made it very unique. And one of the other great things that I personally always liked, you pretty much ran your branch. Of course, it was under the guidance of the company, but if you were doing things right, they left you alone. It was like running your own business, and they paid the bills. It really made it neat. Of course, you learn all facets of the business in that type of an operation. You learn how to ship records, to pack records, to sell records, to do accounting and promotion; you really learn everything from A to Z. It was a great education.

Syd Nathan did not rush headlong into the branch system, which was based on the Decca Records model. By September 1948, there were still only eleven units under the watch of the Cincinnati head office, augmented by five regular distributorships. Within three years, however, *Cash Box* was reporting the number of satellites as "thirty-five" (seemingly a peak) and that Nathan had decided to "switch branch offices from mere order takers to salesmen. In keeping with this new concept, all bookkeeping was taken away from the branches and transferred to the main office. This is intended to give managers and salesmen more time to get out and sell."[2]

For all the inherent benefits, branch offices were an expensive burden that King's indie competitors never copied to the same extent. For a start, the branches were mainly restricted to product on King and its subsidiary labels, Federal and De Luxe, augmented by distribution agreements with labels such as 4 Star, Bethlehem, and Beltone. That meant there had to be a steady stream of commercial-selling records coming out of the Cincinnati studios and elsewhere. Syd Nathan's archrival Herman Lubinsky chided him about the draining overhead in vitriolic correspondence in July 1960: "I'm real happy that you have 11 [records] on the charts, as with the big nut you have you need 20 to break even!"[3]

The individual branches were reliant on the caliber of the local manager, too, but the system did offer an excellent scouting medium. "Every employee was a scout to some degree," said Jim Wilson.

> I was involved in getting a few of the King artists from out of the Detroit area. There was a group called the Royals, [which] became Hank Ballard and the Midnighters; we got them involved. Little Willie John was another artist that I got them interested in and recorded. He was performing around there in Detroit, and being in the business, [my] attention [was] drawn to him through a dee-jay friend, and [I started] paying attention. That's more or less how we got some ears listening and turned up: "Yes, he does have some talent, and he is unique and different."
>
>   That was one of the great things with King. Of all the outstanding artists we worked with, you never had to ask who they were. When you listened to their songs, you knew them; they had an identifiable sound. You didn't have to guess that was Wynonie Harris, no one else sounded like Earl Bostic on the alto saxophone, and you didn't have to guess that was Bill Doggett or James Brown or Hank Ballard. You could listen to them, and you knew immediately who they were.

An essential part of the King branch manager's job was to spot potential hits in order to promote them properly. What was Colonel Jim's strategy?

> Well, I listened carefully to something, and mentally I was like a computer. I evaluated where my market was, where I thought that this would fit, and if it did fit, did it have any kind of potential? So I would normally play it for a few of the record dealers around, and I would go to the one-stops, to the jukebox operators, get a little feel from them and get a little backing to my own feeling. In other words, sometimes I wanted that support, and other times I would have gone after it whether I had support or not, if I felt that strongly about a record. Then I would approach the dee-jays: "Okay, let's give it a shot; I'll give it a play." And we'd start building from there.
>
>   Then get it into the stores and try to get the customers enthusiastic. People would come in, "What do you have new?" And we'd say, "We have this new record!" You would just start developing it. All the positive things that occurred, you would feed that back to the dee-jays and all because they didn't want to be playing "stiffs" or bad records. But you would give them positive reports that were honest, not false. I tried to communicate and feed them as much as possible. Every station was important at that time.

Wilson readily recalled several "very good" Detroit disc jockeys, including the "famous" Jack the Bellboy (Ed McKenzie) on WXYZ and Robin Seymour of *Boppin' with Robin* on WKMH.[4] "I tried to treat them all fairly," said Wilson.

I never tried to give one dee-jay a record to play exclusive before anybody else got a chance to play it. I worked with them all, and I brought artists around to them. Back in the '50s, record hops were big things, and I would bring the artist in, and he would go to the record hops some Friday nights and Saturday nights. I would take artists that were in town on a promotion thing, or maybe they were working a club, but if we could squeeze them into a record hop or something, I'd convince them to go do it. So the fellas, if they could play the record on their show, if it would fit, they would do it. Now, I never asked them to play anything that I felt was in bad taste or didn't fit their show.

The record distribution and promotion community there in Detroit, we were competitive, but we were kind of a close-knit fraternity. I mean, we were all working for ourselves, but we had respect for each other. Bernie Besman and his partner John Kaplan had the Pan American distributing company [founded in the gold rush days, in April 1946]. I think Bernie was more involved in the recording end of their distribution setup, and then later he sold out and moved out to California [in 1952]. But in the early days, he had been instrumental in starting the Sensation label [which had a national distribution deal with King], and originally he had some John Lee Hooker things and some early Todd Rhodes.[5]

At that particular time, along a couple of blocks . . . in Detroit [on Woodward Avenue], most of the five or six independent record distributors were all located there.[6] We used to have a coffee shop where we had coffee in the morning, and we'd lie to each other about all the business we were doing [*laughs*]. We'd compare notes about whose credit was bad and what was going on here. We were all competitive, but we were a kind of a brotherhood.

It was a great era back in the '50s, because you could go to Detroit, and in two or three days you knew if you had a hit. Like, you could come in and get the airplay over a weekend, and by Monday you'd know if you had a record or not because the stations would all be rolling and tumbling. Wherever you went across the dial, you'd be hearing it. If the record had salability, it didn't take you long to find out.

Joe Battle had one of the more successful record shops [Joe's Record Shop] in Detroit, and it was located on Hastings Street right in the heart of The Valley, as we called it. Joe was very entrepreneurial; he wasn't content to be just a record shop per se. He had artists coming in to see him and dee-jays coming and doing broadcasts out of his store. Joe became the lead player in the record industry in Detroit and remained as such for many years. Then we'd get something going. Many times I'd invite his opinion: "What do you think of this?" I respected that he had a good ear for the music and for what the people would go for, and I listened to him many times. I learned a lot from him. Failing health got the better of him, but I enjoyed the association and years of business with Joe.

Known also as Joe Von Battle, he provided Syd Nathan with dozens of masters, mainly blues but some doo-wop, that were recorded in his crude back-of-the-store studio between 1948 and 1954.[7]

Continued Jim Wilson:

Yes, the jukebox operators were very important . . . particularly with a lot of the R&B records that I had difficulty getting played on the pop stations. Some of them—well, let's face it, "Sixty-Minute Man" by the Dominoes was not a hit record to begin with. But that started on the jukeboxes; it became a million seller [in 1951]. Back in those days, you have to remember the lyric was a little risqué. Or let's go to Hank Ballard's "Work with Me Annie"; that was a little touchy [in 1954]. Nowadays it wouldn't mean anything, but we had to start the music many times on the jukeboxes. Sometimes the stations might be a little hesitant to play it, but when it really got such a solid thing, they would maybe get on to it. But you couldn't get any pop play [on the radio], so the coin machine operators were very, very important.

So this type of [risqué] record needed the jukebox operators, and it was bulk sales to the jukeboxes. That was the great thing: you sold a record, and they helped you promote it. Of course, we would work with them sometimes to get a thing started. If the operator had, let's say, two hundred [juke]boxes on his route: "Okay, if you buy a hundred, I'll give you a hundred," or "I'll give you fifty free." I mean, we'd have little incentives. There again, just because he was getting something for nothing wasn't always appealing. It had to have something in the grooves, because if he had a record that was a "stiff" or a "dog," it was taking up a spot on his machine, and it wasn't generating any revenue. It had to have some merit.

The 45 was about coming in when I got into the business in '49, but the 78 was still the dominant thing, and, of course, the LP was starting in the early '50s there. We were one of the last companies to quit making 78s because our customer base still had a lot of 78 record players out there. The black and country record markets were some of the last to get the new equipment, so we didn't just drop those overnight, but they began to get phased out. Then we began to get into the LP biz as the hardware became available in the marketplace. Of course, we tried to cross over into the pop market to promote artists like Earl Bostic. We probably sold Earl Bostic as much in the white marketplace as we did in the black marketplace. He was definitely a crossover artist.

At King we had one of the greatest A&R men in the business, the late Henry Glover. Henry had been a writer and a musician with the Lucky Millinder band and was a graduate music major. In other words, he was not a blues man. He could write charts [and] arrange; he was a professional musician. He headed up our A&R department and not only recorded all of the black acts, the rhythm and blues, he [also] recorded the country acts [making him the first black producer in the genre]. Henry was instrumental in writing such things as "Blues Stay Away from Me," which was Wayne Raney and the Delmore Brothers, and many songs of this nature.

The Delmores' "Blues Stay Away from Me," with its bluesy bass line, was an influence on such well-known records as Hank Williams's "I'm So Lonesome I Could Cry" and Fats Domino's "Blueberry Hill."

In late 1950, Syd Nathan started up the Federal label as a subsidiary to King. Through attorney Jack Pearl, he acquired the A&R services of West Coast–based hipster Ralph Bass, who had learned his craft with Paul Reiner at Black & White and had been scoring

on Savoy with Johnny Otis, Little Esther, and Mel Walker. As a sweetener, Nathan offered Bass a piece of the publishing action through a stake in Armo Music, plus a then-
unprecedented half-cent per record production deal. Back at Savoy, Herman Lubinsky
was probably choking on his cigars at the loss of Bass, his hit-making producer.

In Chicago, King's Sonny Thompson (a former hit act himself with the hypnotic
piano instrumental "Long Gone" for Lee Egalnick's Miracle label in 1948) was to discover blues guitar hero Freddy King, a mainstay in the early 1960s. "Sonny Thompson
not only recorded for us as an artist," said Wilson,

> but he produced a lot of things, and his band was used a lot of times. Sonny was a very
> good writer himself, and at one time he was married to the blues vocalist Lula Reed.
> Again, Henry Glover wrote hits for Lula, "Drown in My Own Tears" and "Let's Call
> It a Day," big, big records. Henry used to write those songs himself, or he'd co-write
> with some, but Henry was a great writer.
>
> In fact, I took the record of "Drown in My Own Tears" to Ahmet Ertegun and Jerry
> Wexler when they were in Detroit. The Atlantic distributor was Pan American, and
> by this time Bernie Besman had left the scene there, and it was John Kaplan. I went
> over and was chatting with them one night, and I gave them a copy of the Lula record.
> I told them, "I think this would be a dynamite record for Ray Charles." Well, they
> went back and cut it with Ray, and of course it became even a bigger hit for Ray than
> it had been for Lula Reed.
>
> I used to get records to Randy Wood, who was president of Dot Records, and get a
> lot of covers on hits like "Hearts of Stone," which we had with the Charms [on the
> De Luxe subsidiary, but not self-published]. Well, he did it with the Fontane Sisters.
> I'd send him copies and say, "I think this would be good" because, as far as I was con-
> cerned, we already had the Detroit market, and that's all I was interested in. Most times
> at King we had the publishing on the songs, so it would help, overall, the company.
>
> So Dot or Mercury were great ones to make a cover. You'd make sure that Randy
> Wood or David Carroll [the Mercury A&R man] or someone would get a copy; Johnny
> Kaplan at Pan American distributed both Dot and Mercury. Of course at King we used
> to cover, too; we had the distribution to do it. If a record was breaking out someplace, if
> it's gonna sell 300,000, we may get 150,000 sales over this side of the country, and they
> can have that side. But covers lost their edge. Communications changed, national TV
> and all, aviation, the shipping of records, etc. Then the recognition of the artists that
> had the hits became more important. For the most part, covering is a gone thing.

Quite clearly, there was an informal mutuality among all labels, majors and independents, in the peak cover-version era of the mid-1950s. It was not just a case of the big
bad majors plundering the poor little indies all the time.[8]

An ingenious King ploy was to record the same self-published songs for the segregated country and R&B audiences. About the best example musically is "Bloodshot
Eyes," written and recorded by Hank Penny. This politically incorrect admonishment
to a partying woman was a No. 4 country hit for Penny in 1950 before blues shouter
Wynonie Harris vibrantly gave the song extra mileage at No. 6 R&B a year later. In
1955, Syd Nathan was milking the same songs through recordings by such as Cowboy

Copas and the Midnighters and by the York Brothers and Earl "Connelly" King. As late as 1960, the Stanley Brothers recorded an unlikely hillbilly boogie version of Hank Ballard's "Finger Poppin' Time." Syd Nathan was still exploiting the dual markets and his copyrights to the full.

The standout King single, "Honky Tonk, Part 1 & 2" by the Bill Doggett Combo, was simply impossible to cover. A No. 2 pop hit (and No. 1 R&B for thirteen weeks) in late 1956, the instrumental tune featured wicked solos and interplay by guitarist Billy Butler and tenor saxophonist Clifford Scott. To his credit, Bill Doggett eschewed an organ solo, concentrating instead on an underlying shuffle rhythm that he had churned out countless times for Louis Jordan. The result was an eternal instrumental that has sold millions of copies. "Honky Tonk" has continued to be a favorite opening number at concerts to get the bands in the groove and the crowds in the mood.

The Bill Doggett Combo played regularly in Detroit, especially at the Flame Show Bar, which was a snazzy black-and-tan club where aspiring young writers Roquel "Billy" Davis and Berry Gordy would hang out with the sharp-dressed, racially mixed clientele. "I'd take friends down to see Bill's group," said Jim Wilson,

> and the whole joint would really be rocking with the songs. Bill could play sweet melodic tunes, or things like "Honky Tonk."
>
> A funny thing about that record: Syd Nathan was always against "Part 1" and "Part 2" records and was very adamant about even cutting them. But Henry Glover insisted and went ahead and cut it. They had been toying with playing this riff at some club where they had been playing [in Lima, Ohio]. Two or three different times Bill and the group had run through it, and the crowd really got with it. So Bill came in and related this to Henry, and at the next session—bingo! They did it, and the rest is history.

"Honky Tonk" is a prime example of a new song getting positive audience reaction prior to recording. It was informal test marketing. The "Honky Tonk" date, of course, was an unforgettable experience for Billy Butler, who achieved an arrestingly warm tone from his Epiphone Broadway guitar with DeArmond pickup and Fender amp. Said Butler in 1989:

> The guy turned the machine on, opened the doors, [and] goes out to take a smoke; he wasn't regulating the controls, he wasn't doing anything, and we went on and just played. So we started to stop, and he said "Keep it up!" So we kept playing, and that's how it became a two-sided record.
>
> When Syd Nathan heard it, he went completely to the moon; he went completely to the moon. He said, "This has got to be a hit!" They put it out, and sure enough, it started to climb, it got on the charts, and the next thing we knew, we were pushing Elvis Presley for No. 1 [the "Hound Dog"/"Don't Be Cruel" coupling]. We didn't know it was gonna be a million-seller, for God's sake—a gold record! Then it becomes a platinum record. It was unbelievable, unbelievable, and then it became a rhythm and blues standard. That's what it is today.

"Let me tell you, it sold plenty!" said Jim Wilson. "I think Doggett should go into the Rock and Roll Hall of Fame and that record should be recognized as such, I really do. It has stood the test of time. That came out in 1956, and [if] you put the record on today, . . . it still sounds just as great as it did then. Yes, it is a timeless classic; it has spanned the decades."

The "Honky Tonk" session was conducted not in Cincinnati but at Les Cahan's Beltone Recording Studios at 4 West Thirty-first Street, New York. This facility had a natural echo within its big room with plaster walls, and with a rate of twenty dollars an hour, it was in great demand by the New York indie record men in the 1950s. When Cahan took the plunge into label ownership with the Beltone Records offshoot, the happy association with "Honky Tonk" would lead to a distribution deal with Syd Nathan. As a result, King was selling through its branch offices one of the biggest smashes of 1961: "Tossin' and Turnin'" by Bobby Lewis. The sales surge was maintained with "My True Story" by the Jive Five (No. 3). Within a year or so, however, a *Billboard Music Week* headline screamed that "Beltone Throws Book of Charges at King, Asks $2 Million Damages."[9] But the case never reached the courts due to more clever maneuverings by Nathan's lethal attorney, Jack Pearl.[10]

Thanks to "Honky Tonk" and those other big 1956 hits, "Please, Please, Please" by James Brown and "Fever" by Little Willie John, King was well positioned to keep pace with the rock 'n' roll explosion, unlike other original independent labels such as Apollo and Savoy. But with King's costly branch network to maintain, that was a necessity. Nathan managed to circumnavigate the Federal Trade Commission payola hearings but sacrificed top A&R men Henry Glover and Ralph Bass on the first rumblings of the inquisition. Then with the music scene ever changing and with Nathan suffering from a debilitating asthmatic condition (not helped by his fat cigar habit), King failed to pick up convincingly on the soul music trend, or indeed the neighboring Nashville country music sound.

James Brown was a noble exception, because he *was* James Brown. By creating a new brand of soul music dosed with funk, he was King's savior in the 1960s. "We can't forget Soul Brother No. 1!" exclaimed Jim Wilson.

A great talent, one of the hardest working, he was "Mr. Dynamite," there's no question of that. James used to cause us a lot of problems, though, and the problems were that he wanted to call the shots in releasing product. Now I can understand that; he would get all excited about something new. An idea came to him, and he was still young: "Let's cut it! Let's put it right out." And I appreciated that from an artist.

But from a company manufacturing standpoint, you have just begun to get the pipeline filled with the last hit he put out, and now we have to back off and start up another one. It was hard to argue with him because, when you're a quarterback like he was and everything he threw was a touchdown, every one was a hit. I mean, it was hard to sit down and reason with him about some of the mechanics of the distribution thing. James's theory probably was, "Well, look, if I've got five hits on the go, they'll play all five of them." But it didn't work quite that way. The dee-jays would get off that older one, even though it was only on release for two or three weeks, and start playing the new one, because they didn't want to be on the old record. The same was true of the jukebox operator, the one-stop, and the retail store. I mean, it presented a lot of problems.

Syd Nathan's failure to spot the popular "Sound of Young America" that was being exploited so brilliantly at Tamla-Motown was particularly galling for Jim Wilson because Berry Gordy's label had started out on his territory. "I think that to some extent, we were dragging our feet at King in moving forward into the Motown-type sound," said Wilson.

> To see a company like Motown who [was], in comparison to King, nothing—I mean, they were like a little fly in a giant flyswatter over here. Then all of a sudden they became real big, and they passed up King and just went right on. I'm not detracting. I think they had a type of a sound that was more mainstream to the entire country and had appeal. They did a great job promoting and marketing and presenting their artists in a very professional manner. I give them all the credit in the world.
>
> So, actually, things pretty much stayed the same until about late '64 when Syd was not in good health. He was gonna close up all the branches and slowly had begun doing so and eventually turned the distribution of King over to the independent distributors around the country.[11] About that time, James really exploded on the pop scene as well as the R&B scene with "Papa's Got a Brand New Bag," which occurred in 1965. That's why all of the distributors really went to work on King. Unfortunately, they neglected the [back] catalog. They were selling just the hits, which was what they were notorious for. But it got Syd back active, although he still wasn't feeling good.

Colonel Jim Wilson was employed by King Records until 1965. He had two short breaks in his sixteen-year service: one was to join Columbia Records as its Midwest distributor, and the other was to start Jay-Kay Distributing Co. with Johnny Kaplan (formerly of Pan American and a certified public accountant). Jay-Kay was destined to become the largest traditional record distributor in Michigan before being swallowed up by rack jobber company Handleman in a relentless repetition of the independent record label takeover scenario. "Both times Syd got on the phone and offered me a better deal to get back to Detroit," said Wilson. "Then our vice president and general manager at King, Hal Neely, had moved down to Nashville with Starday Records and Don Pierce. Hal called me and said, 'Why don't you come on down? I want you to meet Don and move down here to Starday.' Which I did. Within a couple of years, Syd died [in 1968]. Hal had the first option to buy that company, and we immediately bought King and merged it into Starday-King."

As we wound up our interview, Jim Wilson reflected on the legacy of Syd Nathan's labels. "King has had a fantastic impact," he said. "I think that just many great things occurred with King that opened up areas within the world of music." Typically, he made no reference to his own important role. Literally, there were hundreds of dedicated individuals like him who have been forgotten but who made the independent record business tick in its prime.

"I had the greatest admiration for Colonel Jim Wilson from Detroit," said Seymour Stein of Sire Records. "He was an all-around music man and a wonderful guy." Stein also recalled other King branch managers: "Mario DiLario, from Philadelphia, could get a record on the radio as good as the best local promo guys, Matty Singer or Harry Finfer. I have fond memories of Miami's Marvin Novack, nicknamed 'Falsie' by Syd Nathan, and the guy who ran the New York branch: Hy Penzell, an older more experienced guy, and a lovely man." In effect, the branch system took out the reliance on the independent distributors—they *were* the distributors.

Henry Stone: De Luxe Records

Henry Stone had a fragile, fleeting relationship with Syd Nathan when they set up the Crystal Recording Corporation in 1953. Stone's job was to scout artists and record masters for King's revived De Luxe subsidiary label. The biggest hit to come out of this uneasy liaison was "Hearts of Stone" by the Charms.

After leaving California for Florida in 1947, Henry Stone started working for Taran Distributing, which had branches in Jacksonville and Miami, as well as in Atlanta, Georgia. Owner Sam Taran was an important jukebox and record distributor with acknowledged personal connections in Chicago and elsewhere. Both Mercury and Modern were important Taran record lines. There, Stone was involved with pushing the biggest indie hit to date, "Near You" by Francis Craig (Bullet), and worked Jack McVea's original version of "Open the Door, Richard!" (Black & White). In 1949, he started Stone Distributing from 505 West Flagler, Miami.

"Then I started picking up all the other little East Coast labels here in Florida like Apollo," said Stone.

I got in my little car, my little Dodge, and drove up and found the labels myself. The labels didn't know I existed because Florida was the asshole of the world; it really was. There was nothing but everglades down here. It was so early, you know. I guess there was only one little record store when I got here that sold music [in Miami]. I sold records in the Florida area to the jukebox operators, always jukebox operators. That was the *beginning* of the record industry.

There were normal business problems in the early years: the lack of money and the building of inventory constantly. The banks had never heard of the record business. One thing I always did in this business was build up a good credit thing, even if people would say I was slow in paying. But that was the record business. Eventually, everybody got paid, starting right from the very beginning. At this time, it was all 78 records. There was a problem with breakages, and then there wasn't a problem. Records were basically insured when they shipped them, so you would crack them a little bit and put them up for insurance [*laughs*].

Music and recording were like my little hobby, instead of playing golf. When I was distributing in Miami, I was always on the street looking for things. I had a little recording studio in the back of my distributing business. That's when Ray Charles came to Miami in 1951. I picked up on him at one of the hotels, and he needed a little session because he needed a little money for whatever he was doing [*laughs*]. It was easy to record. You'd take an Ampex tape machine, put a mic on it, and he cut those four sides including "St. Pete Blues." He was fantastic.

Those Ray Charles recordings, which were released originally on Bob Shad's Sittin' In With label out of New York, have been the subject of many ownership claims through the years.

By 1952, Henry Stone had formed Seminole Distributing and set up his Chart label. He had already encountered the redoubtable Syd Nathan. "He used to come to Florida all the time," said Stone.

> He had a brother down here. Again, I was the only record music man down here. He found out about me, and we started hanging out together. What happened in the '50s, boom, the explosion came with the 45s and the LPs. Just before that the record business did a dip again; people didn't know what to do. Things weren't too good even with the little distribution thing I had.
>
> Syd said to me, "You're so talented; why are you wasting your time? Why don't you come with me in the manufacturing business?" So I thought it was a good idea. I gave up the distribution. I had these little masters like the Ray Charles thing, a bunch of spiritual things, some of the blues things that I had cut. We restarted the De Luxe label with my stuff. It put Syd right back on the top.

De Luxe Records was a pioneering label formed in 1944 by the Braun brothers, David and Jules, out of Linden, New Jersey, and it released everything from race music, gospel, and jazz to pop and polka. The biggest artist was Roy Brown, whose breakthrough hit, "Good Rocking Tonight" (No. 13 race in 1948), was covered lucratively by Wynonie Harris for King (No. 1 race); New Orleanians Paul Gayten and Annie Laurie were other good-selling 1940s acts. Before long, cash flow problems forced the Brauns into the arms of the wily Nathan, and after a troubled liaison, a bitter legal battle ensued.[12] With the ubiquitous Jack Pearl leading the charge, Syd Nathan acquired full control of the De Luxe assets in 1951.

The De Luxe imprint was reestablished in the charts in late 1954 with "Hearts of Stone" by the Charms (No. 15 pop, No. 1 R&B). "That was one of the first crossover records to hit the pop charts," said Henry Stone, before bursting into song: "Hearts made of stone, do do wadda, do do wadda . . ." He continued: "I couldn't complain about Randy Wood's cover by the Fontane Sisters because I covered 'Hearts of Stone' from a group in California; I was one of the first culprits [*laughs*]. It was by the Jewels [on R and B]. I wasn't the writer on that, but I was the writer on 'Two Hearts' [the follow-up by the Charms].I had eleven covers on that: Pat Boone, Frank Sinatra, Doris Day, a lot of covers."

The Nathan/Stone relationship had collapsed in predictable disarray by November 1955. "I sure did fall out with Syd!" said Henry. "When we came to divvy up the money [that is, the assets], that's a whole story. We never did get to court. We made a settlement, but it was a hell of a battle. He was a good, old-fashioned businessman: very gruff, big cyclops glasses, big cigar, typical thing . . . like you see in the movies about a record executive. He was one of the first brilliant guys in the music industry."

Seymour Stein: Apprentice at King Records

Another vocal supporter of Syd Nathan's is Seymour Stein of Sire Records. Short and stocky, this friendly and immensely wealthy record man was working in an impossibly hyperactive environment in 2004 with a backdrop of constantly ringing telephones and staff interruptions. During our interview at his office at Rockefeller Center, New York, Stein mentioned his Sire act the Ramones but once and his other stars Madonna and Talking Heads not at all. He was more intent on talking about his own musical awakenings in the 1950s and the golden age of the independent record scene.

Incredible as it might seem, Stein had served an informal apprenticeship under Syd Nathan's wing at King Records in Cincinnati while on vacation trips that were the equivalent of summer camps. Soon afterward, Stein took up employment at *Billboard*, followed by a stint as a promo man at Red Bird Records for George Goldner ("the greatest of them all!") before forming Sire Records in 1966. A favorite Stein party piece continued to be a rasping imitation of the inimitable "Sydney."

"I just loved music," said Stein.

It totally took over my life when I was just a kid. My sister Ann was a teenager when I was seven or eight years old. I used to listen to the music she listened to, in the days before rock 'n' roll, artists like Guy Mitchell, Patti Page, Les Paul and Mary Ford, Johnnie Ray, Peggy Lee, Eddie Fisher, Kay Starr, Tony Bennett, Perry Como, and Frankie Laine. We would listen to Martin Block, the pioneering disc jockey who had a daily show, the *Make Believe Ballroom*, and on Saturdays would play the Top 25 from the *Billboard* chart. Later on he started playing the Top 5 country and the R&B hits as well. This was probably my first exposure to those two fields.

I was influenced by Martin Block but soon started switching to the black music stations at the high end of the dial, like WLIB, WWRL, WNJR, and WOV (Jocko Henderson). I used to love Jocko's patter: "This is WOV, the power tower station of the nation's sensation, 1280 on the dial, *Jocko's Rocket Ship* show, hey diddly opp, this is the Jock."

Alan Freed came to New York in September 1954, which was monumental. I mean, he played the best doo-wop and rhythm and blues, and that really mesmerized me. I just wanted to be in the music business. I was twelve years old.

I was born in Brooklyn where all the great live rock 'n' roll shows were held. Alan Freed would have his shows at either the Brooklyn Paramount or the Brooklyn [Fabian] Fox Theatre on Flatbush Avenue over the ten-day school breaks at Christmas and Easter. They were star-studded, and it was heaven. I would take a few salami sandwiches, go early, and stay for two or three shows. There were separate tickets for each show, but like [a] roach motel, I checked in and never checked out. They would have had to get me out with a crowbar.

It was just great, I mean, Fats Domino was overwhelming, pushing that piano across the stage. Sam Cooke was so original, and his songs were the absolute best. Jackie Wilson was an amazing performer; he was a professional boxer, and did these sensational splits (until he got shot) while he was singing on stage. James Brown was equally if not more sensational. I particularly like him in the early days; people today don't realize what a great voice he had with all that screaming, but if you listen to "Try Me" or "Please, Please, Please," his voice and the emotion in those songs is simply amazing. Bo Diddley, what a performer he was. And the women: LaVern Baker, Etta James, Ruth Brown, also Shirley & Lee, they were in a category all their own. Then you'd have the great black doo-wop groups: the Five Satins, the Heartbeats, the Moonglows, the Flamingos, the Harptones, Lee Andrews and the Hearts, the Paragons, the Jesters, the Diablos, the Nutmegs. . . . Later on you had white groups like Dion and the Belmonts, the [mixed] Crests, and the Skyliners.

One evening, young Seymour was invited by *Billboard* music editor Paul Ackerman to attend a weekly record review session.

I said, "No, I've got a test tomorrow at school; I've got to study." He said, "Look, I don't want to get you in trouble, but one of the most interesting men I've ever met in the music business is coming up tonight. And you should meet him. You will not believe this guy, and I think he will see in you what I see in you."

That was Syd Nathan, and he was correct. I mean, I was in awe of him. This man spoke his mind, he held nothing back, and whatever he felt, he would say it. He said, "Look, when I come to New York, I love to have some corned beef, and after I leave here I'm gonna get a sandwich at The Stage. I'm inviting all of you to come with me, I wish you would." And some said yes and some said no.

If a record man was at the *Billboard* sessions, the usual practice was that his records would be reviewed last of all. "They made them sit through the entire listening process," said Stein.

Toward the end, that night, one of the reviewers said, "Oh look, these records are on Jubilee. I hear that company is going out of business." She said, "Syd, why don't we listen to your records and wrap it up?" So he says, in his guttural voice, "What if this was me, and you were talking this way about me . . . *listen* to his records!" So another guy, I believe it was Bob Rolontz, said to him, "Syd, I never knew you were such a good friend of Jerry Blaine," who was the owner of Jubilee and Cosnat Distributing as well. Syd replied, "Jerry Blaine, I'm suing that son of a bitch, but what's right is right." As I recall, one of those Jubilee records became a big hit; I think it was "White Silver Sands" by Don Rondo [around June 1957]. Then they played Syd's records, and we went out. The next day he invited me round to his branch office here in New York and gave me lots of great albums and singles. By the way, Bob Rolontz was a great friend and in between stints at *Billboard* ran RCA's Groove label.

Then when the summer vacation came, Syd invited me to spend a few weeks with his family in Cincinnati. My parents, very hardworking, lower-middle-class people from Brooklyn, were somewhat dubious. So they called Paul Ackerman, who they had met. He said, "Look, perhaps you should meet Syd; he comes to town every few weeks." I think that Sydney was a little annoyed that such a wonderful offer was being scrutinized. He called my parents, and they arranged to meet at *Billboard*. By that time I was working there part time.

They put me in a conference room. Syd saw that my father had a cigar that he had put out. He said, "Take one of mine." It was a Cuban cigar; it was one of the best Cubans my father had. Syd said [*gruffly*], "You've got two choices. This boy has got shellac in his veins: either let him come with me to *Cincinnata* or else get him a newspaper route, 'cause he's not good for anything else" [*laughs*]. In my parents' minds they wanted me to become a pharmacist and go into business with my brother-in-law. I mean, their heads were spinning around, but they said, "Fine." And I went and learned so much.

Cincinnati was interesting. It was in the South and it was in the North; it was at the crossroads. You go over the L&N Bridge and you're in Kentucky—the airport is Erlanger, Kentucky. It's a whole different world. There was another record company there: Harry Carlson's Fraternity Records. Lonnie Mack was on that label with "Memphis" and Bobby Bare, where he was released under a different name of Bill Parsons, had "The All American Boy": "Gather around, cats, and I'll tell you a story / About how to become an All American Boy."[13] Fraternity had other things [including Jimmy Dorsey's swing-era relic "So Rare" No. 2 in 1957], but music-wise, Cincinnati belonged to King Records.

I went out for two summers, '57 and '58, so I would have been fifteen and sixteen. Syd had me doing *everything!* Pressing records, things that they never should have had me doing, but it was great. I was a bit klutzy, you know; the "turd" (biscuit) would come out, [and] you'd put it in. The one thing I wouldn't do and he didn't want me to do was the plating, because acid was involved; I didn't want to go near that. But I worked in the studio, I worked in the shipping department, I worked everywhere. I did A&R with him. He even had me checking expense accounts from his branch offices. And then he said to me, "Now, look, when Bob Krasnow, the San Francisco branch manager [later a driving force at WEA], when his expenses come in, don't even open the envelope." He says, "I don't want you to be *contaminated* by it." Bob Krasnow was a big spender! He was one of the best people there, a great, fabulous A&R guy, too. Syd says, "You send it right up to the controller, Jack Kelley." I mean, I just had the time of my life. It was just an amazing, amazing adventure.

The studio had a great sound. It wasn't that much of an upkeep; that's why Syd was not really interested in renting it out. The studio he felt always paid for itself. He had Eddie Smith, who was a great engineer. Some of the musicians worked in the shipping department, then when there was a session, Syd would pull them out. The head of sales hated that; his name was Johnny Miller. "You know, Syd, we've just got in big orders today." Syd didn't care and gave the men extra money for playing. King had a studio in Chicago, where Sonny Thompson would record, at the branch on South Michigan Avenue. A lot of demos were made there but also a lot of records; the Freddy Kings were made there and kind of upgraded and sweetened in Cincinnati. There was even a studio in the branch office in New York on 146 West Fifty-fourth Street, which in 1966 became Sire Records' first home.

Sydney was a drummer. He wrote lyrics and co-wrote songs like "Signed Sealed and Delivered," which was probably the most successful song that Cowboy Copas ever had, and Copas was one of the biggest country artists on King. King's artists mostly came from the *Midwestern Hayride,* broadcast over WLW in Cincinnati. It was a rival of WSM's *Grand Ole Opry* and the *National Barn Dance* show over WLS in Chicago. In addition to their stellar R&B roster, King had the best country roster of any indie, which included Moon Mullican, Grandpa Jones, the Stanley Brothers, Reno & Smiley, the Carlisles, Wayne Raney, and Hawkshaw Hawkins.

"I learned everything from Syd," said Stein. What exactly?

I learned that you really have to watch how you spend your money and that you had to go with your gut and act fast, but you couldn't and shouldn't be influenced by anyone else. Listen to people, take their advice, but in the end, when it came to artists, you had to make your decision on the music and the songs . . . and on your own.

Syd was probably the first to have business relationships with his A&R people, where they got a share of the profits on acts they brought to the label. A&R men like Ralph Bass, Henry Glover, and Henry Stone also owned a part of the publishing on their artists. If something is going to be very big, like James Brown or Hank Ballard, you don't know it ahead of time. Syd believed that a piece of the pie was better than nothing, and he had these types of arrangements to lure some of the best A&R men over to King.

Almost all indies understood the value of publishing. Atlantic had Progressive Music, the Chesses had Arc, Specialty had Venice, Imperial had Commodore, and on the pop side, Liberty had Metric. Lois Music was Syd's company, and it was the umbrella for all the joint venture companies he had. Lois was named after an old girlfriend, Lois Friedman, and Sydney would write under the pseudonym Lois Mann. Jay & Cee was his company with Henry Glover. When they formed the company, Syd said, "Henry, I'm gonna make an honest and rich man out of you. I'm gonna take you out of jail and put you in the church." That's what Jay & Cee stood for: jail and church. Along with Ralph Bass's company, Armo Music, they were the two most successful joint ventures.

The resourceful Henry Glover had built up an impressive array of New York–based black songwriters on Syd Nathan's payroll in the mid-late 1950s period, including Rudy Toombs (who had R-T Music), Rose Marie McCoy, and Julius Dixson. Dixson, a persistent song peddler, wrote "Begging Begging" for James Brown and "Love, Life and Money" for Little Willie John. Shortly after leaving King, discontentedly, Dixson co-composed the international smash hit "Lollipop." He recalled:

It was between Henry [Glover] and Rudy [Toombs] that I was introduced to Syd Nathan. Henry was the A&R man for New York; he liked the way I wrote songs. It's a funny thing how Syd Nathan began to yell about how Julius Dixson was the greatest songwriter in the world. He told Henry, "Tell him he's the greatest songwriter; tell him I said hello."

So Henry squeezed my hand and leaves four or five fifty-dollar bills in my hand. I'm thinking I want to meet this guy; he's leaving that money in my hand. But Syd Nathan didn't want me to go nowhere else; that's what he was doing. I couldn't catch on to that. I was looking at them fifty-dollar bills; back then that was a lot of money. So naturally he was trying to keep me there at King Records. He signed up the songs to his publishing companies, R-T and Jay & Cee. So he licensed his company King Records a penny a record on the publishing, one cent, when you're supposed to get two cents a record at that time.[14] Oh man, these guys were so busy taking back what they give you.

Sydney Nathan died in Miami on March 5, 1968, an old man at sixty-three. His heart had given out after his cigar-ridden, asthmatic lungs had succumbed to pneumonia. Just before Nathan passed away, Don Pierce, a longtime friend, was on the verge of taking his country music enterprise, Starday Records, public with a stock offering when his investment adviser introduced him to the Nashville division of growth-minded LIN Broadcasting. Over a meal at Shoney's restaurant (probably on Music Row), Pierce asked $2 million for his debt-free company that had a good earnings record, cash reserves, and a remunerative publishing arm but few hits. And he would keep the real estate.

Upon Nathan's death and before the Starday contract was signed, LIN Broadcasting promptly offered $2.5 million for the assets of King Records as well. In a clever transaction, which presumably had tax advantages, Starday and King were merged ahead of LIN's acquisition of the new combine. As Colonel Jim Wilson had already indicated, King's Hal Neely was also involved in the negotiations.[15]

And so majestic King Records and Lois Music, with James Brown the hottest soul brother on the planet and with standout copyrights like "Fever," was worth a mere half-million dollars more than hayseed Starday Records.

"I tried to do everything I could for Syd," Pierce said. "First thing I did, I gave him all my album pressing business in Cincinnati. I had eight hundred albums in the marketplace by the time I sold out, and Syd Nathan pressed 'em all and did all of my jackets and everything. And he would be paid. Well, anytime he had trouble making payroll for thirty-two branches [sic], he knew he could call me on the telephone and I'd send him money. And I'm proud of it. When Syd died, I'm happy to say that I made it possible for his widow [Zella] to sell out to LIN Broadcasting, because I bought King, put it together with Starday, and sold the whole package to LIN. And so I feel that I helped to take care of Syd's widow."[16]

In the end, the takeovers went through with bewildering speed. *Billboard* announced on October 26, 1968, that "Don Pierce and Hal Neely have assumed management and operation of King Records." Then in the November 2 edition, a story read, "Starday Records late last week confirmed that it had acquired the King Records operation. The holdings include the record and distribution operation and masters, Lois Music and its publishing subsidiaries, the Royal Plastics Pressing operation and the long-term contract of James Brown." Finally, on November 23, a big feature was headlined "Lin B'casting Buys Starday-King For $5 Mil; Execs, Policy Retained." The executive lineup was listed as "Don Pierce, president; Hal Neely, vice president; Jim Wilson, vice president marketing; Johnny Miller in charge of the Cincinnati office; Henry Glover, manager of the New York office, and Harlan Dodsen, general counsel."[17]

But concerned at upsetting the FCC radio overlords, LIN soon divested itself of the King-Starday corporations. First, in July 1971, the James Brown masters and recording contract and his share of jointly owned publishing companies were offloaded in a deal worth in excess of $1.3 million with Polydor Records, King's European licensee. Then the residual assets were sold "for $3.5 million" to the new Tennessee Recording and Publishing Company (formed by New York music publisher Freddy Bienstock and producers/songwriters/publishers Jerry Leiber and Mike Stoller).[18] The day-to-day record company operations were placed in the hands of Hal Neely, but it was an uneasy alliance that hemorrhaged cash.

Recalled Johnny Bienstock, Freddy's brother: "I was at the Gavin Convention, and I saw this guy [Neely] having a lavish party and everything else. I said to Freddy, 'Starday-King Records must be doing phenomenally.' He was treating jockeys like I've never seen; he was having bigger parties than Atlantic Records. Freddy was furious." And so Freddy Bienstock and his partners wanted out of the record company, quickly, whatever the paper loss. The prize for them, of course, was the song publishing catalog.

"I bought the publishing from Don Pierce," said Freddy Bienstock. "I think he was quite successful—he was a young man in a hurry. He made a mistake. The reason why they wanted to sell was because they had a guy [Neely] running it in Nashville who wasn't very good, so I made a good deal there, including the 'Fever' copyright. I liked Don Pierce, though; he was a nice man. I think it was $1 million. At the time, it was quite a bit of money, and I didn't have it, so we had to go to the banks and so forth. But it turned out to be a very good deal. We were partners with Leiber and Stoller."

The King-Starday masters were hived off in 1975 and sold, so said Don Pierce, for a mere $375,000 to present owner Moe Lytle of GML Inc., Nashville.[19] Much later, in 2003, Leiber and Stoller offloaded their 45 percent interest in Fort Knox/Trio Music (including the King/Lois Music songs) for $60 million, according to Bienstock.

All this hectic trading proved, if any proof was needed, that Syd Nathan was right to grab every song copyright he could lay his hands on and that his King masters had undeniable value, historic and monetary (even if not fully realized). In the end, King suffered like any company that was overdependent upon an autocratic founder for its position in a changing marketplace and that did not have a viable management succession plan in place once the leader's physical powers began to diminish. It was also hamstrung by its extensive branch office network for too long. Consider, though, that the label had started out most modestly with working-class race and hillbilly music in the Midwest backwoods. Syd Nathan had confirmed in his special, blustering way that there sure was gold in those regional sounds.

King-Queen trade show booth, 1947: Syd Nathan *(left),* Al Sherman, Al [unknown], and M. Levin. Courtesy Gusto Records, Inc., Nashville.

Bill "Hoss" Allen pulling 78–rpm discs at Radio WLAC, Nashville, c. 1950. Courtesy Bebe Evans, with thanks to Michael Gray, Country Music Hall of Fame.

Radio WLAC disc jockeys John "John R." Richbourg, Gene Nobles, Bill "Hoss" Allen, Herman Grizzard, and Don Whitehead *(standing)*, 1960s. Courtesy Bebe Evans, with thanks to Michael Gray, Country Music Hall of Fame.

Leonard Chess, c. 1958, by Don Bronstein. Courtesy Stan Lewis.

Leonard Chess, Marshall Chess, and Phil Chess, c. 1964. Courtesy
Showtime Music Productions.

King branch office, Nashville, early 1950s. Courtesy Gusto Records, Inc., Nashville.

Gold record for "Honky Tonk." Syd Nathan, King Records *(far right)*, with Bill Doggett's Combo: Bill Doggett, Clifford Scott, Billy Butler, and Shep Sheppard, 1957. Courtesy Theo Zwicky.

Sam Phillips at the console, Sun Records studio, Memphis, 1958. Courtesy Colin Escott.

Lester Bihari, with possibly Leona Wynn, outside Meteor Records office at 1914 Chelsea Avenue, Memphis, 1956. © Jody Chastain, courtesy Jim Cole.

Hillbilly-turned-rockabilly act Charlie Feathers *(bottom left)* with his band and Lester Bihari *(top right)* at Meteor Records studio, Memphis, 1956. © Jody Chastain, courtesy Jim Cole.

Stan "The Man" Lewis, early 1950s. Courtesy Stan Lewis.

Stan's Record Shop ad, 1954. Courtesy John Broven.

Cosimo Matassa in his studio with Ace Records teen star Jimmy Clanton, c. 1958. Courtesy John Broven, with acknowledgment to Alvin "Red" Tyler.

Eddie Shuler's first store: Eddie's Music House, Lake Charles, Louisiana, 1944. Courtesy Johnny Shuler, Goldband Records.

Goldband Records and the Quick Service TV fleet of trucks and staff, Lake Charles, Louisiana, 1955; Eddie and Elsie Shuler in foreground (right). Courtesy Johnny Shuler, Goldband Records.

Floyd Soileau in stockroom at Floyd's Record Shop, Ville Platte, Louisiana, 1967. By Mike Leadbitter, courtesy John Broven.

J. D. Miller standing proudly next to gold record of Kitty Wells's "It Wasn't God Who Made Honky Tonk Angels" (written by Miller in 1952), Crowley, Louisiana, 1979. Courtesy Paul Harris.

Slim Harpo *(left)* with Excello-Nashboro Records executives at Woodland Studios, Nashville, c. 1968: Ray Funk, Bob Holmes, Freddie North, Shannon Williams, and Bud Howell. Courtesy Rob Santos.

9

CHAPTER

Behind the Southern Sun

CAST OF CHARACTERS
Sam Phillips, Memphis Recording and Sound Service and
   Sun Records
Joe Bihari, Modern-RPM Records
Rosco Gordon, RPM-Chess-Duke artist
Lillian McMurry, Trumpet Records
Stan Lewis, Stan's Record Shop and Jewel-Paula-Ronn
   Records
*also featuring Lester Bihari, Meteor Records; and Buster
Williams, Music Sales Co. distributor and Plastic Products
pressing plant*

The Sun Records story is yet another that has been honored and dissected many times.[1] Sam Phillips has earned forever his celebrity in rock 'n' roll history as the inspiring Memphis record man behind Elvis Presley, Johnny Cash, Jerry Lee Lewis, Carl Perkins, and a slew of rockabillies—even Roy Orbison, fleetingly. And if that were not enough, Phillips merits a place in the upper pantheon for his myth-like debut recordings of Rosco Gordon, Howlin' Wolf, and Ike Turner. One of the first artists to record at Phillips's new Memphis Recording and Sound Service studio at 706 Union Avenue in the summer of 1950 was willowy youth Riley "Blues Boy" King.

Sam Phillips: Memphis Recording and Sound Service and Sun Records

I spoke to Sam Phillips in June 2000 while gathering stories and information for the book accompanying the B. B. King box set, *The Vintage Years*, released by Ace Records of London. After many dry years, Sam was more open to interviews, probably with the immortalization of his legacy in mind. Over the decades, he must have discussed Elvis, Cash, Jerry Lee, and company until even his prolific verbal capacity was tested. But I gained the distinct impression that he welcomed the opportunity to talk about those early blues years because it was a subject that was close to him and on which he had not been overinterviewed.

Before we spoke, Phillips asked to listen to those near-freshman B. B. King recordings again.[2] The original 78s released by Modern Records' subsidiary RPM were not hits, and it was unlikely that Sam had heard them in half a century. I was impressed at this desire for accuracy in his reminiscences. With Phillips in full flow, he added privileged insights into his recording techniques, the battles with the brothers Bihari and Chess, and his desire to find that white rock 'n' roller with a black sound. The interview presented a striking portrait of a record man starting out in 1950 with the blankest of slates and with an uncertain future ahead of him. Here was the glorious preamble to Sun Records.

"I didn't meet the Bihari brothers [Jules and Saul] until they actually came to town in the summer of 1950," said Sam Phillips. "I knew them indirectly through Dewey Phillips, who was a disc jockey here on a show called *Red Hot and Blue* on Radio WHBQ. I believe Don Pierce of 4 Star Records may have mentioned them to me."

Sam Phillips's first commercial recordings appear to have been with blues pianist "Lost" John Hunter. Cut around May 1950, two singles were released by 4 Star through the ubiquitous Don Pierce (who was using Buster Williams's Memphis-based pressing facilities). Almost immediately, Sam set up the (It's The) Phillips label with disc jockey Dewey Phillips, but there was only one release, by one-man-band Joe Hill Louis. Then B. B. King and Rosco Gordon arrived at the new studio on Union Avenue and Marshall.

"I had B. B. in a time or two for demos and Rosco Gordon also," said Phillips, "and I was very interested in doing some things with B. B. Of course I didn't have a label then, and actually when I found out about the Biharis and talked to them on the phone, I told them about B. B. and Rosco. I told the Biharis [that] if they were interested, I might send them sixteen-inch acetates from Memphis Recording and Sound Service on some things I'd cut on them to see what they thought, and when they came to town we could do a session on them. So that's how it began."

Jules and Saul Bihari had arrived in Memphis flush with a capital injection of $78,000 from the sale of their ARA pressing plant to Mercury, which enabled Modern to move to new offices in Beverly Hills. Apart from seeking out Sam Phillips, the brothers needed now to make arrangements with Buster Williams's Plastic Products company to press their discs for the southern territory; similar outsourcing deals were struck in Hollywood and New Jersey for the West and East Coasts.

"The first sessions for RPM we did were on B. B.," continued Phillips.

I used tape but did dub them to acetate. Now [with] the quality of the dubbing at that time, I wasn't prepared to cut masters to acetate from tape. I didn't have what I wanted in the way of equalization that you [need] to compensate for going through the [tape] head, and I didn't have a heated stylus for cutting purposes. So I didn't attempt to cut a master until much later on, after I got proper equipment. I did my own mastering because a lot of people have a formula and that didn't satisfy me, but these I did not master. The acetates were not the very best in the world because I didn't have an equalizer or a limiter or a compressor.

The Biharis were likable people, especially Saul and then later on Joe. Jules was, too, but he was a kind of warhorse. I was sorry they didn't treat me right, but there were things back then that just went on that I was totally ignorant of. I just thought when people told you something . . . to this day I have no earthly idea [what went wrong] except B. B. was supposed to be my artist and we were going to sign a contract. I was supposed to get a royalty for records sold and on Rosco's, too. Now honestly I did not have B. B. under contract. This was stupid of me, but not as stupid as it may sound. I was just getting into the business, and I was basically for hire.

And so what happened, they made promises to me, and when we got through the first session on B. B. on what they considered were the first masters, they were so impressed with them that Jules jumped on an airplane and went back to the West Coast. Saul stayed in town and finished up the session on Rosco Gordon, I believe.

In the meantime, they had the acetates that I had sent them—they kept them—and I turned over the tapes. There was no need [for me] to keep them because I had shook hands on a deal. There is no use in getting into the criticism and hurt it caused me not to do any more business with the Biharis. And that's when I went to Chess [with "Rocket 88" by Jackie Brenston and his Delta Cats, aka Ike Turner's Kings of Rhythm]. I felt I had not been done right, and I had given them every opportunity to rectify things. In fact, we did at least another two sessions on B. B.[3]

It was most unusual for a first-time artist, but by B. B. being [a performer and disc jockey] in the studios of Radio WDIA [Memphis], I think that made him a little more at ease in the recording studio. Because you have to keep in mind that all the people I recorded, most of them had never seen a studio . . . well, Howlin' Wolf had done something at a little station in West Memphis. B. B. reminds me to a great extent [of] a black Elvis insofar as demeanor and humbleness and [being] just a sweet guy. He came in, he was just somebody we could easily work with, and we did. I did not feel with B. B. I'd really have a lot of trouble being able to work my psychological magic, although my main magic is staying out of the way. Except if I have a suggestion.

His first few records were not hits. In blues, the identifiable sound is of the person or maybe a band or maybe a studio sound or the way you put it together, and with the blues you can move tempos around and change the keys every now and then. There is no doubt I would have liked to have worked more with B. B. I would guarantee you that we would have had some interesting things that would have developed. He probably served himself well staying with the blues at the time, but we might have done it a little differently.

I probably auditioned ten times as many people as I signed to a contract. I didn't scout on Beale Street; they were coming to me, and they couldn't believe this was a free audition. It took me a long time to convince people; they just knew I was going to hit them with a bill. When this was not so, they were knocking on the door.

I worked all the time; I've always been a worker. I loved working with untried, unproven talent, black and white. And I love sound. What I had in equipment, I made it do. Back then, I could make dubs that were adequate for anything except a master. With recording, you have to capture what's in that studio on tape. Then you've got to transfer it to where you can get the frequency responses that you need for the proper loudness. You do not overdo it and distort it, beyond intended distortion [*laughs*]. All those things are fascinating to me until this very day. My equipment was what I could afford, and when I got a 350 Ampex tape recorder, man, I tell you! Then I was able to buy another one shortly after that. I did my own thing; I could do it with what I had. It was no big thing to overcome. My equipment and I understood each other.

With the first sessions, it was a small Presto [mixing] board. It had an NAB curve on it before the RIAA had a standard curve, and that was something you had to pay attention to in those days.[4] Otherwise, on jukeboxes, the level would be up and down, and somebody would put a nickel or a dime or a quarter in, and if it wasn't loud enough, they would be upset. Yet you didn't want to overdo the thing for loudness and kill some of the actual inflection by over-peak limiting and compression. The Presto board was okay. It only had four inputs, but I got along fine [with it].

The jukeboxes were very important, but you knew that your sales volume had to come from people, the consumers. Even so, you definitely wanted your records on every jukebox you could get on. There was a certain amount of prestige attached to that, because then a jukebox only had twelve to twenty-five slots. It seemed like an eternity before they got to one hundred.[5] You had to earn it, and you didn't always get it, especially if you were attempting a new and different sound. Believe me, that's just one of the many times where patience and persistence came in, especially [in] trying to make it against the unbelievable competition. The competition was not only from other record labels. It was also [from] being able to do the type of [musical] things that were so fantastically different with country, the blues, and southern gospel [white and black] as a bedrock of rock 'n' roll. It was a challenge of a lifetime for all my energies.

In his twilight years, Sam Phillips was able to look back with magnanimity on his tortuous relationships with Modern Records and Chess Records. "I'm not placing all the blame on the Biharis," he said, "I don't feel like that. I'm just saying I was disappointed, and frankly, maybe it turned out all right for me, because the same thing, a very similar thing, happened [to me] with Leonard Chess. I liked him very much, him and Phil both. But then I *had* to form my own label!"

After a false dawn in March 1952, Phillips effectively launched Sun Records in January 1953 with investment support and invaluable business experience from Jim Bulleit (of Bullet Records, Nashville, and a mentor of Dot's Randy Wood). Famously, Sam Phillips dived straight into the prolific black Memphis talent pool. Even if many significant artists were contracted elsewhere, he was able to sign young blues turks Little Jimmy Parker, Little Milton, James Cotton, and Billy "The Kid" Emerson. The first Sun hit of note was "Bear Cat" by Rufus Thomas, another WDIA disc jockey, at No. 3 R&B in the late spring of 1953. By taking the writer credit, Phillips found himself embroiled in a publishing dispute with Duke-Peacock's formidable Don Robey:

"Bear Cat" was not only an answer record to Willie Mae Thornton's "Hound Dog" but was a blatant copy.

The precocious Phillips learned quickly that there were certain ground rules in the indie game that even he couldn't violate. But with his radio background, Phillips knew he had to secure white airplay to establish his label. For that to happen, he needed commercial white artists. The vast teenage market was beckoning, as well as the solidly loyal country market. "I had already started the *Atomic Boogie Hour* on WJLD in Bessemer, just outside of Birmingham, Alabama, with my brother-in-law Jimmy Connolly," said Phillips.

> Although we did not have a black dee-jay [the front man was Bob Umbach], it was so well received. The young people did not have anything they could call their own. There was nothing between kiddies' records and the big bands. Young people just needed something that had vitality that wasn't offered, except in black records.
>
> That wasn't kosher with families until we broke through with Elvis. This unbelievable massive integration of the soul and music that came about was exactly what I'd hoped would happen. I knew a white person had to happen to broaden the base for all those outstanding black artists on the many independent labels available then. It was just a shame, but sales of 50– to 75,000 were big for an R&B record. Believe me, there wasn't a radio station on every corner then. It was tough to get a blues record played.

And so with Elvis Presley's emergence, Sam Phillips's strategic vision netted an early payoff. After Presley's departure for RCA Victor, his fellow southern rock 'n' rollers took up the cause. The impact of these Sun rockers in musical and social terms was far greater than a laundry list of their hits, but it is worthwhile to be reminded of the more pivotal records in three distinct markets:

* Elvis Presley: "Baby Let's Play House" (No. 5 country); "I Forgot to Remember to Forget" (No. 1 country), both 1955
* Carl Perkins: "Blue Suede Shoes" (No. 2 pop, No. 1 country, No. 2 R&B), 1956
* Johnny Cash: "I Walk the Line" (No. 17 pop, No. 1 country), 1956
* Jerry Lee Lewis: "Whole Lot of Shakin' Going On" (No. 3 pop, No. 1 country, No. 1 R&B); "Great Balls of Fire" (No. 2 pop, No. 1 country, No. 3 R&B), 1957–early '58

In this exalted company, it is often forgotten just how big a hit was the Bill Justis instrumental "Raunchy" at No. 2 pop and No. 1 R&B at the turn of 1958 on the Phillips International subsidiary. In addition, "Raunchy" yielded Top 10 hits for Ernie Freeman (Imperial) and Billy Vaughn (Dot). It was quite a windfall for Phillips's Hi-Lo Music, with the added bonus of sheet music being subpublished by Hill & Range Songs.

Together, the Sun releases of the time represented the pulsating spirit of rock 'n' roll in all its regional splendor. After another solid year of hits, however, *Billboard* published in May 1959 a worrying article that stated, "The man who was among the first to light the fuse on the rock and roll explosion, Sam Phillips, is now talking about it in the past tense. It's all over but the mushroom cloud." As perverse as ever, Phillips took the opportunity to talk up the virtues of "authentic rhythm & blues" and country music: "Not long ago if someone was playing a hillbilly record and heard a knock on the door, he'd turn down the volume so nobody would know what he was listening to. Today country music is accepted," he said.[6]

In truth, having put all his considerable energies into Sun Records, Sam Phillips was more or less burned out as a record man. The same *Billboard* feature noted, however, that he had invested wisely during Sun's then-lifespan of only seven years or so, accumulating "two thriving diskeries," "two radio stations," "a recently purchased zinc mine in Yellville, Ark., not to mention some oil properties in Southern Illinois," while constructing a building in Memphis "which will house two of the most modern recording studios in the country." As well, Phillips had an early stake in the rapidly expanding Memphis-based Holiday Inn chain of hotels.

Sam Phillips and Sun Records had put Memphis, Tennessee, on the musical map, and Memphis had made them musical icons, both. The Sun Records story, though, was far from being written out.

Joe Bihari: Modern-RPM Records

Back in the early 1950s, if Sam Phillips had stayed behind the mixing board a little longer with B. B. King, one does indeed wonder how B. B.'s career (or at least his recording career) would have panned out. A hint of what might have been was shown when Phillips recorded him in 1951 for the Bihari brothers on an explosive "Rocket 88"-like romp on a cover version of Tampa Red's poorly distributed "She's Dynamite" on RCA Victor. As a result, King's RPM rendition became a minor *Billboard* territorial breakout in Richmond, Virginia, and New Orleans. This was the first real sales movement for the emerging "Blues Boy."

Following the 1950 handshake deal with Sam Phillips, RPM's Jules and Saul Bihari were satisfied they had first refusal on Sam's productions. Then the perceived double-cross was made. "Sam Phillips recorded B. B. King for us," said Joe Bihari, straightforwardly, "[also] Joe Hill Louis, Rosco Gordon, and Walter Horton. He [Sam] would send the acetate record to us, and if we wanted it, we would pay for it. But when 'Rocket 88' was recorded, Leonard Chess was in town and picked it up for three hundred dollars. And that severed our relations with Sam."

Thus began the explosive rivalry between the brothers Bihari and Chess that would last for nearly two years. After the "Rocket 88" fiasco, the next affront to the Biharis came when Rosco Gordon absconded from RPM to Chess for a one-off session, again recorded by Sam Phillips. Worse, Gordon's "Booted" streaked to No. 1 R&B in the spring of 1952, thereby emulating Jackie Brenston's feat and depriving the Biharis of another hit record. In a mad spell, Howlin' Wolf, John Lee Hooker, Bobby Bland, Joe Hill Louis, and Ike Turner were each having releases on Modern and Chess. Contracts were being treated with apparent wild abandon and disdain. In explanation, *Billboard* stated that "both parties alleged that they had proper pacts, as artists had inked both

AFM and singer pacts with either firm."[7] Here was the entrée for contracts to be drawn up by music lawyers to protect the record companies *and* the artists.

Admitted Rosco Gordon, "I continued to record for anybody with the bucks. I didn't know anything about royalties. All I wanted to do was sing, meet a different girl every night, and play a different city." Added Gordon, "Sam's studio was like a hole; it was just something he had slammed together. The recording equipment had the backs out of it, and Sam was using his soldering iron, pliers, and whatever. I tell you, though, he's the best. He generated enthusiasm and energy; he gives it to you."[8]

Eventually the Bihari/Chess disputes were settled: Rosco Gordon stayed with RPM after receiving a six-hundred-dollar bankroll, while Howlin' Wolf went to Chess. Time proved that Chess had the better part of the deal, by far.

For the Bihari brothers, the first part of 1952 was dominated by B. B. King's "3 o'clock Blues." The memory of his first four slow-moving RPM discs was quickly erased as the record climbed steadily to No. 1 R&B in a long seventeen-week chart residence. The song topped both the jukebox and retail charts of *Billboard,* showing that it was being played and purchased in equal measure. Here was a genuine hit. At last a major artist had emerged as a result of the Biharis' arduous, time-consuming southern trips. B. B. King's remarkable performance, built entirely on atmosphere for a hook, was followed by Rosco Gordon's "No More Doggin'" (No. 2 R&B), which had a direct evolutionary impact on the rhythms of Jamaican ska music.

Earlier in 1952, twenty-six-year-old Joe Bihari, wearing his favorite checkered sports jacket, had embarked on one of his southern field trips with scout assistant Ike Turner in Arkansas and Mississippi. Joe's trusty Magnecord tape machine was tucked into the trunk of his flashy fire-engine-red Lincoln Capri with a Continental kit on back—with chrome spare-tire cover, twin antennas, and dual pipes. Before that, he had a lime-green Cadillac. He must have presented quite a sight as he cruised down Highway 61 and other rural routes from his Memphis starting point.

The record man from Hollywood's main targets were popular Delta down-home bluesmen Elmore James and Sonny Boy Williamson (#2).[9] Only James, who was signed to Lillian McMurry's Trumpet Records of Jackson, Mississippi (as was Sonny Boy), would cooperate. At the time, he was enjoying a big regional jukebox record with "Dust My Broom." After making No. 9 R&B briefly in April 1952, James's "Dust My Broom" (a variant of the Robert Johnson song) would emerge in time as a true blues classic, belying its unexceptional chart status.

Waiting out the twelve-month contract term to have his day with a national label, Elmore James refused to record again for Trumpet. A vengeful Mrs. McMurry duly conspired with the Greenville, Mississippi, high sheriff to have Joe Bihari run out of town during a recording session at Club Casablanca on Nelson Street. Before heading up Highway 82, Bihari had managed to commit to tape juke-joint blues artists Boyd Gilmore, Houston Boines, and Charley Booker, with Ike Turner playing a piano that was horribly out of tune due to the drenchingly humid conditions of summers past.

Promptly, McMurry slapped a million-dollar lawsuit on the Bihari brothers for alleged interference with the contract of her act, Lonnie Holmes and his Darktown Boys. The case dragged on until February 1954, when a token settlement of just $2,500 was made in her favor.[10]

Lillian McMurry presents a fascinating case study. She was recording black men (but not exclusively so) at the peak of the Mississippi segregation era, when whites simply didn't associate with blacks, let alone white *women* with blacks. Wisely, she was careful not to court undue local publicity. Even her close family was not aware of the full extent of her music indulgences, so much so that bookkeeping and administrative matters would often be conducted in the wee hours of the night. Starting out with The Record Mart shop in 1949, she was a hardworking, hard-edged record woman (but not "tough" in the fearsome sense) who was popular with her artists. She was moved by the music and would dance at home while playing the latest acetates. There was, of course, a bountiful wellspring of blues, hillbilly, and gospel acts available to her in the environs of Jackson, Mississippi. The label folded in 1956 on the brink of the lucrative rock 'n' roll era, leaving Johnny Vincent's Ace Records with the winning hand locally.

"What would you do if a distributor owed you $27,000 and you got a dividend of 1 cent on the dollar?" Mrs. McMurry asked of *Blues Unlimited*'s Mike Leadbitter and myself in 1970. Lillian was forced to barter Sonny Boy Williamson's contract to Buster Williams at Plastic Products, Memphis, to pay off outstanding pressing plant bills; in turn, Williams rolled over Sonny Boy's contract to friend Leonard Chess, meaning that the Biharis still didn't get their man. The involvement of Lillian's husband, Willard, in Trumpet Records was limited to the financial aspect, and he used to joke to family relatives that "I lost $100,000 in the music business!"[11]

"We were looking for talent because there was a lot of talent down South," said Joe Bihari.

> Sometimes I traveled with the very famous, young, talented, and vibrant Ike Turner. I hired him in Memphis, bought him a Buick Roadmaster, and gave him some of my custom-made suits, a salary of a hundred dollars a week, and an expense account. He said he made more than the president of a bank.[12]
>
> Other times I traveled alone looking for those country blues singers and musicians. Some were from the cotton fields and plantations, some walking down the highway with an old guitar slung across their backs, others playing in juke joints, nightclubs, and backwoods gambling joints that were sponsored by the local sheriff. There were times that we recorded in living rooms and parlors of some of the artists' houses, or even a Greyhound bus station.

In one of his favorite stories, redolent of the era, Joe was apprehended by the law while trying to locate blues talent—which turned out to be nonexistent—in a black area of Alexandria, Louisiana. At the police station, he was interrogated by a visiting FBI agent and was accused, eerily, of being a Communist. This was the McCarthy era, after all. As uneasy and distressing as these adventures might have been, bachelor Joe was comforted by the fact that his girlfriend, Nina (known gloriously as Honeybear), was the daughter of none other than Chief Justice of the United States Earl Warren. Help, or so Joe figured, was only a quick phone call away to Warren at the U.S. Supreme Court in Washington, D.C.[13]

Joe Bihari's southern wanderings ended with his marriage to Marilyn Mayer in 1956. By then, the traditional blues market was in steep decline. Put under the historical microscope, the prime Modern down-home sessions (which included hillbilly and gospel as well as blues, R&B, and the dance music of the fading territorial bands) were conducted over a mere eighteen-month period between 1951 and 1953.

As it happened, Joe Bihari was following in the blazing footsteps of early record men such as Ralph Peer and Art Satherley, who had to overcome the burden of transporting primitive, cumbersome recording equipment to their chosen destinations. In the 1920s, Peer cut regional records for Victor, famously by Jimmie Rodgers and the Carter Family, primarily to promote sales of the Victrola phonograph machines. As part of the deal, Peer was content to gather song copyrights for his Southern Music firm; he is generally credited with inventing the terms "race" and "hillbilly" music. Meanwhile, eccentric Englishman "Uncle" Art Satherley was expending shoe leather in recording promising young artists such as Roy Acuff, Gene Autry, Bob Wills, and Big Bill Broonzy for Columbia and its offshoots. Working outside of major label commissions, John Lomax (with son Alan) was looking to collect and preserve rural folk music for the Library of Congress while acquiring a few song copyrights along the way. The payoff came when Howie Richmond's Spencer Music published the biggest popular song of 1950, "Goodnight, Irene" by the Weavers (Decca), with writer credits to Huddie "Leadbelly" Ledbetter and John A. Lomax. As for Joe Bihari, he was simply making records to fill the southern jukeboxes and those on the industrial city routes.

In later years, Bihari would smile serenely on those hair-raising, gun-toting episodes that took place in the segregated South of "colored only" rooming houses, eating places, bathrooms, and drinking fountains. There was no bitterness toward Sam Phillips or Leonard Chess over the relentless contractual battles and lost hit records. To Joe, it was all part of the Wild West–like independent scenario of the time.

Lester Bihari: Meteor Records

Eldest Bihari brother Lester continued to be an enigma, even after arriving in Memphis to launch Meteor Records in November 1952. With Bluff City and surrounding areas teeming with natural talent, black and white, it seemed that Lester Bihari (with Sam Phillips) was in the right place at the right time. But the heavens were not in accord with Meteor *and* Sun, and newly divorced Lester was eclipsed totally by Sam. Lester's storefront headquarters may have carried a display sign declaring that Meteor was "The Supreme Achievement in High Fidelity Records," but the label never rose above the down-home level in sonic terms or in operation. His three younger brothers back in Hollywood were not pleased at the paradise lost.

"Lester was a very kind man, a great conversationalist, and well read," said Joe Bihari.

He was a very, very bright man, but he should never have been in our shipping department. He was annoying to everybody. Talk, talk, talk instead of getting work done. He needed guidance in business. So Jules said to me, "Can't you get him started? He likes Memphis; maybe he'll go back there." And I talked to Lester. Elmore James would not sign with the [family] record label or anybody else; he only would sign with me personally. So I recorded Elmore in Chicago and gave Lester a hit called "I Believe" [No. 9 R&B, February 1953]. I was not at all worried about Lillian McMurry suing us; her contract with Elmore had expired. So that's what started Meteor. Actually, Meteor was mine and Lester's, but I let him do anything he wanted with it. And all I did was start him off.

So I said, "Lester, here's a hit record. You go to Memphis. We have some old equipment, recording equipment, we'll ship it up to you there, and you open yourself a little office and studio." And he was happy as hell to do that! He had my old Magnecord that I did most of my field recording on. Lester had seen how I had built recording studios, and he bought the Chelsea Avenue premises. When I went to Memphis, I checked the acoustics and added the baffles and isolation booth for the singers. There was lots of blues and country talent in the area, and Sam Phillips couldn't handle it all.

Actually, the first Memphis label of significance was Duke Records, formed in the spring of 1952 by Radio WDIA program director David Mattis and Music Sales Co. employee Bill Fitzgerald. The purple-and-yellow label artwork, based on the front view of a Cadillac with the "V" symbol, was created by Mattis himself to convey a "royal" image.[14] Here was one of many standout artistic label designs of the independent record era. New Duke Records homed in on several promising local artists who had already been recorded by Joe Bihari but were let go after B. B. King had broken out. Joe found himself in the same overloaded situation as Sam Phillips and freely admitted it.

Duke's opening roster of Modern's rejects was formidable indeed: Johnny Ace, Bobby "Blue" Bland, Earl Forest, and the perfidious Rosco Gordon—all with the collective but fictitious "Beale Streeters" in accompaniment. Immediately, Johnny Ace's "My Song" stoked up strong sales reaction, but the inevitable cash-flow crisis erupted when distributors sat on invoices from the novice label. Bill Fitzgerald disappeared from the Duke operation, and this left the way for David Mattis to be bailed out by Peacock Records' Don Robey—a slick wheeler-dealer and professional gambler who could pass for white but was black.[15]

With Robey's financial backing and strong-armed clout, aided by live-wire sales manager Irving Marcus, "My Song" went all the way to No. 1 R&B in the fall of 1952 after seeing off unwelcome bootleg activity. The new racially mixed partnership (Mattis was white) did not last long. On taking a trip down to the Houston headquarters to discuss business affairs, Mattis found himself ejected from Robey's office at gunpoint. He returned to Memphis with life intact but minus his Duke label, which was relocated to Houston.[16] Under talented A&R men Bill Harvey and Joe Scott, Duke would have extensive success with adopted Memphians Bobby "Blue" Bland and Little Junior Parker.

And so Meteor Records, with Sun, stepped into the Memphis breach. Between 1953 and 1957, Lester Bihari's label went through three stylistic phases in unrestrained scattergun manner: city and down-home blues with a little jazz and gospel; hillbilly and rockabilly; and rock 'n' roll, R&B, and a little pop. When Lester was unable to follow through on the opening Elmore James hit, his brothers gave up on him. After three singles were supplied by New York record man and Bihari family friend Bob Shad (then head of jazz A&R at Mercury), Meteor Records ground to a halt.

It would be another year before southerners Bill Cantrell and Quinton Claunch revived the dormant label by recording "Daydreamin'" with hillbilly singer Bud Deckelman. This beautiful Bill Cantrell–Quinton Claunch song (copyrighted by Meteor Publishing Co.) spread right up to Cleveland, Ohio, and Des Moines, Iowa, and all the way down to New Orleans, as evidenced by the *Cash Box* disc jockey charts of late 1954. With great predictability, "Daydreamin'" was covered by Dot Records through Jimmy Newman, who scored the country hit (No. 7, spring 1955). Just as surely, Deckelman was whisked away from independent Meteor by corporate MGM.[17]

By the mid-1950s, Elvis Presley was tearing up the southern regions with incendiary live performances, his reputation enhanced by his Sun recordings. A whole raft of hayseed musicians threw away their fiddles and steel guitars, turned up the guitar amplification, slapped the stand-up string basses, and, sacrilege, added drums to their bands. Memphis was the haven for these neo-Elvis rockabillies. With Sam Phillips fully occupied over at Union Avenue, a revived Meteor Records was the next port of call. Thus, almost by default, Lester Bihari recorded some of the finest rockabilly of the era with Charlie Feathers, Junior Thompson, Jess Hooper, and Bill Bowen.[18]

Alas, Lester Bihari was not accustomed to handling this raw hillbilly boogie music, and neither were his distributors from the Modern Records network. And so the moment passed. Lester reverted to tapping the under-recorded (at the time) Memphis R&B scene with the help of WDIA disc jockey Rufus Thomas. Despite quality artists such as Fenton Robinson, Little Milton, and Thomas himself, nothing sold, and Meteor fizzled out. Lester Bihari was bailed out by his brothers, becoming sales representative for the new Crown budget LP operation in 1957, first in Memphis and then in Texas. "Then he came back to California," recalled Joe nonchalantly. "He just ran out of money. He hung around with us, but we gave him a salary."

In the right hands, Meteor Records could have been another Sun, another Hi, another Stax. "Lester was the official greeter of everybody in the record business that came to Memphis," said Joe Bihari. "For some reason, he knew everybody when they came in. He just had that type of personality. With Meteor, he had everything right there, and the name Bihari had a good reputation in the music industry. He had every chance to do everything."

Buster Williams: Record and Jukebox Distributor, Pressing Plant Owner

Both Sam Phillips and Lester Bihari benefited by being located in the same town as Leonard Chess confidant Robert E. "Buster" Williams, of Music Sales Co. distributors and Plastic Products pressing plant. Here was a natural entrepreneur and socializer whose nonmusic interests would include ownership of twelve oil rigs in three states and rearing Hereford cattle on a Mississippi farm.

After starting in Monroe, Louisiana, way back in 1926, Williams became the Wurlitzer "automatic phonographs and music accessories" distributor for the Memphis trading area.[19] When World War II ended, Buster Williams founded, with Clarence Camp, Music Sales with branches at 680 Union Avenue, Memphis, under Ed Newell and at 303 North Peters Street, New Orleans, under Robert Wynne. An advertisement in *Billboard* of January 26, 1946, announced that "we distribute . . . records for Louisiana, Mississippi, Arkansas, Tennessee, North Florida and Alabama." Among the lines listed were Exclusive, Excelsior, Gilt-Edge, Juke Box, Mercury, Modern Music, National, Philo, Rhythm, and Sterling.

The genesis of Music Sales as a record distributor was summarized contemporaneously by *Billboard:* "Organized October, 1945, in Memphis Tenn., Music Sales began as a small distributing point for several indie diskeries. Within a few weeks sales mounted sufficiently for the firm to start a program of expansion which recently resulted in the opening of a New Orleans branch office. Wholesaling records and allied supplies, the firm at one time shipped to practically every State in the South and Southwest but lately has confined its deliveries to franchised territories allocated by record companies."[20]

Williams himself dabbled as a record man with the short-lived Buster label. In 1949, he saw a gap in the market for a southern pressing plant and, with an investment of $40,000, set up Plastic Products on Chelsea Avenue (Meteor Records would be based later just down the road). Joe Bihari remembered that brother Jules had a better relationship with Williams than he did: "See, Jules did the manufacturing. So Buster and Jules were quite friendly because he [Buster] came into Los Angeles worrying about the pressing plant; Jules was the one that gave him the advice. Nice, nice man; [he was a] heavy drinker that Jules could stay with [*laughs*]."

By 1956, the now-$750,000 Plastic Products facility, housed in ugly Quonset huts, was literally serving the South. Buster Williams was never afraid to offer credit to aid struggling upstart labels such as Sun and Meteor (and bigger ones, too). He was the record men's southern banker and facilitator.

That Williams did extremely well for himself was illustrated when he was accorded a 1956 profile in *Fortune* magazine, which stated that "last year his Plastic Products pressed over six million records, and made a profit from 2 to 3 cents per record." The article concluded by paraphrasing him: "Rock 'n' roll is here to stay; even if it were to fade he should still prosper—Memphis is sure to come up with some other style every bit as good." With soul music just around the corner, how right Williams's crystal ball was. He exemplified the power and influence of the independent record presser and distributor at the top of his game.[21]

Stan Lewis: The Record Man

Another leading player in the independent southern network was Stan Lewis of Shreveport, Louisiana, popularly known as Stan the Record Man. He operated Stan's Record Shop, which became an automatic stop on any promotional road trip down South for exposure in the Texarkana area and beyond.

Born to grocery storekeepers of Italian heritage, Stan Lewis had his parents' flair for business but even more so. Soon after World War II ended, he invested his savings, at age nineteen, in a variety of coin machines, all in black locations. He said his stock comprised twenty-five gumball machines, ten salted almond machines, ten target practice machines, and five Wurlitzer jukeboxes. In struggling to get the hot hits for his jukeboxes, his interest in the record industry was aroused. He took a small first step in June 1948 when, with young wife Pauline, he bought out the tiny record shop that had been poorly servicing his own jukebox requirements.

The store was ideally located at 728 Texas Street in the heart of Shreveport's lively black community where the customers wanted nothing but the latest race hits. "If it hadn't been for John Lee Hooker and Charles Brown, then Muddy Waters," said Lewis, "I don't think I would have survived. I was a big band lover: Tommy Dorsey, Glenn Miller, Benny Goodman, Count Basie, Lionel Hampton. I just had to learn the blues."

Leaning on his modest coin machine experience, Stan expanded the business with energetic abandon into a one-stop for jukebox operators and mom-and-pop retailers. "Sears[, Roebuck] didn't do R&B," he said.

I saw jukebox operators going to the big "five-and-ten" department stores [such as Woolworth's and Kresge's] to try to find records. They could only get Louis Jordan and Ella Fitzgerald on Decca, and Big Maceo and Arthur Crudup on RCA Victor. So I started calling the operators. I gave them their first discount; they never got a discount before. The first line I got was Chess, starting with Muddy Waters's "Honey Bee" in 1951; then I became a distributor for all the labels. I starting selling to record shops wholesale, and I sold to the jukebox operators [at] the same price as I sold to the record shops.

I was probably one of the first one-stops in the country which serviced all these operators in Texas, Oklahoma, Arkansas, Alabama, Mississippi, and Louisiana. Every time I'd call a jukebox operator, I would ask him to introduce me to another jukebox operator, and he'd give me the name of another one. It just continued steaming on, and I did all this myself. I got a mimeograph machine and started sending out the top sellers [charts] and built up a mailing list. We started calling them, and they said, "Send me twenty-five of this, twenty-five of that," way, way down to San Augustine and El Paso, Texas. Jukebox operators called me because I had records that nobody else carried. I just continued to search for the customers, including mom-and-pop shops.

Aware of just how well Randy's Record Shop was faring through its Radio WLAC exposure, Stan set up a similar mail-order house and began booking time over Radio KWKH, Shreveport. "In 1951, they didn't have any black radio in Shreveport at all," he said,

> no black stations. So we started a fifteen-minute program on KWKH. The disc jockey Groovy Boy was Ray Bartlett; he did my show in the afternoon, . . . the 4:30 show. He'd come up with these little rhymes, some of the old black sayings from years ago: "There ain't nothin' cookin' but the peas in a pod, and they wouldn't be cooking if the water wasn't hot," and "Ain't nothin' shakin' but the leaves on a tree; they wouldn't be shakin' if it wasn't for the breeze." Then he did the night show until he left and he went to Arkansas. He was acting crazy, but he was really a good guy. So Frank Page started doing the show; he was the guy at the *Louisiana Hayride:* Gatemouth . . . he called himself the Mouth of the South.
>
> These little independents, when they had their first records, they wanted exposure. So I bought some time on there, a spot or two. I had the shop and set up the mail-order side. So it went so well I bought a one-hour show at night, 10:30 to 11:30, and was selling records like Randy, Ernie, and Buckley in Tennessee. I played Muddy Waters, Sonny Boy, Howlin' Wolf, Little Walter, all of the Chess stuff; B. B. King and all of the Modern stuff; Joe Turner and Atlantic; Shirley & Lee and all of the Aladdin.

Art Rupe's Specialty Records was promoted heavily early on, too.

"Leonard [Chess] used to come by here about every three months," said Stan Lewis.

> There was Joe Bihari, Art Rupe, Eddie Mesner and Leo Mesner, Lew Chudd, all the guys from most of the small companies. I was very close to Leonard; he was one of the best. He was the first one that came by here; he had Lee Egalnick [of Miracle Records]. I came to find out later they went on the road together so that they could share expenses . . . they were so poor. Lee Egalnick had "Long Gone," the instrumental by Sonny Thompson [No. 1 R&B, 1948]. I knew Henry and Muriel Stone; the first time they came by my shop they had just quit a band they were on. Henry was a trumpet player and Muriel was a singer in the band; they got married. They had a record called "Hearts of Stone" by the Charms, and they were working for Syd Nathan out of King Records, Cincinnati. The record men all treated me real good. They let me have records direct real cheap and helped me pay for all of that advertising.
>
> And so I started calling myself Stan's Record Shop, Stan's One-Stop, Stan's Distributors; I was in all phases of the business. The distributing business slowly grew. Of course, I was just a kid and scared and had no money. I just gradually built it up. It took time; it took about ten years to really get started. I would talk to Leonard Chess every day. We talked to very close people like at Atlantic, then Hymie Weiss and Sammy Weiss [Old Town]. I just thought they were big willies; I thought they were rich guys. I didn't know they didn't have anything. Katie and Leo Mesner [of Aladdin] used to come down here in their big cars, and then later on I found out they were just starting and hustling, too, just like everybody else. A lot of it was image, oh yeah.

Stan remembered that whenever Leonard Chess would take his promotional swings through the South, he would have records shipped to him at various points direct from

Chicago. It wasn't simply loading up the trunk of the car, as legend would have it. And if Leonard had any records left over, he would give them to Stan free of charge.

Quickly, Leonard Chess understood that Stan Lewis, by virtue of his location and hardworking business ethic, was going to be tremendously valuable to the fast-growing Chess network. And so he took Lewis under his wing: "Leonard had a Jewish thing; we'd go to conventions, and he'd put his arm around me. [If] somebody would be starting up a record label, he'd say, 'This is my man; take care of him.' Atlantic did the same thing, Jerry [Wexler] and Ahmet [Ertegun], Joe Bihari . . . that meant a lot to me to be introduced to the right people. So they all became my personal friends."

With this strong bond, Leonard Chess would involve Stan in joint ventures in distributorships and pressing plants through the years. Soon, Lewis became a talent scout and learned how to produce records for Chess and others.

"Shreveport and the surrounding areas have always had great, great musicians," he said, "in Monroe, Louisiana, and Jackson, Mississippi, and Arkansas, East Texas, and South Louisiana. It could have been another Nashville, but we just didn't have a studio and didn't have a record label here. I recorded a lot of blues artists like TV Slim for Checker and Pete McKinley for Specialty. They were playing for the hat down; you'd throw money in there."

Lewis recalled picking up word about country blues guitarist Nathaniel "Stick-Horse" Hammond and driving out with Leonard Chess to the plantation where Hammond toiled as a sharecropper. "Leonard had a big black Chrysler automobile," said Lewis, "and with his black overcoat and hat he looked like a lieutenant in the Mafia." It made no difference to the big boss man, who came out screaming armed with a shotgun. "Let's get the hell out of here," shouted Chess. And as they accelerated away along the dirt road, "Stick-Horse" Hammond's big chance disappeared in that cloud of dust.[22]

Lewis made Chess a happier man after cutting "Reconsider Baby" by Lowell Fulson, a No. 3 R&B hit in early 1955 on the Checker subsidiary. "I produced that in Dallas after Leonard asked me to supervise the session," said Lewis. Not a natural songwriter, Stan was accorded co-writer song credits on two Checker recordings that turned out to be very rewarding: "I'll Be Home" by the Flamingos (No. 5 R&B in the spring of 1956, before being crushed by Pat Boone's international hit for Dot) and "Susie-Q" by gifted rocker Dale Hawkins (No. 27 pop, No. 7 R&B, early summer 1957).[23]

"I introduced hillbilly artists to Chess," said Lewis,

Les and Wayne Walker, Jimmy Lee and Johnny Mathis. . . . But Leonard didn't take them all because it was out of his field. It was the same with Art Rupe, who had Claude King; I sent him an acetate on Slim Whitman, "Indian Love Call," but he sat on it. Then we sent it to Lew Chudd; he was the only one who hit [big] with hillbilly. I cut Jimmy Newman and Mac Wiseman for Randy Wood on Dot.

I had good connections with the *Louisiana Hayride* [notably with Shreveport country star-maker Tillman Franks]. All the guys hung around my place. I sold tickets for the *Hayride*; the auditorium was only five blocks away. I would go to the *Hayride* on Saturday nights, stay for a while and leave, keep in touch with all of the artists.

That's when I should have gone in business with my own label, but I didn't. I could have had Jim Reeves, Floyd Cramer, Jim Ed and Maxine Brown [of the Browns], Webb Pierce, Faron Young. I saw Elvis; oh yeah, he was different. I didn't know that the people would accept him. I was kind of concerned about that, but when he caught on, he was a monster.

I just accepted rock 'n' roll when it happened. I couldn't see anything coming. The business changed constantly. I saw white teenagers coming into the shop to buy black records. The parents didn't want them to buy the records; they called them race records. It wasn't a big problem. Of course, I came to work a few times, and there were a few [Ku Klux] Klan stickers on my door. It had to be in the early 1950s.

The distributorship built up in the 1950s. To be a good distributor . . . you had to have the hits; . . . they were good businessmen, most of them. The New Orleans distributors resented me, and so did the Memphis distributors, because I was so close to them [in mileage]. They saw us as competition. I had a real aggressive bunch of kids that worked for me then; they were something. The Houston distributors were Steve Poncio [of United] and the Dailys [of H. W. Daily]. Pappy Daily was a great man. He was mostly interested in country; he discovered George Jones. The large Dallas distributorship was run by Bill Emerson at Big State. Then you had Mrs. McMurry; she had a big record shop in Jackson, Mississippi. I was one of Johnny Vincent's first distributors for his Ace label [also in Jackson].

Stan Lewis launched Jewel Records in 1963, followed by Paula (named after his wife) and Ronn (after his brother). "I was about ten years too late," he admitted, adding that he was afraid the record men "might get mad at me by starting a label." Assisted by former dee-jay "Dandy" Don Logan as vice president, Stan was able to ramp up his record label activities to offset the declining business in record distribution—just as Henry Stone would do in Miami in the 1970s.

Lewis latched on to the psychedelic mood of 1968 when he scored handsomely with "Judy in Disguise (With Glasses)" by college fraternity favorites John Fred and his Playboy Band (Paula). "I handled 'Judy in Disguise' fine," said Lewis. "Looking back now, I could have done some other things, could have kept it on the charts longer by buying more time or advertising and doing other things. It was still a No. 1 hit. I also had a big hit with Toussaint McCall, 'Nothing Takes the Place of You' [No. 52 pop, No. 5 R&B, Ronn, 1967]. I cut him in Muscle Shoals [at Rick Hall's Fame Studios]. I had a great album on him; it had real horns. All my sessions had real instruments."

Stan Lewis built up an impressive catalog of blues, soul, and gospel. "I was one of the last record men to record the old blues guys like Lowell Fulson, Jerry McCain, Frank Frost, the Carter Brothers," he said, correctly. Lewis also acquired the masters of respected Chicago blues labels Cobra, Chief, Age, JOB, and USA through Allstate distributor Paul Glass. The soul charge was led by Little Johnny Taylor and Ted Taylor, while the gospel series featured many active name acts including the Soul Stirrers, the Violinaires, and the Original 5 Blind Boys of Mississippi.

Stan was still going great guns as the 1960s morphed into the 1970s. "We kept adding on to my building," he said.

I had half a block on Texas Street. There was Jewel Records, the shipping department, and a print shop for the mail-order catalog with two union printers. We were mailing to record shops, distributors, jukebox operators. Every time a label started up, we got them: Arista, ABC, 20th Century-Fox, United Artists, and Stax. I had every label there was except for A&M. It didn't happen all at one time; it just grew over a period of years as I got labels. I had the first Motown record, "Money" by Barrett Strong, and as Berry [Gordy] grew, I grew. As Chess grew, I grew. And as Atlantic grew, I grew. I even distributed RCA and Mercury at one time, their R&B stuff.

A lot of shops and one-stops couldn't get records in their own markets, so they started ordering from me. And I was transshipping all over the country to Chicago, Houston, Dallas. I was in every facet, from retail to wholesale to one-stop to selling to rack jobbers; I even had a professional carpenter shop building displays [for windows and counters]. At one time I was the biggest Delta Air freight user in Shreveport; I'd order, like, 50,000 of Little Stevie Wonder. We had records before anybody; we had great people working for us. We were on top of everything.

In fact, Stan was doing so well that he felt comfortable in rejecting a takeover offer of $5 million, he said, from voracious rack jobber Handleman for the distribution side only: "They wanted all my lines. In that way they could buy direct from the labels and bypass the regular distributors. I was only forty years old at the time [around 1967] and thought the bubble would never burst. It was a big mistake."

As extensive as Stan Lewis's empire once was, he was unable to keep it together into the 1980s. "The mom-and-pop stores had just about quit," he said. It was mostly jukebox operators that [were] left. And then it just dwindled down where it wasn't even worth pressing. Well, they went to CDs, and they just cut the 45s out."[24] In the general chaos, Stan's business practices began to slip, and his reputation was in danger of becoming tarnished. But he managed to retain his record catalog and music publishing company, Su-Ma. He thought he had made the deal of a lifetime when he agreed to a multimillion-dollar sale of his masters to eMusic.com in 1999, but it was not to be. The stock nosedived when the dot-com bubble burst before the expiry of the sale lockup period. "Well, then you wind up getting screwed out of all your money with the company going broke you sell out to. It hurts; that was eMusic. I went down; I lost all my shares. I took the stock and some cash, but until the stock is sold . . . I should never have turned over my masters," he stated forlornly. At least Lewis was able to sell Su-Ma Music separately and hold on to his personal songwriting copyrights, including the shares in "I'll Be Home" and "Susie-Q."

It could be argued that Stan Lewis was never quite the same man following his summons to act as a pallbearer at Leonard Chess's funeral in October 1969. After all, his great mentor and benefactor had gone. "There was a lesson from Leonard I will never forget," said Stan the Record Man, "but I didn't follow his rule: Always think of number one." Then perking up, he added, "I look back on it with pleasure. The record men created a sound, a beat. It was just incredible music that we'll never see [again] in our lifetime. The music will last forever—it was the last classical music."

10
CHAPTER

Louisiana Gumbo

CAST OF CHARACTERS
Shelby Singleton, Mercury Records regional promo man
J. D. "Jay" Miller, Crowley record man
Eddie Shuler, Goldband Records
Floyd Soileau, Jin-Swallow Records and Floyd's
  Record Shop
Sam "S. J." Montalbano, Montel Records
Cosimo Matassa, Cosimo Recording Studios and
  Rex Records
Bert Frilot, engineer, Cosimo Recording Studios

Down in South Louisiana, a bevy of record men were able to tap into the rich cultural heritage of Cajun land and New Orleans. There, J. D. "Jay" Miller, Eddie Shuler, and Cosimo Matassa had started out at the dawn of the independent record era, when the jukebox operators were calling all the shots. Others such as Floyd Soileau and Sam Montalbano joined the fray in the late 1950s, just as the Cajun teenagers were formulating an indigenous swamp pop style (influenced directly by Fats Domino and abetted by the lilt of bluesman Jimmy Reed with the heartbreak soul of Hank Williams and the old-timey Cajun artists). The work of the local entrepreneurs was echoed in regional pockets throughout the whole country, adding color and diversity to the national music scene, especially in the rock 'n' roll era.

Collectively, the South Louisiana record men were regarded fondly by Shelby Singleton, himself from Shreveport by way of Texas. "I think the reason the Louisiana record men survived is that they didn't get greedy," he said. "If that market spread out, it was the gravy. The ones that don't survive are the ones who get greedy; they want to have everything rather than just have their niche. Stan Lewis was a good person and a good record man, but him and others, instead of just working their own territory, they want the whole world. And they're the ones that end up losing. You talk about Floyd Soileau or J. D. or Eddie Shuler, they never got greedy. They just wanted to stay in their own niche."

J. D. "Jay" Miller: Crowley Record Man

The most accomplished of the South Louisiana indie record men was J. D. "Jay" Miller. A first-class sound engineer, he was a sensitive songwriter in the blues, country, and rock 'n' roll idioms. Accordingly, he had the priceless ability of being able to knock into shape the most amateurish of songs, for which he demanded his share of the writer credits, like any good song doctor would.

Miller had played guitar in Cajun bands in the 1930s, when acts played dances behind wire nets for protection from drunken patrons. Armed with this earthly experience, he was a dominant figure at recording sessions. Always a realist about the record business, he saw it as "chicken today, feathers tomorrow."

Jay Miller was based in Crowley, the self-proclaimed rice capital of America. "When I got out of the service, my father-in-law, Lee Sonnier, was doing electrical contracting work," he said in 1995, a year before he died.

> We founded the M. & S. Electric Co., and we were doing industrial work on the rice mills. All of it was heavier-type work, industrial and commercial. I rented a building to house our company, but it was such a large building it looked bare with what we had invested in it. There was so much room, I took an idea to put a little music and record shop in it.
>
> So we bought a few records and a guitar or two, strings. There wasn't anything like today; you had very few basic items. We put in a few records, and the jukebox owners started buying records from my store. Many of the customers, because they were predominantly Cajun at the time, . . . wanted Cajun records. They had a couple of Harry Choates records on the market and a few other things, but apart from that, try as hard as I could, I couldn't obtain any. So I got the idea I'm gonna make some, and I didn't know where to turn to go to a studio. Then I found they had a studio in New Orleans, the only studio in Louisiana: Cosimo Matassa's.
>
> So I called Cosimo and scheduled a session over there to cut three records, six sides. So we go over there; we cut "Colinda" by Happy Fats and Doc Guidry, we cut "La Cravat" by Louis Noel, and a country thing [by Al Terry]. I sent the masters off to the West Coast to be pressed—that, of course, was 78s—and when I got them back, I was so proud you wouldn't believe.

J. D. Miller set up a small studio at the back of the Crowley shop at 218 North Parkerson Avenue where he recorded Cajun and hillbilly acts for Fais-Do-Do and Feature. The blues and swamp pop artists (and his other label imprints) came later. For the first 78s, then, the main customers were the jukebox operators supplying the neighboring small Acadian towns and rural areas.

The turning point for Miller came when he recorded female hillbilly singer Al Montgomery on his song "Did God Make Honky Tonk Angels?" It was a wry answer from a woman's perspective to Hank Thompson's No. 1 country hit "The Wild Side of

Life" (Capitol), itself a cover of Jimmy Heaps's original (Imperial). Montgomery's record was picked up by Kitty Wells, who, with her aching voice, took the song (retitled as "It Wasn't God Who Made Honky Tonk Angels") to the top of the country charts in 1952 on Decca. Even then, Wells had to circumvent a cursory ban from the NBC radio network due to the "indecent" line "It brings memories when I was a trustful wife . . ."

With unerring certainty, an answer-song publishing lawsuit followed, further complicated by the fact that "The Wild Side of Life" carried the same melody as the Carter Family's "I Am Thinking Tonight of My Blue Eyes" (copyrighted by Ralph Peer in 1929). Peer's empirical publishing firm triumphed, but Miller was able to retain the writer's share.[1] In time, "It Wasn't God Who Made Honky Tonk Angels" has become recognized as the first song of substance sung by a woman in country music.

With a No. 1 hit under his belt, Jay Miller was welcomed into Nashville's songwriting establishment with a contract from Acuff-Rose. When lauded publisher Fred Rose and not-so-popular son Wesley were ready to launch Hickory Records in 1954, Miller was the provider of hillbilly artists Al Terry, Tommy Hill, and Rusty & Doug (Kershaw), armed with his songs. It was this Music City connection that led to an agreement a year later for Miller to produce blues and R&B recordings (but not country) for Ernie Young's Excello Records. Already Miller realized that there was little chance of exposing his records properly outside of his home territory. The Excello deal made him an early independent record producer.

From the Excello union came an unsurpassed body of Louisiana swamp blues recordings, which rank in the upper echelon of the postwar blues cannon. Many of the colorful names of Jay Miller's artists were created from his lively mind, including Lightnin' Slim, Slim Harpo, Lazy Lester, and, best of all for a bluesman, Lonesome Sundown. Miller had an uncanny understanding of his performers and their music and was keen to prepare them for sessions by creating an ambience whereby they were never too comfortable but were never stressed by the occasion. His best productions were marked by distinctive echo and percussion in an era when studios had recognizable "room sounds," giving the recordings their own identities.

The increasing availability of portable tape machines was a boon in encouraging young men such as Jay Miller to take the plunge into the record business. He understood quickly the engineering benefits afforded by magnetic tape, including better sound reproduction, immediate playbacks, take edits, echo effects, and techniques such as prerecording backing tracks and postrecording overdubs.

"At that time there wasn't much equipment available," Miller said.

In fact, I had the first tape recorder in Louisiana. When we recorded at Cosimo's, we were recorded with an overhead disc cutter. I went to Houston, Gates Radio Supplies, inquiring about getting me a recorder, and I had in mind an overhead because that was the only one I'd ever seen. They had just got in three Magnecord recorders; it seems to me it was a model PT-6. You could carry it around. So I bought that, I bought three microphones, I bought a high-level mixer, which in reality is just three volume controls, and I came back. I had an amplifier that I used for monitoring and set up what I had as a monitor speaker, just one speaker.

I think I was helped by my electrical background. It wasn't technical as far as audio, but I had a sense of something. I didn't go by the book because I went by these two things: my ears. I've had so many compliments about the sound I got. People asked me how I did it, and I said, "I really don't know."

That's interesting how that echo room where I got that tone came about. Well, before I had an echo room, I had an old Concertone tape recorder. I created my slapback echo with that. That's done by feeding [the signal] through your recorder at the same time as you're recording it, and then you take [the signal] back after it's recorded and feed it into your system again. A very crude [tape-delay] thing, but it worked. Remember "Congo Mombo" [by Guitar Gable, Excello, 1956]? You listen to the drummer [Clarence Etienne], you'd swear he's a wizard, but a lot to do with it was the doggone Concertone. I had many guys tell me, "Gee, that's a fast drummer." You got to understand during that time, that was a new concept. They just figured the drummer was that fast, but what happened with that slapback, it was just repeating.[2]

But through the grapevine I learned that some company could build an echo room in that studio. It was a room by itself, nothing in it but a speaker and a microphone. Well, there's an old gentleman that made the tombstones in Rayne, I got him. I had a room in the studio there that was just used as a storeroom; we took everything out. So we put up some cardboard, screening, anything. That's where the sound came out of.

This special Jay Miller studio was a natural destination for the bountiful talent of Louisiana and East Texas and bustled with activity during the rock 'n' roll era. The studio and office were based at the Constantin Building on Tenth and Parkerson, with the warehouse and shipping department being located downtown near the railroad tracks, at 118 North Parkerson Avenue. Although much time was taken up with the productions for Excello and his second-wave small labels Rocko and Zynn, Miller was producing and engineering for other local record men, including Huey Meaux, Floyd Soileau, and Lee Lavergne (whose Lanor label out of rural Church Point was a true grassroots affair).

Miller had an all-round business acumen, so it was strange that in negotiations he allowed Ernie Young to publish his Louisiana-recorded songs under the Excellorec Music banner. Miller always said he wrote his blues compositions under the pseudonym of "Jerry West" to avoid upsetting the country music fraternity; at Acuff-Rose, he was credited as "J. D. Miller."

While he benefited as writer or co-writer on most of his productions, even here it wasn't plain sailing. After falling into a royalty dispute with Slim Harpo that coincided with an astonishing 1961 Top 40 chart run with a tuneful swamp blues record, "Rainin' in My Heart," Miller was never credited again as a co-writer on Harpo's releases. So when Harpo had the big hit in 1966 with "Baby Scratch My Back," Miller received neither writer's nor performance royalties, just a few pennies per record sold. He was also deprived of the royalty bonanza when the Rolling Stones recorded Slim Harpo's

"I'm a King Bee" because Harpo had secured sole writer's credit on his debut recording in 1957.

Slim Harpo was about the only artist to stand up to Jay Miller. In June 1961, while "Rainin' in My Heart" was still in the Top 100 charts, the Baton Rouge bluesman tried to abscond to Imperial and even cut an illicit session in New Orleans. That was until Miller pointed out to Imperial's Lew Chudd, in no uncertain terms, that Harpo was still under contract to him. Chudd backed off, and an uneasy truce with the harmonica bluesman ensued.

During this action-packed period, J. D. was courted by Randy Wood to work at Dot Records on the West Coast. It was that Nashville connection, again. But Miller preferred to be in total control at Crowley rather than move to California, tempting though the offer might have been.

"I was producing product for Excello, but it wasn't making any money," said J. D. Miller.

> Now, don't get me wrong, I believe that Ernie Young was paying me. But at a nickel [per record] and no publishing, you're not going to make money. I was paying for my equipment, I was paying the musicians . . . but I admit I had some of them that wanted to pay me to record. Over a period of years—years—Ernie and I would argue about the rate. Here he's complaining to me about the cost of the stamps, stamps to send out product he's already sold and made a good profit on, and he didn't want to pay me more money. So we finally got it up to about five and a half cents. It took a lot of talking. The most I got Ernie to do was six and a half [cents].
>
> I was relying mostly on Ernie, 'cause that was the brightest thing I had. Ernie wasn't too interested in rock 'n' roll unless it was a black artist. His business was black-oriented. The South was his bread and butter, and that was his radio audience. At that time, very few white people were listening to what he had on the air. Later it became different; little by little, the white audience became greater. At that particular time, you could walk through a colored neighborhood, [and] if you'd open the door you'd hear Ernie's, Randy's, or Buckley's [shows]. That was the only three black radio programs on big stations: 50,000 watts, WLAC. The mail-order houses were in competition, and they spent a lot of money [on the shows], which Ernie used to cry about, too. He had perfect arguments for not increasing my royalties, from stamps to radio costs. Of course, I am sure it cost him a lot, but, gee, they'd send out packets you wouldn't believe. They made a ton of money.

During these years, Miller was recording black artists with integrated bands in the heart of the segregated South. And he did it without fear. J. D. was a very good friend of Louisiana governor Jimmie Davis, one man he respected greatly, but he restricted himself in politics mostly to campaigning in local elections. To his later regret, he did succumb to recording racially offensive material on the Rebel label that reflected the political divisions of the President Lyndon Johnson years. He argued it was an attempt to keep the studio busy when the blues business was dying on its feet.[3]

Aside from the self-induced Rebel wound, the knife in the back for Miller came after Ernie Young sold out in 1966. Excello's new owners succeeded where Imperial's Lew Chudd failed: they enticed Slim Harpo to sign direct to their label. "Slim Harpo's contract with Miller expired," said Excello's Shannon Williams, "and Harpo vowed that he would not sign with Miller again. It was a matter of money, royalties. In order to not let Harpo escape, Nashboro-Excello made an offer which he accepted. Miller claimed that we had stolen his artist from him. That was the last straw [for him]." In retaliation, Miller would never again send his masters to Nashville, and over the years he tried unsuccessfully to retrieve his Excello production masters through legal channels. He continued releasing 45s and LPs on his Blues Unlimited and Soul Unlimited labels for local consumption through his long-established Modern Music store.

Like almost every record man, Jay Miller had to endure regular accusations from artists concerning royalty payments, notwithstanding the fights with Slim Harpo. In 1979, J. D. showed me his accounting ledger for Katie Webster that revealed an unverified debit balance in excess of $8,000. She was a wonderful blues session pianist but as an artist had no record sales to speak of. A typical example was her 1959 cover of Phil Phillips's "Sea of Love" that sunk without trace, even though Miller had placed the master with Decca for national distribution. J. D. proffered these words of wisdom: "My advice to anybody going into the record business: Don't have a music store, because the artists will break you! I know that. They had to have a guitar, but they didn't have money. You put it on the books tip-top, [but] you'd never collect it. They said, 'I'll pay for it out of royalties,' and I said, 'No, we don't know how much royalties there will be.' They finally got the thing, and I kept the bills."

The custodianship of Jay Miller's own master tapes and song publishing interests remained in the hands of the family, with son Mark operating the recording studio. Quite uniquely for a record man, a museum in Miller's honor was opened in a civic ceremony by the mayor of Crowley in April 2006 at the site of his 1960s-era studio in the Ford building. Good old boy J. D.—he was destined always to remain a big fish in a small town pond.

Eddie Shuler: Goldband Records

Farther west from Crowley, some fifty miles along I-10, lays Lake Charles in Calcasieu Parish. In another time, you could meander through a series of small Cajun settlements stretched out along Highway 90—the Old Spanish Trail—that would disappear into the coastal marshes on one side and the prairies on the other. These were the communities that were devastated by Hurricane Rita in 2005. Nestling on the Texas border, oil-enriched Lake Charles was the adopted home town of Eddie Shuler, who died at the grand age of ninety-two in an Atlanta hospital a few months before the deadly hurricane struck.

Shuler was as down-home and folksy as his Goldband label. Beyond the cheery exterior, however, there was a shrewd, steely, and unbending record man. Goldband was to become a valuable repository of Louisiana music. And in Iry LeJeune (credited on record as "LeJune"), the label had an accordion player who was the Cajun equivalent (with fellow accordionist Nathan Abshire) of crossroads bluesman Robert Johnson and hillbilly hero Hank Williams.

An immigrant from Texas, Eddie Shuler was operating a tiny music store when he started Goldband as a private label around 1945 to promote his western outfit, the All Star Reveliers. "I had this eight-piece band," he said in 1992,

and I had a packed house because I had a radio show down there on KPLC Radio. That was a thirty-minute show in the afternoon. My first store was at the corner of Broad and Reed Street in a trailer house. I started about June of '44. I didn't have too much of a business because I didn't have too much stock. I had no pianos and no sheet music; all I had was accessories like guitar strings, tuning keys. Yeah, I sold records in the store, too, the pop music. Back in those days in Louisiana, country music wasn't all that great. Bob Wills would sell records, but the lesser people didn't do all that good. You had the records like Tex Beneke, Glenn Miller, Benny Goodman, all those big pop bands; that's what sold records. And we were fixing radios, too, on the side. That's back in the radio days.

To help out, I went to work as an insurance company salesman. And, of course, I was already a musician by that time, because I had been playing with the Hackberry Ramblers before all this stuff come about. Then I decided I wanted to make records, so I found an ad in *Billboard* magazine, a place in New York, because I had written to all the record companies and nobody even answered my letter. I said, "Well, that's not going to work; I'm going to do it anyway [myself]." So I saved my money, and with this outfit in New York I made my first record on Goldband. Why Goldband? I was one of those true optimists, I believed [*laughs*], and I had to find me a name. I said, "Goldband!" I could visualize a gold band, a gold mine. Then I had to come up with the logo. I had an artist to draw the logo for me, which we sent to the guy in New York.

I moved the store around 1947 to the end of Broad Street and Front Street, and I had a pretty good music business by that time. But I was still working for the insurance and playing music and fixing radios. We stayed at the end of Broad until '51, and then we came to this location [at 313 Church Street, the site of an Assembly of God church]. By then I had already established myself in the record business and in the radio repair business. There were still no TVs.

Shuler cut his first records using the facilities of two Lake Charles radio stations, KPLC and KAOK, since the nearest dedicated recording studios were in distant New Orleans and Houston. "There wasn't no tape recorders back in those days," he said.

You had to cut the thing on an acetate disc. So you'd go into the radio station and give the engineer ten dollars and a bottle of booze, and he'd make you an acetate. I'd go down to the wholesale supply house and buy a little pack of acetates, Presto, or something like that. Well, if one of 'em had a bubble in it, they'd have to throw it away and put another one on. And that's the way you cut records in those days: you'd put an acetate on a recording machine, a disc cutter, and make your record. I'd take the acetate and send it off to the pressing plant and get the records pressed, what they call direct to disc today.

The first record that I had was a smash hit, "Broken Love." It was in the country field; it was me and my band. But the guy, when he was mastering it, he cut the tail end of the music off, so the thing just stopped in the middle of a guitar note. Well, back in those days, all songs had an ending, so the people would call the jukebox operators and tell them the jukebox needed to be readjusted, 'cause it cut the record off before the music got through playing. So after selling initially quite a few records to the jukebox operators, I go around and they're pulling them all off of the jukebox because they don't want to be aggravated by those customers. They couldn't make the customer understand that the fault was in the record, not the jukebox. The people made all sort of noise and they wanted to hear the end of the record, and there wasn't no end. Well, that took care of that record![4]

Oh yes, I sold a lot of records to the jukebox operators; that was where you sold most of your records in those days. There were not all that many record shops, and then the people didn't have all that much money to buy records, except the richer people. That's where you sold most of those pop records. But the jukebox operators had to have what they called race records and hillbilly records; they had to have that stuff and the Cajun records, too. So we got into the Cajun thing.

The first Cajun record was "La Valse de Meche" by Eddie Shuler and his Reveliers with Norris Savoie doing the vocal in French, and we cut that in KLOE radio down on Clarence Street in the middle of the studio. Iry LeJeune didn't come along until about 1948 to do his thing. He had recorded one record for Opera [owned by Bennie Hess], and nobody could get the records. Him and a fiddle player, Floyd LeBlanc, jumped in the car and decided to go to Houston and make a record. And Iry had all these people wanting his record, and nobody could . . . buy it because Opera didn't have any money or something. I don't know what their problem was, but you couldn't get the records.

So Iry and I had a radio show on KPLC radio, and Iry wanted to make another recording. I said, "Well, I'll tell you what. I'll make one record, and if it's a success, me and you are in business, and if it doesn't, we are out!" And we shook hands. I came to find out that shaking hands was a contract with a Cajun, and I had never heard of that before, either. I thought you had to sign papers for that kind of stuff. The rest then was history.

At one time I thought I would get me a distributor, because I was a big-time operator, you know, like all them other people [*laughs*]. So I talked to the guy in New Orleans that was distributing for Mercury Records, and he said, "Send me some samples; I'll let my salesman take them out on the road." And so I sent him the records. I waited about a month and a half, and I never got any orders.

Well, I stopped off in Eunice, Louisiana, with my wife 'cause they had a record shop downtown there that I'd sold a lot of records to. And the woman said, "Oh my God, am I glad to see you! I've been out of records for three weeks; I've got to have more records." So I sold her my records [from the car] and said, "Have you seen anybody else coming by here with Cajun records?" She said no, and I said to myself, "Huh, what's going on?"

Eddie managed to track down the salesman for the New Orleans distributors, William B. Allen Supply Co., at a record shop in nearby Opelousas.

So I met him at the car and I said, "Do you have any Cajun records?" He said, "I got one of them lousy things in my car. The boss gave it to me, but I can't stand that stuff. Man, that's the most horriblest thing I ever heard in my life. I'm not gonna play that thing; I can't stand it." So I called his boss. I said, "Hey, just forget about this distributing thing; we got somebody else." So I went back to work, okay [*laughs*].

I built the studio in about 1955; my father-in-law designed it. He was a carpenter, so him and his brother built the studio according to my specifications. I was already into the electronics thing because I had been cutting discs for the radio commercials and all that kind of stuff.

Now with its own studio, Goldband Records covered all genres of Louisiana music in the rock 'n' roll era through respected artists such as Al Ferrier with rockabilly, Guitar Jr. and Big Walter Price with R&B, Gene Terry with swamp pop, and Clarence Garlow and Juke Boy Bonner with blues. There were still regular, joyously earthy Cajun singles led by Iry LeJeune. If there were few frills, Eddie Shuler was able to capture southern regional music at its most natural and basic, and that's where his market lay. In his filing cabinets were folders for radio stations, jukebox operators, and retail stores throughout Louisiana, Texas, and Mississippi.

Shuler's most rewarding hit, artistically and financially, was swamp pop anthem "Sea of Love" by Phil Phillips with the Twilights in 1959. Eddie produced the No. 2 national smash in his rudimentary studio for George Khoury, a Lake Charles record shop owner with a jukebox route. Khoury operated the Khoury's and Lyric labels (originally for Cajun and hillbilly recordings) from a single-story building opposite the railroad station, just around the corner from Goldband. After taking off locally on Khoury's, "Sea of Love" was picked up for national distribution by Mercury Records through Shelby Singleton. As part of the recording deal, Shuler had landed the publishing rights for Kamar Music, jointly owned with Starday's Don Pierce (already a friend and associate). Eddie Shuler's brilliant move with "Sea of Love," an eternal song, ensured that he would never have any financial worries, no matter how well or poorly Goldband fared. The label was underpinned by his Quick Service TV repair business, now that television had supplanted radio as the general public's favorite medium.[5]

Chris Strachwitz, the altruistic boss of Arhoolie Records of El Cerrito, California, credited Shuler with ramming home to him the virtues of music publishing soon after he formed his folk roots label in 1961. Strachwitz was responsible for reviving the career of Clifton Chenier, the king of zydeco, in the 1960s by releasing 45s for the local South Louisiana/East Texas jukebox market on the Bayou label. Distribution was handled by Swallow Records in a deal with Floyd Soileau, who also had 50 percent of the publishing through Flat Town Music. "Publishing was the thing that sort of got me interested in doing 45s," said Strachwitz, "because I thought that's a neat way to make a little extra money. I mean, when I met Clifton, that's all he wanted was a 45. None of the musicians cared about LPs, which didn't do them any good because people in the neighborhood didn't hear them." Strachwitz regretted the day when he told Shuler that the Goldband recordings lacked "bottom" due to the primitive studio conditions. Thereupon Eddie proceeded to reissue many of his pristine 1950s recordings, sacrilegiously, with plodding bass guitar overdubs.

The biggest name artist recorded by Eddie Shuler, believe it or not, was Dolly Parton as a thirteen-year-old country wannabe on her very first single, "Puppy Love." This introduction had come from her uncle Robert Owens, who was the Goldband hillbilly/rockabilly artist Little Billy Earl. Young, bubbly Dolly made the long journey with her grandmother from Sevierville, Tennessee, to Lake Charles by Greyhound bus in 1959. In stardom, she never forgot her first chance to make a record. It was a good, self-assured performance, too.

Goldband had just one Hot 100 hit, "Sugar Bee" by Cleveland Crochet. With national distribution by publisher Bill Lowery's NRC organization out of Atlanta, the record crept into the charts at No. 80 in early 1961 on sales of 55,000. Always ready to laud a new trend with maximum hyperbole, Shuler was right on the ball this time when he publicized "Sugar Bee" with its English lyrics as the first Cajun rock 'n' roll record. That extravagant Cajun entrepreneur and politician Dudley LeBlanc (of Hadacol drink fame) would have been proud of Eddie's slick sales pitches.

Shuler would be ready to roll the tape for any would-be star, whatever their musical proclivity. He was willing to give a shot to soul music, even though the form was alien to him. "Soul wasn't huge in this part of the world," he recalled, "but it was popular to the degree that you had to have it to get airtime. You have to be with whatever's happening; that's the way the American music culture works. It always has worked and always will work. You have to stay on top of the trends." That's a good definition of his recording philosophy.

Eddie Shuler continued looking for "hit" records until the end of the vinyl era in the 1980s. Through it all, he ensured that his artist and songwriter contracts (and song copyrights) were in perfect order, aided by devoted wife Elsie. If an artist complained about royalties, he (and she) always had the confirmatory paperwork on hand to rebut any claims. Thereafter, Shuler concentrated on licensing out his old recordings to companies around the world for CD reissues, via Shelby Singleton's organization, and working his publishing catalog.

Into the mid-1990s, Eddie Shuler was still optimistically doing his weekly rounds of the fast-disappearing mom-and-pop stores, selling CDs the old-fashioned way, from the trunk of a car like vinyl records. The circular route from Lake Charles took in the towns of Jennings, Lafayette, Church Point, Eunice, Opelousas, and Ville Platte. How many other record men were on the stump as octogenarians? We shall not see his like again.

Floyd Soileau: Jin-Swallow Records and Floyd's Record Shop

If Jay Miller was the best record man in South Louisiana and Eddie Shuler the foxiest, then Floyd Soileau takes the honors as top businessman. A friendly and articulate Cajun, he celebrated his fiftieth anniversary in the music industry in May 2006, all the while based at Ville Platte in the distant prairies of Cajun country.

Coming up through the disc jockey and record shop routes, Soileau established a successful working model (spearheaded by his Jin and Swallow labels and Flat Town Music publishing interests) to both exploit and preserve the indigenous musical heritage represented by swamp pop, Cajun, country, and zydeco. Whenever there were signs of a record building up steam, he would never hesitate to sell the master for national distribution.

Such singles included "This Should Go On Forever" by Rod Bernard (Argo), "Breaking Up Is Hard to Do" by Jivin' Gene (Mercury), "I'm a Fool to Care" by Joe Barry (Smash), and later "My Toot Toot" by Rockin' Sidney (Epic). Thanks to compilation sales in the CD era, Johnnie Allan's version of Chuck Berry's "The Promised Land," with its arresting Cajun accordion solo by Belton Richard, earned a gold record for one million unit sales.

Floyd's first and biggest hit was Rod Bernard's "This Should Go On Forever," a quintessential swamp pop record that touched No. 20 in the spring of 1959. Written by Bernard Jolivette (the Excello artist King Karl), the song was recorded and produced by Jay Miller at his Crowley studio. Because Excello did not take up Karl's record immediately, Miller was able to retain the publishing for Jamil Music. The story behind "This Should Go On Forever" is a perennial, loquacious dinner-table topic with both Rod Bernard and Floyd Soileau.[6]

Recalled Soileau:

> I was glad to get that thousand-dollar advance check for the master from Chess. We'd already sold maybe 5,000 copies on my Jin label, and I was just starting in the business. I couldn't have handled that nationally, and I accomplished what I thought I could do with it. I had got some money to get married, so it was a good deal all around. I did talk to Rod; I said, "I'm gonna put the squeeze on Chess [Records]." Big deal, I'm putting the squeeze on Chess, right! I said, "We got to get the Rod Bernard record played on WLAC, and you got to get him on Dick Clark's *American Bandstand*." Those were two of the stipulations, and the third stipulation was I wanted a thousand-dollar advance royalty. I got all three, no question about that. I probably could have got more if I'd asked.
>
> I never met Leonard Chess or Phil; I did the business on the phone. I was always watching after what Leonard Chess's companies were putting out because I knew my jukebox operators were gonna use it. Chess was a hot independent; so was Vee-Jay with Jimmy Reed, and the Duke-Peacock labels [out of nearby Houston] had Bobby Bland and Junior Parker. These labels would come up with some hot stuff for the area.
>
> By that time, I was a little regional producer myself, but I was looking out at all these other areas. When Johnny Vincent came up with some things on his Ace label, we were watching for those because he had Earl King there for a while and Jimmy Clanton and all that. So what was independently produced in this southern region, I always listened to it because I figured if it was produced in this area, it was probably done with the people of the area in mind. It should be a good record, and the jukeboxes ought to do well with it.

The key conduit figures for the local record men to the nationally distributed labels were Huey Meaux and Shelby Singleton. Soileau had his ups and downs with Meaux through the years and was fonder of Singleton. "Shelby was working for Mercury Records," said Soileau.

He always told me to send him anything in the area that started to make a little noise; send him a sample of it. I think from living in Louisiana, he was keen on helping to boost any Louisiana talent that started to make a territorial noise.

I remember when I had almost completed my studio in the new Floyd's Record Shop building in 1964 and he came through. At the time, I didn't know too much about acoustics; I just thought you had to deaden the room. And he said, "My God, Floyd, it's so dead my words are dropping out of my mouth onto the *floor.*" He told me to put up some plywood sheets in at an angle and it would brighten the room up a little bit. And I did, and I guess it helped out, 'cause the room had a nice sound after that.

Soileau built up a thriving retail record shop, which proved to be a prolific sales outlet for his own releases. The counter was a big asset to him in picking up on the local noisemakers, particularly in Cajun music, "because I got the feel of what my customer base in my area really liked." By utilizing radio spots, Floyd established a successful mail-order business that, again, was based on the Randy Wood and Ernie Young models. "I was fascinated," he said, "by the fact that Randy Wood, out of Gallatin, Tennessee, had started this little record store and then went to the mail-order thing. It turned out to be pretty big. In the back of my mind I'm thinking I've got a little record shop here, it's in Ville Platte, Louisiana, [and] that's not a big place either. It might not hurt to try that route, and it would help my store, for sure. And at the same time [it would] probably help to sell some of my own records."

Floyd Soileau became the leading one-stop supplier to the jukebox operators in the Louisiana rural area with the help of distributor friend Henry Hildebrand at All South in New Orleans:

Henry wanted me to work the "country," as he called it. He wanted me to sell to the operators down here, which he wasn't doing, but Henry only had certain labels [as a distributor].[7]

Well, Stan [Lewis] had all the labels; one way or the other, he got them. To get your business, he could sell *all* you needed. You didn't have to buy them from any other distributor. That was the whole thing about a one-stop; if they didn't have it, they would get it. How much money they made on certain labels, it didn't make that much difference. Some of them might have been loss leaders for them, but they got the business. You made one call, and you got all you needed. Stan was big at that.

That was one of the things that we had with Stan: If something didn't sell, you could send it back for something that would sell. That was the whole concept of the one-stop. But the competition made them offer lower prices and more guarantees and so on. They offered all kinds of deals: prepaid shipments, overnight shipments, whatever it took to get your business if you had a lot of dollars traveling through your store.

But I was making maybe a dime or so a record from Henry [Hildebrand]. The volume proved good for us, and of course the more records we put out in the jukeboxes, the more people would hear them, and then they would come in and buy them. When a Fats Domino record came out, you got to have a Fats Domino record for them, okay. Now toward the end, not every Fats Domino record was bought, but in the beginning it was a sure sale. You had to have the latest Elvis Presley, but you had a lot of other smaller stuff that made big impressions over the years. They wanted the Merle Haggard record maybe, or the Buck Owens, or whatever it was that would make that jukebox jump. They had to have it.

As with Stan Lewis, Floyd Soileau linked the decline of the jukebox to the fall of the 45 single: "I think probably the last nail in the coffin for me on the music end came with the demise of the 45–rpm disc. When it was a popular thing, the kids, for less than a buck, could buy their favorite music. But for the industry, the jukebox was like a small radio station over the area in drive-in restaurants, in barrooms, in clubs. And so we really did wrong when we abolished that 45 rpm. Not only did we put a lot of jukeboxes out of business, but we destroyed a medium to get independent music heard by the masses in a very effective way."

In his time, Soileau, forever entrepreneurial, operated pressing plant and printing facilities and even marketed a "revolutionary" rice cooker ("non-stick *guaranteed*," he would say). He admitted that for all his achievements as a record man, it was the music publishing side that kept him in business: "I quickly learned from my association with radio [as a teenage disc jockey at KVPI in Ville Platte].[8] When I started licensing the Jivin' Gene record to Mercury and so on, I realized that, hey, there was almost as much money in the publishing license as there was in the master license. I knew then that I had to get involved in it to stay in business, and it's been a very good thing for us. Now we've got about 3,500 songs that we administer. We never know when we can get one in a movie or a commercial or whatever TV series. Whenever we do, it usually continues to bring in some royalties and keeps us alive." If anyone wanted to license any Cajun song (or master), it was hard to avoid writing to Flat Town Music in Ville Platte. Floyd's biggest copyright has been Rockin' Sidney's "My Toot Toot."

As we concluded our latest interview in 2005, Floyd Soileau stated with realism, "We're on our last hayride." Then he added with childlike wonder, "I really appreciate having my name and my quotes in the same book with Mr. Ertegun of Atlantic Records. Man, that's something else." Ahmet Ertegun, no doubt, would have admired the accomplishments of Monsieur Soileau.

Sam Montalbano: Montel Records

The only No. 1 national pop record to come out of South Louisiana has been Dale & Grace's "I'm Leaving It Up to You" for Montel Records, of Baton Rouge, in November 1963. It caught the dreamy boy-meets-girl romantic theme as portrayed in Paul & Paula's earlier No. 1, "Hey Paula" (Philips), but the gloss was dimmed when its place in pole position coincided with the assassination of President John F. Kennedy in Dallas, Texas. Although the hit disc came at the tail end of the golden independent era, the song itself had been written and recorded by Don & Dewey for Specialty, without charting, way back in 1957 (and published by Art Rupe's Venice Music).

How did label owner Sam "S. J." Montalbano pick up on this obscure record? "I invested in the neighborhood M. & S. Record Shop in Baton Rouge," he said, "and we prided ourselves in having some of the obscure West Coast regional records." The Don & Dewey disc "was one of my favorites back then, so that was my familiarity with it."

Montalbano, a live-wire operator, launched Montel Records at the tender age of twenty-one in November 1958 while still attending Louisiana State University. He was already booking acts into a dance hall for band battles, and when he started taping them he realized that "some of the stuff I was taking down might make great records." Montalbano was ready to roll after learning the rudiments of the record business by sitting in at meetings in New Orleans with Cosimo Matassa and Johnny Vincent (he knew them when he was the touring manager of Baton Rouge resident Jimmy Clanton). Montel had a No. 82 national hit record in early 1959 with "Shirley" by John Fred and the Playboys, the same band (under a slightly changed name) that would score with "Judy in Disguise (with Glasses)" for Stan Lewis a decade later.

Sam Montalbano showed public relations savvy by securing an interview feature on the genesis of his label in Ren Grevatt's "On the Beat" column in *Billboard* in June 1959 in which he claimed that his John Fred chart record had sold "100,000 copies."[9] The reality check for the rookie record man came after "Shirley" was a radio turntable hit in Chicago. "That would normally represent sales of 40,000," said Montalbano, "as long as you could get them to the distributors quick enough." A Chicago distributor submitted an order for 13,000 records (including the regulatory 3,000 free copies), and so Sam billed him for 10,000 singles, which had cost eleven cents each to press. Imagine his surprise when, instead of a check for some $5,000, he received 18,000 45s as returns. That was 5,000 more than he had shipped! Montalbano was encountering firsthand the twin scourges of the industry: nonpaying distributors and bootleggers. He was saved by financial support from his family, who was building up a prosperous wholesale fruit and vegetable business.

By his own admission a good talker and hustler "who always had a buddy somewhere," Sam had the right ingredients to be a record man (but did admit to failing to sign future Imperial star Johnny Rivers). He learned from past mistakes when he guided to the top national spot Dale & Grace's "I'm Leaving It Up to You," which was recorded at Carol Rachou's professional-sounding La Louisianne studio in nearby Lafayette. It was such a natural hit that Montalbano managed to sell 330,000 copies through his own southern network of distributors, forcing many of them to settle up on old debts before letting them have the hot record. "They begged for product," he said, adding with pride that the overdubbed strings were his idea. He explained that the strings were double-tracked by three girls at Bill Holford's ACA studios in Houston to create the equivalent of a six-piece "orchestra." After an introduction from the tireless Huey Meaux, Montalbano turned over the record nationally to the Philadelphia-based Jamie-Guyden Distributing Corporation, whose owner, Harold B. Lipsius, became a respected friend. "I'm Leaving It Up to You" was the last independent No. 1 hit before the Beatles onslaught on the American charts in January 1964.

Sam Montalbano accumulated a sturdy catalog of South Louisiana music on the Montel and Montel-Michelle labels well into the blue-eyed soul era of the mid-1960s, scoring locally with the brassy fraternity and sorority dance band the Boogie Kings. He stopped recording because "I was used to Otis Redding; I didn't understand the Rolling Stones."

Cosimo Matassa: Studio and Label Owner

From 1945 until 1972, Cosimo Matassa's recording studios were the monopolistic cradle of the New Orleans R&B sound, out of which had grown rock 'n' roll music. Just think Fats Domino, Little Richard, Lloyd Price, Professor Longhair, Roy Brown, and the rest. A little earlier, young Cosimo had joined J. & M. Amusement Services, run by his father, John (a 1910 immigrant from Sicily), with Joe Mancuso at 838–840 North Rampart Street. There, Cos helped service their large jukebox route spread over sixty locations and extending throughout the Big Easy. On a whim from Mancuso, the J. & M. recording studio was opened at the back of the store with the bright Cosimo in charge.

Thus, "recordings" was added to the multiple goods and services provided by J. & M. "When we opened the store, we sold kitchen and bathroom appliances, like washing machines," said Matassa, "and radio as well—TV came along shortly after. The reason for it was that during the war, people couldn't get appliances, so there was something of a backlog, so the presumption is that there'll be a demand, so it's worth doing. It was the same with records." At the same time, the Matassa family continued to operate a grocery store, founded in 1924, in the heart of the French Quarter and proudly still in business in 2008.

With New Orleans awash with musical talent and rhythm, Cosimo Matassa's studio was an essential destination for independent record men throughout the nation seeking the hit sound of Fats Domino. It did not seem to matter that the facilities were behind the technological curve, or "two steps down the hall," as Matassa would say. A haughty January 1953 feature in *Down Beat*, the jazz epistle, concurred: "J. & M. Music, local retail outlet, is the scene for most R&B sessions, with a setup sufficient for the less discriminating tastes of the average R&B buyer. Full scale recording activities [in New Orleans] would require the setting aside of one studio for just that purpose by WDSU or some other radio outlet; expansion and improvement of the J. & M. facilities; and/or creation of a new studio designed for commercial recording a la Putnam's Chicago studios."[10] At least New Orleans's potential as a recording center was recognized, even if this optimism would turn out to be frustratingly unfulfilled over time. The locals would always cast envious glances toward Nashville's rapid growth.

The reference to Bill Putnam is interesting because he was the prime mentor of Cosimo Matassa and a leading figure in the studio game. "Bill Putnam, I admired him for his accomplishments," said Matassa.

Although he had a very large business—he was probably one of the top two or three people in the business—if I called him, he would take my call and give me time on problems I had. I learned a lot from him, including his approach to recording and how he approached the clients. He started in Chicago and moved to the West Coast. I went to Chicago once, I forget what about, and I dropped in to see him. And there was this gorgeous six-foot blonde girl [as] his receptionist, and I teased him about it. He said, "No, nothing's happening with me, but you'd be amazed how much advertising business I get, guys that just want to come over and talk to her."

He also made and sold a fantastic line of recording equipment, equalizers, compressors, and things like that. He licensed patents from the telephone companies and the movie studios and incorporated the stuff for use in a regular audio studio. He was instrumental in loudspeakers, too; he developed a loudspeaker that was the best and most widely used loudspeaker in control rooms—he built one that was similar to the Altec but better. He was a great practical person.

In 1956, Matassa relocated to Cosimo Recording Studios at 525 Governor Nicholls Street in the French Quarter. This was the studio where the New Orleans R&B sound came alive. Jerry Wexler remembered traveling down to New Orleans to supervise a Guitar Slim session at the upgraded facility for Atco Records in March of that year. "Now there's a big commotion because when he hit the first chord of the bridge," said Wexler, "Slim blew all the tubes on Cosimo's new board! So Cosimo never had any spare tubes; he didn't believe in it. He had a little kid that used to run down to the electric store and get one more tube, and we had to wait while he came back. But Slim kept doing this, blowing an amp. Finally we got everything except for this tag. So I go up to him and say, 'Slim, you gotta do the coda.' And he said, 'Motherfuck the fucking coda, I'm here to sing "Plenty of Room at My House"'! The piano, the bottom was all kicked in because Professor Longhair used to kick to keep time. But that was Cosimo's studio, put together with spit and wire. We sweated a lot in those days."

By the late 1950s, an ambitious and restless Cosimo Matassa was part of an Italian American faction in the New Orleans record business that included Johnny Vincent (commuting from Jackson, Mississippi), Joe Caronna, Joe Assunto, and Joe Ruffino. Besides owning the hot Ace label, Vincent was a partner with Caronna in the Record Sales distributors, whose lines included ABC-Paramount and MGM. Matassa was looking for more action, too, so he took up personal management with Jimmy Clanton, whose No. 4 national hit "Just a Dream" had been recorded at his studios for Ace in 1958. According to Matassa, it was not an easy liaison.

He felt more comfortable going into label ownership with Rex, a name derived from the premier Mardi Gras organization. "First of all," said Matassa, "I wanted to record some artists that other people weren't really recording, or they weren't being recorded as I thought they should be recorded. And I just had an itch to play with it, I guess. It did eat a little into my time with the studio, but not much. It's like if you owned a car wash and you wanted to wash your own car, you'd wait until you weren't busy and you'd wash your car. And that's the way I did Rex. If I didn't have something else to do, I could do a Rex thing. But if I had a client, that came first. I didn't do a terribly large amount of stuff."

The Rex catalog included collectible records by Mac Rebennack (later Dr. John), Van Broussard (Grace's brother, of Dale & Grace), ex-Specialty singer/songwriter Earl King, and ex-Trumpet harmonica wailer Jerry McCain, but there were no breakout hits. "It was distributed by Johnny Vincent, to my regret," said Matassa, with unusual and caustic brevity.

Despite the faltering interest of the national labels, indies and majors alike, the New Orleans record scene reasserted itself as a thriving entity in the early 1960s, with Cosimo Recording Studios remaining in the forefront of activity. Enterprising young producers Allen Toussaint, Harold Battiste, and Wardell Quezergue were supplanting old guard Paul Gayten and Dave Bartholomew (whose unparalleled run of hits with Fats Domino was coming to an end).

During this fruitful period, Bert Frilot (who mixed Eddie Shuler's Goldband master tapes and later set up Mickey Gilley's studio in Texas) was one of Matassa's engineers. "There I was at Cosimo's repairing tape recorders," Frilot said.

> He had two engineers working for him at the time, and he had two studios, A and B. There was a third room in an adjoining building that housed the Neumann mastering lathe where we cut the acetate masters. For a time, it was used as an FM classical music studio, which was broadcast from there and transmitted from a riverboat location.
>
>   Then it's about six months later. One of the engineers that's working for Cosimo quit, and the other got fired, so that left Cosimo trying to run all three rooms. And there I went; that's how I got started. I was helping him out on sessions, doing tape copies, and I used to record radio shows, edit the tapes. Then I started with small bands. And Cosimo kept feeding me more and more work until the next thing I know I was into recording full time. So it was like a baptism by fire on how to do the recordings.

Bert Frilot said his hit count at Cosimo's included "I Know" by Barbara George (A.F.O.), "You'll Lose a Good Thing" by Barbara Lynn (Jamie), and "Ernie K-Doe records, Chris Kenner things." Frilot confirmed the genius of his first boss: "Oh geez, I've never seen anyone yet that could outdo him even today. There was nothing anyone ever asked him to do that he didn't know how to do it, or would figure out how to do it. He was so inventive. Yes, there was a special New Orleans sound. I guess it was a combination of the area, the Cosimo sound, and also the producers at the time. Just taking nothing and manipulating it and making it sound like something great."

Cosimo Matassa was the king of mono as he folded his 2– and 3–track master tapes into the monaural format. There is a view that New Orleans's recordings never had quite the same rich, rhythmic attack once stereo took hold in the 1960s.[11]

From World War II on, the highs and lows of the Louisiana experience were being repeated by independent record men in different states all over the nation. Said Floyd Soileau, "The regional sound, to me, was the beautiful part that kept this industry alive and kept the blood flowing. You had all these independent labels and regional producers going into little studios and trying out some song that was written, or trying out some band that was put together and checking it out on the jukebox [and the radio] to see if the public would like it or not. This was happening all over the country. Then if it happened, there was always somebody bigger that would take it on a national ride. It was feeding different pies to these pie-loving audiences all over the country. You had fresh, new material [and] fresh, new sounds coming out every year from different parts of the country. But then when the big-money guys come in and they buy all this up, they put the squeeze on it too hard. Well, then, you wouldn't have that anymore."

The Hustle
Is On

11

Billboard and *Cash Box:* Stars and Bullets

ELVIS PRESLEY with Scotty and Bill
(Sun 209)

B+ "THAT'S ALL RIGHT" (2:43)
[Wabash Music BMI — Arthur
Crudup] Elvis Presley sings a middle
tempo bounce southern type blues.
His feeelingful vocal with a more than
just a backer-upper bass and guitar
support by Scotty and Bill looms like
a potent piece of wax. Listening and
re-listening convinces one that the
deck could make a great deal of noise.

B "BLUE MOON OF KENTUCKY"
(2:45) [Peer BMI—Bill Monroe]
Presley sings a rhythmic country
ditty with an interpretation that has
that country feel all the way through.

CAST OF CHARACTERS
  Jerry Wexler, *Billboard* reporter
  Seymour Stein, *Billboard* staff
  Marty Ostrow, *Cash Box* editor
  Irv Lichtman, *Cash Box* editor
  Ira Howard, *Cash Box* country music editor
  also featuring Paul Ackerman, Billboard *editor*

Billboard and *Cash Box* were integral pillars of the independent record era. These trade papers were, effectively, the support force of rock 'n' roll by supplying chart data and record reviews, feeding news stories, and providing vital advertising platforms. In a fast-moving music industry, the weekly arrival of these journals was awaited eagerly throughout the country by the music establishment and indie hustlers alike. Essentially, *Billboard* was the elitist organ patronized by the major labels, whereas *Cash Box* was the young upstart endorsed by the independent labels. *Billboard* survives to this day.

Billboard

Billboard Advertising was founded in 1894 by William Donaldson and James Hennegan out of Cincinnati, Ohio. Originally a monthly publication, it was targeted at the outdoor advertisers, but, under Donaldson, coverage was steered toward the theatrical groups, carnivals, and fairs that were being promoted by the billposters. Hence the early title change to *The Billboard* (but commonly referred to as *Billboard*).[1]

In time, the magazine became a weekly, covering emerging forms of entertainment such as films, coin machines, radio, television, and, of course, records.

Jerry Wexler's freshman working years encompassed a spell as a journalist with *Billboard* at the turn of the 1950s. With typical eloquence and élan, he recalled his apprenticeship:

> Joe Carlton hired me; he was more of a music biz wheeler-dealer. He was a good editor, but his tenure was so short after I came there. Paul Ackerman seemed to come on almost immediately. Joe Carlton was, like, gone; he went to another big job. One of the perks [of] being the head of RCA or Mercury was getting small tokens of appreciation from the music publishers [*laughs*]. Later on, he formed his own Carlton Records, where he had a brief little flurry of success, but it didn't last long.
>
> What happened [was], I was working at BMI, and I was a "hey you" in one of the backrooms. Nobody knew I was there. One of the old-timers at BMI, [Meyer] Shapiro (Shap we used to call him, an old Broadway hand, publicity guy) said to me, "There's an opening at *Billboard*; let me send you over there." So he sent me over to see Joe Carlton, who interviews me. The interview went well enough, except I didn't pass one test. He said, "What label does Nat Cole record for?" I didn't know.[2] But he hired me anyhow. I would say he was probably very happy because I was a very good writer. Nobody else on the staff wrote as well as I did at the time. I did a lot of rewrites; I was highly involved. I knew how to use semicolons.

Wexler was full of admiration for Paul Ackerman, who joined *Billboard* in 1934 as a reporter and became its respected music editor almost continuously from 1949 until 1973: "He was very educated. He had his master's degree in English literature, and his specialty was the Lake Poets. He was just a very compassionate, wonderful human being. Also, I turned him on to country music when I gave him some Jimmie Rodgers records, the Singing Brakeman. Paul then became very knowledgeable; he really dug into it. Later on, he became very friendly with Sam Phillips. In my [1978] eulogy to Paul in *Billboard*, I end with a quotation from Tennyson [the poem "Crossing the Bar"].

Paul Ackerman with Jerry Wexler featured prominently in an important event for the record industry. In June 1949, *Billboard* updated the designations of its minority charts: hence the terms "folk" and "hillbilly" became "country and western," and "race" and "sepia" became "rhythm and blues." It was the coming of the new. Ackerman coined the country (C&W) notation, while Wexler is acknowledged as the creator of the R&B term, even if he seemed reluctant to take full credit.

"Paul called us all together and we discussed," Wexler recalled.

> I don't know who originally brought it up, Paul or one of the staff, the fact that "race records" seemed a little retro as the proper nomenclature. "Let's change that!" It was just the way they changed "hillbilly" to "country and western"; they found it pejorative. So we used to close on a Friday and come to work on a Tuesday. Paul said, "When you all come in on Tuesday, maybe you'll have an idea." So I came in Tuesday, [and] I said, "Rhythm and blues!" And he said, "That's okay; let's use that." That's how it happened.

But I must tell you, people are entitled to the designation of their choice. For example, the various changes in the designation from "Negro," "colored," "black," "Afro/African-American" . . . the rubric keeps changing. And it's the privilege of the people concerned to choose the way they should be designated, whether or not other people think so. There's no academy here, as there is in France, to approve or disapprove. However, I know that the word "race" at that time was a very noble designation. When you called a black man a "race man," you meant that he was totally committed to being who he was and that he felt his negritude [and] expressed it. One of the greatest compliments you could give a man is to say, "He's a race man to the bricks." That means from the top of his head to the floor; it's a very fine designation. So I never disapproved of it. However, I'm not the registrar of this ballot.

Over time, *Billboard* and *Cash Box* have proved to be invaluable research tools for music historians, especially as rock 'n' roll music was woefully ignored by the academic community of the period. Bob Rolontz, a staffer at *Billboard*, showed in his well-observed stories a fine appreciation of the independent record scene that was developing rapidly under his watch. "He was a good reporter, an intelligent and pleasant man," said Wexler. "I hired him away from *Billboard* [in the 1960s] to do our publicity and promotion at Atlantic."[3]

Young Seymour Stein was a precocious devotee of both magazines before joining the staff of *Billboard*. "I was very well received at *Billboard* in the beginning," said Stein.

Tom Noonan, who was head of the chart department, put me in a room.[4] I went through bound volumes of *Billboard*, wrote down everything that happened, and copied the charts. I went all the way back to the late 1930s and '40s. The thing I didn't realize was that all this knowledge was being thrown out the window. We were right in the middle of the rock 'n' roll revolution, and the established music biz of Tin Pan Alley was fading fast. I was very glad I did the research and it wasn't a waste. But the business was re-inventing itself. Tommy was great and gave me my first job at *Billboard*.

I also met Paul Ackerman, who is legendary and was inducted into the Rock and Roll Hall of Fame. He is responsible for bringing rhythm and blues and country and western music to the forefront, and he took me under his wing. Every Wednesday night there were record review sessions, right before the deadline. Reviews were much more important back in those days because the charts were so slow, up to six weeks behind. A *Billboard* spotlight could immediately sell upwards of 50,000 records to jukebox operators who used this as a guide. This was very important to the major companies, but especially to the struggling little indie labels. If they had an important record that they felt might be overlooked because it was by a new artist or something, they would bring it up personally on Wednesday night and present it. I must say it didn't influence the panel that much, but at least the label heads were sure their record got listened to. *Billboard* was quite unbiased. That's not to say that they weren't wrong sometimes. As we all know, this is a business where fortunately you can be wrong far more often than right and still be a winner.

Cash Box

My own initiation into the world of *Cash Box* came on one of my regular Saturday morning visits to Davis's record shop in Terminus Road, Eastbourne, Sussex. I inquired of the manager about a pile of magazines gathering dust in the corner of his office. "They're *Cash Box*," he said. "Do you want them?" Somewhat taken aback at this generosity, I became the proud possessor of the *Cash Box* issues from May 1960 through March 1961. By then, rock 'n' roll was supposed to be in its death throes in the immediate aftermath of the payola scandal. But I could tell from reading the magazine that the U.S. music scene was fighting back, with rhythm and blues in full flow and the twist craze providing further resuscitation.

Subsequently, I subscribed to *Billboard Music Week* (as the magazine was titled between January 1961 and December 1962), based entirely on its lower subscription price. *Billboard Music Week*'s cheap-looking newsprint at the time did not endear it to me, nor did the seemingly casual reviews, and even its superior news stories did not have the personal resonance they should have had. Somehow, *Cash Box* seemed to be much more alive to the independents' world, especially with its well-laid-out charts, sparkling reviews, and glossy advertisements. Then there were "PoPsie" Randolph's art-quality photographs of artists, record men, distributors, disc jockeys, and jukebox operators adorning front covers and inside pages alike.[5]

The mastheads of those 1960–61 *Cash Box* magazines carried these accreditations: "Joe Orleck, president and publisher; Norman Orleck, vp and managing director; George Albert, treasurer; Bob Austin, manager New York—music (advertising); followed by . . . Editorial—music: Marty Ostrow, editor-in-chief; Ira Howard, editor; Irv Lichtman, associate editor." Little did I know that some forty years on, I would be meeting the three music editors, who were still living in the New York area. Not only would I be listening to their still-fresh stories from when they were tyro music journalists, but I would be getting privileged insights into a relatively unexplored part of the independent record makers' world. All three men had arrived at *Cash Box* in the early to mid-1950s by way of a senior year work-experience program that involved college graduation credits from the Baruch School division of City College in downtown New York.

Marty Ostrow: Editor

By 2004, Marty Ostrow had retired from a distinguished career in music journalism, which also embraced a period with *Rolling Stone*. A man with a clear, precise mind, he had started full-time with *Cash Box* in 1952, just as the explosive upheavals in music history were taking place. The magazine itself was trying to shake off its image as simply a jukebox industry organ.

"In 1951, I went to work at *Cash Box* as a messenger," said Ostrow.

I was picking up some advertising, picking up some press releases, and handling the stamps and mailing of letters to the post office, things like that. At that time, *Cash Box* was just a young beginner in the music business; it wasn't established well in the music business at all. It was still struggling because it was not a paper for the record business originally. It started as [a] publication for the coin machine field [the magazine was launched formally in Chicago in 1942].[6]

Bill Gersh, whose idea the *Cash Box* was, had said, "I think there is a business in informing the people throughout the coin machine world, all of these operators all over the United States, how much a machine is worth." How do you determine that? Very much like a stock market. So what he did was this: he found out the names of the coin machine operators in all of the key cities of the United States, got their phone numbers, and what he would do every week was call them. "What did you sell this week?" he would ask. It was a single man's operation. Day and night he would call; that was his work. He would compile a list of every machine that every manufacturer had that was still salable, and once it had stopped selling, it was just erased from the list. This list gives you an indication of the highs and lows. We used to do these kinds of calls when I started with the paper; I'd make notes of all this, and I had this grid in front of me.

What did Bill Gersh name it? *The Cash Box* because there was a "cash box" in every coin machine—the jukebox, the pinball machine. *Cash Box* was the big answer to everything, but the paper did not have anything to do with music. Bill Gersh's mimeographed, stapled sheet was sent out like a newsletter. It was vital information that nobody else was giving, so necessity was the mother of invention. The guys hated underselling. At least they had a value, something to refer to.

Of course, it was going to all these coin machine operators all over the United States. Remember, for example, that a coin machine operator in New York may have had three hundred machines in different locations; this is his business. Some of these guys were really well-to-do guys because it was all a cash business; they never had to report exactly what [their takings were]. So they liked that business. Some said the mob was in it. I never really knew that, but it sounds like their thing: dealing with taverns and alcohol, luncheonettes. There is so much room for theft [and tax avoidance].

Then Bill Gersh, who fancied himself as a writer, . . . loved doing editorial commentary about the coin machine business, which he knew. He didn't know the record business at all; he was not affiliated with the record business. In talking to these operators, he would find out that while they were giving him details of used equipment, they would say, "This new machine is unbelievable what it's doing in coins." So of course Bill Gersh, as a reporter and having a publication, put in a page about news [on] what was happening: "Hottest machine in nation, doubling weekly take." Then advertisements followed, and this is how it continued to evolve. So our bailiwick was the jukebox operators; *Billboard* doesn't even service them.[7]

We were "the jukebox paper"; [that's] the way they referred to us. Our ads were really telling the one-stops that somehow we had an "in" with the little retailers and the jukebox operators. All of those three, that's where an ad was aimed at in our publication. Then Bill got an assistant to work for him: Bill Gersh stayed in Chicago, and Joe Orleck went over and handled the New York operators; then Bill hired a freelancer for the West Coast. Before you know what had happened, everybody was supplying news. So you had a publication developing all about the coin machine world.

For many years, the central focus of the magazine remained "The Confidential Price Lists," also known as the "CMI (Coin Machine Industry) Blue Book." This weekly list was studied by jukebox and other coin machine operators as avidly as investors would imbibe the daily stock prices. In 1954, based on the models listed in *Cash Box*, the biggest turnover in jukeboxes (new and used) was consistently in Wurlitzers, followed closely by Seeburgs, then the Rock-Ola, AMI, and Evans machines.

Through the demands of the jukebox operator lobby (yet again), *Cash Box* evolved into a music publication. "We're talking about operators all over the United States who owned all of the jukeboxes," said Marty Ostrow.

Now when you think about it, anyone that had a jukebox . . . needed records for it. When he called to these guys asking what jukeboxes they were selling, what kind did you buy, which ones are doing well, which ones get the most coin, they would say, "Bill, you know you can help us a little bit. We have been looking at *Billboard* because that's the only publication around that has a best-seller list of records. And that helps us a little in determining what records to put into the machines. Because, hey, I'm a machine operator, I don't know good music from bad." So Bill Gersh would say, "Let me see what I can do. I can ask all of these operators, when I call them about what they're paying [for machines], what records they are using."

So what happened was Bill Gersh went to a guy called Jack "One-Spot" Tunis, a man in Oak Park, Illinois. He was doing his own compilation list by calling retail shops, and he was doing exactly what *Billboard* was doing. The "Top 10" was what Tunis gave us; it was a national analysis.

As early as 1946, Bob Austin was headhunted from *Billboard* after a decade on its sales staff to become general manager of *Cash Box*. His job was to create a music section of the magazine and bring in ads from the record business. Under Austin's important stewardship, the magazine's slow ascendancy began. Even then, the issue of January 1, 1949, still pronounced that "*The Cash Box* Is the Operator's Magazine." The contents reveal just how segmented, and comparatively small, the music scene was at the time.[8]

But with Bob Austin's push, the advertisements began to flow in. "We were starting to get ads from the record industry that were coming in over the transom," said Ostrow. "In other words, you don't have to sell it. So if you're an enterprising boss and you see the ads are coming in, you think maybe there's more of them out there if you make a little effort. Tell people about who we're reaching, what we're doing. Visit them, take them out to dinner, take them to a ball game, let's go to a Broadway show with them and do the usual advertising sales [pitch]. If they become friendly, they may run two ads in our paper and only one in *Billboard*. It's part of the selling aspect."

However, *Cash Box* subscribers were starting to complain that the Tunis charts were too slow and too late. The work had to be done in-house. "That's where I got involved," said Ostrow, "because I was the first full-time editorial employee at *Cash Box* under the editor, who was Sid Parnes when I came in. Joel Friedman was the editor of *Cash Box* for five or six years during this growth period."

Sid Parnes was another alumnus of City College and joined *Cash Box* as music editor in 1951, the year that Marty Ostrow had started his work-experience program. Rising to become editor in chief, Parnes left in 1959 to start his own firm, Sidmore Music. Later with Bob Austin, by then another exile from *Cash Box*, Sid Parnes founded in 1964 a strong rival publication, *Record World*, out of the remnants of the languishing *Music Vendor*.

"So I stepped into the *Cash Box* editorial office," said Ostrow.

I did some record reviewing and story writing. I would take many of the press releases that would come in from all of the different record companies and rewrite them with Sid's guidance. I loved the music, which was the basic thing; if you had that in your soul, it was great. And the rest was learning how to write. Sid taught me how to write because, oddly enough, I was a math/science lover rather than a writing academic.

By 1954, the magazine was still very much segmented into pop, R&B, and hillbilly. And what segmentation did they give me, the boy from the Bronx? The rhythm and blues section! I knew nothing about it. I said, "What is rhythm and blues?" "Go listen to it; you'll hear it." I was listening to rhythm and blues stars like Faye Adams, Ray Charles, Ivory Joe Hunter, a whole bunch of Fats Domino, Billy Ward and the Dominoes. Okay, I liked it, but it wasn't "in my bones" kind of music. This is new to me; this is what the black people listened to. But as you started to be a reviewer, you threw yourself into it. And that was my category.

Then there was the phone calling for surveying the charts, which was another part of my job, because once they found out that Tunis was slow, it was agreed upon that "we have to hire another guy, and you, Marty, will help him. You'll do the surveying all over the country."

We sent the magazine free of charge to every one of the distributors just so that they would have *Cash Box* on their table when the record company went in to sell to him; [we sent them to] the distributorships, the one-stops. So you made free distribution; we just got our thing expanded. We went to the dealers. I sent to Colony Record Shop [on Broadway, New York] a free copy because, "Hey, I'm going to call you every week and ask you for what are your best sellers, and you're going to spend a little time with me."

We did a lot of phone calling. But we knew if we were going to make the record division have some significance, that chart is either going to have to be better than *Billboard*'s or as good as *Billboard*'s. We really devoted a lot of time and effort into it and hired more people. We had at many different times five and six people calling all over the country all day long. So it was a big phone expense, but we got a reading.

Then we found out something that was unique to *Cash Box*, which we had to move in on. We didn't realize it at the beginning. The big record companies were tied up with *Billboard* because that was the big publication that was going to the retailers, the record shops. *Billboard* had much more advertising than we had at that time; we were the young upstart. But the majors threw us a bone; RCA gave us the new Perry Como [advertisement] with this record and that record. They knew that we helped because we reached the jukebox operators.

Somewhere down the line, we found out that there is a whole group of record companies . . . following *Cash Box*, and they were called the indies: the independents. *Billboard* was too expensive for them [to advertise in]; they were little record companies. They didn't have the kids [teenagers]; they sold to the black audiences, they sold country records, they sold gospel records, they sold polka records. These were little companies called Atlantic Records, Chess Records, Duke-Peacock Records, Savoy Records, and Imperial; and [there was] Lew Chudd, Art Rupe [with] Specialty, the Biharis of Modern, King and Syd Nathan in Cincinnati.

So being a fledgling, we opened up our editorial pages to more than it should be proportionately for your advertising. We ran the majors' stuff, but we devoted pages each week to all of these little companies, like, "Fats Domino has a hit with 'Ain't It a Shame' [on Imperial], and Pat Boone is covering it for Dot Records out of Gallatin." That's the way it was developing, and of course we weren't against selling advertising to those guys also. We established what we called a "little rate holder" so that each one of these little companies every week would send us $32.50. They would buy a two-inch ad, and in it they would write "New Fats Domino hit . . ." I'm talking about every week. It went all over the country, and all the operators saw it. If they were jukebox operators of black records, they would turn to our paper and not to the *Billboard* because of our coverage.

The continued relevance of the jukebox industry to *Cash Box* (and to *Billboard*) was reflected in the colorful terminology used in the record company advertisements in both magazines, such as "3 for the Money," "Still a Colossal Collector of Coins!" and "Want a Money Maker?"

"But this was the ace in the hole," said Marty Ostrow. "We had created what we called the 'Hot R&B' charts [back in the 1940s]. While we were doing the survey, we'd contact the black areas in each of the cities or find out which ones are the black stores in the cities. I knew New York, but I didn't know Chicago. Which one was the store on the South Side? It was called Central Record Shop. How do you know what area it's in? . . . When you call and ask the clerk, 'What are you selling?,' he says Fats Domino, Johnny Ace, Ray Charles. When there isn't a Perry Como, Patti Page, or Doris Day mentioned in the lot, you know who they're selling to. So we built up a series of 'Hot' charts that nobody else had, and it was a city-by-city analysis of the Top 10 rhythm and blues records in each of twelve cities."

The "Hot" charts had evolved out of the "Burning the Jukes in Harlem" Top 10 chart, which was compiled from reports submitted weekly "by leading music operators in New York City's Harlem" and were clearly inspired by *Billboard*'s "Harlem Hit Parade" listing (dating back to 1942). By 1948, there were four "Hot" listings in *Cash Box*: "Hot in Harlem," "Hot on Chicago's South Side!" "Hot in New Orleans," and "Hot on Central Ave. in Los Angeles." These were the major centers for rhythm and blues (race) music, but there were no charts for gospel/spiritual music.

"I brought up the subject of gospel music charts to my editor once or twice," explained Ostrow, when a gospel record was so hot that I thought it should be put on the rhythm and blues charts. He told me to try to compile something. But I found it too difficult, mainly because the gospel records were so varied from one territory to another. There were not enough sales. One problem was that when we called the R&B stores to get sales results, our minds were all focused on R&B records. So even if there was a big gospel seller, it wasn't mentioned. Yes, there was always some gospel star such as Mahalia Jackson who sold a lot of records when a new one was issued. But no storekeeper would ever think to mention it in the same breath with R&B hits. So we never followed up in this area.

Remember, also, that radio play was very fragmented. Even in the R&B field, you could have a Top 10 in New Orleans that was completely different than the Top 10 in Cleveland, or maybe three or four of the Top 10s were the same. But so many local charts were different because each station played its own favorites. If not for *Cash Box* and *Billboard* spreading the word about the big hits in other cities, the charts would have been even more varied. Each R&B station in each city was owned by a different person; there was no multi-station ownership. When R&B records started to cross over into the pop field, the charts in different cities began to look more and more alike.

At *Cash Box*, we kept on debating how to review new releases by black artists as well as country artists, because at one point in time we were living through an era which saw the dividing lines between black music [and pop] or country music [and pop] steadily vanishing. Nat "King" Cole was the most obvious example of a black artist who was always reviewed in the pop category. All of this confusion came about because radio [traditionally] had a clearly drawn dividing line between one kind of music and another. And that resulted in us having separate R&B charts and separate country charts.

There was a time when the R&B radio stations would never play a pop record, and pop radio shows, like Martin Block's *Make Believe Ballroom* on WNEW in New York City, would never play any R&B record. It was a clear, sharp, acceptable division. To a degree, it was somewhat like the nation's acceptance of a baseball league made up of only white players and another league of only African American athletes. It's amazing that it appeared to be okay with most of the people.

Then came Alan Freed: he made a point of playing records like "Sincerely" by the Moonglows, an R&B hit, to show his audience what "soul" meant. Then he would play the McGuire Sisters' version of "Sincerely" to show the difference, even though the McGuire Sisters' version was a big hit in the pop field. Without specifically saying so, he was telling his audience that one version had soul and the other was a "copy" lacking that soul quality. All this resulted in a change in the charts and the development of the word "crossover" that described a record that went from the R&B or country charts onto the pop charts. It was a very difficult time for the trade papers, which were in the habit of categorizing all new releases. And it was a dramatic time for change in the music business.[9]

The inaugural Top 100 chart was actually launched by *Billboard* on November 12, 1955, before becoming the Hot 100 on August 4, 1958. With the "One-Spot" Tunis handicap, *Cash Box* lagged behind. Its Top 50 Best Selling Tunes on Records chart was not instituted until August 4, 1956, and crept up to a fully fledged Top 100 only on September 13, 1958. As from 1959, the *Cash Box* Top 100 chart was made from cardboard stock. "That's something else *Billboard* didn't do," said Ostrow. "We had perforations on a cardboard so that it makes you tear it out; *Billboard*'s chart wasn't able to be torn out."

Marty Ostrow's masterstroke was the introduction in 1959 of the "bullet," depicting the fastest-moving records on the charts. There have been several bullet claimants through the years, but Ostrow must take ultimate credit. "One of my big jobs before becoming editor was doing the Top 100 chart," he said,

> and supervising the surveyors to tally it all up. A number of people called and said, "Do you know what the problem is on your chart? When a record moves up from 30 to 20, and another record moves up from 15 to 12, you have to read on the right side what its position was previously in order to see how much of a move it made, because all you have [are] the numbers 1 to 100."
>
> So I said to Sid Parnes, "We can emphasize certain things. How about we go to the printer and we get a circle printed? We're gonna do categories: if something in the bottom quarter of the chart, from 75 to 100, . . . moves twenty-five points, we'll put a circle around it; . . . from 75 to 50, if it moves fifteen points, we'll put a circle around it; from 50 to 25, if it moves up only eight or ten points, we'll put a circle around it; and from 25 to 1, if it moves up over three or four points, we'll put a circle around it to emphasize." So he says, "Good idea; do it."

So Marty Ostrow contacted the magazine's printer, who said, "Use a bullet," to which Marty replied, "You got something that looks like a bullet? Perfect. You're talking about like a Lone Ranger bullet, like something shot out of a pistol?"

> He said, "You're dumb; you don't know anything about printing. A bullet is a *dot*; that's the printer's terminology."
>
> So this "red bullet" indicates a sharp upward move. I had the art director take a compass and make a circle, and underneath I wrote in red, "Introducing the red bullet! It's designed to call your attention to anything that is really moving quickly." It became something that we never really ever imagined, or I would have imagined, anyway. It became . . . industry terminology: "No. 1 with a bullet." Clive Davis and others used to say, "The record bulleted up the chart without a stop," or, "From the moment it was released, it bulleted into No. 1." It was used as a verb.

Part of the *Cash Box* editors' job was to present annual award trophies. On one occasion, Marty Ostrow was driven to Philadelphia to make a presentation to the Clovers at the Uptown Theater. The journey from New York was made in Ahmet Ertegun's MG convertible with Jerry Wexler as the other passenger: "Three of us in a two-seater," Ostrow noted drolly.

The story behind Marty's rude initiation at the Apollo Theatre, New York (also with the Clovers) was prompted by Wexler. Here's Ostrow's take:

The Clovers won a *Cash Box* vocal group award [around 1954]. I called up Jerry Wexler at Atlantic and told him that I wanted to bring the award over to his office so that he could give it to the Clovers or their manager. Jerry said, "Why don't you come up to the Apollo where they are appearing this week, and I'll make arrangements for you to present the trophy to them on the Apollo stage?" I was a new kid with *Cash Box*, and that seemed like a pretty cool thing to do. So I put on my pale blue suit and met Jerry with Ahmet Ertegun up at the Apollo. They took me in to meet the Clovers in their dressing room.

The Lucky Millinder Band was playing onstage. Jerry and Ahmet told me to go to the stage and wait in the wings with the trophy until Lucky was finished with his set. Lucky finished, took a bow, thanked the audience for the applause, . . . and looked to the wings. I walked out toward the microphone in the middle of the stage, [trophy in hand,] all ready to say, "Ladies and Gentlemen . . . ," when I see Lucky walking over to me. He was saying, "What da *fuck* are you doing onstage, man? Get da *fuck* off this stage!" And he started to push me off the stage with his body and his baton in hand. As Lucky was talking to me, I could smell the alcohol on his breath.

I immediately made the assumption that he either forgot that I was supposed to present an award to the Clovers at this point, or someone else forgot to tell him. I walked or was pushed, I don't exactly remember, into the wings, and Jerry Wexler was coming toward me with the Clovers behind him. Jerry explained to Lucky what was going on, and I finally did the presentation. It was another rite of passage for a young music journalist!

Ira Howard: Editor

The second member of the bright, young editorial team was Ira Howard, who was at *Cash Box* from 1952 until 1965. His tenure encompassed a spell as country music editor and innovative record reviewer. "We had a small office down on 26 West Forty-seventh Street in the diamond-buying district of New York," remembered Howard.

It was over some shop. I originally started in '52 running around as the errand boy and the office boy. I said, "Gee, this is great; I may not have to go into the advertising business," which is what I was gonna do. I was added to the staff full-time in 1953 when I graduated college, so I started my whole career right out of college, just a little bit before rock 'n' roll, so I was there right in the middle of it.

My first job was doing the coin machine charts. I used to go with the boss, Joe Orleck, who was one-third owner of the magazine; Bill Gersh owned two-thirds of it. This was before George Albert bought them all out. I'd get the prices of all the pinball machines and the jukeboxes and get the highs and lows and put them into a chart. That was half the magazine at the time, the coin machine industry.

I did that until about 1954 when Charlie Lamb, who was the country music man for the *Cash Box*, started *Country Music Reporter.* All of a sudden, there was a void. They didn't have anybody in Nashville other than Charlie, and they said, "You do it." I said, "Me? From the west Bronx! I don't know anything about country music." They said, "Learn!" Which I did. It took me a couple of months, that's all. I got into it and really enjoyed it because I really liked a lot of the songs. The lyrics were so different from the nice, easy ballads that we were listening to in the '40s and '50s prior to rock 'n' roll.

Then in country, I was getting these reports about this new artist out of Mississippi that was really shaking up the world with his hips and his songs, and of course that started bringing country out of the darkness. Elvis Presley's impact on country charts was unbelievable; he had around one hundred [country hit] songs, all told. So he helped bring country to the fore just as much as anybody, although for pure country it was Eddy Arnold and of course Hank Williams. A lot of things were converging at the time.

The young turks at *Cash Box* were the first to pick up on Elvis Presley's regional stirrings in the issue of August 14, 1954. His debut recording, "That's All Right" (written by Delta bluesman Arthur "Big Boy" Crudup), was reviewed in the rhythm and blues section. Ira Howard is almost certain he was the writer: "Elvis Presley sings a middle tempo bounce southern type blues. His feelingful [*sic*] vocal with . . . more than just a backer-upper bass and guitar support by Scotty and Bill looms like a potent piece of wax. Listening and re-listening convinces one that the deck could make a great deal of noise." The flip side was "Blue Moon of Kentucky," Bill Monroe's bluegrass classic.

In the same issue, a related news story, headed "Sun's Unusual Country and R&B Pairing Creates Excitement," confirmed the primeval buzz surrounding Presley. It was written that "Music Sales Company, Memphis distributor for Sun[,] reportedly has sold 4,000 copies in the first week" and that "Sun reports the record is being programmed for airplay on all types of programs and operators are spotting the record in all types of locations."[10] Even so, distributor Henry Stone remembered that Presley's Sun singles did not make that much noise for him in Florida and sold mainly to the hillbilly sector.

"So country music during those mid-1950s years started to pick up a little steam," said Ira Howard.

> But . . . if a song was No. 1 on the country charts, the most it would sell would be 100,000, compared to a million-seller popwise. We changed the name to just country by 1960, which was when we dropped the country and western term.
>
> Bob Austin used to give out the country awards, but in my second or third year he said, "You're the country guy; you give out the awards," which I did. That was at the WSM *Grand Ole Opry* annual affair. The magazines used to give out the awards; that's before the CMA [Country Music Association] was started in 1958. I met all the great stars of the time, every one. I have pictures with Patsy Cline, George Jones, you name them.
>
> I had arguments with [publisher/record man] Wesley Rose all the time, especially when it came to Hickory Records. At one time, we'd have all the hits under one song's name, whatever the record was. His song would be on two different labels; one of them would be Hickory. And if we had the other label higher than his, he'd be pissed off. Then we started separating the records [on the chart] according to what each one was doing [saleswise].
>
> My best friend, other than Shelby Singleton, was a guy named Herb Shucher. He was Jim Reeves's manager. He also managed the Browns, who were very big in the

late 1950s, and later on he co-managed Brenda Lee. These were key people for me: Herb used to introduce me to everybody, [and] so would Shelby. Herb was originally an executive with Imperial Records in New Orleans; he worked with Lew Chudd. He used to tell me stories about Fats Domino.[11]

For a while, Ira Howard was in charge of the rhythm and blues charts. He felt genuinely, unlike many others, that the much-denigrated Pat Boone helped to open up and popularize rhythm and blues with his cover records and cited specifically Boone's "beautiful version" for Dot of the Flamingos' "I'll Be Home." Howard could have mentioned, too, Boone's serene rendition of Ivory Joe Hunter's "I Almost Lost My Mind."

"Everybody loved *Cash Box*," said Howard.

I had good relationships with most of the people, because the one thing I never did was review the really bad records. If something was a C or a D, you'd rarely see it in the magazine. You'd only see the B+s and the As. Also, I would get everybody into the "Country Round Up," no matter who they were, with at least one line, whoever sent in anything. And we had the disc jockey [Top 10] record reports for the week.

All the stars that used to come up to the *Cash Box* always felt at home. They said over at *Billboard* it was a little bit of "business as usual" type of thing. I remember the day when Dion and the Belmonts came up, when we were at Fifty-fourth Street and Broadway. We had a big, big room where we played stickball with them, where you use the broomstick and a rubber ball. It was a bit like Grand Central Station; you really felt everyone wanted to come up to the *Cash Box* to say hello. We really had a good thing going with the entire music industry.

Howard remembered that Jerry Wexler would telephone regularly to ask, "What's breaking?" Among the *Cash Box* staff, the Atlantic record man was known laughingly as Mr. Purist for his rhythm and blues bias—that is, until he had his next pop hit.

"I really wish I could have appreciated it then like I do now," said Ira Howard. "Looking back on it, I used to be with those people all the time. We would cover all the events, all the rock 'n' roll shows, the Murray the K shows, Alan Freed shows, every place possible. I was at the Warwick Hotel in 1964 [a year before he left *Cash Box*] when the Beatles came in. I didn't understand how monumental it was at the moment. I was just having a good time."

Irv Lichtman: Editor

In 2004, Irv Lichtman was enjoying a relaxed retirement in Oceanside, Long Island, after a lifetime of deadlines at *Cash Box*, where he established his editorial credentials, and at *Billboard*, where he was deputy editor. An expert on Broadway shows and the great standard writers, he penned at *Billboard* "Inside Track," the widely read news feature, together with the respected "Words and Music" column chronicling the often mysterious world of songwriters and music publishers. As well, he had a spell in music publishing with the *New York Times* division until these interests were bought out by Freddy Bienstock's group.

After lunch at Lichtman's local diner, I handed him a musty issue of *Cash Box*, for old time's sake as much as anything else. Never mind the editorial content; the first thing he did was to look at the advertising makeup, especially the split between the major labels and the independents. That's a professional journalist at work. He took up the story of *Cash Box* from his vantage point, while making sharp observations on the overall independent record scene.

"When I got there, Marty was my immediate boss," Lichtman said,

so that's 1955. By that time he'd had a lot of responsibilities, including the charts and running an editorial. *Cash Box* was not a structured place. You didn't have an organization with four people doing this, four people doing that. Everybody did everything.

As far as I could determine, being a very young person on the staff, the price lists were very, very influential. The magazine was aimed at jukebox distributors. I don't think [it was targeted at] the venues or locations themselves; it was in the distribution end. The fortunes of the jukebox industry helped *Cash Box* grow, but within a few years the music industry coverage (and importance as an advertising vehicle) far outstripped that of the jukebox industry. While we every so often would run photos on the cover of *Cash Box* that included the introduction of new jukebox models, where a very famous recording personality would be standing next to it, the basic thrust of the magazine (certainly by the early 1960s) was toward the music industry.

At a point, Bill Gersh had left. The exact circumstances I'm not aware of; I don't know if not on friendly circumstances. Joe Orleck maintained a presence at the magazine, but he had far less influence in determining music industry policy, which again became the bulk of our coverage and the reason why we existed.

An important mentor for Irv Lichtman was Bob Austin, then music department general manager. "Bob Austin was one of the great music industry salesmen," said Lichtman.

He was a classy dresser with a pencil-thin mustache and a great meet-and-greeter. The line, always said warmly, that "he'd attend a manhole cover opening" may have had its origins in the Bob Austin style. As a young intern at the *Cash Box*, I was more than a bit shy, and Bob, noticing this, took me aside one day. He told me in a very sincere way that I should open up more often and engage fellow staffers and industry folks in conversation. I took it to heart and really worked at it. I learned the ad man's meet-and-greet style with a vengeance and became so comfortable at it that I would often take laidback fellow staffers, even those I reported to, and introduce them to the biggies of the business. Down through the years, I always reminded Bob of his vital advice. For several years before his death, I served with Bob on the board of the Songwriters Hall of Fame.

The [other] personality who was there in 1955 was Sid Parnes. Sid was editor in chief to some degree in name only because he was not that much of a journalist. [He was] a very smart, intelligent man, but in those days I think the practicality of shoring up your advertising base was the way *Cash Box* basically operated. The stories were less meaningful in terms of objectivity, or getting exclusives, or creating a weightier magazine, than to create *charts*. There's no question about it; the charts were the heart of *Cash Box,* just as its price list was the heart of our jukebox coverage. I think editorial coverage took second place by a long shot, even when I got there.

We began to get a little more serious as the music industry grew, but in my view not serious enough. By the time the rack jobbers came along to greatly expand the availability of music and obviously expand the revenues of the industry, it was a much more complicated industry in terms of retail chains, coverage of nonmusic retail chains, and stores that carried music. Artist contracts became more complicated, and the industry just grew by leaps and bounds. It just required a little more extensive, objective news coverage than *Cash Box* was doing at the time.

Cash Box for all its parochialism started some interesting firsts in the music industry, and of course probably the most notable first would be the bullets on the charts. That was a *Cash Box* invention. The industry lived to regret that [*laughs*]. The guy who articulated the idea to me was Marty Ostrow, who actually compiled the charts. He was the basic chart compiler with other people helping him out, like myself at times. I have to admit I was very reluctant; I just didn't like that area much. But there were others: Ira [Howard] was a chart person, then Ted Williams and Mike Martucci.

Basically the charts were made up from retail reports that were graded on a 1 to 10 basis. . . . During the disc jockey scandal, and I think it was referring to *Cash Box* as well as *Billboard,* the word "intuitive" cropped up during testimony at one time [*chuckles*]. I think the person that said it had his eye on the ball. Because a lot of the chart was intuitive; it was projecting based not on actual statistics necessarily but perhaps a buzz, perhaps something more concrete. So that was coupled with actual returns by retailers. The top record is ten points, No. 2 is nine . . . that's how you compiled the chart. IBM was not a part of the process.

There were slips of paper coming from all directions. Marty, Ira, and Mike were good at collating all that stuff into a feasible chart. I think there was practicality to assembling the chart, too, and that to me was a logical progression of movements up and down. Because radio was dependent on using your charts to play songs and retailers, distributors, or anybody else that bought records were dependent on your chart, . . . you did not want chaos. That is, you didn't want a record that you gave a bullet to one week drop down so far that the guy would say, "What the hell did I buy that record for? I bought 5,000 copies; it's worthless." So there was a certain usefulness in that intuitive nature of the charts, plus other practical considerations to keep the chart from being not chaotic. So if you introduced this practicality of logic, you're also introducing something that is not necessarily statistically correct. But it was orderly and perhaps more important than actual precise numbers and spots on the charts.

If the latter-day bar code scans removed many doubts concerning chart manipulation and human error, the introduction of computerized technology in 1991 created a different problem. Said Lichtman:

I think when *Billboard* underwent a major chart restructure based on actual over-the-counter sales through [Nielsen] SoundScan, there was havoc because there was incredible chaos in the charts. Titles would move in and out weekly; a record would go to, say, No. 50, which is a pretty high number for a first-time entrant, and then disappear. You had to settle down the charts so they had a certain logic.

In my view, though, the bullets became an evil because of the demand. Once you set up the criteria of a bullet, you obviously got the pressures from the industry: "I want that bullet; you['ve] got to give me the bullet or the record's dead!" . . . As the pressure increase[d], the margin of point movement up became less and less, to an extent where I think there were times when closer to the top of the chart you could move up one [point] and get a bullet. There was such intense pressure on that reach of the charts so that by moving up one point you had significant sales for that week. That was the so-called evil to me of creating the bullet, but it created a new industry pressure, a new industry guideline of success. *Billboard* picked up on it, but they used a "star." They couldn't use a bullet.

Due to these "industry pressures," the number of bullet allocations per chart increased as the years went by, particularly in the lower reaches of the charts. More than ever, the hit was the Holy Grail of the record business. Forget the art! Advertisements were known to be withdrawn truculently by record companies if their new record didn't get a bullet or a "pick hit" review. And there were occasions, inevitably, when the young editors were subjected to payola-type inducements. Lichtman admitted that his editorial team used to eye *Billboard* charts to ensure there were no serious discrepancies with the *Cash Box* charts, and no doubt their rivals did the same. His feeling was that the listings for the Top 25 records were fairly accurate, but that was all.[12]

As the weekly releases surged, *Billboard* set up in 1959 the "Bubbling Under" chart, which covered local hits in regional markets. "That was a *Billboard* invention," said Lichtman.

We had "Looking Ahead." Remember, the nature of the chart is really to offer as many alternatives to the industry as possible. You can't have just the Top 10, because that's not enough; you have to have a Top 25. Then the burden is "Where was I this week, No. 26?" and so on. Now, what's a "bubbling under"? Bubbling under is like you sold twelve copies; . . . you deserve to be not on the national chart but below the chart. The promotion man at a record company or the owner of a record company would say, "We're bubbling under; see, we're happening." But encouraging advertising was a natural progression. If a record company saw some representation on the charts that it would want to promote the record, hopefully it would be more than willing to use *Cash Box* as a vehicle. You naturally expanded the chart. That's something to do with the growth of the industry.

I can't validate the numbers that were there to make any record No. 1. But I can tell you that with any record in the Top 5, there was a great expectation on the part of the record company involved: "Are we going to be No. 1?" I think there were times that we would give that No. 2 or No. 3 record a shot—it could be a one-week shot—just so they could say they're No. 1. But in a sense, who is to say that a record may not have been the No. 1 record in that particular week?

In the old days, records seemed to last longer. That could be the result of radio using charts more than maybe radio did later on. A record being No. 1 for four to five weeks of course was a great goal that people would have, even for ego's sake. It goes back to the old *Your Hit Parade* show, which was a program that started on radio in 1935.

Radio didn't want rapid change unless some novelty came along which they couldn't avoid, like Dickie Goodman [in the name of Buchanan & Goodman with "The Flying Saucer" in 1956]. Novelties, of course, raced to No. 1 and backed off almost immediately; they had no staying power. That was the problem with novelties. The record companies would wish that you could keep them up there. But what happened was they had a very short life. They got tremendous play, and once the novelty faded after several weeks, they're gone. The more substantial pop, R&B, and country records of course became favorites. And you wanted to hear them.

By the late 1950s, thanks to the great advances by the independent labels, *Cash Box* was being seen in more or less equal terms with *Billboard*. However, there was still an inferiority complex among the *Cash Box* team. "It's almost a noncompetitive way of dealing with a monster," said Irv Lichtman.

That monster was *Billboard,* which had basic chart music coverage from the mid- to late 1930s and had become the powerhouse. It was really a question of *Billboard* absorbing whatever majors existed at one time: RCA, Decca, Capitol, Columbia, and the major independents had 90 percent of that business. So the idea is, it's always good to have an alternative in any trade. In terms of a magazine, *Cash Box* provided an alternative for the guy who was just a small independent.

Believe me, they didn't envy us as much at *Billboard* as we envied them for being able to get the Capitols and the RCAs and the Deccas. . . . These were the stable companies that were bound to advertise every week, almost, because they had so much product. It was not just product introducing new artists but promoting the next Frank Sinatra, the next Bing Crosby record, or the Christmas season when tons of that stuff was coming out.

In those days, you have to understand that the industry had greater control of its product. [It] could determine when it would release product. It knew it had to have its biggest guns out there by August in terms of availability so that the retailers and the distributors could take orders. So record companies could command artists: "I want you to do an album in January and February so we can put it out in the fourth quarter," which is of course the best quarter of all. But it changed; it was not a seasonal business anymore. By the way, summer was always dead; nobody released major albums in the summer. It just wasn't done. The industry eventually became nonseasonal: "Get it out now; we need money rolling in now!"

There was management turmoil at *Cash Box* after George Albert's loud arrival. Said Irv Lichtman:

George Albert, I would say, joined *Cash Box* in '56, '57, around there. He was a self-proclaimed financial wizard; maybe he was. *Cash Box* was going through financial difficulties, serious ones, and he found a way of funding the magazine, giving it an infusion of funds, which gave him a place in the firm as the treasurer. But he, being George Albert, . . . didn't stop there. He was able to take control of the magazine, eventually forcing out Bill Gersh [and] Norman and Joe Orleck. I'd say within seven to eight years of George coming, the savior of *Cash Box* became "The Savior" [*laughs*].

He was a diamond in the rough. Actually, I don't know about diamond; he was just rough—he was a crude man. He had friends from the Latin Quarter days or something, friends who were on the seedier side of our society [laughs], not that he was anything himself to my knowledge. There was a wonderful evening where I spent dining with George. I just remember going into this Italian restaurant on the East Side; it was after eleven o'clock, and the shows were out. I see these beautiful girls going to their assigned seats next to some hoods: "Hey, take a look at that!" He had this *gravel* voice.

Of course, he had judgments about the music business that didn't make any sense most of the time. It was as if George might take credit for Al Jolson, insisting he perform and record "Swanee" (Jolson had recorded "Swanee" probably before George was born). He was a difficult guy to deal with. When he wanted you to be part of something, he gave you the world. He'd take us, Marty and myself, to the clothing store, pick out sharkskin suits. But he would turn on you, as he did with several people and to some degree myself. He didn't have the guts to fire somebody. What he'd do, he would eliminate you from being part of the mix. You didn't go to conventions anymore: "Nah, you gotta stay home. We need the advertising; what's gonna happen if you go?" The person would usually catch on.

The congressional payola investigations of 1959–60 caused a reporting quandary among the *Cash Box* management team and editorial staff. *Billboard*, under Paul Ackerman (himself a major witness at the hearings), was much more objective. At *Cash Box*, the reluctant party "was not George Albert; that was Joe Orleck," said Lichtman.

During the disc jockey hearings, the payola hearings, people in the industry were testifying, and some of them were admitting to payola. Joe Smith himself admitted, as a disc jockey in Boston, that he took payola. It was the policy of *Cash Box* not to have that kind of testimony in the magazine. It would make them look bad.

Forget that you're supposed to be covering this thing as news, so that people who weren't at the event would know about it. Well, of course, their excuse was: "We don't have to hurt our own people; the readers can see it in the *New York Times*." I said, "But Joe, this is our obligation, we're a trade paper, we've got to put all kinds of testimony in. This is what we're here for." "No, no, I don't want to hear about it. No!" I thought he was gonna fire me. Instead, he called me back about ten minutes later: "Irv, don't take this personally, even though you were wrong" [laughs].

Joe Orleck came from the school of hard knocks also. He had a rough New York accent and all that, and he was basically a very nice man. But he had this point of view: "Don't say bad things about people in the business who either we like or may be advertisers." I was just shocked, and I wasn't getting that much support from other people on the staff, to be honest about it. But I'll never forget. He got angry, about as angry as he could get: "No, don't want to hear about it." Then true to his basically sweet nature, he comes back.

I had never ever written an editorial that didn't come from my own head, or maybe from Marty Ostrow or Ira. But it wasn't from a person who was promoting a record. It was a person who was observing the industry like I was supposed to do. A lot of the ideas were just hearing from people. Tuesday night I'd give it to Marty Ostrow, who always found a little grammatical mistake. I used to write too fast, but the worst editor is the person who wrote the piece.

Writing the singles reviews involved a great responsibility, with dozens of new records seeking chart action each week. At *Cash Box,* the pressures were relieved to some extent by the reviews being written in a novel manner that somehow befitted the color of their subject. *Billboard* was unable to compete in this department.

"Oh, we invented [the language]," said Irv Lichtman, "particularly Ira, because we had to think of synonyms for the same things. Remember, we'd run like eighty pop reviews. You can't call a singer a 'singer' in every review; we'd say a 'lark,' 'songbird,' 'thrush.' These are words that still pop into my head. I think Ira was the guy that invented 'rockabilly.' Of course, he also invented, when the cha-cha was big, 'rock-a-cha.' It was really part of the fun [*laughs*]."

Ira Howard backed up Lichtman's recollections: "By the late '50s, I was also doing some of the pop stuff, too. As a very young writer, I stole from previous reviewers such silly phrases as 'money-in-the-bank for all concerned' and 'surefire hit for jocks and jukes.' When I branched out, I began coining my own simple yet to-the-point stuff such as 'rock-a-ballad' (Connie Francis), 'rock-a-rhythmic' (Fats Domino), 'rock-a-thumper' (Gary 'U.S.' Bonds), and 'rock-a-string' (the Drifters, with 'There Goes My Baby'). When I put together the country terms, I referred to one of them as a 'rock-a-billy,' and Irv credits me with being the first one to coin it. It may have been a Jerry Lee Lewis or a Carl Perkins record, one of those types of artists. Rockabilly, because of the hillbilly name, . . . was a good term. That's all; just by chance, I think I was the earliest one to say it. But deadline demands had me knocking them out mass-production style."

"Sometimes Ira would come in with a major release at the last moment," said Lichtman,

and I'd think I was finished. He'd say, "This new Ames Brothers has just come in; you gotta do it." And they'd come in on acetates; they didn't come in finished form. That's how quick it was; that's an important point. But in those days, you'd get the acetate that came from the studio so we could review it and rush it in as a "Pick of the Week" because the label was priming its promotional guns and needed a review if you were gonna pick it. So Wednesday [at] three o'clock was the deadline; sometimes it was four o'clock. I'd get so angry: "I thought I was finished with this, Ira." Actually, it was the printer who put pressure on us to not submit further reviews, but they learned to go along with us on matters of urgency. The magazine was published on a Friday.

After the "Pick of the Week" reviews, there was the "Best Bet" section. It was a record that was close but we were unsure of. It was also a way of highlighting a record so that somebody got a piece of the action, so that someone could show something. Again, there was a lot of pressure, and sometimes we caved in: "At least give us a 'Best Bet'" [at one time there was also "Sleeper of the Week"]. Or a label would say, "We're putting tons of money behind this single; it's from a movie, from a show." Then I think it was legitimate to maybe go overboard a little, because maybe that kind of promotion and funding (and having a source of an important picture) could make it a hit.

There were a lot of factors going into reviewing a record. It wasn't simply the gut feeling [of] whether you think this was going to be a hit now; at the back of your mind, there were other things at play. You only had a dozen words or so with the regular reviews, but you made the "picks" a little more fluffy. Norman Orleck used to do singles reviews before I got there; one of them was a Tony Martin review, the crooner. I think it was Norman who said, "The gals will cream in their pants when they hear this new Tony Martin record"—not thinking, Norman being Norman, that this was not something you said in magazines. His other one was where he claimed, "Each side was better than the other."

As a pop reviewer myself of singles—and Ira knows—I would hear a country single, and in three seconds I'd say, "Ira, it's for you." Or I'd hear a blues record: "Ira, this is not pop; it's blues," some Excello recording or one of the country labels at the time where the blues sensibility was so apparent from the get-go of these recordings, or the twang was so apparent. Ira would love doing the country records, loved doing the R&B; he had a real feel for it. There was no way these records were going to get any exposure outside of country or R&B or blues markets, no way.

That was the time when the [latest] Fats Domino, Little Richard, or Lloyd Price [would come in]. We just wanted to hear that sound, what they'd come up with, what song have they done now. We'd gather round and listen, especially the new Fats Domino. It was a time when rock 'n' roll had its tongue in its cheek, a sense of humor, with the Coasters and all these other acts. It was something that rock 'n' roll has lost that kept me interested.

There were piles of records, literally. I did almost all the album reviews for a while, and eventually I gave up albums and singles. It was part of the growing up. Look, it was a wonderful experience. I really learned what a single was like and . . . that you do need those five to ten seconds up front to establish whether you've got something. I'm not claiming that now. Of course, there was always something that came along that defied the odds. The left-field hit was always the most intriguing thing about the music business.

Irv Lichtman remembered that one of his best random picks was "Since I Don't Have You" by the Skyliners, a totally obscure group on the equally obscure Calico label (owned by Lou Caposi and Bill Lawrence as an offshoot of Alanna Distributing Co. of Pittsburgh). With soulful lead vocal by Jimmy Beaumont and lush orchestral backing, the record fell just short of Top 10 status in the spring of 1959. On the other hand, were there any famous hits that were missed in reviews? If so, Lichtman didn't recall them. But the reviewers, by the very nature of their job, were always putting their reputations on the line. There was no benefit of hindsight to counter the gaze of distributors, one-stops, jukebox operators, disc jockeys, and retailers (or indeed of future music historians).

For a spot-on contemporaneous review (July 12, 1958), try the call on Peggy Lee's Capitol recording of "Fever," now regarded as an all-time classic: "Veteran Peggy Lee takes hold of a tremendous R & R oldie, wraps it up in a slick new rhythm arrangement, and hands in what should be her biggest money maker since 'Lover' [No. 3, 1952,

Decca]. The lark is just great on the vocal, and the backdrop (bass, drums and finger snapping) is fabulous. You can bet your bottom dollar jockeys will wear the grooves off of this hit."[13]

It was hard to gauge the weekly sales of *Cash Box* because the figures were not subject to official audit. "If the sales were declared at 20,000, they [were] more likely to be 8,000," said Lichtman, adding that "if a black artist was featured on the cover in the 1950s, the street sales would drop perceptively, especially in the South." In May 1961, *Billboard Music Week* was bragging that its "total paid circulation" per issue was 21,863, a figure that was "2½ Times the Circulation of the Next Magazine!"[14]

As the 1960s began to swing, *Billboard* sensed the new pulse better than *Cash Box*. "The downhill signs for us probably started, say, in the Beatles era," said Lichtman. "We covered it and all that, but again the business was getting very complicated. We weren't giving the nuts-and-bolts financial news about the industry that we should have been doing. And we were content to be a chart and reviewing magazine, run pictures, occasionally run some decent stories and an editorial, which it was my pleasure to have to write for ten years. I was associate editor in 1960 and became editor when Ira left in '65."

Irv Lichtman and Marty Ostrow stayed on into the mid-1970s, when George Albert left for the West Coast. *Cash Box*'s decline was sad to behold and ended mercifully on November 16, 1996, leaving *Billboard* as the outright winner in a battle that had been very competitive in the peak independent label era.

"It was a wonderful team because we were young," said Lichtman. "We had a wonderful time, we just loved the business, and we loved what we did. Looking back, however, we should have established a more serious tone to the magazine in terms of its coverage. But the industry let us be, because we represented that alternative."

In a similarly reflective mood, Ira Howard said, "In the '50s and '60s, *Cash Box* was really influential and really strong in all areas, even though it did not have the resources of a *Billboard*. I don't mean to put *Billboard* down; they are *the* magazine now. But there was a very, very good race in those times as to who was number one. I think we had the edge on the charts. People looked to us a little bit more, especially when it came to the bullet: 'Hey, I'm 27 with a bullet in *Cash Box*!'"

12
CHAPTER

A-Hustle and A-Scuffle at Old Town

CAST OF CHARACTERS
    Hy Weiss, Old Town Records
    Sam Weiss, Old Town Records and Superior Record
        Sales Co.
    Jerry Wexler, Atlantic Records
    Joe Bihari, Modern Records
    Richard Barrett, Old Town artist (The Valentines)
    Harold "Mr. Blues" Ladell, Radio WNJR and Essex
        Record Distributors
    Ruth McFadden, Old Town artist
    Milton Love, Old Town artist (The Solitaires)
    Billy Bland, Old Town artist
    also featuring Jerry Blaine, Cosnat Distributing Corp.
    and Jubilee-Josie Records; and George Goldner,
    Tico-Rama-Gee and End-Gone Records

Hy Weiss came into my life by accident. In May 1993, I had arranged to meet Shelley Galehouse to discuss the licensing of her father's masters of the Wailers on the Golden Crest label on behalf of Ace Records of London. In particular, I was looking to land "Tall Cool One," a double Top 40 hit (in 1959 and 1964) for Ace's prestigious *Golden Age of American Rock 'n' Roll* series. The meeting was set up at the Country Kitchen restaurant in picture-postcard Cold Spring Harbor, Long Island, near Shelley's family home.

I had no idea that Hy Weiss, of Old Town Records, would be present. In fact, I had no idea that Shelley knew him. Damn it! Her adviser was none other than this battle-hardened veteran from the mythical

New York street-slugger element of the record business, who just happened to live in the neighboring town of Woodbury. If there was a redeeming factor, Hy had an ongoing licensing deal with Ace Records, so there was a relationship of sorts. Negotiations were not made any easier by the fact that the ownership of the Golden Crest masters had fallen into confusion following the death of founder Clark Galehouse in 1983.[1] After discussing the possible whereabouts of the master tapes, which took in all points from Boston to New Jersey and featured a wide spectrum of characters (ranging from hallowed American composer Gunther Schuller and New York music man Mack Wolfson to many others), Hy declared, "Do it!" That was it—no buts, no maybes. The great Hy Weiss had decreed that she should license the masters to Ace.

Shelley did not rush to judgment. In fact, she had already told the wily record man, sweetly, "Hy, I love you, but I don't trust you one iota." He replied, "That's all right; your father didn't either."[2]

Here was an original record man making a snap decision, one of the many thousands made in his long, colorful career. At once, he was clinical and breathtakingly quick. Apart from his strength of personality, wit, and street talk, what was most evident was his grasp of music business law (unexpectedly) and "the deal" (expectedly). He gave the impression that the only worthwhile agreement was the one where all the odds (and benefits) were stacked in his favor; he did not appear to subscribe to the standard business ethic of both parties emerging from negotiations with mutual honor and satisfaction. "I don't know mathematics, but I know figures pretty good," he would say.

Although never in the same exalted league as his friends Leonard Chess and Jerry Wexler, Hy Weiss was the epitome of the hustling, second-division independent record man. That is, he would start something from nothing, supervise the session, hype the record, and try to collect, all the while "busting his chops" to make a "little dollar" here and there.

As an accessory to his armory, all manner of irreverent street banter would cascade from his lips. One of his better one-liners was: "He knows as much about this fucking business as an ant on the wall!" With his natural, rapid-fire humor enhanced by that magnetic smile, pronounced cheek dimples, and wagging cigar, he could have been a borscht belt comedian with a permanent residency in the Catskill Mountains if he had so desired. But the record man in him called.

For such an apparently carefree character, Weiss was frugal with the dollar in his pocket to a fault. Such innate monetary caution, which he would never admit to, may partially explain his longevity in the business. What is not in doubt is the support and sage counsel he received from his wife, Roz, throughout their marriage of more than forty years.

In his prime, Hy Weiss possessed an intimidating exterior: brash, abrasive, arrogant. With a tank full of nervous energy, he upset many innocent people in his lifetime with unnecessarily brusque tactics. But at heart there was a caring family man, a loyal friend, a common man in the best way possible. One of his favorite sayings was, "The street is where it all lays. Respect the street and the people in it." That epithet applied as much to the rap and hip-hop generation as it did to the doo-wop and blues acts back then.

Jerry Wexler met Hy probably around 1953 when Hy was a salesman for Cosnat, Atlantic's main distributor. "One day he materialized," said Wexler,

> and I was aware of him as being a lovable roughneck. Also I became aware that part of his shtick was to pose as a tough guy, which of course he isn't. Not that he couldn't handle himself if need be, 'cause he's a brute of a man, but he would let people have the idea that he's not the kind of man you want to mess with because of his connections. He didn't have any [laughs].
>
> Hy got along well with Morris Levy; certain people got along with him. Morris had a little coterie of straight friends: Juggy Gayles, Jack Hooke, Henry Stone. . . . It was sort of paternalistic, certain handing out of favors and so on, like a don capo, you know. Morris was my peer in one instance: you see, he was not Sicilian; he was Jewish [chuckles].
>
> Hy and his brother Sam started together, and Sam became very successful as a sub-distributor or a jobber. Then Hy did rather well with Old Town Records. The over-arching rubric for Hy would be scuffle, always a scuffle: a-scuffle and a-hustle. I have a little drama of Hy in the studio. Now, he's in a studio after midnight, very low rate or maybe nothing at all. Maybe he slipped the engineer some few bucks on the side? And all he'd need would be maybe a drummer, a pianist, and a saxophone player. There'd be four or five groups waiting in the wings, and Hy would say, "Next!" Out would come these bedraggled kids off the street or the subway. The piano player would say, "Where's the music?" "We ain't got no music, man." "Well, what key?" Hy used to talk back, "We don't study keys, motherfucker; play the music!" I describe this as the Golden Age of A Cappella.[3]
>
> I guess I knew him best when he was a salesman for Jerry Blaine. Hy would be promoting our records, and somehow we became good friends; there was some kind of affinity. I saw past the aura of a tough guy, and somehow he cottoned to me and we became friends through the years. It was very collegial back in those days; it was collegial and cutthroat at the same time. I remember Hy telling the story of his following Leonard Chess into a radio station, passing through the various departments and [seeing] the various disc jockeys. And Leonard would be paying his people a little bit of payola, and Hy would be going in on the backwash. In other words, he was creating the assumption that he was part of the team, and when the Old Town record came along, this was part of it. He'd go to the radio station and take a coin and nick the edges of all the competitors' records.

Old Town's major hits are inscribed in the annals of rock 'n' roll: "There's a Moon Out Tonight" by the Capris, "Remember Then" by the Earls, "So Fine" by the Fiestas, "Let the Little Girl Dance" by Billy Bland, and "We Belong Together" by Robert & Johnny. The principal Old Town musical style was doo-wop, but the releases encompassed a good helping of blues and almost every other popular music category, even folk and jazz.

Hy Weiss: The Early Years

Hyman "Hymie" Weiss was born in Romania in February 1923. Sometime during the next year, according to the 1930 U.S. Census, father Max (a carpenter by trade) and mother Rachel—both Russian-born in the industrial city of Podolsk, near Moscow—joined the final throes of the Jewish exodus from Eastern Europe just as the U.S. immigration doors were closing. And so, carrying their baby son, they headed for the new Promised Land. The family moved into an apartment house in the Bronx on 169th Street between Third Avenue and Fulton Avenue, facing a brewery and the hospital. Some parts of the Bronx were beautiful, but the Weiss's section was not.[4]

Still, with movie theaters, dance halls, amusement parks, swimming pools, and public beaches, there was much to do. The various ethnic groups all contributed to the community dynamic. Certainly, the Bronx was an energetic part of thriving New York before the Depression hit and was a far cry from the decrepit, drug-infested war zone it would later become, its heart and soul split asunder by a combination of urban renewal and the construction of the Cross Bronx Expressway. Many music industry figures emerged from within the boundaries of the Bronx.

The Weiss family was entranced by the magical sounds emitting from the static-ridden Zenith radio. Among the dramas, serials, and variety shows, mother Rachel was fond of Cab Calloway "because he sounded like a Jewish cantor," according to middle son Samuel. Hy and Sam, with young George, were brought up in a strict religious environment and were very respectful of their parents. Unlike many other immigrants, the Weiss family did not appear to anglicize their last name. Nevertheless, the children were embroiled subconsciously in the battle of the Jewish generations as they freed themselves from old European expectations and values to become sturdy all-American citizens.

Hymie attended DeWitt Clinton High School, where he participated in athletics and played football. Schoolmate Cy Leslie, later of Pickwick Records, described Hy as "gregarious, fun-loving, assertive, but not an academic." Morris Levy came from the same locale and went to the same dances as Weiss. After wartime army service and a dull job in the rag trade, Hy became a bouncer throwing out "whiskey heads" at the White Rose bar on Thirty-fourth Street and Third Avenue in Manhattan.

It was 1947: brother Sam was working for Runyon Sales Co., already a muscling jukebox operator and independent record distributor out of Newark, New Jersey, and New York. Important Runyon lines were West Coast–based Leon Rene's Exclusive Records, the Bihari brothers' Modern Records, and Bill McCall's 4 Star. After Exclusive opened its office/distribution warehouse in New York, Sam telephoned Hy to advise him that the new arrival in town had a vacancy for a salesman. Sam knew that his brother appreciated his daily Runyon hours of 11 A.M. to "whenever." Moreover, the infant record business was the place to be.

So Hy Weiss rushed over to Exclusive and was hired on the spot. Meanwhile, it was pandemonium back at the White Rose. On Hy's return, the boss asked how he could possibly leave the place in the middle of the day. Customers were pouring themselves drinks, and the whole joint was like a free giveaway. Happy hour had started way too early. Knowing he was cornered, Hy quipped that everyone was celebrating his new job and he was quitting anyway.

Thus Weiss started selling records to the rough, tough jukebox operators. "I had them tied up in my fingers; they loved me," he would say, then boast that he could sit on a telephone and sell more merchandise to the operators than any man walking in the city. And he probably did. Another important sales channel was to the record stores that were not franchised to the major labels, especially in Harlem. According to the Weiss doctrine, the nucleus of the independent industry was "black records bought by black buyers." On one occasion he acknowledged that "the Negro is responsible for a lot of white folk making a lot of money" and for record men like him being in business. To his credit, Weiss would cite regularly that Leon Rene's Exclusive label was "the original black-owned record company."[5]

Hy and Sam had only one car between them. The brothers solved this problem, so Sam said, by working the same territory for their two companies, enabling them to claim double expenses while using the same vehicle.

With Exclusive Records going into precipitous decline and Runyon Sales concentrating on the coin machine market, Joe Bihari drafted both Hy and Sam Weiss as salesmen operating out of the Modern Records office at 412 West Forty-second Street. According to Hy, a vague promise of a distributorship was made, but it never happened. Bihari readily recalled employing the Weiss brothers. "Runyon Sales in New Jersey became a record distributor and a jukebox operator that went out of the record distribution business," he said.

> That's when we started our office. Runyon Sales were terrific, Hy can tell you. I remember having dinner with Pat Moran, and he was part of Runyon Sales; I think he might have run it.[6] It was in Newark. I don't know if it was Murder Incorporated, but it was part of the mob, some place. They controlled all the [New] Jersey jukeboxes; I don't know how much of New York they controlled. The Runyon people couldn't be nicer, but look out if you fell on the wrong side of them![7]
>
> So in [July] 1948 I went to New York. Lester Sill was running the Modern Records distributing company in Los Angeles, and he needed a break. So I said, "Why don't you go on to Chicago with me, and you can fly back with Saul [Bihari]?" So Les came along. During the convention, Saul said, "When this is over, Joe, why don't you go and check the New York office, see what's going on there? And why don't you go ahead and take Lester with you?" So I took Lester.
>
> Bob Duberstein and Gloria Friedman [a sales manager with both Runyon Sales and Exclusive] were running the office at the time, and Sam and Hy Weiss were the two salesmen. After a couple of days, eventually I said to Bob or Gloria that I wanted a pad of paper. [One of them said,] "Go look in my drawer." Well, when I looked in the drawer, there were a bunch of gin rummy scores, a whole drawer full of them [laughs]. And I guess the next day I just changed the locks on the door, and they wanted to know if they were fired. I said, "Yes!"

We had a meeting together. I told Hy and Sam that I was going to be running the office and Lester Sill would be working with them as a salesman. They were very happy with that; there was no problem at all. They were as young as they could be, probably in their twenties. They were good salesmen, but of course we had good records, too: Pee Wee Crayton, we had a hit on him ["Blues after Hours"], and Hadda Brooks. We had a pretty good catalog of selling stuff in 1948, that early. We did about $3 million a year, and that was a pretty darned good amount of business in those years. You had your hits, and you had your misses, too. In January 1949, I did more business out of New York than they did out of L.A. That was wholesale distributing, going directly to record stores with Sam and Hy. Then I came back to L.A. a month later.

Hy was a darned good salesman. We revamped the territories: I think Sam took upstate New York, Hy took Jersey all through that part, and Lester Sill took Harlem. I think the rest, like Broadway, was split between Sam and us. There was a lot of records sold on Broadway. In the Times Square area, it seemed like there were record stores, one right after another: Colony Records and the jazz stores. One of my favorite distributors was Jack Mitnick [of Runyon Sales], and in Boston there was Sam Clark [of Music Suppliers of New England and later president of ABC-Paramount Records].

We never pressed on the East Coast because we had the factory. We shipped everything from California to New York; we used to ship whole truckloads at one time. With the [Modern Records] ARA factory, we had plenty of production to distribute to the East Coast distributors. I don't ever recall returns on 78s, and there were no free records. You see, in those days there weren't the dee-jays, either; you couldn't get records played. There was a station [WHOM] where Willie [Bryant] and Ray [Carroll] played some blues records in New York, but there were very few.

Hy did get into a little problem in New Jersey one day. He gave me a call; he said, "I'm in jail." "What happened?" It was in Newark. He said, "I got stopped by a cop for running a red light, and the cop called me a *dirty Jew.* And I slugged the cop." Hy was like a boxer, man; he was built like a prize-fighter, as strong as he could be. Anyway, I got him out of jail right away; I called Herman Lubinsky. Now Herman was a police commissioner of Newark, New Jersey, at that time. So of course he got him out of jail right away, and all charges were dropped and everything.

That story was endorsed by Hy many times. As for Lubinsky's appointment, Savoy A&R man Lee Magid said witheringly that Herman "would buy anything, including a police chief star."

"Herman had Savoy Records," continued Joe Bihari.

He also had a radio repair shop and a record store, and he sold a lot of Modern records. Now Herman took a liking to me, and I used to go in his store to see him quite a bit. He used to have a home down on the Shore in New Jersey, on the water with a boat. Herman used to pick me up and take me there on the weekends; we'd go fishing, talk about the music business. He had Charlie Parker, and he had gospel things, too. Herman was very kind to me.

But the Weiss brothers were terrific. They were different: Sam was a little softer than Hy; he was a redhead. They were both good salesmen, never had a problem with them. The family was very religious. I remember they would not work on the

Sabbath—you know, Friday nights or Saturday. Hy was especially good; I always felt comfortable with Hy because I felt protected with him. And Hy was good at getting paid [*laughs*]. I had no negatives with Hy; he was always a positive person, and Sam, too. I loved those guys.

Joe Bihari, still only twenty-three, adored the glamorous role of a record man: going to the clubs and shows, mingling with the artists, getting the girls. After returning home to Los Angeles, he hired Cy House to run the New York office for a short while before the Modern Records line was transferred to Major and then Cosnat. Confidently run by Jerry Blaine with his brothers Ben and Elliot, Cosnat Distributing was already a leader in its field on the eastern seaboard.

With Modern Records closing its New York office and distributorship, Hy Weiss hopped over to Major distributors before joining forces with Bob Green and Hy's brother Sam to set up BHS distributors to handle Apollo, Trumpet, and Colonial (the Modern subsidiary). The office was next door to Apollo head Bess Berman's, and Hy remembered "driving her crazy" by playing archaic organ records that "went right through the walls." It was enough to drive any *man* mad, he said. As well, Weiss recalled Ike Berman (Bess's husband) threatening to torch a lower Manhattan pressing plant that had been bootlegging Apollo records. This was literally a baptism of fire for Hy Weiss, who was observing the ruthless business instincts that were a prerequisite for survival in the fiercely competitive independent record game. He also acquired an inbuilt hatred of bootleggers, seeing them as the vermin of his industry.

Weiss's best moment at BHS was to urge "Bessy" Berman to cover an emerging blues hit by Sonny Boy Williamson, "Eyesight to the Blind," on Lillian McMurry's Trumpet label (distributed by BHS). With a New York push, the Apollo recording by the Larks advanced to No. 5 R&B in July 1951, overwhelming Sonny Boy's original version in the process. While Hy was displaying his feel and awareness of the developing blues and vocal group markets, he was showing a less-principled side of his character. Yet while Mrs. McMurry lost out on the record, she benefited from Weiss's chutzpah as she remained owner of the song copyright.[8]

Hy Weiss took his increasingly well-honed and conniving selling skills to Jerry Blaine at Cosnat, which was stoking the independents' fire with hot lines such as Atlantic, Herald, and Chess. Weiss told Blaine that he was ready to go to work, and, incidentally, he was the best salesman in the country. How could Mr. Blaine refuse to hire him? The liaison was an experience for both men.

Weiss said he was allotted the territory for Long Island and Harlem and handled all the jukebox operators' accounts. He swore that Blaine beat him out of commissions, so he would compensate for any shortfall by selling Cosnat records for cash out of the back of his car and copping the proceeds (but never more than he was owed). In effect, Jerry was stealing from Hy, and Hy was stealing from Jerry; on balance, there was no honor lost. One of Hy's many ruses was to place his records at the front of the record shop racks. Not only would the records be publicized, but there was an even chance that they would be stolen, which would mean reorders and extra remuneration.

By mid-1953, the Cosnat-affiliated Jubilee Records seemed to be dead in the water, and Weiss maintained that he "saved Jerry Blaine's ass" by recommending that Jubilee should cover a country recording by Darrell Glenn on the Valley label, way down in Knoxville, Tennessee.[9] At least Blaine was a good listener (he had "wide-open ears," so Hy said) and duly covered "Crying in the Chapel" with erstwhile chart-makers Sonny Til and the Orioles. As well as making No. 1 R&B, the Orioles' record touched No. 11 pop, thus helping to accelerate the R&B incursion into the national popular music charts (subsequently Elvis Presley cut the most famous version of the song). Another Hy Weiss "breaker" in New York was Willie Mabon's "I Don't Know" for Chess in early 1953.

Well managed and well organized, Cosnat Distributing would hold sales conferences weekly on Monday nights. One evening, Weiss was en route to a scheduled meeting when he ran into a vocal group named the Five Crowns, which had already recorded for Eddie Heller's Rainbow Records. The entourage was waiting to be auditioned by Jerry Blaine, but Hy managed to coax them into a recording studio for *his* first session. And so Old Town Records was born as a part-time operation, with Hy and brother Sam as partners. The Five Crowns, a sapling branch of the Drifters' family tree, saw the first Old Town release, "You Could Be My Love," in August 1953. Distributed by Cosnat despite Hy's hijacking of the group, the record enjoyed immediate airplay through dee-jay friend Tommy Smalls, thereby eliciting a few orders from the shops to the distributors. With glorious bravado a full half century later, Weiss reckoned the Five Crowns record sold "5– to 6,000 copies."

For Hy, the hustle was on with a vengeance. He had the gall to pitch "You Could Be My Love" to Mitch Miller after impersonating, over the telephone, the owner of the Triboro Record Shop (an important Columbia outlet). Mitch took the bait by recording the song with Lu Ann Sims, but TV host Arthur Godfrey hated the record and wouldn't let her sing the song on his show. According to Weiss, he informed Leonard Chess's publisher Gene Goodman at Arc Music that Columbia was covering his record and obtained an advance sufficient to pay the pressing bills to Jack Caidin's Empire Record Corporation. For the time being, Weiss was content to double as Cosnat salesman and Old Town record man.

The evocative record company name was derived from Sam Weiss's then-employer, the Old Town Corporation, manufacturer of duplicating machines and carbon paper. At the start, Hy and Sam were operating from a makeshift office at the Triboro movie theater at 165 East 125th Street. It showed the "worst pictures you ever saw in your life," quipped Hy, but it was a good base to audition the prolific local vocal groups. Along the same drag were many Harlem music hot spots: the Apollo Theatre, the Baby Grand club, Bobby Robinson's Record Shop, the Rainbow Record Shop, and the Theresa Hotel (where the Apollo stars stayed). It was these Harlem roots that were at the core of the classic New York sounds of Old Town Records.

At the start, releases were only dribbling out; it was a cautious buildup. In July 1955, the Weiss brothers formed the Paradise label (possibly named after the popular

Bronx theater or even their first stillborn label, Parody) with record shop owner Leo Rogers, who was impressed by the Weiss's reputed friendship with disc jockey Alan Freed. Rogers had wanted a piece of Old Town, but Hy and Sam would not allow that, so Paradise it was for the joint venture. The talented Harptones arrived with Rogers from the recently disintegrated Bruce label, and, over time, the Willie Winfield–led group's very first Paradise release, "Life Is But a Dream," has become a firm New York doo-wop favorite.[10]

Within a few months, in summer 1956, Frankie Lymon and the Teenagers' "Why Do Fools Fall in Love" was spreading worldwide and representing a symbol of hope for a generation of youthful New York doo-woppers, black and white, male and female. Hy Weiss boasted that he "gave" the Teenagers' hit to George Goldner at Gee Records as a friendly gesture. This story was hotly contested by Richard Barrett, who claimed credit for discovering the act. A strong, commanding black man who was not to be messed with, Barrett was an early Old Town signing with the Valentines. Before long, under Goldner's wing at End Records, he produced the Chantels ("Maybe") and Little Anthony and the Imperials ("Tears on My Pillow").

Of his travails with Weiss (and Goldner), Barrett stated trenchantly:

Hy's a guy I met [in 1954] under strange circumstances. At the time [with] Hy . . . wanting a hit record and the Valentines just needing a good record, we both almost got what each other wanted. If you know Hy, you know there was turbulence and drama: He being bullheaded and then me being hardheaded, it was a formula for a perfect marriage. As in life, this was short-lived and ended in divorce.

I guess without Hy giving us that opportunity to record our first record, who knows what might have been? Through him I got a foot in the door. Then with my hard head, I got my whole being in this business. Hy seemed to always be somewhere in the background as a thorn in George Goldner's side, because that's who I went with after the Old Town experience. Then one dark day in the '50s, Hy and I engaged in some heavy drama at a Goldner record session which secured his respect for me.

To get money out of Hy Weiss was like pulling teeth out of a chicken. Yet to have him as a friend, Hy would give you the shirt off his back. Hy was, in business, miserable[,] but you couldn't find a better friend. He's a good man; I will always care for him.[11]

The vocal group era was coming of age. Having spotted this voracious market, the Weiss brothers (like other New York record makers) were busy signing up teenage vocal groups that proliferated on street corners and subways from Brooklyn to the Bronx. The Old Town stalwarts were the Solitaires, who were introduced by disc jockey Hal Jackson. This class act gave the label another regional hit with "The Wedding," featuring the vocals of Herman Dunham and Milton Love. According to Sam Weiss, "The Solitaires became the Kings of Sugar Hill [in Harlem] and had the ability to communicate the feeling of being lonely and downhearted in the big city of New York."

After a recommendation from Alan Freed, who had ridden into town in September 1954 to shake up radio in New York and the rest of the nation, Archie Bleyer covered "The Wedding" for Cadence. The much-respected Bleyer saw his top harmony act, the

Chordettes, secure a minor Top 100 entry with the dreamy ballad in January 1956, but everyone felt it should have gone higher. Hy claimed he obtained $5,000 for the song from Hill & Range Music and then advanced those monies to Freed for a house purchase against a promissory note.[12]

At the time, Weiss was living with new wife Rosalyn in an apartment development in Whitestone, which was loaded with "bookmakers, shylocks, thieves, any kind of shit you can find," he said. She almost threw him out of the house for making the loan to Freed, but as Hy would say, succinctly, "It was a gamble; it was worth it." Later, this transaction was exposed by the *New York Post* in its investigative stories on payola, but there was nothing illegal in the loan itself. Weiss's main embarrassment was in having to face his riffraff neighbors, who had written him off "like a thief."

Encouraged by the Harptones' local hit "Life Is But a Dream," Hy Weiss felt confident enough to leave Cosnat in September 1955 to work full-time with brother Sam in record manufacturing. Hymie never stopped reminding anyone who would listen that Jerry Blaine's wedding present was a miserly twenty-five dollars (twenty-five dollars!), and that was the beginning of the end for him at Cosnat.

Ironically, Blaine's twin daughters had a "no-expense spared" joint wedding with "more than four hundred guests" just a year earlier that emphasized not only the rewards of the independent record business but its already close-knit nature. *Cash Box* reported that it was "somewhat like a record industry convention" with many guests being "officials of record companies and record distributors," including "Mr. and Mrs. Randy Wood from Gallatin, Tennessee, Mrs. Miriam Abramson, Mr. and Mrs. Ahmet Ertegun, Mr. and Mrs. Milt Salstone who came in from Chicago, Dave Miller from Philadelphia, Mr. and Mrs. Larry Newton and many others."[13]

The Old Town Records office was installed anew in central Manhattan at 701 Seventh Avenue, just off Times Square. This address doubled for the Old Town publishing company, Maureen Music (named after the baby daughter of Hy and Roslyn). Distribution was placed with Alpha Distributing for New York, temporarily, with Essex Record Distributors handling New Jersey.

Harold "Mr. Blues" Ladell: Disc Jockey and Record Distributors Salesman

Another prominent disc jockey latching on to the Solitaires' "The Wedding" with Alan Freed was "Mr. Blues" of Radio WNJR out of Newark, New Jersey. In a familiar practice of the time, in-house Top 40 charts were published in conjunction with the radio show and, without surprise, "The Wedding" was featured prominently. The stenciled handout "Mr. Blues Hits of the Week," printed by Essex Record Shops of Newark, urged everyone to listen in on "Station WNJR, 1430 on your dial, Monday through Saturday 9:00 P.M. to 10:30 P.M."

Essex became the largest independent distributor in the Garden State after Runyon Sales had opted out of the New Jersey record market by 1948 to concentrate on dealing in jukeboxes, pinball and coin machines, and parts.[14] The effervescent chief salesman for Essex was Harold Ladell—the disc jockey Mr. Blues.

Strictly a family-owned concern, Essex distributors was run by Abraham "Pop" Cohen and front-men sons Irv and Joe Cohen (who happened to be very friendly with Freddy Mendelsohn over at neighboring Savoy Records, which used to take fifteen-minute spots on the *Mr. Blues Show*). Pop, known as Mr. Credit, had a built-in instinct for spotting potential bad debts as well as hit records while overseeing the distributor's bread-and-butter roles of stock-keeping, filling orders, billing, and collecting accounts receivable before settling the record companies' invoices over "30–60–90 days." A columnist of *Cash Box*'s "Rhythm N' Blues Ramblings," with tongue in cheek (or even mouth open wide), reckoned there was another factor in Essex's success in acquiring so many different lines: "Mom" Cohen's cakes, knishes, strudels, and blintzes for visiting record men![15]

The *Mr. Blues Show*, dating back to October 1949, was among the first to feature rhythm and blues records in the New York area. "When I went to work with the Cohens," said Harold Ladell,

> I used to sell more than a fair amount of country and western, considering we're talking New Jersey [*laughs*]. We handled a line called Stella owned by Bernie Witkowski, which was polkas; there were a lot of Polish people in New Jersey. You sold the classical and the Latin as well. Now remember, in 1949 the Cohens could hardly give away a single rhythm and blues record, only a few pieces down South because we were mail-ordering them. We would offer jukebox operators (or piccolo operators, as they were referred to in those days) fifty or a hundred records free of charge just to put them on their different jukeboxes. They wouldn't listen to us: "Get the hell out of here. I'm not going to waste this spot on the jukebox with that." Well, that was the reason the *Mr. Blues Show* was created: to create exposure.
>
> I should point out that from midnight Saturday until midnight Sunday, the only thing played on WHBI [the first station to broadcast the show] was black gospel music. So *Mr. Blues* coming on for fifteen minutes at night was a natural; the show just fitted in right with the audience. After every record that I played, I announced that you could get this record at Essex Records, and I gave the address. And that following Monday morning, there were two mounted policemen outside of Essex Records on 91 Springfield Avenue, keeping the crowds up on the sidewalk, with the phones jumping off the hook. I played five records: Amos Milburn['s] "Chicken Shack Boogie" was one of them [number 3014, he recalled], and "Mother Fuyer" by Dirty Red was another; both were on Aladdin.

After just three broadcasts with Radio WHBI, the Cohens contracted the *Mr. Blues Show* to rival Radio WNJR, Newark, for a thirteen-week stint of forty-five minutes each night at 9 P.M. It was as good as prime time. But WNJR mainly reported farm and financial news to a white audience. With this alien black music hitting the airwaves in New Jersey and New York City from their station, the WNJR management wanted to cancel the show, until it was pointed out that the *Mr. Blues Show* was already No. 1 in the ratings.[16]

The show was the making of Harold Ladell and Essex distributors, while the independent record makers had found a vital outlet in the vast New York metropolis. "By the end of 1950, you can't name a label that we weren't the distributor of," said Ladell. "There was Specialty, Aladdin, Modern, Peacock, Imperial . . . later, we used to look at *Cash Box* and *Billboard* and say, 'How do you like that: we don't have a hundred of the Top 100, we only have ninety-eight!' We had major, major labels. The rhythm and blues industry, the record business, came alive in my estimation on a Sunday night in October 1949 at the end of the first fifteen minutes of *Mr. Blues*. There was no stopping it after that."[17]

Continued Ladell:

I met Hy Weiss when he and his brother Sam would visit Essex Records. It had to be in the early to mid-1950s. Hy was a very outgoing individual, as most of the indie record manufacturers were in those days. You had to be outgoing, or else you got stepped on. Hy made his presence known. You heard him before you saw him, but he was a very interesting person. Strip through the opening salvos of Hy Weiss and you had a nice man, a very, very nice individual. My recollection is that I liked the man from the get-go; he was a no-nonsense individual. He would meet the Cohens in New York on occasion, but he would always come running out to New Jersey with new records that he would release on Old Town. Hy used to stand in the doorway with the newest release, exclaiming, "Here's the latest hit!"

He had an ear for the New York sound, if I may, but that's what it was. It was good groups, good arrangements, well-recorded numbers. And he would come out and ask us to play the record. It wasn't a case of keeping your fingers crossed: "What is this thing gonna be? Is it going to be a plonker or what?" No, he came in with good recordings.

Another record man favorite of Harold Ladell's was George Goldner. "Reminiscing about George Goldner is always a pleasant experience," said Mr. Blues with a big smile.

Tico Records, which was a company that George owned, was strictly a Latin label. That started in 1948 [initially with radio personality Art "Pancho" Raymond]. . . . We talk about the record industry and the people in the record industry (you mention the Chess family, a delightful family), but when we talk George, that's a different story. This man was truly one of the lovable characters in the record business. This was a fun man, an absolute fun kind of guy. To spend time with George, you never knew what to expect next.

Essex distributors had moved from a sort of hole-in-the-wall on Springfield Avenue to a beautiful building on Fenwick Street in Newark in 1958. For our grand opening we invited a lot of customers, record dealers, and everyone else. The Cohen family threw a big party, and Joe, being very, very friendly with George, asked George if he could get somebody to come over perhaps and play the piano. And we were also friendly with a guy by name of Teddy Reig, who used to own the Roost label. Joe asked Teddy if he might know of somebody that could come over for our grand opening party, and he brought Johnny Smith, the jazz guitarist. Well, George just happened to walk through the door with *sixteen* musicians and a guy I was introduced to by the name of Tito

Puente, the mambo king! Probably my all-time favorite song by Tito, and one that I played many, many times on the *Mr. Blues Show*, is one called "Babarabatiri."

Why was it that Hy and Sam Weiss, George Goldner, the Chess brothers, Teddy Reig, and their fellow Jewish record men had such an affinity with black and other minority cultures? Said Ladell, poignantly, "You've got to understand, you're talking about Eastern European Jews that were persecuted. Now, my grandchildren's generation is so far removed from that. I'm saying that the business was the Chess boys and the Bihari boys and the Cohen boys and their fathers. So they're not ones to look down upon the blacks; they'd just come out of persecution. Chess Records may have been one of the Cohens' favorite labels because there was Pop Cohen, Joe Cohen, and Irv Cohen, and it was Pop Chess, Len Chess, and Phil Chess. The Chesses would fly in together, and it was like old-home week with them. They would all hug one another, especially the two fathers. They were from the old country: the Cohens and the Chesses were from Eastern Europe."

How did Essex distributors determine whether or not a record had hit qualities? "Believe it or not, it was a case of 'rate the record,'" said Harold Ladell.

Play them, weigh in our own minds, in discussions, that this thing has great potential. We would play a record [on the show], and the next day if the phone calls would come in from six to ten record stores, well, we had a few records on hand for them. When the phones would be jumping off the hook, we knew we had ourselves a hit, and then we would order them by the thousands.

. . . Hy Weiss was one of many manufacturers whose records we'd play. Aladdin and Specialty were very big in the early days, and Chess and King were very strong, but not like Atlantic—all through the years, they were consistent. It was to all our benefit to create, if you will, as many hit records as we possibly could. It was a partnership, absolutely. The more records that the labels had as hits, the more we would sell. And we all benefited from it.

Ruth McFadden and Milton Love: Old Town Artists

After the promising reception to "You Could Be My Love" by the Five Crowns and "The Wedding" by the Solitaires, Old Town began making regional noise with "Tonight Kathleen" by the Valentines, "Chicken in the Basket" by Billy Bland, and "Darling, Listen to the Words of This Song" by Ruth McFadden with the Supremes.

Ruth McFadden, vocally Old Town's answer to Frankie Lymon, had fond memories of Hy and Sam Weiss and appreciated their attempts to make a national hit out of "Darling, Listen to the Words of This Song." Ruth's story was a cameo of a raw teenage artist at the time. In one sense, her experience was one of exploitation, but in another, it was unforgettable. Her promising debut record also hinted at a developing relationship between the Weiss brothers and Alan Freed's organization.

In Alan Freed, Hy and Sam Weiss had found a willing promotional ally. The fledgling record men expressed their gratitude by giving Freed a writer's share on "Darling,

Listen to the Words of This Song" along with Johnny Brantley (Freed's right-hand man) and bona fide writer Julius Dixson. Alan Freed's onetime manager Tommy Vastola admitted to helping get Hy's records aired: "If Alan played your record, it would bust wide open." Vastola first met Hy in an office lobby as he fought with "partner" Teddy Reig in a furious argument over "$5,000 payola." Presumably this was the very same advance that helped to finance Alan Freed's house purchase.[18]

Even *Billboard* referred to the Freed connection in its review of the Ruth McFadden single in the "New R&B Records" section on January 28, 1956: "The thrush sings this opus with uninhibited charm and interesting vocal styling. Tune was co-authored by Manhattan deejay Alan Freed, and is bound to get plenty of airing in that area." With this first-class radio support, Old Town managed to fight off a cover version by established Varetta Dillard on Groove, a subsidiary of major label RCA Victor. Interestingly, just one week after the McFadden review, the august trade magazine gave a "Spotlight" accolade to "Why Do Fools Fall in Love" by Frankie Lymon and the Teenagers, noting that "jockeys and jukes should hand it plenty of spin, and it could easily break pop." Which it did, handsomely.[19]

Ruth McFadden had made a nervous debut on the famed Wednesday *Amateur Night* show at Harlem's Apollo Theatre in late 1955, when she was placed second behind a hot mambo group. The Apollo management had an agreement with a record company to sign a vocalist as the winner, so the mambo combo was eliminated. After gaining first prize for the next four weeks, Little Ruthie got her reward: a recording contract with Old Town.

"I seem to remember Sam taking more of a role with me personally," said Ruth McFadden,

> with Hy being the record person. But then that'd change; they both had an interest in me. And I tell you the truth, I am very grateful to both of them, because the record was done while I was still in school, and it became very, very popular very, very fast. . . . Alan Freed, who had the No. 1 radio show at the time, . . . had something to do with the record. So he played it when his show came on, he played it in the middle, he played it at the end, he played it! So, . . . from being absolutely unknown in school, in one week I was THE person. I wasn't comfortable with that at all, because I was very shy. And then, all of a sudden, I felt like I was expected to be something else that I wasn't prepared for, nor sure if I wanted to be.
>
> After doing record hops, I did this huge show, the Alan Freed revue at the Paramount Theatre in Brooklyn [actually *Alan Freed's Easter Jubilee of Stars* in late March through early April 1956]. Everybody who had a record was on that show. I'm standing there and I'm watching everybody: the Platters, the Teenagers, the Flamingos, the Cleftones . . . [and Ruth's fellow Old Town act the Royaltones, among others]. Alan Freed goes out and says: "And now, if you've been listening to the radio show, I know you can't wait to hear this young lady. Here's Little Ruthie McFadden!" I'm standing there [*laughs*], and there are all these lights, and the band is playing. Someone had to come and push me out. I went out and I stood absolutely straight and [sang] "Hut hah, darling, listen

to the words . . ." I couldn't wait until that was over.[20] The show was for ten days, and I guess by the fourth or fifth day I'd gotten pretty comfortable with it. By the end of the run, I'd really started to enjoy it.

Throughout 1956, the Old Town (and Paradise) releases were averaging only one per month, indicating that the label was still a grassroots operation. Most of the recordings were being cut at Bell Sound studios with engineer Al Weintraub. Already several of the new singles were featuring scorching sax solos, as popularized on the Chords' "Sh-Boom" and the Teenagers' "Why Do Fools Fall in Love." But in truth, Hy and Sam Weiss were not embracing rock 'n' roll in the same hip way that Ahmet Ertegun and Jerry Wexler were doing over at Atlantic.

There was a danger, too, of the Weiss brothers becoming ensnared in the menacing Morris Levy organization, which, according to street rumors, was already controlling Alan Freed. Under the headline "Levy-Kahl Expansion," *Billboard* reported on October 6, 1956, that "the Morris Levy–Phil Kahl interests continued to expand last week when the combine purchased a half interest in Maureen Music, a Broadcast Music, Inc. affiliate. Maureen is an adjunct of the Old Town record operation owned by Hy and Sam Weiss. Simultaneously, the Weiss brothers handed local distribution of their disks to Tico Distributing, adding to the complexity of the Levy-Kahl network."[21]

How Hy and Sam Weiss extracted themselves from Morris Levy's grasp is not known, but escape they did, with Maureen Music in tow. Still, the three parties were to remain on very good terms. It was during this rocking and rolling period that Levy snared George Goldner's Tico-Rama-Gee operations and was getting ready to spin Roulette Records into the independent arena.[22]

Old Town still did not have a solitary national chart entrant. Was there a payola problem, or was the material not good enough? The net was cast wider with a dedicated "pop" series (including folksinger Oscar Brand), but the deadlock should have been broken by the Solitaires' "Walking Along." Released in January 1957, this cheerful romp is viewed in New York as a doo-wop classic but did not make the R&B lists, let alone the Top 100. In late 1958, at the tail end of the cover version era, the Diamonds (Mercury) took the song into the Top 30. Immediately, Hy Weiss licensed the Solitaires' original to buddies Leonard and Phil Chess for national distribution on their Argo label, but yet again the record failed to engage the attentions of the chart compilers.

Milton Love, still lead singer of the Solitaires into the new millennium, said that he was recruited to give the group a more rhythmic approach in contrast to the stereotypical ballad style that had dominated their first recordings. Love claimed to have written the upbeat "Walking Along" and never understood how the Hy Weiss–Winston Willis combination ended up as the accredited writers. In fact, the first pressing of the record carried credits to "Love-Willis-Baylor-Owens-Gaston" (the Solitaires).[23] It would appear that Weiss, with Willis, arranged to buy out the other individuals' shares.

Of the "Walking Along" session, Milton Love said:

Yes, the foot stomps were by Hy and Sam; they were having big fun stomping their feet on the floor. It was an impromptu thing, and they left it on the record. Sam was the quiet one; Hy was the vocal person. Old Town was mainly Hy.

In the studio, he was a nervous wreck [*laughs*]. Running up and down, sometimes he would do twenty-two cuts. [If] we were getting tired, he would take what he'd like best from each of the tape cuts and put something together as far as the record is concerned. He'd encourage you as far as saying, "Let's get this music done," rather than, "You guys are great." He was aware of the clock, dollarwise. It was rush, rush, rush, rush, rush . . . he was a cheapskate. He had very good musicians, but I think we could have used a better quality type of music. I don't understand it, either, why "Walking Along" never made any charts.

If you weren't a group like Frankie Lymon and the Teenagers or the Platters, you got left on the wayside. I would have loved to have traveled the way these groups did, play the places that they played. We never got the chance due to the fact that Hy Weiss didn't have that distribution to put our name out there. Everything happened with the Solitaires on the eastern seaboard. We never went to Mississippi, Tennessee, Georgia, or the West Coast.

On the Charts

The Old Town output was low-key throughout the important rock 'n' roll year of 1957 due principally to the upheaval caused by a mutual partnership split between the Weiss brothers. In June, Sam Weiss set up Superior Record Sales Co. at 424 West Forty-ninth Street and Tenth Avenue. His heart was clearly more in the distribution game. Within a year, Sam would tout his firm as "New York's 'Superior' Record Distributor" with significant indie lines including Ace, Argo, Coed, End-Gone, Kent, and Vee-Jay along with Old Town.[24] Sam Weiss, a shrewd operator who was keenly aware of the radio promotion game and the jukebox market and more of a social climber, was to remain a major player in the New York game in the decades ahead through his Win Records Inc. one-stop business (where brother George Weiss was manager). Hy retained the record company alone but had Sam's valuable support as a distributor (who ensured Hy was paid) and as a confidant.

At long last, the Old Town imprint graced the national charts when "We Belong Together" by Robert (Carr) & Johnny (Mitchell) clawed its way to No. 32 pop and No. 12 R&B in the spring of 1958. It was a genuine sleeper, growing in sales all the time, and was to stay on the *Billboard* Top 100 chart for an impressive twenty-two weeks. Progress was not impeded by the tuneful melody being carefully cloned from the duo's earlier "You're Mine" or by the song being published by Figure Music, Alan Freed's company.

With Robert & Johnny on the national listings, Old Town Records had moved in May 1958 into 1697 Broadway, which also housed Herald-Ember Records. Herald's Doug Moody remembered that Hy would have his records pressed at the Silver-Park plant (affiliated with Herald) and would supply a set number of preprinted labels, thereby ensuring that there would be no production overruns. Usually, he would provide exactly one thousand labels, meaning that the initial press runs were for five hundred singles only.

The Weiss strategy was quite clear. If the Old Town singles inspired little or no reaction, even with the benefit of the celebrated clout of Alan Freed at WINS and Hoss Allen at WLAC, then the records would be dropped quietly. As Milton Love implied, Old Town's distribution was limited mainly to the East Coast. In effect, this was classic test marketing before investing in national promotion. Exclaimed Hy, "There were no returns! I had my records out only if they sold. I knew my business. My head tells me only to go with a record if it starts to go."

Record men Morty Craft and Roquel "Billy" Davis were quick to attest, by the way, that it was easy (and cheap) to produce records in those days with simple rhythm backing. If nothing happened, you would just move on to the next release in the hope of landing the big one.

In October 1958, Hy dribbled "So Fine" by the Fiestas into the marketplace. Costing just forty dollars to make, according to legend, the record took six months to pick up enough steam to pierce the Top 100, eventually climbing to No. 11 in a sixteen-week run (also making No. 3 R&B). Weiss attributed the overall strength of "So Fine" to the assist from the exceptional doo-wop flip side, "Last Night I Dreamed" (which *Cash Box* had reviewed as the "A" side while calling it, deliciously, an "ultra-lovely fish-beat romantic item").[25] The critical pushes for "So Fine" came from Old Town's Houston distributor, H. W. Daily, with an order for five thousand records, and from Hoss Allen. For constant plugs over Radio WLAC, Nashville, Hoss was offered a share of the publishing.

The champagne turned flat when an unwelcome letter arrived on Hy's desk from bandleader Johnny Otis and his manager Hal Zieger. It was claimed that the Fiestas' song (with credits to Hy Weiss and the group's manager, Jim Gribble) had plagiarized the copyright registered by Eldorado Music. "So Fine" had been recorded in 1955 on the West Coast by the Sheiks (featuring Jesse Belvin) for Federal, which promptly reissued the single after the Fiestas' version had charted. Though usually not a person to back down without a fight, Weiss was forced to settle in this instance. And Hoss Allen lost his publishing kickback.

It was a smart lawsuit directed against not only the infringing publisher, Maureen Music, but also Old Town Records, Superior Record Sales (Sam Weiss's distribution company), the Fiestas, and "various stores which marketed it." As a result of the inevitable capitulation by Maureen Music, the action against the other defendants was dropped. Included in the settlement was a nonrefundable advance of $4,500 against future royalties, while Old Town paid legal costs of $1,500 to Eldorado Music.[26] The Fiestas' lead, Tommy Bullock, insisted that none of the group nor anyone in the Old Town camp had ever heard the Sheiks' obscure record.[27] Weiss's final words on the subject: "Johnny Otis was afraid to walk the streets after that!"

To Hy's further dismay, the Fiestas' manager, Jim Gribble, probably in a huff, set up a rival deal with Laurie Records. This new label was headed by Philadelphia distributor Allen Sussel and Gene Schwartz, who had a background in music publishing. Gribble introduced the hit-making Mystics and the Passions to Laurie, which was already scoring with Dion and the Belmonts. The Fiestas remained with Old Town.

If Weiss was not cavorting around Manhattan and environs in a smart dark blue Cadillac, he was on the road with all the related attractions and distractions. The telephone was worked continually. Maintaining friendships with radio personalities everywhere was all-important, especially with Alan Freed, Mr. Blues, and Hoss Allen. Then there was the powerful black New York dee-jay lobby of Willie Bryant ("the Mayor of Harlem"), Douglas "Jocko" Henderson, Hal Jackson, Tommy Smalls (the second "Doctor Jive"), and Jack Walker (the "Pear-Shaped Talker").

Allegedly and rather tiresomely, Weiss was said to be the instigator of the fifty-dollar disc jockey handshake. It was an image-making accolade that fitted his record man persona, and whether true or not, he was content to let rumor translate into fact through the years. No doubt about it, though: Weiss was an ardent supporter of the *concept* of payola, declaring it was the greatest thing in the world. He would much prefer to give a disc jockey a lump sum as a payoff and tell him "to fuck himself" rather than waste time wining and dining "the schmuck" four days a week. Here was the "beautiful" system that gave every record released by an independent label a chance, albeit at a price. Like other record men, Hy Weiss managed to duck the payola firing squad without any harm.

Once the payola inquisition had begun, Henry Glover was forced out of King Records (with Ralph Bass) in an act of self-protection by Syd Nathan and immediately formed his Glover label in association with Old Town. The Weiss-Glover partnership had a minor No. 83 hit first time out in late 1959 with songwriter Titus Turner's "We Told You Not to Marry," an answer to Lloyd Price's "I'm Gonna Get Married."

A follow-up Titus Turner session was scheduled by Henry Glover with a catchy novelty tune, "Let the Little Girl Dance." A vocalist of limited range, Turner was having difficulty in getting an acceptable take despite the presence of stalwart session men Buddy Lucas (saxophone) and Mickey "Guitar" Baker, with the Miller Sisters as background singers. Longtime Old Town artist Billy Bland, a former stand-up singer with the Lionel Hampton and Buddy Johnson orchestras and a member of the Bees, was in the studio and picked up the song without any fuss. Titus Turner was dismissed from the session, only to see his grief compounded when the record became a national hit.

Billy Bland's prance with "Let the Little Girl Dance," with its Latin lilt, was typical of the Brill Building sounds of the time. It was a No. 7 hit in the spring of 1960 and No. 15 in England on London. "'Let the Little Girl Dance' was done in two takes," Bland recalled.

> I knew the song, but the other one [Titus Turner] couldn't feel it. I said, "Is this the way you do the song?" And they said, "Do it again, Billy; try it." So they got together

and set it up, pushed the buttons, [and] when they said, "One, two . . ." I went into it. Then they'd bring the girls in, then they'd take the girls away and make me sing again. And the boy would just stand there; Titus Turner would just stand there. When it was over he said, "I haven't did the record yet . . ."

Then I was in a carwash and this record come on the air, "Let the Little Girl Dance." I jumped on Hy Weiss and I said, "This is my record?" Hy said, "Yeah, sure, we have a contract ready." So I said, "If this is my record, I want a new Cadillac with this record." So they wrote a check out to me for $1,400, man.

Billy Bland was able to get spots on the popular telecasts, including *American Bandstand* and *The Clay Cole Show*. On one occasion, Bland was booked for Jocko Henderson's show out of Philadelphia, and his story illustrates how rampant and virulent payola still was:

I didn't like the TV shows because you didn't get paid. You do a show, you sign a check, and they keep it. I'm halfway down the stairs [at Jocko's] with a check for eight hundred dollars, then I'm waiting. They said, "The show is over. You're a nice kid, but now you gotta get out." I say, "This is it?" They said, "Yeah, what's wrong?" I said, "But I signed a check for eight hundred dollars." They said, "Don't worry about that. You got a new record coming out next month, right? We'll play the record. If we return the eight hundred dollars, you won't hear your record on the air. You got a choice: eight hundred dollars or play the record."

But Hy Weiss was like a father to me. I missed a lot of shows, and he would cover for me. Hey, I was young and stupid, man. I was making money, and money didn't mean nothin' to me, you know. But "Let the Little Girl Dance" was a very big story because I sounded white on the record and because the girls behind me had a white sound.

Blues guitarist Larry Dale recorded for Hy Weiss under the Glover Records banner. Prior to that, Dale had made several good records himself and played guitar on many sessions, including Champion Jack Dupree's classic drug-themed Atlantic LP *Blues from the Gutter*. Dale claimed plausibly to have accompanied Frankie Lymon and the Teenagers on "Why Do Fools Fall in Love," having been contracted to the session by saxophonist Jimmy Wright. The guitarist saw little glory or pride in participating in such a major record. "At that time you'd meet groups everywhere," he said. "To me the Teenagers were just another bunch of little hoodlums."[28] A very capable guitarist and underrated vocalist, Larry Dale performed gigs, weddings, and other social functions with Bob Gaddy and the House Rockers around the New York area. Gaddy, a tasteful blues pianist, enjoyed regular releases on Old Town of a consistently high standard. In 1960, folk blues artists Brownie McGhee and Sonny Terry made some of their last commercial recordings for the R&B market courtesy of Old Town. "They were the best," said Weiss, showing his genuine affinity for the blues, adding that with him "they weren't folked up!" Renowned gospel quartet the Fairfield Four had a single and album on Old Town through the Hoss Allen connection in Nashville.

Around 1960, Jimmy Gilbert, a native Frenchman, joined the Old Town staff to bring order to the office administration. He arrived from Cosnat Distributing, where he had been in charge of accounts under general manager Elliot Blaine. By then, Cosnat had expanded from its New York base to open branches in Cincinnati, Cleveland, Detroit, Newark, Philadelphia, and Pittsburgh. With this network, the firm was able to buy in bulk at a discount and push local hits that had not yet spread from city to city. In a 1960 advertisement in a *Billboard* directory, Cosnat described itself as "the fastest growing independent record distributor in the country." Jerry Blaine was pictured giving a presidential salute, looking for all the world like Commander in Chief Dwight "Ike" Eisenhower.[29]

Jimmy Gilbert had started at Cosnat two years earlier after impressing Jerry Blaine at a gambling junket in Puerto Rico, of all places. Gilbert remembered the gruff-speaking Blaine as a dapper, well-dressed man who could "light up any room"—just like Hy Weiss, in fact. While Gilbert was at Cosnat, Weiss telephoned him once to demand a check from the Cleveland branch. "But you haven't had any new releases lately," said Gilbert. "That doesn't matter," yelled Weiss jokingly. "Where's my money?"

The Brill Building scene and the oldies-but-goodies movement gave comforting respites to the New York indie labels reeling from the payola scandal. Sensing the doo-wop revival, Hy Weiss reissued Robert & Johnny's "We Belong Together," which bubbled under at No. 104 in early 1961. Any chance of the record breaking Hot 100 again was thwarted when Weiss found himself promoting what turned out to be Old Town's biggest record: "There's a Moon Out Tonight" by the Capris. He had picked up this failed 1958 master, on obscure Planet Records, for "two hundred to three hundred dollars."

In a fractious story, Times Square Records started selling a hundred copies per week of the original pressing during 1960. At this point, four aficionados associated with the record shop, led by Jerry Greene (later of Collectables Records) and Al Trommers, made a deal for the record's reissue on a new Lost Nite imprint. Word of the new action reached Sam Weiss at Superior distributors, prompting him to place an order for 10,000 copies. Unable to cover the pressing costs, the four young label owners had little choice but to hand over the record to Hy Weiss upon the recommendation of brother Sam. It needed a real record man to do the job.

Following such an assured start second time out, "There's a Moon Out Tonight" climbed to No. 3 in the first part of 1961, easily eclipsing a cover version by Dot's Pat Boone. Since Old Town's distributor network was focused toward the black market, the Capris' record made No. 11 R&B, regardless of the Queens group's Italian American background. Master ownership issues continued to rumble through the years, but Weiss boisterously defended his corner to retain a share, with Greene and Trommers, in what has become a doo-wop standard.[30]

Hy Weiss kept the tills ringing with the Edsels' "Rama Lama Ding Dong," another rescued 1958 "dead" master that became a No. 21 novelty hit as a one-off release on the Twin subsidiary in the summer of 1961. Once again, Sam was involved in the record's referral to Hy; indeed, the label was named after Sam's wife, Twinnie, a former Latin Quarter dancer. Then Larry Finnegan's jaunty "Dear One," an oddball pop release for Weiss, climbed to No. 11 in the spring of 1962. At the turn of 1963, the Earls, with lead vocalist Larry Chance, contributed another Old Town fixture with "Remember Then." Peaking at No. 24 pop, it caught the final throes of the doo-wop revival prior to the British Invasion.

Hy Weiss did not have the inclination or intuition to sign or mimic the English beat groups, even though at the time he had an overseas licensing relationship in London with EMI Records, home of the Beatles and the rest. Instead, he made a valiant attempt to enter the soul market, where Atlantic Records was already head and shoulders above the competition. Here was a real hustling scene for smaller labels, artists, writers, and producers alike, especially in the New York area.[31]

Hy Weiss: The Later Years

Showing where his musical heart really lay, Hy indulged in recording veteran blues and R&B stars Rosco Gordon, Buddy and Ella Johnson, and Tarheel Slim & Little Ann. But these artists were well and truly sidelined by the difficult market conditions that prevailed in the mid-1960s. The Johnsons, brother and sister, were the subject of a favorite if irreverent Weiss joke: "Ella tells me that she speaks to Buddy in heaven every day. I say to her, 'Well, that's good, but make sure he doesn't try to call collect.'"

At this time, Hymie Weiss pooled all his resources into Buddy Johnson's vocalist from the Savoy Ballroom days, the svelte-voiced bass-baritone heartthrob Arthur Prysock. It was a bold move that paid off. Five Prysock Old Town LPs all charted around the "100" mark in the 1963–65 period, while on the singles front the gorgeous ballad "It's Too Late, Baby Too Late" hit No. 56 in the summer of 1965. But with the winds of change blowing against the independent labels, Weiss realized that he had better find a big company for national distribution and promotion—and quick. He would chuckle at the "enormous" advance he elicited from MGM in the Arthur Prysock production deal, which included the sale of all the Old Town masters. For his part, Jerry Wexler avoided "a costly Prysockian mistake" when Hy advised his friend at Atlantic *not* to sign the ballad-singing nightclub star, whose style was becoming outmoded. Somehow, as only he could, Weiss was able to reclaim the Old Town masters from MGM for just five hundred dollars (excluding Arthur Prysock's recordings), according to him.

In 1970, Hy fell into bed temporarily with Atlantic, resulting in the release of the *Solid Gold Soul* album on the Cotillion subsidiary. From a misty recall, Jerry Wexler seemed to think that Atlantic did the deal more as a favor to an old friend rather than for any commercial reasons, perhaps as a "thank you" for the Prysock escape. Weiss always respected the Atlantic outfit: the partners, the records, the staff, and especially engineer Tommy Dowd.

During the early 1970s, Hy Weiss was taken on as a consultant for Stax Records. Despite his vast experience and personal friendship with Stax president Al Bell, he was unable to save the stricken Memphis label from its dark demise. Generally, the 1970s period, with its overwrought soul and disco productions, was a musical no-no for Weiss (although his brother did well with disco with the eponymous Sam Records and at Win Records Inc.).

Still, Hy held on doggedly to his masters and publishing assets, so much so that he almost missed the lucrative LP reissue market of the 1970s and 1980s. Thanks to the enthusiasm of researcher Bob Hyde and tape engineer Walter DeVenne, Old Town masters began appearing in 1985 on Murray Hill Records, a poorly distributed arm of a New York book publisher. In England, Ace Records made a more promising licensing breakthrough due to the dogged perseverance of consultant Ray Topping with director Roger Armstrong, both of whom impressed Weiss with their interest in the untapped blues masters as much as in the desirable doo-wop sides.

In 1996, Hy lost wife Roz, his pillar and strength. Within three years, he accepted a takeover offer for the Old Town masters and publishing from Music Sales of New York that made him, a poor kid from the Bronx, a millionaire. After retiring to Miami, Florida, he died in 2007 at the age of eighty-four. Fulsome obituaries appeared in such establishment newspapers as the *New York Times*, the *Boston Globe*, the *Los Angeles Times*, and London's *The Times* and *Daily Telegraph*. The old swashbuckling record man would have been tickled pink at this societal acceptance.

Happily, the Weiss tradition in the record industry was continuing through son Barry, who guided Jive Records through its spectacular international run at the start of the new century with Britney Spears, NSync, the Backstreet Boys, R. Kelly, and Justin Timberlake. In April 2008, Barry was promoted to chairman and chief executive officer of the BMG label group, in succession to none other than fabled Clive Davis. In turn, Sam Weiss's family was running Nervous Records, a rap and hip-hop label, in New York. Sam didn't want to discuss his Old Town days, explaining that "I don't want to be known as being associated with a label fifty years old."

Hy Weiss reveled in his art to the end, talking a huge game and never being shy to promote his label or himself. "I knew how to make my moves. We were strong on the East Coast; I was the boss!" he stated bluntly, without expecting or receiving any contradiction. He saw the record business as a game (a big gamble!) and never thought that it would represent his life's work.[32] Could Old Town Records have outgrown the one-man independent operation that it essentially was? Lazy at times by his own admission, Weiss acknowledged that he could have promoted certain records better. But he was never a corporate animal at heart. No, he had taken Old Town, as it was structured, to its limits and beyond.

Weiss understood the independent record business from the inside out. "I know where too many bodies are buried," he would say. And he probably did. He was constantly badgered to give the lowdown on Morris Levy, the toughest record man of all, but Hy always refused, saying quietly, "He was a good man." Then with a rasp he would add, "I know *why* they want to talk to me!" He wasn't going to sell out on his buddy Morris or any other industry figure. In any case, Hymie's conception of an interview was a quick-fire string of funny stories and one-liners with little historical analysis, followed by that whimsical smile. It was all a camouflage to protect the innocent and the guilty.

What cannot be denied is that throughout his long, unique career, he straddled and empathized with three distinct cultures: African American, Italian American, and his own. Larry Chance, of Old Town hit-makers the Earls, told me that "if Damon Runyon had known about Hy Weiss, he would have written one more book."[33] It would have been a best-seller, too. Despite the hubris of hustle and hype, the sounds of Old Town from the streets of New York City have stood the important test of time. Above all else, Hy Weiss never strayed from being Hy Weiss, independent record man.

13
CHAPTER

Mercury Rising and the Roulette Wheel

CAST OF CHARACTERS
Luigi Creatore, A&R man with Mercury, Roulette,
and RCA Victor (with Hugo Peretti as Hugo & Luigi)
Jean Bennett, Buck Ram's secretary, Personality
Productions
Shelby Singleton, Mercury Records vice president
also featuring Jerry Leiber and Mike Stoller,
independent record producers and record men;
and Morris Levy, Roulette Records

In the monochrome culture of the early 1950s, the better-managed pioneering independent labels were adding welcome color to the musical landscape because they had the energized rhythm and blues sector more or less to themselves. R&B music was evolving into a catchall term covering everything from raw gutbucket blues and cool after-hours sounds to booting sax-led band blasters, rhythmic novelties, slinky instrumentals, and melodic doo-wop ballads.

Attracted by annual sales spikes of up to 40 percent, new indie entrants were popping all the time. By 1953, there were around one hundred active labels, yet the market share for rhythm and blues was still relatively small at an estimated 5.7 percent of the total record business, according to perceptive *Billboard* reporter Bob Rolontz. In addition to pop music, the categories for classical, children's, and country were all bigger than R&B. Only jazz, Latin American, and international music lagged behind.[1]

Rolontz embellished his report by stating that an R&B hit "can go over the 300,000 mark, but such hits are most rare." Any record that exceeded 40,000 was considered a "hit," and one that touched 100,000 was a "big hit." However, "a so-so R&B record has a rough time selling over 1,000 platters," a poorer average than elsewhere. He concluded by observing that "the r.&b. field . . . remains alive, exciting and precarious."

Specifically, there were those conspicuous trends of R&B discs breaking into the main pop markets and of southern distributors seeking R&B product for white teen demand.[2] The industry at large, therefore, was starting to take notice of the way rhythm and blues music was developing in the hands of the independents. This monopoly-by-stealth situation could not prevail for long in a market that was preparing itself for explosive growth with the onset of rock 'n' roll (itself a loose amalgam of rhythm and blues, country and western, gospel, and pop music of all denominations). At the start of 1955, *Billboard*'s Bob Rolontz, again, highlighted the benefits of the predominant R&B trend when he wrote: "A lot of pop a.& r. men are thankful to the r.& b. field for many new songs, new artists, and new musical ideas and arrangements."[3]

"Rock 'n' roll's time had come," said Johnny Otis. "There was a tremendous campaign by the white establishment against the blacks when rock 'n' roll became big. They pointed to the effect of degenerate black lyrics on white youths. It was racism at heart. Not only Basie and Ellington but 'slum' bands like mine and Roy Milton['s] were playing ballrooms and drawing large crowds. Whites and blacks were rubbing shoulders together. This is what rankled."

Smelling the rock 'n' roll cash bonanza, the big corporations began reviewing their strategies with haste. With the exception of Capitol, the majors proceeded to organize or ramp up separate R&B divisions: RCA Victor with Groove, Columbia with OKeh, Decca with Coral and Brunswick, and Mercury with Wing. Mercury's vice president Art Talmadge, now A&R chief, summed up the prevailing mood by saying that Wing's musical policy was "anything with a beat."[4]

Were the independent label owners aware of this looming threat from the majors? King's Syd Nathan was, for one. While riding high with the 1954 crossover hit "Hearts of Stone" by the Charms, he implored his A&R staff to monitor the majors' R&B releases. Citing two different vocal group records on Capitol, he said that King should "stop the majors" by covering their breaking hits on back-to-back singles. "We do not have the resources of the major companies," admitted Nathan, "so we've got to get there in a Ford while they're trying to get there in a Cadillac."[5]

Regardless, the major labels began to prey on their independent brethren to head-hunt select name artists and record producers. For all their resources, the majors were missing out on two vital ingredients: the intuitive feel of the indie record men for the music and their inimitable way of doing business.

Jerry Leiber and Mike Stoller: Record Men
and Independent Record Producers

Among the first independent record producers the majors targeted were Jerry Leiber and Mike Stoller. Endlessly creative, this was the same young team that would concoct a potent cocktail of hip hits and smart songs that are the wittiest of the rock 'n' roll era. Both barely twenty-one years old, they endured an initial foray as record men with the Spark label out of Los Angeles in March 1954 in conjunction with their mentor Lester Sill and two other partners: Jack Levy and Stoller's father, Alvin. Sill was the former sales manager at Modern who would become the experienced hand driving the Duane Eddy phenomenon with producer/songwriter Lee Hazlewood and who would be behind Phil Spector's later rise to fame at Philles Records (Sill was the "Les" in Philles).

Spark Records was set up after Leiber and Stoller were angry at being "screwed out of our royalties" for Willie Mae Thornton's "Hound Dog" by Peacock's Don Robey.[6] By that November, after only eight releases, the Spark owners were approached for a masters buyout by Decca, which had plans for Leiber and Stoller to take up A&R positions with the major. This farsighted deal never materialized, much to Decca's detriment.[7]

Spark survived until the fall of 1955 but was unable to get distribution "past the Rockies." The label had one West Coast regional breakout, "Riot in Cell Block #9" by the Robins, before it handed over to Atlantic (through then West Coast–based Nesuhi Ertegun) a future No. 10 R&B hit in "Smokey Joe's Café" by the same group. Now it was all change. In the course of setting up a nonexclusive independent production pact with Atlantic, Leiber and Stoller instigated the formation of the Coasters from the nucleus of two defecting members of the Robins. This union would lead to those unforgettable national hits from 1957 through 1959 on the Atco subsidiary headed by "Searchin'" (No. 3), "Yakety Yak" (No. 1), and "Charlie Brown" (No. 2). Biggest of all for Leiber and Stoller was Elvis Presley, who recorded their eternal songs "Hound Dog" and "Jailhouse Rock," among quite a few others from their prolific pens.

At the end of 1957, Jerry Leiber and Mike Stoller, now twenty-four years old, moved to New York with sky-high reputations. On the back of the Presley connection, the duo landed a production deal with RCA Victor under the supervision of Steve Sholes. Their major label obligation was to make records with the indie sound. But the liaison was annulled amicably within a year after the producer-songwriters became becalmed in a sea of middle-of-the-road mediocrity. Nevertheless, the partners would be called the gold-dust twins after sparkling at Atlantic, Bigtop, and United Artists. To general surprise, including their own in hindsight, they took flight again into label ownership in 1964 with George Goldner at Red Bird in what is a full and eventful story in itself.

Songwriter Doc Pomus was among Leiber and Stoller's many admirers. "First of all, they were real geniuses," he said. "I mean, they put comedic ideas into pop songs, and in that genre I thought they were phenomenal. Also, they were very helpful to me as songwriters; they gave me a lot of hints, and they were great collaborators. When we worked with them on records, they were always wonderful because Jerry and Mike always structured the arrangements for the arrangers as well. A lot of arrangers took complete credit. But I would sit with them sometimes while they were telling the arranger what to write for the horn parts, what to write for the rhythm section. They were two of the greats that I've encountered and, not only that, wonderful, talented guys."

Pomus gave a glimpse of the camaraderie that existed in the New York music community at the time in the course of relating his own adventures in the song royalty minefield. "I used to give away percentages on songs," he admitted, "especially to arrangers. You'd always do that with songs 'cause it's like one poem to a poet; it's [just] one song to a songwriter. So I've given away pieces of songs down the line. I sometimes lived to regret it, you know? But, then again, there is the generosity of other songwriters. For instance, I have a third of 'Young Blood' [by the Coasters]. I don't think I really wrote a third of that song; I think that Jerry and Mike probably wrote three-quarters of the song. I had maybe a concept; that's all I had. They were so generous, but that was the way we all were toward each other."

By gradually assuming creative control, the independent record-producing brigade was eroding the all-consuming power of the traditional A&R men. With the old-time cliques breaking down, there were opportunities afresh for artists, composers, musicians, and publishers alike. Naturally, in this sea change, the new freelancers would try to negotiate a piece of the master royalty action and attempt to copyright the songs for their own music publishing companies as extra income streams. Lessons were being learned quickly across the industry.

Luigi Creatore: Mercury Records

Hugo Peretti and Luigi Creatore followed Jerry Leiber and Mike Stoller into independent production roles at RCA Victor after treading the indie label path. Both sets of production teams had a commercial attitude, but Hugo & Luigi (as they were known professionally) had a more pop-oriented, hit-or-nothing approach. The Peretti and Creatore story embraced the children's records market, a stint with Mercury at the peak of the cover version era, the launch of Roulette, tenure at RCA Victor, and more.

While enlisted in the navy, Luigi Creatore witnessed firsthand the horrors of the Japanese attack on Pearl Harbor in 1941. "It was a terrible, terrible experience, but that was war, you know," he said, quietly. Back in New York, he was to see the record industry unfurl and prosper from the mid-1940s on.

Some sixty years later, in 2004, Luigi Creatore was living a very comfortable existence in Boca Raton, Florida, with his wife, Joyce, a one-time member of the Chordettes. As a sprightly eighty-two-year-old, he was getting ready to pitch a new Broadway show to investors. During his long recording career, he worked inseparably with his cousin, Hugo Peretti. "We were always known as Hugo and Luigi," said Creatore.

Most people didn't know our last names in the business. To this day, I can't read a lead sheet, can't read music, nothing to do with music. I do lyrics, but I hear music in my head. I produced records with Hugo, who was a consummate musician and conductor and arranger. He was my cousin, but he was my partner, more important.

I was born in New York in 1921. There's a picture on my wall of a symphonic band that my father brought over from Naples, Italy, in 1912. You can see the name "Creatore," and that band got rave reviews. They traveled the whole country and became a rival of John Philip Sousa with that group. My father, Giuseppe, was known as The Great Creatore; he became very famous, very wealthy. However, by the time I was born and started to grow up, all . . . changed because the Great Depression came in, and of course nobody was hiring a fifty-piece band, a symphonic band especially.[8] So my formative years from around eleven years old until I joined the navy was spent at Hell's Kitchen in New York, which is the west side of New York above Forty-second and below Fifty-ninth. There were lots of Italians, Irish, Greeks, but not so many blacks, because blacks were pretty much in Harlem then. It was a rough, rough neighborhood—the name will give you an idea!

After the war, Luigi was writing short stories, poems, a novel, and speeches at the United Nations, including a tour de force for Eleanor Roosevelt that began: "There is a child on the doorstep of the world . . ." "She loved it," he said. "I was a kid, but I was mingling and doing good things." On the record front, Luigi was impressed by Nat "King" Cole's "Nature Boy," a massive hit for Capitol in 1948. Peretti and Creatore gained experience in the music business by writing advertising jingles and making children's records for Harry LaPidus's Peter Pan label. "He had no intention of paying royalties; he paid us a fee, and then you're gone," said Creatore. Hugo had already been involved with the Mayfair children's label with Herb Plattner in 1947.

Through the Peter Pan and Mayfair recordings, Hugo and Luigi came to the attention of Mercury's Irving Green, who invited the partners to produce children's recordings for the Chicago label. Now they had a toehold in the Mercury organization. "Mercury had a small office in New York on Broadway around Fifty-second over a car salesroom," recalled Luigi, "not any fancy stuff. He said, 'You can continue to do any work you want with the jingles or the children's records. I've given you the office, I'll be back and forth, maybe we'll come up with something.' We said, 'Okay, great.'"

Before long, the Mercury president had fired the incumbent A&R director, Richard Hayman. Remembered Creatore, "Then Irving Green said, 'Why don't you take that job?' We made a couple of records and they didn't make it, but he knew we could make pop records as opposed to children's records. So he said, 'I'll give you $75 a week each . . . Jesus to God, I got to pay two of you. That's $150!'"

At Mercury, Hugo and Luigi were treading the same A&R trail blazed by Mitch Miller. Said Creatore, "It was Mitch, followed by a chubby guy who went to RCA, Joe Carlton. Then came Richard Hayman, who was a good arranger, good musician, but he wasn't making hit records. Mitch was probably the top A&R man. He was a producer, but we didn't call them that then; he had his pulse on what the public would buy, very commercial. And I think we were commercial, too. Because to a lot of us, when you lean back, there is something artistic in our business, and that's fine, but it was and is a business. You know, you don't make records to sit back and enjoy them yourself. As we used to say, 'What's a good record? A record that sells!' That's a good record [*laughs*]. If it doesn't sell, I don't care how much you admired it; it's not a good record. So that was our philosophy."

The new Mercury A&R team took up its duties at the beginning of 1954 and had a dream start when "The Little Shoemaker" by the Gaylords, with one chorus sung in Italian, shot to the top of the pop charts during that summer. "That had the optimum number of takes [for us as producers] that I remember distinctly," said Creatore. "They couldn't get [the words] out of their mouths, and we did nineteen takes just to get through. The first one we finished we said, 'That's it!'"

The producers consolidated this success by covering current R&B hits, a field in which Mercury was the leader, along with Dot. "Oh yes, this was pre–rock 'n' roll," said Creatore.

> You can tell by the tunes. It was the same year out of Chicago that the Crew-Cuts did "Sh-Boom" [a cover of the Chords' original]. So Mercury had two big records. The next person we did was "Her Nibs," Georgia Gibbs. A lot of artists have managers; they come in and the artists are just nice. The manager demands, negotiates. [But] Georgia took care of herself! She was brought up with big bands, did the road and the buses. She was tough and with language to match, but a good singer. Before we got her, her big hit was "Kiss of Fire" [No. 1, 1952].
>
>   So there was a thing called "Tweedlee Dee"; it was a black record by LaVern Baker [on Atlantic]. So we said to Georgia, "We want to cover this record." She said, "Well, I don't sing like that." I said, "Yeah, you can sing like that, you do rhythm stuff, you can do this. That's what we want to do, we're in the business, we're in the A&R." So she left in a huff, and we called Art Talmadge, our boss in Chicago. The next thing we know, she calls [and] she says, "I was told to get my ass up there and do whatever you say." Much against her will, she made "Tweedlee Dee" [as "Tweedle Dee"] and stormed out of the studio. That was the end of that. Out comes the record, and in two weeks it was up the charts [hitting No. 2, early 1955], and she came by and said, "I knew it was a hit, sweetie" [*laughs*].[9]

How did Creatore view the cover version controversy at the time?

I wasn't aware so much of Fats Domino versus Pat Boone. It was just that if there was a record breaking (and it didn't have to be a black record, it could be any record by an unknown), you could cover it with a name. And these black records, as they started making it, you knew there was going to be a barrier for them. So if you make it with a white act, the white stations will take it because they knew that there was a record making it. But they weren't going to play it [by the black artist].

  Of course, Mercury had very good distribution, and we immediately got to know jockeys. We were on the phone to them; we went on road trips to promote the acts.

We didn't stay in the studio all the time; we were out: active. Those jockeys always came into New York, and then you'd take them out to dinner, maybe pick up their hotel tab if Mercury approved. You got a relationship.

Both cover version smashes by the Crew-Cuts and Georgia Gibbs enjoyed enormous jukebox sales (and plays) in the white areas.

Hugo Peretti and Luigi Creatore recorded "Her Nibs" again for the follow-up to "Tweedle Dee," and this time "Dance with Me Henry" made No. 1 in May 1955. It was a cover of "poor thing" Etta James's No. 1 R&B original, which was anemically titled "The Wallflower" (Modern). "But it's business; if there's a path, you follow," said Creatore. "So rock 'n' roll was coming in right at that time of those Georgia Gibbs records. I remember they had articles about rock 'n' roll, and the magazines would call up and ask, 'What do you think of this rock 'n' roll thing?' I told somebody on *Billboard*, 'Well, it's coming in, but it'll go out,' and of course it didn't [*laughs*]. There was no panic; rather there was a lot of talk: 'As soon as this is over, we'll get back.' But then, of course, the pop and the rock 'n' roll coexisted because a pretty tune well done, and appealingly done, by a good artist is always going to make it."

With the disc jockeys and general public becoming more attuned to the big beat, there was a growing call for the original versions by the creators and not the cover versions by the copyists. The independent distributors, especially, were happy at this development, since this meant more sales outlets for their indie label lines.

The "divine" Sarah Vaughan was far removed from this rock 'n' roll "nonsense" but represented a big test for Hugo and Luigi. "There was this guy Bob Shad, another A&R man," said Luigi Creatore; "he just did jazz. Bobby Shad was doing her for jazz, and he said, 'I hear you're gonna do Sarah for a pop thing.' I said, 'Yeah.' So he said, 'You know, she's *impossible.* If you're starting to look for material for her, you'd better have ninety pieces of material because she comes in . . . she's a wonderful musician, she sits at the piano, *da da*, and she says, 'No, no, no!' I go crazy trying to find material for her.' So I said, 'Okay, thanks for the tip.' On the next day when Sarah Vaughan came into the office, Hugo and I took a gamble. I told her, 'Listen, we've been looking and looking for songs; there's just crap out there.' She says, 'I know; it's terrible.' I said, 'Yeah, we couldn't even find four songs, we only found *two.*'"

And so "Make Yourself Comfortable," written by master songsmith George David Weiss, was a No. 6 hit at the turn of 1955. Hugo and Luigi had further hits by Sarah Vaughan with top Broadway show tunes "Whatever Lola Wants" and "Mr. Wonderful." "We were doing records all the time," said Creatore. "We did a couple of children's things with Patti Page, too; we had a nice relationship with her. Also we did Rusty Draper records, but the main ones for Mercury were the Gaylords, Sarah Vaughan, and Georgia Gibbs."

Even with these big hits on their resume, Hugo and Luigi were still receiving the same weekly retainer. "So at one time we got on a train and went to Chicago," recalled Creatore.

We were getting the $75 a week each, so Irving Green said, "Okay, I'm gonna give you $125 each, but I don't want to hear anymore; that's it." We said, "We've got three things in the Top 10," and he says, "That's what I pay you to do. If you don't do it, I'm gonna fire you." So we came back. I remember sitting in the office, and I said to Hugo, "You know, we're making these hit records, there's a lot of money involved, and we're not getting any of it. They're screwing us!" And he said, "Let them screw us for another six months. We're going to be very big in this business."

So we stayed for a while; we were doing great. Then our names started to get around. The publishers would come up to the office, and we had two desks. We had a little sign saying "Hugo" on one and "Luigi" on the other so they would know [who was who]. And it started to get around, "We're going up to see Hugo and Luigi." So we got a reputation with our first names in the industry out of New York and L.A.: It was Hugo & Luigi!

Jeanie Bennett: Publicist for Buck Ram and the Platters

If Brylcreemed Elvis Presley was the early face of rock 'n' roll, so was kiss-curled Bill Haley, until his birth certificate let him down in an increasingly teen-oriented business. It wasn't all rebels with a cause. The Platters were true rock 'n' roll flag wavers but with a smooth showbiz panache that harked back to the pioneering days (and professionalism) of the Ink Spots and the Mills Brothers. Under the wise guidance of Buck Ram, the Platters fueled the dreams of teenage vocal groups everywhere while stoking up the temperature at Mercury Records.

The Platters' breakthrough Mercury record was "Only You (and You Alone)." The song had been produced nondescriptly in 1954 by Ralph Bass for Syd Nathan's Federal label but, quite rightly, was not deemed to be worthy of release at the time. Buck Ram rerecorded his composition majestically for Mercury as a rock-a-ballad and transformed "Only You" into one of the most recognizable anthems of the rock 'n' roll era as it made No. 1 R&B in late 1955 (but only No. 5 pop as an early crossover hit). However, "The Great Pretender" was the perfect follow-up and became a dual market No. 1, enhanced by West Coast bandleader Ernie Freeman's evocative and much-copied piano triplets.

Much credit for the running up of "Only You" to hit status was due to the hard promotional work of Jeanie Bennett, Buck Ram's bubbly head of public relations and management. In her later years known as simply Jean, she continued to send out on tour Buck Ram's Platters from her Las Vegas base. As well, she administered the masters of Buck Ram's Antler Records.

"I met Buck around 1953 after I had been in California for a while," said Bennett.

My husband and I moved from Missouri. Mainly we moved out there because I wanted to try to get into the music business. I had been working in an office as a bookkeeper, typist, stenographer, all that stuff. But I won a contest of local singers to do Rosie, the lead role in a musical play, *Up in Central Park*. That started off my musical career.

So I started working for Buck. He had Personality Productions at that time, but he didn't have a secretary. He was mainly finding young artists and a few country artists that he took on . . . [and] helped with recording and so forth. Prior to that, of course, he had a musical career up in the East because he graduated from college in Chicago. He was also a sax player and worked his way through college playing in various bands. He became a lawyer because his mother wanted him to, but he never had any intention of practicing. But it sure did come in handy when he began to handle other artists and we got entrenched with all the battles with the people imitating groups that were making it.

Buck played and arranged in New York; he arranged for Count Basie. He worked for a publisher for quite a long while, and he would make out arrangements of new songs coming in. Then he'd take them around to the various orchestra leaders and try to sell them on the songs. He was a song plugger at first, and then later on he did travel with the Dorsey Brothers and Earle Warren, who was [a] tremendous sax player. They would go on these winter dates with the open touring cars. His first management assignment was when he signed the Three Suns and he wrote "Twilight Time." That was one of his first conquests as far as becoming a songwriter [in 1944].[10] Buck wrote "I'll Be Home for Christmas" [for Bing Crosby] and a number of other songs that went pretty well.

Buck Ram, therefore, was a well-seasoned music veteran from the big band era when he signed the Platters in late 1953. "Around that time we had the Penguins, the Flairs, and the Platters that he was working with," said Jean Bennett.

Buck had tried to record "Only You" on Federal, and it turned out that [Platters members] Zola [Taylor] was sick and Tony [Williams] was out of sorts, and so it went off terrible. So he said, "Oh, forget it, erase that, today is not the day for this song."

But Federal released that darn thing after it became a hit on Mercury. Buck had no intention of ever releasing that terrible version, because it didn't come off. Some of the Federal and Mercury distributors were selling it side-by-side. I can imagine those people, after hearing constant play on the jukebox of the right version, and then picking that up in the wrong place and putting it on their record player. They must have had heart failure!

Syd Nathan was the owner of Federal, but we never had any really close contact with him. It was mainly through Ralph Bass. Syd was back east, and we were in California. We heard some fabulous stories. Some guys came in one night and wanted him to put this kid's record out and press it and said they would take care of the sales and not to worry about it. So Syd said okay and pressed it up and distributed it and everything. Then when it came to royalty time, he wrote that there was no royalties. Well, they had bought tons of the darn things and put them on their jukeboxes because they were big jukebox operators. And boy, were they furious when he told them this. They came into his office that night, and they just wrecked the place. They told him, "You'd better straighten out your royalties statements from here on in and give us an honest account, or we're going to do the same thing to *you*." He was shaking in his boots [*laughs*].

Buck liked Ralph Bass; he was a nice hipster guy, but he was strictly for the rhythm tunes. David Lynch was doing most of the leads on the rhythm songs before Tony Williams. Ralph wasn't interested in the ballads, so Buck was kind of disappointed in that. Then Mercury wanted the Penguins, who had just scored with "Earth Angel

(Will You Be Mine)" on Dootone [No. 8 pop, No. 1 R&B, early 1955], thanks to a big promo push from distributor Sid Talmadge at Record Merchandising Co., Los Angeles. Buck said, "On one condition: you have to take the Platters. I want the Platters on the Mercury label." We finally got "Only You" recorded and released on Mercury.

We liked Irving Green very much; Irving was terrific. Art Talmadge was a little bit of a stuffed shirt and wanted to get into the act with the Platters. So he and Buck had some clashes. Art and Irving Green got along fine, but Green vetoed him when he wanted to: Green was the president. Art made several suggestions that he thought we ought to record something besides just the ballads. Green finally told him, "Look, Buck Ram is in charge of the Platters, and he can record anything he wants to as long as he's making gold records for the company." Art was dying to get in there.

Bobby Shad wanted to be involved, oh definitely. He was the very first one to come after Buck; he was out to do the sessions and everything. Then Bobby went behind Buck's back and was trying to approach Tony Williams as well. He was a crafty one, but Buck was always one step ahead of him. Bobby said, "Buck, we've got to get together." You could tell Buck was so ticked off about it. Joe Glaser, our booking agent, put a stop to that. Their offices were in the same building, so all he had to do was take an elevator and go up to his office. Joe asked Bobby how many fingers he had. "Ten." "And you want keep 'em? I hear you're trying to take over Buck's boy, Tony Williams. Leave him alone!"

"Only You" was out quite a while before it became a hit. My husband, Ben, wanted to go back to Detroit to visit his parents during a vacation time. By the time I got in Detroit, it was a dead issue. The promo man hadn't done his work at all and was on vacation. I told the distributor [that] this record can be a hit because we were starting to get some reaction in Seattle. Well, I was pretty down, but I thought, "I'm gonna stop in Cleveland to see what happens." When I told them I was [there] to promote "Only You" by the Platters, why, they rolled out the red carpet for me, because it had been picked up by several of the dee-jays there. And they liked that gimmick [Tony Williams's *uh-oh* vocal phrase]. I really got the royal treatment for the first time.

Cleveland, Ohio, was known for making the most hits, because they had a very strong collection of top dee-jays there. Bill Randle was one, and, of course, Alan Freed had been there, but he had just made his move into New York. Radio station WERE Cleveland was a very big station, and every one of the stations were playing that record, too. I called up Buck and said, "We've got us a hit!" And he said, "Well, I've got the same old news from Seattle; Bob Salter is just crazy about it, too. We've got two cities now that we know, and it should be enough to kick it off." And it did.

"Only You" really fitted well on the popular stations; the scene wasn't integrated then. But Mercury almost threw a monkey wrench in the whole thing by putting it on a purple label, which was for the black artists. We found out about it right at the beginning. There was a big convention in Chicago, and they really proudly announced they had put it on the purple label. Buck just hit the ceiling. He said, "How dare you do that without even consulting me? The white stations will boycott it! The Platters will get black radio play, but they won't get pop play. This is a pop record as well as R&B." There was *Billboard, Cash Box*, dee-jays, and people there, and they all unanimously agreed with Buck that night. We were really grateful that it came up the way it did, because right away Mercury dumped the purple label and put everything out on the black popular label.[11]

Alan Freed tipped off Mercury Records about the Hilltoppers, who had recorded "Only You" [Dot]. He said, "You'd better get off your cans and get that thing promoted, I mean PDQ, or you're gonna lose it to a white group." And they really went to work. Well, it was a good song.

The Hilltoppers' creditable cover version also made Top 10, further benefiting Buck Ram as songwriter.

After "The Great Pretender," the Platters had another No. 1 with "My Prayer" in August 1956. With this extraordinary success for Mercury and for his own organization, Buck Ram opened up a New York office in 1957. "We were given quarters by Ralph Peer, the big publisher," said Jean Bennett.

Ralph had a big office up there in the Brill Building, and Buck had signed with him on his publishing. That's when things really started happening, because Ralph Peer was a millionaire, and he knew the music business. He traveled all over the world picking up copyrights for as little as twenty-five cents apiece, and he knew how to make money with music. He had signed so many foreign countries over as part of his organization. So between Ralph Peer and the fact that the Platters were taking over, everything began to happen. Everything just fell in place.

The Platters were attractive. There were either all-girl groups or all-guy groups, so they were the first to have this cute little girl, Zola Taylor; she was actually about fifteen years old when we first met her. She was foxy when she got her confidence. There were five of them, they were right in their prime as far as their youth was concerned, and it just looked really, really good. Tony's voice was fresh. . . . They held their liquor pretty good for about the first four to five years, [but] after that, it was nip and tuck all the way.

In New York, Jeanie Bennett started a promotional newsletter. "For some reason or other, the music business was filled with pluggers at that time," she said,

different songs, different artists, different this and that. So I got the idea of *The Personality Plugger* [from] Buck's name of Personality Productions. We ran it on a mimeograph; we addressed hundreds and hundreds, licked stamps, to get it out. There wasn't a whole lot of ways of communicating other than that in those days. About every other week I'd put out a new one.

I began to get a lot of response from the disc jockeys; they'd be writing me cards and letters. It really grew. Then when I'd go on [the road], I would never go to a radio station when I didn't give them the bright yellow-and-green *Personality Plugger* for the latest news on the artists that we were plugging. It was a great time because that was the time of the disc jockey, and they would make hits for you right and left if they chose.

I had good connections with Alan Freed and Dick Clark. Dick and I were very close when he had his big show [*The Dick Clark Show*] in New York City on Saturday nights. There was no trouble with the Platters being a black group. They were always class; they were more of a pop group than R&B, really, especially with the type of songs that Buck chose for them, which put them head and shoulders over most of the rock 'n' roll stuff. Dick Clark was happy to have them. They looked good.

Oh yeah, we did the Alan Freed rock 'n' roll movies. The Platters got a chance to do several numbers in those two or three movies that were exhibited around the world, too. As I say, for bookings we had Joe Glaser, ABC. Buck used to tease Joe unmercifully that the Platters were bigger than Louis Armstrong! There was nobody bigger and better in Joe's mind than Louis Armstrong [*laughs*]. He played fair with us; we were with him a long, long time. He was rough and rugged and everything, but by golly, when he was for you, he was for you 100 percent.

As a measure of the Platters' success, a fall 1957 report in *Variety* noted that Joe Glaser was negotiating a five-month European tour booking at "$15,000 weekly plus percentage." No wonder the Platters were the role models and envy of vocal groups everywhere.[12]

"Mercury assigned a number of great arrangers to Buck," said Jean Bennett. "There was Hal Mooney; he did one of the albums. But David Carroll was Buck's favorite. David had that beautiful way of arranging with strings. Mercury didn't spare any expense on their sessions. In fact, we recorded several times over in Paris; Irv Green and David Carroll both came over. That was 'Smoke Gets in Your Eyes' [No. 1, January 1959]."

The Platters' eponymous first album reached No. 7 on the *Billboard* LP chart in 1956, making it one of the first rock 'n' roll LP hits—and by a black act, too. With the album market gaining strength, the group had an even bigger smash in 1960 with *The Encore of Golden Hits* LP, which was on the charts for more than three years. "By this time, the Platters had more than enough to keep going with the albums," said Bennett. "Mercury didn't stint us; they kept things flowing. [With] all the traveling we did, and all the different countries, we built up a tremendous following that very few U.S. artists had."

Before long, the rigors of the road had torn apart the original lineup. The Platters' brand name, however, was far too strong and valuable to be lost among sex scandals and a haze of booze (bass singer Herb Reed excepted, said Jean Bennett). Replacement members would be groomed as and when necessary.

Meanwhile, Buck Ram had set up the independent Antler label in 1956. "He had a lot of young artists that were coming to him," said Bennett. "He was always trying to help them; he was always recording. It wasn't easy, but at least we made enough noise that we got attention for our stable of artists, including Johnny Olenn, Benny Joy, and the Teen Queens. They were artists that he couldn't get to bite on the big labels, so he put them out on our own label. Walt Maguire of London Records, nice guy, he got us the 'Foot Stomping' hit by the Flares [No. 25 on Felsted, a London subsidiary, 1961]. We were hoping to do more, but it didn't come off quite, because London was a pretty staid label. But we got good distribution overseas."

In 1966, Buck Ram had a final fling with the Platters at Musicor Records. This New York label was headed by Art Talmadge, who had quit Mercury in the summer of 1960 due to "policy differences" with Irving Green and moved to United Artists Records as vice president before migrating easily to president. United Artists distributed the early

Musicor hits by Gene Pitney. "Musicor was Art Talmadge's label; that was the Platters' connection," said Jean Bennett. "He tried to take me from Buck as his secretary, but I told him, 'I don't take dictation, I give it!'"[13]

In assessing Buck Ram's qualities, Bennett said, "Buck's secret was that he was consistent. Music was his life. He really loved to write; he was always thinking of ideas for songs. He loved talent, he could spot talent a mile off, and he was very good at developing talent. Oh yes, he liked rock 'n' roll. It's an era that's gone."

Jeanie Bennett's job was to make friends with everybody in the business, whatever their persuasion, and Morris Levy was no exception. "I didn't know him from Adam," she said,

> but I'd been hearing a lot about him. I went up to his apartment one night—oh man, what an apartment that was! It was in the heart of Manhattan. It was beautiful . . . and he had a Japanese houseboy. Morris was very nice, and he gave me a martini so big I could have taken a bath in it. He was showing us around the apartment. He opened up his closet, and it was just suits upon suits upon suits.

> He came to see the Platters on one of their first debuts in Brooklyn, a nice big dinner nightclub, and he sat there at our table to watch the Platters. After they came on and he saw them, he took out a roll of bills that would choke a horse and threw it on the table. He told Buck, "That's for that girl's contract"; he wanted Zola's contract. Buck tossed it back to him and said, "Uh-uh, she belongs to the Platters. I have no intention of taking her away from the Platters." We were aware of Morris's reputation. Buck never was scared of anybody, and I wasn't very much, either, not as long as he was around anyway [laughs].

Hugo and Luigi: Roulette Records

In late 1956, Moishe "Morris" Levy was planning the start-up of Roulette Records. Still only twenty-nine years of age, he had been rapidly accumulating music-based assets. Soon he was being dubbed "The Music Octopus" by *Variety* magazine on account of his expanding, tentacle-like empire.[14] Some say that Levy's rise was rooted in the early control of Alan Freed in New York through a circuitous route that included Tommy Vastola's appointment as Freed's manager in October 1955.[15] Although Morris Levy was not a music man as such, he would have been alerted by Freed to the opportunities that rock 'n' roll offered. Moreover, Levy became aware of the rewards from music publishing through the large performance royalty collections paid by his nightclubs to ASCAP, in particular.

Levy's most famous nightclub was Birdland, located at 1678 Broadway (and Fifty-second Street) and immortalized in blind jazz pianist George Shearing's signature tune, "Lullaby of Birdland." "Oscar Goodstein really ran the place," said George Avakian, of Columbia Records. "Levy made money for the club, not the musicians. Morris's brother Irving was shot and killed in the club by mistake; the killers thought they were nailing Morris. He was best at his forte, strong-arming artists to work cheap—like Count Basie, who borrowed money from him and ended up working many weeks a year at Birdland for peanuts." Basie recorded for Roulette, as did other high profile jazz acts Pearl Bailey, Woody Herman, Sonny Stitt, and many more. Jazz was Levy's favorite music, not rock 'n' roll.[16]

Levy was rising meteorically in the music industry through strength of personality, canny vision, brilliant deal-making, and, it must be said, his virulent business approach. Reputed to be associated with the Mafia underworld through the Genovese crime family via childhood friend Vincent "The Chin" Gigante, Morris Levy was a control freak renowned for crushing the little guy. He didn't know where to stop and often would refuse to settle debts for the sheer hell of it, according to Tommy Vastola.

Then Levy made an inspired move for brand-new Roulette Records by landing the A&R services of Hugo Peretti and Luigi Creatore. "When we left Mercury, we got a call . . . [from] Morris Levy," said Creatore.

> He had songs that he wanted to submit for Sarah Vaughan, which we didn't want. He came up one day and said, "Look, when you guys are tired of being here, . . . not making any money, I'll back you for a record company." So we didn't pay any attention, because we had the chart action, too. Now after a while, we were sitting there and not doing what we wanted to do. I said to Hugo, "What about this guy Morris Levy?" He said, "I don't know about him; Morris has a reputation as kind of connected, you know, the hoodlums. I don't know about that." I said, "There's a lot of crap: people, rumors, and stuff. The guy is a guy; let's talk to him."
>
> So we talked to him, and he said, "Look, why don't you come over?" He had a label [Gee] with George Goldner, and Frankie Lymon [and the Teenagers] had a big hit right around then, "Why Do Fools Fall in Love." And that was '56. So he said, "I'll make a label for you, and we'll split it fifty-fifty. You get 50 percent. I'll take care of all the investment; I'll put up the money." We put up some money, too, very little. He said, "We have distribution, I'll give you an office—let's go!" So we went over, and we started, and we had nothing.

If Roulette's name implied the label was a huge gamble, that was not apparent in the professional way it was launched in January 1957. Clearly, there was big, big money in the background, helped in part by the windfall from the Teenagers' "Why Do Fools Fall in Love" on Gee. Located at 220 West Forty-second Street, Roulette Records was never going to be a flash-in-the-pan, cash-strapped indie start-up. Morris Levy was the autocratic president supported by ex-Disney music publisher Phil Kahl, whose brother Joe Kolsky was head of sales. The directors' first act was to take full control of a ready-made back catalog by completing the buyout of George Goldner's remaining 50 percent interest in Rama, Gee, and Tico. With this cash, Goldner was free to launch his End-Gone combine.

Roulette enjoyed a spectacular run of chart records in its first year of trading, by which time the label was employing over a hundred people, with field staff all over the country. To keep up with demand, the company was ordering product from four indie pressing plants as well as the custom operations of Columbia, RCA, and Capitol. As for Levy, he was profiled in an advertorial in *Billboard* as having "achieved success in a tough, tough field that separates the men from the boys. Forward-looking and enthusiastic, he is able to spark the rest of the operation. It was not by mistake that Morris Levy was chosen president of Roulette organization."[17]

The very first spin of the Roulette wheel hit the jackpot, thanks to the Texas rock 'n' roll of "Party Doll" by Buddy Knox and "I'm Stickin' with You" by Jimmy Bowen, both with accompaniment by the Rhythm Orchids. Picked up for the sum of one thousand dollars, the masters were recorded for Triple D, a minuscule Texas label formed by the young musicians themselves and named after the local Dumas KDDD radio station. A pedestrian back-to-back cover single of both songs by 1940s R&B star Roy Brown for Imperial was easily fought off.

"We bought 'Party Doll' and 'I'm Stickin' with You,'" said Luigi Creatore.

That record was made in Texas, and it was one single with both those sides on it. When we got it, we said, "Hey, they're playing both of them. Why do we have them on one record?" So we split it—it was a good move. Why waste them? So they both sold. Buddy Knox had a big No. 1 record, and Jimmy had a Top 15. Jimmy said, "I'm not a singer," and I said, "You can't quit now; you're a star!" Those were the first records on Roulette. Then we did "Hula Love" with Buddy Knox [a No. 9 hit in the fall of 1957 with a big assist from Knox's appearance in the movie *Jamboree!*]. The rest by him were nice records, but as I told you, a good record is one that sells. Jimmy Bowen never took off after that, but he went in another direction; he became a producer and a very good one.

We recorded Frankie Lymon [for Roulette] as a single. Morris was in contact with him because he had been with the other label, Gee. He said, "Why don't you guys record him?" We said, "Fine." Then I forget what the circumstances were; he'd broken away [from the Teenagers]. We didn't request anything, he showed up, we went over some stuff. And we came up with "Goody Goody" with really a swing band arrangement; it had nothing to do with rock 'n' roll. It was great, and he *did* it great [No. 20, late summer 1957]. I can't tell you, he just got up and sang, and his arms would go. He just had it, a natural gift.

When Hugo Peretti and Luigi Creatore were working out their last weeks at Mercury, they auditioned a young singer from Seattle, one Jimmie Rodgers (whose name, curiously, was spelled identically to that of the country music legend). "We made a demo with him, and we sent it in," said Creatore.

We couldn't just sign people. You had to get approval from Chicago, and they said, "We like this guy; do a couple of sessions with him." Then the word came back that "we have enough boy singers. We don't need him." So we forgot about it; we couldn't hire him.

When we got over to Roulette, we started looking for people. I said to Hugo, "What about that Jimmie Rodgers? I loved his sound. Where is he?" He was in some place in Washington State. We put a private detective on him: "See if you can look up this guy." He found him in a lumber camp up outside of Seattle. And he was playing guitar there for the people, a one-man entertainer; he probably danced and sang a little. And I loved that "Honeycomb."

For Rodgers, the hummable folk-pop rock of "Honeycomb" went to No. 1 in late 1957, followed closely by "Kisses Sweeter Than Wine" (No. 3) and "Oh-Oh, I'm Falling in Love Again" (No. 7 in early 1958). The Playmates' "Jo-Ann" and "Beep Beep," which had a marketing tie-in with Nash-Rambler car dealers, were other Top 20 hits in 1958.

"We did albums with the Playmates and Jimmie Rodgers," said Creatore, "and Count Basie, because Morris had brought him in. We were making money, but not huge by today's standards, because albums were a secondary thing then—they weren't the big thing. The single was, and there's a limited amount of money you can make on a single. If they sold for a dollar, you had to sell it for forty to sixty cents to the distributor; there was only so much money in a single. Albums you did better [in profit terms], but albums didn't sell, not million-sellers like today."

Thanks to the hit streak at Roulette, RCA Victor became interested in hiring Hugo Peretti and Luigi Creatore through the record division's general manager, Viennese-born George Marek. "He was saying, 'Hey, at RCA, we have Presley, and then we have Presley, and then we have none,'" recalled Creatore.

He decided the key was the producer, because he saw us at Mercury and at Roulette. We didn't have a big label and big distribution like they had, and we were making hits. So it's the producer. We started getting wooed by RCA.

So we offered that we would come over, and I had a great idea. I said, "Why don't you *buy* Roulette; then we'll come. We'll make money, all the guys will make money there, and everybody will be happy. We would leave, [and] we'll bring you the tapes of Jimmie Rodgers, everything that we have. It's an asset, and we will be running it." He thought it was a great idea. I think they came up with $3 million or something; in those days, that was a lot of money. Then the lawyer at RCA said, "Oh no, you can't do that, because that's monopoly. You see a little company coming up and you buy it; you take it off the market. That's the definition of monopoly. We're not going to do that." So that ended a nice dream.

I think Morris would have gone along with that because he would have got his share; also because he went over [owning more than] 50 percent of that company. As time went around, Morris called a meeting and said, "Look, instead of you having 50 percent of that company, we have the Goldner company"—which Goldner had left by then—"and we have a distribution company that we own. I'm going to give you 10 percent each of everything, and then you give up 50 percent of that company [Roulette Records]." So we went along with that. Actually, it was not that great an idea as time went by. So we only got 10 percent; we came in with 50.

But anyway . . . RCA kept wooing and wooing us, saying, "What will you take to come over?" And we said, "Okay, we'll give you a program."

Luigi spelled out the demands: their own promotion staff, "because you guys don't know how to promote"; six men in the field under them; offices and secretaries; a certain amount of money for salary; and 1 percent of every record sold.

"So they mulled over the deal and mulled over the deal," he recalled,

and they came back and said, "We went to the board of directors with the deal, and the board said, 'We don't need partners.'" Today a producer gets a percentage like everybody else; he gets a good percentage and pays the acts. In those days, it was unheard of. We asked, and we didn't get it.

But soon the guy says, "I'm going to make you an offer that I think you will accept. I will give you the staff that you want, everything that you want, and we want a five-year contract, and we'll give you a million dollars." A *million* dollars? That's a lot of money in 1958. So we said, "Hey, this we can't refuse." So we went back to Morris and said, "Morris, we have an offer for a lot of money to go to RCA; what do you think we should do?" So he said, "Look, I don't want to stand in your way. If you think that's good for your career and you're satisfied with that, everybody's got to make their own way. Go ahead."

Then we gave it back to him [our shares in Roulette] for what we paid, which was very little at that time, and we were on our way. We had a million dollars [from RCA]; we didn't need that [from Roulette]. And then when we left, we said, "But we want our publishing company back; we don't want to leave it with you." So he gave it back.

In effect, Hugo and Luigi walked away from Roulette with minimal reimbursement, and they probably had no choice, given Levy's reputation. Joe Kolsky, executive vice president at Roulette, attempted to put a good spin on the duo's exit when he told *Cash Box* that "we are winding up matters in an atmosphere of complete cordiality and all of us at the company wish both boys the best of luck in the future."[18]

There has been a perennial curiosity about Morris Levy, his connections, and his one-sided business practices. Tales of Levy continued to enthrall gatherings of record people and collectors in New York and beyond through the years. Yet whenever his name cropped up in conversation with his contemporaries, often as plain "Morris," invariably there was a guarded response. Luigi Creatore knew him better than most and did not falter in his observations:

You get all sorts of stories; of course you do. He was our pal, he was our partner, he was very generous and very likable, smart. He didn't know music, but he knew business. He knew how to make deals; he made deals all over the place. Now, he had a reputation of being connected with the mob, but I never saw that. He may even have said, "I'll reach out for this guy." He was like a fan of the mob, in my opinion. He admired these people that ended up in jail [*laughs*]: "I've got a connection; I can reach him." But nothing ever happened.

Roulette was struggling; we struggled. I know what we made and what we didn't make. And after we left, Roulette was struggling and didn't make it as a company, really. If he had been connected with the mob, they would have supplied him with all the money he needed, and they would have made it. So that's my definition. If we had to struggle here and you're connected, what's going on?

Hugo & Luigi: Independent Producers at RCA Victor

And so Hugo Peretti and Luigi Creatore arrived at straitlaced RCA Victor in February 1959 with a mission to expand the pop catalog beyond Elvis Presley, after the comparative failure of Jerry Leiber and Mike Stoller to shake things up. The reporting line was through Steve Sholes, pop A&R chief, to George Marek, general manager. Over the next five years at RCA, the cousins were to ignite the career of Sam Cooke and create big hits for Della Reese, the Isley Brothers, Ray Peterson, Little Peggy March, and the Tokens. As independent producers, they even had their own logo: cartoon head profiles with the legend "A Hugo & Luigi Production."

"So we went to work," said Creatore,

and we were getting all new people. We started making records, and we had a *terrible* first year, nothing, couldn't get a bite. I think the first record that we broke with, . . . right at the end of our first year there, was Della Reese, "Don't You Know" [No. 2, fall 1959]. Finally we got a big record that was irresistible. If RCA were panicking, they couldn't tell us; I mean, we had a five-year contract. Well, we felt the pressure because we're here; the "big guys" were here. It was in all the papers the big deal that we made, *Billboard* and *Cash Box*. Our pictures were on the covers; they took a picture with Hugo and [me] on our knees with the RCA dog [Nipper] in between! That kind of stuff. There was a lot of publicity. And here we are, sitting doing nothing.

The Della Reese hit was like the first olive out of the bottle. Then we started to get some hits there like "Shout—Part 1" with the Isley Brothers [No. 47, fall 1959, and No. 94, March 1962]. But the Isley Brothers had a one-year contract, and by the time they had "Shout" out and it was a hit, their contract was about up. Actually, I felt they were not understood at all. They went off and did very, very well.

"Shout" was a very influential record, certainly in their career, and also it went on to become "Twist and Shout," all that stuff. We put, like, . . . little bleachers in the studio, and we got a lot of their friends to come in, because they played to the audience. The Isleys were wonderful, full of enthusiasm. It was not really like making a record. When we did "Shout," it was the custom at RCA for the producers to come to a meeting with the advertising people, the promotion people, and the president. They would listen to the records that we made that week, and they had the Nashville records [produced by Chet Atkins], too. Sometimes they'd say, "We don't want to put this record out," or, "We'll get behind this record." Certain decisions were made. So we came, and we played "Shout," [and] there was silence [*chuckles*]. The general manager said, "I didn't understand the words." So I said, "With all due respect, if you were sixteen years old and black, you would understand them." He said, "I see your point. Would you play the other side?" I said, "Certainly." He said, "It's the same [kind of] thing!" . . . So we put it out [with two different parts in the fashion of Ray Charles's "What'd I Say"], and of course it was a smash, it was a smash.

With more than a decade of experience behind them, Hugo and Luigi were very comfortable operating in the ultraprofessional New York recording studios. Luigi recalled the working conditions during their first years in the studio:

You had to get the balance and everything in the studio, 'cause there was no messing with it. You took that tape, and you made the "mother," and that was it. You didn't rebalance; you didn't do anything. When you were in the studio, that was the job: to hear what you wanted to hear, right now. Later, there was a famous excuse: "Fix it in the mix." But in the early days you did it.

Engineers are, of course, very, very valuable—unsung heroes, some of them—making something out of nothing, especially the more technically advanced we got with the [increased] tracks and all that. Remember when the first 2–tracks . . . came in, everybody wanted to do "ping pong" [bouncing from track to track] because it's such a novelty, from here to there? "Isn't that great?" But that's not the song! You can't succumb to the technique and the technology and not do the basic thing, because the kid who is going to buy the record doesn't know anything about this. He'd better hear the song; it had better appeal to him. Every time those technical advances came in, you'd lose some of the spontaneity. Sometimes it's better with a little mistake. Say if Tony Bennett gets a little frog in his throat, that's fine; that's an expression, that's what he's doing. If you get it to perfection, it loses something.

The New York musicians were very good, very good. Like the guitar player Billy Mure, that caliber of a musician was what you had all the time. Of course, it made the sessions go easier because they had no trouble. They never saw this song before, [but] they'd come in and read it. Bom! One run down because [they would] change this note, there's a mistake here and there, and you're ready. You didn't have trouble with the band; you had trouble with the singers in the early days. In the later days, you made the [backing] track, then the singer could stay and go over and over again.

The artist that justified RCA Victor's big investment in the Hugo and Luigi production team was Sam Cooke, who was looking to break out from what he saw as the restrictive R&B and gospel sectors to become a pop star. From RCA's viewpoint, Cooke was the Nat "King" Cole–type figure to replace the unfulfilling if talented Jesse Belvin, the West Coast singer and songwriter killed in a February 1960 Arkansas automobile tragedy.

"Sam Cooke had one big hit, 'You Send Me,'" said Luigi Creatore, "and then he was quiet for about a year. Now they say he had this and he had that, but to me it's all bullshit. He didn't have a [follow-up] hit. He'd done the gospel stuff, so he was big in those circles, but he was not a big act except for the one record that he had. There was a year of silence, really, in the pop field. Again, we thought this was a talented guy; let's work with him. So we made a deal with his agent [the William Morris agency]." That deal, in late 1959, was reported to include an eye-popping "guarantee of $100,000" following the expiration of Sam Cooke's contract with Keen Records.[19] There was no way that any independent label could compete with this sort of largesse, whether the sum was exaggerated by press spin or not.

The first Sam Cooke records for RCA were disappointments: "Teenage Sonata" crawled to No. 50, but the follow-up "You Understand Me" failed dismally (wiped out by Cooke's Keen release of the magical "Wonderful World," a No. 12 hit). Then at the next RCA session, Sam presented Hugo and Luigi with a new song. On asking Cooke what it was like, Creatore recalled him saying, "'It's called "Chain Gang": "Hear the sound of the man, ugh, ah, ugh, ah, hear the sound of the man working on the chain gaaaang." It's not finished.'[20] So I said, 'Well, finish it then' [laughs]. We put that out, and that was his first hit with us [No. 2, late summer 1960]. But he wrote for himself, so he knew exactly what he was doing, [for example] when the breaks would come. Again, he was a wonderful, natural talent; we had a string of hits with him. Now the trick with Sam [was], he wrote a lot of stuff which we didn't think could be a pop hit, so we started seeing our job as picking out [the hits] from him. We'd say, 'Okay, we'll do it, but we've got to do this other one, too.'"

"Chain Gang" was selected by RCA as part of a "Be a Hit at School" campaign in conjunction with Remington typewriters, along with singles by Henry Mancini, Neil Sedaka, Jeanie Johnson, Della Reese, and the Browns. Already Sam Cooke was touching on a new world of corporate sponsorship that was almost unknown to the artists (and record men) of the indie labels.

Continued Luigi, "The first couple of things he did in New York, but then he said, 'You know, I'd like to record in L.A.' I said, 'I don't care; we travel a lot.' There were some musicians he liked to work with in his act, and Rene Hall was the arranger out there; Earl Palmer was the drummer. I remember going out to California to record 'Cupid.' I said, 'Okay, I've got what I came for; now do whatever you want.' I did the sound effect [belly laugh]; I went into the studio and overdubbed the *sssssssh* of the arrow. That's my contribution!" "Cupid" was a No. 17 hit in the summer of 1961.[21]

Sam Cooke had a great run of records with Hugo & Luigi, notably "Twistin' the Night Away" (No. 9, early 1962), "Bring It On Home to Me" backed with "Having a Party" (each with an unforgettable duet with Lou Rawls; both made Top 20 in the summer of 1962), and "Another Saturday Night" (No. 10, early summer 1963). "By the way, Sam didn't sell albums in great quantities," added Luigi.

> He sold *some*. Matter of fact, the president of RCA said to me, "Do you know that Sam Cooke in sales is second only to Presley?" I said, "I know that; we make the records!" It was not a revelation to me, [but] it was to him. I'd say singles sales were 600– to 700,000, but they did not make a million.
>
> We had left Sam Cooke before he died [December 11, 1964], and he was playing the Copacabana. There was a big sign on Forty-second Street: huge. Allen Klein was then handling him. At the opening night party [July 7, 1964], when Sam came out, he starting singing, and he stopped. He said, "Hugo and Luigi, thank you."

Other production triumphs for Peretti and Creatore at RCA included the "death" record "Tell Laura I Love Her" by Ray Peterson (No. 7, summer 1960) and "I Will Follow You" by Little Peggy March, the producers' second RCA No. 1 (spring 1963) with a song that prominent publisher Lou Levy had pitched to them.

The first RCA chart topper under the Hugo & Luigi banner was "The Lion Sleeps Tonight" by the Tokens at the end of 1961. Recalled Luigi Creatore, "The Tokens said, 'We'd like to record this,' and I said, 'What do you mean, record that? It's got no lyrics.'

So they said, 'We think we can just do it.' I said, 'I don't, but I'll tell you what I'll do: we'll write some words for the session. I'm not going to make a record of "wimoweh, wimoweh, wimoweh." First of all, it's very nice, but it's a folk thing. We're making pop stuff.' But it was a fun record to do, and then it was a smash."[22]

Back at Roulette

Hugo and Luigi left RCA in late 1963. "They didn't want to pick up the five-year option," said Luigi. "We wanted to leave anyway. We were writing with George David Weiss, we were writing well [including the perennial Elvis Presley "wedding song" "Can't Help Falling in Love"], and we wanted to do a musical show, looking for Broadway. Then Morris Levy called us and said, 'Why don't you come back with me?' We said, 'We really want to do something else.' The company was in a terrible state, they weren't selling, the distributors all owed them money. It was in a bad state."

The drought period at Roulette had crept up after Levy's deftness in capitalizing on the twist craze with Joey Dee and the Starliters' "Peppermint Twist—Part 1." This No. 1 hit in early 1962 was produced by Henry Glover, who had cut Hank Ballard's original "The Twist" for King, only to see it buried as a "B" side. In the summer of 1963, Glover and George Goldner (in temporary residence as vice president following the sale of his End-Gone labels to Levy a year earlier) took production credits for another Roulette No. 1, "Easier Said Than Done" by the Essex. Possibly it was this hit record that caused the distributor payment problems.

"So we went there . . . for about a year," said Creatore. "We tried, put this out, put that out, couldn't get anything moving. So we said to Morris, 'Look, we're not doing you any good; we're not doing us any good. We can't do it with these acts. We wanna write a show.' So we left, and we went to the Brill Building, our office."

In Morris Levy's later years, with Roulette limping along, he built up the Strawberries retail chain while seeking redemption through many fund-raising ventures, charitable and political. But he couldn't resist a quick whack-up in a bottom-feeding LP cutout racket and was exposed, along with sidekick Tommy Vastola, by stupidly brave Philadelphia record merchant John LaMonte. And so in 1986, the long arm of the law finally caught up with Morris Levy. To his utter shock, he was found guilty of "conspiring to extort" and was sentenced to ten years in jail. The federal authorities described him pithily as the "Godfather of the American Music Business."[23]

Shelby Singleton met Levy while working for Mercury Records in New York:

Oh yeah, Morris and I were very good friends. He was the type of person that if he said he was gonna do something, shook hands with you, then you didn't need a contract. You knew that was going to happen. The things that Morris did . . . I guess the thing with John LaMonte and some of that stuff, you can't blame him, really; here's a guy that's trying to jerk you around. I've seen other people get in fistfights in bars, arguing over a woman. But that's just part of being in business, I guess. Not only in the music business; it's in every business.

I think he was a businessman first and probably a record man second. He was always very good to me. I could go to New York City, and if I had a problem with the AFM, if I had a problem with anybody, Morris would say, "I'[ll] take care of it." He'd get on the phone; he'd call up [and] blast them for this and that and the other, make 'em leave me alone.

Morris Levy died of cancer in 1990 at the age of only sixty-two while appealing the jail sentence. Prior to his death, he sold the Roulette Records group, including the music publishing interests, for a total of $16.5 million. In his later years, as the self-appointed banker to distressed indie labels, Levy had picked up Jerry Blaine's Jubilee-Josie group and Henry Stone's TK enterprise to enhance the core Roulette and early George Goldner catalogs, among others. Even more intriguingly, Morris acquired a stake in Chess Records by way of Joe Robinson, who had purchased the iconic label from GRT in 1975 for a reported giveaway price of $950,000 before hitting a financial brick wall.[24]

All told, Levy's assets were estimated to be worth in excess of $75 million, including a rambling 1,700–acre horse farm with an English-style manor house in verdant upstate New York.[25] It was a world away from his humble upbringing in the bustling Bronx. Assuredly, Morris had left a permanent imprint on the independent record business for better *and* worse. It had served him and his cohorts very well, if not those record men, artists, and other unfortunates who had fallen under his spell and into his grasp.

Hugo Peretti and Luigi Creatore had a final fling as record men by purchasing the Avco-Embassy label from its aircraft corporation parent with a loan of $2 million from Dutch-based Philips, the electronics giant that had purchased Mercury Records in 1961. After a promising start, Avco turned out to be a hair-raising ordeal. "They knew we had the Stylistics' hits," said Creatore,

> so they knew there was money in the pipeline, and we had the Van McCoy disco hit, "The Hustle" [No. 1, 1975]. So we bought Avco out, and we had some money left over to operate. So it started to work; it worked pretty good.
>
> Then we had a tough time around this time. We had the Stylistics going, and we did well with them, but we couldn't get much more going. Then there was a period of time, like six months, when the entire United States . . . the record business, the record stores, decided to return their merchandise. It was flooding in to every place, every company. Now at RCA and Columbia, they could weather the storm, but we couldn't. Everything was coming back, and nothing was selling much.
>
> We were really in dire straits. I said to Hugo, "Look, we've made good money in this business. I'm not giving it back. Let's just close. But we can't close immediately, because anybody that we owe money to will sue, and anybody that owes us money . . . will not pay us." So little by little, we just stopped making records, stopped this, stopped that. And we let it die down, and then we closed [in 1979].

That was the end of the musical road for the independent producers, songwriters, and record men. Luigi Creatore continued to express fond gratitude to cousin Hugo Peretti (who died in 1986) for their business success: "My rapport with Hugo was fantastic. We had thirty years together and never fought, never had any problems at all. I remember we met Leiber and Stoller at a party, and they were introduced to us by Julian Aberbach [of Hill & Range Music]. Then he said, 'They were so happy to meet you,' and I asked, 'Why are they happy to meet us? We're competition for them.' He said, 'Oh, but wouldn't any young baseball player like to meet Babe Ruth?' So that was very flattering."

14
CHAPTER

Tin Pan Alley and Beyond

CAST OF CHARACTERS
Irv Lichtman, *Cash Box* and *Billboard*
Gene Goodman, Regent-Arc-Conrad Music
Freddy Bienstock, Hill & Range Music and Bigtop Records
Johnny Bienstock, Bigtop Records
also featuring Julian and Jean Aberbach,
Hill & Range Music

It is easy to understand a favorite refrain of the music publishing fraternity: "There is nothing better than earning a fortune while you sleep—like from a good song." By the mid-1950s, the music publishers' cozy world of sheet music sales, song plugging, and royalty collections was under threat from the new order being created by the lively independent labels. The ongoing trench warfare between upstart BMI and blue-blooded ASCAP, which in a sense climaxed in the congressional payola hearings, was evidence of that battle. Was the answer to fight rock 'n' roll or to join the revolution?

"Of course, the established publishers were certainly very dismissive of early rock 'n' roll," said Irv Lichtman of *Cash Box* and *Billboard*, with a chuckle.

> They would say, "It's junk, nincompoop music." The smaller publishers that picked up these copyrights, some of them were just not out there in the hinterlands, like Don Kirshner, Al Nevins, and many others who were creating a stable of great rock 'n' roll writers that were dismissed by the great old-time music publishers like Chappell Music, Warner Brothers, Harms, E. B. Marks, Shapiro Bernstein, and Bourne Music. Remember, in 1955 through 1960, you still had a tremendous carryover of people: executives, owners, even promotion people who went back to the 1930s. If you were twenty years old

and got into the business in 1930, in 1955 you were only forty-five. You may be running the firm at the time; you weren't old. And they were totally dismissive.

Another group that was totally dismissive was ASCAP. BMI was picking up on the country and blues area and got its feet wet in the music that would be the mainstream music fifteen to twenty-five years later. As the music gained traction, the million-sellers became more commonplace than not. That was unheard of in the era they came from. You had to go along with the trends.

If you look up the album charts in '55, what are you going to see? Sound tracks, Broadway, Perry Como, and Frank Sinatra . . . they were going great guns. That was the mainstream music, even though rock 'n' roll was making tremendous inroads. I think the old-school publishers didn't understand aesthetically what the [new] music meant. They were more in tune with what they thought it was. Publishing support, for the most part, consisted of a cadre of often colorful song pluggers, who later were known as professional managers. But it was a lessening of the great standards of old Tin Pin Alley and Broadway, both the lyrics and music. It just broke it apart. Yes, revolution is a good word; it was a revolution. But don't put [the old-style publishers] down too much.

Gene Goodman, Music Publisher: Regent-Arc-Conrad Music

Among the earliest music publishers to home in on the potential bounties offered by the independent labels were Gene and Harry Goodman at Regent Music. The Goodman brothers were independents in their business as well but had the inestimable good fortune of being the siblings of Benny, who was the Elvis Presley of his day to the jitterbuggers in the swing band era of the 1930s. The coup de grace for Gene and Harry was to secure the joint publishing rights to the Chess catalog in 1953. This Goodman-Chess family relationship has endured for more than half a century.

Thanks to Arc Music executive Kenneth Higney, I was able to meet Gene Goodman in 2004. An imposing man with something of an air of former secretary of state Henry Kissinger about him, Mr. Goodman was living with wife, Gloria, at their Huntington summer home on the desirable waterfront overlooking Long Island Sound. Then in his late eighties, he was still driving a car and taking thirty-minute daily strolls to keep fit; in between times, he would digest the stock market reports on CNBC-TV. After summer, the Goodmans would retreat to their Manhattan apartment prior to spending the winter as "snowbirds" in sunny Naples, Florida. These were the trappings of the rich and famous, yet Goodman came from an impoverished background in Chicago with Russian Jewish roots.

Still involved, Gene Goodman was content to leave the day-to-day operations of Arc Music, Regent Music, and Conrad Music in the capable hands of Marshall Chess, Leonard's son. "Even now, they'll call me up to discuss contract details," said Goodman. "I was always a fine detail man." Known affectionately as Mr. G., his favorite phrase is "nose to the grindstone." In his active business days, he was a workaholic, traveling from Huntington to Penn Station on the Long Island Rail Road early in the morning and getting back late at night. Adored by his staff and with a reputation as a quick-witted and tough dealmaker, Gene Goodman and his outgoing brother Harry could not have been better publishing partners for Leonard and Phil Chess. Some still ask why the Chesses had to have publishing partners. In fairness, the record men were simply too busy developing the *record* company. In addition, they must have been awestruck at the prospect of joining one of music's royal families, with the attendant elevation in social status.

"I became aware of Chess in the early 1950s," said Gene Goodman. "I was coming back from some meeting. I remember seeing a fellow I was very friendly with; his name was Juggy Gayles, who everybody in the business knows. He told me there were two young men in Chicago who were interested in getting somebody in New York to be in the publishing business with them and to take care of the publishing of all the songs they recorded. Then I gave up my baseball tickets to meet Leonard and Phil Chess in Chicago for the first time. That very day we made a deal, and I flew back to New York and went to my attorney [and] had the papers drawn up."

The early days of Chess Records were summarized with brevity by Goodman: "Leonard had a bar, he had a three-piece band, and his first record [on Chess, the successor to Aristocrat] was a copyright I didn't own, 'My Foolish Heart.' It was a big smash for him by Gene Ammons. That record made Leonard Chess, more so than Muddy Waters. That was the actual *beginning*—I wasn't there yet."

Initially, the Chess publishing was administered in the name of Burton LTD. "John Henry Burton was a black lawyer," said an exasperated Goodman. "He had a room in their office building. He didn't know from shit. He also had a publishing company. Leonard didn't know very much at that time. How he found John, I'll never know."

And so Arc Music was incorporated by the Chess brothers with the Goodman brothers on July 8, 1953. An ASCAP division, Sunflower Music, was set up on November 27, 1953.

Why Arc Music? "I just juggled the RCA letters, that's all I did!" said Goodman, beaming.

> I could see the Chesses were in business as record men the way I was as a publisher; they had their noses to the grindstone. Those artists they had, they recorded their own songs, and from then on when they had a session, they would get a songwriter's contract and a recording contract. Chess Records would direct all the contracts and a copy of the demo to me, and I would in turn have somebody copy it off the record to make a lead sheet. I would have the song registered at the Copyright Office, and I did all the administrative work.
>
> I don't think they were as aware, nor was I for that matter, as to how important a copyright could become through the years. At that time, we didn't put the value on it that we do today. And remember, at that time, the publisher was only getting two cents a record. If it sold a million, we're talking of $20,000, and half of that had to go to the writer. It wasn't that much money then. . . . As the years went on, . . . the publishers as a whole got together and went to Congress, and we asked for raises in relationship to what was going on in the world.[1]

Leonard Chess, if you go back and look at his life, he was not only a record man. He was a distributor, he had a radio station, . . . he saw what was happening in every field. He had the foresight to do it, and later on, of course, he had his own records played on his own radio station, which was a big help. Phil worked hand-in-hand with Leonard. Leonard perhaps was on the road more than Phil at that time and knew more, I guess, of what was going on. While they were in Chicago, I was actually the delivery boy to Alan Freed [in New York], you might say. I would take him his copies [of the latest Chess releases and also other labels with Arc and Regent songs].

Did Goodman have a big vision of the potential of infant rock 'n' roll music in 1953?

No, I think you might call it an accident that I affiliated myself with the Chesses. I was always searching, looking, right since I was thirteen years old, selling newspapers in Chicago. See, I was also from Chicago. The Chess brothers liked me, and I knew the city as well as they did. My parents came from Russia and Romania, part of the big Jewish exodus, and they got burned because most of them didn't have very much. But they put it together: "Get six dollars a night and we'll be able to live." Growing up in Chicago in the 1920s, you had nothing, but you had everything. Nobody had anything to steal; we were all broke together. My mom would give me seven pennies to take a streetcar after school to help my dad selling his papers; that was his job. We lived on the West Side of Chicago, three blocks from Cicero. My mom and dad had nothing to give me, except food on the table and a big kiss when he came home.

Benny was older. As I was growing up, I could sing the theme songs of the radio shows, like Eddie Cantor's. We were all neighbors together; someone had a radio, and we all listened. I didn't become aware of records until later on, sixteen or seventeen. When I moved to New York, I worked in a drugstore for seven dollars a week; [you could] help . . . your mom with something, but you couldn't buy anything. We went to New York to bring the family all together to save money. Benny was already here; Harry was here. We had twelve in our family.

At the beginning, I was a bandboy for Benny Goodman.[2] I drove the truck, and I took care of the instruments for [drummer] Gene Krupa and for my brother Harry, his bass fiddle. When we got to the hotels, I would see all these publishers come in. They sat down; they drank and played songs. And I said, "What a marvelous way to make a living!" I talked my brother Harry into quitting Benny, and we opened up a little office in the Brill Building.

Benny was king of swing, absolutely! We'd come into a place like Chicago, where we were born, and they treated him like a king. He had just made the big hit at the Palomar Ballroom in California [in 1935], but prior to that he had some bad times try-ing to make this new type of music go. He had one booking at the Roosevelt Hotel [in New York], and the first request was "Please Mr. Goodman, by contrast, do something soft and sweet." He kept doing what he was doing [*laughs*]. Remember, we were get-ting rid of that era of poverty at that time, and the people were looking for something: to come to hear Benny Goodman.

Then the ASCAP strike came along. So we were fortunate that we had some songs to give to BMI at that time. Our first Regent Music application to ASCAP was turned down; I don't know for what reason. But it left us open to hear through the grapevine that there was a thing called BMI coming along, and we joined up pronto. That was a big feather in our cap at that time.

Gene and Harry Goodman registered Regent Music Corporation on January 1, 1940. The BMI affiliation was effected on April 1, 1942, making Regent one of the pioneering BMI members. "We got that name from your famous street in London," said Goodman.

We had a company in ASCAP called Harman [registered on December 5, 1941], and we acquired Jewel.

Early on, you had to have a piano player and play [a song] on the piano, and people would gather around and buy the sheet [music] if they liked it. That was the only way, because the kids weren't listening to radio much, and records didn't mean very much then. We had to go to nightclubs and try to get the big bands to play a song. I'd go to see Tommy Dorsey, Artie Shaw, Charlie Barnet. At the beginning, a record had no sales; the income was minuscule, really. Once they became the Benny Goodmans of the world, then you wanted a record by them.

People song pluggers would come to Benny. If you came into the hotel where he was working [and] put your song on the piano, it didn't matter who the publisher was, who the writer was; he wasn't concerned with that. He was more concerned about how well it matche[d] the band. If he made the arrangement and if it happened to be "King Porter Stomp" or "Big John's Special," he played it over and over again. He looked at the bottom line to see who owned the copyright, to see who wrote it, to see if his brothers owned the song. But he was interested in the vehicle [taps fingers].

If you had a big hit, you'd sell a lot of sheets plus the performance royalties you got. Also [there was] the record companies' [income]. It all added up. Both BMI and ASCAP have their way of calculating their performance payments [from films, radio, television, and so on] and adding on those monies which they'd bring in from establishments such as restaurants and hotels, and it all gets added to the pot. Each hotel pays a certain rate, still does; it's based on its class or how many seats are in its bars. It can be a live band; it can be any form of music that is played for profit.[3]

With phonograph records, there are two *song* publishing royalty streams: mechanicals (from record sales) and performances (from public play). The performance aspect was rarely disclosed by the first wave of independent record men to innocent young artists who happened to be songwriters. Even worse, the *exclusion* of performance royalties would be embedded within contracts. For example, a standard agreement drawn up by Aladdin Records in 1952 incorporated the categorical phrase "no performance payments to writers."[4] By 1957, the Modern and Imperial contracts were more specific and even used identical language: "All recordings and/or records and reproductions made therefrom, together with performance embodies therein shall be entirely the property of First Party [the record company], free and clear of any claim of any nature whatsoever by Second Party [the songwriter]."[5] If an artist was desperate to make a record with his new song, with the potential prestige and undoubted financial rewards involved, who cared about this strange thing called "performances"? Then, when the artist understood the implications, he would be locked into the contract until renewal. At the root of it all, the size of those "BMI checks" could be considerable.[6] A gradual resolution to this contentious issue was made when BMI registered "affiliated" song-writers individually and started to make payments direct to them.[7]

The personal acquisition of song copyrights has been another damming accusation levied against record men generally. But who knows exactly what deals were struck behind closed doors? Indeed, what agreements, fair or foul, were made by the entire music industry community, from the Tin Pan Alley era on (and beforehand)? With so much potentially at stake, it is not surprising that song litigation has been rife through the years. It's a safe bet, however, that the vast majority of music publishers' filing cabinets will never reveal their bulging secrets. If so, the statute of limitations laws will come to the rescue of any alleged miscreants if negotiated settlements cannot be made.[8]

Regent Music lifted off, literally, with "Flying Home," a composition by Benny Goodman and Lionel Hampton. Hampton's 1943 remake for Decca, with Illinois Jacquet's standout sax solo, presaged the full-throttled excitement of the rhythm and blues era. In those early days, the Goodman brothers would sell sheet music through jobbers (the equivalent of record distributors), who were an essential part of the song publishing and plugging business. Direct sales were made by the Goodmans to those stores within walking distance of Regent's office at the Brill Building, including next-door Colony Records and Sam Ash and Manny's Music on Forty-eighth Street. But the galloping popularity of gramophone records would change the business irrevocably.

"After the records came in, we went to see the disc jockeys," said Gene Goodman. "And we went to the record company, [to] what they call the A&R men, and they were always on the lookout for material. When my brother Harry went to see Mitch Miller, he picked 'I Saw Mommy Kissing Santa Claus' by an artist, Jimmy Boyd [on Columbia, Christmas 1952], and it became an instantaneous smash. We had another big song [also in 1952] called 'Takes Two to Tango,' which Milt Gabler cut with Pearl Bailey [Coral] and Louis Armstrong [Decca]."

Flushed with these publishing triumphs, the Goodman brothers were in a strong financial position to negotiate with the Chess brothers for the administration of the Chess-Checker publishing rights in 1953. Gene Goodman remembered that Leonard told him he wanted the Chess publishing split three ways "because I have a brother." Retorted Goodman, "Well, I have a brother, too!" So four ways it was. The Chess deal was to take the Goodmans rapidly from one era to another.

"While I thought records were going to take over and jukeboxes were also going to take over," said Gene Goodman, it came so *fast* at that time. Some of us gave things away, which many years later we were sorry for. In my own way, perhaps, I made the Chess publishing business better because I heard all their records. For instance, they had a little record called "See You Later Alligator" [by Bobby Charles], and I took that to Milt Gabler at Decca. They did that with Bill Haley; he made mincemeat out of the Chess record. Then Coral had the McGuire Sisters. They covered "Sincerely" [by the Moonglows]; that hurt Chess. "Goodnite Sweetheart, Goodnite" [by the Spaniels with Pookie Hudson], I bought that from Vee-Jay, another label in Chicago. I called them on the phone, [and] I said, "I want to buy half that song." It was a great song; it had the message. Words were so important. I was a "words" man.

Goodman could have added that "Goodnite Sweetheart, Goodnite" was translated into a country hit by Johnnie & Jack for RCA Victor in 1954 and that the Flamingos' Checker outing of "I'll Be Home" was covered by Pat Boone as a family favorite for armed forces everywhere throughout the world.

In effect, the cover version craze was another form of song pitching, except that the songs originated from the indie record label publishing companies, not Tin Pan Alley. These were the new-wave songs that the old-guard publishers and songwriters were unable to supply.[9]

"Leonard understood I was doing what I had to do," said Goodman. "Nobody covered Chuck Berry's records, basically, because he would get such a big play immediately out of Nashville; WLAC, it would cover immense territory. Nobody could cover Chuck Berry records or Bo Diddley's. . . . Why was Al Freed's name credited as a writer on 'Maybellene' [with Russ Fratto's]? I won't touch that one with a barge pole! We were having hits. It was just one after the other."

Chuck Berry's "Maybellene" was the record that took Chess Records out of the ghettos into the big chart league after nudging Top 5 pop in the fall of 1955. The duck-walking guitarist eased "School Day" to No. 3 in the spring of 1957, followed within twelve months by "Sweet Little Sixteen" at No. 2. A few years later, Gene Goodman showed his fiery competitiveness on behalf of songwriter Berry and the Chess brothers when he became aware that the Beach Boys had borrowed the melody of "Sweet Little Sixteen" on "Surfin' U.S.A," a No. 3 hit for Capitol in 1963. There was no fifty-fifty publishing compromise here, just winner takes all as Mr. G. secured the entire copyright of "Surfin' U.S.A." for Arc Music.

Back in the late 1950s, the art of recording demonstration songs as "demo" acetates was becoming an integral part of the business. In particular, Allegro Recording Studio at 1650 Broadway was situated centrally for New York's publishers, songwriters, and aspiring artists. This basement studio would be well patronized by the Brill Building school of genius tunesmiths and Florence Greenberg's Scepter Records acts, among many others. Harlem record man and songwriter Paul Winley, of Winley Records, said that Gene Goodman would always be willing to audition his songs and for demo recordings would pay five dollars per song to pianist Dave "Baby" Cortez (who recorded "The Happy Organ" at Allegro). Cortez and Winley even recorded a Chess album track as a tribute to Goodman: "Mr. Gee." Another black writer, Billy Dawn Smith, affirmed that Gene Goodman would encourage promising young songsters and, best of all, would ensure they were paid.[10]

Goodman had a knack for picking up from tiny independent labels the publishing *and* masters, including several classics of the rock 'n' roll era. With full support from the Chess brothers (and Harry) and without any interfering line management, he was able to move swiftly to conclude deals for both Arc and Regent.

Goodman related the background stories with proud zeal, starting with "Over the Mountain, Across the Sea" by Johnnie & Joe [Chess, No. 8, summer 1957]: "A disc jockey made that record, and he called the Chesses. Zell Sanders purportedly was a security guard [with a license to carry a gun]. She made this one record [for her J & S label in the Bronx]. Zell was a lovely, sweet, big woman; she didn't have this much of a bad bone in her. I would kid her, because in the lyric it says 'you passed the wind.' I said, 'You're always passing wind!' We had more laughs, but it was just the music business. Today it's a money business."

"Happy, Happy Birthday" by the Tune Weavers (Checker) was acquired from Frank Paul's Casa Grande Records and made No. 5 in the fall of 1957. "I went to Boston to buy that," said Goodman.

> Joe Smith [a prominent disc jockey at WMEX and WILD], who was at Capitol Records later on, said, "Why are you trying to get that record for? That doesn't mean anything." I said, "Joe, I've got a job to do, and I've got to find the owner." He said, "He's back in New York." I had checked into the Boston Sheraton at 3 P.M. and was out again at 4 P.M. to come back to New York, to catch the next plane. I knew the owner was trying to shop the record to a distributor called Jerry Blaine [of Cosnat Distributing and Jubilee Records], and I had the chutzpah to call Jerry Blaine's office: "Can I speak to Frank Paul?" I said, "I get in at 8 P.M.," and I took him to Gallagher's. He was so nervous about signing to me, and he had two guys with him; they were tired. They said, "Please go back to his office and take the $2,000 he's offering you for half the song." I called Leonard that night; I said, "Leonard, I'll send you the record." He said, "Stick your record up your ass; I already have 10,000 on the floor pressed and ready to go!" That's how sure he was of my getting the record. The appeal of the song was that it had a story: "Happy, happy birthday baby . . ." It's universal.[11]

The Goodmans almost went into the record business when they purchased the master of "Silhouettes" by the Rays, but they sold it on to Philadelphia-based Cameo Records, which commandeered a No. 3 hit in late 1957. "'Silhouettes' was two songwriters coming to my office, Frank Slay and Bob Crewe," said Goodman.

> They played me two songs, "Silhouettes" and "Daddy Cool," and I said to these two songwriters: "Here's $2,500; call me cordial." They bring me this record [on their XYZ label], and then everybody is gung-ho on a song called "Daddy Cool." I took the record up to Buffalo to a friend of mine; he said, "I'll play this record provided you don't give it to the fat man at the other radio station." He called me [and] said, "Come up to Buffalo." I said, "Why?" "I'm having a dance at a high school, and I want you to hear

something." He put the record on, and every kid on that floor sang "Took a walk and passed your house . . ." I couldn't believe what I was hearing. A distributor, who was a friend of Leonard's, said "Ship me a thousand!" I don't know about the record business: "What do you mean, ship you a thousand? Don't you want to *buy* them?"

That's when I first found out that you ship them records on *consignment,* plus you gave them for every thousand ordered three hundred *freebies* to promote it. I'm not going to do this. So now I want to sell the record, and nobody wants my record. Finally, one day, I get a call from Dick Clark's office. He said, "Gene, I'd like you to sell the record to Cameo." That's when I first found out that Dick was in bed with Cameo [*laughs*]. We had a big smash; that was with Kal Mann and Bernie Lowe at Cameo. Chess didn't want it; nobody wanted the record. I told Leonard it was good. I did what a publisher does: I promoted my record.[12]

The scourge of promo records presented a real problem to publishers. "They pressed records that were royalty-free, those records which they gave away," said Gene Goodman. "They wouldn't appear on their books for royalties for the publishers or for the artists. It went on a lot; it was impossible for publishers to track down." Even worse, alluding to the bootleg problem, he said darkly, "Some of them had their own pressing plants."

"At the Hop" by Danny and the Juniors was tailor-made for the teen record hops of the day. "I bought 'At the Hop' by Danny and the Juniors after it was a hit," recalled Goodman. "The publisher wasn't doing correct by the two writers, and they were going to sue. In order not to sue, he needed some other publisher to buy the song from him. And I got the writers to agree [that] if I bought the song, they would come along with it. Dick Clark had a share in 'At the Hop.' It was not on the label, but it was copyrighted."[13] When the master was acquired by ABC-Paramount and with a massive push from Dick Clark (encouraged by his "silent" stake in the song), "At the Hop" stayed at No. 1 for seven weeks in early 1958, making it one of the biggest and most recognizable records of the rock 'n' roll era.

"Book of Love" is another top-notch Arc copyright, inspired by the renowned "wonder where the yellow went" Pepsodent toothpaste jingle. The Monotones' recording was picked up from Bea Kaslin's New York–based Mascot label and became a No. 5 hit in the spring of 1958 on the Chess brothers' Argo subsidiary.[14] Then, as an indication of the expanding nature of the music business, the song was an even bigger hit abroad when covered by an English act. "A publisher had called me from London to say the Mudlarks had cut it," said Goodman, "so then I flew over to do my deal. That was Francis Day & Hunter, which today is EMI Music. From EMI, we got one thing that was very important: we got Django Reinhardt from France, and we publish all of Django's works here for the U.S." Later in 1961, the Goodmans acquired "Apache," a big U.K. instrumental hit by the Shadows written by Jerry Lordan that became a No. 2 U.S. success for Danish guitarist Jorgen Ingmann (Atco). Then, illustrating an unimagined source of future publishing income, Gene Goodman said, "Just a few years back, a record company in Jersey, All Platinum [owned by Joe and Sylvia Robinson], put it inside of another song, and I never knew about it. We just got to settling the lawsuit with them." Welcome to the world of hip-hop and rap and the rewards (and controversies) of sampling.

Continued Goodman:

> In the 1950s, most of us were told by lawyers here—we were misguided . . .—[that] we couldn't have our own publishing in London. And that worked for Chappell's, they got a fifty-fifty, they were the subpublishers. We didn't realize how big the overseas market was; it grew. There was so much we learned in time. We didn't know that when our Australian publisher bought a song from us, there were indigenous records in Australia. We learned that [there was a prosperous local scene] through tears, you might say.
>
> Jewel Music in London published the Chess hits. The fact that Chuck Berry was selling in Europe took him by surprise. We did make frequent trips to London to see how things were going, because at that time Chappell had everybody; Chappell had *every* company under some sort of a deal. Burlington Music was Decca, Sir Edward Lewis; I wish I had gone with him. Sir Edward was a prince; he was just a nice man who was in business. He never had a bad deal.

The acquisition of the publishing of "Tell It Like It Is," the early 1967 No. 2 hit by Aaron Neville (Parlo), confirmed the inspired genius of Leonard Chess even in the final throes of the original indie record game. "That was in New Orleans," said Gene Goodman. "They had a disc jockey who wanted to get rid of this song and we, *we*, gave him $10,000. It was a lot of money. It was before it was a hit. You didn't have that kind of foresight; of course you didn't. It was payola, but that turned out well. Now we have a great, great copyright. It was another way of Leonard doing business." The song's title, "Tell It Like It Is," was a prominent catchphrase during the civil rights era.

"Was payola rife?" queried an incredulous-looking Goodman at our interview. "Absolutely! These disc jockeys were coming in here, dressed up and pulling up in big cars; they knew what was going on. There was money to be made. I don't remember the names, but Phil Chess and I were in Memphis, and he gave a disc jockey a record. The jockey held the album up like this, [and] he said, 'Phil, nothing but a *record* fell out of it.' Even the fellows who work at the BBC took it to get a record played. It goes on in *every* business, somewhere, somehow. On the coast, Capitol Records, in order to get a record, the publisher had to tip the A&R man $3,000. In truth, when it was all over, it paid to give him the three. But I didn't want to be a part of that kind of deal. And the big publishers didn't give a penny to them."

Gene Goodman went out on the road with Leonard Chess from time to time: "We would visit the two or three [Radio WLAC] Nashville disc jockeys that would play the Chuck Berry records. By the time they got over the mountains to Charlotte, Leonard's distributor there would say, 'I need your new Chuck Berry record!' He had heard it; the calls were already coming in. Then we'd go from there down to see Stan Lewis, set up the playing there, [and] we'd go to the disc jockeys in New Orleans. We'd go to see Zenas Sears in Atlanta; we'd go to see the distributor there, Jake Friedman, who had a lovely girl, and she'd put the records in the jukeboxes for Leonard." This lady was almost certainly Gwen Kessler, whose great sales pitch was that a record was so hot that "people who don't even own a record player are buying it."[15]

"Leonard just knew his way right through that whole territory," said Goodman.

He knew it better than the back of your hand. Yes, we'd go to Henry Stone in Miami. He had that big hit group, KC and the Sunshine Band. Then he was also a distributor; he would distribute all over the world. It was transshipping [*laughs*]. Leonard said, "What the hell does he need 20,000 records in Miami for?" There weren't 20,000 people there at that time. He was selling them all over the *world*. As long as they paid, nobody cared where they sent them.

We'd be away ten days. Leonard was welcomed with open arms; it was fun, it was fun. We'd come to see the people, and these people knew that a successful manufacturer was coming in. They'd treat him like royalty, and because I was with Leonard, they all knew me then. I really wasn't into it then as much as I was into being with Leonard.

I would help a record myself. I would make a circle with Capital Airlines through Cincinnati, Pittsburgh, Chicago, and Detroit. We'd do a big circle and get disc jockeys to play the records—in a friendlier way, not with any ulterior motives, it was just if you had a good record and they played it.

I only went to a couple of Chess sessions. I spent my nose to the grindstone. Some of the artists like Willie Dixon would allow you to be friendly. Some of them didn't want you to be friendly; they had their own personal life, and they wanted to keep it that way, be it Chuck [Berry] or Bo [Diddley]. They'd come up maybe to the office to say hello, but that's as far as it went. I'd go to a show at the Apollo, but I didn't go backstage.

With the escalating worldwide popularity of the Chess recordings adding considerable value to Arc copyrights, royalty payments to artists and songwriters have come under inevitable scrutiny. "We had an understanding," said Goodman, quietly.

Anything that Leonard had a record on, he paid the artist direct or the writer direct: Chuck Berry, Bo Diddley, "Book of Love," or anything else. He would combine the artist royalty and writer royalty as one. I would only pay those writers when I got a cover record or foreign royalties would come in.

Lillian McMurry [of Trumpet Records], in Jackson, Mississippi, I was very friendly with her; we had things together [by Sonny Boy Williamson]. She was a little god in her territory. She had a furniture store; she was a tough lady. But she did a lot of good in her own territory, helping these artists to get a break.

That was the cue for a big rebuttal against royalty complaints by artists, in support of the record men and women. "A lot of these artists shouldn't have any compunction about what they lost in royalties," opined Goodman,

because they made up in their personal appearances. I don't know whether or not or how much, if anything, they were cheated by these record companies, because these [record] people worked *hard* to get a record played.[16]

But I had no dealings with those things. It was no more than I did when Leonard and Phil started another publishing company with Roquel "Billy" Davis, Chevis Music [an amalgam of Chess and Davis]. [Was it] a bit strange? I don't want to touch that; it was against the rules and regulations.

Goodman was objecting to Chevis Music being used for Billy Davis's Chess production copyrights instead of Arc. If Chevis, later bought out by Davis, represented something of an open sore to the Goodman brothers, then Vee-Jay Records' Conrad Music was a big gain.[17]

"I got a call from Ewart Abner," said Gene Goodman. "He told me he wanted x number of dollars for it [Conrad], and I flew right in. I didn't even do due diligence, looking at the contracts, because I knew the copyrights were great. I bought them. Yes, Vee-Jay [was] closing up. By putting out that one album [*Jolly What!*, incongruously with Frank Ifield, and a second single], the Beatles gave them 'Thank You Girl,' and I publish that; I have one Beatles song. It doesn't make any sense [to have just one McCartney-Lennon copyright]. John Lee Hooker, Jimmy Reed . . . oh yes. Abner was a big gambler; he would take a whole suitcase of money to Las Vegas. When Vee-Jay moved from Chicago to the West Coast, it was over by that time." Conrad Music was acquired by the Goodmans on November 19, 1965.

With song copyrights becoming due for renewal twenty-eight years after registration at the Library of Congress, songwriters were able to claim the publishing on their songs but for the United States only. In the cases of Muddy Waters and Willie Dixon, their songs have been lost forever to Arc Music and its overseas subpublishers. Goodman was still livid about these defections: "Chess kept recording through good times and bad times. You know, I went to see Muddy with my stepson in Roslyn [Long Island] maybe a week before a suit came out accusing us of nonpayment of royalties. We had a bite to eat together, and Muddy was telling me how great Leonard was, how great I was. And he was preparing a lawsuit. Scott Cameron became a partner with Muddy and Willie in their publishing businesses!"

Goodman quickly put his disgust aside, adding, "You see, I've always been happy with whatever I'm doing. I don't want to fight with people. I have a saying, 'I'm an old settler.' I just want to settle things and put my mind toward the future, not going backward."

Goodman had fond memories of the transition from the old to the new in the New York music publishing scene as he kept pace with the latest trends and personalities. "I knew young songwriters like Carole King," he said, "but they were already tied up by Don Kirshner. They were at 1650 [Broadway]; it's another Brill Building, if you will, where Slay and Crewe recorded 'Silhouettes.' Al and Dick's was on Fifty-fourth Street, a steakhouse. We'd all meet [there] at night, a clan of publishers who were all *friendly* to one another. We weren't in competition with each other, because we each had a different song. Without a song, you couldn't make a record," he said, starkly.

All the publishers were together in one building. If they didn't take your song, you walked into the next office and played it for me. If I didn't like it, they played it for the next one. Of course, if you were a big songwriter, you went to the big companies. We couldn't get a Sammy Cahn, for instance, to come to us, no more than we'd get a Cole Porter to come to us. They went to . . . Chappell's, they went to Warner Brothers. That's how we started, by taking in songwriters who would walk in with any song, and we'd print it. Hopefully, the writer would try to get a record.

Yes, with sheet music diminishing, publishers started their own labels. Perhaps Leiber and Stoller were successful for a little while with theirs [Red Bird], Hill & Range had Bigtop that didn't do anything at all,[18] and Acuff-Rose had Hickory. There wasn't a stampede. You had to be a certain type of person to be in the record business. The publishers were what I'd call a straight man; the record companies were rough and tumble. First of all, in order to be as successful as they were, the record men had to have ears as to what was coming. Like Ahmet [Ertegun] and Jerry [Wexler], they had their ears to the ground. They had a fellow with them also who I used to admire: Herb Abramson. Quite honestly, I was concerned about people like Morris Levy. I stayed an arm's length away from them. He had a reputation, whether it was true or not. I was very careful, that's right.

Gene Goodman and brother Harry felt comfortable enough with Jackie Wilson's manager, Nat Tarnopol, an office neighbor in the Brill Building, to jointly form Merrimac Corporation to administer Wilson's profitable song copyrights.[19]

"But the indie era was fun," said Gene Goodman.

You had a disc, a 45, run to people and [got] it played, especially over and above the majors, who didn't even know how to go out and get a record played. The indies opened the doors and let us [publishers] in, so to speak. The majors asleep at the wheel? Absolutely. The rock 'n' roll era . . . gave me everything I have today. That's sort of special. And I enjoyed any kind of music except when it becomes not being music—rap, I can't stand rap. A lot of these things are passing fancies, like hip-hop, but they're going to take a span of years. . . . [Because] of the great, great standards of George Gershwin, the Cole Porters, they'll be around after all of this, as far as I am concerned; Chuck Berry [copyrights] will not be the same in the gross amount. Everything comes to an end. As I say to my children, even a train stops. Fortunately for us, our songs like "Boom Boom" [by John Lee Hooker] are being used all over the world. I feel I was a keeper of the musical family.

Give me a story line: Muddy was great, and so was Willie Dixon. Those were the quality artists, because I was always looking for a song. Chuck appealed to the teenagers; you can see why after the fact, but not before. Sure, I liked Howlin' Wolf, Sonny Boy [Williamson], Little Walter: all those were the storytellers I liked. We made a lot of money with those artists, and they made the record company exist. Arc Music is one of the biggest independent publishers; there are very few independents left.

Gene Goodman's final comments were reserved for Leonard Chess, who else? "Oh, I admire him so much; I looked at him as some kind of a god. He knew what was going on all the time, every day. People would call him and say, 'I would like to be in the distribution business with you.' He put down the telephone and would say, 'He's a cheat; he's not of my family tree. Why do I need him to be in the distribution?' He was really sharp. And he saw radio coming. If he had been alive today, he could have been the radio king."

As we concluded, Goodman said, "Music has always been important; it's brought people together," before adding in almost the same breath, "That's the first interview I've given, and it will be the last!" Thank you, Mr. G., for your consent; it's a wonderful story.

As a postscript, in the summer of 2006, Arc Music and Conrad Music were on the block for sale at a cool $65 million until summarily withdrawn. Compare this asking price with the $6.5 million that the Chess record labels fetched some four decades earlier. There was certainly value in those song copyrights, as Gene and Harry Goodman (and Benny) had long understood.

Johnny Bienstock and Freddy Bienstock: Music Publishers and Bigtop Records

Sheet music sales were in patent decline in the 1950s, as Gene Goodman had observed, with the pop crooner/big band/live radio era slipping into oblivion. Income from records (mechanicals and performances) was assuming extra importance for the stand-alone music publishers. Early in the decade, *Billboard* had noted that publishers were prepared to pay or part-pay for record dates of their songs, even press up a few promo discs, or as a last resort give away a piece of a song to have it released on record.[20]

Recognizing the changes being wrought in the music business landscape, several publishers went whole-hog and formed their own record labels. Fred and Wesley Rose, of Acuff-Rose, were publisher/record company pacesetters in 1954 with Hickory Records out of Nashville. Equally dominant country music rivals Hill & Range would join the circus with Bigtop Records.

Launched in June 1958, Bigtop notched up several big hits over a six-year period, led by "Lavender Blue (Dilly, Dilly)" by Sammy Turner and "Runaway" by Del Shannon. Under the control of majority stockholders Julian and Jean Aberbach, the label was managed by the affable Johnny Bienstock, while his brilliant younger brother Freddy was executive president with redoubtable Hill & Range general manager Paul Case in support. The Aberbachs and the Bienstocks were described by Johnny as "double second cousins."

The Bienstock brothers, born into a privileged Austrian-Swiss family of Jewish descent, almost suffered the ultimate tragedy in the Hitler-ravaged Europe of the late 1930s. Said Johnny Bienstock, "I was born in Vienna; I grew up there and went to school there. Then . . . [came] the unfortunate happenstance that the Nazi German troops marched in, and we who were Jewish had to leave if we wanted to stay alive. Fortunately, Dad [a doctor] was born in Zurich, he was a Swiss citizen, and because of that, my mom, my brother Freddy, and I . . . were all Swiss citizens as well. And that's what really saved our lives and saved us from having to go into concentration camps. But Freddy and I had been in a jail overnight. After we were there for maybe sixteen hours, scared out of our wits, this guy came in and took us out in Vienna, put us on the street, and . . . said [*in German*], 'We made a mistake, sorry.' That was in 1938."

Freddy and Johnny came to the United States with their parents in January 1939, making the ten- to twelve-day transatlantic crossing in a Cunard-line boat. Uncle Sam, their father's older brother, lived in Newark, New Jersey, and he guaranteed that the family would not become wards of the state or ask for any benefits.

After the German occupation of France, Julian Aberbach had escaped to join his brother Jean, who by then was working for Max Dreyfus at Chappell & Co., the biggest music publisher in America. "Julian was hobnobbing around Nashville and on the West Coast," said Johnny Bienstock. "He got to meet people like Lefty Frizzell, Ernest Tubb, Eddy Arnold, and people of that ilk. In New York, you didn't hear these country artists. Julian was a fifty-fifty partner with his brother Jean in a company that they had created in 1945 called Hill & Range Songs. It was all the hillbillies and all the western stars: 'Hill' equals 'hillbilly'; 'Range' equals 'Home on the Range.' They had certain subsidiaries like Ernest Tubb Music and things like that. What they had done was . . . let their artists cut into their profits. That was the idea so that they would get good songwriters."

Hill & Range Music was the first independent music publisher to come to grips with the rock 'n' roll age in a big way. The Austrian-born, aristocratic, art-loving, and aloof Aberbach brothers were the unlikeliest facilitators of hillbilly, rockabilly, and rock 'n' roll music, but the track record speaks for itself. Their entrée into the world of western music came in early 1945, when they published the huge Spade Cooley No. 1 "folk" hit, "Shame on You" (OKeh). Soon they were devising those clever publishing deals that gave prominent country artists not only songwriter entitlements but also partnership stakes in the associated publishing companies. Eddy Arnold, Lefty Frizzell, and Ernest Tubb apart, such deals were done with breakthrough country acts Red Foley, Bill Monroe, Hank Snow, and Bob Wills. Johnny Cash was signed up later, in 1958. Then, of course, there was Elvis Presley.

"With Elvis Presley, the very big one," said Johnny Bienstock,

the fact is that Julian really had a whole lot to do with it. Hank Snow told him, "Listen, I've got the kid warming up for me, and these young people just scream; they'd rather hear him than me." Julian said, "What's his name?" He said, "Elvis Presley. He comes from Tupelo, Mississippi." And Julian said, "I'd like to hear this guy." With Elvis there was a special deal, because Jean and Julian decided he had become so important that they were willing to give Colonel Parker and Elvis Presley 50 percent of what they made; they were fifty-fifty partners. As you know, Elvis "the King" is selling now more dead than when he was alive. It's really hard to believe how much music he is selling.

Once Julian and Jean became partners, whatever they did was fifty-fifty, regardless of who got what. Julian in my humble opinion—I may be all wrong; it's being disputed by the Jean interests and heirs—was the more creative guy. Jean would be able to contribute about certain business ways of handling things. But Julian—the mere fact that Colonel Parker was running this [publishing] thing was a *fantastic* idea.

In a way, Elvis Presley's success signified that a song's portrayal on record was now more important than its publication on sheet music and that the publishers as a body were no longer in total control of a song.

The Aberbachs also recruited some of the rock 'n' roll era's key songwriters, including Jerry Leiber and Mike Stoller, Bernie Lowe and Kal Mann, Doc Pomus and Mort Shuman, and Phil Spector. "We had the whole of the eleventh floor at 1619 Broadway; it was the Brill Building," said Johnny Bienstock. "We had songwriters hanging out in the office and writing songs day in and day out, publishers, demo studios, you name it."

Brother Freddy Bienstock, suave and debonair, has always had the air of a successful man fully in charge. His impressive aura was enhanced further by a distinguished Austrian accent, similar to that of film-star-turned-California-state-governor Arnold Schwarzenegger. In 2006, the Bienstock family's Carlin America offices were located just off prestigious Park Avenue in midtown New York. Bedecked with modern art, the place had an art-gallery quiet that reeked of privileged grandeur. It was a far cry from the bustling, rambling rabbit warrens of the former offices at 1650 Broadway and the Brill Building, only a few blocks away.

Freddy Bienstock started out in the stockroom of venerated publishers Chappell & Co. in 1941 and joined Hill & Range in "1953 or '54." Natural talent apart, he benefited from a line of masterly teachers: Chappell's Max Dreyfus, Julian and Jean Aberbach, and not least Colonel Tom Parker (Elvis Presley's woefully misunderstood manager). With these top mentors behind him, it is no wonder that Freddy acquired an unparalleled reputation for deal making. One of his biggest coups was buying the music publishing of King Records for $1 million in 1975, "a lot of money in those days." Syd Nathan's song catalog has been a marvelous asset for Bienstock.

On the other hand, even the best deal makers don't win all the time. Freddy admitted he missed out on acquiring Morris Levy's publishing interests when he had the one chance: "I was friendly with Morris. Eventually he wanted to sell me his publishing company, and I should have bought it. I remember I had lunch with him, and he said, 'I want $10 million, but if you're interested, you can have it for nine.' And I should have bought it [*taps table*]. But my lawyer said, 'You shouldn't do it because he hasn't been paying the writers and once you take it over you will have nothing but lawsuits.' So I didn't do it. It was a big mistake."

Brother Johnny Bienstock retired from the family company in 2004 following heart problems and never recovered his health. Johnny, more of a *bon viveur*, more outgoing, more relaxed but always in Freddy's shadow, was in charge of the day-to-day workings of Bigtop Records.

Explaining the strategy behind the launch of Bigtop Records, Freddy said a little impatiently, "Yes, yes, in the 1950s sheet music was declining, and the Bigtop label was set up to offset the lost income. Johnny, my brother, ran it. He had a number of hits, so he was involved because Hill & Range, after all, had that label. The Bigtop name had to do with the fact that one of the things that the Aberbachs were dreaming of was to try and get Elvis to come. Since the Colonel used to be involved with circuses, Bigtop was based on an idea about carnivals and so forth, and we thought this might be appealing to Colonel Parker. There was some discussion about signing Elvis at one time. The Colonel was unhappy with RCA and would have considered maybe coming to Bigtop. But it was very nebulous."

This almost fanciful story was confirmed by Johnny Bienstock: "Why 'Bigtop'? Oh, Colonel Parker, he was the man who gave us the name because he was a circus man. That's how we got the name for the pink label with a circus tent on it. So it was not far-fetched when he [Parker] said that Elvis should be on the label, because he gave it the name. We would have to give up half, because the only way the Colonel and Elvis together would do it would be to own 50 percent of Bigtop Records. And I was overjoyed. I wouldn't mind Elvis and the Colonel having half of Bigtop Records, because with him on that label, it was going to grow overnight like a huge tree." But it never happened.

The Elvis Presley–Colonel Tom Parker partnership was patterned loosely on trend-setting personal management alliances such as the one Joe Glaser had with Louis Armstrong and other acts. The Presley dream team, with the Aberbach brothers and Freddy Bienstock, was completed by RCA Victor with its massive marketing resources. "Jean and Julian were, of course, the owners of Hill & Range, and they set the policy," said Freddy.

The Aberbachs had dealt with Colonel Parker, since he was also the manager of Eddy Arnold, with whom they had a deal. When they were able to make a deal with Elvis for publishing, they felt that I was closer to Elvis's age than they were. So they introduced me to Colonel Parker. He was really an extraordinary man; we became very close. And Elvis would relate to me much easier than he would have related to the Aberbachs.

The Colonel wasn't mad about rock 'n' roll, but he recognized it as the trend and that Elvis would do very well. He was to convince him to record the religious albums, which did very well, and Elvis liked gospel music. The Colonel was always concerned about money and his motion picture career. Elvis, after all, made thirty-two films; it's a lot of films. After a very good start, it got to be like, you know, a production line. I must say that the quality of the music declined. The '68 [NBC] television special, that really put him back up.

Sam Phillips sold Elvis's Sun contract before I got there, but I got to know Sam Phillips very well. And I represented [Phillips's] Hi-Lo Music. Sam was terrific, and so were the artists that he had besides Elvis. Yes, Atlantic did try to buy Elvis's contract, but they didn't have enough money at that time, and they weren't really being seriously considered by the Aberbachs. The one thing was that the Colonel would deal with certain people. Of course he dealt with RCA Victor with Eddy Arnold and then with Hank Snow. So it wasn't going to be anybody but RCA to sell to.[21]

Freddy Bienstock attended the defining "Hound Dog" Presley session but without any earth-shattering memories. However, he did recall that "with Elvis, many sessions were magical. When he did 'It's Now or Never,' it was magical."[22] Freddy continued:

Elvis liked Otis Blackwell's songs; he had a few big hits such as "Don't Be Cruel" and "All Shook Up." Otis Blackwell used to produce his own demos, and Elvis's records of them were all based on the demos, as far as the arrangements go. Elvis always had the final word, but I tried to push some [songs].

It's very funny: I had a Picasso drawing, it was rather cubistic, and Otis was in my office. I was coming down and I overheard him saying to Winfield Scott, who was his co-writer, "I think this kid [Bienstock] must have done this." He wanted to give me an opportunity to brag, and he says, "Hey man, who did this?" And I said, "Well, Otis, it is a Picasso" . . . I wasn't quite sure that he knew who Picasso was. He said, "Oh yeah, what does it mean?" Then he looked at it and said, "Beautiful broad!"

I think that Otis made an awful lot of money from us and from Presley, even to this day. Besides, he had another song that we published in a company that we bought called "Fever." It was a huge song, but he wrote it under a pseudonym, John Davenport, [who] was really Otis Blackwell [with Eddie Cooley]. When we acquired the King Records label publishing, we inherited that song of Otis's, and it's still making a lot of money. The Peggy Lee record was huge.[23]

Freddy had met his future wife, Miriam Abramson, at Atlantic Records in 1954, thereby accelerating his awareness of rhythm and blues music and establishing a good business link between the two companies. A subsidiary of Hill & Range Music had already purchased from Progressive Music "Sh-Boom," one of Atlantic's hottest copyrights, for a reported "substantial" sum of money.

"I was pitching another song [for Monument Music]," recalled Freddy Bienstock. "Jerry Wexler and Ahmet [Ertegun] were out, so Miriam came down to listen to my song, and she liked it. She gave it to Jerry, and Jerry recorded it; 'Mambo Baby' became a hit for Ruth Brown. That was the song written by Charlie Singleton and Rose Marie McCoy, who became very fond of me and I became very fond of them. They would take me up to Harlem. I was the only white man in some of those clubs, and they were very proud of having me around. I had the feeling that what then was called rhythm and blues—it became rock 'n' roll later—it was becoming more and more popular. I thought that was going to be where I would start to operate, because all other fields were taken. I mean, the Aberbachs had the country field here, [Max] Dreyfus had the stage and theater, so I decided to go into rhythm and blues. It was a success."

When the Aberbachs appointed Johnny Bienstock to head Bigtop in 1958, he had no idea how to run a record company. So he went down to Philadelphia to pick up tips from former Hill & Range writers Bernie Lowe and Kal Mann, who had jumped out of the gate quickly with their Cameo label. As well, Mann and Lowe had just written a No. 1 hit in the summer of 1957 for Elvis Presley, "(Let Me Be Your) Teddy Bear." "They let me come by and look over their shoulders," said Bienstock, "because I didn't know how to handle certain things production-wise, inventory-wise." It was also his introduction to creative independent label royalty accounting: "I said to myself, 'Look, this is very good, but I'm not erasing things and putting new numbers in. But I'll sell a few records.'"

The first semblance of a Bigtop hit came in November 1958 when young Bobby Pedrick Jr. (later known as Robert John) scored modestly with the bright teen rocker "White Bucks and Saddle Shoes," written by Hill & Range staffers Doc Pomus and Mort Shuman: "That's what the kids all choose . . ." sang Johnny enthusiastically. "That record came out at exactly the same time as Bobby Darin [with "Queen of the Hop," a follow-up to "Splish Splash"]," he said. "They were both on the 'try-out' [called "Rate a Record"] that Dick Clark had. He used to try out new records for the kids to react to, and Bobby Darin overwhelmingly beat 'White Bucks.' Although 'White Bucks' was never really a hit [peaking at No. 74], it was big enough to sell records. I thought it was a very good record."[24]

Bigtop was established by Sammy Turner's "Lavender Blue (Dilly, Dilly)," a No. 3 hit in the summer of 1959. "That was a very, very big record produced by Leiber and Stoller, who were songwriters of ours. They wrote for Elvis and other people," said Johnny Bienstock.

> There was nobody in our office that knew anything about the record business. Freddy didn't, Jean and Julian didn't, and so we had to rely on them [Leiber and Stoller]. They were making records not only for us but for Atlantic and others. We were very friendly with them, and later on we became partners [in Fort Knox Music/Trio Music Co.].
>
> Then television shows became big, such as Dick Clark in Philadelphia; you had this *American Bandstand* show. I used to drive down on every Wednesday once he became prominent. He had a guy by the name of Tony Mammarella who was his assistant, and he screened you before you got to see Dick Clark. I personally got very friendly with Dick right away. He liked Sammy Turner's "Lavender Blue (Dilly, Dilly)" a lot but . . . I said, "Dick, but *what!*" He told me that when he was a high school kid, he used to work in a post office at Christmastime, like most teenagers do, and next to his desk was another guy who constantly used to sing "Lavender blue, dilly dilly."[25] It drove him *bananas!* Dick said, "I got to hate that song with a passion, but I'll tell you something, Johnny, this is a good record. If I didn't hate the song so much, I'd put it on the air of my dance show right away because I think it will sell. But if you can get that record played elsewhere in my town, I'll play it."
>
> Jocko Henderson ["Your ace from outer space"] and Georgie Woods ["The guy with the goods"] were at the black station WDAS; there were two or three black stations in Philadelphia. I made sure that all those black stations played the record, particularly since Sammy Turner was a black artist, and he had that very soulful rendition of "Lavender Blue (Dilly, Dilly)." Then when we got on WFIL, I saw Dick Clark a week later, and I said, "Look, I got you surrounded. . . . Without you playing it on the big *nationwide* show, I've already sold about 100,000." "Wow," he says, "I'm going on

it." It was Sammy's only big hit; he had other little things like "Always" [No. 19], "Paradise" [No. 46], and "Sweet Annie Laurie" [No. 100].

Dick didn't ask for a piece of the action. At that time, he was not as forward, even though I know from certain people that he would make deals of that sort. But I figured it was a bit rash and early [to give payola]; I would rather bring some goodies. I would hate to give money to them. Like if a jockey has a baby, I used to buy the baby a birth gift, became a godfather, and things like that. . . . Hopefully . . . they would like me. And that way I got records played.

Even though "Lavender Blue" was a Top 3 record, Jean Aberbach was not happy back at the Hill & Range ranch. "The interesting part is that the record company was supposed to make up for the loss of the sheet music sales," said Johnny Bienstock. "And Jean was mad at me that 'Lavender Blue (Dilly, Dilly)' didn't belong to us; it belonged to another publisher and became a big hit. He said, 'What's the matter with you? That's not the idea, to have just record sales; the idea is to promote our copyrights.' I said, 'Look, there are certain things that happen in the record business that you may not understand. I can give him [Sammy Turner] all the Hill & Range songs to sing, and if he can't do it, what good is it? You can't force it. But if there is a thing that you can do well that can be a hit, I don't care whose copyright it is, we'll make money out of the record.' That's what record companies do . . . Atlantic Records doesn't care who has the copyright."

The biggest Bigtop hit was the No. 1 international best-seller "Runaway" by Del Shannon in the early summer of 1961. "Well, Del Shannon was the product of a guy that I was very, very friendly with in Ann Arbor, Michigan," said Johnny Bienstock.

His name was Ollie McLaughlin; he was a disc jockey. He first took me to Johnny and the Hurricanes, who came out of a stable [run] by two partners named Irving Micahnik and Harry Balk [they were connected once with Al Green at the Flame Show Bar in Detroit and operated in the name of EmBee Productions]. Harry Balk was the music man in the record business, and Irving Micahnik, a Russian name, was the money man. They bought me this solid gold Swiss watch when I had "Runaway," and they bought a mink cape for my wife. They were so delighted about this big hit.

The record was done and cut in Detroit, but then Harry Balk brought the stuff to New York. We mastered in New York, usually at Atlantic Records if I could get Tommy Dowd to let me into his studio; and I was very friendly with Tommy Dowd. Oh, he was a fantastic engineer! I said to Harry [Balk] in the studio: "It ["Runaway"] is so bad, so flat, we've got to speed it up." And we speeded it up a full ten seconds, so then the sound was pleasant to the ear. But when Del had to do it live, he couldn't go up that high. It was a terrific sound in the bridge that suddenly helped the record along. A guy by the name of Maximillian Crook . . . had this crazy instrument like a Moog that he played [actually a Musitron]. He wanted to protect it; it was his invention and everything.

At this time, I didn't even know of Del Shannon. His real name was Charlie Westover. To tell you the truth, when I first met him, I saw a guy that was about twenty-six years old with a big cigar in his hand, and my heart fell in my pants. I was doing a record hop with him in Teaneck, New Jersey, and I said, "You gotta get rid of that cigar; you got to lose at least five to eight pounds. They'll think that you're a father. You're not a kid that's running away; you don't sound like a runaway when they look at you." That record was the *only* natural record in my career. That record got on the air, and orders would come in by the tens of thousands in every territory in the United States. It was No. 1 here and No. 1 in England, too.

· Johnny Bienstock credited his disc jockey friend Bob Bartel of Radio WLOF Orlando, Florida, with breaking "Runaway" literally overnight. "The next morning, Henry Stone in Miami called me up," Johnny added.

> He said, "You got a record out, something 'Running Love' or whatever?" I said, "'Running' . . . ?" "C'mon, I have so many calls." I said, "Could it possibly be 'Runaway'?" He said, "Yeah, I think that's what it is. I'm your distributor, and I haven't even got a sample: send me 20,000 records! I've had so many calls, and I haven't even heard the record." That's his story, absolutely true. And our New York distributor, Gladys Pare [of Portem], ordered 30,000 copies.
>
> We did not publish "Runaway," but I bought the copyright from Ollie McLaughlin. It took a while, and he needed some money. I got a $12,000 bonus from Jean Aberbach— not even Julian; it was Jean—because that's one thing he did do when we brought [a good song] in.

Other big singles by Del Shannon were "Hats Off to Larry" (No. 5) and "Little Town Flirt" (No. 12). All told he had nine Hot 100 hits on Bigtop between 1961 and 1963. The Del Shannon *Runaway* album, like so many by indie hit acts at the time, fared poorly, but the follow-up LP, *Little Town Flirt*, made No. 12 in 1963.

Johnny and the Hurricanes preceded Del Shannon as a Bigtop-EmBee signing. This popular rocking instrumental group was on a roll with Morty Craft's Warwick label, but after a royalty fiasco, Johnny Bienstock stepped in on behalf of Bigtop. "We had a pretty good run," he said. "They were not those monster hits they originally had on Warwick, but some pretty good records. Harry Balk would get public domain songs and arrange them and they were copyrighted: 'Rocking Goose' [No. 60, fall 1960] was one of those which we published." Of the five Johnny and the Hurricanes chart hits for Bigtop, only "Down Yonder" broke into the Top 50. Bigtop did better in Britain, where the sax-organ combo, fronted by Johnny Paris, notched up four Top 20 hits on London.[26]

In the fall of 1960, still in an expansionary mode, Bigtop, through Hill & Range's Paul Case, financed and distributed on a fifty-fifty profit basis the Dunes label. This was owned by manager Stan Shulman and singer Ray Peterson, who had just come off the "death" hit "Tell Laura I Love Her," produced by Hugo & Luigi for RCA Victor. There was immediate but fleeting Top 10 success for the Dunes-Bigtop combine with Peterson's "Corinna, Corinna" and Curtis Lee's "Pretty Little Angel Eyes." Both records were made under the aegis of ambitious young record man Phil Spector, who already had one No. 1 hit to his credit in late 1958 as a member of the Teddy Bears with "To Know Him Is to Love Him" (Dore).

Bigtop itself was to score big again, somewhat fortunately, with "What's Your Name" by Don & Juan (No. 7, early 1962). "On the other side of that record was the song that I was working on, 'Chicken Necks,'" said Johnny Bienstock. "When Clark Grayson [a Pittsburgh disc jockey] went to a record hop one night, by mistake he put on 'What's Your Name,' and the kids went crazy. I listened to see what they reacted to, and at the end of the record, they [Don & Juan] would say 'shoo be doo, wop wa da.' The kids couldn't wait until it got to that part; they loved to hear it. That made the record. Before any other city had any semblance of sales, Pittsburgh had already sold 30,000 to 40,000 records."

Johnny Bienstock introduced this regional breakout to his main distributors in the rest of the country by using a new concept, a telephone conference call.

It took a little while, [but] it was a Top 10 in the end: "What's Your Name" by Don & Juan. It's a real rock 'n' roll oldie; it's a classic. Everybody knows: "What's your name, is it Mary or Sue . . . shoo be doo."[27]

I had roughly between twenty-eight and thirty distributors throughout the country. Some were better than the others. Milt Salstone [M. S. Distributing Co.], he was one of the best guys, and he had a very good relationship with many jocks, personal, in the city of Chicago. Some of them would even be partners in some of the side businesses, and Milt himself would call up and say, "Listen, I've got a record here from Johnny Bienstock, Bigtop, you gotta play it." And those guys would do it. Each distributorship had one or two or three promotion men, depending on how many different lines they had. And he [Milt] had, of course, a whole bunch of salesmen that went out and sold. The important thing was to augment your promotion with sales. So you went into these various territories and made sure the jocks played the records. That was the important thing. If it was on the air and didn't happen, you'd think it wouldn't sell. My ear was pretty good, and I always had a pretty good idea.

I increased the pressing orders all over the country. I used Specialty Records (Art Rupe), and in Memphis I used Plastic Products (Buster Williams). Buster was a very close friend of mine; he had a home, almost a small mansion, in the middle of Memphis. With "Runaway," I hadn't paid him for the longest time; he just kept pressing them, you know. He gave terrific credit. I had such a good relationship with him. And then I had of course MGM Records [custom pressing] and Al Massler's pressing plant; I used that when I ran short. There were pressing plant problems in the industry. Fortunately, I did not have it happen to me, but there was a fairly large amount of bootlegs. It affected publishers, everybody, no question.

Then Johnny jumped into the future, adding, "I get scared looking at the Internet. I say, 'My God, we are so unprotected.' What are you going to do? This is the twenty-first century."

Bigtop was to enjoy further quality hits: Miss Toni Fisher's evocative "West of the Wall' (No. 37, 1962) was inspired by the Berlin Wall crisis, while another girl singer, Andrea Carroll, scored with "It Hurts to Be Sixteen" (No. 45, 1963). The final charting act was classy soul balladeer Lou Johnson, who was produced by Burt Bacharach.

Even with a commendable list of hits and several near misses, Bigtop was not deemed to be a raging triumph. Johnny Bienstock, well versed in the art of public relations and a gregarious attendee at conventions, had done his best. "Well, the most important difficult problem was to get the records played," he said. "Everybody who was competing tried, and there was just so much airtime. You used to meet everybody [*chuckles*], all those different jocks in all these different territories. Whether it was Chicago or New York, or whether it was a small territory [for pop] like Nashville. But you take territories like Richmond, Virginia. Nothing! You sell a few records, but so what? Philadelphia was important, New York was very important, L.A. was very important."

With the Beatles overturning the musical landscape, even the bigger markets became out of bounds. And so the circus ended at Bigtop. This is how Freddy Bienstock saw the not-so-grand finale: "I think the Aberbachs lost interest in promoting Bigtop. They were more concerned about their publishing business, and they thought Bigtop took up too much time of mine and Paul Case's and so forth. Johnny was actually in charge of Bigtop, and Paul Case would only spend extra time on it, just like I did. My main job was really Hill & Range and Presley Music." If Bigtop, supported by all the Aberbach resources (financial and intellectual) could not succeed at this juncture, what chance was there for most other indies? Very little, it must be said.

With the collapse of Bigtop, Johnny Bienstock was hired immediately as "executive assistant" to Jerry Wexler. "I was never really out of a job," said Bienstock. "Julian was very unhappy, but he never contradicted his brother. That's the one [area in which] I thought that he was weak." And so Johnny went to Atlantic during the era of Aretha Franklin and Percy Sledge and became head of the Atlantic subsidiary Cotillion Records. During his tenure, the Cotillion label scored big with Brook Benton's "Rainy Night in Georgia" (No. 4), followed by *Woodstock,* a No. 1 soundtrack three-LP album from 1970. "That's when I got my first Lincoln automobile," said Bienstock, "because I was doing so well. Ahmet [Ertegun] told me not a Rolls Royce, but I could get a Lincoln." After Cotillion, Bienstock worked closely with Eric Clapton and the Bee Gees at the Robert Stigwood Organization before returning to brother Freddy's publishing fold and heading the venerable firm of E. B. Marks Music.

Johnny Bienstock, despite a commendable résumé as a record man, always saw himself as a music publisher first: "Jean Aberbach kept saying, 'I'm not interested in the record business; why doesn't he shut up with this record thing?' He was only trying to create copyrights, and from [his] point of view, . . . he was not wrong. And I tell you why. Record *masters* on every one of the hit records I had are laying somewhere in the vault and are not worth very much.[28] I mean, if somebody reminisces and once in a while plays one of my old records, there are no big sales of any of those things. But the *songs* on those records, they live and live and live, and they keep earning money. That's the real story."

15

Hillbilly Boogie

CAST OF CHARACTERS
Ira Howard, *Cash Box* country music editor
Don Pierce, 4 Star and Starday Records
Fred Foster, 4 Star record producer
Floyd Soileau, Starday custom client
Shelby Singleton, Mercury and SSS International–
    Sun Records
Margaret Lewis, SSS International songwriter
*also featuring Bill McCall, 4 Star Records; and H. W.
"Pappy" Daily, Starday Records*

By the early 1940s, through regular exposure on Nashville's national barn dance on Radio WSM, the *Grand Ole Opry*, country acts such as Roy Acuff (OKeh) and Ernest Tubb (Decca) were selling millions of records. The powerful Texas-Mexico border stations were important factors in the spread of hillbilly music, too. Another catalyst was the broadcasters' block on ASCAP-protected songs in 1941 that led to top pop acts like Bing Crosby recording BMI country songs such as "You Are My Sunshine" (accredited to Louisiana governor Jimmie Davis) and Al Dexter's "Pistol Packin' Mama." Through necessity, therefore, tuneful, well-written country songs were seen as pop material for radio and jukebox purposes. Then, in quick time, came the enforced but temporary interruptions from the declaration of war, shellac rationing, and the Petrillo ban.

"Country music started to spread, believe it or not, in the army in World War II," said Ira Howard, *Cash Box* country editor.

Everybody from all over the United States was thrown together. A lot of people who never heard country music all of a sudden started hearing it because somebody from one of these small towns (whether it was Nashville, Bakersfield, or whatever) was playing it on the radio.

It was the early 1950s when country started to take hold. There were guys like Eddy Arnold, the guy that bridged the gap between country and pop, and later on Jim Reeves did it even more successfully. But Eddy Arnold was the guy, because his music (not nasal and not twangy) was easier to accept, although in the early days he was a little bit twangy. He could sing the ballads, the pretty stuff, and people started listening to it. Then came Hank Williams.

This is the world that publishers Hill & Range Music and Acuff-Rose (which Roy Acuff founded with Fred Rose) had tapped into profitably.

In the hillbilly-cum-country realm (also incorporating honky-tonk, bluegrass, sacred, western swing, and initially cowboy), the indie labels were already up against much tougher major label opposition compared to the wide-open rhythm and blues sector. The secret of the majors' success in the country sphere was rooted in their shrewd development of the Nashville scene through the skills of several inspiring men: Steve Sholes and Chet Atkins at RCA Victor; Paul Cohen and Owen Bradley at Decca; and Art Satherley and Don Law at Columbia.[1] Over on the West Coast, Capitol was mopping up under Lee Gillette and Ken Nelson (who would get the feel of what was happening by listening to jukeboxes at Greyhound bus stations and restaurants on trips to the South). With country music, it must be noted, the majors were dealing with white artists rather than with blacks, as in rhythm and blues.

Ironically, Nashville's potential as a recording hub was unlocked by a pop record on an independent label. The impact of Francis Craig's "Near You," a freak No. 1 hit on Jim Bulleit's Bullet label in 1947, was as seismic in Tennessee music circles as Cecil Gant's "I Wonder" was on the West Coast.

Back in January 1944, the activity that had helped country music to achieve critical mass led to the introduction of "Juke Box Folk Records," the first-ever country chart, in *Billboard*. Then in 1945, a supposed "million-seller" was notched up by Arthur Smith with "Guitar Boogie" on Super Disc out of Washington, D.C. This toe-tapping instrumental record, mirroring the boogie-woogie piano craze, was the catalyst for the hillbilly-boogie style that evolved effortlessly into rockabilly. Super Disc was owned by the Feld brothers, Irvin and Israel, who earned their fame and fortune as impresarios of the big rock 'n' roll touring caravans of the late 1950s (for a short while with *American Bandstand*'s Dick Clark) and then as owners of the venerable Ringling Bros.–Barnum & Bailey circus beginning in 1967. The Felds' Super Disc label (along with Arthur "Guitar Boogie" Smith's contract) was acquired in the summer of 1947 for MGM by Frank Walker, who needed product for the new quasi-major label, launched in March 1947. Just before the Arthur Smith deal, Walker nipped in nimbly with vision to sign Hank Williams after his debut stint with Sterling Records.

Of the leading independent labels, Syd Nathan's King Records was able to establish itself in the country music genre through its location in the heart of hillbilly terrain, abetted by the presence of the Radio WLW jamborees and the attendant pools of talent. But of the remaining stalwart imprints, only Imperial (with Slim Whitman heading an extensive roster) and Sun (with its made-over artists Johnny Cash and Carl Perkins) reaped any substantial reward in country music. Most of the other leading indies, including Chess, Modern, and Specialty, found themselves picking up the bread crumbs left by the majors. Atlantic had on its books in 1950 a promising western-swing type outfit by name of Bill Haley and his Saddlemen and even went as far as purchasing twenty "folk & western" masters from Lillian Claiborne's DC Records before the series was abandoned.

Typical of the mainstream independent labels was Flair Records, which was set up by Joe Bihari in December 1952 as a dedicated Modern hillbilly subsidiary before soon reverting to the tried-and-tested R&B format. Under a contemporary report titled "Biharis' Flair Disks Enter Country Field," *Billboard* noted that "[Joe] Bihari and his brother, Saul, will make a three-week tour of the South, seeking talent to make up a 10–artist roster, starting mid-January. Modern distributors will handle Flair."[2] Joe admitted, "Our distributors weren't geared to the hillbilly market; also, we didn't have the right songs or the right artists. Hank Williams, MGM, was about as big as you could get in those days, while RCA had Eddy Arnold and Decca had Ernest Tubb. There were plenty of good hillbilly artists around being showcased on the *Louisiana Hayride* and the *Grand Ole Opry*." With a final flourish, Bihari added, "Country was the easiest thing in the world to record."

By the mid-1950s, the confluence of hillbilly music into hillbilly boogie and then rockabilly had taken place. Arise King Elvis! An aspiring young record man who was aware of the Hillbilly Cat almost at the outset was Joe Johnson, assistant to Don Law at Columbia Records in Nashville and later head of Challenge Records. "Don sent me to Texas to check on what was happening with this 'cat music,'" remembered Johnson.[3] "I went down to Dallas to Big State distributors, which was also [the] distributor of Columbia, and Alta Hayes was in charge of singles sales. And I asked her the question, 'What's going on with cat music, what are we talking about here?' She said, 'I can't tell you, but I'm gonna show you. If you get ready tonight, I'll pick you up, and we're going to a show.' We went to see Elvis Presley at a high school gym. I met Elvis backstage, and he was walking the floor, very nervous, with the crowd out in front of me. The place was packed. The people outside couldn't get in, and the kids were actually sitting in the rafters of the gym. The other act was getting booed off stage. 'We want Elvis!' they were yelling.'"[4] Soon RCA Victor, not Columbia, had secured Presley's Sun contract.

Don Pierce: 4 Star and Starday Records

Despite the major label takeover of country music, there was still a niche market for enterprising labels such as 4 Star and Starday. That irrepressible record man Don Pierce was the link between both operations.

Easily the most important indie hillbilly imprint on the West Coast, 4 Star Records was formed by Dick Nelson in August 1945. The label's immediate fortunes were tied to its race music affiliate, Gilt-Edge, which had been scoring monstrously with Private Cecil Gant's "I Wonder." After this triumph, Dick Nelson enlisted record miller William "Bill" McCall Jr. as an investor in both labels. In addition, Cliff McDonald and Don Pierce were drafted into the fold as 25 percent stockholders each in 4 Star only, along with Nelson and McCall.

Viewing Cecil Gant, the "G.I. Sing-Singsation," as a one-way bet, Gilt-Edge flooded the market with no less than twenty singles in quick succession, but there was nothing else with the winning magic of "I Wonder." Within a year, the overextended group was facing bankruptcy. Bill McCall, already gray-haired and walking with a limp, stepped in to buy out Nelson and McDonald to give himself ownership of Gilt-Edge and a majority stake in 4 Star. He was never a popular record man.

McCall's dashing young sales manager, Don Pierce, was now an unequal minority stockholder in a record label teetering on the brink of oblivion. But 4 Star Records survived, thanks to McCall's artful leadership, Pierce's saucy, slick salesmanship, and a series of welcome hit records. In joining the label, Pierce was stumbling by chance upon the lively Californian 1940s "folk and western" scene, which had been fostered by the migrant communities from Oklahoma, Texas, and Arkansas. And as an investor, he was displaying his commitment to the future of the independent record business.

At the Starday Studios outside of Nashville in 1992, with longtime producer Tommy Hill by his side, a dapper Don Pierce recounted his story of many parts to researcher Ray Topping and myself. Small in physical stature (but that's all), Pierce was immersed in the independent record game almost from its inception. A businessman first, he developed many interesting sales and marketing techniques in country music. For all the accolades heaped upon him as a record man, he was called once by his Record Row competitors a carnival huckster "with a Madison Avenue accent."[5]

Going back to his start in music, Don Pierce said:

> I'm originally from Seattle. I don't play any instrument or have any real knowledge of music. But when I got out of the army in 1946, I went on a golfing trip with a couple of ex-caddy friends of mine that were also just out of the service. We had a chance to play Pebble Beach and Cypress Point in the same day coming down, and, being in uniform, they didn't charge us any money. So, when I got to Los Angeles, I decided I didn't want to go back to Seattle, because the sun was shining all the time down in Los Angeles.
>
> Then I needed to find something to do, and I answered an ad in the newspaper that said something about 4 Star Records. They were to be involved with many millions of record sales. I found out that it was started by a fellow named Dick Nelson that [originally] did little things for the armed forces, who let people make little messages to send home. I had accumulated a few bucks up in Seattle, and I invested it there for a minority position.
>
> Bill McCall got into the record business because he was supplying materials to a Decca pressing plant, and so then he had his own milling plant. When the war was over and shellac was still hard to come by, they would try to make a record that would sound good but with as little shellac as possible. In those days he was running that milling plant twenty-four hours a day, and he was furnishing the "biscuits" to the fifteen or twenty little record pressing companies around town. They would have the

record presses, but they didn't have biscuits, and he would sell them the biscuits. And so he's making this money from running this milling plant. It was owned by 4 Star.[6]

I was encouraged to be a salesman by Al Sherman, and he became a branch manager for King Records down on Pico Boulevard there. He said, "Now if you want to have some fun, you go on up the San Joaquin Valley, and all you have to do when you walk in the store is say that you're from 4 Star and you've got a new release by T. Texas Tyler." And that's what I did. I started in Bakersfield—I remember the dealer—and I started out with [pop artists] Ted Fio Rito and Henry Busse. No interest. I said, "But I've got a new record by Tex Tyler." We just had an acetate at the time. She listened to about eight bars and said, "Send me a hundred copies of this!" Well, that made me a Tyler fan right away, and I started to say, "What is this with hillbilly music?" Then we got into Sears, Roebuck mail order. That was a big thing, and it went on from there.

The biggest early 4 Star hits, all by T. Texas Tyler, were "Remember Me" [in 1945]; that lasted for several years and probably did 200,000 pieces on 78 speed. I would say "Filipino Baby" [in 1945] probably did 90,000 in there, but it took maybe two years; it wasn't a thing that you did in four months. Then when we had "Divorce Me C.O.D." [in 1946] and "So Round, So Firm, So Fully Packed" [in 1946], they went quicker and probably did 50,000 or 60,000. When we had "Deck of Cards" [in 1948], of course, we had a monster on our hands, and it was just spread all over. We did, I think, 700,000 pieces on that, which was a very, very big country record in those days.

While I was on the road, I picked up Cousin Ford Lewis in Fresno, and he was successful for us. I got acquainted with the Maddox Brothers [and Rose] in Modesto where I sold a lot of records, and we were very active with their career. I would arrange for in-store appearances for these people, and I would go to their shows from time to time. Then I'd work with them in the studio.

Already the major labels were monitoring closely the hillbilly indie label regional artists and their breakout hits. In the spring of 1947, the expanding and predatory Capitol Records tried vainly to sign Tyler to a five-year pact through his manager, Cliff McDonald, the early 4 Star partner. McDonald claimed unsuccessfully that 4 Star's contract was null and void on the basis of Bill McCall's alleged late payment of royalties. One year later, in glorious retribution, 4 Star enjoyed a huge No. 2 "folk" hit with T. Texas Tyler's "Deck of Cards" (a soldier's morality tale) by trumping Capitol's cover version by Tex Ritter. As well, Tyler managed to make No. 21 pop, hardly a common hillbilly crossover event at the time.[7]

"The records were bulky," explained Don Pierce. "We were shipping from Los Angeles by truck and then finally by Flying Tiger airplanes, and then we had to start pressing in Memphis and Chicago to take care of it. There was some bootlegging. The first bootlegging that I became aware of was when 'Near You' came out of Nashville on Bullet by Francis Craig [in 1947]. They didn't have good control of all the stampers that they shipped around; they were shipping stampers to anybody that would press their records. The guys that would press the records would send them a bill for what they pressed, but the number of records that went out the back door was another matter. It was the first hit that Bullet had, and it was hard for them to police it and control it."

Bootlegging was a debilitating presence, particularly for the poorer-resourced independent labels. It was a cancer that would never go away. *Billboard* highlighted the parasitic problem in a June 24, 1950, dispatch: "Bootleggers are reportedly operating in Los Angeles, with bogus biscuits cropping up here, in Florida and spots along the Eastern Seaboard. Label heads say it's easy to spot bootlegging by studying sales. Any disk, they find, normally builds for a hit, reaches its peak and tapers off in sales. When bootleggers cut in, a hit-riding disk drops suddenly from its peak, with total elimination of the tapering off period."[8]

By the new decade, Don Pierce was operating on the national stage. "I would go coast to coast in my automobile," he said.

A lot of times I would fly to Detroit, pick up a Ford, and go on into New York and then work all the way back down through the South. I called on radio stations, I called on jukebox operators, I got acquainted with the distributors. I looked for talent, I looked for songs, and did the whole thing. It's a great way to learn the business.

I became very friendly with Pappy Daily [in Houston]. At that time, there was very little representation of any record labels in Texas, but Pappy, being a distributor for 4 Star, which had country records, attracted people like Webb Pierce and Hank Locklin to the label.

In Washington, D.C., future Monument Records head Fred Foster was receiving his initiation as a record man guided by Ben Adelman. "We did a little demo tape with Billy Strickland," said Foster. "Ben sent it off to King Records, and they took it." Another demo tape, by Jimmy Dean, was sent to 4 Star, Pasadena, California. Bill McCall was the owner and president; he never paid anybody—the original crook."

McCall was interested enough in Dean to call for a session in Washington, D.C., and sent along a 4 Star copyright, "Bumming Around." "The record came out in August of '52," said Foster.

Unbelievable, it took us two days because nobody had ever produced a record. The engineer had never done a session, the band had never done one, I'd never done one, and certainly Jimmy had never done one. It was a recording studio that did mostly government work, and they taped conferences, speeches, and things. So we were all over our heads, but we plunged in.

So then it starts breaking after all those months. And then Bill McCall, to show you what kind of a guy he was, covered his own record with T. Texas Tyler [for Decca]. When we asked him why he did that, he said, "Well, I didn't know if Jimmy was going to make it all the way." But Jimmy did.

He hit No. 5 country in the spring of 1953 and later scored a No. 1 pop hit with "Big Bad John" for Columbia in 1961.

Don Pierce was never happy with Bill McCall's self-centered business methods, among them McCall's penchant for taking songwriting credits as W. S. Stephenson (a name supposedly inspired by William Shakespeare and Robert Louis Stevenson, no less).[9] Pierce would have left 4 Star earlier than he did, in 1953, had he not been tied to McCall through the stock investment and a loan. All his eggs were in the one 4 Star basket.[10]

"The only way that I was ever gonna get repaid was if Bill was gonna be successful with 4 Star," said Pierce. "I will give Bill McCall a lot of credit; he was a very astute businessman. When I got the loan paid off, I then said, 'Look, Bill, I wanna sell my stock [by now reduced from 25 percent to 10 percent after Pierce was placed on a regular salary], because you have your daughter, your son, your wife all on the payroll. My chances of ever doing anything in a family thing are not much.' And he said, 'I don't wanna buy your stock because you won't stay with me then.' Of course, I knew all the distributors, and I knew all the artists, and I was pretty important to the label at that time. He was smart enough to know that by keeping me invested there, why, he would have my services. And he played that card. But a thing happened, a thing happened!"

That "happening thing" was the arrival of a tape reel of "Don't Let the Stars (Get in Your Eyes)" by Slim Willet, a dee-jay from Abilene, Texas. Willet already had one failed single for 4 Star, and at first Bill McCall refused to take the new record, offering instead to custom press the discs. Willet went as far as to hire a salesman to promote his recording, whereupon Paul Glass, then at Big State distributors in Dallas, implored 4 Star to pick it up. Released in June 1952, the melodic song was strong enough to blossom over Willet's routine western crooning but with spirited rhythm accompaniment.[11]

"The guy sent it in with enough money to press three hundred records for his own use," confirmed Don Pierce. "He did it all himself. But I got the paperwork done so that we owned the masters [and publishing], and it became No. 1 on the *Your Hit Parade* with Perry Como [on RCA Victor in January 1953]. Buddy Morris [of E. H. Morris Music], who was a big publisher in New York and had the sheet music rights to 'Don't Let the Stars (Get in Your Eyes),' was instrumental in getting the Perry Como recording of it."

For the time being, 4 Star was saved, and so was Don Pierce's investment in the label. Slim Willet's song "Don't Let the Stars (Get in Your Eyes)" represented hillbilly heaven. "So I finally negotiated with Bill's lawyer," said Pierce, "where he agreed: Yes, he would either buy my stock, or he would give me a bonus of $15,000 because I had found the song—Perry Como went to No. 1, and all of that. Well, I kept working month after month, and I kept saying, 'Bill, when are you gonna buy my stock?' and he says, 'Well, I'll talk to you about it next week. And when are you gonna hit the road and go selling records?' I said, 'I'm not leaving town again on any trips until I conclude this matter.' And when he wouldn't finalize it, I gave him notice and gave him the keys to the car. I resigned from 4 Star."

So how did Don Pierce get his money back? "It just went on and on with Bill," he said,

and Syd Nathan found out about that. He called me on the phone and he says, "Don, I'm selling 4 Star Records for Bill, and I understood that everything was all settled between you?" So I said, "No, he didn't complete the deal." He says, "I'm sending Jack Kelley, my vice president, out to see Al Sherman [the King branch manager in Los Angeles] anyway. I'm gonna have him sit down with Bill McCall and see if I can help. I'm gonna tell Jack to say this: 'Bill, if you don't complete what you agreed to do as a part of the deal when we took over distribution of 4 Star after Don split, . . . I'm not gonna distribute your records.'" And he held his feet to the fire! Bill signed the papers and finally completed the deal. Now that's what I call a friend; that's Syd Nathan.

And another guy that was an angel to me was Ralph Peer of Southern Music. He was an absolute angel to me, because when I was unable to draw a salary at 4 Star, he made me a song scout for his company. Well, now, that's crazy. I've got my own publishing company, I'm his competitor, and he asks me to be his song scout! And I said, "Well, Mr. Peer, you know if I find a good song, I'm gonna keep it myself." He said, "Yes, but I see in you something that I used to have. When I started in the business for RCA [Victor], they didn't pay me a salary. They told me I could record but keep the copyrights, so I recorded the Carter Family and I recorded Jimmie Rodgers. But I got the copyrights; that was reward enough. Now in your case, here's what we're going to do. I just want the film rights and the sheet music rights, and any time I get you a record of your song, I want half of that record." I said, "This I can do for you."

Upon leaving 4 Star in September 1953, Don Pierce invested $333 for a one-third share in Starday Records, a hillbilly diskery located in Houston, Texas. His new partners were nightclub owner/booking agent Jack Starnes (from Beaumont) and experienced coin machine/record distributor friend H. W. "Pappy" Daily; the "Starday" legend was derived from the last names of these men. With his colleagues based in Texas, Pierce handled sales and manufacturing from Los Angeles. "When Starday came along," he said, "we essentially replaced 4 Star, which had given its distribution to King and then eventually sold out to Gene Autry. And Starday became the [country music] supplier to the independent record distributors."

Initially, though, Don Pierce spent time building up Hollywood Records as a rhythm and blues outlet in partnership with John Dolphin of Los Angeles. Only four months later, in January 1954, Pierce had bought out Dolphin's 50 percent interest in Hollywood and acquired more than 140 copyrights from his ex-partner for Golden State Songs.[12] Dolphin, incidentally, ran the important open-all-hours Dolphin's Record Shop in Los Angeles and would found the Lucky, Cash, and Money labels (which were manufactured and distributed by Pierce's Hollywood Records organization). Dolphin suffered the ultimate fate of any record man when he was shot dead in February 1958 by an angry songwriter, Percy Ivy, over a disputed royalty advance for four unpublished songs.

By late 1955, Jack Starnes had quit Starday. "At that time, Jack Starnes didn't like the way I was running the record company," said Don Pierce. "He wanted to do it on a basis where he had an artist that he was promoting, so he wanted records there. He wanted to release whenever he wanted, regardless of what you think. If you didn't give in, even if he didn't have a release time, he'd go direct to Buster Williams's pressing plant in Memphis and just say: 'Press up some records!' Which is hardly a way to run a record company. We were, you know, kind of estranged over that, but he said he would sell his shares for $7,000. So Pappy and I, well, we had 'A Satisfied Mind,' and so Pappy gave him $7,000, and he turned around and let the company repay him the $7,000. And that way it left Pappy and I fifty-fifty owners, and Pappy and I went on from there."[13]

Starday's major discovery and the reason for its stable ascendancy was the masterful honky-tonk stylist George Jones from Saratoga, Texas. By now, Don Pierce was displaying his talents as a salesman and promotion man of the highest order, based on his unparalleled experiences with Bill McCall at 4 Star. Following the latest in a run of George Jones's country chart entries in 1955 through 1956, headed by "Why, Baby, Why" (No. 4, late 1955), Pierce sent an upbeat marketing letter to his distributors:

This is the break that is needed to assure sales.

This listing should enable you to move this record to all your accounts, so be sure you have enough stock on hand.

The record is in stock and available for immediate shipment from Paramount in Philadelphia, from Plastic Products in Memphis and from Superior in Hollywood.

Another development that will help you get sales on this record is the fact that George Jones won the *Cash Box* magazine fourth Annual Disk Jockey Poll. He was selected the most promising country artist in the nation.

George Jones is exclusively with Starday and his last four releases have made the charts. We believe we are justified in asking our distributors to get in and pitch to keep George Jones in the national charts.

Order today—Don't Delay! George Jones has the hits on Starday![14]

Interestingly, in the midst of this country hit streak, Starday released one of the best-ever rockabilly records, "Rock It," under George's alias of Thumper Jones so as not to alienate his loyal country fans. Without any name recognition and possibly with minimal promotion, the record bombed.

However, Don Pierce and Pappy Daily were able to tap seriously into the nascent rockabilly boom by setting up a custom record-pressing service for the many would-be Elvis Presleys throughout the South. Based on the Bill McCall concept that had been utilized by Slim Willet, records would be pressed and shipped following receipt of a tiny tape reel with cash up-front. Label names were chosen randomly by clients, but as part of the package deal, Pierce and Daily, crucially, would secure the song publishing for their Starrite Music arm. The record was the important thing to the starstruck performers and their financiers, but the wily record men knew where the real money potential lay: it was in the publishing.

In late 1957, Louisiana's Floyd Soileau utilized the Starday custom-pressing service after deciding to get into the record business through Cajun artists Milton Molitor (Big Mamou) and Lawrence Walker (Vee-Pee). With local jukebox operator Ed Manuel in the background, Floyd felt confident enough to order three hundred 45s and two hundred 78s of each single at a cost of just under three hundred dollars respectively, including mastering. "I worked at this radio station [KVPI Ville Platte]," he said,

and the Starday samples would come in with this sheet of paper that said, "If you need to have a record pressed, we can handle it for you." The only hitch was they were claiming publishing rights to anything that was pressed . . . without any contracts or knowing who the actual writers were.

I went ahead and had a couple of records done through him [Don Pierce], but we never signed anything. Their brochure sheet only said that the original songs [would] be published by Starrite BMI. It was just an understanding in his leaflet that if he did the custom pressing, he was gonna take the publishing rights. A lot of people, I guess, were unsuspecting at the time and figured it's okay. Later on I realized that we shouldn't have agreed to anything—actually we agreed by virtue of his sales bulletin. . . . I imagine the biggest benefit for their publishing company was in performance royalties with BMI.

On the bright side of the thing, I'm sure that [through] Don's services with his little leaflets going out, a lot of people who had access to a tape recorder or a radio station studio room probably used his services to get some records done. Because they could say, "Well, I had my records pressed by Starday Records," which was a popular country and western label, although it was an independent.

It did provide a service, and I'm sure a lot of people took advantage of it. . . . It was a bona fide way of getting material sent to him, and he was providing a service for guys like me that didn't know where to go to get a record pressed at that time.

In early 1958, Pierce set up the Dixie label as a Starday subsidiary to formalize under a homogenous banner the best of these custom recordings.

Meanwhile, on January 1, 1957, Mercury inaugurated an unlikely if intriguing deal with Starday after being dissatisfied with the performance of its country music division under Walter "Dee" Kilpatrick in Nashville. And so the Mercury-Starday label was set up with Pappy Daily in charge of A&R and Don Pierce heading promotion and sales.[15] Once Mercury had landed George Jones, the hit country act it was looking for, through this deal, and with the company near to major label status, a continued liaison made no further sense. Accordingly, the contract was not renewed upon expiry in July 1958. Pierce and Daily would go their separate ways, too, in a frenzy of activity.

Don Pierce, who had moved offices from Los Angeles to Nashville on the Mercury tie-up, took full control of Starday as his share of the partnership split. The song copyrights were divvied up. In turn, Pappy Daily formed D Records and continued to supervise George Jones's recordings for Mercury under Art Talmadge's general direction. Pappy's firm, H. W. Daily, Inc., was retained as the Mercury distributor for Texas. Soon, Daily had discovered a hit artist—and songwriter—for D, and then for Mercury: Beaumont disc jockey Big Bopper (J. P. Richardson).

The year 1959 was a good one for Don Pierce. He was elected secretary of the Country Music Association, he started constructing a "modern stereo recording" studio in nearby Madison, and he enjoyed a publishing half-share in the international hit "Sea of Love" through his friendship with Goldband's Eddie Shuler. To cap it all, he was elected as Country & Western Man of the Year in *Billboard*'s twelfth annual C&W disc jockey poll.

As forward-looking as ever, Don Pierce saw that albums were the future, not the trusty 45s. He hit upon the kitsch concept of commissioning simplistic jacket designs with garish colors so that the Starday LPs would stand out in the racks, particularly at truck stops. As well, he instituted annual country music sales campaigns that were backed up with dealer point-of-sale items, including "four-color posters, browser boxes, streamers, catalogs, etc."[16] Then Pierce set up a mail-order company, Country Music Record Club of America, and began exploiting the vast international market potential for country music. And if that were not enough, he would "bring owners or representatives of all our distributors to Nashville, and we entertained them with the remarkable cooperation of the [m]ayor of Nashville, Beverly Briley[,] and others."[17] Don Pierce's Starday Records was no hick operation, and he was no hick operator.

By now, country music was well and truly dominated by the major labels through big-league producers Chet Atkins (RCA Victor), Owen Bradley (Decca), and Don Law (Columbia), who were taking a country-pop direction through artists such as Jim Reeves, Patsy Cline (originally a Bill McCall signing), and Marty Robbins, respectively. Don Pierce, swimming against the tide of the "Nashville Sound" with a roster comprising unknowns and supposed has-beens, stuck primarily to authentic honky-tonk, bluegrass, and sacred music: "the mountain sound," as he once put it. One of his marketing ploys was to send packets of sample records each month to the many small rural radio stations. No wonder he was popular with the country disc jockeys in the heartland. He was rewarded with steady sales of his deep catalog, interspersed with occasional big country hits such as "Black Land Farmer" by Frankie Miller (1959), "Pinball Machine" by Lonnie Irving, and "Alabam" by Cowboy Copas (both 1960).

After his friend and Starday record presser Syd Nathan died in 1968, Don Pierce leaped in with Hal Neely (a ten-year King executive) to arrange a buyout of King Records.[18] Thus, the group became Starday-King. Within a short while, Pierce had cashed in his chips. His original meager Starday investment had grown to more than $2 million, justifying one of his favorite sayings that "the music business is a floating crap game, and money is the name of the game."[19]

Pierce kept hitting the lucky sevens. After leaving the music arena, he went on to amass a further fortune in real estate development and other canny investments while hosting many pro-celebrity charitable golf events. Even then, to no great surprise, he was still earning songwriter royalties in the name of William York, "a pseudonym that I used for things that I could claim." A real charmer and always invigorating company, Don Pierce was willing to talk about his rich—and sometimes controversial—career as an enterprising record man right to the end of his life, in 2005. In the final analysis, the country music and independent record scenes would have been far poorer without his colorful presence.

Shelby Singleton: Mercury and SSS International–Sun Records

If there is a consummate, durable record man, it has to be Shelby Singleton. Continuing to puff cigars in time-honored fashion and based in Nashville, Tennessee, he was still heading in 2007 the Sun Entertainment Corporation. Here was the repository for Sam Phillips's Sun catalog, much of George Goldner's Red Bird–Blue Cat group, Singleton's own SSS International masters, and many others.

Singleton was hired by Mercury Records just as the company was peaking in the late 1950s. After starting out in the business as a junior promo man, with Pappy Daily and Don Pierce as his mentors, he commuted for many years between Nashville and New York. He was able to flesh out the Mercury-Starday saga and bring into focus his own career path at Mercury and beyond.

"I was an industrial engineer for Remington Rand in Shreveport, Louisiana," Shelby Singleton said.

> Of course in those years, the early 1950s, the *Louisiana Hayride* was one of the most popular radio shows, right next to the *Grand Ole Opry* here in Nashville. My wife, Margie Singleton, became a member of the *Louisiana Hayride* later on, after we did some promotions [and] made some records that were recorded for Starday out of Houston with Pappy Daily and Don Pierce. That's what really led me to become an employee of Mercury Records. I was doing all the promotion on Margie on a part-time basis while I was still working, and . . . a job opening came at Mercury Records for a promotion man. Pappy Daily recommended that they hire me.
>
> So as a result of an interview we had in Nashville, they hired me in October 1957. The country music division of Mercury had basically shut down when Dee Kilpatrick left. It became a link between Mercury and Starday, where Mercury was actually the national distributor for Starday Records. At that time, it was called Mercury-Starday. Mercury had made a deal with Don and Pappy Daily, and they took all the country acts that Starday had and put them on Mercury-Starday. We had George Jones, Benny Barnes, and a few other acts. It was a combination distribution deal.
>
> And then, at the end of '57 or beginning of '58, Pappy was telling me [that] one of the top brass at Mercury [the curmudgeonly Art Talmadge] decided we didn't want that deal to carry on anymore, or something went wrong. It was only for a certain period of time, and Mercury decided they could establish their own staff and do it better themselves than what was happening. George Jones was part of the settlement agreement. I think Mercury evidently paid a sum of money, and they kept George Jones and let all the rest of the artists go back to Starday.
>
> Don Pierce was actually my first teacher in the record business. I drove up here from Shreveport, Louisiana, [and] went on the road with Don. I think our first stop was at Knoxville, Tennessee, to see a rack jobber there. Then we drove to Richmond, Virginia, saw a distributor, and we went from there to Washington, D.C. We were in my car, and Don borrowed my car to go someplace. . . . Some guy was crossing the street, and he [Don] ran into him, but I don't think it hurt the guy very bad. Don was so appreciative that when we got back to Nashville, he sent the police a bunch of albums for them being so nice to him.
>
> Don's the one that taught me that you should never go to a restaurant to eat that doesn't serve liquor. If they've got an ice cream sign in the store or in the window, then you shouldn't go in that restaurant and eat. If they serve liquor, then they can make more money off the liquor, so they serve better food.

Pierce remembered that first promo trip with Shelby Singleton:

> Pappy Daily got Shelby Singleton . . . his job with Mercury. And Shelby came up from Shreveport, and we got in the car together, and we drove to Washington and we drove

to Detroit and into Chicago. I carried him in there for one of those all-day sessions at Mercury, where you get in there at eight o'clock in the morning and they send out for lunch and have it brought in. You lock heads, and, I mean, you learn something about the business, and you either cut it or you're gone. And Irv Green ran a hell of a ship. Well, Shelby learned quick, he was a fast study, and he hit the road for the South. Mercury was smart enough to know that a lot of the people in the South didn't like them very well, because they were pretty tough to deal with. They had Patti Page; they had the Platters. If you didn't do a real big, strong job for them, they were liable to move in and open up their [own distribution] branch in your town right away. And you would lose the line.

Singleton added:

Irving Green was really the owner of Mercury at that time; he owned the majority of it. There was a man who was head of A&R, Art Talmadge, and he was really the one that was responsible for signing the artists and developing the acts during those years. I'd say the majority of the hits came through his efforts more than anybody else's.

Irwin Steinberg was an analytical type of person and really a genius at Mercury when it came to that; he was the money man. Dinah Washington used to call him "Mr. Steinmoney." He would get all this research information from the government. The buying power index meant the amount of dollars that people had in certain leisure markets—that is, money to spend on movies, television, radio, concerts, records, anything that was a leisure-time product. If we had a record that sold a million records, then you could take it and break it down. Like, how many did it sell through Stan's Record Shop in Shreveport? Or how many did it sell through Big State in Dallas? How many did it sell through All South in New Orleans? It was different markets, but 90 percent of the time, it was right on the money. The perfect record to have is the one that crosses *all* ages.

We had people like Ralph Marterie, Rusty Draper, and a lot of acts that I guess in today's world are not really that well known or that remembered. Oh, I worked on records like "Love Bug Crawl" by Jimmy Edwards, "The Stroll" by the Diamonds, "Smoke Gets in Your Eyes" and "Harbor Lights" by the Platters, and Brook Benton, Dinah Washington, Sarah Vaughan. . . . I started out just in the state of Louisiana, and after about six months I covered all of the Southeast, from Louisiana over the Carolinas. And then later on I took over Texas and Oklahoma, Ohio, and other markets.

I used to go to the *American Bandstand* all the time, take acts there, get Dick Clark to play different records, [like] "The Stroll" and some of the other records we had then. Basically, it was during the era of Chubby Checker and the local Philadelphia acts that were all broke on *American Bandstand*. It was just a job; it was part of what you did—do whatever you could do to make a record a hit. We didn't really deal with Dick. He had a manager or a guy who was the pre-screener of everything; his name was Tony Mammarella, and he'd be the guy you had to deal with. He was a tough guy, oh yeah, oh yeah. You had to kind of figure out what it would take to get the record played. That was basically it.

You have to realize that a record company or the people that own the masters themselves are probably the only businesses in the world that get free advertisement for the product they are selling. So if you can get the record played, that's like free advertisement for what you are selling. You're not like an automobile company or a service station or anything else that has to advertise [its] wares. So your advertising money was your promotion dollars that you used to go and take the disc jockey out to dinner, or send his wife roses, or whatever you had to do to get a record played. Payola is in every business; there's always been some form of payola, whether it's a car dealer or a clothing business or whatever. It's like you give some free goods to get this play, or you do whatever you have to do to get the exposure originally.

I was in promotion for maybe a year or two, and then Mercury [made] me into what they called a regional manager in charge of sales and promotion. Then I accidentally got involved in A&R when there was a snowstorm in Chicago and the guy David Carroll was supposed to come to Nashville to record Rusty Draper. I happened to be in Nashville, and they called me and said I would have to do the recording sessions. I said, "I don't really know whether I can do that or not." They said, "Well, if you've got the experience to get the radio to play it and the people to buy it, then you ought to know how to make it."

So the first record I did for Mercury was two covers by Rusty Draper. It was "Mule Skinner Blues," [on] which we covered . . . the Fendermen [Soma], and then the other side was "Please Help Me, I'm Falling," on which we covered Hank Locklin [RCA Victor]. So, this being the first record, I got on the telephone, then on the airplane, and went to all my friends and the markets where "Mule Skinner Blues" was a hit by the Fendermen. Then we made a hit out of "Please Help Me, I'm Falling" [No. 54, late summer 1960]. So, as a result, we had a record that sold maybe 150– to 200,000 copies. It was a good beginning, yeah.

I could make a record, cut acetates on it, and be on the road the next day, taking it to disc jockeys, getting it played. A good promotion man was one that could stay up for two or three days, could outdrink everybody, still be up when they were all on the floor, could outeat everybody. Just complete workhorses, that's what we all were. You'd go into a town, and there was forty records on the radio station charts during those years. There was also the odd [local] record on there on an odd label that was on the chart, and it was No. 1 in that market because they knew the disc jockeys. Well, then, you knew there was something commercial about it. And you'd chase down who it belonged to and see if you could make a deal on buying the master.

During those years, it wasn't like it is today, where radio is almost like a machine [dominated by Clear Channel Communications]. There was a lot of personalities, [a] lot of guys that had their own record hops, as we called them. They went out and played records on Friday night and then had a live dance, and all the kids came to it. So I would go to all those things. For instance, "Sea of Love" by Phil Phillips, which was on the Khoury's label, was originally selling in Lake Charles, Louisiana. You'd go to the record hop, and all the kids were requesting it. You knew it wasn't a hype; it was something real. And then I would usually check it out through the pressing plant that was pressing the record to find out how many copies they had actually pressed and shipped. Oh, there were a lot of masters during those years that we bought.

Singleton hooked "Sea of Love" for Mercury, even though the Khoury's recording was recommended to Syd Nathan at King Records by his New Orleans branch manager,

Gene Burley, according to local record man Floyd Soileau. "Shelby Singleton always had his ears to the Louisiana sound, being from Louisiana himself," said Soileau. The acquisition of the Phil Phillips master would have endeared Shelby to Irving Green even more.

"I always did whatever I wanted to do," said Singleton.

After the first couple of years, they gave me a complete[ly] free rein. I could go where I wanted to and sign whoever I wanted to, record whatever I wanted to. I guess as long as you're successful . . . It's kinda hard for somebody sitting in an office all day long to tell what's happening out in the field. So the only real test was: Could you make a record that would sell, and would it give you a return on the money?

Huey Meaux and I became friends back during those years; he was a barber in Winnie, Texas. He's the one that I got the master of Jivin' Gene from, "Breaking Up Is Hard to Do," and he used to get things like "I'm a Fool to Care" by Joe Barry [both acquired from Floyd Soileau's Jin label]. A little later on, when Huey and I became friends, I did a lot of other deals with Huey and for Huey. He was a unique talent, he was a master promotion man, and he could get records played in Houston and Beaumont and Port Arthur, through that area. He'd get something started [on Crazy Cajun, which was his nickname, Tribe, and other labels], then he'd lease the master to Jamie or to Mercury or to Atlantic or some of the different labels. Huey was smart enough to know that he didn't have the resources or the clout to carry a record on a national basis, but he could discover the talent, for some reason.

Everything was coming through Bill Hall in Beaumont, and we all thought that Bill Hall had something to do with this stuff. Then later on we found out it was really Huey Meaux that was doing everything. So we started dealing, after a few years, direct with Huey rather than through Bill.[20]

Two prominent Mercury hits from East Texas were the Big Bopper's "Chantilly Lace" via Pappy Daily (No. 6, fall 1958) and "Running Bear" by Johnny Preston (No. 1, January 1960, written by the Big Bopper). "I think we worked on 'Running Bear' for almost nine months before it ever became a national hit," said Shelby Singleton.

"Sea of Love" probably took five or six months. You'd go through one market and you make it big in that market, and then you go to the next market. You just keep going, one after the other. But we didn't really look for records that were just regional records. If the record didn't have national potential, we didn't wanna fool with it. Those records became really national hits after we bought the master, and then we developed the acts on a national basis. It was the kids' [teenagers'] market; they just weren't interested in LPs in them days. They bought 45s, which were really disposable, you know. It wasn't something that you put up on the shelf and that you pull out every once in a while and play. [In] three weeks the 45 was gone, and they was on to the next 45.

We always felt that the R&B and country markets were pretty much the same, that the country market and the black market were really not fickle like the pop market. In the pop market, you could have one hit record and never be heard of again. But if you established an act in the country field and you have a hit, well then, every record you come out with would sell a certain amount of records. It's the same thing with the black market. Once you had a hit record with Fats Domino, or with any of those types of artists, the second record seemed to sell, and the third one, maybe not as big as the first hit, but they always had a market for them. I think that's still true today; I don't think that's changed at all.

In New Orleans, I was very much friends with Henry Hildebrand. He had All South record distributors, and he was Mercury's distributor. And the one-stop people like Joe Assunto and his wife, they sold to probably 90 percent of the jukebox operators in that town. Joe had a brother-in-law [Joe Ruffino] that had a record label called Ric [and Ron]. It would be nothing for us to be down there at midnight with jukebox operators coming in buying records. I used to take acetates down there sometimes of things that I had recorded, and we would play 'em for jukebox operators. Most of the guys would be in there shopping, pulling out their title strips, and buying their records and stuff. We'd play things over the speaker just to see if we could get a reaction.

People tend to forget just how important jukebox operators were. It was a good selling point for a start, wasn't it? . . . Take an established artist, George Jones or somebody like that. . . . You knew you could sell 20,000 immediately to the jukebox operators, because he'd come off a previous record that [had] made 'em money. If you have that kind of track record, well, at least you got a good listen. The jukebox really was a good barometer in those years; it was a good indication a record was a hit.

We gave the free records basically to the one-stop, and the one-stop would take a record if he liked it. They had standing orders, say from maybe forty or fifty operators that may represent 3,000 jukeboxes, and they wanted, say, twenty-five each of every new country record that came out that was good. So the one-stop knew automatically he could ship maybe 1,000 to 1,500 of a record. And certain jukebox operators just trusted 'em [regarding what they were selling], 'cause they were in small towns, and they didn't get to town but once a month, maybe. That was true not only in the New Orleans area but [in] all of the United States.

But jukebox operators were probably the best A&R men around, because they could listen to a record and tell if it was going to make them any money. There was just something in their minds. Pappy Daily was an old jukebox operator, and a guy like Finley Duncan down at Minaret Records [in Florida], he was a jukebox operator. Quite a few record men developed through that.

What made a good distributor was . . . clout with the local disc jockeys and the local record stores and . . . the right sales people that would call on the jukebox operators and the one-stops. The reason the distribution changed is because of technology. I mean, you didn't have to go in a backroom and look and see how many records you had left to see if you needed to order some more. Computers tell you all that now.

In the spring of 1961, Shelby Singleton was involved in the launch of Smash Records, a Mercury subsidiary headed by Charlie Fach. "There was a reason for it," said Singleton.

Basically, if you had more than five or six records in the radio station's Top 40 chart on the Mercury label, a disc jockey would say to me, "Now look, I know the record's great, but I can't put it on because you got too many records on the play list." So we just started another label, Smash. Columbia did the same thing when they started Epic and [a revitalized] OKeh, and RCA did the same thing [with Groove, "X," and Vik]. We all did the same thing to stop getting the disc jockey in trouble.[21]

So we started putting some artists on Smash. Yes, I signed Jerry Lee Lewis; I also signed Charlie Rich, Roger Miller, Joe Dowell with "Wooden Heart," Dickey Lee with "Patches." A lot of the big hits on Smash were all mine, but Jerry Lee was always one of my favorites.

Among the pop crossover records coming out of the Mercury country music division were "Walk On By" by Leroy Van Dyke and "Ahab, the Arab" by Ray Stevens. The Texas connections paid off again when "Hey! Baby" by Bruce Channel was acquired from Major Bill Smith's Le Cam label out of Fort Worth and went to No. 1 (March 1962, Smash). Soon, the idiosyncratic Major Bill rewarded Mercury's new parent Philips with another No. 1 in February 1963: "Hey Paula" by Paul & Paula.

As Mercury's eastern and southern recording chief, Shelby Singleton was nominated Man of the Week by *Billboard Music Week* on June 23, 1962, with the accompanying feature noting that "at age 29 [actually 30], Singleton has become a fireball among A&R men."[22] Shelby was rewarded that November when he was appointed a Mercury vice president by Irving Green. One of Shelby's enduring accomplishments, along with Buddy Killen at Dial and Fred Foster at Monument–Sound Stage 7, was to help raise the profile of rhythm and blues sessions in Nashville. "We cut some great records with Brook Benton," said Singleton.

We cut "Lie to Me," "Hotel Happiness," "True Confessions," [a] lot of big hits. Rhythm and blues has always been around in Nashville, but I guess it was a kind of secret society, because Nashville has always been known as a country haven rather than [one] for rhythm and blues. Most of the acts that were recorded here during my years . . . Brook Benton, Clyde McPhatter, or Ruth Brown, all of them, were very appreciative of the fact that we would take time to bring a New York act to Nashville. I used to keep Brook Benton and Damita Jo out at my house 'cause there was really nothing but just rattrap-type hotels down in the black section of town. It was still the segregation era.

Clyde Otis recorded most of his stuff with Brook Benton and others in New York City. And then, later on, I replaced Clyde Otis in New York. I had Jerry Kennedy, Jerry Reed, and Ray Stevens all working for me, and whenever I left for New York, I put Jerry [Kennedy] in charge of the office here in Nashville. I used to supervise both New York and Nashville and basically spent a lot of time in England, France, Germany, and all those markets. Mercury was probably one of the five biggest companies in the United States in the record business. Irving Green sold Mercury in 1961, and that's when Philips wanted to get into the American market.

Philips, the Dutch electronics giant, had its own sizable European record label, which had been built up through a shrewd but expiring licensing agreement with Columbia Records. The acquisition of Mercury, as with EMI's purchase of Capitol, was a strategic necessity.

In 1967, Shelby Singleton, after a ten-year career with Mercury Records, went "independent" by setting up SSS International Records, with brother John giving vital backup administrative support. The expensive publicity splash accompanying the launch indicated that Shelby meant business. As he recalled,

> I said to myself, "If I can do one-tenth for myself what I've done with them, then I've got to be successful."
>
> In the beginning, SSS concentrated on southern soul, because I knew that the best—the southern black market. Oh yeah, [WLAC disc jockeys] John R. and Hoss Allen were two of my best friends. If the record was commercial, I would immediately begin getting orders out of Mississippi, Alabama, Georgia, Louisiana, all over the place. Most of the labels . . . had a different producer in charge . . ., where we furnished the money. It was kinda like what the majors are doing today. We furnished the money, and somebody else actually ran the label, like Finley Duncan in Florida with Minaret and Lelan Rogers with Silver Fox. We owned the label, and we were the exclusive distributor of it. But the black records during those years sold absolutely no LPs.

Although SSS International's sales were primarily in the black markets of the South, Singleton had decent-sized national chart records by Mickey Murray with a version of Otis Redding's "Shout Bamalama" (No. 54, late 1967), "Lover's Holiday" and "Pickin' Wild Mountain Berries" by Peggy Scott & Jo Jo Benson (No. 31 and No. 27 respectively, 1968), and "Reconsider Me" by Johnny Adams (No. 28, summer 1969).

"Reconsider Me" was written by the talented team of Mira Smith and Margaret Lewis. Mira was another rare record lady (and guitarist) who had operated the tiny Ram label out of Shreveport at the cusp of the 1960s, while effervescent Margaret was the principal Ram artist (she is the current custodian of the masters). "Mira had closed Ram Records, primarily due to the closing of the *Louisiana Hayride*," said Margaret Lewis. "That took all the musicians out of Shreveport to Nashville, where there was work on the *Opry* and in the studios. Shelby called Mira and asked if she would like to write for his publishing company, and they called me, and so that's how the team began. The songwriter-producer relationship was great fun. Working with Shelby was never boring. He would have a traditional country artist on one session, and then there would be great R&B artists to work with on the next. Shelby was a true 'record man,' as they called them back then. These guys were people like Ahmet Ertegun and Sam Phillips, who simply loved and had a 'feel' for the business that gave it a realness and excitement."

Meanwhile, Singleton had started a country division with Plantation Records and hauled in a ripe harvest with the label's third release, "Harper Valley P.T.A." With Jeannie C. Riley dishing the dirt in Tom T. Hall's steamy southern tale ("This is just a little Peyton Place and you're all Harper Valley hypocrites . . ."), the record went all the way to No. 1 pop in September 1968.[23] Some say that Jerry Kennedy's standout Dobro lick was borrowed from Reggie Young's hilarious guitar line on Joe Tex's "Skinny Legs and All." Kennedy and Young were master Nashville session men (Young's work was always the epitome of good taste, especially in union with bassist Tommy Cogbill). As it happened, "Harper Valley P.T.A." completely transformed the working model of Singleton's fledgling organization during a difficult period for independents.

"We sold about 7 million copies of the single," said Singleton.

The LP and cassette and everything probably sold 5 or 6 million worldwide. I'd get orders for, like, 900,000 records in one day from the distributors, the rack jobbers, and everybody. I was lucky. I had a banker that understood what I was doing and why I was doing it. He actually loaned me the money to get the pressings done. It was really a gamble, but with that particular record, I don't think I got two back in returns. We got paid every dime that was ever owed to me, [except for] those who went bankrupt on me.

We'd made a lot of money with "Harper Valley P.T.A.," and I paid the government a ton of money. What I was trying to do was to spend the money in acquiring assets in order to avoid paying taxes. So that's the reason I bought Sun, that's the reason I bought Red Bird–Blue Cat, and I bought [1950s country labels] Fabor and Radio from Fabor Robison. We bought just tons of stuff through the years by continually reinvesting whatever profits I had. If there's something they want to sell and it's fairly priced, it's not overpriced, well then, I usually buy it.

The Sun deal did not happen overnight. Shelby Singleton recalled the tortuous negotiating process that had begun while he was at Mercury:

Throughout my last few years with Mercury, probably the last five years, every time I was in Memphis I would spend half the day and all the night with Sam Phillips trying to buy the Sun label for Mercury.[24] We never could make a deal. Sam had gone through a lawsuit with Philips. He sued Philips for putting out a label with his name on it, because he had a [subsidiary] Phillips International label, and he not only sued 'em in the United States, he sued 'em in Holland. Sam was pretty bitter. Although he won the lawsuit, he had to agree to give up the name and let them use the name. Even though he and I were friends, I just think that he knew that the big company would take all of his "children" and put 'em on their own label, which he didn't want. He wanted the Sun label to stay alive.

That's how later, in [July] 1969, I was able to buy the Sun label. I had to promise Sam that I would continue to promote it and all this kinda stuff; well, that's part of the contract. Everybody tried to buy it; Atlantic tried to buy it. . . . I don't know whether Sam got bored with the business or what it was; he was more involved in Holiday Inns and that stuff. He just kinda semi-retired from the music business and concentrated on his radio stations and his other business interests.

It took me about six months to work out all the details of all the paperwork, and he came over here to sign the papers. I thought the night before [that] he was probably going to back out. But he didn't; he went through with it. We formed a new corporation, and Sam maintained 20 percent of it; I had 80 percent. I got all the money back in the first year, mainly from Johnny Cash LPs. It's just been a continuous growth.

I bought the Red Bird and Blue Cat labels from George Goldner in the same month that I bought Sun. As usual, George was in trouble; he loved to go to the horse track. I got a call one day from somebody that said, "George is trying to sell his record labels." "Which ones?" "Red Bird and Blue Cat, that's all he's got left; he wants to sell all the masters." I said, "What does he want for them?" He told me, and I said, "Better tell them to go see Paul Marshall"—who's my attorney in New York—"Paul will be able to pay for this whole thing." So I sent a van up to New York, [and] he went to Bell Sound studios and loaded up all the tapes. That was in 1969.

At the time of Blue Cat, nobody was buying masters; in those years, everybody was buying publishing companies. So therefore, the masters were cheap compared to the publishing. I almost bought King, too. In fact, I went to New York to sit down with Freddy Bienstock and [Jerry] Leiber and [Mike] Stoller, [and I] got to looking at all the contracts, and Hal Neely was involved in it then. And the contracts were so bad and so poorly written, . . . [and] Syd owed everybody that he ever recorded—he owed royalties. I was just fearful of all the lawsuits that I would get into.[25]

Without any regrets, as he said, Singleton walked away from acquiring the King masters.

"So I was putting out Johnny Cash and Jerry Lee Lewis LPs like crazy into the marketplace," Singleton continued.

We kinda dropped the ball on the black market when we got involved in Sun; we just quit concentrating on it [just as Sam Phillips had done in the mid-1950s]. Then the company [SSS International] got so big that we got to the point where I felt like I couldn't handle it right, so I started selling things and shutting 'em down. We had printing plants, big warehouse distribution things, and all that kinda stuff. It was like having 155 children. You became their mother, their father, their financial adviser, and their everything else. It just got to the point where I got mad one day and started selling stuff and got rid of it all. I just started to concentrate on other things, particularly Sun.[26]

Everything relating to Sun, it's always all centered around Elvis more or less, and just every year it gets bigger and bigger. Of the independent record labels, Sun is probably the best-known record label in the world because of the logo. Roy Orbison, Johnny Cash, Jerry Lee Lewis, Carl Perkins, and Elvis have grown it; they're all just superstars worldwide. We mostly sit here and just answer the telephone or answer the e-mails; we get so many requests for different things.

As we finished the 2004 interview at the Nashville headquarters of Sun Entertainment Corporation (a company quoted in Canada on a speculative stock exchange, no less), I asked Shelby if "Harper Valley P.T.A." was his biggest hit ever. "Yes," he said, before adding in his slow, thick southern drawl, "So-o-o far . . ." Now that's the talk of a real record man, from Nashville or anywhere else.

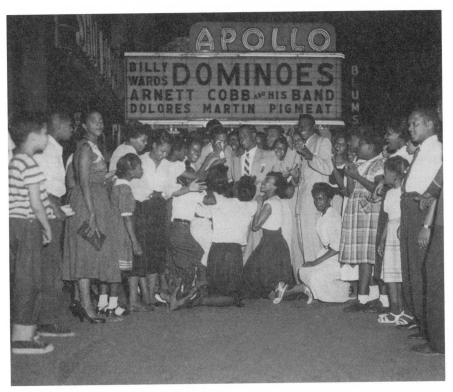

The golden age of R&B with its excitement and innocence: Billy Ward and his
Dominoes (with Clyde McPhatter) at the Apollo Theatre, Harlem, 1952.
By PoPsie, courtesy Michael Randolph.

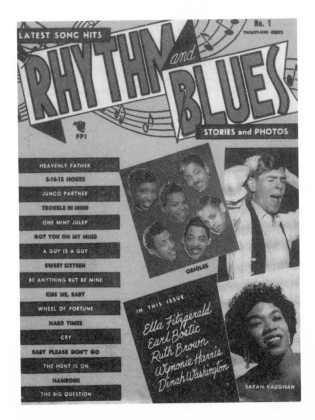

First issue of *Rhythm
and Blues* song magazine,
1952. Courtesy Gordon
Skadberg.

Cash Box staff at
ARMADA convention,
c. 1962. *Standing:* Norman
Orleck, Marv Schlachter,
Marty Ostrow, Ira Howard,
George Albert, Bob Austin;
kneeling: Alan Berzofsky,
Irv Lichtman. Courtesy Irv
Lichtman.

Hy Weiss *(second left)* nightclubbing with Arthur Prysock *(second right)*
(others unknown), c. 1965. Courtesy John Broven, with acknowledgment
to Hy Weiss.

Record men conferring: Berry
Gordy *(left)* and Hy Weiss, 1960s.
Courtesy John Broven, with
acknowledgment to Hy Weiss.

George Goldner *(center)* Gee
Records, with the Crows, 1954.
Courtesy John Broven.

Hugo & Luigi: Luigi Creatore *(left)* and Hugo Peretti at work in the studio, mid-1950s. Courtesy Showtime Music Productions.

Spark Records' Jerry Leiber, Lester Sill, and Mike Stoller with Lou Krefetz (manager of the Clovers, *front*) at Atlantic's West Coast office, c. 1956. Courtesy John Broven, with acknowledgment to Lou Krefetz.

Buck Ram, the Platters' guiding light, and Jeanie Bennett, his publicist, 1954. Courtesy John Broven, with acknowledgment to Jean Bennett.

Modern Records' Joe Bihari *(left)*, B. B. King, disc jockey Hunter Hancock, and editor Joel Friedman with *Cash Box* award, 1954. Courtesy of Ace Records Limited.

Gold record for "Rockin' Robin": Googie Rene, Bobby Day, and Leon Rene outside the Class Records office, Hollywood, 1958. Courtesy of Rafael "Googie" Rene and Tony Jones, Leon Rene Family Partnership.

Harold Battiste (left) with Art Neville, Specialty branch office, New Orleans, c. 1958. Courtesy Harold Battiste, A.F.O. Foundation.

The Champs with Dave Burgess (guitar, *front left*) and
Danny Flores (sax), 1958. Courtesy John Broven.

Gene Goodman *(top left)*,
Harry Goodman *(top right)*,
Nat Tarnopol, Jackie Wilson,
and Brunswick A&R man
Dick Jacobs, 1960. Courtesy
John Broven.

The Flame Show Bar, Detroit, c. 1956, including Nat Tarnopol *(kneeling, bottom left)*, Billy Davis *(left, middle row)*, Colonel Jim Wilson *(third left, middle row)*, Bill Doggett *(next)*, Berry Gordy *(far right, front row)*, and various local disc jockeys. Courtesy John Broven, with acknowledgment to Jim Wilson.

Clark Galehouse, Golden Crest Records, c. 1950. Courtesy Golden Crest Records.

Business card. Courtesy Golden Crest Records.

Joe Battle *(left)* outside his record shop still selling 78s, Hastings Street, Detroit, 1959. © Jacques Demêtre, courtesy *Soul Bag.*

Joe's Record Shop, Hastings Street, Detroit, 1959. © Jacques Demêtre, courtesy *Soul Bag.*

Shelby Singleton
(Mercury Records, *left*)
with Robert Burton
(BMI), 1964. Courtesy
John Broven.

End of an era: Bobby Robinson
standing in doorway of his
original store, 301 West 125th
Street, Harlem, 1986. Courtesy
Paul Harris.

16

CHAPTER

West Coast Rockin' and Rollin'

CAST OF CHARACTERS
  Joe Bihari, Modern-RPM-Flair and Crown-Kent Records
  B. B. King, RPM Records artist
  Roddy Jackson, Specialty Records artist
  Harold Battiste, Specialty Records branch manager
  Art Rupe, Specialty Records
  Rafael "Googie" Rene, Class Records
  Dave Burgess, Challenge Records
  Joe Johnson, Challenge Records
  *also featuring Leon Rene, Class Records; and Gene Autry,
  Challenge Records*

Out west in California, a handful of the original indie labels from the "78 era" were nicely established by the mid-1950s, namely Aladdin, Imperial, Modern, and Specialty. There had been a few important 1940s casualties along the way, such as Exclusive, Excelsior, ARA, and Black & White, felled by a dearth of hits and changing trends coupled with over-expansionistic ideals.

From 1950 on, R&B newcomers popped up, including Swing Time (Jack Lauderdale, Franklin Kort), Recorded in Hollywood (John Dolphin), Combo (Jake Porter), and Dootone (Dootsie Williams). In the pop field, there was Era (Herb Newman, Lou Bedell) and Liberty (Si Waronker), soon to be joined by Randy Wood's Dot label relocated from distant Tennessee. In jazz, there was Verve and Clef (Norman Granz) and Pacific Jazz (Dick Bock). Then along came a resuscitated Leon Rene with Class Records and cowboy movie star Gene Autry with Challenge.

Several first-class independent recording studios would help to feed the West Coast frenzy. The leaders were Radio Recorders (dating back to 1936), Master Recorders (run by Bunny Robyn, a specialist at the speeded-up rock 'n' roll record, particularly for Imperial and Specialty), United Western Recorders (Bill Putnam, by way of Universal, Chicago), and Gold Star (Stan Ross). The futuristic $2 million Capitol Tower, opened on April 6, 1956, was a shining symbol of the Golden State and of Capitol Records itself. The glorious thirteen-story building was designed as a "stack o' records," a name that stuck, with facilities that included impeccable recording studios. California was more than ready to rock and roll.

Joe Bihari: Modern-RPM-Flair Records and Crown-Kent Records

Modern Records, in particular, seemed to be well positioned for the rock 'n' roll era in terms of hit records and business development. In 1953, the Bihari brothers' combine was basking in a brace of B. B. King R&B chart hits for RPM: "Woke Up This Morning" (No. 3) and "Please Love Me" (No. 1). B. B. went off the boil for a while until coming back strong at the end of 1954 with "You Upset Me Baby," another No. 1. The interim R&B chart slack was taken up by the pre–rock 'n' roll teen offerings of the coupling "Tick Tock" (No. 9) and "Cherry Pie" by Marvin & Johnny (Modern), and "Oop Shoop" (No. 8) by Shirley Gunter and the Queens (Flair). There were surprise successes on the national pop charts for the first time, on the subsidiary Crown label, with "Angela Mia" (No. 23) and "That's What I Like" (No. 14) by Don, Dick & Jimmy (led by future A&R man Don Ralke).

Impressed and comforted by this action, the Biharis invested $15,000 in the summer of 1954 for the construction of recording studios and office space adjacent to their Cadet Record Pressing Company building (which housed ten presses) in Culver City. The new studio was equipped with Ampex tape machines, Altec-Lansing sound systems, and an RCA mixing panel. To facilitate management of the expanding organization, Jules Bihari was now president of Crown Records and the Cadet pressing plant, with Saul and Joe presidents of Modern-RPM and Flair, respectively.[1]

The Bihari brothers kept up the pace by scoring a No. 1 R&B hit with "The Wallflower," the auspicious debut by Etta James on Modern in April 1955. Etta, who was just sixteen, was introduced to Modern by bandleader Johnny Otis, who had just come off an eventful stint with Don Robey at Peacock Records. However, her record, based on the tune of "Work with Me Annie" by Hank Ballard and the Midnighters, was unable to cross over into the pop charts because of the powerful cover version by Mercury's Georgia Gibbs (who duly waltzed to No. 1 with the song retitled "Dance with Me Henry").

The Biharis charted pop again at No. 82 on *Billboard*'s debut Top 100 chart of November 12, 1955, with "Why Don't You Write Me?" by the Jacks for RPM, a group that reinvented itself as the Cadets for Modern. The ruse paid off when the Cadets' "Stranded in the Jungle" pipped the Jayhawks' original from neighboring Vernon Avenue–based Flash Records by making No. 15 pop (against No. 18) in the summer of 1956. Yet again, cover versions were not the prerogative of the major labels.

By now, Maxwell Davis was in charge of the Modern sessions and, with a coterie of high-caliber musicians, was giving the productions an indelible stamp of class. His arrangements owed much to the swing-band era sounds of Fletcher Henderson (for whom he played tenor saxophone), Duke Ellington, Jimmie Lunceford, and Artie Shaw. Recalled Joe Bihari, "Maxwell had been in Florida where Louis Jordan had lost his book of songs, all his arrangements. So Louis called Maxwell to rearrange all his songs. When he came back, somebody rammed Maxwell's car head-on. He was okay, but he was in [the] hospital for a while . . . not good for a black man in Georgia. It wasn't his fault; he was all cut up. He needed a job, and that's when I hired Maxwell. We had used him before. He did the arrangements for Gene Phillips [Modern] in the late '40s, he did a lot of Amos Milburn things for Aladdin, and [he] played sax on Ray Anthony's 'Idaho' on Capitol [in 1952]. Maxwell had a very definite sound with the saxophone, [a] great big sound. He was a very fine musician and a wonderful man, wonderful family."

The value of Maxwell Davis to the Bihari organization cannot be overstated, even if at times, said Joe Bihari, he coasted lazily on his abundant talent and did tend to hit the bottle. But in assimilating rhythm and blues music with rock 'n' roll, he was a black A&R man who was making as much creative impact as Henry Glover at King, Jesse Stone at Atlantic, and Dave Bartholomew at Imperial. B. B. King was Maxwell Davis's premier assignment. "He was so good at writing [arrangements], so good," said King. "I don't think I've ever met anybody that could write a blues [song] like Maxwell Davis, before or since. He was unknown outside the industry, but he made a lot of records for a lot of people." B. B. King's music, too, was starting to influence an entire generation of aspiring young blues guitar players.

In 1956, the Biharis had further national hits with "Eddie My Love" by the Teen Queens (No. 14) and "The Girl in My Dreams" by the Cliques (No. 45 for one week only, a real chart aberration). Much of the high school talent was centered on Richard Berry, a vocal group specialist and budding songwriter, later of "Louie Louie" fame. Then B. B. King had his biggest R&B hit for some time at No. 3 with the bel canto ballad "On My Word of Honor," which, despite its R&B chart status, was part of a valiant attempt to find a new pop market for King (the Buck Ram co-write was a No. 20 pop hit shortly afterward by the Platters). The year finished well for Modern, thanks to the first take of Jesse Belvin's dreamy No. 7 R&B hit "Goodnight My Love," enhanced by an orchestral string section and heavenly choir courtesy of the Don Ralke Singers, which were unusual adornments for an independent company production of the time. The record's future was assured when Saul Bihari's good friend Alan Freed chose it as the sign-off theme for his nationally syndicated radio show.

The majority of these chart breakthroughs were published by Modern Music, providing welcome additional revenue streams. The Biharis' publishing house was a beneficiary of the cover version syndrome through pop renditions of "Oop Shoop" by the Crew-Cuts (No. 13), "Eddie My Love" by the Fontane Sisters and the Chordettes (No. 11 and No. 14, respectively), and of course the No. 1 "Dance with Me Henry" by Georgia Gibbs (where the publishing was shared with Syd Nathan's Lois Music because Hank

Ballard's original melody was borrowed). Later, "Cherry Pie" was another good publishing earner through Skip & Flip's No. 11 hit on Bob Shad's Brent label in 1960 and
as a much-recorded oldie. However, Jesse Belvin's "Goodnight My Love," covered by
the McGuire Sisters (No. 32 pop, Coral, 1956), was not published by Modern Music.

The song credits for writer or co-writer on the Modern self-published releases would
invariably show the fictitious names of Jules Taub first, and then later Sam Ling and
Joe Josea. Explained Joe Bihari, "Of course, I'm writer on a lot of the songs because
of . . . my recording them and making deals with the artists. Jules was 'Taub,' which
was my mother's maiden name. Saul liked that song called 'Ling, Ting, Tong,' and he
said, 'I'll just use "Ling"'—he was funny, yeah. And why I used 'Josea' was because
my sisters used to call me Joseph [laughs]."

Initially, self-published songs and those in the public domain were seen by record
companies as a bottom-line method of reducing statutory royalty commitments—and
not as future nest eggs. The return was even better when a label owner was a designated songwriter. At best, the system, which was feudal in nature, did encourage the
writing and use of new songs. However, through the years, there has been a growing
perception of injustice at writer shares accredited to record men.[2]

"The writing and the publishing and all of that, we don't wanna talk about that,"
said B. B. King, with ironic laughter, when the topic was raised with him. "Well, I've
seen the same writers' names on [the records of] many of the artists the Biharis had. I
don't know who Ling was, Josea . . . I never knew who Josea was, or Taub. I never met
them, so how could they write with me, you know? But I didn't know anything about
it. Me, I just wanted to get a good record out."

B. B. King had flirted with label ownership himself by launching Blues Boys Kingdom Records in December 1956. "I thought that at the time, I had gotten good enough
to know and be able to help other artists," he said. "So I started my own little label in
Memphis [at 164 Beale Street]. It made two or three things that was pretty good. My
pianist, Millard Lee, had 'Waughely's Boogie,' and Levi Seabury, a harmonica player
that I think would have really went well, did one record and got killed in an automobile accident."

Supervising a record label proved to be impossible for the popular blues artist, who
spent 342 days on the road in that year. "Well, I had to get other people, yeah," said
King. "I had a guy named James Wilson that ran the company for me, a sister-in-law
that worked with him, Roberta Snyder, and Robert Garner. They ran it, did pretty good,
but it didn't make no money, really." Oddly enough, Joe Bihari was quite relaxed about
this extracurricular activity as long as B. B. did not record personally for his own label,
which he did not. B. B. King's destiny was to become an international icon after Louis
Armstrong and not a record man.

Joe Bihari was convinced that he had found the right artist for the rock 'n' roll era
when a pushy fifteen-year-old Canadian kid, Paul Anka, begged to be recorded while on
a California family vacation. One single was released, but Jules Bihari refused to sign

him to a permanent contract, and so ABC-Paramount was the immediate beneficiary of this unfortunate myopia. Curiously, Modern was unable to get its artists into the rock 'n' roll movies, despite being one of the larger independents and being based in the Hollywood area. Joe Bihari admitted that his family did not fully understand rock 'n' roll music.

But the Bihari brothers did understand payola. Joe claimed that brother Saul and himself were among the first record men to grease the palms of favored disc jockeys. Yet when the federal authorities began eyeing record companies, the Modern Records group had a clean bill of health. Said Joe:

> One reason: we never wrote a check to a dee-jay; we paid them in cash. It was never a check that could show up. And when the government audited our books for all the years, there was never a check written.
>
> We sure had good airplay. It was like a marketing expense; we just paid in cash. I mean, I'd go see a dee-jay and hand him a hundred dollars, like in a handshake [double the alleged generosity of Hy Weiss!], and that was it. And you didn't have to say anything at all, not a word. They knew what it was.
>
> There were a few favorite dee-jays that we had all over in the big cities. We didn't pay quite as much in the little towns, but we saw as many of the black dee-jays as possible to hand them something. We took certain dee-jays and said, "Look, we're gonna send you free records. Get yourself a little record store. You're still on the air; play these records and you'll create a demand in your city, for your area, and you sell 'em." It would be 500 or 1,000, whatever it was. They thought that was a hell of a good idea, so they played the records. We might have four or five releases, they'd get 4,000 or 5,000 records, and they made $4,000 or $5,000 by the time they sold them. Well, they created a certain amount of demand; the records weren't all hits, but they could sell those and put that money into their pocket. And we did that in as many large cities as we could."
>
> Drugs, however, were never among the Biharis' payola handouts: "Oh, [we] never touched a drug. If we were approached by a man who would say, 'We can get drugs,' it was, 'No, I'm sorry!'"

In March 1958, worried by the impact of rock 'n' roll music and associated upheavals in the industry, group president Jules Bihari made two startling announcements: the corporation would concentrate on the "low-price" LP market with Crown Records, and Modern and RPM would be folded summarily in favor of a new-look "pop singles business only" label, Kent Records. According to Joe Bihari, the Kent name was probably inspired by the famous cigarette brand. Nevertheless, to discard such recognized brand names as Modern, RPM, and Flair to the trash can, like butt ends, appeared to be an exercise in folly. In fairness, Jules Bihari was possibly revamping the family web of companies to take advantage of the same excise tax reduction scheme that Arthur Shimkin's accountants were employing at Golden Records.[3] And in the light of subsequent events in the indie record business, who could say that Jules was not right to change strategic direction?

Now the Bihari brothers were seeking the bargain-hunting "impulse buyer and traffic builder" through the "fast turnover, low price" route. Crown's new competition was Pickwick, Harmony (Columbia), Camden (RCA Victor), and many others, wherever the cheap racks were located. "That was a disaster in one way, and yet it was good in another way," said Joe. "The disaster was it took us out of the record business, really, but it put us into the budget merchandising business."[4]

With Maxwell Davis as arranger, Joe Bihari embarked proudly on a series of big band albums for Crown using members of the orchestras of such hallowed names as Benny Goodman, Stan Kenton, and Woody Herman. Bihari also recorded country music and surf/hot rod instrumentals—in fact, any musical style that would bring traffic to the racks. By continuing to use tunes from the Modern Music catalog and those in public domain, the slim profit margins on the low-priced products were protected, helped further by cheap in-house pressings.[5]

In addition to the Los Angeles base, there were sales forces and warehouses in Chicago and New York, indicating that Crown was a substantial nationwide operation. The office work, incidentally, was still in the capable hands of Bihari sisters Florette, Rosalind, and Maxine.

For the new Kent singles label, the Biharis hired old friend Lester Sill, with Lee Hazlewood, in a valiant attempt to get a toehold in the rock 'n' roll market. The independent producers recorded Don Cole and the Barker Brothers, but there was no Elvis Presley—or indeed a Duane Eddy, the guitar star whom the "Sill & Hazlewood" team was producing concurrently for Jamie. Interestingly, the royalty statement of one Kent rocker, Lee Denson, has survived, and it makes for fascinating reading:

Table 16.1

300 Records @ .85 ea.	255.00
90% of $255	229.50
Artists royalty—3% of $229.50	6.89
Artist Draw & Expenses	
March 3, 1958 session	
Session Salaries	247.50 [6 x $41.25]
21% of Salaries to Union	51.98
Vocal Group	75.00
Guaranteed Advance	50.00
TOTAL DRAW AND EXPENSES	(424.48)
OVERDRAWN BALANCE AT JUNE 30, 1958	(417.59)[6]

So was this the loaded dice in favor of the independent record companies? It was hardly a profitable bet on Denson, with his promisingly titled "High School Hop." An analysis of the data confirms that the Biharis did pay advances (with a royalty rate at 3 percent of 90 percent of "total gross receipts"), did conduct union sessions, did carry the recording costs (even if there were no studio hire fees, as Kent had its own facility), and did issue royalty statements (with session cost deductions). In accordance with the standard contracts of the time, it was only when the various costs were recouped that artists would start earning royalties. Theoretically, the detail of a contract was always subject to bargaining. Every record company worth the name, by necessity, had an attorney in the background, but the artists' representation was more piecemeal in an industry where the law of the jungle was still not fully repealed.

Kent Records, although operating in the shadows of the Biharis' budget LP operation, did make its mark in the 1960s R&B and soul markets (not pop as originally envisioned) by becoming one of the last labels to focus on the stores and jukeboxes in the black enclaves. The charge was headed by B. B. King, thanks to regular reissues from the vaults long after he had signed for ABC-Paramount in 1962. Jules Bihari had a chance to retain his star artist (with whom there was mutual respect) but preferred instead to invest the proposed $25,000 advance in new equipment for the pressing plant.

Ironically, one of B. B.'s archive recordings, "Rock Me Baby," managed to break into the Top 40 on Kent in 1964 while ABC-Paramount was still struggling to find any kind of market for its expensive acquisition. Kent's deceptively strong roster also included Lowell Fulson, Z. Z. Hill, Johnny Otis, and Ike & Tina Turner. The Modern name was resuscitated in 1964 with a string of solid 45s by the Ikettes and Little Richard. This time around, the label lasted until 1969, and there was even a singles oldies series.

A casual nod toward rock music was made with Pacific Gas & Electric, under the direction of Freddy DeMann (formerly a young promo man with Cosnat Distributing and later manager of Madonna), before Columbia stepped in to sign the group. Much to Joe's progressive disgust, the Biharis' business was resorting more and more to re-packaging budget album after budget album and pressing records for other labels. There was no creativity at all, although "in 1972 or one of those years, we were the largest-selling budget company in the country," said Joe. He amused himself by indulging in motocross racing and setting up a motorcycle import business. In turn, according to Joe, brother Jules owned a string of racehorses and would visit the track every day. Their competitive, gambling instincts were never far from the surface.

Joe Bihari left the family company in 1978 after heated disputes with Jules and went into construction in the Beverly Hills area, "where I made more money than I ever did with records." Saul Bihari, always admired by his peers, was in his element selling the budget product but retired around 1971 after suffering a serious stroke; he passed away in 1975. Elder brother Lester, never a partner and with Meteor long extinguished, lived until 1983. Then Jules died a year later, a cancer victim. Earlier in 1984, Jules had given away the Modern crown jewels to a newly formed Kent record corporation for about $375,000 (including $170,000 only for the publishing), according to Joe Bihari. Having no voice as a minority stockholder, he saw the sale as a brotherly spite issue.[7]

Soon the Modern Records catalog, so underrated and undervalued at the time, was purchased by the Duck Soup Music Group (owned by Michael Jackson's then-manager Frank DiLeo) before it was sold on in 1990 for around $1.8 million. The buyers, in a tripartite agreement, were Ace Records (for Europe), Virgin (the Americas), and Blues

Interactions (the Far East), while Modern Music was purchased by BMG Music. Thanks to thoughtful CD reissues by Ace (U.K.) and P-Vine (Japan), the Modern group is belatedly recognized as the crucial independent record operation it always was.

Art Rupe: Specialty Records

Contrasting with Modern's uneven experience, Art Rupe's Specialty Records managed to change gears spectacularly to cruise into the rock 'n' roll age. First, "Lawdy Miss Clawdy" by Lloyd Price of New Orleans (with Imperial's Fats Domino moonlighting on piano) was one of the first genuine crossover records in 1952. Then Guitar Slim's blues-drenched "The Things That I Used to Do" (with Ray Charles on piano) was an amazingly popular record, staying at No. 1 R&B for all of fourteen weeks in early 1954 and making No. 23 pop. Finally, Specialty managed to break out of the segmented R&B and gospel markets due to one singular standout talent: Little Richard.

Between January 1956 and May 1959, Little Richard had no less than sixteen Top 100 hits, classics all, including four Top 10 entrants: "Long Tall Sally" (No. 6), "Jenny, Jenny" (No. 10), "Keep a Knockin'" (No. 8), and "Good Golly, Miss Molly" (No. 10). After tentative sojourns with major label RCA Victor and indie Peacock, Richard Penniman, from Macon, Georgia, invented the screaming "black rocker" idiom at Specialty. He enjoyed pulsating rhythmic assist from the session men at Cosimo Matassa's studio in New Orleans, where many of his finest records were cut. With none of Richard's many subsequent recordings for multiple labels hitting the same sweet spot, he was to make a lifelong career out of his Specialty portfolio. A salient fact is that every one of his major Specialty recordings was cut within a truly inspired eighteen-month period.

Of Little Richard's many imitators, just about the best of the rest was Larry Williams, another Specialty artist and a former valet of Lloyd Price. Williams will be known forever for his brace of irreverent R&B rockers from 1957: "Short Fat Fannie" (No. 5) and "Bony Moronie" (No. 14).

Young Roddy Jackson was signed by Specialty as a palatable white artist at the tail end of 1957. Accordingly, he had rare firsthand insights into the Specialty Records organization in the peak rock 'n' roll era that coincided with Art Rupe's stand against the payola machine and the ascendancy of Sonny Bono as Rupe's assistant. "It was a big thrill for me to sign for Specialty Records," Jackson recalled enthusiastically,

> because I was a Little Richard fan. He was my idol; I sang all of his songs. Those were different days then. We just called Specialty on the phone, and they said, "Come on down and audition." Sonny Bono, who conducted the audition, stopped us halfway through and brought Art Rupe down. Sonny felt I was going to be their big white star; he said I sang the "blackest" of any white person.
>
>   I wasn't a businessman then; I was a typical artist. All I cared about was that I was going to get to record for Specialty Records, Little Richard's label. At that time, it was pretty much a standard contract, and they didn't treat me any worse than every company was treating the artists at that time. But the artists were getting a horrible deal then. Now that's a matter of record; I don't fault them personally. Ray Charles

made a stand and demanded more, and then the Beatles changed things and made it fairer for the artists and songwriters. We all owe them a debt of gratitude.

Sonny Bono and I wrote "She Said Yeah" together for Larry Williams. He was on his way out as a big star, and he was trying to get another hit with that. It didn't sell, either. The Rolling Stones recorded it as the lead track on an album [*December's Children*], and I received a check for $5,000 at [a] halfpenny a record and then the BMI performance monies. Paul McCartney recorded it again [in 1999] on *Run Devil Run*. Venice Music [Specialty's BMI publishing house] was pretty honest with me.

I liked Art Rupe. He always treated me with dignity and respect, he and Sonny both. When I was there, Art and Sonny seemed to get along very well, and it had a feeling to me like family. I thought Art was an honest guy, decent guy, but he quit because he was disgusted with the corruption. That's why I didn't go on *American Bandstand*. He decided to make his stand; he decided to say no when it was my turn. Sonny Bono and I were going to fly to Philadelphia. It was in all the papers in central California and a great big deal. Then I get a call three days before I was leaving for L.A., saying [the trip's] been canceled because [the producers at *American Bandstand*] had increased the payola. They had kicked it up more, and Art said, "That's it! That's extortion." He had me come to his office, and we sat down, he, Sonny, and I, and he said: "I know this is a big disappointment for you, and I'm really, really sorry, but I just couldn't do it anymore. I can't stand it; I'm getting out of this business. It's so crooked I can't take it anymore."

I wanted so much to be a big star; that was my life ambition. . . . I thought it was a sure thing, but I didn't anticipate him [Rupe] backing out of *American Bandstand*. If I had gone on, I think I would have been a big star. My first record, "Love at First Sight," was No. 1 in central California and Salt Lake City, and the flip, "I've Got My Sights on Someone New," was No. 3 in Baltimore [early 1958]. So what happens is when you get a regional hit in three different places in the country, it's time to go national. That qualified me to get on national television; that was the kind of formula. Then they pulled the plug.

But if I had been a big star at the time, I don't think I would have survived. I would have wound up like Jimi Hendrix, Janis Joplin, and Jim Morrison. One day there would have been a headline that I either overdosed or got shot to death by a husband or boy friend, because I was *wild*. One of the reasons I wanted to be a big star was because I wanted all the booze and drugs and babes.

Sonny Bono had a remarkable gift that never ceased to amaze me. I would stay at his home when we would go down to L.A., and we hung out together, wrote songs together. We would listen to a station that would play all the new releases, and I'd say, "Oh, God, I love that." "Me, too," he says, "but it's not going anywhere." And it wouldn't. Anytime he heard anything on the radio new, he was always right. He had a real sense for that. That's why when he found Cher, that gift of his, he knew what would work.

Bono went on to become one of the few record people to make his mark in politics, becoming mayor of Palm Springs, California, and a Republican congressman in Washington, where he sponsored revisions in the Copyright Act. He died in a tragic skiing accident months before President Bill Clinton could sign into law the Sonny Bono Copyright Term Extension Act of 1998.

Harold Battiste: Specialty Records Branch Manager, New Orleans

During the rock 'n' roll years at Specialty, the confident Sonny Bono worked hand in hand with the more timid Harold Battiste.[8] A future record man with A.F.O., "Bat" was charged with managing Specialty's only satellite office, in New Orleans, in August 1957 at a starting salary of seventy-five dollars every two weeks, plus a quarter-percent royalty on everything that was produced. "My real assignment was to root out more Lloyd Prices and Fats Dominos and all that jazz," said Battiste. For Specialty, he created rocking classics such as "Lights Out" by Jerry Byrne and "Cha Dooky Doo" by Art Neville and recorded (in conjunction with Sonny Bono) West Coast label stars Larry Williams and Sam Cooke.[9]

Throughout the late 1950s, Battiste saw his mission in New Orleans as "Specialty Records is here to stay, and Harold Battiste is there to work with you," not "Specialty Records is in town this weekend, so everybody line up!" Dave Bartholomew was firmly entrenched at Imperial's New Orleans office and had mopped up much of the available local talent. "But Dave was so busy with Fats," said Harold. "He was sort of unreachable by the common little scared person with a little piece of paper in their hand [that] they called a song. So there was room." The Specialty branch office was not involved with record distribution, because Art Rupe was already backing a New Orleans distributorship, A-1.

"I think A-1 probably was the most influential of the independent distribution guys in the 1950s," said New Orleans studio owner Cosimo Matassa. "Early on there was another one, [Buster Williams's] Music Sales, that did real well. But unfortunately a couple of real bad operators, tough guys, got into it, and they were really low-order criminals, frankly . . . burglars, you know. A-1 was really owned by Art Rupe. A lot of people thought Dick Sturgell owned it—he was from Oklahoma—but he had some kind of operating interest in it. It was the same thing with Joe Banashak, who ran it after Sturgell. People thought it was Banashak that owned it, but it wasn't. That was the impression they wanted to give, because they didn't want you to think that one of the labels being distributed owned the company. That would have caused Art problems with the other independents, if nothing else. Why should they help him if he was a competitor? It was a well-kept secret."[10]

One of Harold Battiste's tasks was to keep a watchful eye on A-1's Joe Banashak. It was a new experience for Harold, who was no match for the wily distributor. "Joe was a much better businessman than I was," admitted Battiste. "He had a real warm facade, and he knew that being warm was a part of what it took to keep things right. So when I talked with him for sincere advice about Specialty's business and business in general, I got what I thought was good advice. And some of it was borderline. I was supposed to keep tabs on him to see that he never kept too much stuff on the floor, making sure he didn't do those things that distributors do in ordering. I was supposed to go up and count his stock, but that seemed awfully sneaky. I was accepting Joe as an adviser; I couldn't be going checking on him."[11]

Showing his all-around musical talent, Harold Battiste arranged the sweet vocal harmonies for the Lee Gotch Singers on Sam Cooke's debut smash hit, "You Send Me" (a song that bore traces of Buddy Johnson's "Since I Fell for You" from 1946). After Art Rupe's hasty rejection of the master as pop pap, Sam's producer Bumps Blackwell took the tape down the road to recently formed Keen Records (headed by John Siemas with Bob Keane, who soon departed to found Del-Fi Records and give a hit platform to Ritchie Valens). "Art felt that 'You Send Me' wasn't characteristic of Sam," said Battiste, and "it wasn't characteristic of Specialty. There was something wrong: all those pretty 'oohs' and 'aahs,' Sam singing like Morton Downey or something like that—he was a gospel singer. And I guess Art, having had [Little] Richard and having had Lloyd Price, he had shouters, that may have been a little difficult to make that quick transition. Here's a balladeer; here's a new thing altogether. But Specialty was kind of like college. I had to find out."

Since 1946, Art Rupe had been building up, with quiet certainty, a vertical record emporium at Specialty that also included publishing companies, pressing plants, the Herald Attractions booking agency, the New Orleans branch office, and the distributor networks. In very short order, he was to taste the highs and lows of rock 'n' roll and of life itself. After a phenomenal run of influential hits and earth-shattering music, led by Lloyd Price, Guitar Slim, Little Richard, and Larry Williams, he had to endure Little Richard's religious conversion and retirement and that self-inflicted loss of the charismatic Sam Cooke. On the personal front, Rupe suffered the breakup of his marriage to Lee, who went on to form Ebb Records (and had the memorable 1957 No. 11 hit "Buzz-Buzz-Buzz" by the Hollywood Flames). Then there was the escalating cost of payola and the iniquitous promo record system.[12]

"Eventually, we succumbed to what we were led to believe was called payola," admitted Art Rupe.

> For this, we took the word of our distributors. We began to suspect that our credits given for disc jockey promotion never reached a disc jockey. At least, that was what we learned later from the leading disc jockeys who dominated the larger urban markets. Specialty developed a reputation for being very stingy and tight with the promotional purse because we abhorred payola. It distorted the free competitive marketplace and resulted in the playing field not being equal. In other words, some inferior records or records not necessarily very popular were pushed to the exclusion of really meritorious product.
>
> Free promos were an industry blemish. It really amounted to a price reduction but was not good business. Specialty tried to keep this practice to the barest minimum because distributors wanted "freebies," as they called them, because they could turn

records into cash. It reduced the initial cost of each record that they sold. And I felt if I had a hit record, why should I give it away? . . . We were obligated to pay royalties and at one time excise tax on all records either manufactured or sold. And since promo records were sold by the distributors, we lost. Eventually, we began to make special labels for samples and radio play. The distributors didn't particularly like that, because the label was stamped "For promo use only, not for resale." This helped to stem illicit returns.

The final insult for Art Rupe came when *he* was cited in a payola complaint by the Federal Trade Commission, along with Hugo Peretti and Luigi Creatore of RCA Victor and Don Pierce of Starday Records. In May 1960, *Billboard* reported that "complaints charge payola to radio and TV disk jockeys to push records, by all three firms, with additional charge that Specialty paid the radio station itself, and both Specialty and Starday paid other personnel besides deejays."[13] For his part, Don Pierce told me, dismissively, that all he did was give a New Orleans disc jockey "a twenty-five-dollar Christmas present."

Let Art Rupe have the last words on this touchy subject: "I not only thought payola dishonest and unfair (no free access to the market), but I resented many no-talent disc jockeys judging music they would play according to how much they squeezed in bribes from record companies. By way of comment, I was really a Don Quixote fighting a winless battle, although Sonny Bono finally made our early excursion into payola, albeit on a very limited basis."

Morally affronted, Art Rupe withdrew from the front line to pursue outside business interests in oil and real estate, lucratively. It was almost as if he knew instinctively that the glory days of the independent record men were over. But he held on to his Specialty goldmine, unlike his Los Angeles neighbors the Mesner brothers, who faded badly before selling their Aladdin catalog (with the publishing as the prize) to Imperial in 1961, or indeed Lew Chudd, who proceeded to cash in his Imperial stock in 1963. Rupe would benefit particularly from recordings of his Venice Music song copyrights by the Beatles and the Rolling Stones. After dabbling in the 1980s vinyl reissue business through daughter Beverly Rupe, he made multimillion-dollar deals for the sale of Venice Music to ATV Music and later Specialty Records to Fantasy Records in 1990.[14]

The Specialty label—printed yellow, black, and white and favored by collectors with the early "wavy line" design—is rightfully seen as the hallmark of quality in the fields of rhythm and blues, gospel, and rock 'n' roll. Yet Art Rupe, always a superior record man, still has not been elected into the Rock and Roll Hall of Fame at the time of writing (nor has Joe Bihari or many of their contemporaries, for that matter).[15]

Leon Rene: Class Records

Genuine pioneer Leon Rene had three key, self-published hits in the peak rock 'n' roll era with the talented Bobby Day: "Little Bitty Pretty One" (No. 57, late 1957) and, in the fall of 1958, the back-to-back coupling "Rockin' Robin" (No. 2) (titled "Rock-In Robin" originally) and "Over and Over" (No. 41). As it happened, Day's "Little Bitty Pretty One" was outpaced by a note-for-note version from Thurston Harris and the Sharps on Aladdin at No. 6. Still, the coffers of Rene's Recordo Music bulged accordingly.

Class Records seemed to have a metronomic rocking sound all of its own, whether on solo, duet, vocal group, or instrumental releases, with the catalog featuring a regular flow of grooving piano-led singles and three albums (eventually) from Leon's son Googie Rene. The bedrock rhythm section comprised those imperious studio professionals Plas Johnson (tenor saxophone), Rene Hall (guitar), and Earl Palmer (drums). With this trio of musicians hailing from funky New Orleans, Leon Rene was utilizing the second-line street-beat culture of his youth to great effect. Other West Coast record men, notably Art Rupe at Specialty and the Mesner brothers at Aladdin, recognized the prize credentials of these session men, who were each performing in blissful anonymity for the record-buying public at the standard union rate of $41.25 per date.

Although Leon Rene's record labels may have come and gone (he also had a tie-in with Rod Pierce's Rendezvous in the early 1960s),[16] the great songs kept earning. "Over and Over" provided Britain's Dave Clark Five with a No. 1 U.S. hit in 1965; "Rockin' Robin" helped Michael Jackson's solo career take off in the spring of 1972 when it flew to No. 2 (again); and a few weeks later, the Jackson 5 had a No. 13 hit with "Little Bitty Pretty One." Always there was the regular income from the classic standards "When It's Sleepy Time Down South" and "When the Swallows Come Back to Capistrano."

Leon Rene lived until 1982, aged eighty. He was able to look back with pride on his founding work as a musician, songwriter, publisher, and record man, even if there were a few obstacles along the way. The very names of his labels, Exclusive and Class, hinted at the high standards he set himself in the music business. "We were independents, you're right," said Googie Rene. "Leon took a chance and did the whole thing. My dad always believed in goals; he always did his best. Everything was going to be perfect."

Dave Burgess and Joe Johnson: Challenge Records

Challenge Records of Hollywood had one of the preeminent hits of the golden age of rock 'n' roll with "Tequila" by the Champs, the instrumental group led by Dave Burgess. Beautifully recorded by Stan Ross at the Gold Star studios with perfect instrument separation and just the right amount of echo, "Tequila" was a wild concoction of rock 'n' roll with a dash of Mexican rhythmic firewater that stayed at No. 1 for five long weeks between March and April in 1958. Later, Burgess was to become a partner with Joe Johnson in the Challenge organization. Here is a tale of two record men who made it big on the West Coast with Challenge but were unable to find happy endings to their stories.

Singing cowboy hero Gene Autry was the principal investor in Challenge Records, founded in early 1957. At first sight, he was the unlikeliest of record men. After all, he was a major movie star and best-selling country and western artist, from the Depression era until World War II, succeeding Jimmie Rodgers. Yet here was the shrewdest of businessmen who saw a record company as a means of promoting his song publishing interests as well as his own recordings.

Autry's right-hand man was Joe Johnson, who had joined the Nashville division of Columbia Records under the revered Don Law in 1953. "Don was my mentor," said Johnson.

> When I started in the business, I was a promotion man for Columbia working the middle Tennessee area basically as assistant to Don Law. I understudied Don and learned to produce and deal with artists and so forth by watching his technique, and he was very good at it. He was English, a wonderful man. He taught me a great deal, and he was very good to me.
>
> After I did the promotions for about six months, I got five . . . Top 10 [country hits] in my territory on Columbia Records. So Don called me one day; he was in Bridgeport, Connecticut [the Columbia headquarters]. He said, "Little Jimmy Dickens is coming into town. I want you to get with him and do a session." At that point I had done some sessions with Don, and he had confidence in me. So I got with Jimmy and recorded one of his hits called "Y'All Come." That was my first session and my first hit [at the turn of 1954].[17]
>
> Then Gene Autry [a longtime Columbia recording artist] expressed an interest in hiring me to do some mass publicity for him in Canada for a tour. At the end of that tour, he asked me to go to California to run his music companies and "I'm making you a partner with 25 percent." I think he had in the back of his mind that he wanted to start an independent record label.
>
> I went out west in '55, and we got a couple of hits, mainly "Just Walking in the Rain" by Johnnie Ray [No. 2, Columbia, fall 1956]. It was written by two prisoners. I took Gene out to do a show for them at the prison [in Nashville], and I met Johnny Bragg and Robert Riley, who told me they had written a song. It started to rain, so they looked at each other: "Let's write a song about it." That's how it came about. We picked up the publishing [from Red Wortham] at that point for Gene's company, Golden West Melodies. The song had been recorded by the Prisonaires and released on Sun Records. It got some action; it wasn't a big hit, but it was on the jukeboxes and sold some. The record was a little out of tune, but I don't think that really killed it [laughs].
>
> But I got several covers on it after we picked up the publishing [including a version by Gene Autry]. Finally Mitch Miller recorded it with Johnnie Ray, who was in a cold slump at that point, but this record brought him back. I pitched it to Don Law, and he gave it to Mitch. With "Just Walking in the Rain," I think we had a net in the coffer of about $58,000. Gene says, "Go start a record label!" So I started Challenge Records in January or February 1957.

The seed capital for Challenge Records had come, therefore, from the publishing windfall from Johnnie Ray's hit record. Gene Autry took a 56 percent stockholding in Challenge, augmented by the 20 percent stakes each of Joe Johnson, A&R chief, and Johnny Thompson, head of sales. The balance of 4 percent was held by Bernie Solomon, secretary, who would later become president of Everest Records. Showing how quickly Gene Autry had become attuned to the world of rock 'n' roll, some six months later he was in negotiations with disc jockey Alan Freed for a possible, albeit aborted, TV film series under the banner of Flying A Productions.[18]

The first Challenge signings were Dave Burgess and Jerry Wallace. Back in 1954, Burgess, after making a series of impressive demo recordings of his country-based songs, was introduced by studio owner Stan Ross to Seymour Heller of Gabbe-Lutz-Heller. This firm, which managed establishment artists such as Lawrence Welk, Liberace, and Frankie Laine, signed young Burgess to a long-term management contract and set up a deal with Columbia Records.

"They called a session at Radio Recorders in Hollywood," remembered Dave Burgess. "There were twenty-six musicians and a big vocal group with six voices. I said, 'Wait a minute, there is an arranger here, right?' 'Yeah, Harry Geller is the arranger.' 'I'm just a country boy; I need a fiddle and steel and a couple of guitars.' He says, 'Oh, they have an idea in mind for you.' So I cut, and it was not what I wanted to do at all. One of the songs was called 'Don't Put a Dent in My Heart.' My heart really had a dent in it after that because I was heartbroken." One stillborn single was issued by OKeh, the Columbia subsidiary.

"So I got my contract release," said Burgess.

I wrote some more songs and went back to Gold Star, and I was doing some more demos. Stan Ross is in the studio, and there's another really nice-looking, clean-cut guy. When I got through with my songs, he came out and introduced himself. He said his name was Joe Johnson: "I work for Gene Autry; I manage his company. Do you have a publisher? Do you have a record contract?" I told him about the Seymour Heller story. Joe said, "Well, I'd like to meet with you. We have a new record company we're just starting called Challenge Records. I'd like to produce you, and I'd like to sign you to a publishing contract." They signed me, and I got to meet Gene Autry, which was a big thrill.

Gene was about as down-to-earth as you could ever expect anybody to be. You'd never know he was worth all that money and was so successful. He was an absolute delight, and he taught me so much; he took me under his wing. He was very tight with the dollar, extremely tight with the dollar. I learned about business, what to do and not what to do, 'cause he had come through the school of hard knocks. He was very open in that he was willing to teach me. He was like a second father to me. I really appreciated that.

Gene Autry told me something one time; I have to pass it on. He said that honesty and integrity are the most important things a man can have: "It's like being a little bit pregnant; you either are or you aren't" [laughs]. What a classy gentleman! He really was a hero in real life. In the beginning I was nervous, of course; I had to be. He was an icon, a true legend.

I think Gene really formed Challenge Records for Joe Johnson and saw it as a way to get his older stuff repackaged and released. This is all pre–Republic Records. Joe saw it as a chance to develop an independent record label; he was very bright in his thinking, too. I recorded a couple of things that didn't do a whole lot, and then I did a song called "Maybelle," which was going up the charts.

I had been working with my guitar, playing around with a thing called "Train to Nowhere." So I came in to Joe and said, "Look, I've got an idea for an instrumental." This was after "Honky Tonk" had hit. So I played it on my guitar, and he said, "I think that's worth cutting; that's great. Let's get a band together." I said, "Well, I don't have a band to do this. I need a rock group." He said, "Well, Charlie Adams [a music publisher and Columbia recording artist] took me out and had me listen to a funky sax player the other night by the name of Danny Flores. I think he'll be great." So we went over to 6920 Sunset Boulevard; they had a little rehearsal room in a building that Gene Autry owned at the time. We started rehearsing, and we got "Train to Nowhere" down just the way we wanted it. Danny played sax, and we overdubbed him on piano. Joe Johnson came in with Johnny Thompson, who was the sales manager.

Johnny Thompson had been with Coral Records. He had a lot of experience in the sales department but not in marketing record labels and things like that. He was looking to Joe Johnson for guidance, and Joe Johnson was looking to Johnny. It became a comedy of errors, and it took a while for everybody to learn how to do it. I think that was true with a lot of labels in those days.

So Joe Johnson and Johnny Thompson said, "That's a smash, absolute smash, but we gotta have a 'B' side." I said, "Give us a little while; we'll come up with something." So we had listened to a guitar player from Tijuana, Mexico, by the name of Little Joe Washington, who had mixed this R&B/Latin rock thing. I started playing that riff on the guitar, and Danny started playing this melody on the saxophone, which was just a great melody, and the bass player Cliff Hills fell in with it; so did the drummer, Gene Alden, and the guitar player, Buddy Bruce. I said to Danny, "Why don't we do a bridge on it and stop and let you say 'Tequila!'" because he had this raspy voice. Everybody said it was a great idea, so we did it. I called Joe Johnson back in to listen to it, and he said, "Great 'B' side; that'll work."

We set up a session at Gold Star. In those days, you could do [up to] four songs in three hours. We spent two hours, fifty-five minutes on "Train to Nowhere," getting it perfect, just the way we wanted it. Joe said, "Well, we'd better hurry up and get that 'B' side." So we did one take of "Tequila," one take. There's a big mistake in the middle of it which nobody ever noticed. It's just a guitar lick—*de dada dede da pow*—the second *pow* was gone. Buddy Bruce forgot to do it.

They released the record under my contract as Dave Burgess. We were going to call ourselves the Champions, but there was a Marge and Gower Champion who were dancers at the time, so we decided to name it after Gene Autry's horse Champ. His horse was Champion, but they called him Champ. Unfortunately, everybody thought we were an Olympic boxing team, but that's okay.

They put the record out, 100 percent on "Train to Nowhere." Then a radio station in Cleveland flipped the record over and played "Tequila." Immediately ABC-Paramount went in and rerecorded the song with Eddie Platt [initially for Bill Buchanan's local Decor label], and they got off our record and started playing the Eddie Platt [eventually a No. 20 hit]. Well, when that happened, the other station in town started playing our record twenty-four hours a day, nonstop. In those days, radio stations had a habit of doing that, so all you heard in Cleveland was "Tequila." I mean, those poor people in Cleveland, no wonder they're confused.

Joe Johnson took up the fast-moving story:

The guy that broke it was Bill Randle in Cleveland [at Radio WERE]. He played it on his show one night, and the phones lit up like a Christmas tree. So he called his friend Eddie Platt, who had just signed with ABC-Paramount: "Hey, there's a record out here on a small independent label, and you ought to cover this and get it out right away." And that's what he did. Fortunately, I had the publishing and was able to put him on a compulsory license. They had a lot of the same distributors as I did, and they were giving two records free for every one they bought on ABC-Paramount. They were trying to knock mine out of the marketplace. But by being on a compulsory license, they had to pay me on every record they pressed for dee-jays or for any purpose whatsoever, and they had to pay every thirty days in cash. So ABC-Paramount kind of backed off a little at that point. They sold about 200,000 while we were selling a million.

Continued Burgess, "Anyway, the record took off instantaneously, worldwide. It was just an instantaneous hit. Immediately the lawsuits started coming in! Danny was under contract to the Bihari brothers. Then a big movie music producer, Les Baxter, said, 'I wrote "Tequila"; that's my melody.' What Danny had done without realizing it, subconsciously he just played that song. He'd have heard it in a movie or on television."

"Tequila" was released with the record and sheet music credited to "Chuck Rio" (Danny Flores) and published by Jat Music (the initials of the last names of Joe Johnson, Gene Autry, and Johnny Thompson). The Les Baxter song in question was "De Rain" from the movie *Bop Girl Goes Calypso*, a last-minute "rock 'n' roll" cash-in on the calypso craze. "When Les approached me [and said] that he was gonna sue on the basis of the melody," recalled Joe Johnson,

I said, "Well, send me a copy of what you got." So he sent it over. In that little clip of the movie was this girl in the islands with a basket on her head walking through the rain, and they were playing that song. It was note for note! The movie was released in '57, and Chuck [Danny Flores] had seen the movie. But I don't think the song was original. [Claimant] Les Baxter lived in Mexico, and he probably picked it up down there. Incidentally, I am told "Tequila" was played in Tijuana in the clubs as a "break" song, just before they'd take a break, to get everybody to the bar and drinking tequila.

Anyway, I asked my attorney, Bob Myers, how much it would cost to fight the lawsuit. He said "Well, you got to figure to spend at least $10,000." I said, "Well, offer him $10,000, and we'll settle with him." He settled just like that, so that tells me he wasn't too strong on his suit.

Another sidebar to the story is that as Danny Flores was contracted to Kent Records, Modern Music ended up with 25 percent of the publishing, according to Joe Bihari.[19]

"I still have great appreciation for the fact that Chuck Rio brought me the song in a timely fashion," said Joe Johnson. "I would never have got it without him. So I never questioned his writer's interest for that reason. We paid him writer royalties right up until the mid-1960s, somewhere in there. He was on drugs . . . cocaine and I don't know what else; he kept coming to me for advances, and I kept advancing him money way beyond his earnings. Finally, he said, 'I need $12,000.' I said, 'Good God, I can't give you another $12,000 advance.' He said, 'Well, buy me out.' So I bought out his interest in royalties for $12,000. After that he turned bitter."

"It was tough managing a hit like 'Tequila,'" confessed Dave Burgess. "It wasn't a lack of funds as much as it was a lack of knowledge. Nobody had great experience. For example, we came out with an album after 'Tequila' that [was titled] *Go Champs Go!* It didn't mention 'Tequila' on the cover, and nobody knew who the Champs were yet. That was a gross error."

As well, it would have been better to separate "Tequila" and "Train to Nowhere," which could have been a hit single in its own right. "The Champs' follow-up was 'El Rancho Rock'; it did very well [No. 30]," said Dave Burgess.

> We had a lot of records out that dotted the charts but weren't real hits; then we came back with "Too Much Tequila" [No. 30, 1960] and "Limbo Rock" [No. 40, 1962], which was an even bigger hit [No. 2] for Chubby Checker (Parkway). But along in there came the Tijuana Brass (A&M), who picked up right where we left off, and we have competition with Herb Alpert; he did all those great Latin rock records. A&M Records was so tremendously successful [for its partners]; you had a great musician [Alpert] and you had a great record promoter with Jerry Moss. Those guys were magic.
>
> I have a great respect for Dick Clark. We were on his shows a lot of time. In fact, when "Tequila" started to happen, it was so quick; it sold so many records so fast. All the different booking agencies called me, everyone from MCA to GAC. I said, "I tell you what, you're all good, but I want the *Ed Sullivan Show* on Sunday night followed by *Dick Clark,* the Saturday night show. And I want a gold record on each." A guy by the name of Jack Gillardi of GAC came up with that; he became our agent, and he did a great job. Rock 'n' roll was just starting, and Ed Sullivan didn't quite know how to handle it.
>
> The real excitement, of course, was doing the concerts. That was a big thrill. But you had to watch the gate very carefully with some of the promoters. The fees ranged from $500 to $1,000 [per night]; in fact, $2,500 was a lot in those days. We told agencies, "We're out there on the road; we've got a traveling overhead. Get good money for us on Fridays and Saturdays, and the rest of the weekdays get whatever you can. Just keep us working." The youngsters loved it, and the parents hated us! We were the bad guys; we were gonna corrupt their kids with rock 'n' roll. You had to look the part, and we did it twenty-four hours a day [*laughs*]. You had to look glamorous and be different from the guy next door. Gene Autry said, "They're not performers when they dress like tramps." We traveled in a station wagon pulling a trailer, six sweaty guys, traveling all over the "world." But things were going on at home we weren't aware of. Then came the problem of Joe Johnson and Johnny Thompson buying Challenge Records from Gene Autry.

With "Tequila" barely off the charts (in a twenty-week run), the sale of Challenge, Jat Music Co., and Sunset Artists was announced hastily in October 1958. Under the arrangement, Johnson and Thompson shared 91 percent of the new stock, with Bernie Solomon's stake being upped to 9 percent. The price was not revealed but was thought to be "in the six-figure bracket, to be paid off on a term basis depending upon company profits." It was a generous deal favoring the beneficiaries, the official line being that Gene Autry would be allowed "to concentrate on other investments." Even so, there can be little doubt that he was unnerved by the flurry of "Tequila"-based lawsuits, which were attracted to some extent by Autry's deep pockets.[20]

"Gene wanted to help Joe and Johnny, and help us," said Dave Burgess. "So he started Republic Records [acquired in November 1959]. It got him going good again, and that was distributed by Challenge. That's what he really wanted, a vehicle for his own records." Gene Autry was primarily intent on building up his publishing operations, a far better bet than record label ownership. In 1960, he paid a reported $150,000 to Bill McCall for the 4 Star music publishing company, which included the prize copyrights "Don't Let the Stars (Get in Your Eyes)," "Release Me," "Lonely Street," "Am I That Easy to Forget?" and a current hit, "Hot Rod Lincoln."

"Gene became a little disillusioned with the record business," said Joe Johnson.

> He didn't realize that you had to spend money to make money. After "Tequila," he wanted to concentrate on his other businesses; he was into radio and hotels very heavily. Then Bob Burton [soon-to-be president of BMI] came to California [and] asked Gene and [me] to have dinner with him at the Hotel Bel-Aire. At dinner, after several drinks and a good meal, he brought up the reason why he wanted to see Gene and me together. He said, "I want you to buy out Bill McCall of Pasadena. This guy is giving the music business a bad name. We want him out of the business. Don't worry, Gene, it won't cost you anything; I'll advance the money. Good-bye." And Gene turned to me, [and] he says, "If I go negotiating with my big white hat on, they'll double the price on it. You go and see what you can do." It took me about six months to negotiate to buy it [4 Star Sales Co.].
>
> BMI paid for the [publishing] purchase of McCall; they advanced all the money. That was back when BMI could advance it. So we bought 4 Star [Sales Co.] from Mc-Call without any risk whatsoever. That's why when we found out about the flaw in the copyrights through due diligence, . . . it didn't stop us because we weren't taking any gamble. The fact is we were being totally banked by BMI, and Gene said it was no problem. We bought the publishing company first in 1960 and the record company in 1961.[21] Gene took 70 percent, and I took 30 percent.
>
> When we were negotiating to buy 4 Star, I met with Patsy Cline. She said, "I am so glad to hear that you and Gene Autry are buying Bill McCall out. I hate his guts. I won't re-sign with him, but I'll re-sign with you. But I need about $4,000; I've got a cash problem."

However, Gene Autry refused to advance the money for the contract of the country star, whose recordings were being released on Decca. "So we passed on Patsy Cline and the rest of her catalog," said Johnson. "Anyway, we got the first half. That's been good for us."[22]

Alas, all was not well with Challenge's top act, the Champs. "When Joe Johnson bought the label," said Dave Burgess, "it became a problem for us to get paid. He would say things like, 'Well, the session cost too much.' I said, 'The session didn't cost anything. We don't even get paid as musicians; all you paid is the studio time.' It cost $500 for an album; that was unheard of. We got a pittance here and there, never a big check in spite of all the sales. 'Tequila' probably did 1,500,000 to 2,000,000 records in the first run, and the album probably sold 100,000 copies. They should have put a 'Tequila' sticker on it at the very least."

More fundamentally, Burgess said he was aggrieved that he did not receive a co-composer's credit for "Tequila," along with guitarist Buddy Bruce in addition to listed writer Chuck Rio. He continued: Anyway, Joe came to me one day: 'Gene has made it possible for us to buy 4 Star Music. Would you like to come into it?' I said, 'Absolutely. I am really interested in getting off the road.' I had gotten married, and I wanted to get into the business end of this thing more than performing. It's not glamorous like people think it is. So I settled into being executive vice president and general manager of 4 Star Sales Co. Immediately we had success. We had [the publishing for] four songs in the Top 10 country and four in the Top 10 pop at the same time."

One of these songs was the Ricky Nelson 1961 No. 1, "Travelin' Man" (Imperial), which led Challenge to tender for Ricky Nelson's contract. "I was in on the production of 'Travelin' Man,'" said Joe Johnson. "I had five hits with him. It was my crew—Jerry Fuller, Dave Burgess, and myself—who was actually doing the studio work. Jerry Fuller taught Ricky line for line how to sing 'Travelin' Man.' I was really involved in production, and I thought we could really carry on Ricky's hits with our writers and his popularity. We guaranteed him $500,000. Well, Decca came in, [and] I couldn't compete."

Gene Autry bowed out finally after a typical entrepreneurial assist from U.K. Decca's Sir Edward Lewis. Remembered Joe Johnson, "When I bought out Gene's interest in '63, I more or less deemphasized my activities in the record business to concentrate on the publishing. I had to pay off Gene over a certain period of time, and I did it in a three-year period, 29 percent down. Actually, Sir Edward Lewis of Decca showed up in my office in Hollywood. I told him about Gene wanting to sell 4 Star Music after he had cash flow problems in the hotel business. Sir Edward Lewis said, 'Why don't you buy it?' I said, 'Well, gosh, if I had the money, I sure would.' He said, 'Well, I tell you what, I'll give you an advance, enough for a down payment, and you can pay the rest of it out of profits.' So that's what I did. Sir Edward Lewis was the guy that made that possible. He was a *brilliant* man."

By then, with original rock 'n' roll mellowing, Joe Johnson had bucked the popular music trends by entering the country music field. "The indie distributors had a hard time," he recalled. "They were saying, 'Don't fool with that country stuff. We got to work as hard to make a hit in country, and we sell about 10 percent of what we do on pop and rock 'n' roll hits.' They discouraged country music. In the face of that, I went ahead and did the Wynn Stewart and Jan Howard stuff and made a success of that in spite of them. That was one of the reasons why I switched over to a major distributor, Warner Bros., for the country exposure."

Challenge had racked up solid sales with Jerry Wallace and would score, too, with artists such as Jan & Dean, Jerry Fuller, and the Knickerbockers. But with policy differences accumulating in the new rock music era, Dave Burgess sold his stakes to Joe Johnson. Following a failed distribution deal with MCA, Johnson moved back to Nashville, where he planned to build an overambitious Brill Building–type production center on Music Row to make records and music videos. After breaking ground in 1974, his partner died a year later, and following a Chapter 11 filing in 1977, "the bankers took the project down, took the record company and publishing company." In effect, Joe Johnson had run head-on into the wall of the old Nashville establishment. He lost, too, the writer's share of "Tequila," a song that had been recorded "hundreds of times" and performed countless times.[23]

Dave Burgess was also submerged in the aftershock of the Challenge collapse. "I sold out in '72 and moved to Montana," he said. "I got a down payment, and I was set for life, except for one thing: I never got another payment. But I got my song catalog back, and that enabled me to come to Nashville and start over again." Although stunned at seeing his dreams of a new life in Montana evaporate in the mountain air, Dave was able to pick up the pieces by starting a career managing the publishing interests of Hank Williams Jr., the country music legend's son.

Of the West Coast record men that Dave Burgess encountered, he admired most Lew Chudd at Imperial Records and Al Bennett of Liberty Records (which in Eddie Cochran had a raunchier teen equivalent of Ricky Nelson). Coincidentally, the Imperial masters and publishing were sold to Liberty (then owned by Avnet Electronics Corporation) for a sum "estimated at in excess of $2 million" in August 1963.[24] "Lew Chudd sold out at right time, brilliant!" stated Burgess.

Everything he did was brilliant. He was a great guy; he stayed up on that building on Hollywood Boulevard and dickered around in the stock market. That was his passion, not the record business. They were gamblers in a sense. He and Al Bennett, it was the old school. They knew timing was of the utmost importance.

The business was so passionate in those days. You'd write a song, hear a singer, you'd go in, do a demo. You could do a session for two hundred dollars, [make] a deal with the recording sessions and the musicians. You could get everybody to work with you; the union wasn't breathing down your neck. Everybody was taking part of a gamble. You bet your time and effort and your talent—at two hundred dollars a session, you could take a chance. Today you can't afford to take a chance; you know you've got to sell product.

My first hit came from "I'm Available" by Margie Rayburn [No. 9, late 1957]. Al Bennett was just coming in it at Liberty; it was basically Si Waronker [in charge]. The record became a big hit. That was my first production. I had written the song by myself, and Gene Autry published it. After the record became a hit, Al Bennett called me, [and] he said, "Look, Dave, we're close to being out of business here. We've got pressing costs, promotional costs, and if we pay you, we can't pay them. We *will* pay you, but you're going to have to wait." I said, "Al, I'll trust you; I'll wait." "Witch Doctor" [by David Seville] came along and then the Chipmunks. I mean, how do you get bigger than that? That's how he was able to pay me for "I'm Available."

But Al Bennett, who was with Dot at the beginning with Randy [Wood], was the consummate businessman. He had a great talent for picking people like Snuffy Garrett, Dick Glasser, and Scotty Turnbull [aka Scott Turner], whom he'd turn over a division of his record company to: "You do it; I trust you. We'll release what you say." There were many things about Al, but one of the things he used to do, . . . I've never forgotten. He had an enormous staff all across the country at United Artists–Liberty [merged from 1968 by the Transamerica parent], and every morning he'd call one of his field people on the phone personally. Somebody maybe he'd never met, somebody in a little town in South Texas that was doing promotion, and he'd say, "I just want you to know that I know what you're doing, you're doing a great job, and I appreciate it." Well, that made people love you. I mean, how many CEOs of corporations today do something like that? You can't name one, I don't think. That was Al Bennett. We need those kind of people at record companies.

A music business Mr. Nice Guy, Dave Burgess can take solace in the fact that during his unexpectedly bumpy journey from artist and songwriter to record man and publisher, he gave us with the Champs the all-time classic "Tequila." It had the whole world rocking in 1958 and has continued to be played everywhere since then. "We had, I guess, altogether nine chart records," said Burgess, "which is good for an instrumental group. 'Honky Tonk' paved the way for rock instrumentals, and if you look back at Bill Doggett and all those groups, most of them just had one hit. Like Bill Justis with 'Raunchy' [Phillips International], the follow-up record usually got in the charts, and then that was the end of that. I felt very fortunate that we were able to sustain it for five years, a long time. It's a wonderful experience. I've been very blessed, I know." Those late 1950s rockin' instrumentals by the Champs and others would inspire a whole generation of young do-it-yourself instrumentalists, particularly on the West Coast, leading to the surf/hot rod movement headed by the Beach Boys and Dick Dale.

In the end, Challenge Records was a challenge for both Dave Burgess and Joe Johnson, in real life as well as in business. With hindsight, Gene Autry had done the right thing to ride away in the opposite direction on Sunset Boulevard. While Challenge ground to a halt, just like Modern, Specialty, Class, and other indies, the corporate record labels kept the West Coast rockin' in its own laidback way into the 1970s and beyond. As Burgess noted, it was a drastically changed music business and social scene compared to the "good old days" of the independents.

17

CHAPTER

From Motown
to Manhattan:
In Almost
Perfect Harmony

CAST OF CHARACTERS
Roquel "Billy" Davis, Anna and Chess Records
Gene Barge, Chess Records arranger and producer
*also featuring Joe Battle, Joe's Record Shop and
J-V-B Records; Leonard and Phil Chess, Chess Records;
and Berry Gordy, Tamla-Motown Records*

It was always a privilege to be in the company of Roquel "Billy" Davis. Forever warm and welcoming, with a constant chuckle, he had an intelligence level that was inspiring. Over lunch or in front of a tape recorder, he was always willing to talk about his many accomplishments in the music business but with a disarming modesty. Could this natural humility be a plausible reason why most history books have not properly conveyed his integral role in preparing the groundwork for Tamla-Motown Records with Berry Gordy?

Billy Davis learned his trade as apprentice to four record men: Joe Battle, Syd Nathan, Leonard Chess, and George Goldner. What teachers; what an education! Starting out in Detroit, oozing with assembly-line talent, Billy Davis had a stellar resume that included singing with the first incarnation of the Four Tops vocal group; writing, with Berry Gordy, the career-launching songs of electric R&B entertainer Jackie Wilson; founding Anna Records in Detroit with Gwen Gordy; becoming A&R director of Chess Records and easing the iconic blues company into the soul era; and changing direction to become a Madison Avenue advertising executive. Davis wound up a dedicated music publisher. His final destination was a highly desirable brownstone building, nestled in the heart of Manhattan, housing the corporate offices and demo studio of Billy Davis Enterprises.

This location was light years away from the Detroit ghettos where he contentedly spent his childhood days in the 1930s and 1940s. "Detroit became a haven for a lot of immigrants from the South," said Davis, "like people from Alabama, Georgia, parts of Florida, and Mississippi. You found a lot of black families came up to Detroit because there was work available in the automobile plants. There was not just Ford Motor Company, which was the largest; my grandfather worked there. It was to Detroit and Chicago primarily that they came." Nevertheless, the northern industrial city of Detroit, with a prominent Ku Klux Klan chapter, still had its share of early racial strife.

Billy was born in 1932 to Willie and Catherine Davis. His father did not feature in our conversation, but "my mother was a dancer on stage. She and another young lady were dancing partners, and they performed around the Midwest, mostly in the Detroit, Ohio, [and] Illinois area, I understand. The name of the act was the Chocolate Drops. They might look at it a little differently today, but that was the name then [laughs]. It wasn't a strip dance or anything like that; they were routine dancers (like tap dancing), and I guess they felt as if they were pretty successful for female dancers. That's what they did for a living until she stopped doing it, I guess after I was born. I put an end to her career!"

The glamour of show business rubbed off on the youngster. "I started out in school learning to play cornet and then trumpet," he said. "I also took up the drums, but in my heart I really wanted to sing. So I was part of the glee club in school, from elementary school on, and I became a vocalist rather than a trumpet player." Davis, the first grandchild, was raised by his grandmother (she was "Mama") in a happy house teeming with the children, including his cousin/second grandchild Lawrence Payton (later of the Four Tops). Family entertainment was provided by way of a Victrola phonograph, which was a rare commodity in the neighborhood.

"Yes, my name is Roquel Davis," he said, "and Tyran Carlo . . . and Billy Davis! It sounds complicated, but it really isn't. In school I was Roquel, and when I got outta school, I was Billy. Roquel was a difficult name to pronounce, and it was totally unusual. My mother said she named me after reading a magazine in [the] hospital after she gave birth to me, and it was [the name of] a French movie actor. She loved it, and so I was handed, branded, Roquel."

Billy explained how his songwriter "nom de plume" came about:

I wouldn't call myself Roquel, and Billy sounded too kid-like for me, so I chose the name Tyran Carlo. As a kid I loved a movie actress named Yvonne De Carlo, [but] I certainly couldn't call myself Yvonne. I also liked Tyrone Power, so I took a combination of those two names and changed it slightly and came up with Tyran Carlo. That stuck primarily because my first big writing success was the Jackie Wilson thing, "Reet Petite."

My career started during the doo-wop craze in the 1950s, and so we were along with all the doo-wop groups. A little bit prior to the doo-wop craze, the bird-group era, were groups like the Dominoes, the Ravens, the Four Buddies, and a few other groups that were big, and so that's who you loved. I also loved, on the other side of that coin, Frank Sinatra and Nat "King" Cole. Oh God, Nat influenced a lot of acts, singers especially. In my opinion, he was probably one of the all-time greatest male vocalists; he also was a gentleman and he had class. So you looked up to him for more reasons than being just an entertainer.

There was a big theater in Detroit that used to bring in top black talent called the Paradise Theater. It was located on the main drag down Woodward Avenue. Could be anybody from Cab Calloway and his orchestra to Louis Jordan, Lena Horne, Lionel Hampton—even Sammy Davis Jr. played there. Generally, the groups were at the Paradise Theater for a week, but when their last shows were ended on the weekends, some of them would play the Flame Show Bar. They had a double gig going that way, and they were able to play the show bar for less money because they were already in town. So the Flame Show Bar became very popular. In popularity, the club was huge; in size, no. I imagine it might have seated, bulging from the seams, with people sitting at the bar, maybe two hundred people. Even from the bar you had a good view.

The house band was led by Maurice King, who was another person that was very influential [to] me and helped us a lot. Maurice actually started me to really get involved in music and writing music down. The very first song I ever got copyrighted was because of Maurice King. He said, "You gotta copyright your songs; this is what you gotta do." He taught me some of the basics of the other side, the business side of things as well as musically. Everyone loved Maurice because he was like a father to all the entertainers who came through there.

King would become the musical director of artist development at Tamla Motown during its 1960s heyday.

Joe Battle: Joe's Record Shop and J-V-B Records

Young Detroit hopefuls would gather at Joe's Record Shop at 3530 Hastings Street. Sometimes adding "Von" as a middle name like an aristocratic German baron, Joe Battle (a black man) had run his business in a solid manner since the mid-1940s. "This dealer is known for having the largest selection of r. & b. records," reported *Billboard* in a 1954 business survey of then recession-hit Detroit.[1] Battle operated the tiny J-V-B and Von labels from the store, where he had set up a makeshift recording studio in the back room, primarily for demos. Critically, he was subject to charm offensives from the leading independent record men, not only to promote and sell records but to discover new talent that often patronized his shop and studio. As the pivotal regional kingpin in Detroit, Battle was as important to the indie label network as were record shop owners Stan Lewis in Shreveport, Ernie Young in Nashville, Randy Wood in Gallatin, John Dolphin in Los Angeles, and Bobby Robinson in Harlem, among others.[2]

In Billy Davis, Joe Battle had discovered a gem. "Joe used to record local talent," said Davis, and he had connections with some of the key record companies around, the independents in those days like Chess, Savoy, King–Federal–De Luxe [and others]. His was probably one of the first record shops to get records directly from the manufacturer at a wholesale price. He would promote their records and so forth because he got a lot of free goods, so to speak, and as a result he would send them artists and do things in return. Oh yeah, he got local radio exposure because everyone knew Joe Battle in town, so he had the connections with local station WJLB.

In the back of Joe's Record Shop—it was sort of like his storage room—he had this little microphone (one mic) and this Ampex recorder set up, where he used to do demos. He also recorded some of the old blues artists back there. John Lee Hooker and some of the guys in the Detroit area used to record back there, and pretty soon he put in an upright piano, a bass, and a drum. There wasn't any space for anything else, and of course, in those days, they [the record companies] didn't use anything else but a rhythm section either!

Joe recorded Reverend C. L. Franklin [Aretha's father]; he used to take that same little portable tape recorder to the New Bethel Baptist Church on Hastings Street. He used to record the choir there and Reverend Franklin's sermons, which were released on Chess 78 records. It was excellent business because he [Reverend Franklin] was not only popular in the Detroit area but Illinois, Ohio, those areas as well. He dressed very contemporary-looking, and he was, as we'd say in those days, very *sharp*. If you didn't know who he was, he didn't look like he was a reverend at all. Oh yes, he was definitely a star. But he was a very likable man, and he didn't allow Aretha to sing [professionally] too early to get out of the church.

Billy Davis credited Joe Battle with encouraging him to focus on the songwriting profession:

He used to tell me, "Billy, you want to concentrate on writing. You are a much better writer than you can sing. Anybody can sing! Look how many groups there are in Detroit, all over the place. They're in here every day. How many of them have their own material? How many can write? You become a writer. Let them do the singing; you just write songs." He used to preach this on me, every day.

Anyway, behind my back he took one of my songs, and he sent it to a company in California called 4 Star: Bill McCall and Don Pierce. They recorded it with some country and western act, and apparently it sold records, because one day Joe called me in and handed me a check for $54. It was the first check I'd ever had with my name on it for $54. Wow! That was like giving me $54,000 today. Of course, I didn't take much more convincing that perhaps I could make more money writing than trying to sing. It is true that R&B and country aren't that far apart in the simplicity of the music. Basically the chord structures are similar in a lot of R&B songs, and certainly the subject matter.[3]

Did Joe educate me about the need to copyright a song? No, no, no! No, he didn't go that far; that would've been stepping into his territory there. That's something that we had to learn the hard way, the real hard way, because in those days, in order to get your songs recorded, you had to cut everybody in. I had more co-writers on my songs than you can shake a stick at. It was years before I had a song with just my name on it!

Being interested in poetry at school, Billy learned his craft by studying the song lyric magazines that proliferated in the 1950s. In particular, he would have read *Rhythm and Blues*, published by The Onyx Publishing Co. of Charlton Buildings, Derby, Connecticut. Known affectionately as a "Charlton" magazine, the publisher had a stable of music titles, including *Song Hits* and *Hit Parader* for the pop market and *Country Song Roundup* and *Folk and Country Songs* for the hillbilly market.

The first issue of *Rhythm and Blues* was published in August 1952 with a brightly colored front cover featuring photographs of the Orioles, Sarah Vaughan, and uncredited Caucasian Johnnie Ray (who was discovered in Detroit).[4] Intriguingly, the magazine's credits indicated the big presence of the Atlantic and Decca record companies, together with talent agencies Gale, Shaw, Universal, and MCA. This was the all-embracing world of rhythm and blues and popular jazz—but not way-out bebop—that still abided by the dress code, discipline, and professionalism of the swing band era, the "It's showtime!" ethos.

The target audience for *Rhythm and Blues* was the teen-and-twenties crowd, still mostly black, who were buying the latest hits. These young adults would descend upon the record stores and convert them into great social-gathering centers. There was excitement in the air as they would hear the new releases in listening booths. But the shop assistants had to be alert, because pilfering was a constant problem. Even if a shop catered to the rhythm and blues trade, certain pop artists were in demand with the black clientele, including Frank Sinatra, Patti Page, Frankie Laine, Johnnie Ray, and "jump specialists" Bill Haley and his Comets.[5]

"Now in those days, either you heard something on a jukebox or the radio," said Billy Davis.

> And you'd go in with your favorite artist in mind and say, "What have you got new by the Dominoes? When is their next record coming out?" So the record shops would have these little posters sitting around letting you know when to expect the next release by such-and-such artist. So there really was quite a pent-up demand then, once a group was hot or an artist was hot.
>
> Joe's Record Shop was a tiny space, actually. It was sort of narrow and long. I guess it was no more than about eighteen feet wide and maybe forty-five to fifty feet deep. In the front was the counter, and behind the counter they had shelving on the wall where records would sit in different slots with the name of the artist under each slot. They were definitely 78s, the ones that would crack if you looked at 'em hard! All right, you'd buy one at the record shop, and before you got it home, it had a crack in it if you weren't careful. But, yeah, those were 78s.

Billy Davis was aware of nearby Fortune Records, run with weird abandon by Devora Brown and her husband, Jack, but Davis's allegiance was strictly to Joe Battle. "Fortune had a group called the Diablos," said Billy. "I can hear one of their songs in my head right now, a great song called 'The Wind' [*sings softly*]. I have met her [Devora], but I've never had any dealings with her. She had another one of those back-of-the-store studios, and she was probably inspired by Joe Battle's setup.[6] But Joe was monumental in getting me jump-started in the right direction."

Billy's first vocal group, the Thrillers, was recorded in 1953 by Joe Battle, who orga-nized the custom-pressing and distribution arrangements through his connection with Bill McCall and Don Pierce at 4 Star. "To record, period!" Davis exclaimed. "I mean, it wasn't happening every day to everyone. Joe Battle was very inspiring to a lot of the young groups there in Detroit, because he was an outlet. We had a big local hit by the Thrillers called 'Mattie' ["Mattie Leave Me Alone"]. He put out a special record label; in fact, he decided to call the label Thrillers. We were the Thrillers on the Thrillers label put out by Joe Von Battle through J-V-B [and 4 Star's Big Town subsidiary], all right [laughs]."

King–De Luxe Records

After the Thrillers were relaunched as the Five Jets, Joe Battle contacted Syd Nathan at King Records down in Cincinnati. "That was the first real record recording studio that I was in," said Billy Davis. "We did an answer to a record called 'Shake a Hand' by Faye Adams, called 'Not a Hand to Shake.' In those days, for every hit record, there was an answer to it that came out." With Berry Gordy, Billy later wrote "Jim Dandy Got Married" (No. 7 R&B, 1957) for Detroit's own LaVern Baker as a sequel to her No. 1 Atlantic R&B hit, "Jim Dandy."[7]

"So Syd recorded 'Not a Hand to Shake,'" continued Davis,

and a few other songs by the Five Jets [for the De Luxe label]. It was an adventure. Syd Nathan would sit up there in the control room. It was sort of set up high looking down into the studio, which later became a model for the Chess studio at 2120 South Michigan. In later years, I discovered there were studios in Europe, in London espe-cially, where the Beatles recorded hits [at EMI's Abbey Road facility], and the situation is the same with the control room up above the actual studio.

Syd Nathan certainly didn't look friendly at all! I don't know whether I was in awe of him or just frightened of him [laughs], because he was an overweight, big fellow, and he had these thick glasses on. The lenses on his glasses had to be, without exag-geration, three-quarters of an inch thick; they were the thickest lenses I have ever seen . . . real Mr. Magoo. But he was a mean man; he didn't pay. Forget it! He was the first real big thief I ever met in the business. Oh yeah, he dominated the industry a little bit in those days.

He had Henry Glover, who was a black A&R man. Ralph Bass, who later became A&R director for Chess, worked for Syd Nathan in those days as well. Henry was one of the pioneers in the business, very sharp guy. He was out there; he contributed a lot. He was pretty popular as an A&R director, but he was one of those guys sitting there looking out for *Henry*. And he was a thief, too; he was the first black thief I ever met. I remember precisely signing the songs away. Henry had his name on some of my songs, very quickly! "Well, I think you ought to change this word over here . . ." It didn't take long [for me] to begin to put the pieces together. But in those days, you just wanted to get recorded and get a recording out in the market so that you could go out and show off to the girls!

Oh yeah, your record on the jukebox, that was it. Oh, it made your day! Because there was more jukebox play, of course, than there was radio play; there was very little radio play until the mid-1950s. But before that, jukebox was the exposure, so if you got a recording, then the next thing you wanted was the jukebox to pick it up. Of course, the jukebox suppliers were not stupid. They'd put all these local groups' records on the jukeboxes, especially in their neighborhoods and so forth, and they'd make a fortune, 'cause every nickel we got was put in the jukebox to hear *ourselves*. Yeah, so it was a big thing. That's how we learned how to really sing and to mimic the big name groups, from these records from the jukeboxes. A lot of exposure came from the jukebox.

Joe was able to get our records on the jukeboxes. I think they were a little bit controlled [*laughs*] from Chicago, the South Side perhaps, or so the story goes. But it was a big thing when you got your record on the jukebox, and if it was successful, of course they put it on more jukeboxes. It was guaranteed sales as well, oh yeah, not that you saw any royalties from it! But somebody got paid something. There were people making money from it, but not generally the artists or the writers.

Did Colonel Jim Wilson, King Records' branch manager in Detroit, give the Five Jets any support? "He was a nice man," said Billy Davis.

He was one of the few I met, on that side of the business, that I really liked, that I felt was a nice person. He would help us, and he was very helpful in helping us to get airplay and telling us what to do.[8]

I know locally our records were pretty big in the area of Ohio, Illinois, [and] Pontiac and other parts of Michigan, but I don't think they got big anywhere else. We certainly played at a lot of high school hops in those days. That's how the disc jockeys made their money. *You* didn't make any money, but you got exposed; you got a chance to go onstage and have the girls scream [*laughs*]. You'd lip synch—you'd stand up and the record would play and you'd sort of pantomime to the music. When you were lip synching, you had to do it the same way every time, and it was difficult. But when you are up onstage and moving around and dancing and singing, it didn't make much difference to the teenage girls in the audience anyway.

So we had the Thrillers followed by the Five Jets. Then the Four Tops came along. My little cousin Lawrence Payton, he was like my first brother, wanted to sing in this group. So he joined this group; they called themselves the Ames: A-m-e-s.[9] The others were in the neighborhood; we were *all* family. When they first got together as a singing group, it was my grandmother's insistence that I looked out after Lawrence when he started. And so I became very involved with the group and became a fifth member, originally. We'd sing, and I began to write songs for them.

Then I said, "Look, first of all we got to change your name," because there was a big white group called the Ames Brothers. That's why they called themselves the Ames, because they wanted to sound like the Ames Brothers, the Hi-Los, and the Four Freshmen. They wanted to sing close harmonies like those groups. They wasn't really into R&B and the stuff that in later years made them very successful. That's not where they wanted to be originally. Reluctantly they gave in to the name change. I started singing with the group as a fifth member, to help get them out of that pop bag they were in. I got them their first recording, a deal which was on Chess.

Songwriter for Chess-Checker Records

So how did Billy Davis get involved with Chess Records? "Well, Willie Mabon played the Flame Show Bar in Detroit," said Davis.

He had a very big hit, "I Don't Know." He had heard the Four Tops sing, and he told Leonard Chess about the group. Willie urged me to send my songs to Chicago, because I was sending my songs around [to] the different recording companies. So I sent a tape of my songs, and Phil Chess responded. He added a handwritten note on the end of my letter; it said, "Like your songs, give us a call," and he mailed it back to me. It was in 1956, that's when it was.

So I called and, sure enough, Phil Chess came to the phone and told me that he loved my songs and that he wanted to use some of my songs for his groups. And my response was, "What about my group? What about the Tops?" He said, "Well, Billy, you got a good group, but you got to understand, we got a lot of groups. We got the Moonglows and we got the Flamingos; we don't really need a group right now. But we need songs, and you got some great songs. Why don't you come to Chicago and let us do a few of your songs and you'll make a lot of money." I heard that before, about my songs making money, from Joe Battle earlier. But this time I said, "No, no." However, he [Phil] convinced me to come to Chicago. He said, "Come out; we'll talk about it. We'll send your bus fare." I went from Detroit to Chicago on the Greyhound bus.

By 1956, Chess was a little company on fire with new signings Chuck Berry and Bo Diddley, those slick vocal groups the Moonglows and the Flamingos, and hot bluesmen Muddy Waters, Little Walter, Howlin' Wolf, and Sonny Boy Williamson. So Billy arrived at the Chess office located on Chicago's South Side, at 4750 South Cottage Grove Avenue, for the meeting with Phil Chess—and Leonard Chess.

Davis's memories of that visit provide a clear insider's view into the workings of the fastest-growing independent record company of the time. "It was like a storefront deal," he said.

It was not even in a huge building. It was like, "Well, is this it?" I remember walking up to the front door and going, "This can't be Chess Records." But sure enough, there was a sign on the door that said "Chess Records."

I went in, and there was this little foyer area that must have been maybe five-by-six, big enough for two people to stand in. There was a door on the left and a door right in front of you and a sliding window with a secretary behind it who said, "Can I help you?" I told her who I was, and she said, "Okay, they're looking for you." She went out the back and came back through the other door, which led into another small office where what looked like bookkeepers and accountants were sitting. I walked right through that into a back office, which is where Leonard and Phil were. I found out later that back office also doubled as a control room to the studio, which was also the stockroom [laughs].

The studio had records stacked up on each side and an old upright piano sitting off to one side. That's where Chuck Berry and Muddy all recorded, right there in that room, and all on this upright Ampex. They had also one of those portable jobs like Joe Battle had in a big leather-looking case that folded up, and you could carry it around to do remotes. The record boxes were the baffles! Acoustics? Hey, Phil didn't know what the word meant [*laughs*]. Forget it! Oh no, no, no, no, no, no baffles. So I was in for a lot of surprises on that trip.

But Phil did most of the talking and tried to convince me to give up my songs for their groups, and he tried for almost two hours. He offered me money: "I'll give you fifty dollars as an advance on each song." I thought, "A hundred dollars, my life." It was a lot of money; it was like someone offering me a thousand dollars today. And I said, "No, I'm sorry in that I came to Chicago, but I really wanted to get my group recorded." It wasn't just allegiance to the group; I was part of the group.

So Phil was beginning to get a little disgusted and give up. Then Leonard, who had said very little, he just sat there—and you knew he was there. His presence was there because Phil would reference him every once in a while and look at him a lot. But Leonard didn't say a lot; he looked at me, and he listened to the conversation. He listened to Phil, and then, when he did interrupt, he said, "Okay, Billy, I'll record your group. But look, *motherfucker*, I want two of your songs!" And I kind of looked at him. It was the first time anyone had called me [that]. . . . I didn't quite know how to take it originally, and he smiled. I probably had a look like "I don't believe you" on my face.

He said, "Look, if I tell you I'm gonna do something, I'm gonna do it! I said I'd record your group [and] buy one or two of your songs: I want 'A Kiss from Your Lips' and 'See Saw.' I'll record your group, we'll send for 'em, you can bring 'em to Chicago." And for some reason, I believed Leonard, you know?

When I was ready, he sent me the money to bring the group to Chicago. He put us up in a hotel; we recorded. The Four Tops still wasn't thrilled because it wasn't the type of songs they wanted to sing, as far as they still had their minds on being their [pop harmony] idols. But we recorded four songs [actually five], and Leonard kept his word; we recorded downtown at Universal [owned by Bill Putnam]. It was an excellent studio; wow, I was very impressed. Yeah, after Joe's place and then the "famous" Chess Records studio, Universal was, gosh, it was wonderful, it was like going into Radio City Music Hall [in New York].

Prior to recording we became the Four Tops. I was trying to figure out a name for them, because they [weren't] typical of all the bird groups that were out there. And I loved the little spinning tops that you used to wrap a string around. I thought it was catchy and cute and spinning. Never stopping was the object; it all made sense to me. And they liked it. I bounced it off Maurice King, the bandleader and arranger at the Flame Show Bar. He loved the name the Four Tops; he thought it was great, and he loved the group.

The Four Tops' first record ["Kiss Me Baby" and "Could It Be You"] got a lot of local action, but it was not a hit nationally. Leonard didn't want to know the group in the first place, but he kept his word to me; I got to give him that. So, when the first record didn't happen, we didn't push rerecording, and they didn't push recording us [after a second session with no releases]. Leonard gave the Tops a release, without any problem, and so we never recorded anymore for Chess. After the Four Tops recorded in 1956, my two songs were hits: "A Kiss from Your Lips" by the Flamingos [No. 12 R&B] and "See Saw" by the Moonglows [No. 25 pop, No. 6 R&B].

Leonard Chess, ever on the ball, saw Billy Davis as his protégé. "Leonard used to have me come to Chicago to sit in on his recording sessions," said Davis.

He liked my ideas and thoughts. He used to pay for me to come to Chicago just to be there when he had his recording sessions, and, of course, he would pick my brain. I would add my two cents into the recording sessions from Chuck Berry to Bo Diddley to Muddy. I was involved in all of them.

Oh yeah, I was on a lot of the great sessions to a point that Chuck Berry found it in his heart to record one of my songs. It was probably the only song he ever recorded that didn't belong to him [on a single at the time]; it was a thing of mine which he reluctantly did. He felt obligated because I'd helped him out on so many of his sessions, thanks to Leonard, who said, "Why don't you do one of Billy's songs?" Chuck didn't want to do it. "I don't need Billy's songs; I got a lotta songs." Leonard shamed him into doing "Too Pooped to Pop" [No. 42 pop, early 1960]. And the record sounds like he didn't really want to do it [*laughs*], which he didn't, so he sort of flopped it. But I made a few coins as a result of it.

So Leonard had me come there and get involved, and pretty soon I was actually producing sessions. In those days, you didn't call it "producing." There was the A&R director, who was the person in charge of the "artists and repertoire" and the songs that the artists recorded. But this whole thing as a record producer, that didn't crop up until long years later. So in those days, if you had a song on a session, it was to your interest to have as much input as you could, regardless of what it was. And so you find yourself writing, arranging, and producing when you are only getting part payment for writing. Well, in this case, Leonard would pay me whenever I would come to Chicago to help him out in any way.

Of course, I was at the sessions for the Flamingos and the Moonglows, who did my songs there, and it was fun. Willie Dixon was there at just about every session [standup bass] and [Lafayette] Leake, the piano player [with Otis Spann and Johnnie Johnson], and Freddie Below, the drummer. There wasn't too many other pieces. Don't forget, in those days, that was about it. Once in a while you'd have a guitar player there or a sax playing a solo in the middle. Those pieces were there, but you didn't want to hear too much of them, basically.

Chuck Berry, for instance, would have his songs all worked out, just about, on his guitar. He would come in, and he would sing his songs down to Willie and to Lafayette until they would work out the changes, which were most likely the same changes. It was "Follow me! Follow what I am playing, on my *untuned* guitar." It was his sound; maybe it was on purpose, I don't know. But you can't knock success, can you?

But I have to give it to Chuck; he was an expert with words. He would come up with things that rhymed [so] that you would scratch your head: "How in the hell did he think of that?" It was very unique: "The rainwater blowing all under my hood, / I knew that wasn't doing my motor good . . .," you know, phrases like that on "Maybellene."[10] I found out later, from Chuck, that he used a rhyming dictionary when he wrote lyrics. It was his bible; that's how he was able to come up with all those unique rhyming words. He used to carry it with him all the time. It helped, it made a difference, it really did.

If Chuck came into Chicago to do a session, he wanted an advance of money up front, not after the session: "Before I go in the studio, I want to know how much money you're gonna give me to record." And that's the way Chuck was. When he went on gigs, he was the same way; before he went onstage, the promoter better have a sack full of money waiting for him. That was his thing.

Chuck and Leonard had a very good relationship. But I must preface it by saying Leonard had a very good relationship with just about everyone that you witnessed him with, whether it was a Chuck Berry, a Bo Diddley, a Muddy Waters, or an Etta James, or the program director from some big pop station. He had the personality; he had a way about him that he came off—in those days you would say "straight." Whether he was or not, he gave you the feeling that he was being straight with you and leveling with you. He didn't say a lot of things, and he was one of the people where his word was his bond, to a great extent.

With a few of the blues artists who had bad habits of drinking a lot, he realized what they were doing. I used to see them come there juiced up and looking for money, every few days. And Leonard would argue with them and call them "mothers" and so forth and end up givin' 'em money, and they'd come back for more. That was his argument: "If I give 'em every penny that they got coming from me now, they gonna be back tomorrow broke lookin' for more!" He knew that they made him a lot of money. He knew that they made him; he didn't deny that fact. But he also told me, . . . in reference once to Muddy Waters, . . ."Muddy is never gonna have to work on anything." I didn't quite know what he meant at the time. I said, "What do you mean?" He said, "Muddy is gonna be all right 'cause Muddy is one of the people that helped make me. All he's got to worry about is stayin' alive." In other words, Leonard had a lot of respect for the old blues artists.

He went out of his way to help a lot of the artists; I know that. Etta James should be a witness to that, if she will. I'm still surprised at what artists remember and what they don't remember. I'm sure that some of the things that are coming out are true, that Leonard Chess cheated the artists out of royalties and didn't pay them all the money they should have received. But how much he actually *stole*, that they never got, I don't know. In those days, all the independent record companies were raking off the top.

I think that if Leonard Chess bought an artist a car—he used to do things like that, buy 'em a car or an instrument and so forth—he was paying for it with *their* own money. I don't think he was going in his pocket and going in the hole advancing them money. But at the same time, I am sure that some of those artists got every penny they had coming to them; in the later years, which you never hear when the blues stopped selling, those same artists [still] used to come around. And Leonard used to give them money, hand it out to pay bills and stuff, and they didn't have any records selling. You never hear that part of the story. Certainly, the artists received benefits from it, and Leonard Chess received benefits and made a lot of money. He just knew more what to do with his money than a lot of the other people.

Basically, you knew that Leonard and Phil were partners. You also knew that Leonard was the boss. Phil let you know that, in his actions and what he said, in reference to his brother; it was his *older* brother. He had a lot of respect for Leonard, and you always knew that Leonard had the last word. But Leonard would never disrespect Phil in front of anybody, ever. So they had a good relationship in that sense. As far as their roles, in the beginning, when I met them, you couldn't define who did what. They were both doing everything from selling records off the back of a station wagon to being in the studio, so there were no clear-cut, defined roles. Later on, Leonard became more of the business executive, especially after the purchase of the radio stations. After moving from 2120 South Michigan to 320 East Twenty-first Street, Phil was still dabbling in the business. He was playing the same role when I left the company around '67 as he did the day I met him on Cottage Grove in '56.

I don't think anyone had any idea that history was being made to the extent that it was made. I wish I had known or had an inkling. I would have kept a lot of things that I didn't keep. No, I had no sense of it. There were very few people with cameras. Pictures, forget it!

Berry Gordy with Jackie Wilson and George Goldner

After being introduced to the Chess brothers, Billy Davis struck up a partnership with Berry Gordy, another talented young Detroit songwriter with unlimited determination and ambition. "We met through Al Green, of the Flame Show Bar [owned by Morris and Sally Wasserman]," said Davis.

Al was at that time managing LaVern Baker, Johnnie Ray, and Della Reese. I had taken Jackie [Wilson] to him. So I was working out of Al Green's office on Woodward Avenue, not too far from King Records [where Colonel Jim Wilson was branch manager] right there on "record row," it was called. The Flame Show Bar was located a block east of Woodward Avenue.

Al Green sent Berry to see me because of Berry's sister Gwen, who worked as a photographer at the Flame Show Bar. Berry came in one day, and we met. Well, I didn't have an office; it was Al Green's office. I had been introduced to Al through, I guess, Alonzo Tucker; he was a writer who co-wrote a lot of Jackie's hits after Berry and I stopped writing. Alonzo had the connection with Al Green and Nat Tarnopol.

Yeah, they saw me as a writer who had had a couple of hit records, and so that brought me into the loop. Al Green had these artists that he needed material for, and they were just making their connections to record labels in New York. Al was planning on a big independent thing himself, but unfortunately he had a [fatal] heart attack soon after that [December 18, 1957].

So he sent Berry up to see me. Berry wanted to get some songs recorded, and I listened to them. I recognized [that] Berry was a good writer. He was more jazz-orientated and wasn't quite as commercial as far as writing poppy songs, with hooks and so forth, as I thought he should be. But he was very stubborn as well; he didn't want to change anything. I couldn't talk him into making any changes in any of his songs, so he left.

But he came back a week later. I happened to be in the office by myself on a Saturday, and he came up and with a slightly different attitude. He was more willing to listen constructively to what I had to say. And I said, "Berry, I don't want to put my name on any of your songs, if that's what you're thinking. I have no interest in that type of thing at all." We talked, and to make a long story short, we ended up sitting down and writing songs together that day. And we discovered one thing: that we had a good relationship. It could work because now he was opened-minded; he was willing to listen.

Berry wasn't bad at lyrics; he [just] wasn't as good as I was at lyrics. But he played piano better than I, so some of the chord things he came up with, I probably would not have come up with. I was very melodic. Everything had to have a melody for me; I wasn't one of those "da-da-da-da-da-da-da-da" boys. Don't forget, I was influenced by singers from Sinatra to Nat "King" Cole, very melodic singers, pop music, and so the melody had to be there. And the hook!

I was good at coming up with ideas, the seed of the idea, the phrase that you would hear repeated throughout a pop song. It was called the "hook," the little phrase that you will remember that was catchy. There are lyrical hooks, and then there are musical hooks, and there are melody hooks. All these things you will find in pop music. You may not remember the whole song, but you remember something about it—that's the hook.

For Billy Davis and Berry Gordy, Jackie Wilson was the perfect artist to complement their songwriting skills. He was a mesmerizing talent who seemed to inject every word and every note of a song into his body and limbs. "Jackie Wilson wasn't one of those people that you could easily control," said Davis with a smile.

He didn't last too long with Billy Ward and the Dominoes for a lot of reasons. It had nothing to do with his singing ability! He showed up one day in Detroit and said he had quit the group; Billy Ward was too much for him, and he wanted to record on his own. I introduced him to Al Green. So Jackie signed with Al, and I started to write songs for Jackie with Berry. That's the way we had the very first song we ever did with him, which was "Reet Petite" [Brunswick].

During that process, Berry and I decided to become songwriting partners and then [business] partners. Unfortunately, as I say, Al Green died somewhere right in there, just after Jackie had charted with "Reet Petite." Nat Tarnopol had everyone thinking he was Al's partner, so he signed Jackie. That's how Nat got in, because Jackie and everyone thought that Nat was Al's partner. He really wasn't Al's partner at all.

When we started doing Jackie's things, we realized that we were not only writing the songs, but we were actually working out the arrangements. I used to teach Jackie the vocal parts because I was more the vocalist; Berry couldn't sing a lick, you know, so I would have to teach the artist the songs and put 'em on tape, send 'em a tape. The "brrrrr reet petite," that bit came from me to Jackie. There was a little girl who was, shit, really stacked and shaped very well. But she was small, she was very short, she was petite . . . she was "reet petite." And that's where the phrase came from. I was sort of secretly in love with this little girl, and it was one of my very first songs, but the song was never completed. So I had part of it written before Berry and I completed it, maybe a couple of years later. It actually was created around a boogie-woogie riff.[11]

It became a big hit, a big hit for us in those days, anyway [No. 62 pop, late 1957, but not an R&B hit]. I never will forget the first time hearing it on the air. Berry and I were at one of his sister's houses, Lucy, on Hague in Detroit. It came on one of the local stations, and we were thrilled. It was Berry's first record release—I'd had several prior to that—and so he was especially thrilled. And I became really thrilled because Dick Clark played it on TV, so it was on the radio and TV at the same time, and we were jumping for joy! Yeah, it was a big thrill. I remember that like it was yesterday."

At first, Davis and Gordy had no idea that "Reet Petite" (recorded at Decca's Pythian Temple studios in New York with a bright pop orchestral backing courtesy of Dick Jacobs, overseen by pioneering record man Bob Thiele) was also breaking overseas. After being plugged on *6.5 Special*, the new teen TV show in England, it made No. 6 U.K., much higher than in the United States.[12] Throughout 1958 and into the summer of 1959, the partnership of Billy Davis (as Tyran Carlo) and Berry Gordy wrote the critical follow-up songs that fully established Jackie Wilson: "To Be Loved" (No. 22), "Lonely Teardrops" (No. 7 pop, No. 1 R&B), "That's Why (I Love You So)" (No. 13), and "I'll Be Satisfied" (No. 20).

Then in acrimony, Davis and Gordy severed their ties with Nat Tarnopol, who was now based in New York. "Nat was using us, misusing us!" exclaimed Billy.

We were writing, arranging, producing, but were only barely getting credit for writing. When we approached him to get songs on both sides of Jackie's records, he said he'd rather get new writers: "Huh, who needs you now? I've got a star. So if you guys don't like what you're getting, I'm sorry." We took the attitude, "Screw you, too! We'll do it for ourselves. If that's the name of the game, we'll find our own artists." We were doing everything anyway. "We'll sign 'em, and we'll spend our own money and record 'em, and we'll release our own records." Initially, of course, we knew nothing about running a business or anything, but you can learn fast when you have to.

Yeah, there was a vast pool of talent in Detroit. Jackie Wilson opened the door, being a Detroiter, and he sort of inspired a lot of the young people there. Jackie was a forerunner of the group era when all the doo-wop groups started popping up, and by him singing with the Dominoes (this was all before becoming a solo artist), he was an inspiration to a lot of young people. For instance, Eddie Holland of Holland-Dozier-Holland, Berry and I signed him up and managed him as well. He was gonna be our answer to Jackie Wilson because we were pissed off at Nat. So we found the next best thing. But he was no singer in comparison to Jackie Wilson; no one has been since Jackie, actually.

We approached Reverend C. L. Franklin to allow Aretha to record for us. We were gonna put her on Chess Records, but he refused to allow Aretha to sing [secular songs] at that time. She was a great vocalist even then, without a doubt, and she played a wicked piano as well. As a result of him not allowing Aretha to record right then, we decided to record Aretha's older sister, whose name was Erma Franklin. It was amazing; out of the two or three songs that were written for Erma to record, two of them became very big hits by other artists later on. We walked Erma through the material and got her ready to record, but she decided she wanted not to do R&B music; she wanted to do sort of jazz. One of the songs made an artist called Marv Johnson, "You Got What It Takes" [No. 10, United Artists, late 1959]. The other one was later recorded by Etta James, "All I Could Do Was Cry" [No. 33, Argo, 1960]. It was Etta's first big [pop] hit. And so Erma didn't want to do the type of songs we had written. So that fell through as well.

Billy Davis and Berry Gordy, smart but still learning, almost fell into the contractual clutches of George Goldner. Even so, Billy was full of praise for the ubiquitous New York record man:

> He used to come through Detroit a lot promoting his other artists on End and Gone. He got wind of Berry and [me] and wanted to hear our songs and material. We went to [Joe Siracuse's] United Sound studios, Second Boulevard at Antoinette, and we played and sang a lot. Berry played piano; I sang, I don't know how many . . . maybe fifty, sixty, seventy songs for George. And he was really flabbergasted at the abundance of material. He wanted us. In fact he pulled out contracts there on the spot, and he wrote checks out for Berry and [me].
>
> We signed the contracts to a lot of songs with George. To George's credit, in spite of his reputation, he later gave them all back to us. He realized that it wasn't fair that we had hope in him and the whole bit and that he really took advantage of a couple of kids. This was after our success with Jackie Wilson, too, during that process. George relinquished the rights he had to a lot of those songs that became hits later; he didn't have to, actually. But that's how I met George Goldner. And so when I started Anna Records, of course I went to George, and he was interested in distributing. Berry also placed an early record by the Miracles on End ["Got a Job" in 1958, an answer to the Silhouettes' "Get a Job"].
>
> George was another character in the business. As far as I am concerned, he was one of the good guys, in spite of how he handled his business otherwise [laughs]. George had a reputation, and rightfully so, of recording just lots and lots of groups. You'd come to New York, and outside of his office and down the hall there would be all of these groups waiting to get in to sign his recording contracts. George would sign just about anybody who was recommended by anybody; he'd sign you up, and then he'd make arrangements for you to go into a studio. You'd go back home, 'cause they were from all over the country—they wasn't just from New York—and you'd practice your songs. Then you'd get a call or a letter from End and Gone Records. They'd send your bus fare or whatever to get to New York. And you'd have two or three hours in the studio, if that long, to record two or four songs.
>
> George Goldner used Sammy Lowe to do the arrangements. Now, you gotta keep in mind this was right back there in the late 1950s or early 1960s, and most of the songs use the same group of changes and maybe a little deviation from that. You could play on the piano the same set of chords and sing a hundred songs in those days.[13] One group after another would come in and sing their songs, and George would record them. You'd get a chance to run it down a couple of times and then record it: "Next!" Next song, next group. George had a sound of what he did because he

recorded all his stuff there at Regent Sound Studios [he also used Bell Sound and un-doubtedly others]. So when he did get a hit or two, and he did have his share of 'em, there was a consistent sound there . . . a sound that the general public had accepted. He knew what he liked and what he didn't like. And he'd surround himself [with] a lot of people who knew music.

George was a businessman, and he knew that in the record business, there was no set formula for what's gonna make a hit or not. So he tried to get stuff from all these groups that were current and in the trend of what was happening at the time. George maybe released ten or twelve records at the same time, or more. He would send pro-motion men out with 'em, and they would talk the disc jockeys into playing these records, one way or the other. Whichever ones caught on, that's the one he would zero in on, and the rest of 'em would just fall right into the garbage can. You wouldn't hear 'em, and he wouldn't care anything about it.

A very special George Goldner release by the Flamingos on End had a big influence on Billy Davis: "I Only Have Eyes for You." This was the same group that had recorded Davis's "A Kiss from Your Lips" for Leonard Chess in Chicago. "Looking back on it, in hindsight," said Davis,

a lot of the magic was that the studio technology at that time had just graduated from mono recording to 2–track or 3–track recording. It was from natural echo to electronic echo, so a lot of records came out with this sound. People would ask, "This sound, where's this sound come from?" Well, it was the electronic echo chamber that was set on two or three seconds' delay that you never heard before.

All of a sudden, George Goldner was one of the pioneers in using that sound. It gave you a lot more production flexibility and creative play. It improved the quality of the sound; it made the sound different. The echo and the sound became part of the hook of the song, so that attracted the attention of the listener. Before you even know what the [Flamingos'] song was about, you heard this sound, *doo wop, doo wop* . . . It echoed, like, for three seconds. Oh, it certainly did influence me. So you had to real-ize what all the mechanisms are that you can use. But he was a real character. I liked George, and I was very sad when he passed away. We had a pretty good arrangement, Berry and I both, with George at that time. He was one of the bad-good guys!

Berry Gordy launched Tamla Records in January 1959 with a family loan of eight hundred dollars followed by Motown Records in September—but without Billy Davis's direct involvement. Soon parading under the banner of Hitsville U.S.A, the Tamla-Motown records became known as the "Sound of Young America" in the 1960s. "We knew what we were trying to do," said Davis.

I speak quite often in reference to the Motown concept, which is really the concept that Berry and I had after we had the rejection from Nat Tarnopol. We realized that you sign the artist, control what they sang (the songs), carefully select the songs for the artist, and create a sound. We also realized that, in those days, if you had violins and horns, your chances were enhanced, by 50 percent, of it becoming played on the pop stations. So, in that sense, there was a concept in mind around what we did.

We made sure the songs were songs, not just funky blues. The productions had to have the R&B with a dance rhythm. Regardless of how funky it got, it had to have a melody so the songs could be sung by anyone. And, when we could, dress it up, put icing on the cake, which was the strings and horns. . . . . If you check back, just about all of it had those elements. That's why those songs survive today. The name of the game was the song, not the artist.

The first release on the yellow-and-black Tamla label was "Come to Me" by Marv Johnson, but it was placed prudently with United Artists Records for national distribution, becoming a No. 30 hit in the spring of 1959.[14] Explained Davis:

Certainly we didn't know enough about the record business to start a record company. We were talented young kids, learning about the business part of things. We knew how to write, arrange, produce, and record a record, and we knew it wasn't difficult to get records pressed or to start your own label. But we knew very little about distribution and the rest of that stuff.

So the formula we had, we would release a record locally in Detroit; we would have it pressed up and released. We might press up five hundred records, and we'd take a box of twenty-five for promotion around to the stations that were there to try to get it played. And we'd get the group to play all the record hops and so forth. So in other words, we released it locally, then if it became popular and created a demand, then of course all the major companies would want it. You could shop it very easily. And that's what happened in the case of Marv Johnson.

Anna Records with Gwen Gordy

Shortly after the launch of Tamla Records, Billy Davis formed the Anna label in April 1959 with a Gordy family member—but not Berry. "At the time, Gwen Gordy and I were close," Davis said. "We were boyfriend and girlfriend, whatever you wanna call it in those days. So Gwen became sort of my partner in the label. The label was named after Gwen's sister, who was a close friend of mine as well, Anna Gordy (who later married Marvin Gaye). Anyway, 'Anna' was just as good as anything else as a name for the label."

The first release, "Hope and Pray" by the Voice Masters (a group that had links with the Thrillers and the Five Jets), was duly distributed nationally by George Goldner's Gone Records, but Chess soon took over Anna's distribution through its network. In fact, Anna Records became the equivalent of a baseball farm team for Chess. Veteran New Orleans artist and Chess promo man Paul Gayten stepped up to the plate with a cover of "The Hunch" and hit the No. 68 spot in late 1959 (doing marginally better than the original of this bluesy instrumental by the Bobby Peterson Quintet on V-Tone of Philadelphia).

"Paul wanted to record it," recalled Davis,

so Leonard said, "Why don't you have Billy record you on it?" Paul gave me a call and said, "I got this song, and it's gonna be a hit, man. It's gonna put Anna Records on the map! I wanna go back to the same studios that recorded the [Peterson] original."

So we went to Philadelphia. Paul just played piano; they were local musicians [with him]. Oh yeah, there was a big clash with Bobby Peterson's record because Bobby's record [had] been out for a couple of weeks before Paul's came out. Our version was just as good as Bobby's was. But primarily because Paul knew a lot of disc jockeys in key stations who got a lot of action, it probably did so well. . . .

It was not difficult to handle the orders. A lot of them were handled out of Detroit, then when the tune became really, really big stuff, it was sent out straight from the record-pressing plants, but there was no problem. And because of Leonard's distribution, we got *paid.* We never had a follow-up, because Paul was not a real artist in the first place. This "Hunch" record was a real hunch! Paul figured he'd get a big record, make some royalties, and forget it. Putting a band back together and going back on the road, no. He had seen that day already; he was not interested in doing that anymore. It sounds a lot more glamorous than it really is. Being an R&B artist was not all fun. So he was happy being a promotion man, I believe.

Anna's biggest record was "Money (That's What I Want)" by Barrett Strong in the early spring of 1960. Actually, it was only a No. 23 hit (albeit No. 2 R&B), surprisingly low considering the song's subsequent fame by way of the Beatles' torrid version. Remembered Davis: "I said to Berry, 'Look, we'll put "Money" on Anna, Chess will distribute it, and that'll make it a national hit. You keep it on Tamla in Detroit, and you publicize the fact later that it started on Tamla. That'll give you your boost for your next record, and then you won't need that distribution [by another label].' So we talked it out; Berry and I were very close. Even though we still did things together, we did things separately."

Previously, in the late summer of 1959, Berry Gordy had cut a deal for the very first record on the Motown label to be rereleased by Chess: "Bad Girl" by the Miracles. The group's lead singer/songwriter, William "Smokey" Robinson, was another important cog in Tamla-Motown's machine. "But Berry had a little problem with Chess for some reason," said Davis.

I think Phil rubbed Berry the wrong way the very first time they ever met. Berry had been to Chicago a couple of times with me, originally to try to get them to sponsor a label for us. This was before Anna was set up. But Berry and Phil Chess just didn't hit it off. [Because of] Phil's attitude and the way he was accustomed to dealing with blacks, he approached Berry totally the wrong way. Especially in his use of the word "motherfucker," even though it was like saying "Good morning." When Phil and Leonard used the word, it was a term of endearment, almost; they didn't mean any offense by it. But Berry took offense by it, and I could understand why. So they didn't hit it off too well.

But I had nothing to do with the recording of "Money." It was strictly Barrett Strong's idea, and I have to say that Barrett was the reason that song was a hit more than anybody else. It was a great song, and it had a real funky sound. If you compare "Money" to the sound of any other record that came after that, from Tamla or Motown, it would still stick out. A big part of it was because it was over-recorded, definitely over-recorded. It was loud, but it gave it its soul; it gave it its own sound.

Strong's follow-up, "Yes, No, Maybe So," was a disaster. It did not chart at all. "Nah, it was just too different," said Davis. "I don't know what we were thinking about, or what Berry was thinking about, either. I thought about that, and I am sure he has as well: How could we follow 'Money' with *this* song? It might have been a great song in its own right, but not as a follow-up to 'Money.' The people who bought 'Money' [weren't] gonna like Barrett Strong doing this other type of material; it just wasn't gonna fly. So that was a mistake. He was a great songwriter; he definitely was a better songwriter than he was a singer." Barrett Strong's co-write of "I Heard It through the Grapevine" was testimony to that.

With Anna hitting the Top 100 with "The Hunch" and "Money" in short order, how was Billy working with Gwen Gordy, his label partner and companion? "She knew very little about the business," said Davis, without malice or emotion.

> Gwen was not musically inclined in any way. She was not a writer, not a singer, not a performer of any type; she was just a beautiful young lady in every other way, but very ambitious. The whole Gordy family was very ambitious, and most of them were pretty successful in their undertakings. But Gwen and I got along pretty well, I felt, for the most part.
>
> After the record company label was started, I was on the road a lot at the time, promoting new records when they came out. We picked up other masters in the process, and then along came the Joe Tex thing. Joe Tex was an artist that had been kicking around for a long time and was a heck of a performer and a person. I mean, you couldn't beat Joe Tex. He was doing a combination of James Brown and Jackie Wilson put together. He was a hell of a performer, and he had had records prior to the ones that came out on Anna. He came to Leonard, and once again, Leonard said, "Why don't you go to Billy?" That's how we got involved with Joe Tex with "All I Could Do Was Cry" [a two-part rework of the Etta James hit song] and "I'll Never Break Your Heart" [a two-part answer to Jerry Butler's "He Will Break Your Heart"]. Joe was a fun artist to record and work with; his style was totally unique.

Billy Davis had a potent artist in Ty Hunter but just couldn't break him. This was the other side of the record business; it wasn't all hit acts, by any means. "We kept trying until you sort of get disappointed after awhile and lose confidence," said Davis. "Of course, the record company and the producer blame everybody but themselves, and the artist blames everybody else . . . as to why it's not being successful. But the fact of the matter is that no one really knows, and if something doesn't happen, it doesn't happen. Is it because of the artist, the song, the producer, the promotion man? And what makes it a hit? If it's a hit, you just accept the fact and give credit to anyone who had anything to do with it." Anna also released noncharting singles by David Ruffin, later of the Temptations, and songwriter Lamont Anthony (Dozier).

Nevertheless, there was a general awakening of R&B music on the national stage that augured well for companies like Tamla and Anna. "John Richbourg and a few of the other disc jockeys . . . played a lot of R&B records," said Davis, "and helped force other pop stations who did not play R&B records to start playing it. That was a big changeover that happened about 1960." Unlike Tamla, Anna Records was not a long-term beneficiary of this broadening market. The label was wound up summarily in 1961 when Billy Davis split from the Gordy family for good. It was not an easy parting.

"We had never talked about it until it was time to do it," said Davis. "In the very beginning, Berry and I worked hand in hand. I think the split came when the realization came that Gwen and I were partners. Berry wanted to cut Gwen in on everything. That's how her name got on all of those songs—she didn't write any of them. But Berry felt obligated to cut his sister in because she had financially helped him in the beginning. And I felt obligated to her because she and I were going together. So we agreed to put her name on stuff and cut her in. After a while, of course, that meant, like, we were getting two-thirds and he was getting one-third, and so it wasn't quite equal anymore. So he and I were not partners as we had been. So, if I look back on it, it probably was the beginning of the departure."

For the only time in our interviews, Billy Davis hesitated: "When we parted . . . friends . . . you know, for reasons, umm . . ." Asserting himself quickly, he said:

> I went on to become the A&R director for Chess. Then when I decided to leave [Detroit], I said, "First we are gonna divvy up the artists." We had all of us signed the Miracles, the Marvelettes. . . . I was partners in all of that. And he was gonna take one; I was gonna take one. In fact, we went through that whole motion, and then I decided, "Hey, have it; you just take 'em. I'm going with another company; I don't need 'em."
>
> At that time, Gwen['s] and my relationship was a little on the rocks, too. I think she had fallen in love with Harvey [Fuqua, of the Moonglows] in my absence [*laughs*], or something like that. So that didn't help, and that probably would've helped me make my decision to go to Chess as well. But, primarily, I had made up my mind to help Leonard because he had helped me so many times. So when I went to Chicago, I decided to leave all the artists, to leave Anna, to leave everything behind: a new challenge.

If there were other underlying reasons, Billy Davis would not disclose them. Even so, he hasn't deserved to be written out of the opening script of the fabulous Tamla-Motown story.

Chicago was calling again. Already a steely negotiator, Davis landed an amazing deal with Chess Records whereby he was appointed head A&R director and was accorded a 50 percent share with the Chess brothers in a song publishing venture: Chevis Music. Over at Arc Music, Gene Goodman was totally disdainful of this interloper taking a piece of the Chess publishing action.[15] For a while, Davis ran the Check-Mate label under the Chess umbrella.

With Billy Davis in the A&R driving seat, Chess made a seamless transition from 1950s blues and R&B to 1960s soul.[16] Biggest of all was Fontella Bass's "Rescue Me" (No. 4 pop, No.1 R&B, 1965), considered to be an anthem for soldiers in Vietnam and a fabulous earner over the years through use in movies, commercials, and television shows. Another huge Chevis-published song was the 1967 Jackie Wilson classic "(Your Love Keeps Lifting Me) Higher and Higher" (No. 6 pop, No. 1 R&B, Brunswick).

Saxophone player, arranger, and producer Gene "Daddy G" Barge arrived at Chess in 1964 during Billy Davis's reign at 2120 South Michigan Avenue. Barge's track record included a one-off 1956 single for Checker, blowing those distinctive sax lines behind Chuck Willis's hits "C. C. Rider" and "Betty and Dupree" (Atlantic), and co-writing and playing on Gary "U.S." Bonds's "Quarter to Three" (No. 1, Legrand, 1961).[17]

In describing his relationship with Billy Davis, Gene Barge painted a stirring portrait of Chess Records in the soul era. There was some competitive tension between the ambitious colleagues. "Billy Davis was the A&R man," said Barge.

He wasn't an arranger. He had a good feel for the music, and he was a very thorough kind of a producer, but he was sort of protective of his turf. In other words, he tried to keep everybody so they wouldn't threaten his position as A&R man, especially guys like me. We were at odds a lot, on a friendly basis, but at odds. But he was good.

Billy was a good songwriter; so was Berry Gordy. Actually, Billy was supposed to have been Berry's partner, but [in] some kind of way he was undermined. I have no idea how. But he took the job at Chess Records; Chess gave him a shot. He helped Chess form Chevis Publishing Company. All the R&B stuff went to Chevis. Chess didn't have a really good R&B department until Billy got there.

The big, brassy sound at Chess started when I got there. I brought in a guy named Charles Stepney—he was a vibraphonist and a piano player—to do some copying, because all of Chevis's music was a mess. It hadn't been copyrighted, and records hadn't been released. So I started to write lead sheets and make copyright forms, but I had to have help. We were backlogged. And I got Stepney; we became writing partners. We did Muddy Waters's *Muddy, Brass & the Blues* LP, we did Buddy Guy['s] *Left My Blues in San Francisco*, we did several projects on the side. Then he [Stepney] and I split up as arranging partners, and he went on to do the Rotary Connection and the Dells. I did the Little Milton stuff, but Little Milton got cold.

We brought in Phil Wright to do most of the arrangements. Before that, he was with the Red Saunders band at the Regal Theater, just gigging around Chicago as a pianist. We used Riley Hampton and Johnny Pate; they were the arrangers of note in Chicago before I got there. Ralph Bass was the A&R man. He did the Etta James stuff; he did some [Howlin'] Wolf and a little bit of Muddy. Later I did some Etta James stuff, but not the early stuff. We had a great rhythm section: Maurice White on drums [later of Earth, Wind & Fire] and Louis Satterfield on bass; the piano was Raynard Miner, a blind kid, who wrote "Rescue Me" with Carl Smith.

I was put in charge of gospel, because Billy Davis was trying to get rid of me anyway, so he put me over there in gospel. The first group I recorded was the Soul Stirrers, then they brought in a group from Detroit (Wilson Pickett used to be in it) called the Violinaires. I had some gospel hits on them guys. It went on and on and on until I went on vacation. And when I came back, I was taken off of gospel, and they gave it to Ralph Bass [laughs].

With *Muddy, Brass & the Blues*, I just overdubbed the horns; I didn't see Muddy.

What happened was Ralph Bass did that album, and he grabbed me and Stepney [and] asks me, "Man, we've got to put some horns on it." So we took the tracks and ran with it. Why horns? At that time, Muddy's run had ran out; the whole world was turning away from blues and going into rhythm and blues [that is, '60s soul], which was the thing. Motown had begun to make its move, and all this stuff coming out of Motown was peaking. So we were trying to compete.

But with Leonard Chess preoccupied with his radio operations (centered on the very successful WVON station) and with the independent record business facing an uncertain future, Billy Davis moved on once more. In 1968, with Leonard's blessing, he took up an unusual post for a record man as music director with McCann-Erickson on Madison Avenue, New York. Billy was headhunted after the advertising agency became aware of his production talents through the Fontella Bass recording of "Rescue Me." There, with marketing man Bill Backer, Davis helped to introduce real songs into advertisements instead of nonsensical jingles. The real highlight, among many, was the Coca-Cola campaign with the famous "hilltop" scene featuring the song "I'd Like to Buy the World a Coke" (credited to Billy Davis, Bill Backer, and British tunesmiths Roger Cook and Roger Greenaway). In a reconfiguration as "I'd Like to Teach the World to Sing (In Perfect Harmony)," it became a smash record in its own right. Through his extensive network of industry contacts, Davis was able to call on the services of top artists to sing on the commercials, including Ray Charles, Aretha Franklin, Glen Campbell, Dusty Springfield, and Dottie West. From Billy's Chess days, there were vocals by Fontella Bass, Little Milton, and the Dells.

By the 1990s, Billy Davis was heading his eponymous music publishing company and administering his song catalogs with the proverbial rod of iron. "If they don't pay what I want, they can't have it," he would say of the many inquiries for synchronization licenses for movies, TV, and advertisements. With gold-plated songs such as "Higher and Higher," "Reet Petite," "Rescue Me," and "I'd Like to Teach the World to Sing" he could afford to hold out for his asking price. Never one to rest on his laurels, Davis was supervising an album by an Australian soul singer in his basement studio in the summer of 2004 when he was overtaken by prostate cancer. He died at his home in New Rochelle, New York, aged seventy-two.

Roquel "Billy" Davis was a brilliant record man and songwriter who had come from the most modest of beginnings, with race as an added adversity, to achieve the pinnacle of the American Dream. The journey from Motown to Manhattan had been in perfect harmony, almost. One last thing: Billy managed to secure the publishing to "I'd Like to Teach the World to Sing" and other ad copyrights for his Shada Music firm. Almost certainly, Joe, Syd, Leonard, and George would have been impressed. And maybe Berry, too?

18
CHAPTER

Harlem Hotshots and the Black Experience

CAST OF CHARACTERS
Bobby Robinson, Fire-Fury-Enjoy Records
Ahmet Ertegun, Atlantic Records
Paul Winley, Winley Records
Marshall Sehorn, promo man Fire-Fury Records
Henry "Juggy" Murray Jr., Sue Records
Harold Battiste, A.F.O. Records
Joe Bihari, Crown-Kent Records

In May 2005, Bobby Robinson, still located in his beloved Harlem, had just turned eighty-eight. Sporting a fetching straw boater hat perched on the gray locks that flowed to his shoulders, he was wearing a bright red jacket, multicolored waistcoat, and white pants with bright red shoes. Here he was all show, relishing in his celebrity as *the* local record man as we meandered down 125th Street for lunch at Sylvia's soul food restaurant on Lenox Avenue. Walking past the Apollo Theatre, still in business, Bobby remembered "the great music, the entertainment, and the jokes." Hotel Theresa, where all the top artists stayed (and partied), loomed across the road. Farther on down 125th Street, Robinson shouted out, "All right, babe!" and the happy lady recipient gave a cry of "Daddy-o!" It was a flavor of Harlem as it used to be.

The family record shop, Bobby's Happy House, run by daughter Denise Benjamin with loyal assistant Bootsy at 2332 Amsterdam Avenue, was operating valiantly just around the corner from the original store on 125th Street. In a more innocent age, Bobby Robinson's Record

Shop, as it used to be called, was a mecca for artists playing the Apollo and for their adoring fans. Record men and promo men would drop in regularly to check on the discs that were being snapped up by Bobby's discerning clientele.

An external speaker still blared out R&B and gospel oldies onto the street, but not the latest hits, as of yore. Inside, CDs representing the distant golden age of black music were lined up in racks, but the shellac and vinyl discs were long gone. On the walls were faded photographs of Bobby with Jackie Wilson, Bobby with Fats Domino, Bobby with Sam Cooke, and Bobby with assorted black entertainers, boxers, and politicians of varying degrees of fame.

With Harlem enjoying a renaissance, the locale was becoming visibly gentrified. Big retail corporations were moving to 125th Street, the neighboring brownstones were being bought up and renovated, and President Bill Clinton had an office a few blocks down the road. Romantics may have objected, but with investment dollars flowing into the area, there was a vitality about the place that hadn't been there when drug dealers and heroin addicts had ruled the streets with brooding cynicism not too many years before. Occasionally, a street vendor would play a record like Jackie Wilson's "Baby Workout" on a portable player, and it sounded great. But the world that Bobby Robinson knew as a record shop owner and independent record man had all but disappeared. Harlem's creeping gentrification caught up with him when his new landlord's eviction order took place on January 21, 2008—Martin Luther King Jr. Day.

Over a series of lunches, Bobby told endless stories of the "good old days" with natural storytelling ability. He was a perfect candidate for a biography, but, frustratingly, for too many years he had been intent on writing his autobiography without any outside help. Fortunately, he had always been a willing interviewee, and there was no lack of documentation on his fascinating life.

With a spiritual air that could be traced back to his Cherokee Indian heritage and with a photographic memory, he recalled how his grandfather farmed his "own" land, "which was rare for coloreds." According to Robinson, the three hundred acres of pasture, woodlands, and swamp was situated some five miles from Union, South Carolina, toward the north of the state between Spartanburg and Columbia, the capital. The work, from sunup to sundown, was harsh. "We didn't get rich, but we were free," said Bobby, adding that "Lincoln was the greatest!" He recalled the long daily walks to and from a small country school along dirt roads and the South Carolina house parties with homemade musical entertainment featuring harmonica, tin tub for percussion, and the "sexy" guitar (in the style of Blind Boy Fuller, Brownie McGhee, and Sonny Terry).

Looking to break out from a life of struggle on the land, Bobby Robinson at age twenty took a Carolinian's natural migratory route to New York. He recalled the exact date of arrival: June 10, 1937. Then he saw his first escalator and wondered to himself how people could go up "the stairs" standing still. It was like being on the moon; it was a universe apart. Bobby sweated in the garment district in midtown New York "but not for long." He met his wife, Thelma, a maid in one of the grand mansions scattered along Long Island's North Shore. "I took her to a place where the jukebox was jumping all the time," he said. "I gave her three plays of her choice." And so with those nickles in the slot the romance started with Thelma—and with the music.

In 1942, Bobby was drafted into the army. As Corporal Morgan Robinson, he became an entertainment officer in Honolulu. Taking a little piece of the action here and a little piece there, this is where his music hustle began. Upon returning to New York, he found that "everything was great after the end of the war; everyone had lots of money." As for Harlem, "everywhere you looked there were nightclubs; it was the greatest dancing place in the world." An expert lindy-hopper and an unabashed ladies' man, Bobby was a regular patron of the Savoy Ballroom. Here he soaked up the Harlem beat that would manifest itself proudly in his recordings. He would become the nimblest of dancers in business, too.

With capital derived from his army service, he opted to join the long-established Jewish shopkeepers in the area. "I had to make up my mind what kind of store I wanted," he said. "I really wanted a 99–cent store, but the floor area was too small. At the time, there was a liquor store on every block in Harlem and guys would go there like flies, but there were no drugs. I was the first black owner on 125th Street."

Bobby Robinson's Record Shop opened on August 20, 1946, at 301 West 125th Street. "I took a shot at records," said Bobby, "but I didn't know anything about it. I bought anything that came out. There were few record manufacturers . . . and no [local] black manufacturers. The time and place couldn't have been better; it was pure luck. The Apollo Theatre was open seven days a week, six shows a day, from 11 A.M. to 1 A.M.[1] It was so close, and people were passing the store all the time. Everyone was dressed up; it was like Times Square. The artists would stay at the Hotel Theresa and would drop in all the time; the Baby Grand club was only a few doors away." Bobby's first big seller over the counter was "Drifting Blues" by Johnny Moore's Three Blazers with Charles Brown. As a means of attracting customers from the street, Robinson started playing records through that now-famous exterior loudspeaker.

"Everybody was heading for the Apollo," said Robinson.

That was the epitome for black artists. They'd go past my door to go eat or something, and I met everybody. So when the guys would go on the road, they'd say, "When you're in New York, stop in Bobby's [and] listen to all your records in the store, man; he knows how your records are doing." So I got word-of-mouth recommendation, so everybody started coming in to me. I met all the artists; they stopped by. "Hey, Bobby, how's my record doing?" Later on, Ray Charles, he'd buy a whole lot of records, some gospel records. He'd get the tune and the feeling and change it into rhythm and blues.[2]

Leonard Chess and the other guys started coming in to me, listening to records. Hear this, hear that. Chess had a distributor in New York, but they used to ship me a lot of stuff from Chicago, too. Little by little, this little guy in New Orleans really helped Leonard Chess set that company up, colored guy, Paul Gayten. Leonard and Paul Gayten went all over; he introduced Leonard to a lot of people, and he got him known. Phil Chess stayed more or less in Chicago. So I got very busy just playing records for different people. I hadn't really thought about going into the "record business"; I had a retail store.

As the 1950s progressed, Robinson had several competitors on the same busy Harlem thoroughfare, including the long-established Rainbow Record Shop, Ed Portnoy at the Record Shack, and the lively young Paul Winley with a "great" record concession in the W. T. Grant department store.

Ahmet Ertegun was a frequent visitor to Harlem and saw the 125th Street shops as special sales indicators for Atlantic. With his witty storytelling ability, he claimed to have given Robinson a helping hand in starting his record labels:

We sold to all the big [retail] accounts, but our distributor [Jerry Blaine at Cosnat Distributing] took care of that. The only thing we did was like on 125th Street. There'd be some record shops that had outside speakers, so we'd make a deal; we'd give a box of twenty-five records free if they put the record on the speaker. I put Bobby Robinson in business, but he won't acknowledge it [*smiles*].

Every Friday, there was a new show at the Apollo Theatre, and I'd go every Friday morning to catch the first show. It was never a full house that early, but I'd get to see whoever is on. Most of the time, our competitors' artists were on, so I'd go see Charles Brown, Amos Milburn, or whoever is on; sometimes it was Count Basie. There was a restaurant called Frank's where a lot of white people ate lunch. Next door to that was a shoeshine parlor, very narrow, and it was owned by Bobby Robinson. I used to go there to get my shoes shined because they gave you a very high gloss. The shoeshine parlor also sold records, and then he wants to start a record company.

It's one thing to sell records, [but] you can't just . . . [start a record company] like that. It's a very tough thing. He says, "Would you help me? I need a list of all the distributors." He didn't know that was printed once a year in *Billboard* [and *Cash Box*]. I said, "You've got to have promotion guys; you just can't put out records." He said, "Let me do it my way." After that, I gave him a list of R&B stations. I thought he was crazy. I said, "Look, don't waste your money, because you've got a good business here in Harlem." Then he put out "Kansas City" by . . . Wilbert Harrison [in 1959]; it sold *three million*. It sold more than we'd ever done [*laughs*]. But I gave him everything; I helped him get started.[3]

Actually, Bobby Robinson had set up his first record label, Robin, in late 1951 with younger brother Danny, who had followed Bobby up from South Carolina. As with their indie counterparts, they had spotted a gap in the market. "See, New York was wide open," said Bobby. "All the record companies, like Decca, RCA, and those guys, they [weren't] into [the changing music scene]. Record men used to bring dubs to me and ask if they were hits. I realized I had a good ear, so why not do it myself?"

After only a few months, the brothers Robinson were forced to change the label name from Robin. And so Red Robin came bobbing along, looking for the rich pickings and morsels to be found in the blues, R&B, and especially doo-wop music of Harlem. "Doo-wop music was love music; everyone was making love and getting married!" said Robinson whimsically, adding that "I had so many groups knocking on my door that I couldn't handle them all. But there was no feeling of competition amongst the indies."

In 1956, Bobby Robinson thought he had hit the big time when he launched Whirlin' Disc Records with Jerry Blaine, head of Jubilee Records and Cosnat Distributing. "He was the distributor, but I got waylaid by him," said Bobby, abruptly. Marshall Sehorn, a future promo man with Robinson, thought that Morris Levy might have had yet another of his "silent" stakes in near-hitless Whirlin' Disc, but in any case the partnership was dissolved after just one year.[4]

Fury and Fire Records

Just before Whirlin' Disc had spun out, Bobby Robinson—supposedly "furious" at the actions of Jerry Blaine—formed Fury Records in January 1957. After a commendable series of doo-wop releases (and a local noisemaker with Tarheel Slim's black rocker "Number 9 Train"), the Fury label struck gold when "Kansas City" by Wilbert Harrison became a shock No. 1 national pop hit in May 1959. This basic blues shuffle record was issued by a small independent label operated by a black record man from a tiny Harlem storefront. No wonder Ahmet Ertegun was still incredulous almost fifty years after the event.

Bobby Robinson loved telling the story of this epic feat, which represented in a microcosm the dreams and schemes of the original indie record men.[5] "I cut about fifteen demo discs, acetates," he said.

> I had a couple of doo-wop group things out as well, [and] I was going to take to the road to promote them. We were gone eleven days. We left here and went to Philadelphia, Pittsburgh, Cleveland, Detroit, Chicago, Nashville . . . down here and there, then came back to Atlanta, Mississippi, and New Orleans. We closed the shop. We came back one Sunday afternoon, we got back about 1 or 2 P.M.; it was cold, it was March, light snow. So I got out of the car, went right upstairs. I put the key in the door and pushed the door. It was tight. I pushed again, and there were telegrams waist-high, I didn't know what it was. Have I got the right place here, wrong place? Telegrams *all* over: "Kansas City" had broke!
>
> What happened was I left the disc dubs everywhere I went. And "Kansas City" had broken in Chicago, Detroit; my man in Cleveland was hot on it, [and] so was St. Louis, Missouri.

The "fun" was about to begin. As a start, Wilbert Harrison was under contract to Savoy Records. "He had recorded for Herman Lubinsky in [New] Jersey in 1954," said Robinson.

> He had a fair record with him ["Don't Drop It," an incongruous cover of a major label country hit, no less]. Wilbert Harrison was bugging him; for two years he hadn't recorded. So Lubinsky got mad one day; he was in a bad mood. Wilbert Harrison went in there, [and] he [Lubinsky] opened the drawer and got his gun: "Get the hell out of here. Don't darken this door anymore. Go to record for who the hell you want to record. Record for anybody, just don't come here no more." He meant it; he was serious.
>
> So Wilbert Harrison came to me; he was doing "Kansas City." The song had been

out a few years before . . . but the guy didn't make a hit with it ["K.C. Loving" by Little Willie Littlefield (Federal, 1952).] So Wilbert Harrison picked it up, and he was doing a one-man band out in Jersey. He had a bass drum that he played with his feet: he had two little rods, made it himself, put a mic into the drum and tightened up; over here he had a harmonica, and he was playing guitar. I never saw anything like that. So anyhow, he had sung this thing his way. He did the song not like the original guy did it; nobody had heard this "Kansas City" before. He said, "This thing is so hot, I have to play this thing about every three songs in the nightclub, all night long."

So I said, "Look, I got a rehearsal tonight down at 116th Street, come down there and let me hear what you've got." We went down there. I had a band rehearsing some things, and he sat down at the piano. He started to get off, "I'm going to Kansas City . . .," and the band got carried away; Wild Jimmy Spruill was on guitar.[6] I said, "That thing sounds so good! Listen, I've got a session tomorrow."

We went down to midtown to the Bell Sound studio, the original old studio on Forty-sixth and Eighth Avenue.[7] I cut the Harrison Brothers [no relation to Wilbert], two boys, finished their thing, and Wilbert hadn't showed up yet. So we hung around there for a while. Another white doo-wop group was coming on next. Our time had run out. They were looking in the window there, started looking to do music; the drummer had taken his drums down, everybody was packing up. So in walked Wilbert Harrison.

I said, "The time is up; I can't record you now." He said, "I had a flat on the [New Jersey] Turnpike, I had to go and make a phone call, the guy drove me in and changed tires, this delayed me. *We've* got to do this thing; we can do it just, poop, like that." I said, "Oh, man." So I said to the engineer, "Can you give me another twenty minutes or so? Ask the kids if it's all right." So the kids said, "Yeah, okay, okay." They wanted to listen to us.

So the guys set back up and again, "I'm going to Kansas City . . .," they filled right in on it, funny thing, and everybody felt it. We did it, and we played it back; it sounds so good. I said, "I'll be damned. What else have you got?" He said, "I've got a slow song to do, 'Listen My Darling.'" So in about fifteen minutes we did the whole record, the biggest record I ever had. Fifteen minutes, two takes, boom.

While Bobby Robinson was plugging his acetate of "Kansas City" to ecstatic reaction on the road, a Cleveland disc jockey (possibly Bill Randle) picked up on the record and promptly cut a cover version by one Rocky Olson, placing it with Leonard Chess. "They copied it closely," said Robinson,

and Chess had the record out [and shot] them out all over the country. He was strong then; he told the disc jockeys, "There's another record coming out, but this is the record here; play my record. If you don't play my record, I'll take my line away from you." In St. Louis, Buffalo, New York, Chess threatened these guys. He was big in R&B then.

So the guy in Chicago told me, "Man, somebody is trying to find you; goddammit, Leonard Chess has got this record out. They're starting to put it on the air and playing it. I've got a sample of your [better] record, [and] there ain't no comparison, man. We ain't got your record, and I'm not going to take another record with the same thing." Oh man, I went crazy!

Worse, there was extra competition from established artists Little Richard (Specialty) and Hank Ballard and the Midnighters (King), and King's Syd Nathan had doubled his options by rereleasing Little Willie Littlefield's original Federal version with overdubbed guitar and drums to give the record a "modern" backbeat. Somehow Robinson managed to hold on to his record despite "bigwig" master purchase offers from Liberty's Al Bennett, Dot's Randy Wood, and End's George Goldner (who essayed another inferior cover, by Rockin' Ronald [Hawkins] and the Rebels). Then the first lawsuit arrived at Bobby Robinson's office at 271 West 125th Street.

> A guy walked in one day and said, "Bobby Robinson?" "Yeah." It was a suit for $100,000! Lubinsky had run Wilbert Harrison out of his place with a gun, but when that record came out, he comes running. So now I have to go to court. The best thing was his lawyer from Jersey, but I had a good lawyer, too. He said, "Well, listen, we got this record, the boy had a few weeks to go on his contract, and Lubinsky ran him out." So Lubinsky's lawyer said, "There's a chance of losing the whole thing and nobody would have nothing. Let us have the record and the court will decide. . . ." I looked at my lawyer. The judge said, "Robinson, I'll give you forty-eight hours to open an account in escrow with $20,000 [to fight the case]. Can you do that?" I said, "Well, sir, one thing is sure; I'm gonna try." "I'll give you forty-eight hours to bring that bank account in here, and you can have the record."
>
> I got back on the phone. I called everywhere, "Send me $5,000 today!" Oh boy, I had that $20,000. Lubinsky's lawyer didn't know what to say; he thought they were going to get the record that morning. I got it! They called Lubinsky in Newark, but his lawyer was such a great lawyer. I was pressing in New York and I was pressing in Leonia, New Jersey, right across from the [George Washington] bridge. So they found that out, and they said I was doing production in their state, so that way he got a chance to draw the case to New Jersey.
>
> So I went over to New Jersey, got on the stage. His lawyer was there; he tried to get me on all kind of things. I was ready for him. I said we complied with the court, and I told him what happened: "Wilbert Harrison came to me, I took him at his word, and I recorded him." And so they had us back in court, but they didn't win; they didn't win. My lawyer said, "Well, the fact that [Robinson's] pressing in New Jersey, that company's pressing all over, down south, Chicago. That doesn't mean the company is in Jersey." So we got away with it. And we killed the Rocky Olson [Chess] record.

The case dragged on for almost a year until settled out of court, with Lubinsky accepting just $13,500 to Robinson's great relief.[8] But the legal furor didn't end there. Armo Music's Sydney Nathan, through his lawyer Jack Pearl, had jumped into the fray by insisting that Harrison's "Kansas City" infringed the copyright of "K.C. Loving," written by Jerry Leiber and Mike Stoller. As indeed it did.

Poor Bobby! Pending settlement in both cases, Fury Records was frozen as a trading entity. What to do? "So there I was, just getting off the ground," he reflected. "I mean, it was very frustrating; I was going real strong. So I said, 'Okay, we'll form a new record company.' I was all fired up, so we formed Fire Records. My very first record was called 'It's Too Late' by Tarheel Slim and his girlfriend Little Ann. We had been working on this thing; I was gonna do it on Fury. It was a very authentic crying scene [on the record], you know; when she came back, he wouldn't let her in the door. This record took off very big, so my first record on Fire was also a hit [No. 20 R&B, 1959]. So I was off again." The story behind the new label name made for a good yarn but ignored the fact that Robinson was already using Fire Music as his publishing house for the Fury releases.

Meanwhile, *Billboard* was able to reflect on the wider significance of Wilbert Harrison's wonderful smash record (together with Dave "Baby" Cortez's contemporaneous No. 1 hit with "The Happy Organ") in a story headed "Little Indie Jackpots: Brand-New Label Can Hit It—With Real Hot Disk": "What all this means is that now, with many indie pressing plants able and willing to press records in addition to the major diskery pressing plants; with factors [factoring agents] and other persons available to help finance the pressings, and with indie distributors willing to swing into action on a hot disk, a new label can make it on its own. Of course, the product must be there—and more than that, must be so much there that it practically happens on its own."

The feature noted that "if either Clock or Fury decides to build into a large label, with regular singles releases, and possibly album releases as well, they will probably have to make an affiliation with a large label or major—or else add an awful lot of personnel." Welcome to the world of the small independent labels, 1959 version.[9]

And so "Kansas City" was a wild, wild trip. "Until then, I had most local things that did very well on the eastern seaboard," said Bobby Robinson. "It was a whole new ballgame. I think the final count is four million over a period of time; we did a million right away. But from the business side, it was a *rough* experience."

So how did humble Harlem storekeeper Bobby Robinson manage to handle his monumental hit record? Bear in mind that he had turned down offers for the purchase of the master and had overcome tough competition, too. Well, he needed outside help. Robinson would have chased up distributors for outstanding sums, obtained extended credit from various pressing plants, and taken on loans from whomever. Remember, speed was of the essence. In Bobby's words, "I went to hustlin' and scramblin'. Made a call here and there, had samples made up, [got] the labels printed, rushed it out."

"There was no problem," said fellow Harlem record man Paul Winley a little disarmingly, adding that there was a "natural communication" at the time between the distributors, disc jockeys, and stores such as Waxie Maxie's in Washington, D.C., to facilitate the hit. As for the magnitude of Robinson's achievement, think of those leading independent labels that never had a national No. 1 pop hit, including King, Modern, Specialty, and Sun.

In the background of it all, Bobby had a rarely acknowledged accomplice. "Clarence 'Fats' Lewis was my partner," admitted Robinson. "He had Fats' restaurant on 129th and Lenox."[10] Robinson's promo man Marshall Sehorn described Lewis as "like a Zulu king with a cigar, and with his ego. He always tried to impress you, but there was nothing [there] to impress [you with]. It's like an ugly bitch trying to say she's *purty*."

Typically, Bobby Robinson and Marshall Sehorn were at odds over who should take credit for signing Wilbert Harrison to Fury and for breaking "Kansas City." Sehorn always claimed that he discovered the singer in North Carolina, their common home state. "Bullshit!" Robinson told me. "He had nothing to do with Wilbert Harrison until after 'Kansas City' was a hit." More seriously, the two record men were to have longstanding Fire-Fury licensing issues. Nevertheless, there was a mutual, jousting fondness for one another. "I taught him a record was round!" exclaimed Robinson, laughing. Sehorn had no hesitation in acknowledging that Bobby gave him his first chance in the business as a promo man after a series of rejections from other New York record figures.

"I rapped and knocked on doors," said Sehorn,

and nobody even talked to me. I remembered talking to Bobby Robinson at a Miami disc jockey convention. As I look back, being from the South, I wouldn't say it was prejudice as much as at that time being afraid of the unknown by working with black people in the music business. I knew nothing of them. I got into his office, we got into a rap, and we went up to Frank's Restaurant and we had dinner. I love him for it, but he conned me into going to work as a promotion man.

He said, "You look for acts and be out on the road; it gives you experience [in] the field." Plus he told me outright, "I need a white representative in the South." In those days, there was no such thing as a black promotion man, no black salesman.[11] Poor black people were riding in the front of the bus to the Mason-Dixon Line and then it was "Get in the back"; restaurants were still segregated. A black man lived second, third, fourth class, and that's as far as he could get in those days.

So Bobby said, "I'm not getting any help down there [in the Carolinas and Georgia]. Nobody's playing my records; nobody's selling my records. I can give you fifty dollars a week salary, I can give you fifty dollars a week expense money and that's all, and you can call me collect." So I got the job. I respect Bobby for giving me my foothold. He has that extra sense about him, of being able to recognize something in the raw, and that's very important. See, so many people can say, "That's a hit," after it's a hit. But being able to recognize it and hear it in the raw, and take wishbones and feathers and put it together, that's the greatest talent of our business.

Lawsuits and financial matters apart, the Wilbert Harrison euphoria soon evaporated when Robinson released the appalling "Cheating Baby" on Fury as the delayed follow-up record. It failed to breach the Top 100, wretchedly. After the "Kansas City" episode, Fire Records had further national hits with "Fannie Mae" by Buster Brown (No. 38 pop, No. 1 R&B, early 1960)—one of the last commercial records to be manufactured on 78 rpm—and "There's Something on Your Mind (Part 2)" by Bobby Marchan (No. 31 pop, No. 1 R&B, summer 1960). Marchan was the effeminate member of Huey "Piano" Smith's Clowns, and the Fire hit sparked more contractual controversy—this time with Chess Records and Johnny Vincent's Ace Records.

In the general chaos and confusion, Robinson admitted to missing out on signing future stars Otis Redding and Ike & Tina Turner. Think, too, of the potential hits that were lost because they were released in the same time frame as the chart records. This issue of stretched resources was a common problem for all independent record men, not just Bobby Robinson. During this period, Robinson was using the services of black promo man Wally Roker, who had been a member of the hit-making Heartbeats vocal group from Queens. Roker left Robinson in the spring of 1961 to join Florence Greenberg's Scepter-Wand group.[12]

In late 1961, bigger, more dramatic changes were afoot in the Fire-Fury stable. Symbolized by a fresh Fire label design and a new numerical series, it seemed that Bobby Robinson and Fats Lewis had encountered partnership problems. At this point, Marshall Sehorn's name began appearing on production credits. Still the big hits kept coming, into 1962: "Ya Ya" by Lee Dorsey (No. 7 pop, No. 1 R&B, Fury); "Every Beat of My Heart" (No. 45 pop, No. 15 R&B) and "Letter Full of Tears" (No. 19 pop, No. 3 R&B) by Gladys Knight and the Pips (Fury); and "I Need Your Loving" by Don Gardner & Dee Dee Ford (No. 20 pop, No. 4 R&B, Fire).

The never-distant cash flow crisis surfaced when the hits ran out, the distributors' payments dried up, and the tax man came knocking on the door for a sum in excess of $25,000 (with penalty interest). According to Marshall Sehorn, even accountant Allen Klein (later to found ABKCO Records) couldn't save the day. But, so said Sehorn, a label-saving plan was on the table.

With the help of attorney Paul Marshall, Robinson and Sehorn had "worked out" with ABC-Paramount a distribution agreement that included settlement of the IRS bankruptcy petition, a royalty scale, and promotional funds for Sehorn.[13] But there was no lump-sum payment for Fats Lewis. If that wasn't bad enough, Lewis wouldn't have been best pleased when Bobby and brother Danny launched a new label called Enjoy and had an immediate hit with King Curtis's "Soul Twist." According to Sehorn, Lewis summarily torpedoed the ABC-Paramount lifeboat by withholding his agreement as a partner in Fire-Fury. He continued in the record business with his self-named Falew! label and other activities.

Critically, Bobby Robinson was forced into the hands of Morris Levy at Roulette by borrowing from him against the security of Fire Music and Fast Music publishing rights. Levy emerged with yet more lucrative copyrights. Then, amongst the wreckage, the Fire and Fury masters were picked up by an emergent Bell Records in 1965, probably for the proverbial song.

Marshall Sehorn was to have a roller-coaster, up-and-down career after leaving Fire-Fury Records. He formed a partnership with Allen Toussaint, also in 1965, that led to a welcome New Orleans music revival starting with Lee Dorsey on Amy, the Bell subsidiary, and the Meters on Josie, the Jubilee subsidiary. Alas, in the mid-1990s, Sehorn imploded spectacularly in the courts after becoming entwined in the worldwide sublicensing of the Chess masters. Sehorn had been luxuriating falsely in the comfort of tax shelter deals dating back to the late 1970s with New Jersey's Joe Robinson (no relation to Bobby), then the unlikely owner of Chess Records. The courts adjudicated unequivocally in MCA's favor.

"Joe [Robinson] got into hock to Morris Levy and MCA," said Sehorn. "He didn't get a good price for the Chess masters, no! When he went into his second bankruptcy, Morris Levy came in and bailed him out, and Morris had a big stake in Chess. So when it was sold to MCA [in 1985], Morris got his share; everybody got their share—and Marshall got the commode." Sehorn, who died in 2006, never recovered in business or in personal terms from the catastrophe in the courts. He ought to be remembered for all his good work in reigniting, with Allen Toussaint, the moribund New Orleans recording scene in the post–Cosimo Matassa era. But he did sully his reputation with those unfortunate, inexcusable licensing deals with Chess, Fire-Fury, and other indie masters.

Enjoy Records

Undaunted by the partnership problems surrounding Fire and Fury, Bobby Robinson launched Enjoy Records in 1962 with brother Danny. "Enjoy was a catchy name, short and simple," said Bobby. "I saw a joke book in a store, *Enjoy with Eddie,* and the name hit me. It was a good name for music that is there to be enjoyed; it is my favorite name. I still have the label."

And so the Robinson brothers scored an immediate No. 1 R&B hit (and No. 17 pop) with King Curtis's "Soul Twist." Curtis, prominent as a session man on many big Atlantic recordings, had the hottest band in town while playing at Small's Paradise in Harlem in the early 1960s. Unable to get a solo hit on Atco and other labels, Curtis Ousley agreed to cut a record for Bobby Robinson. The saxophonist wanted to monopolize the lead on "Soul Twist," but Robinson insisted that he come "in and out" and that he give spots to the other musicians, including guitarist Billy Butler (of "Honky Tonk" fame). It was impossible for the Robinsons to retain King Curtis once Capitol intervened with its large checkbook.

Bobby and Danny Robinson ran Hit Town distributors in the late 1960s. "We had six staff and serviced twenty record stores on 125th Street, the Bronx, and Mount Vernon," said Bobby. "It opened from 8 A.M. to 10 P.M." Although now a distributor's promo man, he "couldn't stand it," much preferring the creative side of the industry. During this spell, his wife was running the record shop. Danny Robinson, of whom Bobby spoke comparatively little, was a dedicated if unsentimental man who worked all hours. Whereas Danny did not have the magic recording touch of his elder brother, he was by common consensus a better businessman. Eventually the partnership was split, with Bobby taking the Enjoy label and publishing and Danny taking the distribution arm.[14]

Bobby Robinson continued to make sporadic releases on Enjoy throughout the 1960s soul era. He conducted occasional if spirited sessions for old friends at Mercury (with Junior Parker), Josie (Jay Dee Bryant), and Capitol (Willie Hightower). Even though disco was pushing out soul music in the 1970s, Robinson still kept his ears open to the beat of the edgy streets of Harlem and the Bronx. There, along with 125th Street neighbor Paul Winley of Winley Records and Joe Robinson of Sugar Hill Records, he stumbled upon first-generation rap and hip-hop. Bobby Robinson reaped his just reward in 1997 when diva Mariah Carey sampled his recording of "Honey." He reckoned that he earned royalties in excess of six figures from Carey's rendition.

Donn Fileti licensed many Fire-Fury-Enjoy masters for reissue on Relic. He recalled Robinson fondly: "Bobby has enjoyed his life; he's lived a good life. It's amazing Bobby did as well as he did considering he made some bad business decisions, or he wouldn't have lost Fire and Fury in the early 1960s like that. But on the other hand, he ran a very viable record label [Red Robin] that started with just doo-wop, and he branched out into having some significant national hits [on Fire-Fury]. Then [he did] blues, [as with] Elmore James and Lightnin' Hopkins [Fire], followed by soul and early rap [Enjoy]. It's hard to know about the millions of dollars he could have had if he had run the business right."

Juggy Murray: Sue Records

Henry "Juggy" Murray Jr., another native Carolinian, did not have Bobby Robinson's same pedigree in music. But for a while in the early 1960s, he was jockeying with Robinson as New York's top black record man. Murray incorporated Sue Records on New Year's Day 1957 at 271 West 125th Street, a building that housed the offices of disc jockey Tommy Smalls and Tommy Robinson (who owned the Atlas-Angletone labels). There seemed to be a mutual business relationship among all three of them. From the outset, Murray tapped into the bountiful reservoir of local black talent and songwriters. While still a rookie in the record business, he remembered Leonard Chess giving him useful business tips when they were together on the same air flight. The Sue label took off in 1960 after signing the redoubtable Ike Turner (then based in St. Louis) with vivacious standup singer Anna Mae Bullock, aka Tina Turner.

Juggy Murray, who was raised in Hell's Kitchen, New York, proceeded to take R&B into the soul age with productions that had an energetic, rhythmic beat with a distinct gospel edge. After the formation of a Sue label in England by Island Records under Guy Stevens's watch, Murray's recordings had a big influence on the British "mod" culture of the mid-1960s. But the U.K. relationship was marred when Juggy did not take kindly to Island licensing in other independent label recordings for release on *his* Sue label.

Like Bobby Robinson, Juggy Murray was confident that he knew how to make and recognize a hit record aided by formidable professional skills. His track record bore him out with a string of Top 100 hits.[15] Murray threw himself into the LP market with eye-catching albums of strong content by main acts Ike Turner (with and without Tina), Jimmy McGriff, Baby Washington, Inez Foxx, and the Soul Sisters.

Murray told me he started out in the numbers game, which is where the funding for Sue Records would have come from. The exploitative gambling racket took root in Harlem and other urban centers in the 1930s under mobster "Dutch" Schultz in the years of economic depression. By the late 1950s, the central Harlem area was controlled by one Bumpy Johnson, known as "The Lamb."[16] Paul Winley, of Winley Records, believed the impact of the numbers game in Harlem declined relative to the growth in drug dealing.

Harold Battiste: A.F.O. Records

Juggy Murray's biggest record was "I Know (You Don't Love Me No More)" by Barbara George, a Top 3 hit in 1961. This funky New Orleans R&B outing was procured from A.F.O. Records, which was brought into the Sue fold as a subsidiary label. A.F.O. was the altruistic All For One organization led by Harold Battiste.

Primarily a saxophonist, Battiste began playing the R&B jukebox hits in the New Orleans area in the late 1940s with the Joe Jones band and the Johnson Brothers (led by tenor man Plas and pianist Ray). After embarking on a teaching career that accelerated his sense of racial injustice, Battiste flirted with his prime love, modern jazz, before landing an appointment at age twenty-five as the Specialty Records branch manager in New Orleans in 1957.[17] Prior to the A.F.O. escapade, he took up the A&R post at Joe Ruffino's Ric-Ron Records of New Orleans in a union that led to the great adventure with Joe Jones's "You Talk Too Much" (No. 3 pop, No. 9 R&B, late 1960).

Battiste, a deep thinker and one-time convert to the Black Muslim movement, explained the step-by-step process of translating "You Talk Too Much" into a hit record on the Ric label and the seemingly inevitable brush with the management of Roulette Records:

> Now Joe Jones was the promotion man. He could walk in anywhere, and they remembered him. Nine times out of ten they liked him well enough to do what he wanted; he had that ability. So we hit the road with "You Talk Too Much." Poor Joe Ruffino, man, he had no idea that record had the kind of potential it had. His concept was limited. But after we got to New York, it was really strange because we didn't have any money; the record was big by then. I had never really traveled that much of the country doing that, and due to Joe [Jones]'s adventurousness, perseverance, and cockiness, I was able to get that experience.[18]
>
> In the meantime, I had learned something, theoretically, about distributors in Chicago, Detroit, Atlanta, and other places and [could] see the difference in different cities and how they operated and so forth. It was all valuable experience for what I was planning to do. I kept notes and records of all the cats I'd met; Joe was a real record keeper as well. I kept names of distributors, names of disc jockeys, and what station it is—white station, black station, hillbilly station. There was no question about us not thinking "You Talk Too Much" was not a hit.

Then the Roulette smash and grab was made after "the discovery that a prior recording of the same tune by Joe Jones was in the Roulette file," whereupon "an amicable decision" was made concerning the transfer of rights.[19] "After Roulette got Joe Ruffino's throat there," said Battiste, "boy, I was scared to death. I mean, we had no reason to be afraid, but we were because we were thinking, oh man, Phil Kahl and those cats. That's the Mafia! He had sent Joe Robinson, who was the old man of Sylvia [of Mickey & Sylvia], to the place we were staying to make us an offer. They had taken us out to the Roundtable, some of those places in New York, and gave us the royal treatment. They knew Joe Jones was weak for chicks. We told the people at the hotel not to tell anybody we had checked out in case they came looking for us. We were crazy, but it was okay. We found out that Joe Ruffino had to go up to New York and so, well, it's gonna get settled." Joe Jones confirmed to me in 1975 that "Roulette got Ruffino up there; they just took it. Joe Ruffino didn't get nothin'." Morris Levy had snaffled the master, the publishing, and Joe Jones's contract.

For Harold Battiste, there was already a pattern of high achievement dogged by bad luck. This trend continued after he had put into action his master plan: a record cooperative that was *black*-owned. A.F.O. Records was formed with a collective of like-minded New Orleans musicians known as the A.F.O. Combo: Melvin Lastie (who played the arresting cornet solo on "I Know"), Alvin "Red" Tyler (saxophone), Roy Montrell (guitar), Chuck Badie (upright bass), and John Boudreaux (drums).

Juggy Murray arrived on the scene through an introduction from Sonny Bono, Harold Battiste's erstwhile colleague at Specialty Records. "So Juggy called," remembered Harold.

> I didn't know if Juggy was black or white. He told me he wanted me to be an A&R man for Sue Records, so I said, "Okay, that's cool, too, but let me tell you what I've got going." He said, "Well, look, man, don't tell nobody. I'll be down there." He was down here on the next plane to New Orleans.
>
> We went to the airport, me and Red [Tyler]. Allen Toussaint had a pretty Cadillac, so we got his car to go to the airport! We finally realized that this little black cat that got off the plane . . ."Could you be Juggy?" Oh, wow, because now we could almost complete the chain. We wanted a black business. Now we'd got a cat to handle our national distribution, and he was *black*. I was blinded by that, I mean, he was just a black cat. And Juggy, smart cat, sensed immediately what role to play: the "brother" this, the "brother" that . . ."Yeah baby, right now," "Yes indeed, man," "It's gonna be sweet, man." His records were doing fine with Ike & Tina Turner.
>
> We saw ourselves making a heap out of this. My thinking was, okay, crazy, there's cats in New York with little labels, there's Sue Records, there's Bobby Robinson doing something. But I was thinking we don't have no RCA Victor, and we don't have no Capitol. I'm saying we should be operating at that level of the record business, what eventually Motown turned out to be. We should be a giant corporation, a major voice in the whole record industry.
>
> So I saw dealing with Juggy as an opportunity to bring a coalition thing together that would be a conglomerate entertainment enterprise, where we would incorporate records, booking and management, motion pictures. All of the facets of entertainment that basically they say that a nigger can do—they can sing and dance!—we gonna own it all. There's no reason why [at the] Shaw [Agency] in New York, some Jew's gonna run us all over the country . . . you know, Ray Charles, Ruth Brown running all over the country, and he's sitting on the telephone making a fortune. Let some black cat be sitting there making that fortune. We got the talent; we just need the structure.
>
> So then we did Barbara George and Prince La La at the next record date [in New Orleans]. And everything was going along cool. I used my house at Hickory Street— that was our office—and we used to have little meetings, discuss what we're gonna do. We had our system worked out, got a black attorney, we got it all together. It was

so beautiful, man, that when Henry Hildebrand [of All South distributors] first saw our business cards (it was a black business card with each one of our names on it in gold), he said, "Well, man, if you guys get any hit at all, you're gonna get every artist in town." Well, we thought, so what, that's the way it's supposed to be.

Reality asserted itself quickly. "After we hit with 'I Know,'" said Harold Battiste, "Juggy convinced Barbara to buy her contract *from A.F.O.* Juggy had got pissed after we recorded 'Ya Ya' by Lee Dorsey for Bobby Robinson. I saw nothing wrong when Bobby [contacted] me, although we had made an agreement with Juggy. Bobby Robinson wanted to do the Lee Dorsey thing, okay, crazy, but that's what we're gonna do, man, we're gonna supply everybody with hits. That ain't no problem. You get out there and sell us something. So it was love; we set up an agreement [with Bobby]." Here was a virtual replay of the Bihari brothers/Chess brothers/Sam Phillips scenario of a decade earlier.

"I got really discouraged," admitted Battiste. "We went to New York, pleaded with Juggy not to do that [take Barbara George's contract], it's gonna mess the whole thing up. It took a lot of steam out of us. We had only a half-dozen releases with Juggy, and that was it. I tried to take the object lesson out of that; [I] came back and said, 'Okay, man, all that's black is not black. Maybe it don't make no difference after all. Maybe I have to stop being blinded by color and try to see people better.'" As for Barbara George, she had her Cadillac and fine wardrobe, but another Tina Turner she was not. One album, no more hits, and her time had passed.

In August 1963, Harold Battiste, still with starry-eyed dreams, departed New Orleans for California with his A.F.O. colleagues. He teamed up again with Sam Cooke, who was running his Sar label as well as churning out hits for RCA Victor. "We set up the same auditioning system that I used at Specialty and A.F.O. called Soul Station," said Battiste. "But we're going through this black shit again. Then Sam met with a very unfair death in the midst of our thing [shot dead in a seedy Los Angeles motel]. It was ridiculous, man; of all the cats in the world to die under those circumstances, Sam didn't deserve that."

"Then Sonny Bono met this broad," continued Battiste, "and the first place he brought her to was the Soul Station. He said, 'This is what we can do, man. Cher has got an uncle that's got some bread; let's make a record.'" Thus Sonny & Cher came on the scene with the No. 1 international hit "I Got You Babe" (Atco, 1965), enhanced by Battiste's striking but, at the time, unaccredited arrangement. "In the meantime," said Harold, "[Bob] Dylan's tune came out, 'All I Really Want to Do,' so, okay, [let's record] that with Cher. So they took Cher to Imperial and proved that because Sonny & Cher are signed to Atlantic, that ain't Cher. That's *Sonny & Cher*, another artist. So that's how that parallel thing got going with Sonny & Cher on Atlantic and Cher on Imperial."

Another Californian excursion for Battiste was the relaunch of New Orleanian Mac Rebennack's career in the guise of Dr. John through the *Gris-Gris* album for Atlantic. Yet again, Harold was squeezed out after the Hoodoo Man became the darling of the rock audiences. "That really threw me," said Battiste. "That was as traumatic to me as the Juggy Murray thing was, because then I began to question myself." Harold Battiste, for all his intellectual and musical talent, just did not have the ruthless streak of the old school record men to compete at the highest business level.[20]

If Harold Battiste felt the gods were not on his side, sharp operator Juggy Murray suffered an even worse fate. By 1968, Tamla-Motown was ruling the black airwaves, and Sue couldn't get a look in. With hits drying up and cash flow problems mounting, Murray said that he went to United Artists for a $100,000 loan that was secured by the Sue assets. When the debt became delinquent, United Artists assumed ownership of Murray's Sue Records masters and Saturn Music publishing. Then the valuable real estate—the "Sue building," comprising offices and the Juggy Sound Studio at 265 West Fifty-fourth Street in midtown Manhattan—was off-loaded over his head, so he also said.

Murray was forced to start all over again and reactivated Sue Records independently, using the same name but with a different logo and label design. At the turn of 1970, he had one more Top 40 hit through a resuscitated Wilbert Harrison with "Let's Work Together" (a song that Harrison recorded first as "Let's Stick Together" for Fury and that was picked up subsequently in 1970 by blues-rock band Canned Heat).

Murray agreed that Sue's fortunes rose and fell with Ike & Tina Turner—and, as an aside, perhaps fell even further due to his incurable weakness for the opposite sex. Ike's teacher, the experienced Joe Bihari, was the artist's secret adviser when the Sue contract came up for renewal in the fall of 1962:

> Ike came to me, [and] he said, "Look, Joe, I have this contract, and they [Sue] are gonna give me $50,000, but if you give it to me, I'll come back with you." I said, "[Brother] Jules would never part with $50,000, Ike, but let me look at the contract." So I looked at the contract and, yeah, he [Juggy Murray] was gonna give him $50,000, but he didn't say when he was gonna give it to him. So I said, "Ike, here, let me give you a few words; I'll write them in." One of them was "forthwith," that is, $50,000 right now, and I told him that's what it means, [and] also "cashier's check." So I said, "Now you go tell him that you'll sign, but he's to give you $50,000 right now in a cashier's check." He did, he signed it, and Juggy Murray said, "I never got another recording from Ike Turner!" So Ike thanked me so much. He never would've gotten the $50,000 because he was not gonna supply Juggy with any more recordings [and would have been locked into the contract for its duration]. That was when he was in between contracts [and] he recorded for me "Good Bye, So Long" with Tina [No. 32 R&B, 1965, Modern].

To add to Murray's discomfiture, he was slammed with a lawsuit with Ike suing for $220,000, Tina for $100,000, and the Placid Music arm for $10,000—a grand sum of $330,000. One part of the complaint charges was that Sue failed and refused "to give an accounting and pay certain royalties"; another was that "the label withheld and concealed over $100,000 from the singers' earnings in both the foreign and domestic markets."[21] Here was another example of the potentially inflammatory nature of the record man–hit artist relationship.

In his twilight years, Juggy Murray was living in a respectable seniors' public accommodation on New York's West Side, with an enviable view of the Hudson River. There was always a hangdog air about him that could be traced to the calamitous loss of his original Sue label. Never losing hope entirely, he went into the studio again at the turn of the millennium with his favorite artist, Baby Washington, but nothing surfaced. It was a sad final act for a once-bustling black record entrepreneur who had enhanced the national stage and beyond. He died almost forgotten in January 2005, and, worse, his body lay unburied for weeks.

The contrast with Bobby Robinson, who was still happily parading the streets of Harlem at the time, was total.

19
CHAPTER

On and Off Broadway

CAST OF CHARACTERS
Donn Fileti, Relic Records
Doug Moody, Herald-Ember and Clock Records
Jeffrey Kruger, Ember International Records
Maxine Brown, Nomar, ABC-Paramount, and Scepter-
 Wand Records artist
*also featuring Al Silver, Herald-Ember Records;
and Florence Greenburg, Scepter-Wand Records*

Back in late 1956, with the rock 'n' roll age approaching full bloom, young teen Donn Fileti harangued his father into taking him on a selective tour of the offices of the independent labels in New York. His memories of the trip provide a unique firsthand account of the indie environment of the time from the perspective of a record collector, record researcher, and future record man. It is fair to say that most original record men did not understand the collectors' sensibility toward the music business and the romantic aura surrounding it. After all, business is business, and business conquered all. What did label listings, discographies, artist biographies, and matrix numbers mean to them?

Fileti grew up in Newark, New Jersey (the domain of Herman Lubinsky's Savoy Records and the Cohen family's Essex Record Distributors), and from an early age dreamed his dreams of becoming a record man. He turned his back on a career in law to do just that. In partnership with Eddie Gries, he ran Relic Records in Hackensack, New Jersey, for some thirty-five years, specializing in vocal group reissues mainly from the plethora of indie labels that flourished and foundered in the New York area. Many important recordings were preserved.

"I started listening seriously to records in '55," recalled Donn Fileti.

I had been an avid reader courtesy of my father picking up *Billboard* and *Cash Box* on the newsstand in Newark for two years previously. I was fascinated with the small independent labels. So my father, bless his heart, decided that as an advance Christmas present, he would take my sister, who was twelve—I was fourteen—around to the various record companies in Manhattan.

Of course, I really wanted to see what they looked like, because that was the absolute fascination to me, their day-to-day operation. I had read about these legendary names in *Billboard* and *Cash Box* such as Al Silver, Morty Craft, Hy Weiss, and Jerry Winston. And I really wanted to see what these guys looked like, also. So our ploy was to ask for photos of the various recording artists, because I figured that would be a good way to get inside the companies.

I think we had a bunch of startled people that day in 1956, because most of them said, "Well, how did you find out where we were?" I remember Jerry Winston at Onyx Records, which was supporting local hits by the Velours and the Pearls at that time; he was in the offices of Malverne distributors on West Forty-ninth. He came down and was very amenable, but he asked, "Why do you want a photo of the Chordells?" whose record had just bombed for him. And then I was very arrogant. The Pearls had a local hit with "Let's You and I Go Steady," and it was very popular on the Alan Freed show [and with] Dr. Jive and Jocko [Henderson], all the local R&B dee-jays. Then Winston followed it up with a ballad, the standard called "Tree in the Meadow," and I heard that. I said, "This is a bomb." I told him it wasn't going to sell, and he looked at me like, "Who is this young jerk?" or whatever. But he was nice enough to give us an 8-by-10 photo of the Pearls and was extremely cordial. Of course, I was right: "Tree in the Meadow" didn't sell!

But that day I remember we got a very curt "No" from Morty Craft, who was too busy to even look at us; that was Melba at 1650 Broadway. A lot of these offices then consisted of a small front room, where you might have a secretary and a desk and a piano; in the back there might be some record boxes. I think the rent was $150 a month for a two-room little suite in 1650 Broadway. The thing is, you could walk down the halls, and you could hear different groups auditioning or rehearsing.

At one point we came down the elevator, and there was Cirino of the Bowties, which was a local group that was popular on Alan Freed. Nobody remembers them now. Certainly the nicest of everybody was Mr. Joe Davis, because he took time with us, he smiled, and he took out many photos in his files. Some of them to this day I don't recognize, groups who recorded on Davis in '53 and '54. He was extremely cordial, too.

Apollo was sharing space with Alpha distributors on West Forty-fifth Street. That was an interesting little operation; I can still picture what these people looked like. I was fascinated to see the boxes of 45s sitting in the office. I think Bess Berman had had a heart attack at that time, and she was out of the business in late '56. It was being run by [Bess and Ike's] son-in-law, Charlie Merenstein, who later had a small label called Doe with a couple of New York hits.

We went to Sol Rabinowitz, Baton Records, on West Forty-fourth Street [a label that was doing well on the R&B charts with the Hearts and Ann Cole and would hit again soon with Noble "Thin Man" Watts]. In those days, you could do this. He had walked out of the office to get coffee, and the door was open; we went in, and we waited for maybe five minutes. There was a stack of mailers, and he was mailing records to radio stations. It was just a one-room office, but he had actually left it unguarded [*laughs*].

We had even gone to a couple of the majors at that time. Decca was on Fifty-seventh Street, and Capitol had a big office on Broadway. Yet their offices were by present-day standards hardly impressive, except that they were bigger, obviously, [and] there were more secretaries. I remember hearing really good high-fidelity sounds in popular music for the first time in Decca's office. They were playing Teresa Brewer records that really sounded good.

You could feel the energy of rock 'n' roll coming in by just going down Broadway at that time and seeing [signs such as] "Hull Records" on the window. At 1674 Broadway, another old building, there were lots of different offices. I'd love to go in and just see the directories . . . there or [at] 1619 or 1650; there would just be so many labels. Then you'd go there the next month, and they would be gone. I think what they would do on some of these things is that they would test them in a few markets. If nothing happened, that was the end of it. Basically, if a record didn't sell, three months later it was scrapped.

We didn't go to the distributors on Tenth Avenue; there would be nothing that I could really ask for there. They were in business for one reason, to sell records wholesale. I had a pretty good example of what that was like from Essex of Newark. I guess it was early '58 when they closed their old retail store, so their new store at 114 Springfield Avenue was also their wholesale distributorship. That was an extremely vibrant little place. The records were stacked very neatly on the shelves out of the old Jewish merchant tradition in a way, where they had everything. All the 78s were filed by label on shelves. Even though it was almost a 100 percent black area and they were catering to black customers, they had all young white employees there, except that they had their token black stock manager. They published a chart, so you looked at the list on the counter: *Mr. Blues Hits of the Week.* Of course, it was all their records [that they distributed].

I remember in '56 asking them for an Elvis record on Sun, and they went, like, "What the hell?" I was just curious to see what they would say. I was collecting Jim Reeves records on Abbott, a label they had distributed, which was literally defunct at the time. But the black manager, Ricky, let me behind the counter to look. Then the old guy that was the driving force of the business, Pop Cohen, comes over, and he goes in a Russian Jewish accent, "Vot eez he doing here, get heem out, get heem out!" At that point, you saw the other side of this. That was Joe Cohen, Pop Cohen, and Irv Cohen.

But after the New York trip, going back to my ninth-grade class in West Orange High School was a singular disappointment, believe me, because I was fascinated by what these men were doing every day. Of course, at that time I didn't care or I didn't know anything about the nuts and bolts: getting money from the distributors and invoices, anything like that. To me, it was the most glamorous thing in the world. I mean, you could make a record in the afternoon with a group that was auditioning and have it on Alan Freed or Peter Tripp or Jocko that night. To me, there was nothing more exciting in the world. I guess that's why I made the record business my career.

New York Radio and Oldies but Goodies

Donn Fileti, like most teenagers at the time, was an avid radio listener. "Alan Freed was No. 1, not only in New York but nationally. He had a huge influence. Nobody had any kind of comparable influence except Dick Clark, when *American Bandstand* really started in '57 to take hold nationally. But Freed just created one national hit after another and, of course, his [rock 'n' roll] stage shows were unheard of at the time. You can look at the old *Billboard*s when they would have Frank Sinatra, Eddie Fisher, and Johnnie Ray at the Paramount. But Freed, his grosses were just incredible. Then the lines of kids, they had never seen anything like this," said Fileti.

Freed had Figure Music with his partner Jack Hooke.[1] A lot of times the labels were smart enough to give him the publishing on the song to get airplay. They had no idea that these copyrights would be so valuable some day, but that's why there was a lot of split publishing. He also had a few others that were run with Morris Levy's interests; for example, Jackie Music was named after Freed's wife. It's been well documented when payola got out of hand by the beginning of '59. I remember [that] this small record company in New Jersey gave Alan Freed five hundred dollars to play a record, and he played it once! He was arrogant at that point.

At the beginning, he came to New York from Cleveland in August of 1954 to attract white listeners. For whatever reason, he played Tony Bennett, Alan Dale was a favorite, Don Cornell, and people like that. Are they rock 'n' roll or rhythm and blues? Not quite. I think Jocko Henderson was the first black disc jockey to appeal to a white audience. The pioneers were Jack Walker on WOV and Hal Jackson on WLIB [and] Willie [Bryant] and Ray [Carroll] on WHOM (they had a suit against Freed at one point because they thought, "We're black and he's stolen our music"). The problem was that they were on smaller stations; they were on 5,000-watt stations that had directional antennas so they couldn't be heard in certain parts of New York City. They tended to be aimed at specifically a black audience. So on Tommy Smalls's WWRL show, the dedications were all to people in Harlem or Brooklyn.

I was attracted. I would prefer Smalls's show over Freed's because he would play vocal groups. . . . [Another] reason . . . is because he would play the small companies' records. Tommy Robinson of Atlas-Angletone told me he would pay him twenty-five dollars a week. That wouldn't cut it with Freed [*laughs*]. But what happened a lot of times is that somebody like Jocko or Tommy Smalls or Hal Jackson would play a record sometimes for three or four weeks, and then Freed would pick it up. Then it would become a much bigger hit.

There were many records that Freed originated, such as Jackie Wilson's "Lonely Teardrops" [Brunswick]—he'd play it ten times in a row one night—and "Little Star" by the Elegants [Apt]. These things broke in three days in New York. It would be very interesting, and I've always said this, to see . . . how many copies of some of these records were actually sold at that time. Someone like Hy Weiss of Old Town would just have the numbers in his head.

Already there were signs of a rock 'n' roll oldies-but-goodies movement taking hold in the New York area, with selected back catalog items getting consistent airplay and selling on steadily. In building up and promoting their oldies lines, the record companies were reducing their reliance on current hit records. Observed Fileti, "Around early '59, Freed started once a week for fifteen minutes, maybe thirty minutes, playing oldies, because some of the most popular records from the mid-'50s were still requested. Then Bruce Morrow started something called *The Musical Museum* on WINS; he began playing 'Earth Angel' by the Penguins [Dootone], 'In the Still of the Nite' by the Five Satins [Ember], 'This Is My Story' by Gene & Eunice [Aladdin]."

The 1956 hit "The Flying Saucer Part 1 & 2" by (Bill) Buchanan and (Dickie) Goodman (No. 3, Luniverse) was an interesting catalyst in the oldies phenomenon, featuring as it did snippets of some fifteen hits dressed up in the popular sci-fi garb of the day. Known as a "break-in" record, it was an early example of sampling; it was also a splendid means of spreading the R&B word among the hipper teens. Where else could you hear in quick succession the Penguins (disguised as the Pelicans), Chuck Berry (Huckleberry), the Platters (the Clatters), Smiley Lewis (Laughing Lewis), and Fats Domino (Skinny Dynamo)? The hits that were embedded in "The Flying Saucer" saw visible sales spikes, notably "Earth Angel," "Maybellene," "The Great Pretender," "I Hear You Knocking," and "Ain't It a Shame." But the music establishment was not happy. Publishers, record firms, and artists were all plotting to bring "The Flying Saucer" back to earth for breach of copyright. There was trade speculation concerning the perpetrator(s) behind the Luniverse label. And, yes, the omnipresent George Goldner was forced to issue a disclaimer.[2]

An important institution that helped to establish the oldies market in New York was Times Square Record Shop. Recalled Fileti:

> In September of 1959, Alan Fredericks was a white disc jockey who played a good assortment of rock 'n' roll and rhythm and blues on WHOM. This was a Spanish station during the day, and he had a show called *Night Train*. He was sponsored by this tiny store called Times Square Records on a Saturday night, and so he mentions different oldies and different hard-to-get oldies that were stocked. I think he introduced the concept of bringing in old records for credit. The one most in demand was "W-P-L-J" by the Four Deuces [on Ray Dobard's San Francisco label, Music City].[3]
>
> The next day, supposedly, outside of Times Square Records, when Slim Rose, the owner, and his two young boys came to open the store at noon, there were probably two hundred guys in black leather jackets that were standing in line, waiting for the store to open. That was the power of radio. Also, Slim was the first person to start with rock 'n' roll oldies as far as having a reissue label, Times Square Records.
>
> The interesting thing about this whole oldies thing was that the doo-wop sound then in New York was still fairly strong at the end of the 1950s and early 1960s. Slim was responsible directly for the reissue of two records that had gone nowhere and then became revived as national hits: "Rama Lama Ding Dong" by the Edsels and "There's a Moon Out Tonight" by the Capris. Both records ended up with Hy Weiss! The thing is that Hy was sharp enough to sense there was money to be made out of this.
>
> Art Laboe on the West Coast was active on the air, and he was smart enough to do the *Oldies but Goodies* albums on Original Sound [starting in 1959]. That really gave

a whole impetus to the movement. Anything that was on those albums became an instant standard. I mean, nobody had heard of "The Way You Look Tonight" by the Jaguars [R-Dell] until then.

This trend was the first sign of "remember when" nostalgia in rock 'n' roll. In other words, there was a creeping sense that the new records might not be maintaining the character of old.[4]

Donn Fileti was involved with friend Wayne Stierle in the oldies reissue of "Baby Oh Baby" by the Shells (No. 21, Johnson, early 1961). "That had originally come out in 1957," said Fileti.

The owner of the label was a guy named Hiram Johnson, who was the brother of the bandleader Buddy Johnson. He had cut it with Cliff Driver's Combo in the background—very good piano, very haunting sound—on his own label. Then it was picked up for national distribution by George Goldner, but the rights were retained by Johnson. It was a local hit in just Pittsburgh and New York in '57 and disappeared. But when Times Square Records opened in 1959, there was a demand for the record.

Fortunately in '57, the publishing had been given to Freed [through Figure Music], who in early 1960 had moved to KDAY in Los Angeles, California [after the payola scandal had erupted]. When he saw that he owned the publishing, he started to play the "Baby Oh Baby" record. It broke out in L.A., and it became a national hit as a result of Freed's play out there. Later, Jim McCarthy [Buddy Johnson's publicist] bought out Hiram Johnson's interest in the label. McCarthy had trouble with collecting payments. That was another thing, too, because ["Baby Oh Baby"] was never followed up with a hit record. Consequently, I can believe the stories he told me of shipping 2,000 to Oklahoma City and getting 1,999 back, because the distributors would see it rising on the charts, and they would order something like those numbers. In a lot of areas it didn't get played or it didn't sell. I think they ended up with net sales of about 100,000, which is good, but you don't know how much it cost in pressings and everything else.

Doug Moody: Herald-Ember and Clock Records

Some eighteen months after Donn Fileti had made his bright-eyed trip around the New York diskeries, the trade magazines were reporting breathlessly on the avalanche of new independent record label start-ups. Indeed, there was mounting concern that the market was reaching saturation point. That didn't deter the Lowell Music launch of Clock Records at 1619 Broadway in the summer of 1958. Here was another publishing concern testing out the record waters. Heading operations were English-born Walter "Wally" Moody, an EMI recording manager in London's 1930s dance-band era, and professional publisher George Levy.

Young Doug Moody, Wally's chirpy son, handled Clock's sales and promotion. At the same time, Doug was an executive at Al Silver's Herald-Ember combine that had been hitting the high spots with "In the Still of the Nite" by the Five Satins and "Get a Job" by the Silhouettes. It was through Doug Moody that Clock linked up with Al

Silver's subsidiary companies for pressing and distribution, namely Silver-Park Pressing and Ember Distributors.

The promotional budget of Clock Records was swollen from a capital injection by James Kriegsmann when he was recruited into the Lowell Music lineup. Kriegsmann, a theatrical photographer, had opened a studio in 1929 after arriving in New York from Europe. Trading as JJK Copy-Art Photographers, he was the leader in the New York market for artists' publicity photographs that exuded class. By 1950, he was already promoting his business as "the world's largest producer of glossy photographs in quantity," adding that "We Deliver What We Advertise."[5]

The major Clock signing was Dave "Baby" Cortez, a pianist who was earning his daily bread by recording demos for music publishers and undertaking regular session work. On arriving in New York from Detroit in 1955, he performed with the Pearls and the Valentines and cut the occasional single in his own name for Ember, Paris, and OKeh but without making any real noise. "The Happy Organ" was his second single for Clock. Although the tune was credited to Wood (Wally Moody) and Clowney (Cortez) on the disc label, Kriegsmann's name was added when the copyright was registered.

The record was reviewed by *Billboard* on February 16, 1959, with a top rating of "four stars." Entering the Hot 100 chart exactly a month later, this joyful, whistle-along instrumental raced all the way to No. 1 on May 11 before being toppled the next week by Wilbert Harrison's "Kansas City." In effect, this double-header represented a pinnacle for the small indie labels. The background story to "The Happy Organ" is told with enthusiasm by Doug Moody.[6]

"It was a Saturday morning in the fall of 1958 in New York City in the basement of 1650 Broadway," he said.

> This building housed a lot of music publishers and record companies. It had a cigar stand in the lobby, lots of telephones. It would be fun to stand there and listen to all these people trying to sell their songs over the telephone, and to see these song publishers standing around with big cigars in their mouths. The building was quiet on Saturdays, and that was why we recorded there down in the basement. Also, we got to use the echo chamber, and the echo chamber was the elevator. The elevator man, Joe, was an Italian guy. He would ring the bell twice, and that meant we'd stop recording and rehearse the next song.
>
> Anyway, we were down there in the basement, Allegro Recording Studios, run by a man called Charlie Brave. Charlie was in his seventies, he was a leftover from vaudeville and the circus, and had a glass eye. In the studio, we started off at about ten o'clock, not too early, and Dave Clowney [Cortez] is due to record a song called "The Cat and the Dog." He'd lost his voice this morning, he was hoarse, couldn't sing a note. In the studio was Big Buddy Lucas, he is somewhere hovering between 250 and 300 pounds, blows a mean saxophone; Jimmy Spruill was the guitar player, Panama Francis was the drummer, and David was piano player and vocalist.
>
> We had two tracks: we would lay the backing track and catch the vocal later with the lead guitar. This morning, it wasn't going too well because Dave lost his voice. We were about to call the session when David says, "Let me try out an instrumental."

So he goes over to the piano and he's banging away on the piano, which is interesting, and the guys start picking it up. So Charlie starts yelling through the intercom, "Try it on the organ!" Well, they had a huge old Hammond B-3 in the corner.[7]

So Charlie came out and fired it up, and Dave could only play in the key of C on the organ, so he started playing. Well, what he actually was playing was "Shortnin' Bread." The end of the take was rough; it went on and on, and it was all wrong notes. We didn't fade out because that was the [desired] length of the 45; we faded out because it just went wild and was full of wrong notes. There we had it; there was David playing the organ.

The finished record featured the overdubbed organ of Cortez with his piano part being embedded in the original rhythm track. That early fade came just as Jimmy Spruill was beginning to stretch out on one of his distinctive guitar solos. Spruill, of course, would be featured on the next week's No. 1, "Kansas City."

"My father was in the studio," said Doug Moody.

Wally and I were a team in those days. We took an acetate home—that was in New York City—but we were going to spend the rest of the weekend in Long Island where we had a place and I would go out fishing. We played this thing all Sunday; it kept haunting me. I just walked around whistling and humming, and it just stuck with me.

Well, we got through Christmas. I was due to go on a promotion trip around Washington and Baltimore. A friend of mine, Bobby Joyce, was on a small radio station, WLLY (known as the Willy station!), in Richmond, Virginia. Richmond was one of those areas that even in depression times had two industries that kept people working full-time apart from tobacco: aluminum and peanuts. So Richmond, Virginia, is a haven for people with money in their pockets. You could start a record there on WLLY because Bobby was lenient.

The object always was for WLLY to play the record often enough to activate the big station. That was a 50,000-watter down the road, WLEE, which leaked into Baltimore and Washington, D.C., and would make the other stations pick up. So Richmond, Virginia, started developing into a very hot area to break records.

Well, down the road from the radio station was a one-stop, Pat Cohen's [Pat's One Stop]. He would supply all the jukeboxes, not only in Richmond but a lot of them in Baltimore. And when you got Pat intrigued, he would place an order for two hundred records with our distributor, which was in Washington, D.C. [Schwartz Bros., widely respected as one of the best-run distributors anywhere]. That would always excite the distributor, who would send his promotion man to put them on local radio to test them.

Now, Bobby Joyce played the record endlessly on WLLY and, remember, this was just an acetate. The reaction from playing the record was immense; the telephones started to ring. Bobby's playing records, and every other record is "The Happy Organ." So I'm taking the calls and telling everybody about it. And pretty soon we get an irate call from WLEE saying that they will never play another of our records unless I give them a copy. By now Pat Cohen, who's been listening all over the weekend, said, "Give me two hundred records." I said, "Pat, you can't order them from me; you'll have to order them from Jimmy Schwartz in Washington."

So, of course, the routine had started, and this is how records are broken. I had by now one other acetate, so I had to go to Washington, D.C., to give it to Jimmy Schwartz. Jimmy controlled the radio station in what was called Quality Music Store [owned by "Waxie Maxie" Silverman, old friend of Atlantic's Ertegun brothers]. There was a disc jockey sitting in the window. The store became a chain; it was the place you'd jump off a record in Washington, D.C. People came to hear the latest record, and they'd listen to the disc jockey. They'd see him in the window, they'd listen to him in the car, they'd drive by and hoot and wave. And he starts playing "The Happy Organ." So Jimmy Schwartz calls me on the phone; I'm back in New York at the time. He says to me, "You'd better get me a thousand records right away; you've got something here." Well, Wally and I looked at each other and said, "Well, that's torn it; we haven't got a 'B' side!"

There was a young disc jockey in Buffalo called Dick Biondi; he moved from WHOT Youngstown, Ohio. He had become very famous for following in the footsteps of Alan Freed, playing heavily all the new rock 'n' roll stuff. At nighttime on WKBW in Buffalo, New York, Dick Biondi reached fourteen states right across America; probably in those days he was one of the most powerful disc jockeys. Dick and I were quite friendly, and I brought him this record straight up there from Washington, D.C.[8]

Subsequently, I went to see the two underground dee-jays that were down South: Bill "Hoss" Allen and John Richbourg. They probably were responsible for more black records happening than any other disc jockeys in America. So between WKBW and WLAC you could pretty much pull the country, and other stations just jumped on. That's how "The Happy Organ" reached across the country fast. Although the RIAA has never certified or given a gold record, I can testify that we did over a million. Of course, there were 200,000 that were bootlegged, mainly in the Midwest, the Minneapolis and Indianapolis area [also Chicago], where we didn't sell too many records. But the bootleggers did!

"The Happy Organ" was following in a series of instrumental hits sparked off by Bill Doggett's "Honky Tonk" in 1956. Within a year, "Raunchy" had consolidated the popularity of the sax-guitar lineup with the three Top 10 placings, by Bill Justis (Phillips International), Ernie Freeman (Imperial), and Billy Vaughn (Dot). In 1958, the charts were alive to the diverse instrumental sounds of "Tequila" by the Champs (Challenge), "Rebel-Rouser" by Duane Eddy (Jamie), "Patricia" by Perez Prado (RCA Victor), and "Topsy Part 2" by Cozy Cole (Love).

The Dave "Baby" Cortez 1959 No. 1 presaged further teen-organ hits by Johnny and the Hurricanes (Warwick, Bigtop), Bill Black's Combo (Hi), and, a little later, Booker T. & the MGs (Stax). Other banner 1959 chart-makers were "Guitar Boogie Shuffle" (an update of Arthur "Guitar" Smith's tour de force) by the Virtues (Hunt), "Sleep Walk" by Santo & Johnny (a No. 1 on Canadian American), and a record whose title said it all: "Teen Beat" by drummer Sandy Nelson (Original Sound). On the international front, native languages, of course, did not present any barriers to these American instrumental records.

"Another interesting aspect of this story," continued Doug Moody,

is that I had a friend at RCA Victor called Ben Rosner who worked in national distribution for Steve Sholes. Now, Ben said to me that RCA would love to have some of this independent product and have independent people working with RCA. I never felt like working for a major, although I did subsequently work for Mercury-Smash and 20th Century-Fox. So Ben set up a meeting with Steve Sholes. It turned out RCA was having a difficult time promoting their singles, and they wanted to know how we got around promoting our singles. At the time, the independents were all over the charts. Steve had paid $40,000 for Elvis Presley but found it extremely difficult to promote some of his other artists on RCA.

So I made a deal with them. I said, "You can sell a lot more albums than I can." So we gave them an album of Dave "Baby" Cortez, which was released on RCA Victor, and we also gave them an EP of songs. Steve was going to give us singles to promote on Clock, but his legal department stopped it. We discontinued our deal at that point. Cortez's album on RCA was recorded mainly for sale through RCA's distributors. Therefore, [standard] titles like "It's a Sin to Tell a Lie" and "Red Sails in the Sunset" were a combination of talking to Steve Sholes and his staff, because he could not sell too "R&B-ish" sounds. "Deep in the Heart of Texas" had a special promotional force attached to it by Peer-Southern music company, and they actually forced it out as single.

The official Clock follow-up was "The Whistling Organ," but without the same magic in the grooves, it ground to a halt at No. 61.

Doug Moody was never fond of the majors' corporate approach to business: "My father would say, 'Always do something different; keep ahead of the learning curve.' The majors were always stealing ideas; the major record companies were not in the record business. All they were interested in was getting their logos into homes so they could sell other products like TVs, electrical appliances, and record players."

On the vexed topic of erratic royalty accounting by independent companies, Moody was not at all apologetic. "None of the indies paid royalties on the first 30,000 copies," he said. "The majors regarded the indie record men as thieves and pirates, but we were not. We were like a band of brothers doing the impossible. With promotion, for example, you had to pay dee-jays to break records, had the car costs on trips, and you had to have a thousand records in the back of the car. There were no distributors in half the places in North Carolina or South Carolina. So you helped sell your own records in the stores while living on the road. You'd pay for fried chicken with an all-night disc jockey, had fifty-cent showers at the Greyhound bus stations, and rented rooms . . . and then you'd pay yourself a salary at the end of the week."

Doug Moody, who served with the Royal Air Force in Britain (and remembered the 1948–49 Berlin airlift), was always keen to follow father Wally into the music business and did so in England's lean postwar years. Looking for more opportunity, he arrived with his parents in the United States on January 27, 1953, to discover there was a multitude of radio stations, large and small, awaiting him, in contrast to Lord Reith's monopolistic British Broadcasting Corporation (BBC) back home. After taking up posts with record veteran Eli Oberstein and photographer James Kriegsmann (thereby striking up that relationship), Doug Moody ventured into the realm of song publishing.

In July 1957, he joined Al Silver at Herald-Ember Records upon the departure of Bob Rosen to George Goldner's expansion-minded Gone-End group. Silver's labels were hitting with "In the Still of the Nite" and "To the Aisle" by the Five Satins, "Tonite, Tonite" by the Mello-Kings, and, in the South, "When I Meet My Girl" by Tommy Ridgley. As well as acting as A&R staffer, Moody was charged with establishing connections with distributors and dee-jays and assisting Silver with administrative duties at Herald-Ember. In assuming the role of general professional manager at affiliated Angel Music, the young Englishman was forced to divest himself of holdings in Dorchester Music and to terminate his associations with the Kassner, Schaeffer, and Piccadilly publishing houses.[9]

Doug Moody enjoyed the collegiate spirit in the New York indie record business during this period. "It was like a big family," he said.

> They were mostly Jewish; there were a few Italians. I was probably the only Englishman [with father Wally and London's D. H. Toller-Bond] . . . there. My education was incredibly good by hanging out with people like Hy Weiss, George Levy, and Jolly Joyce in the Turf Restaurant next to Jack Dempsey's. You were in the center of New York's music scene.
>
> We would hang out with a cup of coffee in the morning, and we'd all give information to each other: who was stiffing us, who was giving the best deal, what pressing plants were trustworthy. Then we went and worked. Almost everybody got a sandwich at Hector's; it was two dollars for lunch and you had roast beef, corned beef. It was a great school that continued over an evening meal at Al and Dick's. We all paid our own bills, but we sat in a big circle around a big table and talked. If only we'd taped that in those days! We discussed who picked up what and what disc jockey was giving us a fair deal. We were not antagonistic toward each other; we were never competitors. It was like a school and a club, a men's club. There were no women, but occasionally you met the wives, usually at Jewish gatherings and once a year at the BMI awards dinner.

Soon, in January 1958, the Herald-Ember telephone lines were abuzz: Al Silver and Doug Moody were handling a major hit, "Get a Job" by the Silhouettes (Ember). The record reached No. 1 and sold more than a million copies. Everyone seemed to love the universal message of its lyrics and the gimmicky bass-voice hook: *yip-yip-yip-sha-la-lala-badoo*.[10]

The Silhouettes' master of "Get a Job" was purchased from Junior Records for about $2,500 (including hospitality and hotel expenses, as Doug Moody recalled it). This homespun label was run as a sideline in conjunction with Kaiser Records by disc jockey Kae "Loudmouth" Williams of Radio WDAS, Philadelphia. Williams also offered platforms to quality Philly artists Yvonne Baker and the Sensations, Doc Bagby,

Don Gardner, and Rollee McGill (who played the sax solo on "Get a Job"). There was no time to lose in snaring the Silhouettes' record because Ember had a tip-off from Ed Cohn (of Lesco distributors) that Larry Newton at ABC-Paramount and Morty Craft at MGM were in the hunt for the master. Doug Moody remembered sweetening the deal by handing Williams's offspring bars of chocolate and, for his enterprise, ending up covered in the melted confection.

Later, during the payola inquiries, it was disclosed that following the purchase of the "Get a Job" master by Ember, the publishing was placed in the name of Wildcat Music, in which *American Bandstand*'s Tony Mammarella had a declared interest. The "singing canary" on this potentially incriminating snippet of information was the previously helpful distributor Ed Cohn, who also trilled to the federal authorities about parties for disc jockeys "where various unusual things occur and where orgies took place."[11]

"The publishing ensured the exposure nationally," stated Doug Moody, "and coupled with the help of Kae's circle, the disc really took off. We still had to have some 50,000 records on the floors of our distributors nationwide before Dick [Clark] would play it. If there was not a reaction in the trades to his exposure, he could not keep up the plays nationally. And we backed up his play [with promotion]."

Kae Williams could not possibly handle all this action by himself, which is why the sale of "Get a Job" was engineered in the first place. Moody maintained that Al Silver's operation was part of Dick Clark's inner sanctum of labels for regular spins on the popular ABC-TV teen dance show. As a result of this nepotism, Herald-Ember Records (and Silver-Park Pressing) never had it so good. "We all worked with each other," said Moody, "and we were proud of the way we were successful. We did nothing illegal, even if we did bend every rule possible. To us, it was the 'indie' way of doing business."[12]

And so Doug Moody was picking up many tricks of the independent record trade. Understanding the value of performance royalties through his music publishing experience, he compiled a list of radio stations that reported to BMI. "The society only monitored one station in each town per year," said Moody, "and then multiplied the rest by population. The indies shared this information on which stations were being logged. The librarians were responsible for filling out the station logs, and the librarians became very important." Moody and his colleagues would ply the "girls" with perfume and flowers to encourage radio play on these reporting stations. "The resulting income from broadcast royalties financed many of the indie records," he said.

Moody was well aware that the kids tuned in to the record shows on their transistor radios on the way to school and back, and he continued to target aggressively disc jockeys in primary and secondary markets. "If we went into radio through the back door," he stated, "there was no sign saying 'Do not enter'!" The car salesmen came within his sights, too. "They bought much airtime," he said, "and sometimes we gave them 100 records to give to the first 100 visitors on Saturdays. The car people liked to have the kids come with their parents." A favorite promotional medium was arranging personal appearances by artists at these car lots when autographed photographs were given away as inducements to eager teenagers. It was sell, sell, sell all the time.

Then there was the seamier side of the business. According to Moody, the Mafia took control of night shifts at Al Silver's Silver-Park pressing plant by way of union infiltration, leading to counterfeit records and press overruns. Moody pointed a finger at ubiquitous New York discounter Sam Goody for undercutting the traditional record shops on price. "It affected the business very badly," he said. "That was hard on everybody; that's not the way you do it. The mama and papa store is the backbone of the industry."

Alongside the pop and R&B hits, Herald-Ember was getting solid sales with Lightnin' Hopkins's releases. The great Texas bluesman's "My Little Kewpie Doll" was hyped to the trades in May 1958 as "doing just fine in Detroit" by Moody, who recalled Hopkins telephoning regularly from Houston, saying, "Mr. Herald, I'm broke, send me fifty dollars!" Herald was to release one of the most cherished of blues LPs culled from his singles, *Lightnin' and the Blues.*

Puffed up with pride, Moody remembered attending the infamous May 1959 Miami disc jockey convention and having a No. 1 record for the second year running: "Get a Job" (Ember) and now "The Happy Organ" (Clock, distributed by Ember). Moody's future with Al Silver seemed assured when his boss stated publicly, within one month, that he was rewarding his assistant "because of his tremendous capabilities and the reputation he has established in the trade. Jack Braverman, my partner in the three companies, and I feel that he has enhanced our set-up and has been a tremendous asset." As a result, Doug Moody was appointed as company secretary and made a partner. In the package, he would receive a royalty on all masters acquired and placed through Ember. He was still vice president and stockholder in the associated publishing firm Angel Music.[13]

A June article in *Billboard* under the title "Ember Tests Novel Rack Service Plan" emphasized Moody's creative marketing and promotional abilities and also his awareness of the radical change taking place in the working model of the indie companies due to rack selling. It was a clear sign that the independent record men were becoming, out of necessity, more sophisticated in their business practices.[14]

Suddenly, it all ended just two months later. "Moody Exits Herald-Ember," ran the headline to a terse *Billboard* news item of August 10, 1959: "Doug Moody, youthful British-born veepee of Herald-Ember, has resigned his post and given up his interest in the combine, effective this week. Moody, son of Brill Building publisher Wally Moody, of Lowell and Mecca Music, will take a three-week vacation, after which he's expected to announce his plans."[15] Moody would never discuss the reasons behind his rapid departure. It was an anticlimactic conclusion to a sizzling partnership, just as the payola clouds were looming on the horizon.

Jeffrey Kruger: Ember International Records

Jeffrey Kruger, a buccaneering English entrepreneur from London's East End, had a broken relationship with Al Silver, too. Since 1957, they had a masters and subpublishing agreement, and in anticipation of consolidating that arrangement, Kruger set up the Ember International label in London for releasing the Herald-Ember catalog abroad. Then two years later came the betrayal: Al Silver signed a deal with Top Rank Records, a division of the Rank Organisation film company, which was seeking in vain to emulate the successful international licensing strategy of Decca's London American group.[16] Kruger, despite this setback with Silver, pressed on with his Ember label but without the Herald-Ember affiliation. His most glamorous operation would turn out to be the Flamingo club, a throbbing cradle of the British R&B boom during London's "Swinging Sixties" era.

Jeff Kruger's recollections of his encounters with Al Silver and Doug Moody provided a rare contemporaneous overview of the overseas potential for the U.S. indie labels.

I first became aware of the American independent record scene from my first trip to the United States. It was in 1953 or 1954. All I could afford was a trip over by a noncommercial boat, which was delayed by heavy storms and took eight days to reach the port of New York. I had a chance to go through the record shops and saw all these different labels, which I was not aware of. This initially turned me on to the independent record scene, which was, at that time, totally nonexistent in England. There, the record business was dominated by and comprised of a monopoly with the labels from EMI, Decca, Philips, and Pye with one independent being Oriole Records, who served, via their Embassy label, mainly the Woolworth's chain. There was one specialist Jamaican label called Melodisc, but other than that, the independents had no distribution in the U.K., nowhere to press, and nowhere to promote. So it was refreshing for me to see so many independent labels in New York.

At that time, I was concentrating on the Flamingo club and the management of jazz artists and concert promotions at the American air force bases and starting to build my music publishing company. I had no thought of having a record label. I met Al Silver and his wife, and there was initially a mutual comradeship and friendship. I enjoyed the company of the Silvers more socially than for business at the start. Doug Moody ran the place, but we were not what I would call close, although I knew his father, Walter Moody. Initially, I saw Al Silver as a conduit to add an American catalog to my music publishing—he owned Angel Music, Inc.

Indeed, in August 1957, which was a long time after my first trip, I did sign a deal with Al Silver for me to represent Angel Music ex-U.S.A. and for Angel to represent my Florida Music publishing company in the U.S. We were still not at the stage of my thinking of having a record label. In order to help build the publishing, I wanted to get many U.S. Ember records out onto the British market. Al had then no representation, being busy enough in the United States.

So I took on the task of initially sublicensing what I could until such time as a joint Ember U.K. label could be set up. I was closest in a relationship to Len Wood, then general manager of EMI. Sir Edward Lewis of Decca was a snob! I think he saw my endeavors as an affront to his empire and refused to help or talk, even though I said he could never stop the launch of an independent label or labels.

L. G. Wood reintroduced me to Norrie Paramor, who with George Martin [later the Beatles' producer] was running Columbia and Parlophone. At the time, Walter Ridley was running HMV with a solo strength brooking no interference [his power enforced by overseeing Elvis Presley's early RCA hits]. Norrie saw the potential with Ember, but once Ridley saw something new, he wanted it for HMV. So we issued the first product, "The Joker" by Billy Myles, on HMV in 1957. This was followed by "Get a Job" by the Silhouettes on Parlophone, which then was not a successful label for international acts.[17]

Al Silver was not disappointed that Parlophone did not get a hit out of "Get a Job." Indeed, he was shocked that I'd managed to get a major label to release the recording at all and that it was understood in the United Kingdom and in Europe. The fact that it came out was a triumph for an independent American label, to get its product out via the mighty and monopolistic EMI. I broke the mold and succeeded where others had previously failed; that was the criteria. Then Al did his ill-fated deal with Top Rank in summer 1959.

Of course, he was subsequently upset by my use of the Ember name and at blocking him out. But by that time, he was forced legally to settle with me on both the publishing front and the record front. He knew I would not trust him any further. He made threats, but my lawyer at the time, Benjamin Starr, just made it clear to Al Silver that I would fight him tooth and nail. He would have to fight me on my territory and under English law. Either he didn't have the wherewithal to fight or the inclination, but it was only justice that I finished up with the Ember name.

There is no question that around 1957 and 1958, Herald-Ember was a very successful enterprise. What made it tick was the mutual admiration society between Doug and Al, their entrepreneurial skills, the fact that they never looked at a clock, and they were only interested in the music. If it excited them, then they wanted that record pressed and out and on the air within minutes, as it were, of the session ending. They both had great ears. Whilst Al was the owner, I think that Doug was no less an important part of the operation, and I would say it was a 55/45 endeavor.

The label had success after success after success. Whilst it did its best to cope with paperwork, their first priority was to record and get recordings out and on the air. And the money was rolling in. The reason it collapsed, so far as I am aware, is they made no provision for paying out all of their royalties, although they did pay where they had to. They could not cope with the paperwork, nor could they handle correspondence in a quick manner, and they forgot about a little matter called taxes. Once the Internal Revenue Service leaned on Al Silver, that was the beginning of the end of all his operations. I hope I am not libeling the late Al Silver when I say that he was spending and living at a rate far above his net income. In fact, I think the decline of the independent record scene can be summed up in one word: Greed!

Herald's last big hit was "Stay" by Maurice Williams and the Zodiacs (formerly the Gladiolas on Excello), which made No. 1 in November 1960 but only rose to No. 14 on Top Rank in the U.K. The record was publicized as the "shortest ever" to make the top spot, at one minute, thirty-four seconds. Herald-Ember struggled on until early 1965, after which the masters were picked up cheaply by Bell Records—as Bell did with the Fire-Fury catalog. Angel Music had already been sold off to Murray Sporn, a decision that Al Silver much regretted later on. As Silver told author Arnold Shaw, he was a record man gambling on the next hit record, not a music publisher.[18]

"We had the chance of buying the Herald-Ember masters for around $15,000," recalled Donn Fileti of Relic Records, "because Al Silver didn't pay his back taxes.[19] Oh, $15,000 was a huge amount for us then. But what was the choice for him of dissolving the catalog: selling it, or go[ing] to jail? Al Silver obviously took the easy way out. But what a shame, considering what he could have made with 'In the Still of the Nite,' 'Get a Job,' 'Stay,' . . . 'Story Untold' [the Nutmegs], 'Tonite, Tonite' [the Mello-Kings], and 'When You Dance' [the Turbans]. I mean, in the 1970s they were being used in movies such as *American Graffiti*. And that poor guy had to work in a liquor store."[20]

Doug Moody never accrued the rewards that many record men did, either. After spells with Mercury-Smash and 20th Century-Fox, he moved to California in 1968 where he formed Mystic Records as a niche "thrash" (punk-type) music label. In 2008, he was living contentedly in California but occasionally wondered what might have been. He was selling Mystic CDs and handling licensing deals for the Clock and Mystic masters but, unfortunately for him, not the Herald-Ember catalog. Even though a resident in America for over fifty years, he retained the air of a jovial Englishman who would not be out of place, glass of gin and tonic in hand, at Cheltenham races, Lords cricket ground, or Henley Royal Regatta. Still, he could look back with satisfaction and a smile to the time when he was, as he called it, a "record pie-in-the-sky man."

Maxine Brown: Nomar, ABC-Paramount, and Scepter-Wand Records Artist

Maxine Brown has remained a soul survivor. Coming up the well-trodden migratory trail from South Carolina to New York as a young girl, she did not record professionally until 1960. At this juncture, the independent record companies were trying to come to grips with the aftermath of the payola scandal. It was also a time when sinister influences were taking deeper root in the industry. Nevertheless, Nomar—Maxine Brown's first contracted label—revealed the opportunities that were still open to newcomers in the record business with the right artist, the right sound, and the right song.

The genesis of Nomar Records was unusual, to say the least. Initially, Maxine Brown had no idea that the label was a front for a bookmaker's racket in the Brill Building and remained hazy about its background.[21] "Tony Bruno, I understand, was a writer with his wife, Brenda," Brown said, "and they had a pretty good publishing firm. Tony ran Nomar for a guy who I think owned a pizza parlor in New Jersey [*laughs*].

No one ever saw him! Tony was the company." Probably the last thing that the New Jersey investor (later identified by Bruno to Brown as one Joe Romano) wanted was a hit record to blow the bookmaking cover. But that is precisely what happened when Maxine Brown's charismatic blues ballad "All in My Mind" hit big in early 1961 (at No. 19 pop, No. 2 R&B).

Before relating the Nomar episode, Brown spelled out what it was like to break through at the time from a woman's vantage point—and a black lady's, at that. "It was h-a-r-d," she said.

> Hard! Even though I had been singing during the 1950s [including vocal group demos], I wasn't a hit or anything, because you had just come off the Pat Boone bobby-sox era; you came off the good-looking kid who catches all the girls: Bobby Darin, Bobby Rydell, Frankie Avalon, and Fabian.
>
> I made my debut at the Apollo Theatre on January 1 with Jocko Henderson. That's how I could always remember the date; I really started in '61. I was backed at the Apollo by the Reuben Phillips band. Yeah, it was beautiful. You see, we came from an era where there were musicians live onstage, loved it, twelve to fifteen pieces, yeah. Then you'd bring your own rhythm section. "All in My Mind" was starting to break; it was instant.

The man behind "All in My Mind" was Mal Williams, a hustling booking agent, would-be record producer, and Maxine Brown's soon-to-be husband. They had met by chance at a club on Linden Boulevard in Jamaica, Queens. Quickly appreciating her potential, Williams arranged a split demo session at the basement Allegro studio at 1650 Broadway with a small combo including Jimmy Spruill, the remarkable "Kansas City" guitarist from the Bronx, and a captivating but unknown trombone player. "Oh now, here's the fun," said Brown, chuckling.

> Now remember, I am nobody at that point. So now Mal has to peddle this material to see who would want it, because whoever would want it would rerecord it, probably. He went to all of the major labels, ABC, Columbia, all of 'em, and they said, "I'm sorry, girls are not happening." That's why I said, "Hard!"
>
> So girls were not happening, and Mal was stuck with this demo. One day I was leaning on this parking meter right in front of the Brill Building, and everyone was flowing out of the building. Tony Bruno came out with a crowd of people. The elevator had just emptied out, and he said, "Hey, Mal, what have you got?" And Mal said, "Well, I've got this demo," which he held up, "*and* her." I just thought he said it kinda funny—what do you mean, "her"? So, Tony said, "Well, why don't you bring it up tomorrow and let me hear it?"
>
> When Tony Bruno heard my record, he flipped, and he put that record out instantly. I cut it in September, it was out in October, and it was already starting to make national sales. It was by the flip of a coin that my record made it [due to a quick cover version]. At that time, we used to be able to play a song on the telephone in different cities to let your different distributors hear it. There was a way that you had a phone hookup that you could listen. The people in Chicago must have recorded it, because they taught my song overnight to a young girl.

That artist was Terri Anders (Chief). Then Linda Hopkins (Brunswick) jumped on "All in My Mind," and so did Bobby Marchan (Fire). But Maxine's superior version of her own song prevailed (although she shared writer credits with Freddy Johnson and Leroy Kirkland).

It didn't take long for the knockout punch to be delivered. "We're talking openly here," Brown confided.

Tony Bruno and Mal Williams went to the distributors to get my first pay from the sales of my record, 'cause the record made it, like, phew, overnight. Then I understand that they were backed out of the door *with guns*. My first time saying this! Yeah, whoever those distributors were, they refused to pay and told them they had better get moving. This is the story that came down to me.

The mob was all over the place from the beginning. That's how I didn't get my first royalty. I never got paid, so I never knew what if felt like to be a real star; I had a name, but I wasn't rich. I thought I would get the cars and the houses . . . something, something [*laughs*]. Oh yeah, within the business it was well known who was who. Mal owed them for some reason. And then he had to pay; he had to work it off.

I had no idea about publishing, no! The publishing company was, believe it or not, Alan Freed's and was run by his sidekick, Jack Hooke. It was Figure Music, and Mal peddled the song to them. It wasn't known then, but I was married to Mal. We came off the era when they wanted their stars single, and they did likewise with me. They kept me single publicly; it was the record company's idea. I was married on December 27, 1960, just as the song was being hatched, yeah.

To compound her difficulties, she struggled to get her first BMI writer's check. "Having the name Maxine Brown created a problem from the very beginning," she said. "BMI called me, because I wrote the song, and said, 'You have to change your name.' I say, 'No way! Why do I have to change my name?' They said, 'Because there's another Maxine Brown out there. . . . She's with the Browns.' That was Jim Brown and his sister Maxine [who had] 'The Three Bells.' I got the songwriting performance royalties through BMI, eventually. It took six months to get that check back."

Later, Brown attempted to recover her song from the publisher, who by now was none other than Morris Levy:

He had the "All in My Mind" copyright at one point through Alan Freed, so I said I'd like to buy back the [publishing] rights. He laughed so hard, as if it was the biggest joke ever. I said, "I am serious." He said, "Go home!" [*blows a raspberry*]. You know, we were around [people like him], but it wasn't frightening.

We recorded in the era that you had to renew the copyright every twenty-eight years. So people had to keep their eye on their material. If not, anyone can go along and pick up the material. I went over to EMI Music, [and] the guy over there told me: "You should keep your eye on the material, because it'll be due in another five years." I'm glad he told me, and lo and behold, after Leroy Kirkland had passed, his estate . . . don't you know that they went in and claimed the song? Don't you know that [ex-husband] Mal Williams kept his eye on the copyright, and don't you know he claimed it? And they were all gonna cut me out. I could have lost that copyright. So that's the one legacy that I still have; it's still earning money.

Still on Nomar, Maxine Brown managed to avoid the ignominious "one-hit wonder" tag when the follow-up, "Funny" (written by her guitarist, Sammy Taylor), climbed to No. 25 pop and No. 3 R&B in the late spring of 1961. As an aside, the label of the 45–rpm single indicated that this record was distributed by one Muse Products.²² Was this the distributor that had refused to pay Tony Bruno and Mal Williams? At least the twin hit records created demand for Maxine's services as a top-class live act with superb stage presence.

"The only money I ever got was when I sang," she said.

I guess that's why I lean so heavily on performing, because that's the only thing I could depend on. I was with the Shaw Booking Agency at the time, with Ray Charles, Miles Davis, and so on. Shaw would book you on that chitlin' circuit; that's all they knew. Yeah, down South, all over the country, we made tours that never made sense, travel-wise. We'd be exhausted because they'll send you to Boston today, and you're in South Carolina tomorrow; then you're out in Virginia, and the next thing you're in Oklahoma. They just grabbed wherever the next money was. Until you were on a big bus tour, which was important, you traveled by your car. . . . That's when some interstates were happening. That's why the stars way back then believed in Cadillacs—that was the epitome of "I have arrived."

It was like in the movies—the kids would be running down the street, and you'd have your driver circle the town. Of course, I had my name on the side of the station wagon; the lettering was *The Maxine Brown Show.* So that was the advertisement, and the promoter would want you to roll through town because he's got placards up all over the place, and then you visited the local disc jockey. Oh God, it was like the old circus days [laughs].

Then I left Nomar, and I went to ABC-Paramount. They accepted us, and Ray Charles was over there just before he cut that big country and western song, "I Can't Stop Loving You." I got caught in the backwash of the Ray Charles country music phenomenon. I didn't have a successful time over there at ABC at all.

Enter center stage Florence Greenberg, the fascinating head of rapidly expanding Scepter-Wand Records. Her company was flush with a run of big hits by the Shirelles and was about to score again with Dionne Warwick, through Burt Bacharach. "So one day," said Maxine Brown,

we were all in a restaurant, right downstairs from 1650 [Broadway], right on the corner. Florence Greenberg, some of the Shirelles, and a bunch of writers were all in the back; they were sharing tables and having lunch and talking about the day's events. Florence saw me come in, so she came over to my table, and she says, "When are you going to leave that company who's doing nothing for you"—referring to ABC-Paramount—"and come to me?" I said, "Well, if you want me, go get me" [laughs]. The next day, you know, she did; she did.

She went over there, negotiated a deal with ABC-Paramount, took everything out of their vaults that they had on me, and brought them over to Scepter Records. Her reason for doing that, whether she sold any of those, was unimportant. She didn't want ABC to release them in case she got a hit with me; she didn't want ABC to go along for a free ride. It was a smart move. My ABC contract hadn't even expired; she just bought me out. Now, little did I know, that later everything is charged to me. Whatever deal she made, it still cost me, the artist. So I never got a dime.

Yeah, yeah, Florence was tough; she was tough! Everyone at the company became like a family, because the Shirelles were there first. I knew she came from some sort of money background. She came in with capital but very little know-how, just guts and ambition and determination.

For Wand Records, the Scepter subsidiary, Maxine Brown had ten Top 100 entries during the 1963–67 period, the biggest being "Oh No Not My Baby" (written by Carole King and Gerry Goffin) at No. 24 in 1964. She participated in a string of duets with label mate Chuck Jackson, including "Something You Got" (No. 10 R&B, 1965).

But it was a troubling time for many at 1650 Broadway. "We had an office and we had secretaries and we had all of this stuff, oh yes," said Brown. "I had an office in 1650, which was later taken over by the mob. I am telling it now because Mal is dead, but they are still here. It got so bad with my husband, the way he got in trouble, and the next thing you know, he is hooked on drugs and stuff like that. So every dime I ever made in this business came from my blood, sweat, and tears."

Others were caught up in the crossfire of Mafia turf wars of "Brooklyn people" against "New York people," Brown said. As a footnote, even Florence Greenburg was not immune to the familiar mob threat "to hang her out of the window at 1650." "I don't know too much," added Maxine Brown, "but that's how she was forced into certain situations, and that's why she gave up."

In reflecting upon the many handicaps facing her fellow recording artists, Brown saw their failings, too:

Back then, the artists were kept in ignorance by record companies, and also by some managers. But the males: their egos were so big that all they wanted was to make money, have large cars, and catch women. And the women [singers] were weak for thinking that the man who was controlling her life was so much wiser and stronger than she, when she [was] actually the one who [was] doing the work and . . . [had] the talent.

Yes, it was a social product at the time. It wasn't just in the music and entertainment business. Oh, the men with the alligator shoes, the sea-green suit, the hot red suit, the yellow suit, all of this. The louder you were, the more attention you got; it was almost like a need for that. A lot of this was coming out of their royalties, but at least they had their live performances that came directly to them. All they had to do was pay the agent and/or manager. But where their ignorance came in is that they blew all their money. They lived high [on] whatever they made, they lived on the hog for the moment, or got deeper in debt, because they had to have these suits and cars: the male! Then they find out, when they get in trouble [after the hits dry up], that they have nothing to fall back on. There's nothing; there's no business under them that they can call on if they get sick or someone died. People have to take up a collection for them. So that's the sad part.[23]

Maxine Brown was gracious when she added up the scorecard for the independent record men and women of the 1950s and '60s: "The good points . . . they knew how to pick an artist, get . . . the material, and creat[e] . . . a hit with these people. 'Cause these are 'nothing' people when they're found. A big company would not go out looking for them. And the negative part is that they never played fair with the money. But they were struggling, too, because they had to do all the legal stuff: see that you get a [song] license, see that the songs get to the proper societies. And then they would have returns. Get paid . . . I didn't know how badly they were suffering, but they were suffering. And the era moved on."

20
CHAPTER

Gold Coast Platters and Stock Matters

CAST OF CHARACTERS
Shelley Galehouse, Clark Galehouse's daughter
Dorothea Lorenzo, Clark Galehouse's sister
Joe Dreyhaupt, vice president and pressing plant manager,
    Shelley Products
John Greek, Golden Crest artist (The Wailers)
Art Mineo, composer
Morty Wax, promotion man
Billy Mure, session man, producer, and Valentine Records
Harvey Phillips, Golden Crest artist (New York Brass
    Quintet)
*also featuring Clark Galehouse, Golden Crest Records
    and Shelley Products pressing plant*

Famed for its Gold Coast as portrayed in F. Scott Fitzgerald's *The Great Gatsby* and as the setting for the original suburban dream, Long Island was home to record men Jerry Blaine, Archie Bleyer, Joe Carlton, Bob Shad, Al Silver, Mike Stoller, and Jerry Wexler. "We smell the same sea breeze!" exclaimed Hy Weiss, another noted resident. Nestled off the South Shore is Fire Island, which was the summer playground (long before the Hamptons took over that role) where high-flyers Ahmet Ertegun, Wexler again, and Arthur Shimkin used to party with the Atlantic (the ocean, that is) rolling in.

Yet Long Island was hardly full of indigenous record companies. Realtor Lou Fargo scored a No. 21 left-field hit in 1958 with the mesmeric "You" by the Aquatones on his Fargo label out of Valley Stream in Nassau County after ABC-Paramount took over national distribution. Then Clark Galehouse had Golden Crest Records in Huntington Station, Suffolk County, and that was about it. While there was a strong club network from Queens in the west to Riverhead in the east, there was no identifiable local music style due to the Island's location near New York.

Clark Galehouse: Golden Crest and Shelley Records and Shelley Products Pressing Plant

Golden Crest Records attracted many artists and composers from Long Island itself and from Queens, Brooklyn, and New York City. The core Clark Galehouse business, however, was the Shelley Products pressing plant, which gave continual life support to the record company division. Galehouse described it to his only child, Shelley, as "my bread and butter."[1] Whereas self-owned pressing facilities were an integral factor behind the growth of labels such as Chess, Herald-Ember, King, Mercury, Modern, and Specialty, Galehouse's many noncommercial ventures (even if artistically worthy and well recorded) ensured that Golden Crest Records would never be in the same league.

The output of Golden Crest was akin to that of a musical chameleon, covering many different shades and colors of the American music spectrum that were largely alien to the average teenager. With his broad tastes rooted in the swing band era, Clark Galehouse saw the releases primarily as extensions of his passion for the art of recording and as educational tools. Furthermore, he understood from an early date that albums were the future of the record industry and preferred to build up an extensive LP catalog at the expense of the 45.

Golden Crest was active between 1956 and 1986, well beyond the life span of most independent record companies. Occasional tilts were made at the singles charts, but there were just two Top 100 hits, both by the Wailers from Washington State. Actually, it's three if "Tall Cool One" is counted twice (No. 36, 1959; No. 38, 1964) along with a token appearance from the 1959 follow-up, "Mau-Mau" (No. 68). And if the *Cash Box* charts are included, the grand total is four with "Billy Boy's Tune" by the Three Graces (just No. 100 for all of two weeks, late summer 1959). That's an abysmal tally, considering that the label and its subsidiaries released some two hundred singles.

Still, Clark Galehouse, the son of an Iowan country town jeweler of Germanic origins, was one determined record man. With his musical knowledge, experience, and quick-witted one-liner asides, he was universally liked within the business, even if he had occasional temper outbursts. His early years in music were recalled by his sister, Dorothea Lorenzo, in a written testimonial:

> Clark was active in high school in all sorts of musical endeavors. He sang in the glee club, in a trio, and solo and played clarinet in the band and violin in the orchestra; he won the state contest in violin in his senior year. Clark enrolled at Drake University, Des Moines, Iowa, in the music department. Clark's love for the big bands lured him away from college in his junior year; mom and dad were very disappointed, but Clark had a strong mind of his own. From a local band, he joined Bernie Lowe's group and they started traveling.[2] Clark toured the country with Paul Whiteman, Anson Weeks, Joe Venuti, and Red Norvo and doubled as arranger. From that time Clark entered the

big band world in Chicago.[3] My brother ended in New York where a tight musician's union would not allow an outsider to play publicly until he had been in residence in the city for a year. He stayed at Buck Ram's home that year arranging for Buck, although the arrangements went out in Buck's name. Clark quit playing with bands when he married Aleece [a swing jazz harpist] in 1939. He had seen too many marriages dissolve with the time spent away from home and playing every evening and holidays. He wanted a home life.

Upon becoming a union cardholder, Clark Galehouse played his $148 Conn tenor saxophone on recording sessions in 1939 with great friend and vaunted jazz violinist Joe Venuti (Decca), Redd Evans and His Billy Boys (Vocalion), and the Quintones as a member of Buck Ram's Orchestra that included future jazz stars trumpeter Buck Clayton and drummer Jo Jones (Vocalion, OKeh). Galehouse was also a stock arranger for Mills Music and Paramount Publishers. These traditional Tin Pan Alley connections gained him a foothold in the New York music network and would serve him well in the future. But for the time, Clark Galehouse's budding music career was stopped in its tracks by marriage and by the war.

Continued sister Dorothea: "After quitting music, he spent some time as a salesman selling Boonton Ware plastic dinner services. But he was unhappy and unfulfilled in the job. During World War II he worked for Sperry Rand in Long Island making parts for the military. Clark met Arnold Brilhart, another musician, and together they designed and manufactured the Brilhart mouthpiece for sax and clarinet from plastic. It became very popular and was used by many musicians in big bands. The Brilhart mouthpiece led to a studio in New York where they made and sold high-quality lamps which sold for $150 and up. When he and Arnold parted, he set up his own pressing plant. He told me it was a difficult process because he had no training in math at a high level."

Clark Galehouse raised the much-needed start-up capital for the pressing plant from Mike Friedman, whose family operated large stores in nearby Brooklyn. Galehouse, with a 51 percent stake, was elected president; Friedman took the remaining 49 percent stock and the title of vice president. Named after Clark's baby daughter at Friedman's suggestion, the Shelley Products pressing plant business was started modestly from a garage in Roslyn on Long Island's North Shore. According to Mike Friedman's widow, Eve, the Shelley factory was set up in "1947 or 1948" to manufacture 78–rpm records as contractors for Columbia and RCA Victor. "Everybody was listening to music at the time," she said. The first pressing machine was assembled by IMPCO (Improved Machinery Products Corporation) of Nashua, New Hampshire.

Galehouse's own first releases appear to have been a series of twelve children's six-inch records at 78 rpm pressed in blue styrene entitled *Daddy Lew Lehr Tells a Story* on the Shelley Products label. The accompanying picture wheels, gorgeously printed, show a 1948 copyright date. As the records featured narratives (and not music) by Lehr, famed for his voiceovers on Movietone News, there was no Petrillo recording ban to worry about.

By 1952, Galehouse had relocated his pressing plant operations farther east to larger premises within the industrial zone of Huntington Station, adjoining the railway station at 220 Broadway. The move was timed exquisitely to exploit that promising new innovation: the unbreakable 45–rpm single. By now, Mike Friedman's capital investment had shot up to almost $500,000, according to wife Eve. It was an astonishing show of confidence in Galehouse's abilities and in the future of the record industry itself. Orders to Shelley Products for overspill pressings of 45–rpm singles were pouring in from major labels RCA Victor and Columbia (with its OKeh subsidiary) and also from Capitol and Mercury when their own plants were fully committed. Other customers may have included fast-growing Atlantic, London, Prestige, and Varsity, based on circumstantial family evidence. Clark Galehouse was well on his way to creating a significant one-stop record manufacturing facility.

Still, Galehouse wanted to take his fervor for music to the next logical stage by resurrecting the record label idea. Started in early 1953 with pop and country series, Crest Records was named after his family hometown of Creston, Iowa. The principal artist was Arizona Cliff Martin, a cowboy singer. That was more or less the kiss of death in the New York area, where there were only small pockets of country music— even allowing for the popularity of western movies.

Joe Dreyhaupt: Pressing Plant Manager

By 1955, management problems were mounting at Shelley Products. As a solution, a Kentucky plating company supervisor recommended to Clark Galehouse the experienced, conscientious Joe Dreyhaupt as pressing plant manager. "You know, Clark, your quality is not always the greatest, and you have poor production control," Dreyhaupt remembered his supervisor saying. Years later, Dreyhaupt added, "He had none." At the interview, Clark told Joe curtly, "You're looking for a job. I'll give you a hundred dollars a week, take it or leave it."

Joe Dreyhaupt was an engineer in the Merchant Marine during World War II. When hostilities ended, he became a maintenance man at Pilot Radio in Long Island City, Queens. Running its own Pilotone label, the company manufactured what it called "the *wonder record* of the new post-war world on *non-breakable* vinylite."[4] It couldn't have been that wonderful, because the record division was soon folded. So Dreyhaupt landed a job with Raleigh Records, which made ten-inch shellac records and sixteen-inch transcription discs for radio broadcasting and was located in lower Manhattan on Fulton Street and Broadway.

There, Dreyhaupt could hear the subway trains rumbling *above* the low-rent basement premises. He was quite forthright about pressing plant work. "An important historical aspect of the record business is that in its early days, it was essentially a sweatshop operation," he said. "Sometimes people worked for eighteen hours at a time. It was not good for your health. But vinyl fumes were more dangerous than the shellac." The pressing plant in the dungeons must have had the foreboding atmosphere of an oppressive factory in Victorian times. There was the clang and bang and hiss of the pressing machines, the smell of molten wax, and the steam and the heat. This was pre–rock 'n' roll at its most primeval.

After toiling in the New York pressing plant, Joe Dreyhaupt came up for air when he took to the road as a salesman for two companies affiliated with Raleigh Records that were based in Kentucky. He was hawking products that Shelley Products was using in the record manufacturing process, notably the compounds and the electroplating ingredients for the metal parts. Hence the referral to Clark Galehouse was made.

Galehouse's command of plastics had led him to introduce a four-cavity press for the manufacture of records by injection mold. This revolutionary process, by polystyrene, not vinyl, enabled records to be turned out quickly in volume. A *Billboard* report back in 1950 noted that "one injection mold diskery, Shelley Products, Ltd., of Roslyn, L.I., N.Y., is already set up to press 45 and 33⅓ r.p.m. disks at the market's lowest rates for quantity orders."

Although Clark Galehouse designed a press that operated automatically instead of manually, he did not invent the *process*. That was originated by Bestway Products, which worked closely in the developmental stages with Columbia Records, according to *Billboard*. Yet Galehouse did not patent this or any other of his inventions, according to Eve Friedman.

That same 1950 *Billboard* report indicated that Shelley and Bestway were the only two plants "in the vicinity" using this process, but others were experimenting with it. The story concluded by stating that "Shelley Products, headed by Clark Galehouse, has three larger [than Bestway] multiple units and produces seven and 10–inch platters. Galehouse (who, incidentally, is a former arranger and tenor sax man for Red Norvo, Mildred Bailey and Joe Venuti) claims that his plant can turn out 400,000 seven-inch and 200,000 10–inch discs per month."[5]

Fascinatingly, Joe Dreyhaupt remembered being told by Galehouse that in developing the automatic injection molded idea, he worked "in collusion with somebody from Mercury Records who was trying to do the same thing." It could possibly have been Irving Green, "but Clark had a falling out with them [Mercury]."

The mechanics of the prototype injection-molding machine at Shelley Products, as well as the early trials and errors, were described by Dreyhaupt:

The labels were impressed into the records. Then, hydraulically, pins would move up and puncture the center of the record, it would retract, and the mold would open. A great big air-operated retriever arm would come in with four suction cups on it, pick up the four records, [and] bring them out. That was the theory: you'd drop four records in four separate boxes. With the very first machine, it didn't work too well. It was kind of a clumsy operation; it was slow. It was hard to control the molding process—it made a lot of rejects—but it lent itself very well to 45s, finally.

With the conventional *compression* system, the timing of that operation was very important; otherwise, it would warp or dish the record. The majority of 45s were still produced by compression molding. Finally, an automated compression-molding machine was invented that would make two 45s at one time, but the speed would not compare with ours.

Up until the time that we put in the compression-molding machines with a vinyl operation, we were trying to make ten-inch and twelve-inch records by injection molding machines. That was a disadvantage; it did not lend itself well to those formats. Mercury Records made injection-molded large records; Columbia Records also did it. But we were able to custom-mold for Columbia Records for 45s because they were used to injection-molded polystyrene records. With 45s, injection-mold polystyrene was automated and quicker. You could operate it with very little labor.[6]

The contrasting pressing methods, compression and injection-mold, were summarized beautifully by Golden Records' Arthur Shimkin, who was familiar with Shelley competitor Al Massler's Bestway Products operation in New Jersey. "Regular presses had one press," he said, "with the 'A' side stamper on top and the 'B' side stamper on the bottom. Records were trimmed and placed on a cooling spindle. With a four-cavity press there was no vinyl biscuit, but a powdered polystyrene compound was used instead. The mold came together like a clasp and had a plastic cavity; four records could be pressed every twenty-eight seconds. The labels were [affixed] on the record, and a blue label was best."[7]

The Shelley Products pressing plant may have been Clark Galehouse's cash cow, but he loved producing, engineering, and mixing sessions. He would make regular trips to tape university and college bands on location, giving opportunities for promising musicians to record. To make a record was still a thing of glamour at the time. Clark was quoted by his sister Dorothea as saying, "Give a kid a horn, and he's going to be a good kid and a good citizen." There was a commercial payback, though: the young musicians and their families and friends purchased thousands of the custom-pressed concert recordings from Crest through the mail.

In 1956, Crest Records was supplanted as the singles vehicle by Golden Crest, with Crest being retained as the education division. The prominent early Golden Crest artist was sultry songstress Pat O'Day, but after three 45s and one album, she was whisked away by RCA Victor. Two years later, she had a one-off single release on Chess.

Clark Galehouse was very much part of that pre–rock 'n' roll generation, and this explains why Golden Crest was never chock-full of teen material. "He was disdainful of pop music for the most part," said Joe Dreyhaupt. "I remember discussing with him what had popular appeal, and I brought in a Frank Sinatra record and played it for him. He dismissed it by saying, 'That guy has no talent, he has a terrible reputation, a bad personality.' Even though pop music was what we made most of, he didn't care much for it. He liked quality music, whether it was popular music, orchestral, or choral: ungadgeted."

This aversion to gimmicks placed Galehouse at a severe disadvantage in the singles market of the time. He first stumbled upon rock 'n' roll with Mando and the Chili Peppers after being stranded in a snowstorm during a trip to Denver, Colorado, of all places. This trendsetting Tex-Mex group had come up from San Antonio to play a long club residency. Their debut Golden Crest single in 1956, "South of the Border," made some impact in the New Orleans area and led to the release of their highly collectible album, *On the Road with Rock 'n' Roll.* An evocative cover jacket caught the wanderlust spirit of the period by showing the group studying a map alongside their touring Packard.

The first R&B single on Golden Crest featured ex-Josie artist Calvin "Houn' Dog" Ruffin in a nicely relaxed Fats Domino style. These masters were supplied by Lillian Claiborne, who would dispatch a steady stream of bluesy releases to Galehouse. She owned DC Records out of Washington, D.C., and had been hustling local recordings to other labels since the 1940s to stoke up publishing action, her principal interest. Claiborne's biggest potential discovery was young country singer Patsy Cline, but the record lady and close associate Ben Adelman were outwitted by Bill McCall at 4 Star Records. Claiborne established contact with Golden Crest through Michael Angelo Graham, a master of ceremonies at the Howard Theater, Washington, D.C., and who himself managed a small stable of artists headed by Billy Stewart, of Chess Records.

The Wailers and "Tall Cool One"

In early 1959, Golden Crest made the breakthrough that Galehouse was longing for. It arrived from the opposite coast by way of a bona fide rock 'n' roll band: the Wailers. This was no ordinary four-chord, teenage rock 'n' roll aggregation. Over time, the Wailers have become recognized as the pioneers of the hard-edged Northwest Sound (and in a way, surf music), influencing acts such as the Ventures, Paul Revere and the Raiders, the Kingsmen, the Sonics, and, much later, grunge rockers Nirvana with Kurt Cobain. The Wailers, proficient young musicians all (especially guitarist Rich Dangel and drummer Mike Burk), soaked up a range of musical styles from the wild R&B of Little Richard to the sophisticated cool of Henry Mancini and Chet Baker.

In the summer of 1958, leader John Greek organized a demo session in Seattle through the auspices of local bandleader and composer Art Mineo, who was signed to Epic Records, the Columbia subsidiary. First, the audition tape was offered to Bob Reisdorff, head of promotion at C. & C. Distributing Company, an important indie distributor in the region. Reisdorff was in the process of setting up Dolphin Records, soon renamed Dolton. He was impressed enough to agree to sign the Wailers after first recording the Frantics, but the Wailers, viewing that group as competition, turned down the offer. With Los Angeles–based Liberty Records distributing and then purchasing Dolton, Bob Reisdorff would have enormous success with the dreamy pop of the Fleetwoods, including two 1959 No. 1 hits, "Come Softly to Me" and "Mr. Blue," and also with prolific guitar-instrumental act the Ventures.

Art Mineo had little interest in rock 'n' roll but liked the pushy kids who made up the Wailers and so looked farther afield for a record placement for the group. On his next trip to New York, Mineo took the demo tape to Jim Fogelsong, his A&R man at Epic, and to Richard Mills, his publisher at Mills Music. Fogelsong declined, saying it was not Epic's type of music, but Mills referred Mineo to his pal Clark Galehouse at Golden Crest.

Seeing real potential in the Wailers, Galehouse arranged to tape them during a visit to Seattle in early 1959. The makeshift session for "the record company from New York" was held under field conditions in an empty hall at nearby Tacoma in the wee hours after a dance date. One instrumental tune had been getting special reaction from the excited teenagers: "Tall Cool One" (with its title wisely changed from its original incarnation, "Scotch on the Rocks"). "Gee, I think we've got a hit," Galehouse told Mineo, who soon dropped out of the picture to concentrate on his own musical projects.

"Tall Cool One," with its Mancini-like introduction creating an immediate hook, started to make local noise after the Wailers used the seasoned trick of getting friends and family to inundate local dee-jays with postcard requests. The record broke into *Billboard*'s Hot 100 on May 18 at No. 74, whereupon Dick Clark handed out an invitation for the group to appear on *American Bandstand* on June 11 (a Thursday). The mood instrumental peaked at No. 36 shortly thereafter in a thirteen-week Hot 100 residence and even brushed the R&B charts at No. 24 following the TV appearance. According to John Greek, "Tall Cool One" sold more than 200,000 copies. The follow-up, "Mau-Mau," from the original dance-hall session, was a jazzier instrumental that stalled at No. 68, not helped by its (accidentally) politicized title. Apart from Greek, the Wailers felt that the flip, "Dirty Robber," a thumping Little Richard–type rocker with vocal by pianist Kent Morrill, should have been promoted as the "A" side, and they were right. Both singles were licensed abroad, to Quality in Canada and to London in England and Europe.

The talented teenagers had made the coast-to-coast adventure packed into a '59 Plymouth Fury station wagon. After the *American Bandstand* cameo, Clark Galehouse summoned them to Golden Crest's modern-equipped studio at Huntington Station. The three-day session on Long Island led to the impressive *Fabulous Wailers* LP, enhanced by a striking cover photograph that constituted rock 'n' roll chic.[8] Following an offer from GAC agency, founder John Greek was prepared to leave home for a full-time music career domiciled in New York, but the rest of the Wailers—homesick, parentally challenged, bereft of sweethearts, and college-bound—could not give the same commitment. Without the band's wholehearted support, Galehouse felt it was not worth shelling out valuable promotional dollars, and he let them go.

Upon the expiration of the Golden Crest contract, the Wailers formed their own Etiquette Records back in Seattle. Here was a pioneering artist-run venture headed by recent recruit Buck Ormsby, who replaced the now-estranged John Greek. With new lead singer Rockin' Robin Roberts, the Wailers revamped Richard Berry's "Louie Louie," only to see eternal fame snatched from them by way of a plagiarized version from Northwest frat group the Kingsmen (No. 2 *Billboard* but No. 1 *Cash Box*, Wand, January 1964).

In a quiet moment of reflection while the Beatles were overrunning America, Clark Galehouse mused that the Wailers could have been the American equivalent of the

Liverpool mop-tops. To cash in on the astonishing turn of events, Galehouse relaunched the 1959 LP with appropriate hype from a *Cash Box* story announcing that "Golden Crest re-issues Liverpool Sound album."[9] After a Detroit disc jockey started spinning "Tall Cool One" from the LP, the single was repressed and became a national Top 40 hit all over again in the early summer of 1964. In reality, the special window of opportunity for all concerned had been closed long before.

In 1959, Clark Galehouse was so delighted with the Wailers' original chart action that he launched a teen-targeted imprint, Shelley, named after the main Shelley Products business and in turn his pre-teenage daughter. The Shelley label was off to a splendid start with commercial-sounding singles by New Jersey's Donny Lee Moore (an Elvis Presley clone) and extrovert Northwest rocker Clayton Watson (a fervent Jerry Lee Lewis admirer). However, there were to be no hits among any of the thirty or so singles over a five-year period, and so the label had no identity in the marketplace.

Since Galehouse owned the pressing plant, it was not an expensive process to press up a few promo 45s on Golden Crest or Shelley for disc jockey and distributor consumption. He introduced interesting promotional tactics for singles, including paper picture sleeves and labels bearing artist photographs. If there was little or no reaction to the test marketing, however, the record was dumped. Who remembers, then or now, the Senators, Rick & Rob, the Seven Teens, Cartrell Dickson, or Paul Griffin (the New York session pianist), good as their records were? In truth, Golden Crest was a one-trick pony in the singles stakes.

The gloriously named Morty Wax, of National Record Promotions, did his best with regular quotes in *Cash Box*'s weekly "Record Ramblings" column. Wax, who later promoted Barbra Streisand for many years before going into film distribution, remembered Galehouse as a tough, serious, moral man who respected a job well done but found it hard to tolerate inadequacies. "He was always screaming at me," he said with laughter, adding that Galehouse always had a limited budget, "but then you had to be careful with your own money."

In 1961, Galehouse made a concerted effort to increase the visibility of Golden Crest and Shelley Records. He did so by transforming Golden Crest into a public corporation—a popular strategy at the time that was adopted by Cameo-Parkway Records, Liberty Records, Beltone Studios, and Cosnat Distributing. As such, Galehouse was able to raise vital cash from an initial public offering (IPO) stock issue while redeeming part of his original holdings and those of Mike Friedman and others. *Cash Box* ran a press release from Morty Wax that indicated that Golden Crest "has realized over $200,000 in proceeds following an issue of common stock. . . . The company now has sufficient capital, the label said, to embark on a 'full scale expansion program' and enable the firm to actively promote the Golden Crest line, new labels and further developments." The opportunity was taken to announce the introduction of the Crestereophone, "a recently perfected stereo head-set plus turn-table, amplifier selling for under $100."[10]

"It was failure," Joe Dreyhaupt said of the record player invention, adding that much of the money raised from the stock offering was wasted because the company was trying to act like a sophisticated public corporation, which it wasn't.

As part of the expansion drive, an office was opened at 1697 Broadway, New York, where masters were screened and lines of artists were auditioned (including the Kactties and the Precisions). A distribution partnership was struck up with Ervin Litkei's Olympia firm, utilizing Olympia's extensive field force and rack and chain store connections. A follow-up news story in *Cash Box* confirmed that the company would be specifically targeting the singles market under the A&R direction of Cy Levitan, who had first suggested the IPO.[11]

With cash in hand and a new management team, there was a flurry of singles activity, but there were few signs of a payoff hit, not even on the "Bubbling Under" nor "Looking Ahead" charts. In early 1962, "Altar of Dreams" by Gino and the Dells had the right ingredients for a latter-day doo-wop hit, but the record couldn't fulfill the whimsy of its title. Then "Toy Balloons" by the Oxfords was a turntable hit on the New York stations but failed to convert heavy radio play into sales. "The Oxfords" was in fact busy New York session musician and arranger Billy Mure, who wrote the tuneful instrumental that was a U.K. hit for British housewives'-choice pianist Russ Conway.

Billy Mure: Valentine Records

Guitarist Billy Mure came up through the ranks of the Lester Lanin Orchestra in a bygone era of supper clubs and band boxes, fox trots, and fur stoles. In the course of a long CBS live radio stint in the *Arthur Godfrey Show* orchestra directed by Archie Bleyer (the founder of Cadence Records), Mure became immersed in the New York recording scene, "which was like nowhere else." A staunch union man, he carried out a host of studio duties as a session man, leader, contractor, copyist, and arranger.[12] He recalled arranging at $150 per date for top producers such as Mitch Miller, Jerry Leiber and Mike Stoller, Hugo & Luigi, and Phil Spector.

Until he became too busy with this arranging work, Billy Mure was viewed as a first-call session guitarist and boasted an impressive hit count. One of the biggest records was Perry Como's "Don't Let the Stars (Get in Your Eyes)." Yet Mure's memory was that Como was totally unable to get the "feel" of Slim Willet's 4 Star country hit, and after just two takes at the RCA Victor date, the somnolent crooner couldn't wait to get to the golf course. On the rock 'n' roll front, Billy's standout accompaniment was on Bobby Freeman's "Do You Want to Dance" (Josie).[13] Mure did remember King Curtis playing saxophone on many sessions and that Panama Francis was "the best rock 'n' roll drummer in town, but wanted double scale—and got it." By working at full tilt, Billy admitted that "the sessions are a blur, even the studios."

Billy Mure launched a secondary career as a guitar hero, in the Les Paul mode, with a series of *Supersonic Guitars* albums in "stereo" and "hi-fi" for RCA Victor and MGM. He was sponsored by Gibson guitars. Although record man and distributor Jerry Blaine had tagged him "my hit maker" for his Jubilee-Josie productions, according to Mure, the guitarist was unable to repeat the magic in the 1960s at Golden Crest. There, he produced sessions for the label while operating his own Valentine Records from the Huntington Station base. He called Clark Galehouse "a talented engineer and a very generous man."

After A&R chief Cy Levitan departed Golden Crest in 1963, genial Mack Wolfson arrived to boost the management team. He had a long track record in music publishing and songwriting but, again, not in rock 'n' roll. The appointment of Wolfson coincided with a policy decision to concentrate almost exclusively on albums and to wind down the singles output. Releases on 45 rpm would be made from time to time, but mainly as promotional items for albums. The hoped-for hit singles hadn't materialized, and much of the blame for the poor investment return must be placed with Levitan, whose intellectual abilities were not reflected in his inadequate, dated productions. There was no doubt that the Shelley Products division was keeping the business afloat.

Even here, conditions were getting progressively more difficult, with intense competition coming from the custom-record divisions of the pressing plants of RCA, Columbia, MGM, and Capitol. These major label divisions had long taken a nice chunk of the indies' pressing business—and thus a piece of the independent record sector—having the advantages of bigger plant capacity (a real benefit in dealing quickly with hits), better equipment, assured quality, and, of course, flexible pricing. Not only did the Shelleys of the world have to fight with ingenuity to survive, but they had to keep abreast of the latest technological developments (such as stereo pressings) and fund the associated capital investment. For the smaller fabricators, it was a vivid replay of the ultimately unequal battle between the independent record companies and the major labels.

In 1963, Shelley Products was promoting custom pressing, especially in small runs. A *Billboard* advertisement read:

> We find that the term CUSTOM is loosely used. In Our Complete Plant at Huntington Station, L.I., N.Y. IT IS A REALITY . . .
> SHELLEY PRODUCTS offers a complete CUSTOM SERVICE from YOUR Tapes to a completed product.
> 1– Fairchild Compatible Unigroove Cutter 2– Finest Quality Pressing 3– Mastering 4– Label Printing 5– Packaging 6– Service 7– Competitive Pricing 8– Etc.[14]

Jerry "Swamp Dogg" Williams, a future player in soul music, was a client at the time. According to him, Shelley Products offered a first-class facility for young artists and producers. The master tape would be handed in, a lacquer would be cut, metal molds would be prepared and plated, the labels would be printed, the polystyrene compound would be readied, and the labels and stampers would converge at press. Within twenty-four hours, customers would have a supply of promo singles to hawk around the radio stations. The corporate plants did not give that kind of speedy, personal attention.

Another customer was Libra Records, an optimistic venture launched by songwriters Billy Dawn Smith and Otis Blackwell. Smith recalled that it was a long journey from Brooklyn, but it was worth it: "Clark Galehouse was the engineer," he said. "He made clear records with a good sound. Then it was out of the studio into the pressing plant." Shelley was still pressing custom LPs for educational institutions and others.

By the mid-1960s, thanks to good service and competitive pricing, Shelley Products had accumulated an impressive record company client list, including labels such as ABC-Paramount, Atlantic, Dimension, Double L, Laurie (with Legrand), Liberty-Imperial, London, Mercury, Polydor, Red Bird, and United Artists–Musicor–Ascot. In addition, Columbia, MGM, and RCA (and King with James Brown) were using the plant as an overspill at peak periods. Joe Dreyhaupt would get annoyed when he had to interrupt these profitable jobs for unprofitable small press runs of Golden Crest LPs or custom 45s and LPs.

"We were with them for years," said Bob Schwartz of Laurie Records. "We pressed a lot of records there. They were a good plant, or I wouldn't have been there. They would drop ship to the distributors."

While working in the print shop, Galehouse's daughter, Shelley, admitted she once omitted the "black eye" from the Red Bird logo; she also recalled the misdirection of a drop shipment of 10,000 Red Bird 45s to a distributor in Atlanta instead of Detroit. George Goldner would not have been best pleased, but such problems had to be resolved as part of the day-to-day customer service routine. It was rough justice when Goldner bequeathed a bad debt of $16,000 to the pressing plant after Red Bird went under, remembered Shelley.

Clark's daughter would spot record men visitors at the plant, including Lloyd Price and Harold Logan of Double L (she got Price's autograph) and the suave Al Bennett of Liberty-Imperial, who impressed her most of all. She said that her father was summoned to Berry Gordy's "beautiful house" in Detroit, although no deal seemed to have materialized.

Once, teenager Shelley was approached by a careless "plant," an unauthorized union official, to the fury of her father. Shelley Products was strictly non-union and in theory free from any possible mob corruption. Straitlaced Clark Galehouse would never have countenanced willful bootlegging or backdoor press overruns.

Earlier, in May 1960, it seemed that Shelley Products had been caught up in the ignominious bootlegging racket when *Billboard* reported that legal action against the company was being "pursued at the benefit of publishers," although no details were given. Later, *Cash Box* revealed that the case revolved around just two songs used on "a 69c EP without a license under the Copyright Act."[15] The judgment was duly summarized by *Cash Box* as follows: "The Appellate Court's affirmation of the lower-court's decision makes liable for damages all those involved in the manufacture and sale of illegal disks." The clear message from the courts was that the onus was on Shelley Products (and other pressing plants, right through to the retail chain) to ensure that work undertaken was legitimate and that the paperwork was in order. To compound the insult at

Shelley, a check for $750 from Solitaire Records of Canada was returned for "lack of funds." It transpired that the suit was originated in 1957 by Harry Fox, "the publisher's agent." In effect, it was a test case involving the liability of a subcontractor for copyright infringements by a principal, but the situation was almost impossible to police.[16]

At its peak, the approximately 70,000–square-foot Huntington Station complex was employing around seventy people in the offices, studio, factory, warehouse, shipping department, and printing division. With three eight-hour shifts, there was a pressing capacity of 75,000 discs per day, according to plant manager Joe Dreyhaupt. Clark Galehouse, with his technical expertise, was always on call for any breakdowns in the nine injection molding presses (for 45s) or the four compression presses (for LPs) and would roll up his sleeves to carry out repairs with Dreyhaupt, if necessary.

Dreyhaupt was unaware that in later years, the printed labels would become detached from the records due to heat sealant problems, a fact confirmed by dedicated Golden Crest record collectors. However, he remembered that Galehouse would always reserve the best quality compounds for the Golden Crest albums. It was a twist on the old days, in the immediate postwar era, when pressing plants were known to hold up customers' orders while making cover versions of hits for themselves in order to exploit furious distributor demand.[17]

A total workaholic, Clark Galehouse was known to spend up to sixteen hours a day at the factory and the studio. Despite the heavy administrative overload of running a public corporation, Galehouse was still engineering most of the sessions at the Golden Crest studio, which by now had been moved to larger premises across the road from 220 Broadway. According to tuba virtuoso Harvey Phillips, Galehouse had an infallible ear for detecting wrong notes, as befitted his musical past. As well, he was expert at balancing the correct levels before a session and conjured up an identifiable, pleasing drum sound. Long Island guitarist Paul Hotchkiss, of Paul and the Four-Most, recalled bringing Galehouse an acceptable demo of his instrumental "Tight Spot," but Galehouse insisted on making an improved rerecording at his studio before releasing the single on Shelley in 1963.

And so with Mack Wolfson firmly installed as vice president (sales), Golden Crest was primarily an album label with a bewildering number of releases, musical styles, and series. Artists included classical pianist Grant Johannesen (of NBC-TV's *Bell Telephone Hour*), whose three-volume double-LP series of Gabriel Fauré's works was an adventurous concept for the time; the revered but feared Dr. William D. Revelli with the University of Michigan Symphonic bands; and tuba maestros Bill Bell and Harvey Phillips.

Clark Galehouse gave a willing outlet to the chamber music works of the eccentric composer Alec Wilder, great friend of Mitch Miller, Arthur Shimkin, and Harvey Phillips and author of the respected book *American Popular Song: The Great Innovators*. Galehouse, going back to his formative years on the road, was proud to cut two albums by Joe Venuti featuring the music of George Gershwin and Jerome Kern. As well, Golden Crest distributed Gunter Schuller's classy NEC label from the New

England Conservatory in Boston, with releases including an extravagant five-LP set as a tribute to Merle Evans, the conductor of the Ringling Bros. and Barnum & Bailey Circus Band. Erroneously, however, Galehouse never repackaged the Golden Crest and Shelley singles into albums to capitalize on the golden oldies movement, even with the impoverished hit count.[18]

In discussing the record labels' poor performances with plant manager Joe Dreyhaupt, he gave the impression that he was not happy at the detrimental impact on his Shelley Products division. "Not only did we not have the top notch names on record," he said, "we did not have the promotional organization or the merchandising organization. Golden Crest used to cost Shelley Products a lot of money. I could see the thousands and thousands of records in the warehouse unsold."

The roller coaster–like ride of the pressing business was well exemplified in the late 1970s to 1980: first, Shelley Products received huge orders from RCA desperate to fill the demand following Elvis Presley's death in 1977 and also benefited from a prolonged strike at the Columbia Records plant. By contrast, there was the despair in 1980 of suffering a terrible bad debt of $637,000 from a major customer that had been having national hits until the good times were dashed as the LP market crashed disastrously.[19] It was the beginning of the end. Just around the corner was the technological change to compact disc that would make vinyl—and the existing pressing plant—virtually extinct. Even here, according to secretary Madeleine Pfister, Galehouse was studying the latest technical data direct from Sony in Japan with a view to setting up a compact disc pressing facility. He was as visionary as ever on the manufacturing side.

During the mid-1970s, loyal cofounder Mike Friedman had retired. Somewhat alone, Clark Galehouse was beginning to suffer health problems. Apart from the stress of running the Shelley Products and Golden Crest Records businesses, he was answerable to a board of directors and stockholders (as Bernie Lowe of Cameo-Parkway and Larry Newton of Am-Par had found, to their dislike). Against Galehouse's will, a diversifying film editing business, Take 5 Productions, was launched. Indeed, a group of venture capitalists (originally led by Simon Sheib) were now in majority control and were looking to save their investment.[20] The Golden Crest stockholders were not a happy bunch as the stock price plunged from fourteen dollars a share to a few cents, according to Joe Dreyhaupt. There were cries of misrepresentation, but in reality, the anticipated stock market killing was a symbol of misplaced aspirations in the independent record business: a 1979 Golden Crest company report revealed turnover of $5.7 million giving a net profit of $279,000, but this would be wiped out by the bad debt write-off a year later.

The pressures were relentless. Said daughter Shelley, "When I got to speak to Daddy about slowing down after his first heart attack, he looked at me in a sweetly saddened way and said, 'When you've got a tiger by the tail, you can't let go.'" With cruel inevitability, Galehouse suffered another heart attack on the way to record at the Florida State Music Convention and died in a Jacksonville hospital on January 3, 1983, aged seventy-one. An ensuing obituary in the local *Oyster Bay Guardian* described him succinctly as "a pioneer in the field of recording and record manufacture."

Golden Crest labored on under the management of Mack Wolfson and Jamie Sheib, the young son of major investor Simon Sheib. Joe Dreyhaupt was the frustrated production vice president, and in the general desperation it was mooted, so he said, that the company should become involved in producing pornographic movies through its film division. Galehouse would have exploded at the very idea! With the compact-disc bandwagon starting to roll and with inadequate capital to invest in a CD plant, it was no great surprise when Shelley Products was shuttered in May 1984, followed in quick order by the Golden Crest record division. The assets were stripped, including the real estate, pressing machines, and Heidelberg printers (and daughter Shelley's oak organ, to her dismay). By a miracle, the album master tapes survived, but the singles tapes were dumped, a sad fate encountered by too many independent labels. In 1997, in a tortuous series of events that had been kick-started by Hy Weiss four years earlier, Shelley reacquired her father's record company, having already inherited the family CFG Publishing Company (a BMI affiliate).

During his lifetime, Clark Galehouse gave countless opportunities to musicians of all ages and musical persuasions, yet never did he seek personal glory. In a 1980 *New York Times* article, "Small Classical Labels—The Industry's 'Rugged Individuals,'" he said in a rare quote: "Music is an art form that cannot be sold like McDonald hamburgers. Classical records are not a mass medium and they never will be. It's up to us little fellows to remind the majors from time to time that a classical record can be a very meaningful and a very individual work of art."[21]

In Golden Crest's case, it was more than classical music, and it was much more than rock 'n' roll.[22] In a sense, Clark Galehouse was fulfilling Thomas Edison's vision of recording as a multifaceted medium, even if commerciality was often lacking and ignored. But behind the creaky Golden Crest edifice, the Wailers apart, there was always the reliable prop provided by the Shelley Products pressing plant.

PART 4

Rock 'n' Roll Is Here to Stay

21

The London American Group: Rockin' around the World

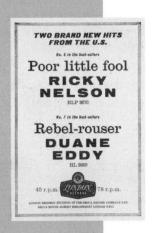

CAST OF CHARACTERS
Mimi Trepel, London Records department manager
and Burlington Music managing director
Johnny Bienstock, Bigtop Records
Freddy Bienstock, Bigtop Records
Ahmet Ertegun, Atlantic Records
Jerry Wexler, Atlantic Records
Fred Foster, Monument Records
*also featuring Sir Edward Lewis, chairman of Decca and
London Records and founder of Decca Records (U.S.)*

In licensing thousands of independent masters for distribution throughout the world, London American Records was the international messenger of rock 'n' roll. Here was the global marketplace in operation years ahead of its time. The New York office of the parent company, Decca Records of London, England, was the conduit for a raft of deals with the indie record men.

The artists indebted to the London American division for their initial exposure on the world stage make up a "Who's Who of Rock 'n' Roll" in its many guises. Elvis Presley was one of the few headline acts missing. Even here, it seemed that his second Sun single, "Good Rockin' Tonight," was being considered for release by London, but the music was thought to be too advanced for its time. When, at last, it was decided to schedule "Mystery Train," RCA Victor had intervened to buy out Elvis's Sun contract. Any sampling of London's accumulated indie label licensors reads as impressively as the artists' list.[1]

It wasn't all big hits, by any means. Buried in the catalog were rare R&B gems that missed the U.S. charts but were targeted at the black immigrant population in England and the armed forces in Europe. Such obscurities included "It's Really You" by Nappy Brown (Savoy), "I Knew from the Start" by the Moonglows (Chess), "So Tough" by the Kuf-Linx (Challenge), and "Some Other Guy" by Richie Barrett (Atlantic). Too, there were rare rockers such as "Bertha Lou" by Johnny Faire (Surf) and "Save It" by Mel Robbins (Argo). The London vision was quite extraordinary.

London American Records had an indelible impact on a whole generation outside of the United States. In England, teenagers would huddle under the bedsheets to catch the latest London releases on their radios by way of the late-night Decca record shows, hosted primarily by Jack Jackson, Pete Murray, and Tony Hall, over Radio Luxembourg of the wavering airwaves. One such youth, Harry Webb—born again as Cliff Richard and then elevated to Sir Cliff—was learning his craft by purchasing London singles by the Everly Brothers and Jerry Lee Lewis prior to becoming the first genuine British rock 'n' roller.[2]

More fundamentally in Liverpool, John Lennon, Paul McCartney (another future knight), and George Harrison would have absorbed avidly the weekly London releases at their local record shops in the late 1950s, as so many of us did in our isolated pockets of the country. So earnest were these future members of the Beatles that they repackaged timeless American and American-styled music for the consumption of the United States' baby boomers in the name of the British Invasion. America's export of rock 'n' roll music was returned with interest.

Sir Edward Lewis and Decca Records

The London American story apart, such is the overall importance of Decca Records (U.K. and U.S. versions) that a brief discourse would not be remiss.

Decca Records was the brainchild of Edward Lewis, who was smitten by the "magic" of the emergent record industry in the 1920s.[3] A stockbroker by trade, he formed the company in England on February 28, 1929, after engineering a takeover of the one-hundred-year-old firm of Barnett Samuel & Sons, manufacturers of musical instruments and the "famous" Decca portable gramophone. Alas, the timing could not have been worse—the stock market crash was just a few months away—but Lewis managed to keep the nascent business afloat. Then he bravely launched a New World counterpart in 1934 during the last gasps of the Depression, after Warner Bros. Pictures had shed its record company assets. Full of independent spirit, U.S. Decca, with ex-Brunswick man Jack Kapp at the helm, was destined to become one of the big three major labels.

So who was this blue-blooded Brit, born a world apart from the traditional record man? And how did he immerse himself so wholeheartedly in the music business, emerging as one of its greatest-ever visionary geniuses? Educated at elite Rugby School and

Trinity College, Cambridge, Edward Lewis came from an upper-crust English family that was involved in the profitable worlds of stockbroking and insurance. With entrepreneurialism to spare, he coerced the "old boy" network in the City of London (and to a lesser degree that of Wall Street) to underwrite the Decca Gramophone Company Limited and Decca Records Inc. Lewis was utilizing to great effect his keen knowledge of the financial instruments of the time—the machinations of ordinary shares, common stock, debentures, convertible shares, preference shares, extended credit from suppliers, and bank overdrafts—a specialty that few (if any) record men had. Private loans were also sought from friends and the Lewis family businesses in an era when gentlemanly trust, usually, was the name of the game.

During the frantic negotiations to form U.S. Decca, the "early bird" commute for Lewis was a transatlantic boat crossing on the *Europa, Mauretania,* or *Aquitania.* The critical key to Decca's rise to major label status was Ted Lewis's insistence on a "one price 35–cent" record compared with the prevailing pattern of seventy-five-, thirty-five-, and twenty-five-cent records. He argued vehemently that at the thirty-five-cents level, not only would business be taken away from competitors, but it would boost the overall industry.[4]

Both Decca companies teetered on the brink of disaster in the dark days of the 1930s, when radio was supposed to have "killed" records.[5] U.K. Decca itself was only three weeks away from being bundled into National Provincial Bank's "breaking up" department but managed to survive to compete with EMI, not only in Britain but literally in every corner of the globe. It goes without saying that EMI's Sir Louis Sterling was another giant in fashioning the record business at large.

Come World War II and in need of cash to fund its war effort, the U.K. company sold off its U.S. holdings. Here, Edward Lewis was making the ultimate patriotic act overlaid with a large dose of the British bulldog spirit. The Decca invention of the radio navigational system, known as the Navigator, turned out to be a startling success at the D-day landings at Normandy. As a result of this wartime research, chief recording engineer Arthur Haddy was able to introduce superior tonal range into the company's recording technology while implementing improvements such as better record surfaces, a reliable stylus for playback, and an upgrading of the electroplating masters in the manufacturing process to accommodate the improved sound.[6] The Haddy team's sonic innovation was marketed as "ffrr" (full frequency range recording) and "true high fidelity," with a logo based on a human ear. The Decca sound was impeccably the best.

Even if the loss of U.S. Decca was a personal blow, Ted Lewis had seen his confidence in the potential of the American division borne out by the market statistics: in 1933, America was buying 10 million records a year, but by 1946, the figure had shot up to 330 million. And Decca's stock prices had soared on both sides of the Atlantic.[7]

The loosening of ties with U.S. Decca led to the formation of the U.K. company's own record division in the United States. With the loss of the "Decca" trademark in America, the U.K. parent was forced to choose a new name for its New York subsidiary: The London Gramophone Corporation. Director D. H. Toller-Bond was quoted by *Billboard* on December 20, 1947, as saying, with the expected military precision of a D-day veteran, that the prime objectives were "introducing English talent here and securing dollar credits for England."[8]

By having access to the U.K. Decca repertoire, London Records was able to make a peremptory strike against James Petrillo's AFM ban. *Billboard* caught the irony of the moment with its January 17, 1948, headline "London Diskery Moving in On Petrillo-Blighted U.S."[9] Records would be imported by boat from Europe, leading to the label's high reputation for the quality of its pressings, particularly in the classical music field. A new English pressing plant was opened in the major port city of Southampton with a manufacturing potential of 18 million discs a year.[10] As early as August 1949, LP albums for export-only to the United States were rolling out of the factory.

London had an immediate chart single with "Now Is the Hour" by English music hall singer and comedienne Gracie Fields (No. 3, 1948). Post-Petrillo, a U.S. roster was headed by Teresa Brewer (who had a 1950 No. 1 hit with "Music! Music! Music!" and would marry record man Bob Thiele), and there were even series for rhythm and blues and hillbilly. Although London wanted to become a major record company, it found that its U.S. competitors had too much of head start with the big name acts. The label decided, therefore, to wind down its U.S. signings and revert to European recordings for sustenance.

Vera Lynn, the British forces' sweetheart, scored a surrogate 1952 No. 1 hit with "Auf Wiederseh'n Sweetheart" during the Korean War conflict, but London's biggest-selling artist would be Mantovani with his orchestral sounds, lush and romantic. An escalating problem was that the U.K. Decca pop catalog was rooted in the dated sounds of the British entertainment establishment, which had no place in the burgeoning U.S. teen market of the 1950s.

A noble exception was Lonnie Donegan, who managed a surprise No. 8 chart placing in 1956 with his compelling skiffle version of Leadbelly's "Rock Island Line," but there was no follow-through because he went with rival Pye. In 1962, London scored its next stateside No. 1 with "Telstar," Decca's space-age instrumental by the Tornadoes produced by Joe Meek. Soon London was to deliver its coup de grace, thanks to the Rolling Stones' spearheading of the British Invasion, along with Capitol's Beatles. Then ladies' men Tom Jones and Engelbert Humperdinck took command on London's Parrot subsidiary.

In England, back in October 1949, the London label was set up by Decca to release the recordings of its U.S. subsidiary. With the American roster being whittled down, U.K. London needed to find masters from other sources. It was slow going until the mid-1950s, when a veritable goldmine was discovered within the ranks of the independent labels. Even then, many of the indie record men were blissfully unaware that there was a market for their product beyond the various regions of the United States.

The U.K. 78–rpm releases would bear the legend "London American Recordings," while the 45 logo, introduced in October 1954, was abbreviated to simple "London." The London pressings, with those fabled tri-centers, were far superior to the U.S. originals due to Decca's technological expertise and immaculate pressing plants. Legend has it that Edward Lewis would make unannounced visits to the factory shop floors to monitor quality control. For example, he was very keen to see that the record labels were lined up correctly on each side of the disc. This attention to detail explains why the London releases, in addition to musical content, have become so collectible.

London American Records was able to act as a clearinghouse for the independent record makers, offering a network of local divisions and agencies scattered throughout the world. Many countries were members of the British Commonwealth, previously the British Empire, where, like Decca, it seemed the sun would never set. Inevitably, the London model spawned imitators and competitors everywhere. Fellow global player EMI used its venerable Columbia, HMV, and Parlophone lines as inward licensing vehicles and then set up Stateside as a dedicated label, but Capitol remained an imperious stand-alone marque. Interestingly, Decca stole a march on EMI when it adopted the LP in Britain far quicker than its archrival, as early as June 1950 (compared to EMI's October 1952). On the other hand, EMI was ahead of Decca with the 45–rpm single, introduced in late 1952 versus October 1954.[11]

Other big U.K. inward licensing players into the 1960s were Philips-Fontana, the aggressive promoters of the U.S. Columbia catalog in the 1950s before buying Mercury; Pye International, notably with Chess; Chris Blackwell's Island with Sue and many small indies; Top Rank, soon acquired by EMI; and also Jeff Kruger's Ember International. Elsewhere there were imitative labels such as Quality and Sparton in Canada, Barclay in France, and Leedon and Festival in Australia. But London Records led the field in supplying the international marketplace with American rock 'n' roll music and remained in pole position throughout the independent record era.

Sir Edward Lewis continued to be the face of Decca Records, and of London Records, into old age. Toward the end, Sir Edward specifically wanted his sadly declining record group to be merged with PolyGram so that the classical catalogs of Decca and Deutsche Grammophon could be united.[12] He died in 1980, just two weeks after PolyGram's acquisition of Decca, his wish granted.

Mimi Trepel: Head of Foreign Distribution, London Records

In better times, Sir Edward Lewis's aide for licensing the U.S. indie label masters for international distribution was a relatively unknown New York lady: Miriam "Mimi" Trepel Jordan. In January 2005, I found myself in Lake Worth, a sprawling town with little apparent heart, just a few miles from West Palm Beach airport, where I met the beautifully dressed and manicured Mimi, fragile in build but with an imposing character and still very alert, if somewhat hard of hearing. Living in a single room of a family home, she was well cared for, but she was clearly a victim of the U.S. health care system by living too long and seeing her assets diminish over time. She was ninety-six years old.

Mimi Trepel was happy and proud to talk about her life and times in drama, in early radio, and especially with London Records. She took a distinctly feminist stance, emphasizing that the radio and record businesses were like glorified men's clubs right up to her retirement in 1975. With tiredness creeping in, she kindly handed me her personal copy of the autobiography that had earned her graduation credits at Fordham University, New York, at the grand age of seventy-three. This unique document allowed the content of our interview to be topped and tailed.

"I was first of all known as Mimi Trepel," she stated in a clear, precise voice that hinted at her theatrical upbringing. "My maiden name was a very, very well known name in the flower business for many, many years until the Great Depression. It was just a question of getting out of high school and going [for] training for business, which I hated, just plain old business. Everything was in New York, because I was born and brought up in Brooklyn, but I lived in Manhattan many, many years."

Despite the rampant effects of the Depression, Mimi's parents were able to send her to the Feagin School of Dramatic Art situated in Carnegie Hall and so give her a chance to pursue a career on the stage. Then radio entered her life, as she recalled: "Well, in 1944, a very close friend of mine told me that she heard about WLIB, that little station in Brooklyn on Flatbush Avenue which two brothers owned. Somebody gave me a very good bit of advice, because they said, 'You will remain a secretary ten years from now if you stay with the large networks. If you really want to go into the profession, you go into a little station.' Independent radio stations were very popular at that time. WLIB had mostly a versatile type of broadcasting, so there I was in radio, in music programming, and production." Mimi Trepel's radio credits included "live" productions of a show with promising young folk singer Oscar Brand and a series of interview programs with Ethel Waters, Ella Fitzgerald, and vaudevillian Belle Baker.

On taking a better-paid post at Radio WMCA, New York, in 1946, Trepel came across the mysterious world of music copyrights. In her autobiography, she stated:

> New to me was the clearance department with an office adjacent to ours. I knew that independent radio stations paid an annual fee to the performance societies (ASCAP and BMI), for which the stations were awarded the overall privilege of broadcasting music material in copyright. BMI required stations all over the country to take turns at keeping a log of every recorded selection programmed during one month, then sending it to the Society so that royalties earned from airplay could be distributed among publishers and composers. ASCAP had and continues to have a monitoring system of its own for this purpose. The clearance department at WMCA had to approve all the music programmed, whether "live" or recorded, and handled all the obligations concerning the performance royalties.[13]

The proximity of Station WMCA to the area known as "Tin Pan Alley," where most of the music publishers were still located in the 1940s [on Twenty-eighth Street between Broadway and Sixth Avenue], gave me the opportunity to become better acquainted with several of these publishers. They would often relate interesting anecdotes and impart valuable information regarding that facet of the business. This experience stood me in good stead during the later years of my career.

In January 1947, Mimi Trepel was invited back to Radio WLIB as head of music programming. "The station had moved to Manhattan," she wrote, "having rented larger quarters on the second floor of an old church building, which Columbia Records had bought for use as a recording studio—acoustically the best kind of area for this purpose. . . . An unforgettable highlight of those later years at WLIB was the witnessing of many Columbia recording sessions. . . . During these sessions, among other things, I was able to observe the new techniques of recording, such as use of the tape, which was rapidly replacing the old method of direct recording on wax, or acetate blanks; and the proper placement of an orchestra, chorus, and soloists to achieve the highest sound quality."

In 1953, Trepel married, happily, her third husband, Murray Jordan, who was a top radio announcer at WLIB (he died nine years later). "They didn't call them disc jockeys then," she insisted. By attending many functions together, Mimi was developing her music industry network. It was just as well, because her radio career came to a shuddering halt when WVNJ, Newark, New Jersey, adopted a chart record format. "Let's say that by 1953, radio got less and less and less and less important," she stated.

> And lo and behold, the records, *the records,* that was the thing. So we were out from there, and I went to apply to a job agency. They said, "Well, we don't have any similar jobs, but there's a job that's open at London Records in New York City. They want somebody to write the back of the albums," that stuff. I had never done that, and I don't know how I talked myself into that, but I got it.
>
> I joined London in December 1954 at a salary of about $4,000 a year, but I was not any kind of executive.[14] A *woman,* never! One mustn't forget that ours was an English company, British Decca. Dear Sir Edward Lewis, that would be terrible [to him] if I was the head of any kind of department. Of all his very good, wonderful secretaries, nobody was promoted. But the elderly person who was the head of the publishing companies, which were subsidiaries of London Records, retired. And they needed a person to be head of that department.
>
> We had a very small office that was granted to us by Sir Edward. It was[in] one of the worst areas in New York. How shall I explain it? It wasn't in the main part, like Broadway; it was way over on the extreme West Side on Twenty-fifth Street. It was an old building. They improved some of it, and we had a small staff there.

The location, however, was very close to the Hudson River docks, where the manufactured product was being shipped from Southampton, England.

Within one year, Mimi Trepel had become managing director of Burlington Music (BMI) and Felsted Music (ASCAP), manager of the copyright department, and manager of the foreign distribution department. "At first glance, this impressive list reads like the numerous jobs of Poo-Bah in *The Mikado*," she wrote. "In reality these divisions in the American company were still small, so that they could conceivably be handled by one executive. But therein lay the beginnings of a multi-faceted learning experience that was to continue for more than two decades."

Even with these added responsibilities, she was still not treated as senior management. "I never went to a meeting of the heads of the different departments," she said,

until Mantovani noticed that my name wasn't on the list. He went in and he said, "Now you just look here, just look here, Miss Trepel has a very important position. Just because she's a woman has nothing to do with it; she can be with all the men." I always thanked him for that.

So I became the head of [the] foreign distribution [department]. We developed foreign distribution where American companies could have their records sold abroad; that was the next job. I stayed all the time in the publishing division because they felt that I had a lot of music publishing experience by that time. I went and got American artists, and the masters were sent over to England. All of our records, really, were manufactured in England because they had all the facilities.

One of the most "challenging" (her word) of Trepel's responsibilities was to negotiate agreements with the independent record men. "At first," she wrote, "negotiating was as awesome as the art of fencing, learning how to lunge with the verbal sword against a clever adversary. But after a while, it became a study in rhetoric and in communication, and sharpened my insights into human nature. When contract terms in each negotiation were decided upon, many of these agreements were prepared in my office, some in consultation with our attorneys."

In her autobiography, again, Mimi Trepel outlined the day-to-day functions of the foreign distribution department:

Upon consummation of agreements, summaries had to be prepared, with copies sent to England, our royalty department, and others. (Lessors were paid in American dollars);

American lessors had to be contacted to set up procedures of transmittal of their product already released, and of new product, upon release;

Upon England's directive, tapes had to be ordered to be shipped to Decca, for manufacture and distribution in various countries included in the lease agreement;

Publicity: transatlantic phone calls had to be arranged between an artist and British press interviewers for print publication or media; promotional material had to be obtained from American licensors on their artists, to be sent to foreign affiliates included in the agreement;

Licensors had to be advised of releases of their recordings in foreign licensed territories.

All this work was being carried in the pre-computer, pre-e-mail, pre-fax, pre-FedEx era when the telegram, the telex, and the telephone reigned supreme. As for regular communications with England, airmail was the preferred method—the transatlantic telephone call was an expensive overhead and used sparingly. A big business obstacle was the inordinately tight exchange controls on international money transfers by the Bank of England, to Edward Lewis's continued frustration and fury.

Around the turn of the 1960s, Mimi's assistant Diana Weller recalled, IBM punch-hole data equipment was installed on the first floor to replace the Burroughs ledger machines to process the royalty statements. The new machines were so sensitive that the room had to be fully air conditioned. Trepel was privileged to have the new IBM electric typewriter in her office.

She would monitor, zealously, the record charts of *Billboard* and *Cash Box* with a view to moving in on new licensing deals. There was no time to lose because the New York music publishers would be relaying information on the hot U.S. hits to their counterparts in Europe, especially those located in the other Tin Pan Alley: Denmark Street, London. Invariably, there would be hasty and inferior cover versions recorded by established British artists that would be advertised weekly in the *New Musical Express* (which launched the first British pop chart in 1952) and the jazz-slanted, vehemently anti–rock 'n' roll *Melody Maker*.

"I became very friendly with some of the English people," said Trepel.

I was a counterpart to Geoffrey Milne. We talked to the English people all the time on the telephone, and I went there and they came to us. Geoff Milne, I was in touch with him very, very much: he knew the business very well; he had a wonderful ear. Marcel Stellman took care of the European side. Oh yes, I loved Tony Hall, I knew all the promotion men, they were just wonderful. I would visit their apartments here [and] had dinner with them many times. We were all fond of each other.

I tried to get publishing at the same time as the masters. There were occasions, yes, we did whatever we could. John Nice [of Decca's Burlington Music arm], I love him; I will never forget him. He is the kindest man and very knowledgeable. He was looking after the publishing deals in London.

The Burlington Music subpublishing contracts were bombproof. The standard royalty split at the time was 50/50 and has since increased to 70/30 or even 80/20 subject to negotiation, but the lower Burlington rate (50/50) holds good to this day. Whoever drafted the contracts was a very smart person because in the standard agreement there was a clause that covered "phonograph records, electrical transcriptions, *and all future developments* for similar uses."[15] Therefore, the contract was not rendered obsolete by the introduction of the compact disc and other paraphernalia of the digital era. Burlington Music is now part of the Warner-Chappell conglomerate.

"[Burlington Music] grew large and successful mainly due to the negotiating skills of Ms. Mimi Trepel Jordan in the U.S.A. and the close collaboration in which we worked," wrote John Nice, by then of the Valentine Music Group. "The company still exists today totally on the strength of those copyrights acquired during our period of joint control. Sad to say, though, it is now in the hands of a multi-national corporation and is no more considered to be a dynamic and progressive company."[16]

With her background in radio and in the record industry, Mimi Trepel was well aware of the social upheavals in music. "History was changing," she said.

This was a real change in history. It's very interesting; we almost signed Elvis. I was asked to go after him. All of sudden, when he was being sold to one of the big companies, RCA, a lot of people talked to him. I just lost him like that. I wanted to get him for us, of course. His recording manager was a doll, too. He was lovely, the first man that discovered Elvis when he walked into his office . . . Sam Phillips.[17]

That's another experience. We were invited with Joe Cuoghi [of Hi Records]—he was from Memphis—on one of those Mississippi boats. Oh well, the liquor never stopped, it was one after another, and everybody kept drinking and drinking. I kept wondering when we were going to eat, because I can't drink without eating. But it got to be pretty far into the night, we'll say. One of the nice men there took me back to the hotel. I got undressed and wanted to get into bed because I was already feeling pretty sick. Silly, but I was. And Sam Phillips called me; I was so surprised to hear from him. He said, "Why aren't you back here? You come back here. You're the best one in that whole place." I thought it was so sweet; he was a lovely man.

Fred Foster [of Monument], I was very friendly with him and the artists, too, including Roy Orbison—I had lunch with him one day; it was lovely. I tell you, I was very, very active, let's say, with the country people and the country artists. They were all my friends. I had lunch with them many, many times.

Of all the labels Mimi Trepel handled, Atlantic was her favorite. That's a tribute to Miriam Bienstock's regimented administrative qualities as much as to the attributes of the other esteemed partners. Trepel remembered a deal in the early 1960s when Atlantic received a total advance of $150,000, she believed, with three annual installments of $50,000. She was aware of Leonard Chess and his star artist Chuck Berry but never met them. The Chess link man was national sales and promotion manager Max Cooperstein, who was known laughingly to the London staff as "Max Cooperation," because he didn't.

Johnny Bienstock, of Bigtop Records, entrusted London with his overseas distribution and was rewarded with the No. 1 international hit "Runaway" by Del Shannon. Recalled Johnny:

I had a deal in England with Mimi Trepel of London Records; from the early Bigtop days, they represented me in England. She was a clever woman, very much. I met her through publishing, but she got into the record end because, again, there were many of the publishers that got into the record business. So she was there, and she had no difficulty to get me with London Records in England. Walt Maguire, he was her boss. Then after years of trying, they had a London Records in America as well.

Yes, London in England did a very good job. I never met Sir Edward, [but I] talked to him on the phone once or twice; he was very friendly, [a] very nice guy. London Records did well for us, there was no question about it. Don't forget, I gave her not just the U.K. but also all of the territories like Hong Kong, Australia, South Africa. She was very happy, and she supervised that from where she was. I felt [she] or her lieutenants were better qualified to do that than [I was] from here. I couldn't do it, and she did. After all, they were real English colonials; they worked that way.

Among the attractions to the record men of being members of the London family were the trips to England to discuss business with Edward Lewis and his assistant W. W. Townsley. The visitors from America were entertained royally in the grand oak-paneled offices at Decca House at 9 Albert Embankment, London. Here, the River Thames was in full flow with the Houses of Parliament and Big Ben in full view. Art Rupe traveled over as an honored guest when Little Richard was at the height of his wayward powers, while ever-visible Don Pierce lapped up the regal treatment as he introduced his many Starday country LPs to Sir Edward. "It happened before the surge for country music," said Pierce, "and they weren't very important commercially at the time. We were just a little bit too ahead of time, yes."

Freddy Bienstock, Johnny's brother, happened to be in town for an appointment with Ted Lewis when Savoy's Herman Lubinsky was visiting England. Lubinsky had a licensing deal with London covering Canada, the British Empire, Germany, and Italy. Recalled Freddy, "I'm sitting in the anteroom waiting for Sir Edward Lewis, and he had somebody in there. The door opens and out comes Herman Lubinsky; he didn't realize that Sir Edward Lewis was right behind him. He was delighted to see somebody from America in London, and he says to me, 'Boy, didn't I put one over on him!' Sir Edward was standing right behind him. Then he said, 'Herman, I'm delighted to hear you say that.' It was very embarrassing. But then I went in to see Sir Edward Lewis, and he was still thinking about that. He said, 'I want you to know that whenever Herman Lubinsky comes to London, I invite him to dinner at my house. And aren't you surprised that I would do that?' I said, 'Come to think of it, yes; why would you do that?' And he said, 'Because I have a feeling nobody else would'" [laughs].

Ahmet Ertegun of Atlantic Records was not one to miss out on a swell party and used to dine with Sir Edward in much more convivial circumstances. "Of course, we became friends," he said. "I mean, he was married, but he had a mistress, and I used to go out with him and his mistress; I also had . . . [hearty laugh]. The overseas market didn't grow overnight. We were always selling some records, and as we had bigger hits here, we got bigger hits there. I think our first really big seller in Europe was Ray Charles, in France [with Barclay Records], yeah."

When Mimi Trepel began traveling overseas in the 1960s, she was content to delegate her work to "my very, very, very capable assistants, whom I trained," including Diana Weller and Helene Blue. "I would say I wasn't strict in that sense of strict in the office," Mimi said,

> because I don't like that word too much. Rather, I was very *particular.* I was very, very particular, and my people had to learn that office backward and forwards right away. I had a good time training them.
>
> I know Sir Edward didn't like my travels very much, but he saw that, if I may say, I was popular with everyone at all the European countries: Holland, Sweden, Denmark, all of those countries. I was very well liked over there. So he allowed me as head of the foreign distribution department to go over. But never, never could I take first-class

travel, until our attorneys had to go—and they insisted on my going with them. I had lunch with him [Sir Edward] once when I went to England. He asked me if I liked seafood; I said, "Oh yes, very much," so we went to this shrimp restaurant. But he wasn't exactly as interesting as some of the other people [*laughs*]; he was *so* serious. A lot of people liked him very much. But you have to admire him for his success; he had tremendous success.

He had personal business, too, you know—his wife [Maisie] was not a well woman; she died finally. Even while she was alive, he had a girlfriend . . . Jean. Yes, very sweet, yes, yes, yes—all those people were lovely.

Sir Edward would make unannounced "royal visits" to the New York office at least once a year. Mimi Trepel's immediate boss was D. H. (Dudley) Toller-Bond, another Englishman of privilege who was addressed as "T. B.," even by his wife, Nancy. "I was working for the president of London Records, Toller-Bond. He had a hard time of it as the New York head; I'm sure he got scolded all the time. I dealt mostly with [division manager] Walt Maguire; I had to," said Mimi, with an uncharacteristic edge in her voice.

One of Trepel's biggest publishing triumphs was in concluding a big overseas deal with Buddy Killen of Tree Publishing of Nashville in 1963. The Tree catalog was a haven for golden country songs. At the time, Killen's Dial Records, headlined by Joe Tex and an outlet for Tree copyrights, was being distributed by London in the United States before Atlantic took over with great success in the soul era.

Nevertheless, the 1960s was a good time at London Records, especially with Decca's British acts producing results at last. Said Trepel, "I didn't know the Rolling Stones; I wish I had met even one of them. I was a great, great fan of theirs. They were Decca's biggest act. Decca turned down the Beatles, and [the management was] horribly upset about it; oh yes, God, I can imagine. I guess they didn't think it was good, sure, but you just hear one thing of the Beatles, [and] that's all you needed. Engelbert Humperdinck was one of our big artists and Tom Jones. I knew all those people, but I didn't deal with the artists. Decca was very successful, oh, very successful. And then Sir Edward had [Decca] Radar, too. He has to be given credit for that."[18]

Nevertheless, storm clouds were appearing on the horizon and were heading toward Mimi Trepel's foreign distribution department. By the mid-1960s, in an accelerating trend, the larger U.S. labels were demanding to have their own imprints overseas. The pattern had been set earlier by Capitol, Mercury, and RCA (with Decca from 1957). At London, the widespread complaint from the independent record companies was that their labels were being "buried" anonymously among all the other indie companies; therefore, individual "brand names" were suffering. Initially, Decca countered this argument by redesigning the standard London record label to incorporate the logos of favored indies Atlantic, Dot, and Monument. Soon, that was not enough. More and more labels wanted their own identities overseas, from Columbia (which was forced to use the "CBS" name for trademark copyright reasons) to Chess and Tamla-Motown. It was the beginning of the end for the London-type licensing model.

In 1966, Atlantic's Jerry Wexler was dispatched to England to sever a ten-year relationship with London after Ahmet Ertegun had expressed unhappiness with the royalty
accounting of the Canadian division. "Our contract was running out, and the English
[beat group] thing was really starting to boom," said Wexler. "And we saw that if we
couldn't get some English records over here, it was going to be very rough. So my two
Turkish partners elected me to go and confront Sir Edward; he's the lion. I would go
over there, and I had the feeling that in his presence he was turning his head away to
avoid some reeking malodorous effluvium coming from this person. He would have
responded better to Ahmet because Ahmet had this aristocratic, cosmopolite overlay.
But here's this street Jew from New York coming over to tell him that they're taking
the line away [*laughs*]. Of course, I put it right to him; I said, 'Can we get product from
you?' But he had London Records [in New York], and he said 'No!' So we wound up
[licensing] with Polydor."

With the foreign department in decline, London became a shadow of its former self.
Mimi Trepel was retired in 1975, much against her wishes. "I was the first one to go,
yes, I was. And that's another thing: I was a *woman,* so who would go first? But it was
a glamorous job in many ways. . . . I feel that was an experience that I really should
appreciate very much. And talking to people like you," she concluded, sweetly.

As I left Mimi Trepel to her one-room confinement in Florida, it hit me: that little
frail lady was responsible, in conjunction with her colleague Geoff Milne in London,
for dispatching the rock 'n' roll message, not just to my contemporaries in England but
throughout the rest of the world. She was aware that her work with London Records
was important, but she didn't realize it was *that* important. Here was the person who
was responsible for sealing the deals and keeping the irascible record men in order so
that their priceless master tapes would end up as 78s, 45s, EPs, and LPs on our Garrard
and Dansette record players. I couldn't help but reflect on her sparky retort to my closing question. "Am I in any hall of fame? Of course not!" She died shy of her hundredth
birthday in September 2006, still without any formal recognition, remembered by her
loyal staff members, a few elderly record men, and, unfairly, not by many others. She
was an unseen heroine of rock 'n' roll.

By the late 1950s, London Records' New York division was still operating under
the stewardship of Dudley Toller-Bond. He led a strong management team that, as of
May 1962, included Leon "Lee" Hartstone, general manager; Walt Maguire, division
manager; Ed Kissack, producer liaison and engineer; and Mimi Trepel, entrenched as
head of her three departments.

"Toller-Bond was [a] very proper . . . Englishman," said Irv Lichtman of *Cash Box.*
"He looked it, dressed to the nines. He was always sartorially resplendent; he looked
like Arthur Treacher to some extent, the actor who plays the butler. I remember we
were invited to hear the London demonstration of stereo [probably in 1958]; they
had offices on Twenty-fifth Street on the West Side. 'What is this stereo everybody is

talking about?' This was the new discreet sound; it wasn't phony or whatever. So we go down there, we're ushered into this room, and the curtain closes. We hear these railroad sounds, music going across, it was *novel.* After it's all over, I said, 'T.B., that was incredible!' In best British accent, he replied, 'It's *fucking wonderful,* isn't it?' And there's no way I could ever expect he'd talk that way. He wasn't a man of music, I would say, but he had the people around him that knew what to do."

Despite the revered classical line, London Records in New York was reeling from the lack of suitable product for the American pop market coming out of U.K. Decca. In desperate need of a new business menu, the London management found it among the heaving cauldron of the smaller U.S. indie labels. With a reputation for honesty and integrity, as demanded by Edward Lewis, the London Group took on the roles of manufacturing, marketing, and distributing certain independent labels within the United States. In effect, the strategy was an extension of the independent producer concept.

Fred Foster: Monument Records

The first significant stand-alone London distribution deal, in 1958, was with Fred Foster's Monument Records, formed originally in Baltimore, Maryland, before moving quickly to Hendersonville, Tennessee, and then to Nashville. There was a dream start, first through Billy Grammer's opening chart maker, "Gotta Travel On," and then by way of the unrivaled class of Roy Orbison's early hits. It is fair to say that London American helped to establish Foster's Monument label and that Monument helped to establish the London American Group.

Fred Foster has had a fascinating career in music. He displayed his entrepreneurial instincts early on while working at a record shop in Washington, D.C. There he cornered the local market in Hank Williams (and Luke the Drifter) discs following the hillbilly hero's untimely death on New Year's Day 1953 and made the proverbial killing for his bosses. At first they were unnerved by this unauthorized exercise, not only from the financial outlay involved but also by having a shop overflowing with boxes of yellow-labeled MGM 78s (which soon disappeared following judicious radio spots on the Connie B. Gay show, WARL Arlington). Foster's further job experiences as distributor's salesman and label promo man, with Ben Adelman as his mentor, were ideal apprenticeships for a future record man. A farm boy from Rutherford County, North Carolina, he was a sparkling Nashville success until he lost his companies in the 1980s following a self-admitted dumb banking investment, which "drained the assets."

In looking back, this colorful raconteur with a nice line in understatement takes up the story:

> After turning down the chance of working for [fledgling] Marriott Hotels and making "lots of money," I went to work in [the] record shop. It was forty-five dollars a week— [I almost] starved to death—but I wanted to learn the business. After a year, I went to a big distributor, a wholesale distributor there in Washington, Schwartz Bros. They handled Mercury, Atlantic, Chess-Checker, Cadence, and lots of big labels. I did take

a [sales] job with ABC-Paramount [and] stayed with them almost two years actually covering the East Coast.

[Before ABC,] I wound up with Mercury as a promotion man directly. I was their second field person; the first was Tommy Schlesinger in Detroit. So we were so successful doing all that, then they finally promoted me to head of country music promotion out of Nashville, nationally. Well, I didn't feel qualified; I'd lost all touch with country music. Anyway, I took the job, [but] it didn't work out. The guy here that was head of it was Dee Kilpatrick, and he had never cut a hit in his whole life. He was so out of step with the times. Anyway, it didn't work out, and I didn't stay there long.[19]

[After ABC,] I went back to Washington where I had a multitude of friends and acquaintances. I wanted to take a break from traveling to be with my wife and my young child, and she was expecting again. So J. & F. distributors in Baltimore were huge in classical; that was owned by Jack Sobel and Frank Bamberger. Frank was one of the most knowledgeable classical salesmen I ever met. London was J. & F.'s big label, but he had no popular product; he didn't know a pop record from a Caterpillar tractor. We struck a deal: I would come in and create a pop department for him and solicit some labels that were in that business, and I would get a piece of the profits and so on. Here I was going to be home and probably making more money.

And so Fred Foster took J. & F. distributors into the rock 'n' roll age. "We had lines such as Apt, which was a subsidiary of ABC-Paramount," he said,

and the first thing was huge: "Little Star" by the Elegants. Then there was Bigtop Records, which had "White Bucks and Saddle Shoes" by Bobby Pedrick Jr. and "Lavender Blue" by Sammy Turner. Big records.

But here comes Walt Maguire. Now I started that job in January of '58. In March of '58, he came down to show off the new catalog with album releases and instigate a promotional program behind them. He did something that really turned me off early on: he got a stepladder out of the stockroom [and] set it up. We were out in the main area, all the salesmen gathering around. He climbed up on the stepladder so he could look down at all of us. I said to myself, okay, well, if you need to do that. Anyway, he finished showing his albums, and there were some great ones, classical things; Mantovani had a new one. So then he turns around to me and says, "You're doing a lousy job." I said, "Well, so are you! You're not sending me anything that I can get away with. People laugh at me when I ask . . . them to play Vera Lynn, David Whitfield, and the Frank Chacksfield Orchestra. Come on, Walt! I mean, Elvis is a smash, [and] so are Little Richard and Fats Domino."

He turned kind of white around the mouth. I thought Frank Bamberger was literally going to have a coronary, because he could see Walt pulling London from the distributors. Walt said, "If you think you can do better, then why don't you?" I said, "I will!" The next day I started Monument.

Now I had to find the song, and I didn't find anything that I could even remotely use until August. It was an old "public domain" that I rewrote: "Gotta Travel On." When I finished it here in Nashville with Billy Grammer, I went back to Washington. I was making some acetates in a studio there in Washington. I called Walt because I knew I wasn't going to be able to handle this distribution; I didn't have the money. I said,

"You asked me to do better, and I did." He said, "What are you talking about?" I told him. "Well, what are you going to do with it?" "I'm gonna let somebody distribute it for me, and I'll be checking in with a label today." He said, "Well, I'll just catch the shuttle down there."

To his credit, he did. [He] flew down, met me at the studio, and listened to it. He said, "It's a smash, undoubtedly a smash. We'll put it on Felsted." [The London-owned Felsted label was named after the English country village in Essex where Sir Edward Lewis lived.] I said, "We won't put anything on Felsted." "What do you mean?" I said, "Man, this is my label. Felsted? I don't even care about it. No, no way, can't have it." He said, "I'll have to get clearance to put it on your label."

Lee Hartstone was his immediate supervisor. Walt went back and asked him; he turned him down. Then he went over Lee's head to one big-headed man, to D. H. Toller-Bond; he was the head of the American company. He was obviously English, [and] he said, "I can't give you the clearance. You'll have to talk to the chairman if you think it's that important." I said, "You call the chairman," Sir Edward Lewis. So Walt called him and explained how London couldn't be a real player in America until they could have proper music. They just didn't have anything soon, and could he please pick up this master? So Sir Edward finally said, "I don't care what label it's on, we need business, give him his label."

That first Monument release, "Gotta Travel On" by Billy Grammer, broke into the national charts in November 1958 and became a No. 4 hit in a lengthy twenty-week chart run.

Monument Records was named after the Washington landmark of the same name that Foster used to see from the airplane whenever he flew back home to D.C. "So we became the first little London group of distributed labels," he said. "I started the company with $1,200, and after finishing I had $80 left.[20] My first check from London was for $46,000. Then we just went on."

Within London's comfort zone, Fred Foster and Monument were to revel in a string of hits by Roy Orbison between 1960 and 1962 that included genuine classics such as "Only the Lonely" (No. 2), "Running Scared" (No. 1), "Crying" (No. 2), and "Dream Baby" (No. 4). By October 1962, Monument was big enough and well financed enough to undertake its own distribution independent of the London Group.

Foster is justly proud of his work in the studio. "If you could produce something that was timeless in nature, you were ahead of the game," he observed.

Gimmicks are okay for the short run but not the long haul. So I always tried to make my productions as pure as possible, well thought out. Anything in there that would ever jar after you heard it a few times, it had to go. Oh, the Nashville "A" Team, as we called them, were wonderful. Now these were guys that were playing pop records for me; they were making hillbilly records—not just country, but corn poke—on other days during the week. Well, they welcomed the chance to be able to really play, not just two or three chords, you know.

It's hard and expensive to rehearse in the studio, so I would usually rehearse in my office. Roy Orbison and I would sit in my office planning out note by note, everything.

We'd call in the arranger, and we'd leave some open spots for creativity. For example, when I did "Oh, Pretty Woman" [No. 1, 1964], that guitar figure that opens the record, that was by Jerry Kennedy. He was a marvelous player and a great producer in his own right: he produced all of Roger Miller's things, the Statler Brothers, Tom T. Hall, and he was head of the Mercury office here for a while. We were running the song through, and Jerry said, "You know what might be worth trying? . . . Just open this the first time through this lick with one guitar, then add another and another as long as it repeats." And I said, "You've just done it." He said, "Well, don't you want to hear it?" I said, "I just did, in my head." Then I added two saxophones to play that lick and buried them in the mix, but it gave it a lot of weight . . . just little things.

It's good to have a hook, of course. Let me give you an example of the opposite: another Orbison record, "Running Scared." Never repeats anything, doesn't have a chorus. It starts and tells the story and then builds all the way to the climax, and there it is. Nobody had done that before. Wesley Rose thought it was awful; he said, "That's not even a song." And he was supposed to be managing Roy. It was fights all the way through [with Rose]; it was awful.[21]

But Monument was the first of the London distributed labels to succeed. I could concentrate on creativity, and London, not having to invest anything on the creative side, it worked for them. They could pay me more than they paid one of their old artists; they didn't have to invest anything, just the distribution. It was a higher percentage royalty than normal. I could have got an advance probably on that first record, but after that first check was $46,000, from then on I was having hit records and the checks were bigger and bigger and bigger. I had a free hand; they didn't tell me anything. "Thank you" was all they ever told me.

Along with Monument, Hi Records was the star performer in the London stable thanks to a run of instrumental hits by Bill Black's Combo and Ace Cannon (before the Willie Mitchell–Al Green soul era of the 1970s). This Memphis label was headed by Joe Cuoghi, a jukebox operator and co-owner of the local Poplar Tunes retail store. In May 1962, *Billboard Music Week* published a booklet celebrating the renewal of the London-Hi deal. The insert described the history and benefits of the London American Group scheme in the United States and revealed the full extent of its network, including an intriguing list of record men clients.[22]

According to the booklet, the London American Group represented "distributors from all over the U.S.A. and assures them of representation throughout the world." There were three basic types of arrangements: purchase of single masters, agreements covering all the recordings of a particular artist, and an exclusive representation agreement covering all the recording activities of a producer. Importantly, said the handout, "The London American Group offers the best national and worldwide distribution and exploitation at its own expense. In addition, the London American Group assumes the complete responsibility for all pressing costs and all billing and collections. . . . The producer and only the producer controls the artist." With time running out for the small independents trying to operate on the national stage, the lifeline offered by the London scheme was well worth considering.

Without any doubt, Sir Edward Lewis's free enterprise spirit is embedded in the portals of the global record industry. Under his enlightened leadership, first Decca Records and then London Records were terrific operations at every level at home and abroad until the rock era of the 1960s. As for the independent record men, they were well versed in Sir Edward's habit of making instant decisions and his cavalier shake-a-hand approach toward deal making . . . until Mimi Trepel produced the cast-iron contracts for signature. The London family was a happy family, and the common bond was the record men's rocking and rolling music.

22
CHAPTER

Teen Scene

CAST OF CHARACTERS
Julius Dixson, Deb Records
Clyde Otis, Mercury Records A&R man and songwriter
Harold B. Lipsius, Jamie-Guyden Records
Bob Marcucci, Chancellor Records
Doc Pomus, Fabian songwriter
Dave Appell, Cameo-Parkway Records
Hank Ballard, "The Twist" songwriter
Paul Evans, Carlton-Guaranteed Records artist-songwriter
also featuring Dick Clark, American Bandstand *host; and*
Bernie Lowe and Kal Mann, Cameo-Parkway Records

By the late 1950s, heavy rock 'n' roll, mixing the harsher
elements of R&B with testosterone-laden rockabilly, had seen its best
days. Or so it seemed. Even Sun Records' Sam Phillips was talking
about rock 'n' roll in the past tense. He was paraphrased by *Billboard*
in May 1959 as saying, "Perhaps never again will pop music be so
dominated by a single style of sound. But the kids 'got tired of the
ruckus' and we are moving into a period of greater variety in taste."
The story noted that "the explosive trend put music on equal terms
economically with other leading entertainment forms and he [Phillips]
credited it with being the miracle drug that saved the life of radio." As
well, "R & r. pulled a coup, where many previous campaigns failed, in
getting young America to dance again." Interestingly, Phillips forecast
"a grand re-entrance of the big dance bands," which showed that his
crystal ball was not always correct.[1]

Now it was the turn of innocent teen idols singing innocuous teen
songs. The smarter record makers were well aware that the first baby
boomers were approaching money-spending age and that the majority of teen buyers were impressionable young girls. The continued
strength of the carriers of teenage music was expressed graphically in

a 1958 year-end *Billboard* report by Bob Rolontz, who stated that "76 percent of all hits" were on indie labels, with "only 24 percent belonging to the four majors, Capitol, Columbia, Victor and Decca."[2]

Fourteen months earlier, that esteemed entertainment weekly *Variety* had chronicled the ongoing majors vs. indies, David and Goliath saga in a ribald feature by Mike Gross that was as relevant as ever, perhaps even more so. Noted Gross, "It's all a matter of 'wheeling and dealing,' a game in which the indies are making their bigtime rivals look like pigeons. Working with hustling freelance distributors, the indies have been able to pile up a long line of regional hits with quite a number eventually falling into the national sweepstakes." The writer hinted that the "indie distribs" were romancing the jukebox operators and dealers with "under-the-counter" giveaways, as well as offering "special" consideration to the disc jockeys. "It's all written off, somehow, by a special process developed by the indies," he opined. "Some of it is written off to promotion and sundry other expenses, while at other times it's just conveniently forgotten when accounting time to the publishers comes around." Gross acknowledged that "the indies continue to move in from left field and take away the play."[3]

RCA's major label intervention into the teen arena with Elvis Presley meant that the writing would be on the wall, eventually, for the independents. A big market leap forward had come in 1956, Presley's *annus mirabilis*, when record sales nationally increased from $277 million to $377 million. It was a massive year-on-year uptick of 36 percent.

Elvis Presley's "Heartbreak Hotel," full of angst and atmosphere, was the perfect record to kick-start his career on RCA Victor after the Sun transfer, and it simply flew off the record shop shelves into teenagers' dens nationwide. In its slipstream came the ultimate back-to-back hit coupling of "Hound Dog" and "Don't Be Cruel," followed through by "All Shook Up." Not only were Elvis's records for RCA selling by the millions, the productions were works of professional craftsmanship. He was also breaking new ground for fellow rock 'n' rollers in the movies and on television: The *Ed Sullivan Show* TV clips, in particular, reveal that Presley was way ahead of the field in terms of brio, bravado, and star quality. Moreover, he was introducing subtly into his repertoire gentle ballads such as "Love Me Tender" and "Love Me." Meanwhile, the hunt was on for the next Elvis by the majors and the indies alike.

Perhaps the best of the rest was Ricky Nelson. Lew Chudd of Imperial Records was alerted to Ricky Nelson's potential after the teenager had covered, lamely, "I'm Walkin'"—a Chudd copyright written by Fats Domino and Dave Bartholomew and published by Reeve Music. Nelson was recorded by Norman Granz's Verve label, primarily a jazz imprint, in response to powerful distributor requests for teen product but without a secure long-term contract. In stepping in speedily and ruthlessly to sign the seventeen-year-old sensation, Chudd was illustrating the newfound clout of the leading indie labels.

Hollywood-based Lew Chudd was widely respected as one of the best businessmen of the independent era. As with Memphis record presser Buster Williams in *Fortune* magazine before him, Chudd was accorded a profile in *Business Week* magazine (September 7, 1957), around the time Imperial contracted Ricky Nelson. This was a rare establishment insight into the activities of a very successful independent record man: "Since he launched his venture in 1945 with a $10,000 investment, Chudd's business has grown into a company with sales that this year will amount to $7.5 million—and possibly double that next year. Besides managing five music publishing concerns, Chudd owns the entire company himself. He knows every phase of the business and directly supervises each of the operations required to put a record on the market." The seal of approval for Lew Chudd and his breed was duly delivered: "Chudd himself is typical of the independent operator in any field—a fast moving, hard-working entrepreneur with an ear for what the market wants in popular music."[4]

With Ricky Nelson, Chudd recognized the importance of the weekly exposure afforded by the teen's popular family TV show, *The Adventures of Ozzie and Harriet*. Unlike the majority of Imperial's artists, Ricky was young, handsome, and white; he also had the talent and feel for genuine rock 'n' roll as well as teen ballads. Moreover, his band, led by guitarist James Burton, really rocked. With Fats Domino under long-term contract, Chudd now had control of two rock 'n' roll headliners. It didn't matter at all that they came from wildly differing musical and social backgrounds.

On the national stage, major label Elvis Presley and indie label Ricky Nelson may have been hyped mercilessly, but at least they did perform quality rock 'n' roll music for eager teen record buyers. Ironically, they were about the only big 1950s stars who did not appear on the influential *American Bandstand* TV show. But then again, they had no need for that outlet, unlike their many followers.

Dick Clark and American Bandstand

It was a landmark day on August 5, 1957, when *American Bandstand*, hosted by the genial twenty-seven-year-old Dick Clark, was nationally networked by ABC-TV from Philadelphia. Now teenagers had their own television show, and hit records (along with future hits) would be heard simultaneously throughout the nation. Within a year or so, *American Bandstand* had the highest ratings of any daytime program on television and, with advertisers lining up, was being screened by 130 stations.[5] The powerful formula was being replicated by TV stations in major cities everywhere, but on the downside, the days of the radio-driven regional record were irrevocably numbered.

Dick Clark, in embracing wholeheartedly the new television medium (even if his show was being transmitted in black and white), put himself well ahead of the disc jockey competition. He proved to be an astonishing, worldly, wise young entrepreneur who grasped, quickly, the inner workings of the independent record business. In particular, he understood the performance royalty aspect of publishing through his early work in radio. Guided by henchman Tony Mammarella, Clark may have profited through his many side companies, but he was the perfect public relations front man for teenage rock 'n' roll with his casual "boy next door" persona.

Clark's rival Alan Freed had a thriving business empire, too, but his demeanor was more furtive and shadowy; there was something of the night about him. It could be said that Freed was hard-edged "Mr. Rhythm and Blues" to Clark's clean-cut "Mr. Teen." Or, as Harold Lipsius of Jamie-Guyden Records put it, Alan Freed was the street hustler and Dick Clark was the altar boy.

Even if they were cut from a different cloth, Clark was every bit as powerful as Freed in breaking and controlling hit records, according to New York songwriter Julius Dixson. He had set up Deb Records after co-writing, as "Julius Dixon" with Beverly Ross, the smash hit "Lollipop" by the Chordettes (No. 2, Cadence, spring 1958). "I got busy with my stuff," said Dixson.

> I had immediate luck with "The Reason" by the Chanels; ABC-Paramount gave me a $5,500 advance altogether just to distribute. I called it [the label] after "debutant," a debut label, and it started clicking. The Chanels went right away to the charts, right away.
>
> A lot of strange things happened back then. You see, Dick Clark wanted that record for himself, to distribute that on Swan Records. Had they did that, Dick Clark would have pushed that across the board to No. 1; that could have been a No. 1. Dick Clark was very disappointed that Sam Clark did the distribution at ABC-Paramount, so I lost out on that. Dick stopped promoting it.

"The Reason" was on the Hot 100 for just one week (No. 98, end of 1958). It was good-night for Dixson's group and for his record label (although he did secure a Top 50 hit in late 1959 with "The Clouds" by the Spacemen on his Alton label).

American Bandstand, with attractive teenage couples sporting the latest fashions and highlighting their own culture, began to make its name by introducing accessible new teen dances. A significant trendsetting record was "The Stroll" by the Diamonds, a No. 4 hit in the first part of 1958, making it the Canadian vocal group's second substantial Mercury smash after the "Little Darlin'" sensation. Promptly, veteran Oakland bluesman Jimmy McCracklin joined in the fun with a clever cash-in, "The Walk," which succeeded because it was a good dance record (No. 7, Checker). The hereditary line could be traced through Sil Austin's slinky instrumental of late 1956 with the promenading title of "Slow Walk" (No. 17, Mercury), itself a child of Bill Doggett's "Honky Tonk."

"The Stroll" was written and produced by Clyde Otis, soon to become Mercury's first appointed black A&R chief in October 1958, in succession to Bob Shad and preceding Quincy Jones. In recalling the genesis of this evergreen line dance at rock 'n' roll emporiums, Otis gave generous credit to the *American Bandstand* host:

> Dick Clark was playing a record, and the dance was that beat. The rhythm was the same as when I wrote the song. Dick had these dancers strollin'. Jack Lee [of publishers Meridian Music and E. H. Morris Music] told me about this record that Dick was playing, and I listened to it and said, "That's nice." So I wrote a song based on that tempo. What I think happened was that Dick had come out with the name; they were strollin'. And that's how it had the name. But the record that he was using, that beat, was not called the stroll.

So Nancy Lee, Jack Lee's daughter, wound up being a third of the writer [credit] because Jack brought me the record. And he told me, "Look, I want a piece of this for my daughter"; she was ten or eleven. So that's how I wound up with two-thirds of me writing and a third for her as a co-writer. You see, Brook Benton did the demo on "The Stroll," and when Jack heard it, he flipped. I was happy with the Diamonds' recording; oh, yeah, they were happy, too. That's made a lot of money, even today. I produced the record.

The professionally made demo record was an increasingly popular tool for song-writers, publishers, and artists to pitch their songs to record companies. Among the Clyde Otis–Brook Benton demo collaborations were "A Lover's Question" (a Clyde McPhatter Top 10 hit for Atlantic, late 1958) and "It's Just a Matter of Time" (Benton's first hit for Mercury, No. 3, early 1959). "Yes, I made my own demos," said Otis. "I didn't sing on them; I brought the musicians in and the singers, and I made the demo. That's how I learned to produce records, downstairs at 1650 Broadway in the basement studio [Allegro]."

The stroll dance was inspired by Chuck Willis's surprise No. 12 hit with "C. C. Rider" (Atlantic, summer 1957), whose mesmeric aura was enhanced by the saxophone interjections of Gene Barge and the charm of Phil Kraus's marimba playing. Most of all, the record's slow-burning groove was perfect for the teen strollers, who had no idea of the song's salty folk roots. For a short while, Chuck Willis, improbable as it might seem, was king of the stroll. On the day of his untimely death on April 10, 1958, the turban-sporting singer's fortuitous contribution to *American Bandstand*'s early success was acknowledged by Dick Clark, to his credit, with an hour-long tribute segment.[6] Within two weeks, Willis's prophetic posthumous double-sider, "What Am I Living For"/"Hang Up My Rock and Roll Shoes," was on the charts.

American Bandstand, in effect, was an on-air record hop with guest stars lip-syn-ching to their latest releases. It also featured the Rate-a-Record voting diversion for new releases that was watched eagerly by record buyers and record makers alike. By being networked across the country's TV screens, *American Bandstand* was putting the spotlight firmly on historic Philadelphia.

The Quaker City's rising industry influence was enhanced by a strong distributors' network involving Harry Chipetz, Ed Cohn, Harry Finfer, Bob Heller, Sam Hodge, David Rosen, and Nelson Verbit. There was an equally vibrant disc jockey lineup featuring Larry Brown, Jocko Henderson, Hy Lit, Kae Williams, and Georgie Woods. Philadel-phia's strength, then, was in its underlying tight-knit infrastructure.

However, there was a strong Mafia presence in Philly with plenty of capital to spare, as evidenced by New York gangster Meyer Lansky's involvement in the "lucrative music box field" there as early as 1945, according to a *Billboard* story. At one point in the 1950s, it was reckoned in the jukebox trade that Philadelphia "sells three times the title strips of the New York market" with "a quarter of the population."[7] The title strips, of course, were genuine sales indicators.

Initially, the City of Brotherly Love had seemed to be too much in New York's shadow to become a major record center in its own right. Pioneering local labels from the 1940s that made some impression were Ivin Ballen's 20th Century and Gotham Records. Then Dave Miller's Essex Records had a freak No. 4 hit at the start of 1953 with Don Howard's bought-in master of "Oh Happy Day." More significantly, Bill Haley and his Comets served their apprenticeship at Essex and charted with "Crazy, Man, Crazy" (No. 12, summer 1953) prior to defining the power and the glory of rock 'n' roll with "Rock Around the Clock" on Decca. Both Ballen and Miller came up through the record-pressing route. Ballen would stay in that line while Miller, who was a big presence in the business, would make a fortune out of the 101 Strings budget album concept.

From the mid-1950s onward, however, Philadelphia would take a more cohesive step forward by playing host to a clutch of new labels, which soon made their respective marks due to a combination of shrewd entrepreneurialism and abundant native talent, massaged by large helpings of cronyism and nepotism. The driving force, of course, was *American Bandstand*, fueled by teen music.

The Jamie-Guyden Labyrinth

Jamie Records was at the forefront of this Philly surge. The label is rightly associated with Harold B. Lipsius, but at one time there were other names in the frame. Importantly, there was Harry Finfer, who had spent his first eight years in the business with Gotham Records. He was still hustling budget recordings of dubious merit at the annual MIDEM music industry festival in Cannes, France, into the 1990s.

In 1955, Finfer went into the distribution game with Universal Record Distributing Corporation, along with Essex Records' Dave Miller and Allan Sussel (later president of Laurie Records, New York). Then Finfer launched Jamie Records in late 1956 with "backer" Sussel and Harold B. Lipsius, a practicing attorney. The first releases, in a hesitant start, were pressed by Miller's plant. At one stage, Dick Clark had a quarter share in Jamie, but label hit maker Duane Eddy's standing joke was that he lost count of the 25 percent owners in Jamie.[8]

Harry Finfer's technique was to play a record continually, and if he didn't tire of the performance, he knew it was a hit. That's how he picked out Eddy's "Rebel-Rouser" that was produced in Phoenix, Arizona, by Lee Hazlewood and Lester Sill, yet another Jamie stockholder. Duane Eddy's twangy guitar instrumental sound was jokingly said to be "like plucking a string over the Grand Canyon" by the Jamie staff, who recognized that a creative force behind the Eddy phenomenon was Phoenix guitarist Al Casey. Such was Jamie's reliance on Duane Eddy and the corresponding exposure on *American Bandstand* that it was always a nerve-racking experience to see if his next record would be a hit, for fear of not being paid by the distributors on the last chart entrant. As the Universal distributorship covered the Pennsylvania and Delaware areas only, national distribution was placed initially in the hands of George Goldner through his Gone Recording Corporation until a friendly split in September 1959. All told, Duane Eddy had a remarkable twenty Top 100 records for Jamie between 1958 and 1961, before he was snapped up by RCA Victor.

By the early 1960s, Jamie-Guyden Records (and then Universal distributors) was under the control of Harold B. Lipsius. With his lawyer's background, he admitted self-disparagingly that he was "tone deaf" and "couldn't spot a hit" but recognized that "record men lived by their wits."[9]

Back in late 1957, the respected Bernie Binnick and Dick Clark's right-hand man Tony Mammarella founded Swan Records to swell the Philly indie ranks. Here was the vehicle that launched Freddy Cannon into the stratosphere, starting with the booming rocker "Tallahassee Lassie" (No. 6, summer 1959), after early hits by Dicky Doo and the Don'ts and Billy & Lillie. Then there were those important labels, Chancellor and Cameo-Parkway.

Bob Marcucci: Chancellor Records

The front man for Chancellor Records was Bob Marcucci, with Peter DeAngelis as the behind-the-scenes music maker. "Peter was a genius," said Marcucci, adding with laughter, "and that enabled me to play around." Between them, they deftly handled the careers of top teen stars Frankie Avalon and Fabian. Much of the two record men's success can be attributed to their early decision to enter into a farsighted distribution arrangement with ABC-Paramount, giving them the freedom to act as independent producers.

Bob Marcucci and Peter DeAngelis became a songwriting team as teenagers, with Marcucci penning lyrics and DeAngelis originating melodies. "But we didn't know what we were going to do with them," said Marcucci. "Then we finally got this one song recorded called 'You Are Mine' by a guy called Vince Carson [Essex, 1953]. At that time, the 'boys' (or the Mafia-type people) came in and wanted to take over the song. We had to give it to them." It was a startling introduction to the record business, but Marcucci was able to recover their marriage song later on.

Bob Marcucci discovered his first teen star, Frankie Avalon, at a club appearance by popular band Rocco and his Saints. Avalon had already recorded trumpet instrumentals in 1954 as a fourteen-year-old sensation for "X," an RCA Victor subsidiary. Recalled Marcucci, "I went there because Frankie asked me to come over and listen to a singer, who was blonde and blue-eyed. But he just didn't hit me as being an idol or being someone who could be a big star. I was about to leave. Then Frank got up and sang two or three songs, and he came offstage. He said, 'Bob, did you like that kid? Isn't he great?' I said, 'Not really; it's you I want to sign. I can make you into a big star. Give me a year.'" Within one year, Avalon had a Top 10 record with "Dede Dinah."

Chancellor's name and heraldic logo design were inspired by the Chancellor Hall Hotel where the label was located, at 206 South Thirteenth Street, Philadelphia. The new imprint had an early regional breakout with a pop ballad by Jodie Sands that was far removed from rock 'n' roll. Immediately, Chancellor was attracting the attention of larger labels. "'With All My Heart' became a hit in Baltimore, Boston, Philadelphia and a couple of other places," said Marcucci.

> Randy Wood, who owned Dot Records at that time, called me up and said, "I want to buy that record." I said, "No, I'm not going to give it to you." He said, "Well then, I'll just cover it." I said, "If you can find somebody that sounds likes Jodie Sands, I wish you all the luck in the world, but mine is doing very well."
>
> At the same time, Sam Clark from ABC-Paramount Records called me up. He asked me to do the same thing. I said, "No, Randy just called me. I want a distribution deal, and I want to have Chancellor. I want to start my own label!" Well, after a long back and forth—the record was getting hotter and hotter and hotter—he then made the deal with me. But the record didn't turn out to be a Top 10 record throughout the country, because girl singers weren't making it at that time.

"With All My Heart" by Jodie Sands peaked at No. 15 in the summer of 1957.

The Chancellor/ABC-Paramount deal turned out to be an industry bellwether. At the start, Bob Marcucci said he and Peter DeAngelis were getting less than 50 percent of the net income as independent producers. "Then it went to 70/30 in our favor, then 80/20," said Marcucci.

> I remember in 1957 when the "Dede Dinah" record was becoming a hit, Frank, myself, and my partner went to New York to see them [ABC-Paramount], and we all got a $2,500 advance for Christmas. From that point on, it was like millions and millions and millions. The albums sold 300,000 to 500,000, which was a *lot* of albums to sell back in that day. Larry Newton was a character at ABC; we loved him. But I was much closer to Sam Clark, who did the deal. He was a very nice man, very classy, very fair, very together . . . wonderful.[10]
>
> As part of the deal, all the masters after I left there would revert back to me. Ray Charles got the same kind of deal [with ABC-Paramount] that I did. Ray was saying to me, "I don't understand how come these records are so successful. I can't sell as many records of mine that you do with Frank and Fabe [Fabian]." It's because they were kids, and the kids loved them! There was nothing for the kids; they were so hungry for music for themselves.
>
> It was very much *American Bandstand* that helped launch Frankie Avalon and Fabian, both. That helped tremendously; I cannot say how much it did. Dick Clark was wonderful then; he's wonderful to me now—we're still the best of friends. I was very close to [disc jockeys] . . . Joe Niagara, Hy Lit, and The Geator with the Heater (Jerry Blavat). But Dick was just a different kind of human being.

Although Frankie Avalon was stirring up interest at record hops, his first two Chancellor releases were flops. "Then me and Pete DeAngelis sat home one night and wrote this incredible dumb song called 'Dede Dinah,'" confessed Marcucci.

> It was the worst song I ever heard in my life. I didn't figure it would ever make it. It was released on December 5, 1957, and within three weeks it sold 250,000 records, which

was a lot of records. It hit No. 7, and that's when we really started our business. We recorded at a little studio [Les Cahan's Beltone studio, New York], and we had to put all the sounds on one track. Pete was just into the producing, and I was into helping Frankie with his voice. If you remember, the big gimmick on that was that he held his nose, and it gave it a real nasal sound. That nasal sound made it a hit record.[11] Every disc jockey would give it an air and say, "Hello everybody, here's Frankie Avalon's new record, 'Dede Dinah.'" And they would hold their noses!

Back in those days, the first two records should be kind of much alike. After "You Excite Me" [No. 49], the next one he did was "Ginger Bread" [No. 9]; he held his nose on that one, too. He could do up-tempo tunes, but he was very good for the ballads, records like "Venus" [No. 1], "Why" [No. 1], "Bobby Sox to Stockings" [No. 8], and "A Boy without a Girl" [No. 10]. They were perfect; that's what Frankie's image was. The kids loved all that, definitely. Then when he turned twenty-one, we got bookings from all the big, big nightclubs throughout the country. We then gave him an album called *Swinging on a Rainbow*, which was all up-tempo Sinatra-type tunes.

Frankie Avalon was taking the well-trodden route from rock 'n' rolling teen star to cabaret artist, just like Paul Anka, Bobby Darin, and Bobby Rydell. In the narrower rhythm and blues sector, Ray Charles, Sam Cooke, Lloyd Price, and Jackie Wilson were seeking similar adult acceptance.

Meanwhile, Bob Marcucci, noting the enormous popularity of Elvis Presley and Ricky Nelson, started scouring the country for an equivalent pinup artist to join forces with Frankie Avalon. Magically, Marcucci was to discover Fabiano Forte, not yet sixteen, in his own Philadelphia backyard. Although the teenager had the requisite personality and heartthrob looks, famously, he could hardly sing a note. With the DeAngelis-Marcucci team having a songwriting mental block with their new signing, they enlisted the services of Doc Pomus and Mort Shuman through the Aberbach brothers' Hill & Range Music. In one of the most amazing conjuring tricks of the rock 'n' roll era, Fabian was transformed into a top-selling record artist, courtesy of the Pomus and Shuman compositions "I'm a Man" (No. 31), "Turn Me Loose" (No. 9), and "Hound Dog Man" (No. 9). It was perfect teen fodder for the likable, nonsinging teen star.

"We made a lot of money with him," said Doc Pomus. "He was a very, very nice kid, you know. He was the last of the 'singers' [*laughs*]. Eventually, he learned how to sing a little, but then his career was over." Pomus and Shuman, of course, wrote the teen classics "A Teenager in Love" for Dion and the Belmonts (Laurie) and "Save the Last Dance for Me" for the Drifters (Atlantic).

With ABC-Paramount taking the business strain, Bob Marcucci and Peter DeAngelis were free to capitalize on the rock 'n' roll era's rich pickings by advancing the careers of Frankie Avalon and Fabian. As ABC's Larry Newton once said, "When most small indies are starting, they're long on creative ideas and talent, and short on cash and business know-how."[12] But it was almost impossible for the partners to develop the Chancellor roster outside of their teen stars. "Our hands were totally, incredibly full," admitted Marcucci. "We did have a couple of vocal groups [such as the Five

Satins], but it was so hard. I couldn't handle any more than those two: being on the road, attending conventions, going to Hollywood, and making movies, doing television. I had to leave all the record stuff up to the people in Philadelphia. We had a hit with Claudine Clark's 'Party Lights' [No. 5, 1962], but Frankie and Fabe were the two big stars. They sold more records than you could imagine. We made more money for ABC-Paramount than they had made with all their artists for the first year we were with them, much more."[13]

Dave Appell: Cameo-Parkway Records

The Cameo and Parkway labels became known as one, Cameo-Parkway, rather like the more celebrated Tamla-Motown. Cameo Records was founded in early 1957, with Parkway entering the fold in December 1958. The label heads were Bernie Lowe, pianist and bandleader, and Kal Mann, comedy writer, with the appealingly modest guitarist Dave Appell as A&R director.

Hailing from northeast Philadelphia, Appell was raised in the 1920s just around the corner from the Stetson hat factory. "Tom Mix, the famous cowboy, used to come down once a year riding a white horse with a big Stetson hat down Fourth Street," said Appell. "We were thrilled; it was a little PR work."

"Before I got into pop and jazz," he added, "I was playing with a Hungarian gypsy orchestra. We used to wear those Cossack outfits [and] played weddings. Cars came in from all over the country; gypsies are tribes, so when somebody gets married, they all come in. You'd open the back door, and twenty kids would fall out of your car. The weddings would go on for days. The guys were wonderful musicians—[they] don't read [music], but they know what to do. It was quite an experience; I learned a lot."

This is where Dave Appell acquired his all-around musicianship, including an acute sense of rhythm that manifested itself in those Cameo-Parkway recordings. Long retired, he was a loyal company man, still, in 2005.

Back in the early 1940s, Dave Appell played jazz guitar with the band of Mike Pedicin (who coincidentally had a minor hit on Cameo with "Shake a Hand" in 1958). "There were a lot of clubs around Philadelphia," said Appell. "In those days, we didn't have drummers in the clubs; it was too noisy. We had vibes, Mike Pedicin played alto sax, we had an upright bass. My idol was Django Reinhardt, who was part gypsy. I guess I was pretty much one of first electric guitarists. Mine was a Gibson, an old L-7; it was a good instrument. They didn't make electric guitars as such; you just put a pickup attachment on the regular guitar, and the amps were funny then. It helps in clubs and changes the sound, too; the concept and feel is different. There are so many effects now, everything is high tech, you can go crazy. We didn't have a name for our band. The guy [club owner] was a mobster; he says, 'You're the Men of Rhythm, that's it, that's your name!' You can't argue with him, you know [laughs]."

During the war, Dave Appell was drafted to Williamsburg, Virginia, where he was inducted into the official navy band. "That was like going to college for me," he said.

"I was learning to orchestrate and do writing, stud[ying] jazz, reading a lot of books. We had a full orchestra." After service, he started the Dave Appell Trio, and "we added drums, got a little bit bigger band." By the early 1950s, Appell's combo was working almost ten months out of the year in the Philadelphia area, where there were many active clubs, and took summer jobs in the New Jersey coastal towns. Appell even landed a regular spot on Ernie Kovacs's show in the early days of television.

In 1954, the Decca Records representative in Philadelphia organized a demo session that led to Dave Appell's first recording contract. "We had two releases on Decca," he remembered. "Paul Cohen was one of the A&R guys; he gave me the name Applejacks. We drove down to Nashville to cut a couple of sessions, and we did one at the Ryman Auditorium where the *Grand Ole Opry* was. We were playing pop, and we didn't have any charts [for the musicians]. The musicians were excellent down there. I think we had six brass; they came in, and they had charts for them. Owen Bradley was the A&R guy. Decca did [mainly] traditional country in those days; they were big then."

The proficiency of Appell's group was such that it was featured in the 1956 Alan Freed rock 'n' roll movie *Don't Knock the Rock*. Along the way, Dave Appell had run into Bernie Lowe and Kal Mann, the founders of Cameo Records. Lowe had been alerted to the tastes of the younger generation after being appointed musical director of Paul Whiteman's *TV-Teen Club* in early 1952. This is where future Philly Cameo stars Charlie Gracie and Bobby Rydell had their grounding.

"I had known Bernie Lowe from a long time ago," said Dave Appell.

He played piano with Paul Whiteman. He had a good musical background. He used to play piano at society dances and weddings; he worked the "outsides"—it's called the outsides when you work that way. When he came out of the navy, he had a GI School of Music for guys to study music in downtown Philadelphia. He wanted me to come over and teach, so I taught composition and things like that. They had GI bills for a lot of different things. Guys would learn a trade—electricians, carpenters, and so on.

Then Kal Mann was working for Bernie, too, in a way. He did parodies; that's how he made his living. He used to write for comics and things like that. Bernie said, "If you can write a parody, you can write a lyric." Kal was my co-writer; he did all the lyrics, and I did most of the music of the songs we've written.

Bernie was a little hard to work for, but he was a great music man. He knew how to merchandise, which is good; he was a good record man. He borrowed $2,000 to start this company. Both he and Kal were working at the time for Hill & Range in New York before they got in the record business. [Actually, Lowe was involved with the Teen and Sound labels prior to starting Cameo.] They were hired as writers; they made a $150 apiece per week. If they ever got a hit, they deducted the money they were paid as a salary from the royalties. That's the way the publishing companies worked in those days. Then they wrote a song called "Teddy Bear," and they got a record from Presley on that thing. So that started them. But they said to themselves, "Why stay here for the rest of our lives at $150 a week?"

So Bernie came back and started this company. He got a kid named Charlie Gracie, who was his first act. He was like a spin-off of Presley at that time, and they did this song "Butterfly." My group did all the vocal backgrounds on that thing. That was our first job together via Cameo.

"Butterfly," by diminutive guitarist Charlie Gracie with Bernie Lowe on rinky-dink piano, made No. 1 for the neophyte imprint in April 1957. Just two weeks earlier, Andy Williams had eased the song into the top spot on Archie Bleyer's Cadence label, making it a double No. 1 payday for the writers and publisher.

In an apparently devilish scheme to secure the publishing, Lowe and Mann released Gracie's record of their song without any writer credits before plumping for one "Anthony September" (the nom de plume of none other than Tony Mammarella, Dick Clark's iron man at *American Bandstand*).[14] Thus, the song was published by Lowe's Mayland Music (which, like Cameo Records, was part of Bernard Lowe Enterprises) and not by former salary payers Hill & Range.[15] Furthermore, Clark was offered a reported 25 percent publisher's share in the song as an incentive to promote the record as the original version to disc jockeys throughout the country. Adding honey to the Cameo publishing pot, Charlie Gracie's flip side, "Ninety-Nine Ways," became a No. 11 hit for screen star Tab Hunter (Dot).

With some irony, Hill & Range associate Elvis Presley clipped the wings of both sets of "Butterfly" when his "All Shook Up" shot to No. 1. Then in a further bizarre coincidence, Presley's next chart topper was Mann and Lowe's "(Let Me Be Your) Teddy Bear" in July 1957.

Charlie Gracie scored again with a Top 20 follow-up record, "Fabulous," written by Dave Appell and Kal Mann. Here was official notice that Cameo Records was an independent concern to be reckoned with. Cameo had the important underlying business supports, too, particularly Bernie Lowe's interests with Dick Clark in Harry Chipetz's Chips Distributing Company and in the Mallard Pressing Corporation. However, Gracie did not participate in the label's bright future. He became embroiled in a bitter royalty dispute with the result that his extremely promising American career came to a grinding halt.

"Charlie Gracie put them on the map," opined Dave Appell.

Then I started to work at Cameo at fifty bucks a week. Bernie had been making a hundred and a half [*laughs*]. At Cameo, I did all the arrangements. In reality, I did the charts, did the engineering, rehearsed the band, rehearsed the singers. I did everything there for a salary. The way I made my money was with Kal, because we used to write. I got more than the fifty dollars a week salary later on, but my real money came when we started to write the hits. I'm still collecting today.

Mann and Lowe wrote together at the beginning. Then Bernie got more involved in the record business, so that's when I started to write for him with Kal. We were AS-CAP writers, but we had some BMI songs. In those days, you couldn't write for both. So my BMI name was Harry Land (Land was my middle name), and Kal's name was Jon Sheldon (his son's name and middle name); Dave Appell was my ASCAP name. [The process] varied how we wrote songs. Sometimes I'd have a melody, sometimes he had a lyric; sometimes we worked together, and sometimes we didn't. There's so many different approaches to writing songs.

In those days, all the independent label companies used to buy a lot of outside records; they didn't produce everything. So Cameo bought "Silhouettes" by the Rays, produced by Frank Slay and Bob Crewe; it was a lot of money.

Acquired from Regent Music's Gene Goodman, "Silhouettes" was a No. 3 hit in late 1957 after fighting off covers from the Diamonds (No. 10, Mercury) and Steve Gibson and the Red Caps (No. 63, ABC-Paramount).[16] With these three Top 100 placements, the song was a music publisher's delight. Slay and Crewe proceeded to produce a run of hits for Swan Records with Billy & Lillie and Freddy Cannon. There was a close relationship between Cameo and Swan, with the labels sharing the same sales manager, Jerry Field, and the same office floor at 140 South Locust Street.[17]

"Dinner with Drac (Part 1)" was served up as the next Cameo hit platter (No. 6, spring 1958). In exploiting the popularity of horror films and high-rated spook-movie shows, this eternal Halloween party record was performed with eldritch authority by John Zacherle, known as the Cool Ghoul. The crowning enhancement was Kal Mann's cleverly constructed lyrics, as exemplified by the line "For dessert there was bat-wing confetti and the veins of a mummy named Betty." It was a controversial and brave release.[18]

"That was my band on 'Dinner with Drac,'" said Dave Appell. "I actually did the guitar background: *de dede de ding ding* . . . that was all me. I never got credit for that. The bass player, Joe 'Macho' Mack, was born in Prague, Joe Sher was drummer, and the sax player was this kid Dan Dailey. I remember we were appearing at the time in St. Louis, and we heard it on the air out of there. I said, 'Gee, that sounds familiar,' and it was a smash. John [Zacherle] was doing one of those spooky shows, radio and TV [WCAU-TV, Philadelphia]. He did all crazy things; he was like a Shakespearean actor, because he knew how to really project himself. He did a great album [*Monster Mash*, Parkway, 1962] for which Kal wrote some great lyrics; he was great for that stuff." "Dinner with Drac" is Appell's favorite Cameo record, principally because of his own standout guitar licks, but it is an astonishingly good all-around performance.

With his Applejacks, Dave kept the Cameo chart run rolling in late 1958 with "Mexican Hat Rock" (No. 16). "A thing happens in Philadelphia on New Year's Day," explained Appell; "people would come out to the Mummers Parade. All these string bands would play *oompah* songs. So we did a medley of that stuff in the clubs; we used to dance around with little umbrellas. Everybody used to love that thing, just instrumental stuff; we used two tenors and a baritone and a rhythm section. It was a smash. All the kids were dancing to it; we played it at all the hops in Philadelphia. As a matter of fact, at the Catholic churches the nuns were dancing around to it! Another thing was 'Rocka-Conga,' which still stands up, I tell you. It was in the charts ten weeks [No. 38, early 1959]. The last hit was 'The Bunny Hop' [No. 70]."

At this point, Mann and Lowe contracted Cameo's very own teen idol in the person of Robert Ridarelli: Bobby Rydell. He had been a regular on Paul Whiteman's amateur TV show, where Bernie Lowe was music director in the early 1950s, and had played drums with Rocco and his Saints, the same band that Frankie Avalon had performed with. After a slow start, Rydell made a splash with his third Cameo record, "Kissin' Time" (No. 11, late summer 1959). The follow-up, "We Got Love," made No. 6, and then "Wild One" became his biggest hit at No. 2 in early 1960.

Illustrating how a hit song could be written spontaneously, Dave Appell recalled: "We were driving up to a show at the Brooklyn Paramount, and we needed some material for him. Bernie was driving; Kal and I were in the backseat. I said, 'We've got to get a couple of songs together.' I had some manuscript paper; I wrote bars down and put chord symbols over the bars. Then I took an old song, 'Ida, Sweet as Apple Cider,' and I used those chord changes for 'Wild One' and wrote a new song. It wasn't a spin-off; it just happened to be that way. By the time we got to New York, we had the song done. Bobby Rydell was the easiest to work with in the studio. He was more 'pro' musically than the other artists."

Bobby Rydell was able to establish himself through exposure on *American Bandstand* just before the payola scandal kicked in. "We had a good rapport with Dick Clark," said Dave Appell. "As a matter of fact, before him was Bob Horn, much older man. It was just a local show; everybody loved that show. They [were] ready to go network, and they said, 'They can't use Bob Horn on that thing.'[19] Dick at that time had a little cubbyhole and did radio. Every time I went down there to see the kids on the show, I always stopped [to] say hello to Dick, and he remembered those things. Then they used him. I guess Dick was involved with payola, but he got through that. Finally the law caught up with that; it wasn't illegal, but technically it was. Everybody had their hands out. It was business practice."

Dave Appell was enlisted as musical director for *The Dick Clark Caravan*, which was organized at its peak by top-notch impresarios Irvin and Israel Feld in conjunction with Clark. Advertised as "featuring many of the nation's top recording stars," the show was booked by Shaw Artists Corporation. "I went as Dick's conductor on a lot of his tours," said Appell. "We took a couple of key guys, a drummer and maybe a keyboard player, and each town we went in we hired. I'd call up the union [and] get a contractor to get the band. We'd need four saxes, three trumpets . . . it was a big band with the shows. I wrote out all the charts; the artists had their charts, too. I remember Anita Bryant, Frankie Avalon, and a lot of black artists."

When Bernie Lowe and Kal Mann constructed their own studio in 1960, Dave Appell was brought into the mix. "I didn't know anything about engineering," he said.

Boom, you're an engineer! The studio was maybe 18-by-18; we used to put seven musicians in there. We did all the tracks there, but we didn't have the capability to do voices there. So we went to another studio in Philadelphia called Reco-Art; technically, it was a very good studio.[20] I think it was two mono machines we had then. You overdubbed while you were there. Emil Korsen, who built the studio, said, "See that meter over there? Before [the needle] gets up [to the red area], everything is fine."

I had three saxes, piano, bass, drums, and a guitar, side to side. So about an hour into the thing, he said, "How are you doing?" I said, "Okay, but I can't get that meter up there [to a satisfactory level]." "Well, how does it sound?" "Pretty good." "Well, forget the meter; that's your first lesson!"

We recorded in the evening because everybody was working in the office building there in the daytime. We didn't have any echo chambers. We took a mic with a long wire and put it in the men's room, because it would give you that *click* sound. Everything was great until somebody flushed the toilet, and that would be the end of that take. But we grew. We built our own studio, our own echo chamber and stuff.

We had a sound, the three saxes. A lot of them just had one sax with rock 'n' roll. Georgie Young played sax, *excellent* man, and Buddy Savitt, a jazz player who worked with Woody Herman, he played the majority of the stuff on sax. We had an old upright piano, didn't have a grand piano. The piano player was Roy Straigis, but on "The Twist" there was a black man, Leroy Lovett; he went with Motown publishing company [Jobete Music]. We had an integrated band; we never had problems. The voicing was a little different—we had ten dollar microphones [*laughs*]—but we had super rhythm. The New York union was very strict, but down here not so much. We had to pay scale, forty bucks a session for a three-hour date [actually $41.25]. That was lot of money for the musicians. I played guitar on a lot of sessions.

Mann and Lowe rarely interfered. Kal would come there if it was his song, and he'd only come there if there was a vocal going on, not when we were doing tracks. That was my baby. Bernie used to call me at eleven o'clock at night [if] we were doing a night session, [and] he'd say, "Play the track!" I said, "Bernie, you know what it's going to sound like over the phone." He said, "Look, I'm a musician, I understand, play it for me." "What do you think, Bernie?" "It doesn't have enough bottom" [*laughs*].

"Let's Twist Again" and Again

And so Dave Appell was producing the backing tracks at Cameo's small studio and overdubbing the vocal parts at Reco-Art studios. With crisp, whip-crack rhythms, the Cameo-Parkway hits of the early 1960s resonate with a comforting familiarity, starting with "The Twist." The dance novelty was launched on Parkway Records by Chubby Checker in the late summer of 1960 after Hank Ballard's original 1959 King version was repromoted by Sid Nathan.

"'The Twist' was a hit already by Hank Ballard," said Appell. "We knew it would hit again because we copied it pretty good as a cover record. Hank in one way . . . was mad, but in another he made his share out of it [as writer]. 'The Twist' got us into the dance craze. All we did was write songs like 'Let's Twist Again,' 'Limbo Rock,' 'The Wah Watusi,' 'Bristol Stomp.' We didn't start the dances, but we did the stroll, the slow dance, and so on, because everybody was doing dance records to get on Dick Clark's show."

As Appell implied, Hank Ballard was not terribly upset at seeing his original recording of "The Twist" being shunted to the side. Ballard explained the background intrigue to me in 1992: "Dick Clark made a deal with King Records: 'If you don't [re]release Hank Ballard's "The Twist" [to compete with Checker's version], I'll make

"Finger Poppin' Time" a hit.' That was the deal. What record company wouldn't like for Dick Clark to be playing *two* songs a day and have the publishing on them? King had the publishing on 'Finger Poppin' Time' and the publishing on 'The Twist.' Now you tell me what record company wouldn't want that on *American Bandstand.* Oh yes, I've always gotten my royalties, big royalties!"

"The Twist" by Chubby Checker proceeded to hit No. 1 in the charts twice, in September 1960 and January 1962; it was a double shared with Bing Crosby's "White Christmas." "Chubby Checker was Ernest Evans," said Dave Appell,

> and he was working as a chicken flicker in a poultry place. When we needed a name for him, Dick Clark's first wife says, "Fats Domino . . . let's call him Chubby Checker." You couldn't say, "Now here he is, Ernest Evans!" Chubby used to come up to our place and used to hang around. He'd sit at the piano and imitate Fats Domino; he knew three chords on the piano. We used to kick him out all the time, and he'd come back every day until finally we got to record with him. Before we did the "The Twist," we did "Schooldays Oh Schooldays"; that got him started on Parkway.
>
> Chubby was pretty easy in the studio. When he knew he had to work, he worked. "Let's Twist Again," that was Kal's idea, the story, and I wrote the music to it. That was a smash [but only No. 8 in summer 1961 despite its subsequent celebrity]. We knew it was going to be a hit because it was so close to "The Twist." If it's working, don't fix it. That was our approach. There was "Slow Twistin'," "Ray Charles Twist," so many of them . . .

The entire record market was given a lift after the post-payola lull as singles sales rebounded on the back of the twist dance craze, which was spreading internationally. "It was like doing the hula hoop without the hoop," said Appell, "and there was no need to attend a dance school. Anybody could do it; it was so natural. I used to do the twist. When I was a kid, I was a good jitterbugger, too."

In between the big twist hits, Checker had another No. 1 in early 1961 with the near-forgotten "Pony Time." The Cameo-Parkway production line became overloaded with dance records, on LPs as well as 45s. But the chart streak continued unabated, so why not? "Bristol Stomp" by the Dovells was one of the biggest hits (No. 2, Parkway, late 1961). Kal Mann went up to Bristol, just outside of Philadelphia, to see the kids "dancing a special dance" and returned to write the song with Dave Appell. "Bernie Lowe said that line with 'sharp as a pistol' will never go," recalled Appell.[21]

> Kal would say, "Uh, uh, uh." The Dovells, we had a lot of problems with them. I used to record them with a police whistle [*laughs*]. Len Barry was the original lead [with] four guys singing doo-wops in the background, and it was too much. Like, one kid would sing a note, and the other guy would say, "You got my note; give me my note back." Boom, before you know it, they're on the floor fighting—and I'm in the control booth recording them.
>
> Joe Tarsia, later of Sigma Sound, was my assistant at one time as an engineer. In those days, the [tape] machines were old mono machines—you had to snap on the gate—and we were recording Jo Ann Campbell's "(I'm the Girl on) Wolverton Moun-

tain" [an answer song to Claude King's Top 10 hit and a No. 38 chart record in its own right, late summer 1962]. At the time, there was a craze for short-shorts. She was sitting on the stool with her legs crossed, and Joe was out there; he's going crazy. I said, "Roll the tape, Joe," and he rolls the tape and she's singing. I said, "Great, play it back, Joe." Nothing . . . he forgot to close the gate of the tape machine.

To cope with the extra workload brought about by the astonishing run of hits and following a stock IPO, Bernie Lowe strengthened his management team by bringing in distributor Harry Chipetz as general manager with Al Kahn as sales executive. The heavy action showed through in net sales of $3.9 million for the first six months of 1962, compared with just over $1 million for the comparable period of the previous year.[22]

In quick succession, through summer 1962 to spring 1963, the Orlons continued the winning streak with "The Wah Watusi" (No. 2), "Don't Hang Up" (No. 4), and "South Street" (No. 3). "The Orlons were pretty easy," said Dave Appell. "In fact, most of the guys were pretty easy to record. We had a relationship with them: they knew me; I knew them. It wasn't complete strangers going into places. The girls that used to sing background on Bobby Rydell—'yeah yeah wo wo wee'—were all grandmothers; they were black gospel singers. Everybody thought they were kids; they had a sound."

Dee Dee Sharp was a strong contributor to the Cameo-Parkway honor roll of hits. After scoring with "Mashed Potato Time" at No. 2, she had four other Top 10 songs in 1962 and early 1963: "Slow Twistin'" with Chubby Checker (No. 3), "Gravy (For My Mashed Potatoes) (No. 9), "Ride!" (No. 5), and "Do the Bird" (No. 10). "Mashed Potato Time" presented a publishing dilemma that was resolved by Tamla's Berry Gordy with common sense.

"In those days, they did business differently," said Dave Appell. "Like, 'Mashed Potato Time' was based on 'Please Mr. Postman' [the first Tamla-Motown No. 1 hit, by the Marvelettes in 1961]. We knew we were going to get sued, so Bernie called up Berry Gordy and said, 'Hey, man, I've got a song here. I know you've got a song there; let's work it out over the phone,' and they did. 'Okay, you've got half the publishing' [for Jobete Music]. Today they'd go to court, lawyers and everything."

Cameo-Parkway did have a little local difficulty with a firm of lawyers who occupied an office one floor below the Cameo studio. According to a tongue-in-cheek front page story in *Billboard* (April 6, 1963), "Some lawyers don't want no twistin' round here . . . but Cameo don't care what Philadelphia lawyers won't allow, they're gonna play the twist anyhow . . . and the whole thing wound up in Judge Leo Weinrott's Common Pleas Court last week. . . . They complained it was impossible to hear themselves think—much less hear clients—with the rumble of the twist, the wailing of the brass and the moans of Checker and his buddies filtering through the floor."

The Tymes' first record, "So Much in Love," was another Parkway No. 1 in August 1963. It was a performance far removed from teen dances, more a precursor of the "Philly sweet soul" movement. "That was Billy Jackson and Jimmy Wisner," said Dave Appell. "They came in to do a vocal on the record, and all they did was add a drum backbeat and maracas, kept it very simple. Jimmy Wisner did some production for us. He worked with Billy Jackson; they were a team. He left and went to work for Columbia Records [and] did a lot charts." Jimmy Wisner had a 1961 No. 8 hit as Kokomo with the pseudo-classical piano instrumental "Asia Minor" (Felsted). Among his biggest production hits was "1–2–3" for Decca in 1965 by Len Barry, the Dovells' lead singer.

Meanwhile, the Cameo-Parkway phenomenon had peaked. It was no coincidence that the labels started to lose their gloss when Dick Clark transplanted his organization to the West Coast in 1964, the very same year that the Beatles turned the music world upside down. For all its success, or perhaps because of it, Cameo-Parkway had a reputation of being something of a closed shop. With little outside input, Bernie Lowe, Kal Mann, and Dave Appell missed out on the burgeoning soul scene in Philadelphia that was hinted at by the Tymes' No. 1 record for Parkway. The way ahead was clear for Jamie-Guyden, Swan, and, famously, for Philadelphia International through Gamble and Huff. By then, Cameo-Parkway Records was yesterday's news.

"My involvement ended when Bernie Lowe sold the place in 1965," said Dave Appell. "His lawyers talked him into going public. They made money, and he made some money out of that thing. A lot of people bought the stock, but he was just fed up with stockholders' meetings. He wasn't built like that; he was a musician. Then he went downhill, got sick, and passed away [in 1993]. He was a little nervous guy, but the record business can really make you nervous. Maybe it got to him? Kal Mann didn't write much after that; he just kept countin' his money, that's all [laughs]. The guys from Texas bought Cameo-Parkway. Neil Bogart [head of ill-fated Casablanca Records in the disco era] came in, and it was a completely different operation; it wasn't for me. I went to New York; that era was over." Dave Appell had further big success in the early 1970s co-producing, with Hank Medress of the Tokens, a series of hit records by Tony Orlando & Dawn for Bell.[23]

A merger between Cameo-Parkway Records and Allen Klein and Co. was announced formally on September 16, 1968.[24] Somewhat belatedly, in 2005, Klein's ABKCO Music & Records commenced a quality Cameo-Parkway CD reissue program.

In a way, Dave Appell could have rested easily in retirement just by being known among his golfing buddies as the co-writer of "Let's Twist Again," an elemental song in the international cult phenomenon. As he said, Chubby Checker's record was still played all over the world—and Dave would have known from his performance royalty statements. Rather, he was the crucial, understated linchpin at Cameo Records. With the immaculate pedigrees of Bernie Lowe, Kal Mann, and Appell himself (and with the solid support of Dick Clark at *American Bandstand*), there was much more to Cameo-Parkway than the twist and other teen dance records.

Paul Evans: Teen Star and Brill Building Songwriter

Back in New York, Paul Evans was thrust into the limelight as a teen star when his first release for Joe Carlton's Guaranteed label, "Seven Little Girls Sitting in the Back Seat," was a No. 9 hit in the fall of 1959. Backed by female duo the Curls, Paul had cut the silly novelty song as a demo, but in typical New York fashion, the recording was good enough to be released as a single. Evans had further big hits in 1960 with a creditable version of Leadbelly's "Midnite Special" (No. 16) and "Happy-Go-Lucky-Me" (No. 10). He was the beneficiary of Joe Carlton's long industry experience as editor of *Billboard* and head of A&R at Mercury and RCA Victor. At the same time, Evans claimed he was a victim of royalty abuse.

Paul Evans turned out to be more than an aggrieved, fleeting pop artist and was able to carve out a lifetime career in music by writing songs (including country) and commercial jingles. His portfolio is headed by the classic co-write "Roses Are Red (My Love)," a No. 1 for Bobby Vinton (Epic, 1962), and four songs for Elvis Presley. With escalating statutory rates combined with Presley's unstoppable popularity, these songs were earning more than ever at the turn of the new millennium.

Evans had an unusual start as a teen recording artist back in the '50s by starting out with a major label. "First of all, I was originally signed to Groove," he said,

> which was an R&B subsidiary of RCA Victor. Steve Sholes and Brad McCuen came to my first session and decided that I would not come out under Groove [but] that I would be a white rock 'n' roller on RCA Victor. And I was! It was a shame that nothing happened with those records.
>
> I learned my lesson quickly when I went on the road with an RCA promotion man. You would go in with the promotion man, and he would say to the disc jockey, "Oh, by the way (very quietly), this is Paul Evans, who has a new record on RCA." And (very loud) "Look what I have for you, a new Belafonte record and . . . I have an Elvis record here!" I mean, there was no chance; there was just no chance. However, if I would have gone in with an independent, they would probably have taken my records a little more seriously.

After three RCA releases, the nineteen-year-old Evans was signed to another major label, Decca. His eyes were soon opened to the scramble to land song copyrights. "You'd walk in at Decca," he said, "and as you walked out [into the studio], all the A&R men would ask if your publishing was spoken for. They had some pretty hefty guys there at the time: Milt Gabler, Dick Jacobs, and Jack Pleis . . . all had a publishing business on the side. That didn't happen at RCA or Columbia. It did, of course, at the independents—they wanted a piece of it—but at Decca, it was more open. I learned fast. You had a commodity, and it was called publishing. And everybody wanted that commodity."

With nonproductive recording contracts for RCA and Decca, Paul Evans signed in 1959 for red-hot Atlantic Records. "It was a disappointment," he admitted, "because before even cutting the record, they forgot about me. I couldn't get in to see Jerry [Wexler]; they didn't bother with me. But I loved going up there. Jerry and Ahmet [Ertegun] were nuts; they were wonderful, funny guys. I played them a demo song once, and I don't know whether it had an Indian motif or something, but the next thing I knew, Ahmet and Jerry were on their knees in their office, underneath a keyhole desk. I am playing my song, and they are making war whoops like Indians. So they finished the song, and, like one guy, they both said, "We're not interested" [*laughs*]. Now, maybe they signed me because they thought "Maybe we need a whitebread artist," I don't know, but Bobby Darin was much "blacker" than I was. Atlantic did record two of my songs: "Dix-a-Billy" by LaVern Baker and "The P.T.A." by the Coasters.

Immediately after leaving Atlantic, Paul Evans signed with Guaranteed, a new "rock 'n' roll" subsidiary of Carlton Records. The parent label's early teen star was the talented Jack Scott, but with his hits drying up, Joe Carlton offloaded his contract to newly formed Top Rank Records in an astute deal worth $50,000, involving a fee of $30,000 for the contract and a royalty waiver of $20,000.[25] The chart slack at Carlton was taken up by Anita Bryant (a Miss Oklahoma and a Miss America runner-up) and by Paul Evans.

"Joe Carlton was certainly one of the top, top A&R men," said Evans, "and he saw [that] the independents were becoming very important and set up Carlton Records. When I went to Carlton Records, Joe understood promotion and publicity. He had three very good promotion men: Juggy Gayles, George Furness, Morris Diamond. Their job was to get your records played on the radio; that's all their job was. There was no more sheet music market, period. Come to think of it, that was a quick deterioration. What a change there was when rock 'n' roll came in, whew! When I got into the business, they really were looking for me. They needed somebody who could write rock 'n' roll, because the big companies didn't have them. It was the independents that sprang this music on us, and it was catch-up for the big companies."

Following the debut hit "Seven Little Girls Sitting in the Back Seat," Paul Evans was snapped up by GAC for the regulatory rock 'n' roll caravan tours. "That was a horrible experience, too," he recalled,

> because they [GAC] were a monopoly. They were your agent, but they were also producing the shows. Where did they make the most money? By giving these "stars" on a big package tour as little money as they possibly could and by pocketing the rest as part of the production. These were my agents. I didn't like getting paid four hundred dollars that first week I went on the bus tour and paying out so much in daily expenses that it cost me money. And here I had the No. 9 record in the country.
>
> But I was so unprepared, because we were kids and it didn't matter. The Crests were on this first tour, Santo & Johnny, LaVern Baker . . . and the Everly Brothers joined us in a couple of spots. But, anyway, I got out of that very quickly; I didn't like it. Later, the Motown acts were choreographed. That was much better; that was much smarter. We were like in a mill. White pop young acts, chew 'em up, and make as much money as you can, and then on to the next artist. I understand that because that's the way it mainly went. How many white pop artists stood the test of time? Most were one-hit wonders; I was a three-hit wonder at that time. I always believed that part of my fall from grace was Joe's habit of playing . . . the Carlton distributors against the Guaranteed distributors. In other words, "If you don't do what I want you to do, I'll pull the label."
>
> Another part of the deal, I guess, was when you went on the road to promote. Truly, I would get in the car with the promotion guy, and he'd ask me what I'd like for "din-

ner." I mean, he was talking about women. What a horrible thing to do to me [*laughs*]. I didn't realize I was paying for the promotion trip, but I paid for it. The disc jockeys would interview me, and then I would go out of town and they would drop the record. I wouldn't know what was going on.

Joe Carlton appeared to spare no expense in marketing his hot new teen commodity. Full-page advertisements started appearing in *Billboard* and *Cash Box*, album promotional campaigns ensued, and even a short tour of the Far East was arranged. It was impressive on the surface. All the time, of course, Evans was paying for this expenditure (including the album recording sessions) as charges against royalties.

"Joe Carlton was a very smart business guy," said Evans.

I am smiling because I had a big dispute, and I sent an accountant in. After my one year or so there, it looked like he owed me over $40,000. Unfortunately, I was told, "If you sue him for the money, he'll go bankrupt." So, what's the point? I just got off the label. That was my big benefit. Joe would drive me home sometimes, as he . . . live[d] farther out in Long Island, and he'd drop me off in Queens. He was like, in a way, another father to me. I loved Joe in a way, I suppose, but he was taking my money.

I really think that they were convinced that it's just the way you do business: you sell 100,000 records, you pay on 40[,000]. After all, you have your wife, family, and house. So, I think that's the way the independents thought: you cheat the artist. Besides, the artist wouldn't have a hit record without the label owner. I can see how you could convince yourself. That's what they call SBP: standard business procedure.

I remember Joe Carlton and a publisher named [Aaron] Goldie Goldmark, who had an office called Sequence Music, which had some of my songs. Joe and Goldie were very good music business friends, and they were typical. I mean, they would have drinks at the bars together, they would eat food together, and they would *cheat* each other. It was a game to them; they played this silly game. I was in Joe's office once, and Goldie was on the phone. Goldie was asking if he was going to do something, and while Joe was "yes"-ing him to death, he was winking at me all the time. I think Goldie knew this, but they were just having a lot of fun. The business *was* a lot of fun. I can't explain how that goes together with cheating the artists, but they were fun; these guys were characters.

In Joe Carlton's case, I think it was street smarts, and I think it was knowing the way the business was manipulated. I think he took the clue from the earlier independent labels. He saw what was going on, and he replicated whatever was going on. But it was always an area with some exceptions. I only can tell you that I always heard that Archie Bleyer [Cadence Records] was the exception to this rule. He did what he thought was right, and I never heard anybody complain about being cheated by Archie. I wish I knew him. He recorded one of my good friends, Johnny Tillotson [also the Chordettes, the Everly Brothers, and Andy Williams].

Growing up quickly, Paul Evans came across the shadier side of the business at the Roulette Records complex. "Well, I used to go up to Planetary Music," he said,

which is where Nat Tarnopol had an office. I walked past Nat; I knew he managed Jackie Wilson. And I knew he was involved somehow with tough people, because . . .

at Planetary, there would be guys literally with a fedora pulled down over one eye [and] a big wad over the chest, which was a gun. It was like a joke, but they would hang out there like that, and I was a little nervous. So, anyway, Nat Tarnopol called me in his office and said, "Hey kid, come here! Paul, I think you could have big hits, and I would like to manage you. Because, kid, if I manage you, I am going to make a lot of money. And, kid, if I make a lot of money, you're going to make money, too." I observed that there was something different about that line of thought. If he managed me, he was going to make a lot of money and *then* I would make money, too. So I knew that I would be caught in a situation I didn't want to get in.

With blanket exposure on radio and TV at the turn of the 1960s, the lifespan of records was getting shorter. A continual supply of new songs was needed in replenishment. And so "1619"—the Brill Building—and 1650 Broadway became the heart and soul of the music business for record labels as well as for songwriters, music publishers, promo men, and assorted hangers-on.

Despite the commercial pressures, there was electricity in the New York air that led to the girl group sound, uptown soul, and rejuvenated doo-wop. The heavy backbeat of first-wave, rebellious rock 'n' roll was being supplanted to a large extent by subtle Latin rhythms and neoclassical violin arrangements. And the lyrics were being written for teens by teens, more or less. Thus began what is known as the Brill Building era via the pens of such teams as Jeff Barry and Ellie Greenwich, Gerry Goffin and Carole King, Barry Mann and Cynthia Weill, and Neil Sedaka and Howie Greenfield. History has decreed that their songs have become far more durable than could possibly have been envisaged at the era's dawning.

One of Evans's favorite stories is of coming across Barry Mann on Broadway when he had three songs in the Top 10, but Mann did not have the time to converse for self-congratulation. Instead, he was rushing to record new demos because that triumvirate of chart songs was on the way *down.*

"So rock 'n' roll opened the way for the young writers," said Paul Evans,

and knocked out the so-called standard writers, although a few of them made the change, such as Bob Hilliard and Hal David. But the old-time writers from ASCAP owned the business, and they must have *really* hated rock 'n' roll. They could see [that] people didn't want their music as much anymore; they wanted this raw kids music.

The older writers always told me, sneering, . . . "Okay, you're having a hit now, but you are never going to hear that song again." They'd say, "Ah, we wrote the standards!" But look, who wins? I win, they lose; their songs are not getting played. Not that they're bad songs, not that my songs were better, but that's what happened. That group just sort of disappeared. Rock 'n' roll was just something else that had come into the business; it changed the whole thing. It was *kids.*

Then Don Kirshner formed this Aldon group with Al Nevins. That was quite revolutionary, to bring all these young writers together. He would have had incentives from BMI, absolutely; all his writers were BMI. That was a scary group of guys and girls, because, suddenly, they started getting all the records. Donny Kirshner was not noted as a music man, but he loved music. I remember [songwriter] Jack Keller once telling me that up there, even if Kirshner was in a conference with record companies, anybody, . . . if a writer had a problem in one of those little cubicles and asked him to come in, he would break the meeting to go in and talk to the writers. So that was probably his success, that he handled his writers very well and with respect. I think another part of the Aldon formula was being competitive. Donny would say so-and-so artist is coming up for a date, and he had an "in" because he was Donny Kirshner with a load of hits behind him. And the writers would all run off to their little cubicles and write for this artist.[26]

Paul Evans's first big writer's royalty check arrived after "When," co-written with Jack Reardon and recorded by the Kalin Twins, was a No. 5 hit in the summer of 1958 (and an improbable No. 1 R&B) before making the top spot in England. This record hinted strongly that the young Brill songwriters were avidly absorbing the latest chart sounds.

"That's how 'When' came about," agreed Evans. "The Everly Brothers were around making hits, and so all the labels decided they needed a 'twins' act or a 'brothers' act or whatever. We wrote 'When' for the Everly Brothers, but we didn't know how to get it to them. So we got into whom we knew. We got it to Jack Pleis; the Kalin Twins were signed by Decca. Creativity is not really respected in our business; it's eaten up right away. I mean, if you come out with a novelty hit, all of a sudden everybody wants novelty songs. Creativity doesn't last long, and then probably the people who are the creators find this is a formula."

Much inspiration for the cubbyholed Brill Building songwriters had come from the Diamonds' 1957 version of "Little Darlin'." With its slick David Carroll orchestration, the record was a template for a host of songs with a rock-a-cha beat, including "Dream Lover" by Bobby Darin (Atco), "Oh! Carol" by Neil Sedaka (RCA Victor), and "Let the Little Girl Dance" by Billy Bland (Old Town).

Paul Evans, as in "When," was influenced by the Penguins' trendsetting 1954 recording of "Earth Angel" (Dootone). He recognized that the same popular "four-chord" sequence was found in many other doo-wop songs, such as "In the Still of the Nite," "Come Go with Me," and "We Belong Together." "The triplet piano *rhythm* accompaniment," added Evans, "that Fats Domino used [and many others did as a rock 'n' roll feature] is often associated with that four-chord progression, but it isn't an integral part of those four chords. The three-note chords can be used with any chord progression."[27] As if to prove there's nothing new in music, Evans noted that Irving Berlin employed a four-chord structure on "Blue Moon," which perhaps is why the song was so easily adapted in doo-wop style by the Marcels for their memorable No. 1 hit (Colpix, 1961). But here's the punch line: even Beethoven used this format. The classical composer, said Evans laughingly, would have made a great rock 'n' roll writer.

Paul Evans arrived as a songwriter when his "I Gotta Know" co-write was recorded by Elvis Presley as the flip side of "Are You Lonesome Tonight?"—a massive end of 1960 No. 1 record that was a follow-up to the equally big "It's Now or Never." "Which wasn't a bad place to be," Evans said.

"I Gotta Know" hit the charts in its own right [No. 20]. Our first royalty check was based on 1,500,000 sales. Even if the publisher made a deal with RCA—maybe they had a deal at 75 percent of statutory or something—I didn't know, and I didn't care. I knew I would make some money if I had success in any form of the business.

If I'd heard that Elvis Presley was coming up for a date, I would try to write a song for Elvis. I remember when I finally discovered how you get Elvis: you have to go to Hill & Range. I literally knocked on the Hill & Range door, and that meant the Bienstocks. Paul Case was there, their song man, who did the first audition of your demos. For a big company that was so important, I found them very friendly, and I liked the people up there. I liked the Bienstocks; I think their reputation was fair. Their reputation was if you signed a bad contract with them, too bad, they are going to make you stick with it. I didn't have an argument with that. Simply be careful with what you sign.

Just as the old-school songwriters were struck down by rock 'n' roll, so the young New York scribes would not be immunized against ever-evolving industry trends. "I remember when the Beatles hit town," said Evans. "I saw their writing, and I got really scared. I was still writing at the time; I was still getting records—I had Elvis. And I saw that along with the Rolling Stones, the Beatles were a self-contained group. Actually, Paul Anka was the first one I ever saw that got me a little nervous, because he was a writer/singer, very successful. I was a writer/singer, but I was really a writer first. But Anka came in and hit the top of the charts so fast and so furiously, he was scary. It meant that they wouldn't need [professional] writers."

In a parting reflection on his time as a teen star and teen songwriter, Paul Evans said, "It's a manipulated business, you know, but we were very naive. We were just, 'Golly, this is fun.' I got some money from my hits, but again the payoff was small. The payoff wasn't the money; the payoff was being in this business and singing and writing. And being happy, right? [laughs]."

Alan Freed dinner, New York, at the peak of the indie era, c. 1957, including Freed *(turning away at top table)* with wife Jackie, songwriters Rose Marie McCoy *(top left)* and Charlie Singleton *(standing next to her, part only)*, A&R man Leroy Kirkland *(second row, fourth from left)*, and Sid Parnes, *Cash Box* editor *(front row, with glasses)*. Courtesy John Broven, with acknowledgment to Rose Marie McCoy.

Gale agency's *The Big Rhythm and Blues Show* poster, 1953. Courtesy Richard Tapp, *Juke Blues.*

The Wailers with Dick Clark on *American Bandstand,* 1959. Courtesy Golden Crest Records.

Sir Edward Lewis, president of London Records Inc. and chairman of the board of Decca Records Ltd., 1961. Courtesy John Broven.

Mimi Trepel, London
Records, with husband
Murray Jordan, c. 1955.
Courtesy John Broven,
with acknowledgment to
Mimi Trepel.

Hi Records–London Records
distributor meeting, Mem-
phis, 1964: Joe Cuoghi, Hi
president; Bill Emerson, Big
State Distributing Corpora-
tion, Dallas; D. H. Toller-
Bond, director, London
American group; and Walt
Maguire, head of singles,
London. Courtesy John
Broven.

Cameo-Parkway Records, 1964. *Standing:* Dave Appell and Bernie Lowe. *Seated:* Kal Mann, Billy Jackson (of the Tymes), and engineer Joe Tarsia. Courtesy Urban Archives, Temple University, Philadelphia.

Fred Foster, Monument Records *(left)* and Roy Orbison in Nashville studio, early 1960s. Courtesy Trevor Cajiao, *Now Dig This.*

Larry Newton, vice president of ABC-Paramount Records, 1960. Courtesy John Broven.

M. S. Distributors meeting, Chicago, 1960. These record company execs were among the many record manufacturers, dealers, and disc jockeys in attendance. *Front row:* Bob Kornheiser (Atlantic), Bob Skaff (Liberty), Milt Salstone (M. S. Distributors), Si Waronker (Liberty), Harry Carlson (Fraternity), Jay Lasker (Kapp), and Ewart Abner and Jimmy Bracken (Vee-Jay). *Back row:* Leonard Chess (Chess), Larry Uttal (Madison), Johnny Bienstock (Bigtop), Bob Schwartz (Laurie), Al Bennett (Liberty), Neil Galligan (Canadian American), Don Sanders (Cadence), and Calvin Carter (Vee-Jay). Courtesy John Broven.

Veteran record men Don Pierce (Starday), Sam Phillips (Sun), and Shelby
Singleton (SSS International–Sun), Nashville, early 1970s. Courtesy Colin
Escott.

John Broven interviewing Bobby Robinson, Harlem, 1986. Courtesy Paul Harris.

23
CHAPTER

Corporate Takeover and Talent Makeover

CAST OF CHARACTERS
  Fred Foster, district sales manager, ABC-Paramount
    Records
  Morty Craft, MGM and Warwick Records
  Dick Alen, Shaw and William Morris booking agencies
  also featuring Sam Clark and Larry Newton,
  ABC-Paramount Records

The entrance of ABC-Paramount Records in November 1955 was another indication that the big corporations were waking up to the growth potential in the record market, to the general detriment and ultimate demise of the original stand-alone independents. This intriguing label was an offshoot of the national network American Broadcasting Company (ABC) and Paramount Theatres, which had been merged in February 1953 under the inspired leadership of Leonard Goldenson (who saw television as the golden prize). Paramount Theatres itself had been spun off from Paramount Pictures in 1949 following federal antitrust activity over theater-chain monopolies.

In the record stakes, ABC was seeking to emulate NBC with RCA Victor and CBS with Columbia. With this corporate might behind the Am-Par Record Corporation, as it was called, here was a start-up that was as near to a champagne-laden, major label–type launch as could be. Affiliated publishing divisions Pamco (BMI) and Ampco (ASCAP) were registered at the same time.

The highly respected Sam Clark was recruited as Am-Par's president with the promise of initial capital of $500,000 and a 10 percent equity stake. What must the likes of Hy Weiss and George Goldner have thought of such largesse, even if they were both incapable of working within large corporations? ABC's strategy toward formal major label status consisted of a two-pronged attack: hiring accomplished A&R men Sid Feller and Don Costa for in-house productions to develop talent, and seeking worthwhile masters to distribute or purchase. ABC-Paramount, with an open music policy, was a real supporter of the independent ethos from day one, thanks in part to Sam Clark's indie industry grounding.

Clark had arrived at ABC after coming off a stint as national sales manager for Archie Bleyer's hot Cadence label, having learned the industry ropes as a successful distributor with Music Suppliers of New England in Boston. Sam's right-hand man was chief administrative officer Harry Levine, the chief talent booker for Paramount Theatres. Even with a fruitful early Walt Disney licensing deal, in the froth of the Davy Crockett cult craze, the lofty aspirations for Am-Par were far from being satisfied.[1] The pop division required much better results than the modest hits provided by Bobby Scott and Eydie Gorme.

Enter Larry Newton, who, like Sam Clark, was well versed in every aspect of the independent record business. The loud yet charismatic Newton was yet another record man who came from a humble Russian Jewish background. He was raised in Philadelphia where his parents ran a fish store, which, with its perpetual stench, was the type of business that only poor immigrants would take on. Starting out as a record picker and packer at the Columbia Records depot in his hometown, Newton went to New York to work as sales manager for Joe Davis's Celebrity label and then Paul Reiner's Black & White imprint before forming Derby Records in June 1949.

While operating Derby, Newton dabbled in artist management with Eddie Heller of Rainbow Records before moonlighting, on a small scale, with the launch of Central Records with Lee Magid in 1953. However, Derby Records represented an uneasy mix of pop and R&B, and there were no substantial hits apart from the first chart entrant of "Wheel of Fortune" by the Eddie Wilcox Orchestra with Sunny Gale (No. 13 pop, No. 2 R&B, 1952).[2] Catastrophically, Derby overextended itself, forcing Newton to file for bankruptcy in October 1954 with "liabilities of $213,090 and assets of $18,935." After indefatigable industry veteran Eli Oberstein had come in with a rejected lowball bid of $3,500, RCA Victor ended up with the dated Derby catalog.[3]

Larry Newton came back fighting in August 1956 when he was recruited by ABC-Paramount as eastern sales supervisor, only to be promoted hastily to national sales manager. Newton's relationship with Sam Clark dated back to Clark's time working for the Boston distributor of Derby Records. A natural-born salesman, Newton could hustle with the best of them. Whenever he wanted favors from a distributor or a disc jockey, one of his shticks was to gift perfume to the various secretaries, according to his grandson Adam Kaplan. Yet Newton showed a professional approach to his trade by keenly analyzing the sales reports. And he endeared himself to his far-flung backroom staff by knowing every one of them on first-name terms, said Kaplan.

Thus, under the assured leadership of Sam Clark and with the relentless drive of Larry Newton, ABC-Paramount strode toward its major label target but with those indie label philosophies. Newton's approach was summarized in his quote to *Billboard* in June 1960: "A real record man should know everything about the business. He can't be a specialist and really make it. He must have an intuitive feeling for a hit and he must have 100 percent distributor loyalty."[4]

Fred Foster: District Sales Manager, ABC-Paramount Records

Replacing Larry Newton in the field, Fred Foster was taken on as Am-Par's district manager for the eastern seaboard covering Philadelphia down to Florida.[5] Previously, Foster was Mercury's promotion man in the Baltimore-Washington area, where he helped to break "Only You" by the Platters. There was early friction between Foster and Newton. "I was promotion and sales manager of ABC-Paramount," said Foster.

> It was September '56 until January '58. It was a marvelous company. Sam Clark was a wonderful man who was president. Larry Newton, who was sales manager, was not . . . my cup of tea; he was always afraid I was after his job. I wouldn't have had his freaking job, living in New York City; I'd already been offered that by a bunch of people. No way was I gonna take the children into New York City and try to raise a family. We didn't get along very well. He was always trying to undercut me.
>
> But Sam was great. He gave me freedom to explore things as his East Coast representative. One night I called him from El Paso, Texas, and said, "Sam, where in the hell does the East Coast end?" He said, "Wherever you are!" I was traveling almost every minute, and I was picking up masters.

Foster remembered ABC-Paramount's uneasy ascent:
They'd never had a Top 10 record when they hired me. I said to Sam, "What you ought to get is a hit," and he said, "Well, get us one!" So the late Buddy Deane, the great deejay in Baltimore, had the No. 1 rated show in the whole area. Matter of fact, when he went on television with *The Buddy Deane* [*Show*, on WJZ-TV], that was the highest-rated [local] show in the history of broadcasting. He had 67 percent of the available audience, on the average. Buddy ran a contest one time, and it burned out so many exchanges on the phone system [that] they got a court order preventing him from ever doing it again. I told Buddy, "You have got to help me find a hit," and he said, "It's not easy." I said, "I know it's not easy. With all of [the corporation's] money, ABC [hasn't] been able to find *one*."

Then one Saturday morning he called me, early; he went on the air about five o'clock. He said, "If you want a hit, you'd better get over here." And the phones started going crazy. He said, "Answer the phone." I did, and they said, "Oh, what is that record? Can you play it again? I missed part of it." Stuff like that. It was just magic. I said, "I must say it's a smash, but I don't even think it's a good record." He said, "It doesn't matter, does it? The people think it's a hit."

It was on a little label called Colonial Records out of Chapel Hill, North Carolina. So I called down that morning for information. "Do you have a Colonial Records?" "No." "Do you have a Colonial anything?" I figured it might be an umbrella company or something. They said, "We got a Colonial Press." I don't know how I found out, but the head of Colonial Records was Orville Campbell. So when he answered the phone at Colonial Press, I said, "Are you in any way, shape, or form associated with Orville Campbell, Colonial Records?" He said, "Well, you're talking to him." I said, "Thank you, I'm interested in picking up one of your masters: 'A Rose and a Baby Ruth,' George Hamilton IV."

Well, the record finally gets up there, [and] Larry Newton called me and said, "You're a sick man, Foster; it's the worst record I've ever heard. It's cost us all this money." I said, "It's not 'all this money.' It's a smash; I don't care whether you like it or not. The bass is out of tune in one place, but who cares? I haven't heard of one kid complaining about the bass." Well, it broke into the Top 10 at No. 6 in *Billboard*; I think it was No. 7 in *Cash Box* [actually No. 6, late 1956].[6]

Larry Newton again: ABC was trying to pick up a master from Lloyd Price in Washington, which is where I was living [in early 1957]. Larry had made him mad; Lloyd just hung up on him: "No deal, no deal." So Sam called me and asked if I could go down and try to resurrect the Lloyd Price thing. I'd already turned the record in to them as one they should try to pick up, the record called "Just Because" [on KRC Records, owned by Lloyd Price with confidants Harold Logan and Bill Boskent].

It was late at night when Sam called me. "You gotta go find him tonight." I had to go on Seventh Street NW below Florida Avenue, right down where the [1968] riots were in Washington. I was the only white person you could find at that time. So I walked in bars and clubs: "Is Lloyd Price here?" Every time I would walk in, people were laughing and you'd hear glasses tinkling, and they'd stop. I was the only white face around. Finally I walked into one called the Jack o' Diamonds. This girl goes along in this inverted L-shaped bar, and in about ten seconds I hear, "My man, send him on back here." And everybody started drinking and talking again.

So I had to talk to Lloyd and his manager Harold Logan for hours, all night, didn't go to bed. Twelve of the next morning I called Sam and said, "We can come up and you can sign the deal, but Larry Newton cannot be visible. You'll have to get him out of the building. First of all, I wouldn't be surprised if they ended up shooting him. I'm serious." So we got up there, and Harold Logan said, "Well, there's a rotten apple in every barrel, they say, but you got one good 'un here." I was real pleased, and we got the deal. Lloyd Price sold millions and millions of records, one after another: "Just Because" [No. 29], "Stagger Lee" [No. 1], "Where Were You (on Our Wedding Day)?" [No. 23], "Personality" [No. 2], and "I'm Gonna Get Married" [No. 3]. Later [in the mid-1960s] he came on Monument.

Harold Logan, to me he was a nice man. You know, he was killed [in 1969]. I don't know if such a thing as a black mafia exists. I heard that there is, and I don't know if he got crossways with some of the wrong people or what he did. He was obviously wiped out by a pro while Lloyd went to the men's room in their office in New York. But Harold wanted to tell Sam what the situation was: "Don't mess around; don't bullshit me."

The record that truly established ABC-Paramount as a force in the industry was "Diana" by Paul Anka, a No. 1 in September 1957 and an international smash hit. "He was from Canada," said Fred Foster.

I think he came down and auditioned. Everybody was going to turn him down, but it was Don Costa who said, "Sam, there may be something here; let me see." And they signed him. Don was a genius: he was a wonderful arranger and producer, and he was a great guitar player—most people didn't know that. So he *thought* like a guitarist. Everything was guitar-heavy in those days, in the beginning of the rock 'n' roll style. It just fell right in his lap.

But "Diana" broke huge. Yeah, Anka was an arrogant little bastard. No, nothing broke naturally; you had to work everything. So he came down [and] did a dee-jay tour with me, all over Washington. He was young, but he acted real bratty: "You got to treat me great because I'm great; I'm better than you." And then this wore on my nerves. So then he came down to play the Carter Barron Amphitheatre in Washington [run by famous promoters Irvin and Israel Feld]. Of course I had to meet him [and] take care of him. He had been driving me crazy for about three hours when he said suddenly, "Hey, how come you didn't get my Coke? You better go and get it right now." I said, "You'd better go to hell; I'm through with you." I went and called Sam Clark: "If you want to fire me you may, but I'm not going to put up with this little prick anymore." He said, "You don't have to. I agree with you; I can't stand to be around him" [*laughs*]. But of course over time Paul matured; he became a nice guy.

But then it was a situation that was really strained with me and Larry. I visited distributors one week, and we had a fall album release. I get into Atlanta and they've got the albums, but I don't know what the program is: [I asked,] "Is there any discount on this?" . . . "Are there any advertisement allowances?" . . . "Well, what's the deal?" So I went in to Sam and explained this to him, and that was in December 1957. I said, "I don't want to work under these conditions anymore." He said, "What would you be interested in? I don't want lose you; you're a valuable employee." I said, "I think I could be productive on A&R." He shook his head and said, "Fred, everybody wants to be in A&R; there's no way I can fix it." I said, "That's fine."

A year or so later I got to a dee-jay convention in Miami [the infamous 1959 affair], and so I'm there with two or three Monument hits under my belt. So Sam comes up to me, and he said, "Fred, why didn't you tell me you could produce hit records? I would have kept you." I said, "Sam, if you say one more word, I'm gonna throw you in the pool!" People got laughing and yelling at me. He said, "I'm really proud of you."

At the start of 1958, ABC-Paramount had already picked up two scorching masters, both of which were heavily promoted on ABC-TV's *American Bandstand*, from the smallest of independent labels.[7] "At the Hop" by Danny and the Juniors was acquired

from Singular and, after staying at No. 1 for seven weeks, became one of the signature tunes of the era. In the same period, "Short Shorts" by the Royal Teens (with
Bob Gaudio, later the brains behind the 4 Seasons) made No. 3 when purchased from
Leo Rogers and Lee Silver of Power Records at a reported cost of $15,000. But ABC,
along with Cameo, Mercury, and others, failed in the scramble to land the master of
"Don't You Just Know It" by Huey "Piano" Smith and the Clowns in March 1958. The
seasoned Johnny Vincent, wisely as it turned out, rejected a cash offer of $25,000 and
kept this eventual Top 10 record for his Ace label (and Ace Publishing) from Jackson,
Mississippi.[8]

The ABC hit momentum was maintained by "Rock and Roll Is Here to Stay," a
first-class Top 20 follow-up by Danny and the Juniors to "At the Hop." Then "Little
Star" by the Elegants shot to No. 1 in July 1958 on the Apt subsidiary, followed closely
by another Top 10 record, "Born Too Late" by the Poni-Tails. Meanwhile, that innovative Am-Par distribution deal with Chancellor Records was reaping big dividends from
Frankie Avalon's hits, inflated further by Fabian's onslaught on the musical lexicon.

In time, a positive raft of labels was to follow variants of the ABC-Paramount/
Chancellor deal model, including Atlantic with Stax, Chess with Anna, Imperial with
Minit, King with Beltone, Laurie with Legrand, Liberty with Dolton and Era, Mercury
with Clock, United Artists with Boyd, Vee-Jay with Ace (disastrously), and Warner
Bros. with Challenge. Then, of course, the London American Group prospered mutually
with Fred Foster's Monument label and Joe Cuoghi's Hi Records. A report in *Billboard
Music Week* in 1961 noted with unease that "some tradesters look on the distribution
of small labels by the large indies as a trend toward bigness in the competitive record
business. Others view it as a stabilizing trend in the singles field."[9]

To the patent relief of the Am-Par executives, 1959 turned out to be a gold-plated
year with no less than four No. 1 hits: "Stagger Lee" by Lloyd Price, "Venus" by Frankie
Avalon, "Lonely Boy" by Paul Anka, and "Why" by Frankie Avalon. Remember: the
ABC network broadcasted shows by Dick Clark and Alan Freed through its radio and
TV affiliates. Rock 'n' roll was indeed Am-Par's rocket fuel.

Even so, ABC-Paramount failed to break Cliff Richard, England's talented teen
equivalent of Elvis Presley. Cliff was bringing the houses down while on a U.S. tour
with Bobby Rydell and Clyde McPhatter but said he wasn't given the necessary backup
support from the ABC management. Once his current record, "Living Doll" (a U.K. No.
1 licensed from EMI's Columbia label) had stalled at No. 30 in late 1959, the chance
of an extensive U.S. career had gone, to his eternal chagrin.

In June 1960, the prestige of ABC-Paramount Records was confirmed by way of
huge advertorial spreads celebrating the label's fifth anniversary in *Billboard* and *Cash
Box*. It was a splendid opportunity to announce ABC's recent arrival: Ray Charles.
Am-Par's star acquisition had been enticed away from his natural home at Atlantic
through a unique artist-producer deal, including the retention of his master tapes. A
full-page advertisement in *Cash Box* must have rubbed more salt into the open wounds
of Ahmet Ertegun, Jerry Wexler, and Miriam Bienstock: Ray's dedication read, "Best

wishes, ABC-Paramount. Glad To Be A Member of The Winning Team." He didn't take long to deliver three enduring No. 1 hits: "Georgia on My Mind" (1960), "Hit the Road Jack" (1961), and "I Can't Stop Loving You" (1962). Then he capped everything with the revolutionary No. 1 LP *Modern Sounds in Country and Western Music* (1962), where R&B and C&W converged. ABC-Paramount's faith, and calculated gamble, in Ray Charles had paid off quickly and handsomely.

As an example of ABC's all-around vision, Impulse Records was launched in February 1961 as an avant-garde jazz imprint under the watch of young Creed Taylor, who was followed by wily Bob Thiele. The parent label, meanwhile, was looking beyond established hit-makers Ray Charles and Lloyd Price. And so ABC proceeded to lure away top-drawer indie artists B. B. King and Fats Domino from their respective longtime guardians Jules Bihari and Lew Chudd with guaranteed advances of at least $25,000 each; the Impressions, led by Curtis Mayfield, were welcome arrivals from Vee-Jay. Together, these signings represented an enormous vote of confidence in the long-term commerciality of black music. Although the singles sector was still important to ABC, the lucrative LP market was seen as the future by Sam Clark and Larry Newton, the more so after Ray Charles's blockbuster album of country songs. At last, ABC-Paramount meant business, big business.

In 1965, Larry Newton succeeded Sam Clark as Am-Par's president, an astonishing feat for a self-made man whose only formal learning had come from the action-packed environs of Philadelphia and New York. Here he was on public company boards, mingling with MBAs and law graduates, and answering to public stockholders. And yet his lack of education bothered him, according to grandson Adam Kaplan, even when he had made it to the top. Still, he had those street smarts that gave him a far better footing in the record business than any Ivy League college degree would have.

Easing himself in as president, Larry Newton led an expansionary program that would include the acquisitions of Lou Adler's Dunhill Records in 1966, Don Robey's Duke-Peacock Records in 1973, and Gulf+Western's record division, with Dot, in 1974. One year later, Newton was gone. In 1979, with ABC seeing other media as better bets and always worried about FCC intervention, the record arm was offloaded to MCA. Known later as ABC/Dunhill, ABC-Paramount Records was history shortly before its twenty-fifth birthday and in the end never achieved the major label status is creators had planned for. The record industry was not so easy to conquer after all.

Morty Craft: MGM and Warwick Records

In the late 1950s, there was an influx of record companies with movie affiliations attracted by the exploding market: United Artists, Warner Bros., 20th Century-Fox, Colpix (Columbia Pictures), Buena Vista (Disney), and England's Top Rank. Moreover, Dot was a part of Paramount Pictures (which was no longer related to the ABC organization), while rumors abounded that Lew Chudd's Imperial label was a takeover target for these well-heeled entrants.[10] Suddenly, the playing field was getting mighty crowded.

Even laboring MGM Records (which was affiliated to the "Big Three" music publishers, Robbins, Feist, and Miller) managed to ratchet itself up a few notches following the appointment of Morton "Morty" Craft with the splendid title of Recording Chief and Director of Single Record Sales. "After a short spell with Mercury," said Craft, "I got this offer to go with MGM [in December 1957], which was a dead company completely. By being with independent labels, I was able to give MGM new ideas. I had to teach MGM a whole new business."

That is not to say that MGM Records had not enjoyed hits beforehand, which it had, and there were always the money-spinning movie soundtracks. But like ABC-Paramount, MGM, with its tremendous resources, never achieved the major-label credibility it should have.

In summer 2004, I sat with octogenarian Morty Craft in the neat gardens within his apartment block on Manhattan's Fifty-eighth Street. Towering above us was the Time-Warner Center on Columbus Circle. "If the terrorists hit that, we're in trouble," said a worried Morty. It could be argued that the AOL merger did an even better job of damaging the conglomerate, which at that time included Warner Music Group (since sold off). An aging Mitch Miller was still residing in the apartment complex, while Seymour Stein was living across the road whenever in town. Allen Klein, another good friend of Craft's, was located just a few blocks away in the ABKCO offices on Broadway.

Morty Craft, networking connoisseur, was once described accurately by the trade magazines as a "colorful mahoff." Certainly, he was well known in the industry but not always for the right reasons. Compared to others in the independent fraternity, his track record was checkered at best. Rather, his proudest personal boast was that he had never dated a woman "over twenty-five." Few of his friends would dispute that assertion as he sailed through his seventies and into his eighties. Now he harped on a familiar theme: things are not what they used to be, in business or pleasure.

A product of the big band era, Morty Craft learned to arrange while playing saxophone and clarinet in Boston, Massachusetts. After heading for New York, he found an early mentor in Philadelphia disc magnate Dave Miller, who taught him how to "run with a record." "So what I did," said Morty,

> I associated with people that had record stores, and that led me to getting into creating and producing records. The guys I did Bruce Records with [were] Leo Rogers, who owned the Whirling Disc in Manhattan, and Monte Bruce. We used the name Bruce [Records]; the three of us were partners.
>
> We had an immediate hit with the Harptones, "A Sunday Kind of Love" [in early 1954]. Well, for us it was big, but in reality it was not that big, maybe 50,000. We were only in a few cities in those days. Then Leo Rogers promised Monte Bruce and myself that he would take care of the taxes, and he never took care of them. And he just stole the goddamn company.

Hy Weiss was at his waspish best when he described the Bruce Records partnership as "an unholy alliance."

Morty Craft had further chart entrants with "Church Bells May Ring" by the Willows (No. 62 pop, 1956) on Melba and "Alone" by the Shepherd Sisters (No. 18 pop, 1957) on Lance, a label named fawningly after Alan Freed's son. Then as director of singles, Morty helped to energize a demoralized MGM with a superb run of smash hits during his electric regime.[11]

By his own admission, Craft had an arsenal of incendiary stories that he could relate, but whether it was his memory failing or a feeling of discretion (or a combination of both), he wouldn't reveal them. He was willing, though, to expand on his time with MGM and on his career highlights as a New York indie record man. "Those were the days," he sighed.

If you were a success with an independent type of record company, what we would call a major independent label like Mercury, you would get offers to go with bigger companies like MGM, Columbia, RCA. That's how Hugo & Luigi got started.

Now Mitch [Miller] couldn't tell a Columbia distributor what to do; he could ask in a nice way. But I could *force* an MGM distributor to help us. I was higher than just an A&R man. You got to understand, Mitch Miller and myself, everybody that ran the creative end of a label, was also into promotion, sales, and making sure the record got played—whatever that took. That's the era we had. So we just didn't do one job; we did maybe ten jobs of making somebody a hit. We could find a master and make it a hit even if we didn't record it ourselves. Today, you need twenty guys to do what you did in those days.

The MGM head was Arnold Maxin. He was out of Philadelphia, an ex-trombone player, and was with Columbia's other labels, Epic and OKeh. His art was the romance of the actors and actresses. He was more into a relationship with artists that way; he wasn't as involved in actually making a record on them. I was in charge of all forms of music, so if something came out of Nashville or California, I still had to give the okay before it was ever done.

I broke "Who's Sorry Now" by Connie Francis [No. 4, spring 1958], but I didn't record it. The only one playing "Who's Sorry Now" was Dick Clark in Philadelphia, but the record wasn't really working. So I went city by city on promotion until it became a hit. We knew everybody, and there were major promotion men like Pete Bennett that worked for independent distributors. The majors all had promotion men, but the independent labels in those days couldn't afford hiring too many people. So at MGM, I okayed "The Purple People Eater" [by Sheb Wooley] and "It's Only Make Believe" [by Conway Twitty]. I made tons of Connie Francis, including "Stupid Cupid"; that's when she caught on all over. MGM became very, very hot.

I recorded and produced "It's All in the Game" by Tommy Edwards. He had been on MGM and did the record as a waltz the first time [in 1951]. It was originally written [in 1912] by one of the vice presidents of the United States way back, Charles Dawes [under President Calvin Coolidge]. I helped to create the triplets on the piano and the backbeat on the second and fourth beats of the drums, which made it very famous. "Making out" dancing become big after that! It was where you accented the second and fourth beat, and that was the style of almost every record in that era; the keyboard would play up-high triplets. All the R&B records were done that way. It was all part of that era that came out of the black scene.

Cash Box acknowledged the achievements of Arnold Maxin and Morty Craft when it reported in November 1958 that they "have established MGM Records as a top label and a top money-maker in the business. MGM's pop singles have jumped from one percent of the total market to seven percent while its album business has more than doubled." The trade magazine noted that the singles were "treated like an indie disk operation."[12]

By January 1959, Morty Craft's lightning-charged tenure at MGM was over. "Well, with MGM they never paid me," he explained curtly. "I was one of the first ones supposed to get a royalty for everything that was put out on MGM, and I never got a penny." Craft was replaced by conductor-arranger Ray Ellis, whose résumé included hits for Columbia and Atlantic.

After exiting MGM, Morty Craft was in the frame for a post at Morris Levy's Roulette Records following the departure of the Hugo & Luigi team. Then on Valentine's Day, *Cash Box* reported that Craft "denied rumors that distributors in ten key markets were buying shares of stock in a record company he was said to be forming." Gossip about a possible liaison with ex-Decca man Paul Cohen at Todd Records was also dismissed.[13] By the spring, Morty Craft was placed in charge of Warwick Records with corporate backing from yet another movie company, this one from Canada. "Warwick came from the hotel on Sixth Avenue and Fifty-fourth," said Craft. "I liked the name, and I had a logo made. Seven-Arts came from the people that backed me. They met me at the Fontainebleau in Miami Beach, and they're the ones who wanted me to leave MGM and start a new label. They were involved in cartoons out of Canada, a lot of Warner Bros. cartoon stuff. That's how I started Warwick."[14]

Morty Craft's involvement with Warwick formed part of a trend whereby prominent music directors left their posts with established companies to head up independent operations. Inspiration for this movement had come from the impact that Archie Bleyer (Cadence) and ex-Decca man Dave Kapp (Kapp) were making with their classy pop productions. The new intake included Herb Abramson (Triumph), Joe Carlton (Carlton-Guaranteed), Bob Shad (Time-Shad-Brent), and Bob Thiele (Hanover-Signature) as well as Paul Cohen (Todd). This desire to be "your own boss" was in part a reflection of the potential rewards of being a record man and also of the high mortality rates in the A&R domain. Alas, the timing was awry for these industry veterans who would face almost impossible challenges in the realms of pricing, distribution, and merchandising; then there was the ascendancy of the revitalized major labels. Of the newcomers, Bob Shad with his operation lasted the longest. The former Sittin' In With owner/Mercury A&R man had a good run of Top 100 hits at the turn of the 1960s, before discovering Janis Joplin (with Big Brother and the Holding Company) and selling on the recording contract to Columbia in 1967.

At Warwick, Morty Craft had immediate hits with rock 'n' roll instrumental group Johnny and the Hurricanes. "Their first record was a semi-hit that I had, 'Crossfire'

[No. 23, early summer 1959]," said Craft. "The group did it in Detroit [on Twirl]; they were out of Toledo. Then I used the studio group: 'Red River Rock' [No. 5, late 1959; No. 3 U.K.] was [performed by] a studio orchestra; it wasn't even the group out of Michigan, never was. Bill Ramal was the arranger and sax player. He was very famous later—he did a lot of Hill & Range stuff, including that big hit on Bigtop, 'Runaway' [by Del Shannon]."[15]

It was Bigtop Records that spirited away Johnny and the Hurricanes from Warwick. "I was upset with the two guys that thought they owned everything," said Craft. "Irving Micahnik and Harry Balk, EmBee Productions . . ." He was hinting darkly that for him, the root of the dispute was an unequal share of profits, especially in the publishing realm.

Against prevailing trends, Morty Craft tried bravely to reignite the careers of several faded R&B stars. Their number included Louis Jordan, Roy Milton, Bull Moose Jackson, Lucky Millinder, Percy Mayfield, and Faye Adams. "I just thought they had great product," said Craft. "There was no such thing as using the expression 'time has gone.' If you had talent, age had nothing to do with it. I redid 'Let the Good Times Roll' by Shirley & Lee [No. 48, fall 1960]. In the beginning, you had associations with your artists in a big way. Everyone was always in touch; they hung out with us. You went into the office, and all you heard was music. Today you don't hear any music; it's all accountants and lawyers."

At the turn of the 1960s, Morty Craft was having trouble connecting with the teen market after losing Johnny and the Hurricanes to Bigtop. A year later, Warwick scored big with "Wheels" by the String-A-Longs (No. 3), a guitar-rich instrumental hit acquired from Norman Petty, who had enjoyed stunning success as Buddy Holly's producer in Clovis, New Mexico. "I wasn't too familiar with Petty," said Craft, "but I liked what he played for me. He came in with a stack of about twenty demo records. 'Wheels' I picked out from that, but it was the other side ["Tell the World"] that I thought would be the hit."

Morty Craft described his generation of record men as "operators," and he certainly fell into that category. "It was a case of knowing everybody," he said,

being able to wine and dine; everybody was romantic in those days. Wherever you went, people got to you. If it wasn't money, it was sex. But there were no drugs; only jazz guys did pot. And only millionaires did cocaine in the 1950s; that was the luxury of the famous rich people.

It was all the deals that went on. If people got away with them, they got away with them. They all did it, I think, even myself. I don't think anybody was 200 percent legal in those days. There was always the opportunity of getting somebody's check by mistake and cashing it [laughs]. But everybody could get an opportunity in those days, right in the street. Every door was open. Today there isn't one door open, especially in New York.

The disc jockeys played what they liked. If they saw it as a hit and they liked you, they'd call you and tell you. Or they'd call a distributor who would then call you. These

were the middle men. Even at MGM, where one time they had their noses in the air
. . . they weren't nice; they had to learn to be "independent" when I took over.

Dick Alen: Booking Agent

The independent booking agencies were operating in a similar cut-and-thrust environment to that of their indie record company counterparts and were able to benefit from
the same niche opportunities. In the early 1950s, the R&B and jazz package shows
would anticipate the popular rock 'n' roll caravans that arrived later in the decade.
The Gale agency packaged *The Big Rhythm and Blues Show* in summer 1953 featuring Faye Adams, the Drifters, the Spaniels, the Counts, Big Maybelle, LaVern Baker,
Roy Hamilton, and the Erskine Hawkins Orchestra. Then Shaw Artists Corporation
followed suit with the *Top Ten Rhythm and Blues Show*. Famously, Norman Granz
had been trawling tours of *Jazz at the Philharmonic* since 1946.

   A constant homily from canny record men on signing awestruck young artists (or
on securing the guardians' confirmatory signatures) was that they didn't make money
from discs. Rather, the riches flowed from live performances; the records were promotional tools. This is where the booking agents came in. Nevertheless, Atlantic's Jerry
Wexler did not feel particularly well disposed toward the agencies. "We had links with
Ben Bart at Universal and Billy Shaw at Shaw," Wexler said. "Billy engineered the Ray
Charles purchase; his contract was purchased from Swing Time [Jack Lauderdale] for
$2,500. But agents never had any significance to us in that era. They didn't help to
nurture the artists—they are agents. In fact, they're commission purveyors who find
work. But we were very close to the managers."

   One booking agent who had seen it all was Wexler's good friend Dick Alen. Even
though in his eighties, he was still working in 2006 for the venerable William Morris
Agency in Hollywood. His book of stars included Aretha Franklin, Chuck Berry, Little
Richard, and Tom Jones. With this long service, Dick Alen was able to give an insider's
view on the work of the agencies leading up to and including the rock 'n' roll era.

   "Moe Gale had the Gale agency," Alen said.[16]

Here was Shaw Artists with Billy Shaw, and Don Robey in Houston; Texas had the
Buffalo Booking Agency. There were a couple of smaller companies in New York. Then
later on, Universal Attractions came along, which became a big company under Ben
Bart, and Queen Booking was Ruth Bowen.

   Of course, the big companies William Morris and MCA, those were the class operations: they controlled the café artists, the big singers, and movie stars. GAC was the
bottom of the big agencies and made themselves by signing a lot of the new music
acts that had more of a white appeal. Associated Booking always had a good jazz list,
of course, and Joe Glaser had Louis Armstrong, always very important. So the touring
business that was open was in both R&B and jazz. Billy Shaw saw that opening.[17]

   Billy Shaw had started up a little while before. He had come from William Morris's
company at the end of the big band era, when the big bands were just falling apart. I

mean, they couldn't do business, they weren't drawing people, they weren't selling records. And the new jazz was just starting. Billy Shaw was a wonderful agent.

Shaw, who died of a heart attack in 1956, had a slogan that would have made Irving Berlin wince: "There's no business like *Shaw* business."

"It's a tough business, the jazz and the R&B business," said Dick Alen.

You're dealing with very young clients, inexperienced, who have no money and need help and need financing right along the way. With the agency, the thing was to find work, and it was just at the time where R&B acts were mainly playing only in R&B locations. In every city there'd be nightclubs in the black area of town or small dance halls, and that's where you would work.

In the R&B [sector] we at Shaw had Arthur Prysock, Buddy and Ella Johnson, Fats Domino, the Orioles, the Clovers. I'd say seven out of the Top 10 R&B acts were with Shaw Artists at that time [with the big package shows being organized by Eli Weinberg and Lou Krefetz]. Most of the artists don't have a shelf life of . . . more than three years; they're just not popular into that time. You [book them], and they leap. Then the artists will leave because there's no work, they go, and you barely notice they're not there [*laughs*].

There was a club circuit and a dance hall circuit that went right across the country. It was very much so down South. In fact, it was one of the best markets down South, and these were black artists playing in front of black audiences. Whether the particular location was owned by black or white, it almost didn't matter; as far as the management was concerned, this was a very integrated system.[18] Of the theaters, that was top of the class when you got to the Apollo and to the Howard in Washington, the Royal in Baltimore, the Uptown in Philadelphia, the Regal in Chicago.

You had to figure who was a talented artist. When you had an artist, you usually had to help them out. A poor kid coming from nowhere suddenly is having a chance to go out. He may have a car or he may not have a car, he may have a local band, or his buddies are on the payroll. Then there were the hotels, and on and on and on. These were all things that they barely had the money to finance. Stagecraft coaches? No! This was a sink-or-swim type of situation: Get out and do it! The good ones lived as artists, and the bad ones didn't.

I came into Shaw Artists around 1954, and I'd come from an independent company. I made a deal with Shaw to sell their acts to television. I think the first sale I made was with a dance team for twenty-five dollars, and we split the money. Television was a completely new medium then: I'd put Ray Charles on TV the first time [as a jazz artist], I put George Shearing on, Erroll Garner, Chet Baker. Shaw was about the top jazz company.

You could barely get on [the] *Ed Sullivan [Show]*. Elvis was a phenomenon; there were always certain artists that got on, but for the most part you did not. Their audience was not Fats Domino's. The advertisers didn't particularly care for a young audience or a black audience. It was all about advertising and ratings.

We'd work together with someone like Hy Weiss. He and I were somewhat friendly; he knew a good agency. He'd call: "I got the Solitaires coming; I got a good record coming. Would you guys take them and put them on the road? Any chance you could put them with the Midnighters?" Or whoever the act is that we were pushing at that time who could sell some tickets. He'd tip you off. You do it or you die.

The record companies were glad for the agencies to have an act. If we could get them out, it would help the act to earn money. Then the artists didn't drive the record companies crazy to borrow money [*laughs*]. I mean, [for] the artists in general, the feeling was "If you could borrow from the man, he'd work harder to make you money."

Remember, the major labels weren't in our business; it was only the independents. There was Hy [Weiss], Jerry [Wexler], George Goldner, the Biharis, Bert Berns [of Shout-Bang Records in the 1960s]. You'd hear a record, or a disc jockey friend of yours would tip you off: "I've just heard a record, and it sounds pretty good to me." "Okay, what label is it on?" And you'd call them.

A lot of artists, though, they had a record that was real good in four cities. And you booked them in those four cities, but no one had ever heard of them in the fifth city. Then the second record didn't sell any copies, and unfortunately the kids were history. They were probably blaming everybody—they're blaming the record man; they're blaming me. But it happens. You take a look at the charts today, read these charts, and look at them in six months. See who's left in business. It's all about the hit records.

That generation of record men invented the business, same as the early rhythm and blues agents are the ones who invented the rock 'n' roll business of *how* to tour. At that time, the big action was with the Sophie Tuckers or the Sammy Davises, the Dean Martins, Frank Sinatras; they were going strong from the Copacabana to the Palladium in London. We couldn't get these acts, and we had to find other places to book our artists.

We did everything. Like, you'd help a nightclub get started, and they needed chairs. You'd phone up the local funeral parlor and made a deal to rent the chairs. That's the way you did it then. The money was far lower for everybody: the artist, the agent, the agencies, the employees of the agencies. There were no multimillion-dollar deals there. And so everyone had to work real hard for their money.

At one time I was working for Universal, and I left and went to GAC. That was when I was brought in by Irvin Feld to help book their rock 'n' roll caravans, *The Biggest Show of Stars*. In fact, I'm looking at a poster in my office right now. On the show was Fats Domino, LaVern Baker, Frankie Lymon, Chuck Berry, Clyde McPhatter, the Crickets, Eddie Cochran, Buddy Knox, the Diamonds, the Drifters and "introducing Paul Anka," with the orchestra being Paul Williams. It was at the Forum in Wichita, Kansas [in 1957], and the ticket prices were $2, $2.50, and $3. You had to make a profit out of that, and we did. The rock 'n' roll era was exciting because we were able to move up.

It wasn't a nightmare to organize; it's what your job is. There were always people who caused you nightmares, but it was part of the deal; it comes with the territory. The managers and promoters, we're in a money business, and nobody had real money in those days. There were times in these shows, you'd drive up and you'd be sitting in the bus, and you wouldn't let the acts get off the bus until you got some money.

By the early 1960s, the world of the independent booking agencies was changing, just as it was for the independent record business. "The big agencies picked off our stars like Sam Cooke," said Dick Alen, "because they could get jobs in the white places. And it made it somewhat uneconomic[al] to keep on running. But the chitlin' circuit was an honorable way to make a living and a good way for the local audiences to see shows. The people who saw the shows at the Audubon Ballroom up in Harlem would not go to the Copacabana down in Manhattan."

The unequal burden between the record men and the booking agents, as expressed by Jerry Wexler, was summarized succinctly by Mercury Records' Berle Adams, a member of both churches, in his book *A Sucker for Talent:* "When you're an agent selling talent, you're convincing another person to bet on the talent you represent. When you're in the record business, the shoe is on the other foot. It's your gamble. . . . What a contrast this was from being an agent, where the only investment was my services, and at the end of each week I received a commission. In the record business I was paying out, paying out, paying out—and waiting for months to get anything back."[19]

Who would be an independent record maker in an industry that was becoming increasingly corporate and ruthless? Even worse, as the momentous decade of the 1950s was drawing to a close, there was a strong smell of scandal in the air. That pollutant was payola.

24

CHAPTER

The Payola Scandal and Changing Times

CAST OF CHARACTERS

Henry Stone, Tone Distributors and TK Records
Ahmet Ertegun, Atlantic Records
Harold B. Lipsius, Jamie-Guyden Records
Alan Bubis, Tennessee-Republic and Hit Records
Stan Lewis, Stan's Record Shop
Fred Foster, Monument Records
Irv Lichtman, *Cash Box* and *Billboard*
Donn Fileti, Relic Records
Shelby Singleton, Mercury and SSS International–
     Sun Records
Jerry Wexler, Atlantic Records
also featuring Alan Freed, disc jockey

For Deejays: Babes, Bribes And Booze

All hell broke loose at that never-to-be-forgotten 1959 Miami disc jockey convention, held May 28–31 and sponsored by chain broadcaster Storz Radio headed by Todd Storz. Laboring under the name of the Second Annual International Radio Programming Seminar and Pop Music Disk Jockey Convention, everybody seemed to be there. It was as if the indie record men and women were having a last hurrah with their radio brethren. The new order, which had only just been constituted, was about to be overturned irrevocably.

Stop the presses! With a dateline of May 31, the *Miami News* carried a front-page story with the now-classic headline "For Deejays: Babes, Bribes and Booze," accompanied by the subhead "Diskers Act Like Tin Gods." The sensational news feature by Haines Colbert read like an end-of-term report for the independent record industry, inter alia:

> The disc jockeys, here from cities throughout the United States and Canada, were given the greatest buttering-up since Nero was

persuaded he was a fiddle virtuoso. There were expensive prizes, free liquor around the clock in at least 20 suites and girls, imported and domestic. And there was constant praise for the apparently unbelievable talent required to put a record on a turntable, play it and sell it to all those wonderful people out there in radioland.

Promotion men and disc jockeys agreed that the strange industry in which they are chained together is plagued by too many companies and too many records—most of the records being hard on the ears. "There are about 2,000 record companies," explained a spokesman for one of the major companies, "and all of them send all their releases to every disc jockey. The only possible way to get them on the air is by giving the jockey personal attention. And that means giving him whatever he wants."

The *Miami News* piece, also notable for the anonymity of the interviewees, confirmed the accumulative, overarching reach of the disc jockey in a music business suffering from excess product, excess competition, excess everything. Here was a terrible public relations disaster for an industry that needed to project a wholesome image, particularly among the teenagers and parents. Something had to be done about the "lousy situation," as described in the Miami story, and Congress duly obliged after looking for answers to the $64,000 question in the TV quiz–rigging scandal.

And so began the "payola" hearings, chaired by Representative Oren Harris of the Special Subcommittee on Legislative Oversight, which targeted the independents' cartel—and in a way, the music that was being championed. With Alan Freed seen as the prime suspect, the "inventor" of rock 'n' roll was axed summarily from his jobs at Radio WABC and at WNEW-TV. On November 25, 1959, a big, bold *New York Post* headline that would have done justice to a declaration of war blazoned: "Alan Freed Telling All About Payola House Problems: Drops TV Shows." The covering front page story, by Earl Wilson, emphasized just how widespread Freed's business web had become:

> The Harris subcommittee investigators started questioning him very soon after he was fired and they also interrogated Johnny Brantley, talent coordinator of Freed's show, and Jack Hook[e], a former associate and onetime booking agent for his dance shows. . . . They inquired about Freed's knowledge of disc jockey involvements in other enterprises, such as record companies, record-pressing companies, record distributorships, talent agencies, "ownership" of singers, record shops and all the varied phases of payola which are now being revealed to the public. . . . He was also interrogated about his rival network star Dick Clark but "I merely answered some of their questions about him."

Perhaps out of self-preservation, Alan Freed was careful not to implicate others in his tight New York network. In a farewell speech on the WNEW-TV *Big Beat* dance show on Friday, November 27, Freed—wearing that trademark plaid jacket—said that he was sorry to leave his fans but "I know a bunch of ASCAP publishers who will be glad I'm off the air."[1] There were industry whispers that New York district attorney Frank Hogan was manipulating publicity for his own political ends. Who knows, too, what pressures were being applied by the various corporate advertisers?

Disclosures continued apace under the guise of investigative journalism, or was it just circulation-driven tittle-tattle? On December 3, the *New York Post* reported that Jerry Blaine admitted granting Alan Freed a mortgage of $11,000 in 1956 but had turned over the loan to Roulette Records with a refund of interest to Freed. In time-honored fashion, Morris Levy was unavailable for comment. Then Hy Weiss was implicated, fleetingly, through his $5,000 "mortgage" to the fallen disc jockey.[2] How much more dirt would be dished? As Art Rupe of Specialty Records had observed, bitterly, payola had gotten out of hand. Satirist Stan Freberg added to the indies' general discomfiture with an establishment-biased lampoon, "The Old Payola Roll Blues," on just-arrived major label Capitol.

A striking example of record company payola was given in an affidavit to the Harris subcommittee by Marvin Cane "with regard to the amount paid by Coed Records, Inc. to disk jockeys etc., for promotion of records." Coed, a comparatively minor New York independent but with thrusting ambition, was headed by Cane with music publisher George Paxton and was enjoying an encouraging run of hits with the Crests, beginning with "16 Candles" (No. 2, early 1959). Cane's staff included as a promotion man young Jerry Moss, soon to be the dynamic cofounder of A&M Records with Herb Alpert.

Among the sworn recipients "with regard to the amount paid by Coed Records, Inc., to disk jockeys, etc. for promotion of records" were Johnny Brantley (probably as a conduit to Alan Freed at $445), Ernie Durham ($175), Don McLeod ($225), Tommy Smalls ($200), Joe Smith ($800), George Woods ($150), and Lynn Tripp (a huge $5,050).[3] The total Coed bag exceeded $19,000.

In May 1960, *Cash Box* reported that WMGM's Peter Tripp, another high profile New York disc jockey, was embroiled in the payola mess and "worked on a royalty basis." According to District Attorney Hogan, two specific hits were caught up in this arrangement: the aforesaid "16 Candles" by the Crests for Coed and "I Wonder Why" by Dion and the Belmonts (a New York doo-wop classic that made No. 22 for novice Laurie Records, summer 1958).[4] Subsequently, on May 15, 1961, Tripp was found "guilty of accepting $34,150 in payola while host of WMGM-New York's *Your Hits of the Week* show in 1958–59." His unaccepted principal defense was that he "received payments not for spinning certain disks, but for advice he gave to labels on how to produce the most commercial recordings."[5]

Meanwhile, Hogan exposed four New York firms as the "chief offenders" in payola, which he described as "graft payments." Any reaction among the New York music-chattering classes in the bars, delis, and restaurants around Broadway was probably muted when several familiar names came into the frame (with the alleged payments): Alpha Distributing ($21,650), Superior Record Sales Co. ($18,200), Roulette Records ($12,325), and Cosnat Distributing with its Cleveland affiliate ($12,950). Nevertheless, the cognoscenti must have been amused when haughty London Records was nailed for an alleged $3,600.[6]

Suddenly, there was a wave of heightened ethical consciousness sweeping through the erstwhile freewheeling independent music community. At first, it seemed that everyone was caught in the sights of the Federal Trade Commission (FTC), but it was the dee-jays who took the main rap. And so whereas payola was handed out by record men, distributors, music publishers, and promo men alike, it was only the disc jockey recipients who were perceived as guilty. The radio stations, however, were startled to learn that they could lose their operational licenses even if ignorant of their employees' indiscretions. The witch hunt had begun: Top 40 radio, here we come!

While the Miami fallout may have hastened the payola inquiries, the conventions in themselves presented heaven-sent networking opportunities. These gatherings led to a cheerful camaraderie among the independent community. "In the early years, we used to go to the jukebox conventions because the record people didn't have their own conventions at that time," said Henry Stone, distributor and record man.

> So the record distributors and the record manufacturers would gather at the jukebox conventions. At the beginning, we just met. We didn't have any stands; those came later on as the market kind of evolved. When we first started, the manufacturers would come up and ask a distributor if he would be the manufacturer's representative, and, vice versa, the distributor would ask about the manufacturer's lines. It was very congenial. We would discuss trends, hit records, the failures, pretty much so. I remember we had poker games between Don Robey of Duke-Peacock Records, Leonard Chess of Chess Records, [Ewart] Abner of Vee-Jay Records, George Goldner of New York, and Hy Weiss.
>
> We decided it would be a good idea for the record people to have their own conventions, so we got ahold of Abner, who was a very organized person. We set up a group of record people, and we formed a group called ARMADA [American Record Manufacturers and Distributors Association]. We all met there, we played cards, just did a lot of crazy things. We had a great time.[7]

The first annual convention of ARMADA was held in Chicago on June 8, 1959, just after the Miami ruckus, with the following hot topics:

* Better Co-operation between the Indie Manufacturer and Distributor
* A Uniform Return Privilege
* The Pricing of Records
* What a Manufacturer Can Learn from a Retailer

According to Washington, D.C., distributor Harry Schwartz, as quoted in *Billboard*, ARMADA was a natural result of the growth of indie labels and distributors, and "we feel we are now strong enough to wear long pants."[8]

"Yes, it was a network of people that really understood each other," said Henry Stone. "They were dedicated people. At that time, it was a young business where everybody was trying to make a good living. Nobody was getting rich; there [were] no multimillion-dollar deals. There was just a good feeling between people who trusted each other pretty much. We had our little fights, but it worked out good between the manufacturer and the distributor."

Atlantic's Ahmet Ertegun was in his practical-joking element at such gatherings. "We had conventions every year," he said,

> and these conventions would be very wild get-togethers. Before the gambling, Atlantic City was a seaside resort that had gone down; everything was run down. And the people that came there were renting cars, and the only cars they had to rent were very inexpensive, cheap cars. There was one distributor from Chicago who was quite an arrogant person and who was very well dressed. He got very angry that he couldn't rent a Cadillac, so he bought a Cadillac. He said, "I'll drive it and I'll give it to my son." Some friends and I bought a fish from the fish market, and we put it under the seat of the Cadillac. It was a very hot summer day, and this convertible Cadillac started to smell, and he couldn't find where it was smelling from. So he took it back and he wanted to return the car. And the man wouldn't take the car back. They were in a big fight, and they couldn't find the smell [*laughs*].

Harold B. Lipsius, of Jamie-Guyden Records and Universal Record Distributing Corporation, saw the serious side of conventions. "We went to them as a preventative measure," he said. "We wanted to ensure that the record labels wouldn't change lines." He had never forgotten how his partner Harry Finfer had lost the profitable Chess account when he blabbed about the conquests of Jamie Records to the exclusion of all else. There were at least fourteen other competing distributors in Philadelphia at the time.

Sadly, this collective unity among the independents, as implied by the conventions and organizations such as ARMADA, was too little, too late in the grand scheme of things.

At the "Rome is burning" Miami disc jockey convention, dubbed as an "all-play and no-work meeting," the fun-loving Henry Stone was in his element. "By 1959, the independent record industry was really coming into its own," he said.

> I remember [that] a gentleman from New Orleans put me in charge of the liquor. I had gathered all these bottles of liquor and stored them in my warehouse for this convention. One of the reasons I was included was because I was the distributor down here in Florida. It was not so much the distributors around the country; [it was] the record manufacturers and the radio people that came here to Miami.
>
> It was quite a convention; there was quite a lot action down here. There were the hotels such as the Fontainebleau and the Americana. I remember Morris Levy bringing Count Basie and Sarah Vaughan to perform, people being thrown in the pool, [a record man's] wife diving nude from a yacht. I mean, there was a real ruckus. A lot of the booze that I brought over from my warehouse was distributed to all the people there. And of course the headline in the Miami paper was quite a headline. It became quite a national thing. I think it brought the payola hearings to light.

Before the scandal broke, payola was not illegal, and afterward it was deemed to be a misdemeanor only—that is, a minor criminal act. Alan Freed's manager, Tommy Vastola, was right when he explained to me that payola represented "collusion" leading to unfair competition. Under New York State law, the term was "criminal bribery," punishable by a fine of five hundred dollars or a year in jail or more. That is how Alan Freed was charged. Eventually, in December 1962, Freed was fined a mere three hundred dollars with a six-month suspended sentence, but the damage had been done. There was also the small matter of taxes, a familiar payola pitfall. The Internal Revenue Service did not relent in its quest against Freed, and on March 15, 1964, he was indicted by a federal grand jury on charges of evading taxable income of $56,652 between 1957 and 1959.[9]

Almost overnight, the payola hearings had diminished the power of the personality disc jockey and hastened the widespread use of the Top 40 rotation format (prompted by the *Gavin Report* tip sheet, founded in 1958). Now those dozens of new weekly releases, from majors and independents alike, were fighting for even more restricted airtime. But payola would never go away, in whatever form. It was, after all, an integral part of the fabric of capitalist society, no matter what industry, being especially rife in politics.

As early as August 29, 1960, *Billboard* ran a timely page-1 lead story by veteran reporter June Bundy hinting at the difficulties of policing payola. "Deejay payola—supposedly a dead issue as a result of the Washington hearings—hasn't stopped," she wrote. "It has 'gone underground.'" In particular, Bundy's article highlighted the lack of clarity in Congress's definition of payola: "Washington has never given a satisfactory (to the music and broadcasting businesses anyway) explanation of just what they consider payola. Is a $75 tab at the Four Seasons as much payola as a $50 check? If it's payola when you send a dee-jay a case of scotch, is it also payola when you pick up the bar tab for spinner and six guests?"[10]

Dick Clark, quick-witted and charming, was able to survive the payola inquisition after divesting many of his business interests and would make a miraculous, enduring recovery after relocating to the West Coast. But Alan Freed was mortally wounded and died a broken man in 1965. Even so, he retained many supporters posthumously. "A great guy," said Doc Pomus. "Now let me explain something about the payola deal. Everybody was on payola, but the difference between Alan Freed and the others was that he wouldn't play a record unless he liked it. Most of these other guys would play anything! Alan really helped people, and he knew a lot about music. He had great instincts. If there was one disc jockey who was responsible for rock 'n' roll, he was the guy. And to me, it was sad. They made him the scapegoat."

The record industry as a whole would emerge stronger from the payola traumas. Even ASCAP realized that the cake was plenty big enough to be shared with BMI. For the pioneering independent record men, however, it would never be quite the same again. As innovators, they were beginning to suffer from collective creative exhaustion, while competition from the majors was intensifying. Plus, in a defeated Alan Freed and a weakened Dick Clark, the indies had lost their crusading champions.

Crucially, the independent distributors were seeing their business undergo fundamental change. As with the disc jockeys, the distributors had been accumulating much power in the independent record game, and for too long, it seemed, they were calling the shots. In a show of retaliatory strength in the aftermath of payola and the signing of the FTC consent decrees, the manufacturers started to squeeze the weaker distributors by curtailing "freebie" promo records and getting them to "order up and pay up." Now the more enlightened distributors had to revert to the "old-time energetic promotion and romance tactics that they used to employ years ago."[11] Within a short while, however, distributors were complaining of having to act as "bankers" due to "ridiculously extended" payment terms demanded by dealers. There was also the grave problem that "more people are cutting up the market."[12]

Henry Stone: King of the Transshippers

Even as the record men–disc jockey–distributor network was crumbling, Henry Stone was carrying on regardless down in Florida. After he had exited De Luxe Records in 1955, Henry went back wholeheartedly into the distribution business with Tru-Tone Distributing and then Tone Distributing from his Miami base with wife Muriel and Milt Oshins. Stone applied himself with such resolution that he saw opportunities to transship records outside of his allotted territory, a process that was encouraged by the record companies' enforced extravagance with free records. Tone was doing well enough to open spanking-new premises in 1960.

"I used to get all the independent labels," said Henry Stone.

> They all came to me. I didn't have too much competition in the state. The distributors were given certain territories and had to stay in those territories. Then I came up with my idea to start transshipping records all over the country. Transshipping is a label that was laid on me. I would order a thousand records [and] get three hundred records [at] no charge. The three hundred records were basically for promotion, and I'd have a good price break on the records. I built up a little network around the country in New York City and Detroit and a few places in the South. I would get these records around to the local stores, and I went to the jukebox operators in those areas.
>
> The first step for a good distributor would be to listen to the records when they came in. I did have some pretty good ears when it came to R&B and black music. The second step is to have disc jockeys in your pocket; what you'd do is to get these records played. Once I got these records played, I knew I had a hit record. The third step was to get paid on whatever records were sold by the record stores, jukebox operators, and the people that I transshipped the records to. I told the manufacturers, "I'm not going to pay for that crap on the floor. If you sent me a hundred and I sold twenty, I'll pay for twenty." It wasn't too much of a problem. That's why I stayed in business.[13]

Did transshipping cause aggravation? "It sure did!" said Stone. "My [allotted] territory was the Southeast. I used to cut the labels from the boxes so nobody knew where they came from, relabel them, and send them back up North as if they came from the West or wherever. The distributors in those areas didn't like that, but, hey, I created a different part of the industry."

The evils of transshipping were spelled out by Dot's Randy Wood in *Cash Box* as early as 1958, when he was reported as saying that the jumping of territorial lines and transshipping of records resulted in price wars and the loss of sales to the rightful franchise holder. Even worse, "distributors would often be snowed under by disk returns from dealers overloaded by the line-jumping distributor." Wood's reaction was to threaten any transgressor in his network with the withdrawal of the valuable Dot franchise.[14]

Jerry Blaine, the commanding head of leading indie distributor Cosnat (which endured transshipping accusations itself), called for "an era of legitimacy" while warning ominously, "Stay in your own back yard or the goose who laid the golden egg will be killed."[15] Bob Adams, of Music Sales in Memphis, felt the distributors' ills could be cured "by the elimination of the 'Three D's': Deals, Discounts and Damn-Transshipping."[16]

"Transshipping led to chaos," said Nashville record man Alan Bubis. "Everybody more or less became a one-stop."[17] Bubis, with Bill Beasley, had launched Tennessee Records in 1950 and Republic in 1952, but their various labels were unable to survive in the competitive, professional Music City environment.[18] Then in 1959, the entrepreneurial pair spotted an opening in a sector that became another industry blight: the big business of buying up overstocked hits at knockdown prices and selling them cheaply in the racks nationwide. In effect, this distressed merchandise was the record industry's equivalent of the European Union's wine lake or butter mountain. Al Bubis and Bill Beasley, now entrenched in the jobbing business, merrily added to the excess by introducing their own thirty-nine-cent budget rack label, Hit, featuring back-to-back chart smashes of the day. The partners did especially well with a rerecording of "The Twist," according to Bubis.

As for Henry Stone, he did not view the rack business as magnanimously as he did his own transshipping activities. "The rack jobbers used to buy records from distributors all over the country," he said, "and they returned most of the records. The rack jobber was, I think, the downfall of the record business, when it went into a little spin for a while [in the 1960s]. I never sold to rack jobbers because I didn't believe in it. Supposedly, they handled the Walgreens and [big] stores like that who didn't buy direct from the record distributors. Basically, they'd buy five thousand of a hit record, put them in the racks, and return four thousand of them: sell a thousand. There were a lot of problems in returning these records for the manufacturer. That really changed the business."

The old-time distributors and one-stop owners were becoming more and more disillusioned. It was a symbolic moment in 1963 when *Billboard* announced that Jerry Blaine, for so long the most visible independent record distributor, was "telescoping Cosnat operations" by closing and consolidating branches "due to current conditions in the market."[19]

And pity the poor traditional retailer who was affected, too, by competition from the chain stores, general merchandise outlets, discount houses, and records clubs, let alone the racks everywhere. In fact, the mom-and-pop record shops were falling by the wayside in droves. Jerry Blaine, again, complained that Cosnat used to supply "hundreds" of independent stores in any given major market in large metropolitan areas, but now there were just "50 or 60 old style mom and pop stores."[20]

In this cold-war situation, it seemed that price and volume were the only considerations, never mind the artistic content of the records. The rack jobbers, along with the transshippers, were undermining the tight-knit, integrated chain of regional record distributors with their exclusive territories and specific label lines. With the disc jockeys being muffled as well, the grand independent record model was coming apart at the seams.

As the 1960s progressed, another gremlin emerged for the besieged independent record distributors: established indie labels were vanishing from the landscape after being taken over, merging, changing strategies, collapsing, or simply ceasing to trade. Among the series of seismic shocks, Lew Chudd's Imperial was sold to Liberty, while Imperial itself had already absorbed ailing Aladdin; the Bihari brothers' Modern Records group had been revamped as a budget album company; Bobby Robinson's Fire-Fury labels were extinguished; and Vee-Jay simply imploded (as did Red Bird and, later, Scepter and Stax). Moreover, Art Rupe wound down Specialty, as did Bob Marcucci and Peter DeAngelis with Chancellor and Sam Phillips with Sun. "The majors could buy you out of it at any time," said Joe Bihari with ironic laughter. "Our day in the sun was fading."

"We started going downhill when the manufacturers started selling out to the majors," agreed Stan Lewis. "The mom-and-pop distributors started going out of business because they were losing so many lines. In the East, a distributor might only have five or six lines, but they would do far greater business. I mean, you take a guy with ABC, United Artists, Atlantic, or Arista, they might do more business than me in the South. Where they could sell 150- to 200,000 of a 45, maybe I was only selling 25,000. So the big [indie] manufacturers were selling out to the majors, and we lost one label by one label. So the distributors went out of business. It wasn't the distributors' fault."

Showing how the independent distribution business was in disarray, the once-mighty (and immaculately run) Essex Record Distributors of New Jersey gave up the fight in May 1973. Head salesman Harold "Mr. Blues" Ladell was pink-slipped with one day's notice after being employed by the Cohen family for twenty-five years. The residual value in Essex was in the real estate, not the record stock.

Just as damaging, the bigger companies were picking off the indies' star artists with offers of large advances and long-term guarantees (including tax benefits and more) that the smaller labels couldn't match. The primary damage was done in the years 1960–63 when Atlantic lost Ray Charles to ABC-Paramount and Bobby Darin to Capitol; Imperial lost Fats Domino to ABC-Paramount and Ricky Nelson to Decca; Jamie lost Duane Eddy to RCA Victor; Keen lost Sam Cooke to RCA Victor; Laurie lost Dion to Columbia; Modern lost B. B. King to ABC-Paramount; Sun lost Jerry Lee Lewis to Mercury, having already lost Johnny Cash and Carl Perkins to Columbia and Elvis Presley to RCA before that; and Vee-Jay lost Curtis Mayfield and the Impressions to ABC-Paramount and the 4 Seasons to Philips following an acrimonious royalty dispute. The jazz field was not immune from this transfer activity, with Jimmy Smith moving seamlessly from Blue Note to Verve (now under MGM's control).

Most originally, Specialty lost Little Richard to his religious conversion, resulting in bemusing label hops to record gospel music to save his soul. Most tellingly, Cadence suffered a triple whammy in losing the Everly Brothers to Warner Bros., Andy Williams to Columbia, and Johnny Tillotson to MGM. Label boss Archie Bleyer had a big consolation prize with Vaughn Meader's *The First Family* LP, voted Grammy Album of the Year in 1962, but it was not enough. In September 1964, *Billboard* reported that Bleyer was throwing in the towel on his Cadence operation after almost twelve years as a "key indie label manufacturer." The reason was "disenchantment"; the asking price was "$300,000."[21]

Fred Foster still had a resigned fury as he remembered events that led to his hit act Roy Orbison departing Monument for MGM in 1965. The sorry tale implicated Orbison's manager, Wesley Rose of Acuff-Rose Music and Hickory Records, and Sir Edward Lewis of U.K. Decca. Foster recalled the deal that Wesley presented to him:

He said, "In order to keep Roy, you have to guarantee him a million dollars, a motion-picture contract, and twenty primetime television appearances in the contract. Three years!" I said, "Well, Wesley, we have a history here, almost five years. I can guarantee a million dollars, no problem, but I can't guarantee motion-picture contracts because I don't own the studios. And any manager worth his salt could pick up a telephone and get him twenty television appearances."

He said, "You can submit your offer, and we'll open it with everybody else who is around the conference table." I said, "No, you won't be opening anything from me after what we have been through, Roy and I, and what we have accomplished. If I am not worthy to be considered separately from the rest of the world . . . First of all I wouldn't submit an offer if I couldn't meet all your terms. And next, I can't and so I won't."

That upset Roy a lot, but he finally came round and sat down in my office [and] just cried: "I don't ever want to leave, but it's easier to leave you than it is to fight Wesley." 'Cause any time they got into any kind of a confrontation, Wesley grabbed his chest like he was going to have a heart attack. They signed the first million-dollar deal for a pop singer: MGM put up $500,000 for the United States and Canada, and Sir Edward [Lewis] put up $500,000 for the rest of the world.

So then I get a call from Sir Edward, probably six months after the MGM deal with Roy. He said, "I need to talk to you seriously; I need help. I can't give the Orbison product away. It's simply horrible, dreadful. Is there any way I can engage you to produce him?" I said, "Well, sure, as a matter of fact, Sir Edward, for you I'll do it for nothing on one condition." He said, "Well, what's that, old boy?" "You can assure me that Wesley Rose will be nowhere near me or the studio. But I can tell you right now I don't think you will be able to get that done." And he didn't. C'mon![22]

Another reason for the indie labels' general discomfiture was the continuing assimilation of upstart rhythm and blues, which had been such an industry driving force, into mainstream popular music. Both *Cash Box* and *Billboard* had reacted to this trend by attempting to dispense unilaterally with their dedicated R&B charts at different times in the early 1960s. The frustration of both trade magazines was understandable, as indicated in a page-3 editorial in *Cash Box* on July 23, 1960: "For a lengthy time we studied both the R&B lists and the Pop lists and found that about 90 percent and more of the R&B best sellers were also Pop best sellers. After much discussion we decided that the time had come to accept an integration that had undoubtedly come about."

"I remember having many conversations with Berry Gordy on the phone," said *Cash Box* editor Marty Ostrow, "when he argued the point that every one of his records on Motown was a record for everyone—and not just for African Americans. The Supremes, the Temptations, Stevie Wonder, Marvin Gaye all helped to break the mold." But following industry grumbles, led by King's blustering Syd Nathan, both *Cash Box* and *Billboard* reversed their decisions to abandon the R&B charts.[23]

Certainly, Tamla-Motown had taken over the independents' baton in exhilarating style. Chess remained in a threatening position throughout the 1960s before losing the end game meekly. Atlantic was roaring on, first with soul (enhanced by distributed labels Stax and Volt) and then rock music.

Jerry Wexler hinted at the common malaise affecting the original indie labels when discussing Atlantic's necessary change of musical direction at the time: "We were in a period of entropy," he said. "We were running down. It didn't look like that, but we were. We kept doing the same thing for more than ten years with the same musicians, same arrangers, same songwriters, and the same artists. The songwriters were out of lyrics, the musicians were out of licks, and the arrangers were out of ideas . . . suffering and tired. And I had Wilson Pickett; I had to do a session with him. I gave it to Bert Berns [in New York], and it didn't work, so just one day I called Jim Stewart [at Stax Records, Memphis], and I said, 'I want Wilson Pickett down there.' I had seen this fabulous way of recording with Booker T. & the MGs. So I got Pickett down there, and one thing led to another. So we went on to the next place, like John the Baptist, and now I found Muscle Shoals [Alabama]," that is, Rick Hall's Fame studios. The South rises again!

Commerciality and quality of product aside, much of the success of Tamla-Motown, Chess, and Atlantic was due to their brilliant use of large and expanded promotion staffs. In the immediate pre-Beatles era, *Billboard*'s Bob Rolontz acknowledged this hidden breed "who have built strong followings in various key markets," naming specifically Sammy Kaplan in Detroit, Dave Siegel in Cleveland, Jerry Moss in California, Jerry Simon in the East, and Joe Galkin in the South.[24] But the promotion men, effectively the labels' "eyes and ears" on the road, could no longer rely on getting indie singles exposed through traditional methods and would see a role diversification, too, in the coming new age of the long-playing record. The times really were a-changin'.

Reflecting on the continual evolution in the industry, Shelby Singleton said:

The music business basically is not unlike anything else. I compare it to automobiles. We don't drive a horse and buggy anymore; we don't drive a Model A or a Model T anymore. And as time changes and technology changes, that's what dictates the changes in the music business. It really has nothing to do with anything except people's tastes change as they modernize. I think as the conglomerates buy into any going business, whether it be automobiles or clothing or whatever, it's like in music; it becomes more sophisticated. And so from decisions being made from the seat of your pants or from your ears, they're making all this scientific research rather than just [relying on] the guts and glory that we used to have.

It's the same thing with the cars. You don't have to get out and hand-crank a car; now you push a button and it starts. [It's the] same thing with making records. You started off with the direct-to-disc [machine], you made them on wire, then we made them on tape, and now we make them direct to computers. So really the business didn't change; technology changed. It caused the business itself to change.

I think most of the record people who developed those things were real characters. They loved to work hard, they loved to play hard, and they were just very determined in anything they did. I mean, you [look at] Don Pierce or Fred Foster or myself or Ahmet Ertegun and Nesuhi or the Chess brothers or any of those type of people. We would do anything to get a record played, within reason. If it was something we believed in, we would not give up on it until we made it a hit.

As editor at *Cash Box*, Irv Lichtman was well aware of the ongoing upheavals in the record industry. "You could see the change," he said.

Part of the change was that we were getting older, too. As the years went by, we got married, had responsibilities. I think your attitudes change about everything; you're not single, you're not twenty-one. And of course the business did get very, very serious. The personalities began to fade from the scene, those great entrepreneurs that we've talked about. Of course, the clichés apply to some extent—a corporation became a corporation, and you had the situation with the accountants and the lawyers beginning to run the show.

The truth is, it was probably totally necessary that some kind of better organization structure [took] place because the industry was growing and there was more at stake than even in those earlier days. Independent production began to feed the music industry, and artists' temperaments became much different. Labels were not in control anymore and became what movie studios became eventually: distributors. They didn't produce or own the product anymore, by and large.

The single existed in its own right in the earlier days, but then the single became a vehicle of promotion in the more advanced days of rock 'n' roll. The money was in the album. A lot of people claimed there was no money to be made on a single, and that almost became a self-fulfilling prophecy. But rock didn't fare too badly. Starting with the Beatles, that made for a more sophisticated, complicated, and expanding industry. The major labels asserted themselves, absolutely, because they bought up the major acts and independent labels.

The effects of time and change were echoed by Relic Records' Donn Fileti:

A perfect example was when rock 'n' roll started to come in. Joe Davis and Herman Lubinsky, who had really tapped the R&B market in the late '40s, early '50s, they were too old. They didn't have the ears then for rock 'n' roll. I mean, they were over fifty at the time, and they just couldn't compete with somebody like [George] Goldner or Hy Weiss, who were guys in their early thirties or even maybe late twenties. So in any kind of music, it's very rare that an artist or certainly a record man, any kind of an entrepreneur, anybody working for a label or owning a label, can have a really long career. The music just changes too much. It's difficult to have that same kind of ear for it. In the mid-1960s, rock started to come in, the Beatles, the [Rolling] Stones, and all of that. Then the Vietnam War was getting that generation of people as draftees, and "oldies" really dropped until the early 1970s. I mean, it really did seem these indie catalogs were dead.

But what about our old friends the jukebox operators, who had done so much to dictate the sound and then to accelerate the diaspora of America's rock 'n' roll records? By 1963, it was clear that their industry had seen its best days. *Billboard* was reporting that within the past five-year period, operators were down by one-fifth in number and were diversifying into other activities. Moreover, domestic jukebox production had dropped alarmingly by two-thirds, and the number of locations had fallen by one-ninth (due in part to many lower-class honky-tonk spots being lost to slum clearance and other urban renewal projects).[25] In effect, the operators' fortunes were tied to the fate of the 45–rpm single. Just as critically, the jukebox was yesterday's technology within the assertive youth culture of the Swinging Sixties. The relentless falloff in business badly weakened fabled manufacturer Wurlitzer, which was undone finally by the 1973 recession; Seeburg struggled on until the end of the decade.

With the volume jukebox record trade falling away in tandem with the vanquished independent labels, the dyed-in-the-wool independent distributors and one-stop owners were losing their traditional life supports. Then there was the increasing stranglehold of the majors' distribution setups. The last straw (long before downloads—that is, digital distribution!) was the introduction of that unfathomable new invention for stock-keeping and accounting: the computer. What to do? For the old-time record distributors, the tough jukebox operators, and the veteran record men, there was little choice but to disappear, cowboy-like, into the sunset—or, rather, to the sun of Florida.

In what turned out to be almost the last roundup, on October 29, 1973, record men and women and their partners gathered at the Hilton Hotel in New York to honor Morris Levy for the United Jewish Appeal. Looking for all the world in a private film of the event like a generic godfather but with an unsuspected coyness, Levy was flanked by thirty-three "founding fathers of this our record industry," including Archie Bleyer, Sam Clark, Florence Greenberg, Cy Leslie, Art Talmadge, Hy Weiss, and Jerry Wexler.

Keynote speaker Joe Smith—Yale graduate, former Boston disc jockey, and then president of Warner Bros./Reprise Records—had an affectionate wit that could have come only from an intelligent insider. "Pioneers!" he exclaimed. "When you think of the Wild West, you think of Daniel Boone and Kit Carson; none of these people have been west of Tenth Avenue." To bellows of laughter, he told how Elliot Blaine and brother Jerry formed Cosnat Distributing and Jubilee Records in 1947: "They introduced the 'four-bookkeeping' system . . . four separate sets of books," Smith said. "It took those guys ten years to find out they were suing each other for distributing Jubilee."[26]

Henry Stone: Disco and the End of an Era

Down in Miami, Henry Stone was far from retirement. With the major corporations tightening their collective grip on the music business, he fought an unlikely rearguard action on behalf of the independents. In the same year of 1973, he launched TK Records to compensate for the falloff in his Tone distribution business and promptly danced into the disco era.

"I was concentrating on my distribution company at that time," said Stone.

Then I started to go back into the studio. Clarence Reid came in to play with Betty Wright; that's when we had "Clean Up Woman" [No. 6, 1972]. When I released "Clean Up Woman" it was a certain smash. Rather than try to take this record nationally myself, I used to work with Atlantic pretty good, so I put my Alston label with the Atlantic distribution. Steve Alaimo was the "Al" of Alston, and I was the "ston."

I had a series of labels, Glades, Cat, and Marlin, which I integrated into TK. I had a little 8–track studio upstairs, which I built because I used to *love* getting in the studio. It was like my golf game. I guess the first hit on TK was "Rock Your Baby" by George McCrae [No. 1, 1974]. It sold about 15 million records worldwide. . . . Then of course KC and the Sunshine Band came along with two No. 1s: "Get Down Tonight" and "That's the Way (I Like It)."

At the time, it was just another job. Every morning I woke up, there was another hit, whether it was R&B or it was disco, because I had twenty-three gold and platinum records in the 1970s. It was one explosion after another. I remember getting a call from Berry Gordy when TK was hot, because I was Berry Gordy's distributor and we had a very good relationship. He said, "Henry, what's happening? I'm not selling records like I used to; you're selling all the records!" I said, "Well, it's the disco era." Motown was not doing too well in the discos because it was a great, wonderful R&B crossover label.

It lasted from 1974 until there was a bust in the industry in the early 1980s. That was when all the returns started coming in from major labels, because everybody thought they had a *Saturday Night Fever* [a massive-selling album, featuring the Bee Gees, that lasted on the charts for well over two years from November 1977]. Basically they said, "Disco is dead!" These record companies started to fold, including TK and Casablanca. The major companies, of course, they didn't fold, because they had a good backing, but they lost a lot of money. Every label shipped like they had a *Saturday Night Fever,* but it didn't work. The returns were expensive LPs, not cheap singles. It affected the record industry badly.

At its pinnacle in 1976, TK Records was accorded an advertorial spread in *Cash Box,* and Jerry Wexler was coerced into writing a tribute article: "A Loving Look at Henry Stone." It was a witty study, hilarious and endearing, which in turn captured the inventive machinations of the independent record men and distributors at large. Here are selected highlights from Wexler's review of Henry's "early works [that] evoke an amalgam of bemusement, awe, and a deep, religious-like wonder":

* Henry Stone set out a shingle as "distributor" and invented the Minotaurian warehouse, a miasmic catacomb into which records returned from retailers disappeared, never to be opened, counted, or sorted. Similarly, mountains of good news sent in by manufacturers in double and triple helpings piled up in unmanageable slag heaps in the nether reaches of this Dantean hell. The nearer outposts were attainable if one were fortified with personal courage, keen night vision, and a working knowledge of Cuban argot, but the inner redoubts proved ultimately unstormable.

* Next came a landmark invention: the unsigned check, or "Muriel" [the name of Henry's first wife] as it came to be known at ARMADA meetings.

* Another breakthrough was the extirpation of the "back order," a chronic nuisance in the record industry. Henry came up with the marvelously simple idea of the Ultimate Solution, or purification by burning of all the slips, memos, invoices, or covering letters referring to back-ordered records.

* In a ten-year contest with Jerry Blaine, he emerged triumphant as "Father of Trans-shipping." His master stroke was the placing of a box of Francis Craig's "Near You" in the first space ship to the moon. The goods are in the Sea of Tranquility, ready for lunar jocks and ops as soon as operations begin.

* In a rush of altruism, Henry extended the hand of welcome to many worthy Cuban refugees, training them in a new cottage industry: the one-press pressing plant. Never advertising his connection with these presses, he kept their location unadvertised in the true spirit of anonymous charity.

* Henry, in the early years, had no peer in his relations with artist, trade and press. Many conventions were held in Miami, and Henry soon developed a subtle, sinuous mix of invisibility and cheap hospitality, e.g., at no cost he might "borrow" an extra suite from Roulette, bring in three bottles of I. W. Harper from a cut rate liquor store, and empower Morty Craft to take over as social director. What a marvelous evocation of the old American tradition of home entertainment! Eager helpers would be found in Normie Rubin, Dave Miller, Wally Shuster and other willing hands in those great early days of "Whose Suite Is It?"

* The Creative Charge Back. On rainy days in slack seasons, Henry trained assembly lines of apprentice clerks in the craft of fiction. Subtlety was the watchword, and verisimilitude the *sine qua non*—nothing crude, vulgar, or obvious—and the results were impossible to challenge or upset.

* The greatest Ploy of all was the negotiation of the 20¢ Freebie. Henry, in the company of the Council of The Elders including Jim Schwartz, Milt Salstone, Sid Talmadge, Paul Glass, Jake Friedman, and other Great Shamans, in the dim reaches of the Pliestocene had invented the three-hundred-free-on-a-thousand to be borne in silent rage by the indie manufacturers. One of the cleverer of these forebearing souls (whom modesty prevents me from naming) came up with the idea that the records cost eight cents to press, copyright royalties were four cents, a penny to Mr. Petrillo, a nickel to the artists, and two cents for overhead, and that instead of being entirely free, the "freebie" would now cost the distributors 20 cents. All of them bit, except Henry, who greeted the move with hearty guffaws. Whereupon a trade was made: he would not pay the 20 cents; in return

he would not tell the other labels what the clever label was doing. (The 20 cent freebie remained exclusive with its originators for a long time).

* Foreseeing the agglomeration, proliferation, conglomerization, and sheer aggravation in store for the independent distributor, Henry thought back to his miserable apprenticeship under the dreaded Syd Nathan. Back in the early fifties, Henry was sweeping the control room in Cincinnati while a group called Otis Williams and the Charms recorded a caterwauling dirge called "Hearts of Stone." Henry hypnotized himself into believing he had produced this minor hit, and as the decades rolled by, he passed himself off as an a&r man manqué who was only fighting with the Chesses, the Mesners and your deponent and his partners as a temporary stopgap until his return to the studio. Circumstances finally forced him to this desperation measure and:

* In some godforsaken limbo in his warehouse, he threw together a closet-sized "studio" and a control room the size of a medium steamer trunk. He sent his janissaries on night patrols to sift through Mack Emmerman's garbage, and from a rag bag of used parts and discarded microphones came up with a "console" and a temperamental mono tape machine. At this point even Dick Clark had given up on Steve Alaimo, and faced with total ruin and starvation, Steve and Henry wallowed about in the "studio" and in spasms of ineffectuality began to "produce" the "Miami Sound." In those days, visitors to a Stone session from the North were known to blench and run for the sidewalk, when they heard those early sounds.

Now look at Henry today.

See Henry going to MIDEM, wallowing in 3-star restaurants! See Henry in the Polo Lounge! Read the Henry Stone issue in *Cash Box*! See Henry being interviewed by *Melody Maker* and *Salut Les Copains*! Here is Henry quoted in the *Wall Street Journal*; Henry savoring the sounds of Betty Wright, K. C., and Gwen McCrae at Regin's in Paris! Here's one: Henry discounting his bills with the printer! Look at Henry peering at a computer printout of sales in California!

It was a long way from Henry Stone's humble beginnings, which were profiled with equal relish by Jerry Wexler in the opening paragraph of his eulogistic fantasy:

In 1946 Henry Stone left California at midnight in a boxcar (something apocryphal about a blood feud with the Bihari clan and a bonded warehouse) and stumbled into the glare of a Miami summer day. He had an attaché case containing a bar of soap, two pairs of jockey shorts, tear sheets of the last 20 "Hot in Harlem"'s, a roll of toilet paper, and Ben Bart's phone number. In his pocket he had eighteen dollars and change.[27]

In a sense, Henry Stone's odyssey, as portrayed by Jerry Wexler, could have been a fictional template for the rest of the independent record pioneers who started out modest in ambition and yet who delivered deliciously. It was only a matter of time before this merry band of mavericks, loaded down with dreams and schemes, was reined in by the unstoppable combination of changing tastes, stiffer legislation, natural economic forces, and technological revolution (what to do with all those multi-tracks . . . 4, 8, 16,

32, 64?). Then there were the unwelcome intrusions from upstart artists, power lawyers and accountants, organized crime (white and black), and resurgent major labels. Simply put, the once wide-open indie record market would mature, as markets of substance always do. And the energetic excitement would drain away, as it always does.

The independent record industry, on the surface so unique, was complying with surprising uniformity to the standard business pattern as described by management expert Peter Drucker: "When market or industry structures change, traditional industry leaders again and again neglect the fastest growing segments. New opportunities rarely fit the way the industry has always approached the market, defined it, or organized to serve it. Innovators therefore have a good chance of being left alone for a long time."[28]

While the independents may have been setting the new rules, the status quo—and accompanying freedom—could not last forever. Big business would assert itself in the end by infiltrating and overwhelming the once-powerful cabal of indie record makers, disc jockeys, distributors, and jukebox operators (along with pressing plant owners and the rest). Inevitably, and not without irony, most of the masters and publishing assets of the independent labels from the Golden Age have been swallowed up and rest profitably in the ownership of the current global major corporations.[29]

Yet for a while, the founding record men and women, who had such a remarkable capacity for innovation and hard work, were smash hits themselves. Their astonishing enterprise in giving opportunities to almost every artist of any merit is evidenced in the veteran recording acts who continued to tread the boards, in the seemingly never-ending reissues from the vaults, and in the many oldies songs that are featured in movies, in TV commercials, on radio (terrestrial and satellite), and on the Internet. Most of all, the legacy and mystique of the "record men" survive in our record collections, whether on 78s, 45s, LPs, CDs, or even computer downloads, iPods, and whatever next. This ingenious body of record makers stumbled upon a product that has sold and sold and sold and continues to sell. If the original audience has aged, the music has not.

The adventurous gamble paid off, gloriously, as the popular independent recordings spread from city to city, region to region, and nation to nation. "You make a record like 'Respect' by Aretha Franklin [No. 1, 1967]," said Ahmet Ertegun in one of his last interviews, "and you go to Copenhagen, to a disco, and that's what they dance to. You go to Singapore, and they're dancing to that same record . . . in Johannesburg, and Des Moines, Iowa. This is the music of the world. It's a wonderful advertisement for America, yes."

With the good fortune of history thrust upon them, the record innovators became inadvertent social innovators by igniting a lasting cultural reformation through rock 'n' roll music and its component parts. Somehow we knew that Elvis Presley, Chuck Berry, Fats Domino, Little Richard, and company would conquer all, but for too long we knew too little about the record men and women working behind the scenes. It has to be said: the artists needed the record makers as much as the record makers needed the artists.

Now the glare of the spotlight is on the "greatest generation" of independent record makers, the saints and the not-so-saintly, whose colorful stories as a body still glitter like their gold records. What a show, what a cast, what characters . . . and what pioneering voices.

25

CHAPTER

End of Session: Art Rupe's New Rules at Specialty Records

In the mid-1950s, Art Rupe wrote up the equivalent of a staff instruction manual based on his personal experiences in the "school of hard knocks." Viewed as a whole, these documents represent priceless insights into the modus operandi of the independent record makers from a faded era through one of its leading practitioners.

The idea came to Rupe when he appointed Johnny Vincent, often a loose cannon, as his southern representative in the spring of 1953. Vincent, who sold his year-old Champion Records to Rupe at the same time, was already acquainted with the region through his posts as salesman for distributors William B. Allen and Music Sales of New Orleans and as a label owner and distributor in his own right. His Specialty duties were described by *Billboard* as "a roving good-will ambassador among distribs, d.j.'s and retailers."[1] After two explosive years, during which time he produced Guitar Slim's huge R&B hit "The Things That I Used to Do," Vincent moved on to start Ace Records out of Jackson, Mississippi, in the summer of 1955. There, he had great success in the rock 'n' roll era with Jimmy Clanton, Frankie Ford, and Huey "Piano" Smith. While running Ace, he was a partner with Joe Caronna in Record Sales distributors of New Orleans at the turn of the 1960s.

In Art Rupe's notes, there are references to distributors, retailers, unions, and disc jockeys, but there appear to be no files on jukebox operators. In order to plug this gap, Rupe added his inimitable reflections on the juke-box topic after a hiatus of almost a half century.

To put the original chronology into perspective, Specialty was about to break out with one of rock 'n' roll's crucial records, "Tutti-Frutti" by Little Richard, accompanied by the New Orleans studio band with saxophonists Lee Allen and Red Tyler. It is worth noting Rupe's serendipitous references to New Orleans musicians and in particular to Earl Palmer, who set the pace impeccably as rock 'n' roll's premier drummer.

On this evidence, the independent record business was becoming more sophisticated in its business approach yet at times still seemed to be barely above cottage-industry status.

I: General Recording Principles

1. Try to record in the following studios whenever possible:
    a. New Orleans (Cosimo's)
    b. Houston (ACA—Bill Holford's)
    c. Memphis (Sam Phillips)
    d. Chicago (Universal—Bill Putnam)
    e. Dallas (Sellers)

2. Otherwise, try to record in a large hall with a high ceiling, or an auditorium, or a large room, or nite club.

3. Remember that a recording session costs money and requires extreme concentration of everybody involved. GET RID OF ALL SIGHTSEERS, HANGERS-ON, etc. TRY NOT TO HAVE VISITORS! That is also the way competitors learn your business. That is also the way such interference keeps you from getting good results.

4. Microphone placement is very important and may require a little experimentation for best results. Generally, it is best to group the rhythm section (piano, bass, drums, guitar, vibra-harp, mouth organ) together. The horns (alto, tenor, baritone, trumpet, etc.) should have their own mic. The vocalist should always have his own mic.

5. Where having heavy rhythm is desirable, it might be a good idea to put a mic on a boom near the piano and also one mic near the drums. You can also get good results by grouping the rhythm together.

6. Place the singer on a separate mic in such a way that the sounds of the rhythm or the band will not feed into the singer's mic. It may be necessary to place the singer in another room, although you can probably get good sound isolation with a little experimentation.

7. The general idea is to control the various elements of sound so you can mix them any way you desire. Just imagine that you have the rhythm in one room, the horns in another room, the singer in still another room, and that you can bring in whatever you want just by turning the dial of your mixer controlling that room. This is called isolation.

8. The most important thing is to bring out the words of the singer. He should be way out in front of the music. However, at no time shall the rhythm be lost.

9. It sometimes helps you get a better balance if you turn all the controls off on your mixer and then listen to the rhythm alone. Repeat this procedure, and listen to the harmony alone, etc. This will help you check on the little details of the music. If the small points are right, the whole should be right.

10. All the above technique does not mean anything if the song is not sung and the music is not played WITH FEELING. As a matter of fact, FEELING AND SOUL is more important than good technique. Put good material performed with feeling and recorded with good technique together—and you have a good chance to HIT!

11. It is also a good idea to listen to former HIT records that are similar in material and tempo to the material you are trying to record. PLAY THESE RECORDS FOR YOUR BAND OR VOCALIST TO DEMONSTRATE WHAT YOU WANT.

12. Be sure to identify each "cut" or "take." Before each selection say the Title of the song and the "take #." For example: WHAT'S THE MATTER NOW, Take #1.[2] If you record another Take on this selection, say WHAT'S THE MATTER NOW, Take #2. Keep a written record of the session as you go along. This is very necessary bookkeeping. Your recording *log* or *legend* should look like this:

> Joe Dyson Band
> King Jones, vocalist
> What Happened To Me?
> Tk#1 2:40 Voice not out enough
> Tk#2 2:35 Maybe good. Check again
> Tk#3 2:38 Probably best take
>
> I'm Blue Again
> Tk#1 3:01 Too long
> Tk#2 2:48 Probably this one[3]

13. Generally, it is a good idea to save all takes. The tape is not wasted, as we can always reuse the bad takes for rerecording at a later date. Frequently, the bad take will sound better than the best take a few days after the session.

14. Do not tire out your vocalist and musicians by trying to do it over and over again. If a number has the FEELING, go on to the next song. If a song does not sound like good material, go on to the next one. MANY A HIT HAS BEEN LOST BECAUSE THE SINGER GOT HOARSE OR TIRED AND LOST FEELING.

15. Generally, it takes a band and vocalist about 45 minutes to really warm up. TRY TO DO YOUR BEST SONG 2nd or 3rd IN THE SESSION, [and] ALWAYS TRY TO DO A FAST NUMBER FIRST. THIS WARMS AND LOOSENS EVERY-BODY UP.

16. WATCH YOUR BEHAVIOR AT A SESSION. Never show anger or disgust. KEEP PRAISING EFFORT. Say things like, "That was pretty good fellows, but it would be better if you could move in on the tenor sax solo, etc. etc." KEEP THEM RELAXED!

17. Remember, you are a Director. Set the mood for a song. Tell a story about the mood you want to create. Gain their confidence by showing them that you appreciate what is being sung and played—and that you feel the song also.

18. Immediately after you have decided to send the Tapes to Hollywood, pack well and send via PARCEL POST, SPECIAL DELIVERY, INSURED. Only send by Air when there is a Rush for release.

19. Protect your valuable equipment and supplies. Nobody touches them!

II. General Policies in Distributor Relations

All our distributors are considered to be exclusive distributors with protected territories. The only thing that your distributors have in writing from us is a letter appointing them as our distributors. HOWEVER, WE RESERVE THE RIGHT TO DISCONTINUE THAT ARRANGEMENT AT ANY TIME. We have no understanding on the return of merchandise in event of cancellation, but we generally work something out to relieve them of their stock.

All distributors are billed at 42¢ f.o.b. our factory in Hollywood or Philadelphia.[4] However, certain individual deals have been made on freight allowances which average about 1¢ per record. Distributors are sent a packing slip, Bill of Lading, and Invoice with each shipment. At the end of the month, we render a statement. We expect all bills to be paid by the 10th day of the month following purchase. We permit a 2% discount for prompt payment. UNDER NO CIRCUMSTANCES ARE YOU EVER TO DISCUSS A DISTRIBUTOR'S TERMS WITH ANYBODY ELSE!

We send each distributor free salesmen samples and free disc jockey samples, if they request disc jockey samples. We also supply quantities of catalogs, Spiritual catalogs, pictures, streamers, etc. at no charge to the distributor.

We grant a 5% return privilege, which is computed twice a year on June 30th and December 31st.

We have different promotion deals with different distributors. Consult each distributor file for the deal applying to them.

The promotional allowance and the freight allowance are given in the form of a Credit Memo which our Hollywood office issues at the end of every month. NO DISTRIBUTOR IS PERMITTED TO DEDUCT ANYTHING FROM OUR STATEMENTS! ONLY OUR CREDIT MEMOS MAY BE DEDUCTED AFTER [BEING] ISSUED BY OUR OFFICE!

If a distributor notifies us that he is ever loaded on a number, we do our best to relieve him of his long inventory. However, we do this only when we can re-route to another distributor. YOU MUST NOTIFY THE HOLLYWOOD OFFICE OF A DISTRIBUTOR'S OVERSTOCK, AND THE HOLLYWOOD OFFICE WILL TRY TO RE-ROUTE IT.

ORAL ARRANGEMENTS DO NOT GO! EVERYTHING MUST BE IN WRITING. In this manner, no distributor can say that you promised this or our office promised that.

SEND OUR HOLLYWOOD OFFICE A COPY OF EVERY LETTER YOU WRITE! WE WILL SEND YOU A COPY OF ALL LETTERS TO YOUR ACCOUNTS!

III. How to Work a Territory

1. Try to discover as much as you can about the distributor's method of representing and distributing SPECIALTY RECORDS. This should include examination of the following points:

   a. How many salesmen does he use to cover his area?

   b. What territory does our distributor actually cover? Make an outline on a map to designate this, so you can check it when you are in the field.

   c. Get a list of all disc jockeys the distributor or his salesmen regularly see in person.

   d. Get a list of all disc jockeys they regularly send samples to. Are our samples included?

   e. How often do the salesmen see all the accounts?

   f. Do they maintain a mailing list and use it? How often do they make a mailing?

   g. What is the distributor doing with the free advertising literature we send him? Should we send him more or less quantities?

   h. Are our records prominently displayed in the distribution office?

2. Check the big retail outlets for our product in all the large cities to see how our product is being displayed. Ask the manager of these retail outlets if they are getting good service. Also ask them what radio programs sells records for them.

3. Particularly check on the 2nd and 3rd class cities in each territory. For example, in Georgia, check on Macon, Decatur, etc.

4. Always check a distributor's inventory. See what numbers of our standard catalog that he should have on order. Also see if he is loaded on any number. NOTIFY THE HOLLYWOOD OFFICE IN WRITING if the distributor is heavy on any number, and we will try to relieve him.

5. Get the distributor's permission to go out into the field with each of the salesmen. Encourage the salesmen to push SPECIALTY RECORDS by presenting the whole catalog. Get them to present SPECIALTY RECORDS ahead of their other lines.

6. If you are able to have breakfast or lunch with a distributor, salesman, dealer, or disc jockey—by all means do so. However, try to avoid dinner engagements or lavish entertainment. AN APPROACH OF FRIENDLY BUSINESS BEHAVIOR IS MORE DESIRABLE THAN THE PLAY-BOY, BIG-SPENDER APPROACH. ALWAYS PICK UP THE CHECK.

7. Try to set up deals with key dealers on our SPIRITUAL line. Emphasize our SPIRITUAL line to the distributors constantly!

8. ALWAYS ASK DISTRIBUTORS, SALESMEN, DEALERS, and DISC JOCKEYS IF THEY KNOW OF ANY SINGERS OR BANDS IN THE TERRITORY.

9. Also, check with colored people in the various towns. YOU NEVER KNOW WHERE YOU MAY UNCOVER A HIT!!

IV. How to Sign Up a Recording Artist

After you have satisfied yourself that an artist has commercial possibilities by listening to ALL HIS ORIGINAL MATERIAL, sign him to an EXCLUSIVE contract.

Union: If the vocalist is also a musician and a member of the union, it becomes necessary to give him a UNION CONTRACT. This calls for $41.25 per side-man, and $82.50 for the leader. You are permitted to do 4 sides in a three hour recording period. Technically, but it is very rarely observed, the rule of the union is that all men must be paid $13.75 for each ½ hr. of overtime. Of course, you are permitted to do 1 extra side for each ½ hr. of overtime.

When writing up the contract you must specify so much per side. It is best to leave this blank as the new contracts which you will get will call for union scale.

Non-union: On non-union contracts, you can set any deal you want. However, USE OUR NON-UNION CONTRACT FORMS.

On all contracts, our standard rate is ½¢ Artist royalty during the first year. We also grant additional 1 year options, raising the rate gradually until the artist is receiving 2¢ artist royalty. We will leave these raises up to you. It all depends on your business ability.

Impress upon the artist that if they succeed, the publicity of having their records played constantly all over the U.S.A. will make them in demand for personal appearances. Impress on them not to look in the records for income, but to the profitable personal appearances.

All our royalty statements are HONEST and ACCURATE, as they are all paid promptly and certified by a CERTIFIED PUBLIC ACCOUNTANT.

V. Song Contracts

We must have a VENICE MUSIC, INC. contract on every original song we record. This calls for ½¢ per side. Also, if the song should be recorded on any other label, we collect the royalties and pay the writer 50%. If the song is good enough to publish, we print and sell sheet music. This pays 3¢ per copy on all songs except gospel and spiritual which pays 1½¢ per copy. If an artist is a good writer, get him to sign the GENERAL AGREEMENT.[5]

SEND HOLLYWOOD OFFICE A COPY OF THE WORDS, and if possible, A LEAD SHEET consisting of a simple melody line with the words. WE WILL COPYRIGHT ALL ORIGINAL MATERIAL. However, if the song is already copyrighted, send us the copyright number.

DO NOT SIGN ANY CONTRACTS AS YOU ARE NOT AN OFFICER OF THE COMPANY. THIS MUST BE DONE IN OUR HOLLYWOOD OFFICE. GIVE US THE CORRECT MAILING ADDRESS OF ALL ARTISTS AND WRITERS.

VI. New Orleans

J. & M. RECORDING STUDIO
838 North Rampart Street
New Orleans, Louisiana

This is the studio to use, and is owned and operated by Cosimo Matassa.[6] Call him COZ.

As soon as you get to New Orleans, look up the phone number of the above studio, and introduce yourself over the phone to Coz. Tell him what you are there for and get him on your side immediately. Tell him that Art Rupe said that he is the guy to steer you properly. If he doesn't answer at the studio because of Sunday look up Matassa in the phone book. It may be listed as *Mantissa*. Coz is very close to Imperial and Dave Bartholomew, Imperial's man; but Coz is also obligated to us. He owes us $500 and also has our Magnecord tape machine, so don't be bashful about asking him for favors and his cooperation.

Musician's Union: It might be a good idea to call up the union and let them know you are in town. Perhaps a visit would be better. Ask them what their local rules are so you can cooperate with them. Coz can also give you the low-down.

Musicians: Try to use the best recording musicians you can. Coz can also help you on this score. Ask for the musicians who back Fats Domino, Smiley Lewis, etc. Drummer—Earl Palmer (was on "Lawdy Miss Clawdy"). Earl Palmer will put you on to the other good cats . . . he really knows the New Orleans beat. Also, get a good piano man who plays the Fats Domino, New Orleans style.

Ask Coz about Alonzo Stewart, a singer who still owes us two sides . . . also, about the band that still owes us two sides.[7]

There's a guy called [Victor] Augustine, who owns a small record shop and a small label [Wonder]. He's very friendly to us and will act as a good bird dog for you. Also, ask Dick Sturgell, our distributor, for the address of that fat lady who writes songs . . . I think her name is Bently.[8]

Frank Panaii [actually Painia]: He runs the Dew Drop Inn, the colored nite club . . . he tries to get his fingers on artists as he had an interest in Guitar Slim, got Price involved with Don Robey's booking agency, and is now trying to control Earl King. *GET INFORMATION FROM HIM BUT TRY TO AVOID DEALING WITH HIM.*

Our distributor is A-1 Record Distributors and the boss there is Dick Sturgell, a very close friend . . . the address is 640 Baronne Street, New Orleans.[9] The phone is Tulane 7147. Get acquainted with him . . . he will introduce you to the important disc jockeys and give you important pointers. IF YOU GET INTO ANY KIND OF TROUBLE CALL DICK AT HOME . . . look it up in the phone book.

PLUG OUR CURRENT RELEASES: ZINDY LOU, TEARS ON MY PILLOW etc.[10]

Jukebox Distributors and Operators

"The national distribution system was an outgrowth of the jukebox distributors who frequently had a jukebox operating division," said Art Rupe, almost fifty years later.[11]

That is, the jukebox operator serviced the restaurants, bars, bowling alleys, and so forth where they located the jukebox. Since the operators needed records for the machines and since the major companies could not always meet the demands, the independents like Specialty Records began to be a source for the jukebox operator.

Since jukebox distributors already supplied jukeboxes and replacement parts, it was natural for the jukebox distributor to also begin to stock records, which actually were like replacement parts for the jukeboxes. The major record companies had their own distribution offices and distributed only their own brand. For example, Victor distributed Victor records, Decca distributed Decca records, and so on. But a jukebox operator needing multiple labels sold any label he could get, so the jukebox distributors were the original distributors for the independent record companies from the mid-1940s through the 1950s. They continued to expand and distribute more independent labels as the industry grew [leading to the one-stop].

Jake Gutshall and Jake Friedman were typical jukebox distributors who distributed independent records. They were so successful that they opened separate divisions just to distribute records. Besides Jack Gutshall in Los Angeles [and] Jake Friedman in Atlanta, some names I recall were Runyon in New Jersey and Sam Taran in Miami. There were numerous others in all the major cities. We had the same distributors generally for rhythm and blues, gospel, and hillbilly records. Occasionally we did appoint separate distributors for Fidelity [a minor subsidiary label] but had most of our success having the one distributor for both labels, because with volume we had a little more clout.

With the independent distributor involved, he serviced jukebox operators, retail stores, and radio stations. Yes, we would give credit to the distributor for evidence that he expended funds specifically for our records in his promotional efforts. In some instances, we gave him a credit to be used for promotion based upon volume.

If you had hit records, problems with distributors were virtually nonexistent; they needed records to survive, particularly records that were in demand, so "no pay" meant "no play." Fortunately, Specialty had minimal difficulties with late payment. Sometimes a distributor would overextend himself and would go bankrupt. In that event, we lost what they owed us, but this seldom happened.

I believe the concept of pay-for-play for music on a machine developed years earlier with the player piano. The marriage of the record changer technology with the 78-rpm record disc along with distributors of the pinball and slot machines accelerated this development. Restaurants and bars were able to now provide music to their patrons and to share the income the jukeboxes earned with distributors, who really owned the jukeboxes and serviced them.

The success of a jukebox operator depended upon the number of locations he could place his jukeboxes in. Each location was a cash generator. If the operator had locations that weren't profitable, or if he had an insufficient number of locations, then his business was not very profitable. With the proliferation of jukeboxes came the related demand for records.

The majors concentrated mostly on the Tin Pan Alley Top 10 records of the period, and the vacuum then was filled by independent record labels like Specialty Records. It was a niche that I found in the rhythm and blues, which was then referred to as race records. Specialty Records enjoyed the best sales in the urban areas where the distributors were located. However, they sold well in the rural areas, but not nearly in the large quantities sold in the cities. In other words, sales followed population. Jukeboxes were ubiquitous even in the rural South.

I feel [that] by the 1960s, the jukebox was in a serious decline, and therefore the record use by the jukebox operators declined accordingly. The percentage of sales specifically for the jukebox industry declined with each decade as record retail stores increased in number. Then the fast food outlets, which didn't feature or even have a jukebox, began to proliferate. So there was just less demand for the jukeboxes. The fast food restaurants seemed to want their patrons to get in and get out in a hurry and not linger to listen to music. Besides, there were now car radios—and radio stations adopted recorded music formats like the Top 40 format. So there was a lot of music which was supplying the need rather than the former jukebox.

Jukebox demand followed the promotional efforts of the radio industry. . . . The key element was the record length: I tried to limit the record length so that it never exceeded three minutes. Radio and jukeboxes preferred short playing time so they could play more records within a time limit. In that way it produced more revenue. But I felt radio play was more significant in breaking a record than the jukeboxes. . . . The sound technique I employed was identical for the two mediums: lots of bass and accented rhythm.

Never stop, rock 'n' roll!

PART

5

Appendixes

Appendix A

U.S. Record Sales, 1921–69

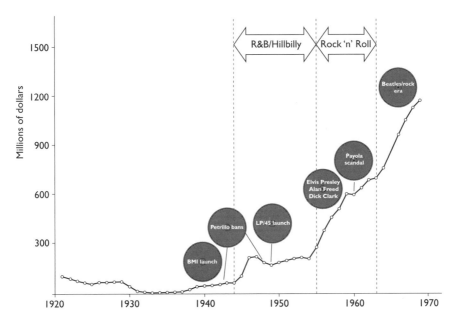

U.S. Record Sales, 1921–69

Year	Sales in Millions of Dollars	Annual Percent Change	Year	Sales in Millions of Dollars	Annual Percent Change
1921	$106	–%	1946	218	+100%
1922	92	–13.2%	1947	224	+2.8%
1923	79	–14.1%	1948	189	–15.6%
1924	68	–13.9%	1949	173	–8.5%
1925	59	–13.2%	1950	189	+9.2%
1926	70	+18.6%	1951	199	+5.3%
1927	70	0%	1952	214	+7.5%
1928	73	+ 4.3%	1953	219	+2.3%
1929	75	+2.7%	1954	213	–2.7%
1930	46	–38.7%	1955	277	+30%
1931	18	–60.9%	1956	377	+36.1%
1932	11	–38.9%	1957	460	+22%
1933	6	–45.5%	1958	511	+11.1%
1934	7	+16.7%	1959	603	+18%
1935	9	+28.6%	1960	600	–0.5%
1936	11	+22.2%	1961	640	+6.7%
1937	13	+18.2%	1962	687	+7.3%
1938	26	+100%	1963	698	+1.6%
1939	44	+69.2%	1964	758	+8.6%
1940	48	+9.1%	1965	862	+13.7%
1941	51	+6.3%	1966	959	+11.3%
1942	55	+7.8%	1967	1051	+9.6%
1943	66	+20%	1968	1124	+6.9%
1944	66	0%	1969	1170	+4.1%
1945	109	+65.2%			

Source: Recording Industry Association of America.

Notes: As a latter-day comparison, for year 2005 the RIAA reported that manufacturers' *shipments* totaled $10.5 billion. *Cash Box* noted on May 15, 1954, that these compilations, based on retail sales, were "valuable as indicating trends but are not a complete reflection of total record sales in the United States" (16).

Major city markets, recording centers, and record label domiciles

Appendix B

Independent Record Distributors' Network: 1946–48, 1954, 1960

Using Exclusive, Modern, Atlantic, and Chess-Checker-Argo as important label benchmarks, these listings illustrate the growth of the independent distributors' network from its early jukebox distributor/operator beginnings in 1946 through the 1960 peak. As such, it is possible to discern the main markets and the key distributors. The principal contacts, where known, are listed in parentheses, but it should be remembered that there were constant personnel—and name—changes. Indeed, distribution companies came and went with regularity, as in any fast-moving and developing industry.

Exclusive Records and Modern Records, December 1946

National Distributor

 Jack Gutshall Distributing Co. (Jack Gutshall), Los Angeles, CA

Common Distributors

 Record Sales Inc. (Leon Levy), Birmingham, AL
 Jack Gutshall Dist. Co., San Diego, CA
 Melody Sales Co. (Tom Moyles), San Francisco, CA
 M. S. Distributing Co. (Milt Salstone), Chicago, IL
 Music Sales Co. (Robert D. Wynne), New Orleans, LA
 Becker Novelty Co. (Maurice Becker), Springfield, MA
 Pan American Record Distributors (Bernard Besman, John Kaplan), Detroit, MI
 Commercial Music Co., Kansas City, MO
 Commercial Music Co. (Jack Stengele), St. Louis, MO
 Runyon Sales Co. (Jack Mitnick, Bernard Sugarman), New York, NY
 David Rosen (David Rosen), Philadelphia, PA
 Music Sales Co. (E. H. Newell), Memphis, TN
 M. B. Krupp Distributors (M. B. Krupp), El Paso, TX
 Standard Music Distributors (H. M. Crowe, Sam Ayo), Houston, TX
 C & C Distributing Co. (Irving Chellin), Seattle, WA

Exclusive Records (only)

 Lion Distributing Co. (Burton S. Green), Louisville, KY
 J. D. Hurst (probably J. D. Hurst), Kannapolis, NC
 Hales-Mullaly Co. (Carter Mullaly Jr.), Oklahoma City, OK
 American Coin-O-Matic (Sam Strahl), Pittsburgh, PA

Modern Records (only)

 Modern Music Distributing Co. (Saul Bihari, Joe Bihari), Los Angeles, CA

Davis Sales (Bill Davis), Denver, CO

Taran Distributing Co. (Sam Taran), Jacksonville FL, Miami FL, Atlanta, GA

J. F. Bard (Julius Bard), Chicago, IL

Mangold Distributors (Manny Goldberg), Baltimore, MD

Commercial Music Co. (Sam Klayman), Cincinnati, OH

Music Distributing Co. (Paul Reiner), Cleveland, OH

Note: In view of the close working relationship between Leon Rene and the Bihari brothers, there is a possibility that there may have been a few more common distributors.

Modern Records, 1948

At the start of 1948, the ever-fluid Modern network also included:

Modern Record Distributors (Saul Bihari, Lester Sill), Los Angeles, CA

Modern Record Distributors (Bob Duberstein, Gloria Friedman), New York, NY

Blue Bonnet Music Co. (Herb Rippa), Dallas, TX

Sunland Supply Co. (M. B. Krupp), El Paso, TX

Macy's Record Distributing (Macy Henry, Steve Poncio), Houston, TX

Tanner Record Distributing Co. (Bob Tanner), San Antonio, TX

Allen Distributing Co. (possibly Joe Sinshiemer), Richmond, VA

Sources: Exclusive Records brochure, Joe Bihari, and *Billboard*

Atlantic Records, June 1954

Central Record Sales Co. (Jim Warren), Los Angeles, CA

Chatton Dist. Co. (Robert Chatton), Oakland, CA

Davis Sales Co. (Bill Davis), Denver, CO

Seaboard Dist. Co. (Bernard Mitnick), Hartford, CT

Schwartz Bros. (Jim Schwartz), Washington, DC

Binkley Dist. Co., Jacksonville, FL, and Miami, FL

Southland Dist. Co. (Jake Friedman), Atlanta, GA

James Martin Inc. (probably Morris Goldman), Chicago, IL

Indiana State Record Dist. (probably Jerry Herman), Indianapolis, IN

A-1 Record Dist. Co. (Richard Sturgell), New Orleans, LA

Records Inc. (Cecil Steen), Boston, MA

Pan American Record Distributors (John Kaplan), Detroit, MI

Roberts Record Dist. (Robert Hausfater), St. Louis, MO

Essex Record Distributors (Joe Cohen), Newark, NJ

Faysan Dist. Inc. (probably Fay Mirti), Buffalo, NY

Cosnat Distributing Corp. (Jerry and Elliot Blaine), New York, NY,
    Cleveland, OH, Philadelphia, PA

F. & F. Enterprises (Bert Fleishman), Charlotte, NC

Hit Record Dist. Co. (probably Izzy Nathan), Cincinnati, OH

B. G. Record Service (Bertha Gribble), Portland, OR

Alco Record Dist. Co., (probably Bill Lawrence), Pittsburgh, PA

Randy's Record Dist. (Gilbert Brown), Gallatin, TN

Glenn Allen Supply Co. (Glenn Allen), Memphis, TN

Music City Record Sales (E. H. Newell), Nashville, TN

Big State Dist. Co. (Bill Emerson), Dallas, TX

M. B. Krupp Dist. (M. B. Krupp), El Paso, TX

United Record Dist. (Steve Poncio), Houston, TX

N. W. Tempo Dist. Co. (Stan Jaffes), Seattle, WA

Source: Cash Box, July 3, 1954

Note: Although Atlantic launched its Cat subsidiary in the spring of 1954, no separate distributor listings were shown.

Chess-Checker-Argo Records, June 1960

M. B. Krupp Dist. (Margo Grover), Phoenix, AZ (Chess-Checker)

Esskay Distributors (R. Kramer), Phoenix, AZ (Argo only)

A & A Record Dist. (Jack Andrews, Mike Akopoff), Los Angeles CA

Chatton Dist. Co. (Robert Chatton), Oakland, CA

Pan American Record Supply Co. (Louis Oxman), Denver, CO (Chess-Checker)

Leslie Dist. of New England (John Recanello), East Hartford, CT

Tone Dist. (Henry Stone, Milt Oshins), Miami, FL

Southland Dist. Co. (Jake Friedman), Atlanta, GA (Chess-Checker)

Dixie Dist. Co. (Jake Friedman), Atlanta, GA (Argo only)

Allstate Record Dist. Co. (Paul Glass), Chicago, IL (Chess-Checker)

M. S. Dist. Co. (Milt Salstone), Chicago, IL (Argo only)

A-1 Record Dist. Co. (Joe Banashak), New Orleans, LA (Chess-Argo)

All South Dist. Corp. (Henry Hildebrand), New Orleans, LA (Checker only)

Stan's Record Shop (Stan Lewis), Shreveport, LA

General Dist. Co. (Henry Nathanson), Baltimore, MD (Chess-Checker)

Records Inc. (Cecil Steen), Boston, MA

Cosnat Distributing Corp. (Charles Gray), Detroit, MI (Chess-Checker)

Coda Dist. Co. (R. H. Dahle), Minneapolis, MN (Chess only)

Sandel Co. (Herbert Sandel), Minneapolis, MN (Checker only)

Midwest Dist. Co. (Paul Levy), St. Louis, MO (Chess only)

Roberts Records Dist. Co. (Robert Hausfater, Sam Rosenblatt), St. Louis, MO (Checker only)

Music Service Co. (R. E. Holm), Great Falls, MT (Argo only)

Essex Record Distributors (Joe Cohen), Newark, NJ

Seaboard Distributors (Bernard Mitnick), Albany, NY

Scan Dist. (Jay Pastor), Buffalo, NY (Chess only)

Alpha Dist. Corp. (Johnny Halonka, Harry Apostoleris), New York, NY (Chess-Checker)

Superior Record Sales Co. (Sam Weiss), New York, NY (Argo only)

Bertos Sales Corp. (Phil Goldberg), Charlotte, NC

A-1 Record Dist. Co. (Richard Sturgell), Oklahoma City, OK

Universal Record Dist. Corp. (Harry Finfer), Philadelphia, PA

Astor-Ajax Dist. (H. S. Cohen), Pittsburgh, PA

Randy's Record Shop (Gilbert Brown), Gallatin, TN

Music Sales Co. (Leon McLemore), Memphis, TN

Ernie's Record Mart (Ted Adams), Nashville, TN

Southern Record Distributors (Howard Allison), Nashville, TN

United Record Dist. & Co. (Steve Poncio), Houston, TX

Great Western Record Dist. Corp. (Ray Peterson), Salt Lake City, UT

C & C Dist. Co. (Lou Lavinthal), Seattle, WA

John O'Brien Dist. Corp. (John O'Brien), Milwaukee, WI (Chess-Checker)

Source: Cash Box, July 30, 1960

Notes: (1) State Record Dist. and Whirling Disc Dist., both of Indianapolis, IN, and Cincinnati, OH, requested that their distributed labels should not be listed. In 1954, State Record Dist. of Indianapolis was handling the Chess-Checker lines. (2) The common view is that subsidiary labels used alternative distributors, but as can be seen with Chess-Checker-Argo, this is not necessarily so. (3) Please note that the abbreviation "Dist." is as printed in *Cash Box* and represents a variation of "Distributors," "Distributing," and "Distribution."

 Appendix C

Pressing Plants, 1946

The pressing plants represented something of a dot-com-like boom industry in the immediate post–World War II years in the scramble to meet the expected demand for phonograph records. On February 2, 1946, *Billboard* published on page 13 a list of the main pressing plants with year-end production forecasts. The trade paper expressed grave doubts that these growth estimates would be met by way of tongue-in-cheek comments such as "absolutely no slide rule used (not much)," and "*Billboard* does not recommend that record retailers or operators base expansion plans on these 'zillions' of records." The presence was also noted, caustically, of "sincere young men" and "sharpies" who "firmly believe they have developed new pressing and stamping equipment, which will enable them to hit production peaks never dreamed of before."

Company	Plant Location	Anticipated Production as of January 1, 1947
RCA Victor	Camden, NJ	100,000,000
	Indianapolis	
	Los Angeles	
Decca	New York	50,000,000
	Richmond, IN	
	Bridgeport, CT	
	Los Angeles	
	Chicago (due to be operational soon)	
Columbia	Bridgeport, CT	50,000,000
	Kings Mills, OH	
	Los Angeles	
Capitol	Scranton, PA	25,000,000
	Hollywood (due to be operational soon)	
Vogue	Detroit	36,000,000
Musicraft-Guild	Norwalk, CT	30,000,000
	Ossining, NY (in name of Jefferson-Davis)	
	Los Angeles	
Continental	New York	2,000,000
Mercury	Chicago	15,000,000
	St. Louis	
National	Phillipsburg, NJ	10,000,000
Pilot	Long Island City, NY	5,000,000
Sonora	Meriden, CT	10,000,000
Davis	Richmond, IN	2,500,000
	(in name of Starr Piano Plant)	
Cosmopolitan	Massapequa, LI, NY	2,500,000
	Subtotal	**338,000,000**

For the 100-odd other manufacturers, large, medium and small, multiply above subtotal by 5 to get:

	Grand total	**1,690,000,000**

Note: The following week, *Billboard* (February 9, 1946, 18) reported glibly that it was "only 4,000,000 shy" on the Cosmopolitan (Cosmo) estimate and that figures for Capitol's new Hollywood plant should have been included (production was forecast at 10 million discs per year "in addition to whatever their Scranton plant produces").

Appendix D

Original Postwar Record Labels: Locations, Launch Dates, and Current Owners

Majors

Columbia, New York, 1889—Sony-BMG (Japan)
Decca, New York, 1934—Vivendi-Universal (France)
RCA Victor, Camden, NJ, 1901—Sony-BMG (Japan)
MGM, New York, 1947—Vivendi-Universal (France)

Super Indies

ABC-Paramount, New York, 1955—Vivendi-Universal (France)
Capitol, Hollywood, CA, 1942—EMI/Terra Firma (U.K.)
Mercury, Chicago, IL, 1945—Vivendi-Universal (France)

Indies

Ace, Jackson, MS, 1955—Demon Music Group (U.K.)
A.F.O., New Orleans, LA, 1961—EMI (U.K.) (early masters), A.F.O. (late)
Aladdin [Philo], Los Angeles, CA, 1945—EMI (U.K.)
Anna, Detroit, MI, 1959—Billy Davis Enterprises
Apollo, New York, 1944—Delmark (R&B), Malaco (gospel)
Atlantic, New York, 1948; Atco, 1955; Cat, 1954—Warner Music Group
Bell, New York, 1952—Sony-BMG (Japan)
Bigtop, New York, 1958—Aberbach Estate
Cameo, Philadelphia, PA, 1957; Parkway, 1958—ABKCO
Challenge, Hollywood, CA, 1957—Sony-Tree (Japan)
Chancellor, Philadelphia, PA, 1957—Digital Music Group
Chess, Chicago, IL, 1950; Checker, 1952; Argo, 1956; Aristocrat, 1947—
    Vivendi-Universal (France)
Class, Los Angeles, CA, 1951—Sid Talmadge Estate
Clock, New York, 1958—Doug Moody
Cobra, Chicago, IL, 1956—Fuel 2000
Coed, New York, 1958—Janus Records
Derby, New York, 1949—Sony-BMG (Japan)
Dootone, Los Angeles, CA, 1951 [Dooto, 1957]—Ace (U.K.)
Dot, Gallatin, TN [Hollywood, CA], 1950—Universal-Vivendi (France)
Duke, Memphis, TN, 1952; Peacock, Houston, TX, 1949—Universal-Vivendi (France)
End, New York, 1957; Gone, 1957—EMI (U.K.)
Excello, Nashville, TN, 1952; Nashboro, 1951; Nasco, 1957—Universal-Vivendi (France)

Excelsior, Los Angeles, CA, 1944—Savoy-Denon (Japan)

Exclusive, Los Angeles, CA, 1944—title chain dispersed

Feature, Crowley, LA, 1947; Fais-Do-Do, 1946—Jay Miller Estate

Fire, Harlem, New York, 1959; Fury, 1957; Enjoy, 1962—Sony-BMG (Japan)

4 Star, Los Angeles, CA [Pasadena, CA], 1945—Sony-Tree

Fraternity, Cincinnati, OH, 1955—Ace (U.K.)

Gee, New York, 1955; Tico, 1948; Rama, 1952—EMI (U.K.)

Goldband, Lake Charles, LA, c. 1945—Eddie Shuler Estate

Golden, New York, 1948—Arthur Shimkin Estate

Golden Crest, Huntington Station, NY, 1953; Shelley, 1959—CFG Publishing Co.

Herald, New York, 1953; Ember, 1953—Sony-BMG (Japan)

Hi, Memphis, TN, 1957—Cream-Hi

Hickory, Nashville, TN, 1954—Sony-Tree (Japan)

Imperial, Los Angeles, CA, 1946—EMI (U.K.)

Jamie, Philadelphia, PA, 1956; Guyden, 1954—Jamie-Guyden

Jewel, Shreveport, LA, 1963; Paula, 1964; Ronn, 1966—Fuel 2000

Jin, Ville Platte, LA, 1958; Swallow, 1958—Flat Town Music

Jubilee, New York, 1946; Josie, 1954—EMI (U.K.)

King, Cincinnati, OH, 1943; Federal, 1950; De Luxe, 1944—King

Laurie, New York, 1958—EMI (U.K.)

Liberty, Hollywood, CA, 1955—EMI (U.K.)

London, New York, 1947—Universal-Vivendi (France)

Meteor, Memphis, TN, 1952—Virgin (U.S.), Ace (U.K.), Blues Interactions (Japan)

Modern, Los Angeles, CA, 1945; RPM, 1950; Flair, 1953; Crown, 1953; Kent, 1958—
    Virgin (U.S.), Ace (U.K.), Blues Interactions (Japan)

Montel, Baton Rouge, LA, 1958—Sam Montalbano

Monument, Baltimore, MD [Nashville, TN], 1958; Sound Stage 7, 1963—Sony-BMG (Japan)

National, New York, 1944—Savoy-Denon (Japan)

Old Town, Harlem, New York, 1953—Music Sales

Red Bird, New York, 1964—Sun Entertainment

Roulette, New York, 1957—EMI (U.K.)

Savoy, Newark, NJ, 1942—Savoy-Denon (Japan)

Scepter, New York, 1958; Wand, 1959—King

Specialty, Los Angeles, CA, 1946—Concord

SSS Int., Nashville, TN, 1967—Sun Entertainment

Starday, Houston, TX, 1953—King

Stax, Memphis, TN, 1958—Warner Music Group (early masters), Concord (late)

Sue, Harlem, New York, 1957—EMI (U.K.)

Sun, Memphis, TN, 1952—Sun Entertainment

Swan, Philadelphia, PA, 1957—Rollercoaster (U.K.)

Tamla, Detroit, MI, 1959; Motown, 1959—Universal-Vivendi (France)

Time, New York, 1958; Shad, 1959—Time

TK, Miami, FL, 1974—EMI (U.K.)

Top Rank, New York, 1959—EMI (U.K.)

Trumpet, Jackson, MS, 1950—University of Mississippi, Marc Ryan

Vee-Jay, Gary, IN [Chicago, IL], 1953—Vee-Jay Partnership

Warwick, New York, 1959—Morty Craft

Notes: (1) The ownership data, from best information available as of December 31, 2007, is of record labels featured in the text. All current owners are U.S.-based unless stated otherwise. (2) Prime labels only in company groups are listed. (3) In Europe, under current EU laws, released masters over fifty years old are perceived as being in the public domain.

 Appendix E

Rock and Roll Hall of Fame: Record Men Inductees, 1986–2008

The honor roll of record men—there are no record women—and associated inductees into the Hall of Fame, in the non-performers category (including some names outside the scope of this book), is as follows:

1986

Alan Freed (disc jockey)
John Hammond (Columbia)
Sam Phillips (Sun)

1987

Leonard Chess (Chess)
Ahmet Ertegun (Atlantic)
Jerry Leiber (Spark, Red Bird)
Mike Stoller (Spark, Red Bird)
Jerry Wexler (Atlantic)

1988

Berry Gordy (Tamla-Motown)

1989

Phil Spector (Philles)

1990

Brian Holland, Lamont Dozier, Eddie Holland (Tamla-Motown, HDH)

1991

Dave Bartholomew (Imperial)
Ralph Bass (Savoy, Federal, Chess)
Nesuhi Ertegun (Atlantic)

1992

Leo Fender (guitar manufacturer)
Doc Pomus (songwriter)

1993

Dick Clark (*American Bandstand* host)
Milt Gabler (Commodore, Decca)

1994

Willie Dixon (Chess, Cobra)

Johnny Otis (Dig, Eldo)

1995

Paul Ackerman (editor, *Billboard*)

1996

Tom Donahue (disc jockey)

1997

Syd Nathan (King-Federal)

1998

Allen Toussaint (Minit, Instant, Sansu)

1999

George Martin (EMI)

2000

Clive Davis (Columbia, Arista, Sony-BMG)

2001

Chris Blackwell (Island)

2002

Jim Stewart (Stax)

2003

Mo Ostin (Verve, Warner-Reprise)

2004

Jann Wenner (publisher, *Rolling Stone*)

2005

Seymour Stein (Sire, Warner Music Group)

2006

Herb Alpert (A&M)

Jerry Moss (A&M)

2007

None

2008

Kenny Gamble (Philadelphia International)

Leon Huff (Philadelphia International)

Appendix F

Record Makers: Biographical Data (Selective)

Joachim Jean Aberbach, August 12, 1910 (Vienna, Austria)–May 24, 1992 (New York)

Julian Aberbach, February 8, 1909 (Vienna, Austria)–May 17, 2004 (New York)

Ewart Abner, May 11, 1923 (Chicago, IL)–December 27, 1997 (Los Angeles, CA)

Herb Abramson, November 16, 1916 (Brooklyn, NY)–November 9, 1999 (Las Vegas, NV)

Berle Adams [Beryl Adasky], June 11, 1917 (Chicago, IL)–

William Trousdale "Hoss" Allen, December 3, 1922 (Gallatin, TN)–February 25, 1997 (Nashville, TN)

Herb Alpert, March 31, 1935 (Los Angeles, CA)–

Dave Appell, March 24, 1922 (Philadelphia, PA)–

Gene Autry, September 29, 1907 (Tioga, TX)–October 2, 1998 (Studio City, Los Angeles, CA)

George Avakian, March 15, 1919 (Armavir, Russian SFSR)–

Estelle Axton, September 11, 1918 (Middleton, TN)–February 24, 2004 (Memphis, TN)

Joe Banashak, February 15, 1923 (Baltimore, MD)–October 23, 1985 (Atlanta, GA)

Richard "Richie" Barrett, July 14, 1933 (Philadelphia, PA)–August 3, 2006 (Philadelphia, PA)

Dave Bartholomew, December 24, 1918 (Edgard, LA)–

Ralph Bass Jr., May 5, 1910 [or 1911] (New York)–March 5, 1997 (Nassau, Bahamas)

Harold Battiste Jr., October 28, 1931 (New Orleans, LA)–

Joe Battle, April 3, 1915 (unknown)–March 26, 1973 (Detroit, MI)

Bill Beasley, December 5, 1927 (Greenwood, MS)–March 9, 2001 (Arlington, TX)

Howard Bedno, May 26, 1918 (Chicago, IL)–May 15, 2006 (Chicago, IL)

Alvin "Al" Bennett, September 21, 1926 (Arkansas)–March 15, 1989 (Sherman Oaks, CA)

Bessie "Bess" Berman, June 3, 1902 (New York)–October 1997 (probably New Jersey)

Bert Berns [Bertrand Russell Bernstein], November 28, 1929 (New York)–December 30, 1967 (New York)

Bernie Besman [Eze Bessman], October 8, 1912 (Russia, USSR)–January 10, 2003 (Los Angeles, CA)

Freddy Bienstock, April 24, 1923 (Vienna, Austria)–

Johnny Bienstock, March 1, 1922 (Vienna, Austria)–January 20, 2006 (Naples, FL)

Joe Bihari, May 30, 1925 (Memphis TN)–

Jules Bihari, September 9, 1913 [or 1914] (Philadelphia, PA)–November 17, 1984 (Los Angeles, CA)

Lester Bihari, May 12, 1914 (Philadelphia, PA)–September 5, 1983 (Los Angeles, CA)

Saul Bihari, March 8, 1918 [or 1919]–February 22, 1975 (Los Angeles, CA)

Bernie Binnick, February 16, 1917 (unknown)–September 5, 1991 (Philadelphia, PA?)

Jerry Blaine, December 31, 1910 (Allenwood, NJ)–March 3, 1973 (Long Island, NY)

Archie Bleyer, June 12, 1909 (Corona, NY)–March 20, 1989 (Sheboygan, WI)

Salvatore "Sonny" Bono, February 16, 1935 (Detroit, MI)–January 5, 1998 (near Lake Tahoe, NV)

James Bracken, May 23, 1909 (unknown)–February 20, 1972 (Chicago, IL)

Daria "David" Braun, April 30, 1908 (New York)–September 27, 1985 (Jacksonville, FL)

Julius "Jules" Braun, July 8, 1911 (Hungary)–February 20, 2002 (Pompano Beach, FL)

Alan Bubis, August 18, 1922 (Nashville, TN)–

Jim Bulleit, November 4, 1908 (Corydon, IN)–December 12, 1988 (Nashville, TN)

Dave Burgess, December 3, 1934 (Beverly Hills, CA)–

John "Lawyer" Burton, September 14, 1916 (Illinois)–November 1985 (Illinois?)

Orville Campbell, August 17, 1919 (Springfield, IL)–June 6, 1989 (Chapel Hill, NC)

Harry Carlson, December 28, 1904 (Holdrege, NE)–March 16, 1986 (Pompano Beach, FL)

Vivian Carter, March 25, 1921(Tunica, MS)–June 12, 1989 (Gary, IN)

Leonard Chess [Lejzor Czyz], March 12, 1917 (Motol, Poland)–October 16, 1969 (Chicago, IL)

Marshall Chess, March 13, 1942 (Chicago, IL)–

Phil Chess [Fiszel Czyz], March 27, 1921 (Motol, Poland)–

Lew Chudd, July 1, 1911 (Toronto, Canada)–June 15, 1998 (Los Angeles, CA)

Lillian Claiborne [née Nichol], March 9, 1898 (Winchester, VA)–April 9, 1975 (Washington, DC)

Dick Clark, November 30, 1929 (Bronxville, NY)–

Samuel "Sam" Clark, January 10, 1910 (Boston, MA)–October 9, 1988 (New York)

Quinton Claunch, December 3, 1921 (Tishomingo, MS)–

Morton "Morty" Craft, August 19, 1920 (Brockton, MA)–

Luigi Creatore, December 21, 1921 (New York)–

Harold "Pappy" Daily, February 8, 1902 (Yoakum, TX)–December 5, 1987 (Houston, TX)

Joe Davis, October 6, 1896 (New York)–September 3, 1978 (Louisville, KY)

Roquel "Billy" Davis, July 11, 1932 (Detroit, MI)–September 2, 2004 (New Rochelle, NY)

Peter DeAngelis, June 18, 1929 (Philadelphia, PA)–September 1982 (unknown)

Tom Dowd, October 20, 1925 (New York)–October 22, 2002 (Aventura, FL)

Ahmet Ertegun, July 31, 1923 (Istanbul, Turkey)–December 14, 2006 (New York)

Nesuhi Ertegun, November 27 [or 26], 1917 (Istanbul, Turkey)–July 15, 1989 (New York)

Harry Finfer, May 29, 1916 (Philadelphia, PA)–March 16, 1998 (Philadelphia, PA)

Fred Foster, July 26, 1931 (Rutherford County, NC)–

Aldon "Alan" Freed, December 21, 1921 (Windber, PA)–January 20, 1965 (Palm Springs, CA)

Milt Gabler, May 20, 1911 (Harlem, NY)–July 20, 2001 (New York)

Clark Galehouse, September 25, 1911 (Pontiac, IL)–January 3, 1983 (Jacksonville, FL)

Paul Gayten, January 29, 1920 (New Orleans, LA)–March 26, 1991 (Los Angeles, CA)

Bob Geddins, February 6, 1913 (Highbank, TX)–February 16, 1991 (Los Angeles, CA)

Paul Glass, May 23, 1925 (Iowa)–March 29, 1986 (Oceanside, CA)

Henry Glover, May 21, 1921 (Hot Springs, AR)–April 7, 1991 (Queens, NY)

George Goldner [Jacob Goldman], February 9, 1917 (New York)–April 15, 1970 (Turtle Bay, NY)

Eugene "Gene" Goodman, August 3, 1915 (Chicago, IL)–

Harry Goodman, June 21, 1906 (Chicago, IL)–October 22, 1997 (Gstaad, Switzerland)

Berry Gordy III, November 28, 1929 (Detroit, MI)–

Albert "Al" B. Green, April 14, 1892 (Brooklyn, NY)–August 6, 1962 (Chicago, IL)

Irving Green, February 6, 1916 (Brooklyn, NY)–July 1, 2006 (Palm Springs, CA)

Florence Greenberg, September 16, 1913 (New York)–November 2, 1995 (Hackensack, NJ)

Frank Guida, May 26, 1922 (Palermo, Sicily)–May 19, 2007 (Virginia Beach, VA)

Jack Gutshall, April 6, 1902 (Missouri)–October 7, 1986 (Riverside County, CA)

Bill Hall, October 23, 1929 (Belton, TX)–April 28, 1983 (Jefferson County, TX)

Rick Hall, January 31, 1932 (Tishomingo, MS)–

Hunter Hancock, April 21, 1916 (Uvalde, TX)–August 4, 2004 (Claremont, CA)

Macy Henry, April 10, 1912 (unknown)–March 10, 1991 (Denton, TX)

Henry Hildebrand, November 26, 1901 (unknown)–May 1977 (Metairie, LA)

Jack Hooke [Jacob Horowitz], August 21, 1916 (Brooklyn, NY)–November 13, 1999 (Queens, NY)

Leroy Hurte, May 2, 1915 (Muskogee, OK)–

Joe Johnson, August 18, 1927 (Cookeville, TN)–

Phil Kahl [Kolsky], October 10, 1916 (Poland)–March 13, 2000 (Boca Raton, FL)

Dave Kapp, August 7, 1904 (Chicago, IL)–March 1, 1976 (New York)

Jack Kapp, June 15, 1901 (Chicago, IL)–March 25, 1949 (New York)

Bob Keane [Kuhn], January 5, 1922 (Manhattan Beach, CA)–

George Khoury, July 17, 1908 (Sulphur, LA)–January 9, 1998 (Lake Charles, LA)

William "Buddy" Killen, November 13, 1932 (Florence, AL)–November 1, 2006 (Nashville, TN)

Bob Koester, October 30, 1932 (Wichita, KS)–

Joe Kolsky, March 20, 1920 (Poland)–May 8, 1997 (Pompano Beach, FL)

Lou Krefetz, January 27, 1907 (probably Brooklyn, NY)–December 20, 1981 (Baltimore, MD)

Jeffrey Kruger, April 19, 1931 (London, England)–

Connie LaRocca [née Sculco], September 26, 1923 (San Francisco, CA)–

Jack Lauderdale, January 28, 1922 (San Antonio, TX)–October 19, 1991 (Los Angeles, CA)

Lee Lavergne, December 10, 1932 (Church Point, LA)–January 17, 1998 (Church Point, LA)

Don Law, February 24, 1902 (London, England)–December 20, 1982 (Galveston County, TX)

Ernie Leaner, August 15, 1921 (Jackson, MS)–April 17, 1990 (Kalamazoo, MI)

George Leaner, June 1, 1917 (Jackson, MS)–September 18, 1983 (Chicago, IL)

Jerry Leiber, April 25, 1933 (Baltimore, MD)–

Joe Leonard, June 20, 1919 (Gainesville, TX)–

Seymour "Cy" Leslie, December 16, 1922 (Brooklyn, NY)–January 26, 2008 (Roslyn, NY)

Moishe "Morris" Levy, August 27, 1927 (Bronx, NY)–May 21, 1990 (Ghent, NY)

(Sir) Edward Lewis, April 19, 1900 (Derby, England)–January 29, 1980 (London, England)

Stan Lewis, July 5, 1927 (Shreveport, LA)–

Goddard Lieberson, April 5, 1911 (Hanley, England)–May 29, 1977 (New York)

Albert Lion, April 21, 1908 (Berlin, Germany)–February 2, 1987 (San Diego, CA)

Harold B. Lipsius, October 12, 1913 (Philadelphia, PA)–March 17, 2007 (Philadelphia, PA)

Mel London, April 9, 1932 (Mississippi)–May 16, 1975 (Chicago, IL)

Bernie Lowe [Lowenthal], November 22, 1917 (Philadelphia, PA)–September 1, 1993 (Wyncote, PA)

Bill Lowery, October 21, 1924 (Leesville, LA)–June 8, 2004 (Atlanta, GA)

Herman Lubinsky, August 30, 1896 (Bradford, CT)–March 16, 1974 (Glen Ridge, NJ)

Lee Magid, April 6, 1926 (New York)–March 31, 2007 (Los Angeles, CA)

Tony Mammarella, September 2, 1924 (Philadelphia, PA)–November 29, 1977 (Philadelphia, PA?)

Kal Mann [Kalman Cohen], May 6, 1917 (Philadelphia, PA)–November 28, 2001 (Pompano Beach, FL)

Bob Marcucci, February 28, 1930 (Philadelphia, PA)–

Cosimo Matassa, April 13, 1926 (New Orleans, LA)–

David J. Mattis, October 1, 1914 (St. Louis, MO)–July 21, 2000 (Wheeling, WV)

Bill McCall, March 18, 1889 (Oklahoma)–June 22, 1969 (Santa Rosa, CA)

Lillian McMurry [née Shedd], December 30, 1921 (Purvis, MS)–March 18, 1999 (Jackson, MS)

Huey Meaux, March 10, 1929 (Kaplan, LA)–

Fred Mendelsohn, May 16, 1917 (New York)–April 28, 2000 (Palm Beach County, FL)

Eddie Mesner, 1914 (New York)–March 26, 1963 (Los Angeles, CA)

Leo Mesner, June 7, 1904 (Austria)–September 26, 1992 (Van Nuys, CA)

Dave Miller [Kleiber], June 30, 1903 (Somerset County, NJ)–June 1985 (Princeton, NJ)

Joseph Denton "J. D."/"Jay" Miller, May 5, 1922 (Iota, LA)–March 23, 1996 (Lafayette, LA)

Mitchell "Mitch" Miller, July 4, 1911 (Rochester, NY)–

Sam "S. J." Montalbano, February 8, 1937 (Baton Rouge, LA)–

Doug Moody, November 3, 1928 (Edmonton, Middlesex, England)–

Jerry Moss, May 8, 1935 (Bronx, NY)–

Henry "Juggy" Murray Jr., November 24, 1922 (Charleston, SC)–January 20, 2005 (New York)

Syd Nathan, April 27, 1904 (Cincinnati, OH)–March 5, 1968 (Miami Beach, FL)

Ken Nelson, January 19, 1911 (Caledonia, MN)–January 6, 2008 (Somis, CA)

Larry Newton, May 7, 1920? (unknown)–January 30, 2005 (Florida)

Eugene "Gene" Nobles, August 3, 1913 (Hot Springs, AR)–September 21, 1989 (Nashville, TN)

Elias "Eli" Oberstein, December 13, 1901 (New York)–June 12, 1960 (Westport, CT)

Clyde Otis, September 11, 1924 (Carson, MS)–January 8, 2008 (Englewood, NJ)

Johnny Otis [Veliotes], December 28, 1921 (Vallejo, CA)–

William "Bill" Paley, September 28, 1901 (Chicago, IL)–October 26, 1990 (New York)

Ralph Peer Jr., May 22, 1892 (Kansas City, MO)–January 19, 1960 (Los Angeles, CA)

Hugo Peretti, December 6, 1915 (New York)–May 1, 1986 (Englewood, NJ)

Norman Petty, May 25, 1927 (Clovis, NM)–August 15, 1984 (Lubbock, TX)

Sam Phillips, January 5, 1923 (Florence, AL)–July 30, 2003 (Memphis, TN)

Don Pierce [Picht], October 10, 1915 (Seattle, WA)–April 3, 2005 (Hendersonville, TN)

Jerome "Doc" Pomus [Felder], June 27, 1925 (Brooklyn, NY)–March 14, 1991 (New York)

Bill Quinn, January 8, 1904 (Amesbury, MA)–January 4, 1976 (Pasadena, TX)

Sol Rabinowitz, April 12, 1910 (unknown)–September 2, 1998 (New York)

Carol Rachou, December 27, 1932 (New Orleans, LA)–January 29, 2004 (Lafayette, LA)

Milton Rackmil, February 12, 1903 (New York)–April 2, 1992 (New York)

Samuel "Buck" Ram, November 21, 1907 (Chicago, IL)–January 1, 1991 (Las Vegas, NV)

Paul Reiner, December 6, 1905 (Hungary)–February 1, 1982 (Los Angeles, CA)

Bob Reissdorff, June 24, 1922 (Seattle, WA)–June 15, 2002 (Modesto, CA)

Leon Rene, February 6, 1902 (Covington, LA)–May 30, 1982 (Los Angeles, CA)

Otis Rene, October 2, 1898 (New Orleans, LA)–April 5, 1970 (Los Angeles, CA)

Rafael "Googie" Rene, March 30, 1927 (Los Angeles, CA)–November 25, 2007 (Los Angeles, CA)

John "John R." Richbourg, August 20, 1910 (Davis Station, SC)–February 15, 1986 (Nashville, TN)

Don Robey, November 1, 1903 (Houston, TX)–June 16, 1975 (Houston, TX)

Lawrence Dwain "Danny" Robinson, June 23, 1929 (Union, SC)–April 17, 1996 (Bronx, NY)

Morgan "Bobby" Robinson, April 16, 1917 (Union, SC)–

Leo Rogers [Levinson], January 16, 1901 (New York)–January 17, 1970 (Los Angeles, CA)

Fred Rose [Knols], August 24, 1894 (Evansville, IN)–December 1, 1954 (Nashville, TN)

Wesley Rose, February 11, 1918 (Chicago, IL)–April 26, 1990 (Nashville, TN)

Art Rupe [Goldborough], September 5, 1917 (Greensburg, PA)–

Milt Salstone, June 16, 1916 (Chicago, IL)–September 1980 (unknown)

David Sarnoff, February 27, 1891 (Minsk, Russia)–December 12, 1971 (New York)

Art Satherley, October 19, 1891 (Bristol, England)–February 10, 1986 (Fountain Valley, CA)

Bob Schwartz, June 29, 1924 (New York)–

Eugene "Gene" Schwartz, December 16, 1920 (New York)–May 4, 1999 (Newport Beach, CA)

Marshall Sehorn, June 25, 1934 (Concord, NC)–December 5, 2006 (New Orleans, LA)

Bobby Shad [Abraham Shadrinsky], February 12, 1919 (New York)–March 13, 1985 (Beverly Hills, CA)

Arthur Shimkin, October 8, 1922 (New York)–December 4, 2006 (New York)

Steve Sholes, February 12, 1911 (Washington, DC)–April 22, 1968 (Nashville, TN)

Eddie Shuler, March 26, 1913 (Wrightsboro, TX)–July 23, 2005 (Atlanta, GA)

Lester Sill, January 13, 1918 (Pennsylvania?)–October 31, 1994 (Los Angeles, CA)

Abraham "Al" Silver, January 9, 1914 (Providence, RI)–March 4, 1992 (Fort Lauderdale, FL)

Shelby Singleton, December 16, 1931 (Waskom, TX)–

Floyd Soileau, November 2, 1938 (Ville Platte, LA)–

Phil Spector, December 26, 1940 (Bronx, NY)–

Seymour Stein, April 18, 1942 (Brooklyn, NY)–

Jim Stewart, July 29, 1930 (Middleton, TN)–

Mike Stoller, March 13, 1933 (Belle Harbor, NY)–

Henry Stone, June 3, 1921 (Bronx, NY)–

Chris Strachwitz, July 1, 1931 (Lower Silesia, Germany)–

Allen Sussel, June 29, 1924 (Philadelphia, PA)–January 25, 2003 (West Palm Beach, FL)

Art Talmadge, July 1913 (Chicago, IL)–May 25, 2006 (Palm Beach, FL)

Nat Tarnopol, January 26, 1931 (Detroit, MI)–December 24, 1987 (Las Vegas, NV)

Bob Thiele, June 27, 1922 (Brooklyn, NY)–January 30, 1996 (New York)

Elias "Eli" Toscano, April 17, 1924 (Cameron County, TX)–September 21, 1967 (Nunda, IL)

Allen Toussaint, January 14, 1938 (New Orleans, LA)–

Mimi Trepel [Jordan], May 7, 1908 (Brooklyn, NY)–September 20, 2006 (Lake Worth, FL)

Johnny Vincent [Imbragulio], October 3, 1925 (Laurel, MS)–February 4, 2000 (Flowood, MS)

Glenn Wallichs, August 9, 1910 (Grand Island, NE)–December 23, 1971 (Hollywood, CA)

Simon "Si" Waronker, March 4, 1915 (Los Angeles, CA)–June 7, 2005 (Beverly Hills, CA)

Hyman "Hy" Weiss, February 12, 1923 (Romania)–March 20, 2007 (Englewood, NJ)

Samuel "Sam" Weiss, September 19, 1925 (Bronx, NY)–March 19, 2008 (Boca Raton, FL)

Gerald "Jerry" Wexler, January 10, 1917 (New York)–August 15, 2008 (Sarasota, FL)

Robert E. "Buster" Williams, c. 1909 (Enterprise, MS)–c. 1982 (Memphis, TN)

Shannon Williams, July 28, 1942 (Lancaster, TN)–October 22, 2003 (Nashville, TN)

Walter "Dootsie" Williams, June 17, 1911 (Birmingham, AL)–August 21, 1991 (Los Angeles, CA)

Paul Winley, July 10, 1934 (Washington, DC)–

Francis Wolff, January 4, 1907 (Berlin, Germany)–March 8, 1971 (New York)

Randy Wood, March 30, 1917 (McMinnville, TN)–

Ernie Young, December 2, 1892 (Giles County, TN)–June 8, 1977 (Nashville, TN)

Notes: This summary, as of August 2008, relates primarily to the individuals covered in the text and is not deemed to be a definitive listing. Some original last names have been added where known, but almost certainly there are more. While every attempt has been made to ensure that the correct information has been filed, there is always a possibility of inaccurate data being handed down. That said, any emendations will be warmly received. I am grateful, again, to Eric LeBlanc for his selfless research and constant support.

Appendix G

Oral History

The interviews for this book are listed below. All were conducted by me, sometimes with others, where noted. The conversations were mainly face to face but were occasionally by telephone. Unless stated otherwise, the interviews were taped, and the tapes are in my possession.

Berle Adams, Beverly Hills, CA, April 6, 14, 20, 2004; March 5, 2005; July 27, 2006 (all by telephone)

Dick Alen, Beverly Hills, CA, May 4, 2004 (telephone)

Bill "Hoss" Allen, Nashville, TN, May 18, 1992

Dave Appell, Cherry Hill, NJ, June 1, 2005

George Avakian, Riverdale, NY, February 11, 2005

Hank Ballard, Utrecht, Holland, November 28, 1992 (with Paul Harris)

Gene Barge, Chicago, IL, June 28, 1999 (with Tony Collins)

Richard Barrett, Gladwyne, PA, July 28, 2003 (faxed letter)

Harold Battiste, Los Angeles, CA, June 30, 1975; New Orleans, LA, November 11, 1997 (notes)

Howard Bedno, Chicago, IL, June 25, 1999 (with Tony Collins and Dave Williams); May 13, 2004 (telephone)

Jean Bennett, Las Vegas, NV, November 29, 2004; February 28, 2005 (telephone); sundry telephone conversations

Freddy Bienstock, New York, September 15, 2004; follow-up September 22, 2006

Johnny Bienstock, Southampton, NY, May 22, 2004

Miriam Bienstock, New York, June 28, 2004

Joe Bihari, Los Angeles, CA, March 2, 2000 (partially with Colin Escott); June 12, 2003 (telephone); October 28, 2004; many conversations, e-mails, and faxes

Billy Bland, Harlem, NY, May 10, 1989

Maxine Brown, Harlem, NY, July 16, 2004

Alan Bubis, Nashville, TN, October 25, 2004 (telephone)

Dave Burgess, Nashville, TN, June 9, 2005

Billy Butler, New York, May 13, 1989 (with Richard Tapp)

Marshall Chess, New York, June 3, 2004

Morty Craft, New York, August 24, 2004

Luigi Creatore, Boca Raton, FL, June 11, 2004

Roquel "Billy" Davis, New York, April 29, May 13, July 30, 1999; March 30, 2004

Julius Dixson, New York, November 6, 2000

Joe Dreyhaupt, East Setauket, NY, October 20, 2000 (with Shelley Galehouse)

Ahmet Ertegun, New York, November 3, 2004; October 4, 2006

Paul Evans, East Setauket, NY, May 8, 2004; follow-up e-mails and discussions

Donn Fileti, Hackensack, NJ, December 15, 2004; February 23, 2005

Frankie Ford, London, England, April 3, 1984

Fred Foster, Nashville, TN, October 26–27, 2004

Eve Friedman, East Setauket, NY, July 2, 1998 (with Shelley Galehouse)

Bert Frilot, Lake Charles, LA, May 3, 1992

Shelley Galehouse, East Setauket, NY, summer 2004; other conversations

Paul Gayten, Los Angeles, CA, June 15, 1975

Jimmy Gilbert, Miami, FL, June 8, 2004

Gene Goodman, Huntington, NY, July 23, 2004

Rosco Gordon, New York, May 19, 1986

John Greek, San Diego, CA, 1996–99 (various telephone conversions)

Ira Howard, Eastchester, NY, April 13, 2004 (telephone); July 20, 2006 (e-mail)

Roddy Jackson, Merced, CA, February 21, 2005 (telephone)

Joe Johnson, Gallatin, TN, September 29, 2006 (telephone)

Joe Jones, Los Angeles, CA, July 2, 1975

Adam Kaplan, New York, November 18, 2004 (notes)

Riley "B. B." King (with Colin Escott), Los Angeles, CA, February 29, 2000

Jeffrey Kruger, Hove, Sussex, England, July 5, August 4, September 8, 2004 (e-mails)

Harold "Mr. Blues" Ladell, Hackensack, NJ, July 2, 2003 (with Donn Fileti, George Lavatelli, and Bill Olb)

Cy Leslie, New York, July 7, 2005

Margaret Lewis, Shreveport, LA, January 2, 2005 (e-mail)

Stan Lewis, Shreveport, LA, January 10, 2005; July 20, September 27, 2006 (all by telephone)

Irv Lichtman, Oceanside, NY, March 31, 2004; follow-up e-mails

Harold and Frank Lipsius, Philadelphia, PA, September 16, 2003

Dorothea Lorenzo, Stuart, FL, December 2001 (typed memoir)

Milton Love, New York, January 8, 2004

Lee Magid, Malibu Beach, CA, July 13, 2004 (telephone); October 28, 2004

Bob Marcucci, Los Angeles, CA, November 18–19, 2004 (telephone)

Cosimo Matassa, New Orleans, LA, April 25, 1973; May 18, 2004 (telephone)

Ruth McFadden, New York, February 25, 1999 (with Richard Tapp)

J. D. "Jay" Miller, Crowley, LA, April 26, 1995

Mitch Miller, New York, February 21, 1998; c. February 28, 2004 (brief conversations only)

Art Mineo, New York, July 13, 2000

Sam "S. J." Montalbano, Baton Rouge, LA, April 29, 2005; New Orleans, LA, April 30, 2008 (notes, e-mails)

Doug Moody, Fort Lauderdale, FL, June 7–8, 2004; many telephone conversations from 1992, also e-mails

Billy Mure, Sebastian, FL, June 7, 2004

Henry "Juggy" Murray Jr., New York, May 19, 2004 (notes)

Marty Ostrow, New York, April 10, 2004; follow-up e-mails

Clyde Otis, Englewood, NJ, April 7, 2004

Johnny Otis, Hastings, Sussex, England, August 1, 1972 (with Mike Leadbitter)

Harvey Phillips, East Setauket, NY, May 10, 1998

Sam Phillips, Memphis, TN, June 29, 2000 (telephone)

Don Pierce, Madison, TN, May 12, 1992 (with Ray Topping); August 14, 2002 (letter); Hendersonville, TN, October 26, 2004 (notes)

Jerome "Doc" Pomus, New York, May 18, 1986; May 7, 1989

Rafael "Googie" Rene, Woodland Hills, CA, October 28, 2004 (with Tony Jones)

Sir Cliff Richard, New York, November 12, 2005

Bobby Robinson, Harlem, NY, May 15, 1986; July 2, 1999; July 2, 2003 (with Richard Tapp); various meetings between 2000 and 2005

Art Rupe, Santa Barbara, CA, March 9, April 19, 2004; follow-up e-mails

Bob Schwartz, New York, October 12, 2007 (telephone)

Marshall Sehorn, New Orleans, LA, April 16, 1973; March 21, 2003 (with Tad Jones)

Roscoe Shelton, Nashville, TN, May 24, 1993 (with Ray Topping and Richard Tapp)

Arthur Shimkin, New York, February 13, 20, 2004; several follow-up meetings through November 2005

Eddie Shuler, Lake Charles, LA, May 2–3, 1992; April 21, 1995; April 2, 2005 (telephone)

Shelby Singleton, Nashville, TN, May 16, 1992 (with Ray Topping); October 26, 2004

Billy Dawn Smith, Queens, NY, July 27, 2004 (notes only)

Floyd Soileau, Ville Platte, LA, February 2, 2005 (telephone); May 15, 2007 (e-mail)

Seymour Stein, New York, October 15, 2004; May 11, 2007 (e-mail)

Henry Stone, Coconut Grove, FL, May 7, 2004 (telephone); June 8, 2004

Chris Strachwitz, El Cerrito, CA, May 6, 1994

Paul Tarnopol, Coconut Grove, FL, July 21, 2006

Ray Topping, Harold Wood, Essex, England, February 13, 2005 (telephone)

Mimi Trepel, Lake Worth, FL, January 25, 2005

Tommy Vastola, New Hyde Park, NY, August 26, 2003 (notes only)

Morty Wax, New York, summer 1998

Hy Weiss, Miami, FL, June 8, 2004; January 26, 2005; many conversations between 1993 and 2005

Sam Weiss, New York, August 12, 2003 (letter)

Jerry Wexler, New York, May 21, 1986; East Hampton, NY, October 22, 2002; Sarasota FL, August 3, 2003, April 13, 2004; March 10, 2005 (telephone); January 17, 2008 (letter)

Jerry "Swamp Dogg" Williams, Porretta, Italy, July 25, 1998

Shannon Williams, Nashville, TN, June 9, 1995 (with Rob Santos); December 1998–January 1999 (e-mail correspondence)

Jim Wilson, Nashville, TN, May 14, 1992

Paul Winley, Harlem, NY, July 2005; January 19, 2007 (telephone)

John Wood (son of Randy), Los Angeles, CA, August 12, 2007 (telephone, after he had conversed with his father)

 Notes

Preface

1. Art Rupe, letter to author, January 8, 2004.

2. With the year 2006 as the base point, dollar inflation rates for the principal period covered in the text are as follows:

1940	14.41: 1
1945	11.21: 1
1950	8.37: 1
1955	7.53: 1
1960	6.81: 1
1965	6.40: 1
1970	5.20: 1
1980	2.45: 1
1990	1.54: 1

(source: Federal Reserve Bank of Minneapolis Web site)

Introduction

1. Jerry Wexler, letter to author, August 3, 2003.

2. Drucker, *Essential Drucker*, 20.

3. Among those many record makers who were not interviewed extensively in their time were Bess Berman (Apollo Records), Jerry Blaine (Jubilee-Josie, and Cosnat Distributing), Leonard Chess (Chess-Checker), Sam Clark (ABC-Paramount), George Goldner (End-Gone), Florence Greenberg (Scepter-Wand), Herman Lubinsky (Savoy), Bill McCall (4 Star), Syd Nathan (King-Federal), Don Robey (Duke-Peacock), and Ernie Young (Excello-Nashboro).

4. See appendix G for full details of interviews featured in the text.

5. The results of the pioneering research on the Coasters can be found in Bill Millar, *The Coasters* (London: Stars Books/W.H. Allen, 1975).

6. Broven, "Southern Record Men," 3–4. See also chapter 10. *Blues Unlimited* was edited by Mike Leadbitter and Simon Napier.

Chapter 1: We're Rolling—Take One!

1. Coincidentally, Stein contributed an article entitled "Independents 39, Majors 2" to the program of the first annual Rock and Roll Hall of Fame Foundation induction ceremony in 1986.

2. This stylistic analysis has been repeated several times in print by Jerry Wexler, but this is the variant as told to the author.

3. SESAC (Society of European Stage Authors and Composers) was a third but much smaller

performing society, which was started in 1931 to handle music licensing for unaffiliated foreign publishers.

4. *Billboard*, July 25, 1942, 92.

5. "This Man Petrillo," *Billboard*, August 8, 1942, 62 and 67 (from original undated article by Daniel T. Smyth, published in the *Chicago Sun*).

6. Interestingly, this scenario was a reversal of fortunes compared with the post–World War I era, when the major labels easily brushed aside competition from independent labels such as Gennett and Paramount in every musical genre. The majors, however, never totally ignored the "roots" markets in the immediate post–World War II era. For example, RCA Victor enjoyed steady sales with its blues releases in a house style known as the Bluebird Beat (named after its budget-price subsidiary label), spawning influential artists such as Big Maceo, Dr. Clayton, Arthur "Big Boy" Crudup, Jazz Gillum, Tampa Red, Washboard Sam, and the first Sonny Boy Williamson. Then Decca, with its Sepia series, had the biggest race artist of the 1940s in Louis Jordan (see chapter 2), along with Lionel Hampton and Buddy Johnson. Columbia had a "Negro Blues" series including releases by Big Bill Broonzy. The potent underlying power of the major labels was shown when they assumed quick control of the hillbilly/country market, in contrast to the rhythm and blues sector. It is not difficult to conclude that inert racism was one of the factors involved in the majors' distancing themselves from black music of all styles at the time.

7. These pop-rock labels included Cadence (Archie Bleyer), Cameo-Parkway (Bernie Lowe, Kal Mann, Dave Appell), Challenge (Gene Autry, Dave Burgess, Joe Johnson), Dot (Randy Wood), Liberty (Si Waronker, Al Bennett), Monument (Fred Foster), and Roulette (Morris Levy). In addition, there were the larger ABC-Paramount (Sam Clark, Larry Newton), Capitol (Buddy DeSylva, Johnny Mercer, Glenn Wallichs), and Mercury (Berle Adams, Irving Green, Art Talmadge).

8. Sanjek and Sanjek, *American Popular Music Business in the 20th Century*, 56; *Billboard*, October 7, 1950, 93–95.

9. The jukebox manufacturers—Wurlitzer, Seeburg, Rock-Ola, etc.—had their own distribution networks for "phonographs," that is, jukebox machines.

10. Poe, "Senate Report Lauds Coin Industry," 81. This story was based on a March 31, 1960, report by the Senate Select Committee on Improper Activities in the Labor or Management Field. See also chapter 7.

11. The jukebox operators founded MOA (Music Operators of America) in 1948, primarily to lobby against tax payments on jukeboxes and performance royalties on records, but also to promote the concept of the "gramophone record." An important part of MOA's mission was to present a cohesive front as a trade organization, including the improvement of the industry's stereotypical poor image.

12. *Billboard*, March 15, 1947, 30.

13. See chapter 25, the "End of Session" section, for reproduction of Art Rupe's staff manual.

Chapter 2: The Super Indies

1. Quoted in Grein, *Capitol Records Fiftieth Anniversary*, 14.

2. See chapter 5 for Avakian's story of Columbia's invention of the long-playing record.

3. *Billboard*, October 13, 1945, 24.

4. GAC's full name was changed from General Amusement Corporation to General Artists Corporation to avoid confusion with a registered coin-machine company, according to Berle Adams by telephone. Headed by Thomas Rockwell, GAC was based in New York with offices in Chicago, Cincinnati, and Hollywood. In 1943, the Chicago branch at 360 North Michigan Avenue was man-

aged by Art Weems, vice president, supported by Berle Adams and two others. *"The Billboard" 1943 Music Year Book*, 137 (accompanying *Billboard*, September 24, 1943).

5. The beer vat manufacturing company, Olsen and Tilgner, was owned by Irving Green and Ray Greenberg.

6. Irving Green, telephone interview by Colin Escott, January 1995.

7. Adams with Cohn, *Sucker for Talent*, 98.

8. Ibid., 117.

9. Ibid., 118–19.

10. The Heilicher brothers, who later owned the Soma label, were to make fortunes with the Musicland store chain and the Pickwick group.

11. *Billboard*, February 20, 1946, 18.

12. Ibid., January 3, 1948, 16.

13. Ibid., April 19, 1947, 23. Art Talmadge, a "marketing and advertising whiz," was another important Mercury personality. He was grounded in show business, having arrived at Mercury after a seven-year stint with Music Corporation of America (MCA). In the 1960s, he headed United Artists Records and then Musicor.

14. See also chapter 21.

15. Back in 1937, Jack Kapp launched a new merchandising concept: the packaging of 78–rpm records into colorful album portfolios. Kapp masterminded Decca's unparalleled servicing of the jukebox operators and supervised Decca's self-owned branch office distribution operation (which differed from the dealer franchise system favored by Columbia and RCA Victor). *Cash Box*, September 4, 1954, 18.

16. Decca's J. Mayo Williams, an African American, was involved with prewar companies Paramount, Brunswick, and Vocalion with artists as diverse as Blind Lemon Jefferson and Ma Rainey. He did not have outstanding success with his own postwar indie labels, Harlem and Ebony, but he is recognized as an early supporter of BMI (along with RCA Victor's Ralph Peer).

17. With the accent on rhythm and dance, the Soundies' featured artists included Count Basie, Cab Calloway, Nat Cole Trio, Jimmy Dorsey, Duke Ellington, Les Paul, Kay Starr, and Fats Waller among many, besides Louis Jordan. The slogan was "See a Soundie: A Wonderful Time for Only a Dime!"

18. Rock 'n' roll music was introduced globally when Bill Haley's "Rock Around the Clock" was featured in MGM's teen rebellion/juvenile delinquent film *The Blackboard Jungle* (1955). Apart from Louis Jordan, producer Milt Gabler was involved at Decca with pioneering "rhythm" artists Lionel Hampton and Buddy Johnson.

19. Adams with Cohn, *Sucker for Talent*, 129.

20. *Cash Box* profiled Jack J. Mitnick as "Man of the Week" in its coin machine section (September 20, 1958, 61). According to the feature, he entered the automatic music business in 1937 as a field man for George Ponser prior to war service: "In 1945 he was sales manager in the New York office for Runyon Sales Company. In 1947 he went up to Boston to open Beacon Coin Machine Company. Toward the end of 1947 he joined AMI, Inc. [the jukebox manufacturer] as eastern regional manager . . . until the end of '55. In April of 1956, he entered the newly created United Music Corporation of Chicago."

21. *Billboard*, October 15, 1949, 18.

22. At this point, in 1950, Berle Adams divested himself of his other active music interests, including the personal management of Louis Jordan.

23. As part of the Decca-Universal merger, MCA agreed to dissolve its talent agencies throughout the world to avoid antitrust problems. *Billboard Music Week*, August 4, 1962, 5.

24. According to his autobiography, Berle Adams negotiated MCA's acquisitions of Lou Levy's Leeds Music and Dave Kapp's Kapp Records and landed the musical *Jesus Christ Superstar* for Decca. After leaving MCA, Adams joined the William Morris Agency before taking an unlikely assignment as Berry Gordy's number two at Motown Records for nine short months in 1974 following the Detroit company's move to the West Coast. Adams with Cohn, *Sucker for Talent*, 292. As for Irving Green, after retiring from Mercury Records in 1969, he went into real estate development in a typically big way and continued in that sector until his death at age ninety in Palm Springs, California, in 2006.

Chapter 3: California Booming

1. The Johnny Otis interview extracts were first published in my article "A Rap with Johnny Otis," *Blues Unlimited* 100 (April 1973): 11–15.

2. Vocalist/pianist Charles Brown fronted Johnny Moore's Three Blazers on "Drifting Blues," which was on the race charts for twenty-three weeks from February 1946 on Philo. The label, founded the previous July, was named after the Mesner brothers' Philharmonic Music Shop in Los Angeles but was changed to Aladdin the following March after objections from Philco Radio.

3. In an Exclusive Records brochure from 1946 (see Rene, *Exclusive Records: Royalty of Records—Crest of Distinctive Music*), it was stated that "Leon Rene has headed Exclusive Records for 15 years," the implication being that Exclusive was formed in 1932. There is no evidence of any Exclusive releases at that time, but it is known that Leon Rene recorded Cleo Brown for Decca in 1935–36. It is possible that Exclusive was the name of the Rene brothers' independent production company. Also referenced is an interview with Leon Rene that appears in Shaw, *Honkers and Shouters*, 150–58.

4. The name and concept of Al Jarvis's *Make Believe Ballroom* show was borrowed and popularized by Martin Block of Radio WNEW, New York.

5. As noted by Steve Propes and Peter Grendysa in their research on West Coast labels (for a book provisionally titled *L.A. R&B Matrix: 1920 to 1949*), the piano-guitar-bass combo format of the Nat Cole Trio was picked up by Johnny Moore's Three Blazers (with Charles Brown), the Flennoy Trio, and the Maxim Trio with Ray Charles.

6. Tony Jones (Rene family relative), e-mail correspondence with author, March 15, 2007.

7. Rafael "Googie" Rene was assisted at the 2004 interview by nephew Tony Jones.

8. Although trumpeter Buddy Petit was unrecorded, he is acknowledged to have been a big influence on the evolution of New Orleans jazz.

9. See Joe Dreyhaupt section in chapter 20.

10. As Googie Rene implied, the record-pressing process involves several stages in which negative and positive images are made alternately from a lacquer-coated metal disc containing the recorded music. This grooved master disc is electroplated to form the ridged negative "master," then a positive "mother" (or "matrix") is created similarly to make the negative metal "stamper" (or "plate") for the press. (See Kernfeld, *New Grove Dictionary of Jazz*, 1019.) The process was further explained by Joe Bihari of Modern Records: "You sprayed silver nitrate onto the master; you put it in a bath with nickel and then nickel plate. Through electrolysis it would build onto the acetate master, probably $\frac{1}{32}$ of an inch thick, and you split that apart. That was your master. Now the plate that you put on the press was the opposite of a record, so when you pressed the two together, it made a record you could play. It was like a waffle iron."

11. See appendix B for list of Exclusive and Modern distributors in 1946, headed by Jack Gutshall as their national distributor.

12. R. Smith, *Great Black Way*, 186–87.

13. "Exclusive Stock Put Up for Sale," *Billboard*, December 31, 1949, 12.

14. "Exclusive Wax Rights to Fox," *Billboard*, April 15, 1950. According to the news story, "Harry Fox, local disk distrib. [with Consolidated Record Distributors in 1946], was granted the right to press and distribute nationally Exclusive Records under terms of a contract made by the defunct diskery's assignee. . . . Fox is currently contacting Exclusive's 38 distribs. explaining the set-up." There must have been problems with this arrangement because Exclusive never reemerged as a stand-alone entity.

15. Randy Wood nipped in to purchase Liggins's hits for release by Dot in early 1951. Wood also bought masters by Cecil Gant and Ivory Joe Hunter, but not the entire Exclusive catalog.

16. Sadly, the widely admired Saul Bihari was never interviewed. As such, his contributions to the Modern Records story have tended to be overshadowed by his more visible brothers.

17. The jukebox factories were converted into defense plants for the war effort as part of what was known as the "Arsenal of Democracy." Krivine, *Juke Box Saturday Night*, 75.

18. The last jukeboxes accepting nickels were manufactured in 1951. Krivine, *Juke Box Saturday Night*, 114.

19. Although Cecil Gant had a No. 1 race hit with "I Wonder," it stayed in the top spot for two weeks only. Emphasizing that Gilt-Edge was a novice indie label (and that the song was paramount at the time), bigger record companies rushed in with cover versions: Roosevelt Sykes had a lengthier No. 1 hit over seven weeks on RCA's Bluebird label, and there were smaller hits by Louis Armstrong (at No. 3, Decca) and Warren Evans, a Buddy Johnson vocalist (No. 6, National). "I Wonder" is published by Universal MCA Music Publishing, with a Raymond Leveen listed as co-composer with Cecil Gant.

20. See chapter 15 for Don Pierce's story.

21. *Billboard*, April 28, 1945, 65.

22. The *Billboard* article of January 19, 1946, was titled "Coinmen Retailing Platters: Trend to Disk Selling Grows: Record Makers Said Eager to Get Sales Push of Coin Business behind Waxings," 76. The "20 Year Club" reference was listed in *Cash Box*, July 3, 1954, part 2 (Coin Machines), 45.

23. These prominent distributors were also early record men: Jack Gutshall with Ammor, 1940; Paul Reiner with Black & White (after a false start in 1942 he began in earnest in 1944 out of New York before relocating to Hollywood); and Julius Bard with Rondo, 1948.

24. For a list of Modern Records distributors in 1946, see appendix B.

25. Leadbitter, *Nothing but the Blues*, 176. Mrs. Henry ran a short-lived R&B/hillbilly label, Macy's, in 1949–51. Steve Poncio became a prominent distributor at United, Houston.

26. *Who's Who in Music*. For Aladdin Recordings, see p. 719; Imperial Record Co., p. 757; Modern Music Records, p. 776.

27. *Billboard*, March 8, 1947, 31.

28. According to Joe Bihari, Modern Records' 78–rpm selling prices at first were 52½ cents to distributors, 79 cents to stores, and $1.05 to customers. In 1948, prices were reduced to 37½ cents to distributors, 56 cents to stores, and 79 cents to customers.

29. *Billboard*, January 17, 1948, 15.

30. Atlanta, Georgia, was an example of a major music conurbation that did not boast a significant independent record company in the immediate post–World War II era. Just think of the local talent that could have been netted: James Brown, Little Richard, Otis Redding, and Chuck Willis. What made the situation even more surprising was that Atlanta was a center well-patronized by record companies in the pre–World War II years. A similar scenario applied in Dallas, Texas. Yet both cities housed influential distributors: Jake Friedman at Southland in Atlanta (with Gwen Kessler) and Bill Emerson at Big State in Dallas (with Alta Hayes).

31. *Billboard*, October 14, 1950, 13. For another aspect of distributors/subsidiary labels, see "End of Session" section (chapter 25).

32. For record man Shelby Singleton's comments on the subsidiary label topic, see chapter 15.

33. Based on research by Billy Vera with Art Rupe, it seems that Rupe's last name of Goldberg (as collectively applied to many immigrants) was wrongly transcribed by U.S. authorities as Goldborough. The Rupe name was adapted phonetically from the real German family name, Ropp. Eric LeBlanc, e-mail correspondence with author, May 18, 2007.

34. *Billboard*, January 11, 1947, 27.

35. Escott with Merritt and MacEwen, *Hank Williams*, 51.

36. Story titled "Portem to Distrib Specialty & Aladdin," *Billboard*, December 3, 1949, 14.

37. Art Rupe explained that the Specialty pressing network comprised Alco Record Pressing (Al Levine and Les Cottrell) in Los Angeles, Plastic Products (Buster Williams) in Memphis, and two plants in Philadelphia, Ballen Record Co. (Ivin Ballen) "for a short while," followed by Sam Hodge's Paramount Record Manufacturing Co., "where we did the majority of our pressing for years." E-mail correspondence with author, December 7, 2006.

Chapter 4: New York: Big City and Little Tiffany

1. *Billboard*, June 5, 1948, 17. The Apollo Records directors were quoted as also including "Commander John J. Bergen, chairman of the board; Mack Kriendler, of '21' Brands; Jules Rubenstein, of the Teentimer dress firm; Jerry Beins, Nat Strom, Dick Taylor and Leo Landberg."

2. *Cash Box*, October 9, 1954, 21.

3. Ibid., June 5, 1954, 24.

4. See chapter 23.

5. Al Green's tenure as president of Painters Union No. 147 in Chicago was at the root of his alleged mob ties.

6. Bob Porter (music historian), e-mail correspondence with author, July 20, 2006.

7. Rolontz, "Tenth Avenue—Street of Hope," 13.

8. See Ertegun et al., *"What'd I Say"*; and Wexler and Ritz, *Rhythm and the Blues*.

9. The National name was used for the pressing plant as well as the record label.

10. In time, Jubilee Records, headed by Jerry Blaine, would establish itself as a prominent New York independent label, along with subsidiary Josie (formed in 1954). Cosnat Distributing Corp., however, was the focal point of the group. See chapters 12 and 24, in particular.

11. *Billboard*, January 17, 1948, 19.

12. See appendix B for a list of Atlantic distributors in 1954.

13. Granville "Stick(s)" McGhee's first recording of the song, titled "Drinking Wine, Spo-Dee-O-Dee, Drinking Wine," was made in 1947 for J. Mayo Williams's Harlem Records. When the Atlantic recording started to break out, Williams sold the original master to his friends at Decca, but Atlantic's superior version managed to fend off this major label opposition.

14. At the same time, Herb Abramson told *Billboard* that Stick McGhee's "Drinkin' Wine, Spo-Dee-O-Dee" had touched the 200,000 mark and that "the diskery anticipated a total sale of 950,000 this year." *Billboard*, December 3, 1949, 18.

15. In hindsight, the sale of Progressive Music was not the smartest of the many decisions made by the Atlantic directors. The price was reported to be "in excess of $500,000" (*Billboard Music Week*, October 27, 1962, 8). An earlier news story indicated that Progressive "is understood to have a guarantee from BMI of over $90,000 per year" (September 29, 1962, 6).

16. *Billboard*, March 13, 1954, 47.

17. Article by Jerry Wexler and Ahmet Ertegun, *Cash Box*, July 3, 1954, 56.

18. Horowitz, "Donut Platters," 30, 90, 94.

19. Among the many Atlantic jazz signings were Nat Adderley, Ornette Coleman, John Coltrane, Hank Crawford, Stephane Grappelli, Herbie Mann, Charles Mingus, and Sonny Stitt, along with Ray Charles in an experimental groove.

20. See also chapter 21 for more on the Atlantic partners' relationship with Sir Edward Lewis.

21. *Cash Box*, February 7, 1959, 28.

22. The Rhythm & Blues Foundation described its origins and mission statement on its Web site in 2006 as follows: "The Rhythm & Blues Foundation had its beginnings in 1987 during discussions about royalty issues between entertainer Ruth Brown, prominent entertainment attorney Howell Begle, and the head of Atlantic Records, Ahmet Ertegun. Recognizing the needs of the artists who brought the rhythm and blues art form into prominence, Mr. Ertegun provided a $1.5 million donation and the Foundation was born. The Rhythm & Blues Foundation was established in 1988 to promote recognition, financial support, educational outreach and historic and cultural preservation of rhythm and blues music through various grants and programs in support of R&B and Motown artists from the 1940s through the 1970s."

23. *Billboard*, September 26, 1964, 1.

24. Jerry Wexler echoed the importance of positive company cash flow when he said that "Jerry Blaine with his labels [Jubilee and Josie] factored all his receivables; the money had to come from somewhere. Our money always came from next month's receipts. We kept selling the records." Blaine's Cosnat, of course, was Atlantic's main distributor.

Chapter 5: The Battle of the Speeds and Golden Records' Seeds

1. "Avakian Leaves Columbia, Gets Piece of World Pacific," *Billboard*, March 17, 1958, 3. Later that year, George Avakian was involved in the agonizing start-up of Warner Bros. Records with Jim Conkling and Hal Cook and helped to establish the label through the No. 1 best-selling LP *The Button-Down Mind of Bob Newhart*. Almost immediately, Avakian joined RCA Victor in 1960 as the pop albums manager. In 2006, Avakian received the Django d'Or Award, Europe's most prestigious jazz honor.

2. At the time, Brunswick was owned by Warner Bros. Pictures, which wanted to get out of the record business and off-loaded the labels to ARC. See chapter 21.

3. In 1938, ARC-BRC was bought by Columbia Broadcasting System to become Columbia Record Corporation. In 1940, Columbia revived the OKeh label in place of Vocalion until 1945; OKeh was resurrected again in 1951.

4. Hal Cook's career included spells with Chicago indie Vitacoustic, which had a No. 1 hit in 1947 with "Peg o' My Heart" by the Harmonicats, and at Capitol, where he was distribution vice president. After joining Columbia as vice president in charge of sales in 1955, he helped launch Warner Bros. Records in 1958 with Jim Conkling and George Avakian. In 1962, Cook became the *Billboard Music Week* publisher. *Billboard Music Week*, June 30, 1962, 4.

5. This amusing tale of retribution was refuted by music historian Charles L. Granata, who insisted that "RCA's decision to use a speed of 45 rpm was based on calculations by Bell Laboratory scientist J. P. Maxfield." Drate, *45 RPM*, 8.

6. "The World's Greatest Artists Are on RCA Victor 45 rpm Records" catalog, 1950, in author's collection.

7. George Avakian, conversation with author, August 6, 2006. Also, *Billboard*, February 25, 1956, 17.

8. See chapters 21–23.

9. Bob Fine constructed the Fine Sound studio out of the main ballroom of the Great Northern Hotel at 118 West Fifty-seventh Street, New York.

10. Arthur Shimkin's description of the inaugural RIAA meetings, based on his memory of the occasions, was remarkably good. The temporary board charged with setting up the organization consisted of Milton Rackmil (Decca), a driving force; Frank Walker (MGM); Jim Conkling (Columbia); Paul Barkmeier (RCA Victor); and Glenn Wallichs (Capitol). *Billboard*, January 26, 1952, 15.

11. "Editorial: Hats Off to RIAA Fine Start for Org," *Billboard*, March 1, 1952, 16.

12. A Golden Records advertisement in *Billboard Music Week* (October 13, 1962, 35) claimed total cumulative sales "of 150,000,000."

13. Shimkin explained the ramifications of the excise tax reduction scheme, which was employed by other record company groups at the time: "There was a federal regulation after World War II called excise tax. All record companies had to pay it; that tax was 10 percent of the first 'arms-length' transaction. That transaction had to be accomplished by the proprietor of the label; that was the party that would be responsible for paying the excise tax. Now the accountants got the brilliant idea that if they established A. A. purely, totally, for the purpose of having an intermediary entity which would buy the records from [Al Massler's] Bestway Products and then sell them to Simon and Schuster's distributing company [Pocket Books], it would halve the [taxable] cost of the fourteen cents [wholesale price] to seven cents [pressing price]. That saved .07 cents in excise tax on each of thirty or forty million records a year." The excise tax was lifted finally as of July 1, 1965, giving a massive boost to the record industry overall.

14. The *Your Hit Parade* weekly survey, so the listeners were told, was based on the best-sellers in the media of the time: sheet music, phonograph records, songs most heard on air, and most-played discs on jukeboxes.

15. Among the early Bell artists were redoubtable band leaders Tommy and Jimmy Dorsey, Enoch Light, and Artie Shaw. Later came the "adorable" Betty Johnson; the teenage Edna McGriff and saxophonist Buddy Lucas, already with a 1952 R&B hit to their credit ("Heavenly Father" [Jubilee]); stocky Barry Frank on a recommendation from Jerry Wexler (with a note to Shimkin saying, "You can't judge a book by its cover"), and a very young Simon & Garfunkel as Tom & Jerry. Bell hired top-line New York session talent and seasoned A&R men such as Sy Oliver and Morty Palitz.

16. In 2006, just before he passed away, Arthur Shimkin was trying to negotiate CD licensing deals for his Golden masters.

17. Cy Leslie's competitors in the budget LP rack market included Eli Oberstein (who sold out to Pickwick in 1960), Dave Miller (who concentrated cleverly on the 101 Strings for Somerset Records), Phil Landwehr (Premier Albums), and the Bihari brothers (with Crown and its successors; see chapter 16). In 1963, the Pickwick annual turnover was reported to be in excess of $5 million.

18. *Billboard*, October 27, 1951, 15.

19. Ibid., October 20, 1951, 12.

20. Jim Bessman, "Aberbach Recalls Presley Dealings with Fondness," *Billboard*, October 5, 2002, 52. In an e-mail to me dated March 17, 2007, Colin Escott stated that "Miller told me that he wanted to record more rock 'n' roll, but the higher-ups wouldn't okay payola, and he knew he couldn't get the records played without payola."

Chapter 6: Riding the Nashville Airwaves

1. Prominent rock 'n' roll–era disc jockeys also included Al "The Ole Swingmaster" Benson (Chicago), Buddy Deane (Baltimore), Hunter Hancock (Los Angeles), Harold "Mr. Blues" Ladell (Newark),

George "Hound Dog" Lorenz (Buffalo), Ed "Jack the Bellboy" McKenzie (Detroit), Dewey "Daddy-O" Phillips (Memphis), Bill Randle (Cleveland), Zenas "Daddy" Sears (Atlanta), Vern "Doctor Daddy-O" Winslow (New Orleans), and Georgie Woods (Philadelphia).

2. See chapter 5 for a discussion on the television rivalry between NBC and CBS.

3. See appendix B for a list of Atlantic distributors in 1954.

4. As with other disc jockeys, John R.'s business activities came under the microscope of the federal authorities during the payola scandal of 1959–60.

5. Advertisement, *Billboard*, July 30, 1949, 99.

6. Dot Records was formally incorporated on April 12, 1950, with stock capital of $10,000. Hawkins, *Shot in the Dark*, 168–69.

7. Rob Finnis, telephone conversation with the author, September 15, 2006. In Randy Wood's twilight years, he did not give interviews but did answer on August 12, 2007, through his son John, my questions on the early days.

8. *Billboard Music Week* quoted Dot Records' sale price as "a reported $2,800,000" (July 28, 1962, 6). Randy Wood's son John told me the sum was "$3 million." On this basis, Gene Nobles would have received about $300,000 from the buyout for his 10 percent stake, as would Al Bennett and Gilbert Brown. After the 1957 sale to Paramount Pictures, Wood cleverly negotiated a management contract and continued to helm Dot for another ten years before forming Ranwood Records with Lawrence Welk.

9. See also chapter 12 for the saga surrounding "So Fine."

10. See also Hawkins, *Shot in the Dark*, 180–81.

11. Ernie Young was notorious for reusing his master tapes to save tape (and a few dollars); he would also use these tapes for home recording. This explains why so many of the early Nashboro-Excello master treasures are missing from the archives, as I witnessed in Nashville, 1992–95.

12. Everybody in the record supply chain had the same "misnaming" identification problems, especially the retailers.

13. Broven, "I Knew Leonard at the Macomba," 10.

14. Jordan Stokes III was the music lawyer of choice in Nashville for many years. See Hawkins, *Shot in the Dark*.

15. *Cash Box*, December 17, 1960, 37. See also chapter 7 for Marshall Chess's observations on Hoss Allen's employment by Leonard Chess.

16. The Gladys Knight original of "Every Beat of My Heart" was recorded for the tiny Atlanta label Huntom and became a No. 6 pop hit (in the name of the Pips only, summer 1961) when picked up by Chess's Chicago rival, Vee-Jay. Bobby Robinson of New York rerecorded the song by Knight for Fury and had a No. 45 hit at the same time (see chapter 18). Interestingly, *Billboard Music Week* indicated that Hoss Allen, "indie promotion man," was actually working out of Atlanta during this period (May 19, 1962, 1).

17. The name was changed from Showcase to Sound Stage 7 because of a prior registration (*Billboard*, May 11, 1963, 10). John Richbourg's first introduction to label management was with Rich Records in 1960.

18. Richbourg reissued many of the Sound Stage 7 masters on his Seventy 7 and Sound Plus labels before becoming a cancer victim. He died in 1986.

Chapter 7: The Chess Game

1. See also Gene Goodman section in chapter 14.

2. See, for example, Cohodas, *Spinning Blues into Gold*, and others.

3. The hit album's full title is *But Not for Me: Ahmad Jamal at the Pershing.* See appendix B for list of Chess-Checker distributors in 1960.

4. An advertisement appeared in *Cash Box,* July 30, 1960, 126, for Chess's Ter-Mar Recording Studios at 2120 South Michigan showing Ron Malo as chief engineer. With a heading "You Never Heard It So Good!", the ad was touting these facilities: four-channel Sel-Sync multiple recording equipment; complete recording services, monaural and stereophonic; new Steinway piano and Hammond organ; and editing/mixing/mastering services.

5. Originally released as "Rocket '88'," the song no longer has internal quotes. See chapter 9 for more on Sam Phillips, Buster Williams, and Stan Lewis.

6. Lee Andrews's "Long Lonely Nights" made No. 45 (Chess, fall 1957), marginally higher than Clyde McPhatter's contemporaneous cover (No. 49, Atlantic).

7. Cohodas, *Spinning Blues into Gold,* 295.

8. "I Can't Quit You Baby," written by Willie Dixon, published by Hoochie Coochie Music.

9. See also chapter 1.

10. "Praise and Scold Coin Industry in McClellan Rackets Report," *Billboard,* April 4, 1960, 81.

11. Stories by Bernie Asbell and Bob Dietmeier under the headline "Lid Off Chi Disk Bootleg Operation; Juke Ops Muscled," *Billboard,* February 17, 1958, 1.

12. Broven, "I Knew Leonard at the Macomba," 10. Paul Gayten, a hit race artist in the 1940s with De Luxe, became a latter-day record man with Pzazz Records in Hollywood from 1968 to 1970. Even with his vast network of contacts, he was unable to overcome the independents' dire distribution and promotion problems of the day. One of the Pzazz artists was Louis Jordan, in the twilight of his career.

13. Mel London formed Chief Records in spring 1957 followed by the Profile subsidiary and was active in the 1960s with the Age and USA labels.

14. See chapter 14 for more on Arc Music and Willie Dixon.

15. Copy of coroner's certificate dated September 28, 1967, obtained by Ace Atkins, who kindly forwarded it to me via Eric LeBlanc.

16. Spizer, *Beatles Records on Vee-Jay,* 4.

17. Pruter, *Chicago Soul,* 253.

Chapter 8: King of Them All

1. "Syd Nathan and Eli Oberstein Address a Sales Meeting, September 22, 1951," released on *The King R&B Box Set.*

2. *Cash Box,* June 2, 1951, 16.

3. Undated letter, part of a series of hilarious mudslinging missives between Syd Nathan and Herman Lubinsky, from June 24 through July 22, 1960, copies in author's possession. This correspondence was initiated by Nathan in an attempt to coerce his fellow record men to pressurize *Cash Box* to reinstate its recently abandoned R&B chart (see chapter 24). Naturally, the curmudgeonly Lubinsky wouldn't play ball, but Nathan was successful in his mission.

4. Other Detroit disc jockeys remembered by Colonel Jim Wilson were Tom Clay, Don McLeod, Casey Kasem, and Clark Reid (all at WJBK) and three black jocks from Radio WJLB: "Senator" Bristoe Bryant, "Frantic" Ernie Durham, and "Rockin'" LeRoy White.

5. In the late 1940s, Bernie Besman had supplied Modern with John Lee Hooker's "Boogie Chillen" hit and King with Todd Rhodes's "Blues for the Red Boy." In 1951, Alan Freed adopted the Rhodes tune as his theme song, referring to it as "Blues for the Moondog."

6. The King branch office was then based at 3725 Woodward Avenue, Detroit, while Pan American Record Distributors was in the same block at 3731 Woodward.

7. See chapter 17 for more on Joe Battle and the Detroit scene.

8. "Hearts of Stone," a breakthrough pop-crossover song, was covered by Red Foley (Decca), the Goofers (Coral), and Vicki Young (Capitol). The fortunate publisher in this instance was Gene and Harry Goodman's Regent Music. See also chapter 14.

9. *Billboard Music Week*, October 6, 1962, 8.

10. Donn Fileti, booklet notes to *The Golden Era of Doowops: The Groups of Beltone Records*, Relic CD 7066.

11. According to the lead story in *Billboard* (December 26, 1964), Mercury Records and rack jobber Handleman Drug Company were preparing bids for a reported $1,250,000 for "King Records, Lois Music, plus the King plant." The Aberbach brothers were among the other interested parties (hence Freddy Bienstock's awareness of the valuable song publishing catalog). A deal with Handleman was aborted at the eleventh hour after contracts had been drawn up.

12. "Nathan-Braun Deluxe [*sic*] Fuss Erupts in Court Litigation," *Billboard*, December 31, 1949, 30.

13. "The All American Boy," written by Bobby Bare, published by Dream City Music.

14. At the time, in the 1950s, the statutory royalty rate for mechanical license fees was two cents per composition, split traditionally fifty-fifty between publisher and songwriter. In Julius Dixson's example of "a penny a record," the songwriter would receive only half a cent per song title of each record sold instead of one cent.

15. Don Pierce, interview by Colin Escott, January 3, 1993, Madison, Tennessee.

16. See chapter 15 for more details on the Syd Nathan–Don Pierce business relationship.

17. *Billboard*, October 26, November 2, and November 23, 1968, all page 3.

18. The sale price of $3.5 million was quoted by Hal Neely. Kennedy and McNutt, *Little Labels— Big Sound*, 70.

19. Aside from King-Starday, Moe Lytle's company (with business affairs handled by Englishman Stephen Hawkins) acquired the important Scepter-Wand, Musicor, and Hollywood masters, among others.

Chapter 9: Behind the Southern Sun

1. See Escott with Hawkins, *Good Rockin' Tonight*.

2. B. B. King's first recordings were for Jim Bulleit's Bullet Records in 1949.

3. All told, Sam Phillips cut four sessions with B. B. King for the Bihari brothers from about July 1950 to June 1951.

4. A fresh set of recording standards was determined by the National Association of Broadcasters in 1949, before the RIAA devised the RIAA equalization curve as an industry standard for the recording and playback of vinyl records in 1954.

5. Seeburg started to break Wurlitzer's industry dominance after introducing the first one-hundred-selection jukebox in 1948.

6. Bernie Asbell, "Sam Phillips Notes: R&R Fading but Imprint Permanent," *Billboard*, May 18, 1959, 4, 21.

7. *Billboard*, July 19, 1952, 21.

8. Early in his career, Gordon's first name was spelled as "Roscoe," but he preferred his chosen birth name, Rosco.

9. Sonny Boy Williamson #2 was Aleck "Rice" Miller. The original "Sonny Boy," Bluebird–RCA Victor artist John Lee Williamson, was murdered in 1948.

10. Ryan, *Trumpet Records*, 69–70.

11. Pat Escott (Lillian McMurry relative), telephone conversation with author, September 15, 2006. Mrs. McMurray quote from "Behind the Sun: Jackson!" by Mike Leadbitter and John Broven, *Blues Unlimited* 78 (December 1970): 4.

12. As a record man and producer, Ike Turner learned his skills well from Joe Bihari. Ike was to find unwanted fame in his subsequent marital discord with Tina Turner that had the unfortunate effect of overshadowing his considerable musical accomplishments.

13. Chief Justice Earl Warren headed the Warren Commission investigations into the death of President John Kennedy.

14. Gart and Ames, *Duke/Peacock Records*, 28.

15. Bill Fitzgerald became general manager of Sun Records in August 1959, staying on until the label faded beneath the horizon in 1967.

16. Gart and Ames, *Duke/Peacock Records*, 35. This book is a well-researched label story. Peacock Records had been launched in December 1949 by Don Robey, who was described by *Billboard* as "Houston talent booker and promoter." "Peacock Disks into Blues, Rhythm Field," *Billboard*, December 24, 1949, 40.

17. Bill Cantrell and Quinton Claunch went on to form Hi Records in 1957 with Ray Harris and Joe Cuoghi, a jukebox operator and partner in the Poplar Tunes record shop. Claunch, with Doc Russell, launched Goldwax as a southern soul label in 1963 and hit with James Carr.

18. Rumors have rumbled on down the years that Elvis Presley was rejected by Lester Bihari for a Meteor deal. According to Joe Bihari, this was not the case. See also booklet notes by Martin Hawkins accompanying *The Complete Meteor Rockabilly and Hillbilly Recordings*.

19. Advertisement for the Williams Distributing Co., *Cash Box*, July 3, 1954.

20. *Who's Who in Music*, 779.

21. *Fortune*, November 1956, 272. Later, Buster Williams transferred the Plastic Products pressing operation to Coldwater, Mississippi, some thirty miles due south of Memphis.

22. "Stick-Horse" Hammond had country blues releases on JOB and Gotham in 1950, the same year that Chess Records was founded. It is likely, but not certain, that the Leonard Chess incident came soon afterward.

23. "Susie-Q" was the first Creedence Clearwater Revival hit for Fantasy Records in 1968. With the LP version being eight minutes, thirty-four seconds in duration, it was a tremendous publishing earner. Along with Dale Hawkins and Stan Lewis, the other co-writer was shown as Eleanor Broadwater, reputedly the wife of Radio WLAC disc jockey Gene Nobles.

24. After the demise of Jewel Records, the southern torch was carried into the CD era by Malaco of Jackson, Mississippi. Very competently run by Tommy Couch, Stewart Madison, and Wolf Stephenson, the label boasted a roster of popular chitlin' circuit soul-blues acts such as Bobby Bland, Z. Z. Hill, Denise La Salle, Little Milton, Bobby Rush, and Johnnie Taylor.

Chapter 10: Louisiana Gumbo

1. Dave Sax, e-mail correspondence with author, December 15, 2006. "It Wasn't God Who Made Honky Tonk Angels," written by J. D. Miller, published by Peermusic (originally Peer-International). On Hank Thompson's "The Wild Side of Life," Capitol assigned song credits to W. Warren–A. A. Carter under the name of Commodore Music, Imperial Records' publishing company (EMI Unart Catalog in 2007).

2. Sam Phillips was another master of the so-called slapback sound, with its delayed echo achieved by using tape loops as described by Miller.

3. Aside from the indefensible racist material, the Rebel releases featured the overlooked 1960s southern political commentary of Jay Miller's original artist Happy Fats (Leroy LeBlanc) with titles such as "The Story of the Po' Folks and the New Dealers" and "Dear Mr. Secretary (Going in the No Hog Raising Business)."

4. Eddie Shuler re-pressed "Broken Love" (originally Goldband 1010) with the full finale on Goldband 1011.

5. By 1955, Eddie Shuler was selling "between 45 and 100" television sets a day, had a fleet of trucks, and was grossing $200,000 annually with Quick Service TV, according to the Southern Folklife Collection Web site (2006). The Goldband tapes and paperwork are held as a collection at the University of North Carolina.

6. For Rod Bernard's detailed story of "This Should Go On Forever," see my *South to Louisiana*, 195–206.

7. According to *Cash Box* (September 20, 1958, 56), All South Distributing Corporation was started by Henry Hildebrand and New Orleans disc jockey Ken "Jack the Cat" Elliott, covering "Louisiana, lower Mississippi, and the coastal region of Alabama and Florida." In late 1963, Hildebrand formed the Watch label (with one-stop owner Joe Assunto), featuring a quality roster with Professor Longhair, Earl King, Johnny Adams, and Benny Spellman under the baton of Wardell Quezergue. Although Hildebrand had all the distributor contacts necessary, he was unable to overcome the post-payola problem of getting satisfactory promotion for national airplay.

8. See chapter 15 for Floyd Soileau's account of getting his first records pressed through Starday.

9. *Billboard*, June 22, 1959, 53.

10. Joe Delaney, "New Orleans Beginning to Challenge Chicago, Nashville as Waxing Center," *Down Beat*, January 28, 1953, 16. See "End of Session" section (chapter 25) for further contemporary insights into the operations of Cosimo Matassa's studio.

11. Matassa's unfortunate failure with the Dover one-stop recording facility in the 1960s is related in my book *Walking to New Orleans*, 197–201. There was a happy ending. In 2007, Matassa received a Grammy award in the Trustees category for "outstanding contributions to the industry in a non-performing capacity."

Chapter 11: *Billboard* and *Cash Box:* Stars and Bullets

1. Through the years, the trade magazine's title has metamorphosed from *Billboard Advertising*, *The Billboard*, and *Billboard Music Week* to the current *Billboard*. In text, *The Billboard* has been abbreviated to *Billboard*; similarly, *The Cash Box* is denoted as *Cash Box*.

2. This is a good story on paper, but with Jerry Wexler's deep musical knowledge, it seems implausible that he did not know that Nat "King" Cole recorded for Capitol.

3. According to *Billboard Music Week*, "[Bob] Rolontz joined *The Billboard* in 1951 as a reporter and served until 1955, when he became a.& r. director of RCA's Groove label. He returned to this publication in 1958 and . . . became Associate Music Editor" (May 12, 1962, 5). Rolontz was appointed the magazine's music news editor in May 1962.

4. Tom Noonan is generally credited with introducing *Billboard*'s Top 100 chart on November 12, 1955.

5. William "PoPsie" Randolph was a freelance photographer who had a studio at 1625 Broadway, New York, right by Colony Records and the Brill Building. He was Benny Goodman's bandboy (after Gene Goodman; see chapter 14) and then his manager, according to son Mike Randolph. Working

all hours, the chain-smoking PoPsie became the paparazzo for the New York music community and died a millionaire at age fifty-seven in 1978. See appendix H.

6. Bill Gersh had been mailing out weekly *Cash Box Price Lists* "for about four years prior to the creation of *The Cash Box* itself" to "hundreds of jobbers and distributors from coast to coast." *Cash Box*, September 20, 1958, 77.

7. When *Cash Box* was launched in 1942, *Billboard* was already carrying an "Amusement Machines (Music)" column. By June 9, 1945, under the zippier banner head of "Music Machines," the "Folk Record Reviews (Hillbilly, Race, Cowboy Songs, Spirituals)" section was clearly aimed at the jukebox operators, however token it might have seemed (p. 66).

8. The *Cash Box* contents for the January 1, 1949, issue were: "Big Point of Ops' CMI Meet Will Be Demand to Halt Direct Sales to Locations," p. 4; "Record Reviews," pp. 6, 8; "Nation's Top Ten Juke Box Tunes," p. 7; "'Round the Wax Circle," p. 11; "Regional Record Report," p. 12; "Race Record Reviews," p. 13; "Folk and Western Record Reviews," p. 14; "Hot In—Harlem, Chicago, New Orleans and Los Angeles," p. 15; "Big 5 Folk and Western Tunes," p. 16; "Disc Jockey Record Reports," p. 17; "Tunis Disk Hits Box Score," p. 18; "Coin Machine Section," p. 19; "Classified Advertising," pp. 26, 27; "CMI Blue Book," pp. 28, 29, 30; and also the "Eastern Flashes, Chicago Chatter, Los Angeles Clippings" columns.

9. See also chapter 24.

10. *Cash Box*, August 14, 1954, 22.

11. Herb Shucher founded Minaret Records in the early 1960s before joining Shelby Singleton's SSS organization, which took over the label in 1967.

12. *Billboard* chart philosophy (as an alternative viewpoint to that of *Cash Box* editors) was explained in a "Music Pop Charts" series on March 20, 1954: "Record dealers, jukebox operators, disk jockeys and program directors are faced with two basic problems when it comes to buying and/or programming records from week to week. The first is the problem of trying to estimate the commercial value of the brand new releases before the records have been exposed to the public. In many of the weeks there are well over 100 new releases. The second is the problem of trying to keep closely in touch with consumer reaction after the public has had a chance to hear and buy the records. . . . To do it, a conscientious attempt is made to follow the life of every record from its release date thru its varying stages of public exposure" (25).

13. *Cash Box*, July 12, 1958, 10.

14. *Billboard Music Week*, May 29, 1961, 28.

Chapter 12: A-Hustle and A-Scuffle at Old Town

1. See chapter 20.

2. Shelley Galehouse, conversation with the author, September 4, 2006.

3. This imagined story has been repeated several times in print by Jerry Wexler, but this is the variant as told to me.

4. Sam Weiss, letter to author, August 12, 2003.

5. From a Hy Weiss taped interview conducted by Bob Rolontz and Jim Delehant for Atlantic Records in 1970, courtesy of Jerry Wexler. This chapter includes several stories extracted from the interview that were well-worn party pieces in Weiss's later years but at the time were still fresh in his memory. The meeting was well chaired by Rolontz, with Weiss being irresistibly at the top of his verbal game.

6. Visible partners of Runyon Sales Co. in the 1940s were Jack Mitnick and Bernard "Shugy" Sugarman.

7. A well-known Mafia front in the local jukebox business was the Automatic Amusement Machine Operators of New York (Bianco, *Ghosts of 42nd Street*, 160). As an example of mob power in this sector, the Wurlitzer jukebox license for New York was held at one time by a company controlled by feared gangsters Frank Costello and Meyer Lansky. The street word was "Play another record; their daughters need new Cadillacs." Tosches, "Hipsters and Hoodlums," 206.

8. "Eyesight to the Blind" continued to earn royalties for Lillian McMurry, first through Sonny Boy Williamson's rerecord on Checker but more significantly from the inclusion of the song in The Who's 1968 rock opera *Tommy* and the subsequent 1975 movie starring Jack Nicholson, Elton John, Tina Turner, and Eric Clapton. Ryan, *Trumpet Records*, 162.

9. Jerry Blaine's Jubilee label was reported to be for sale at various times in the 1950s, indicating the inherent conflict of interest risks in running record and distributing companies in tandem.

10. The poignant lyrics of "Life Is But a Dream" were narrated by Hy Weiss's caregiver, Norma, at his funeral on March 22, 2007.

11. Richard Barrett, letter to author, July 28, 2003. First published in booklet to *Hy Weiss Presents Old Town Records*.

12. Although this large publishing advance of $5,000 cannot be verified, it is known that Hy Weiss did make a "house" loan (i.e., mortgage) in this sum to Alan Freed in this period.

13. *Cash Box*, July 3, 1954, 104.

14. According to Harold Ladell, Essex distributors opened a branch office in Springfield, New Jersey, to supply records for Runyon Sales' jukebox chain in the late 1950s period.

15. *Cash Box*, March 6, 1954, 23.

16. Bill Olb (friend of Harold Ladell's), telephone conversation with the author, September 12, 2006.

17. In 1954, the *Mr. Blues Show* was attracting "hip kids" from the local colleges. Fan clubs were set up in four states: New Jersey, New York, Connecticut, and Massachusetts (*Cash Box*, October 23, 1954, 23). Like other pioneering white R&B disc jockeys, Ladell did not disclose his roots over the air.

18. For background details of Vastola's activities in the music business, see Dannen, *Hit Men*; Douglas, *Lonely Teardrops*; and Knoedelseder, *Stiffed*.

19. *Billboard*, January 28, 1956, 63 (Ruth McFadden review); February 4, 1956, 58 (Frankie Lymon and the Teenagers review).

20. "Darling, Listen to the Words of This Song," written by John Brantley–Julius Dixon–Alan Freed, published by Embassy Music Corporation.

21. *Billboard*, October 6, 1956, 36.

22. See chapter 13.

23. At the "Walking Along" session in late 1956, the Solitaires were made up of Milton Love, Winston "Buzzy" Willis, Bobby Baylor, Monte Owens, and Pat Gaston.

24. Detail from original trade magazine advertisement. Gart, *First Pressings*, vol. 8, 58.

25. The *Cash Box* review of "Last Night I Dreamed" appeared in the soon-to-be abandoned "R&B Reviews" section on November 22, 1958, and was accorded an "Award o' the Week." "So Fine" did not break into the *Billboard* national R&B chart until March 23, 1959, followed by a Hot 100 entry on April 6.

26. Story headed "Eldorado Wins 'So Fine' Suit," *Billboard*, May 25, 1959, 8.

27. Seamus McGarvey, "Those 'So Fine' Fiestas!" *Now Dig This*, February 1995, 14.

28. Broven, "Larry Dale," 6.

29. "Record Industry Source Book and Directory," *Billboard*, April 25, 1960, 106.

30. The diverse background stories to the master of "There's a Moon Out Tonight" were related to Nadine DuBois by Al Trommers, Jerry Greene, and collector Wayne Stierle for her book *The History of Times Square Records*, 107–14. The song publishing rights are owned by Embassy Music, a division of Music Sales.

31. This soul sector, with many nonselling singles that became instant rarities, effectively spawned the fevered "Northern Soul" collectors' market in England and elsewhere. Weiss used the Barry label, named after his son, as a soul outlet. See also the Maxine Brown section in chapter 19.

32. Streissguth, "Old Town," 188.

33. This oft-repeated but apposite quote was given in this instance by Larry Chance to me following a Long Island concert by the Earls in August 2003 and first published in the booklet to *Hy Weiss Presents Old Town Records*.

Chapter 13: Mercury Rising and the Roulette Wheel

1. Rolontz, "Mushrooming R.&B.'s," 14, 18. Since there were few reliable statistics being declared by the rhythm and blues manufacturers of the time, it is likely that the actual R&B market share was higher than the quoted estimate.

2. Critical crossover recordings from 1952 through 1955 included "Lawdy Miss Clawdy" by Lloyd Price (Specialty), "Hound Dog" by Willie Mae Thornton (Peacock), "Shake a Hand" by Faye Adams (Herald), "Money Honey" by Clyde McPhatter and the Drifters (Atlantic), "Shake, Rattle and Roll" by Joe Turner (Atlantic), "Earth Angel (Will You Be Mine)" by the Penguins (Dootone), "Sincerely" by the Moonglows (Chess), "Pledging My Love" by Johnny Ace (Duke), "I've Got a Woman" by Ray Charles (Atlantic), "Ain't It [That] Shame" by Fats Domino (Imperial), "Maybellene" by Chuck Berry (Chess), "Only You (and You Alone)" by the Platters (Mercury), and "Tutti-Frutti" by Little Richard (Specialty). Notice that many of these songs were included in Elvis Presley's early repertoire onstage and on-record.

3. Bob Rolontz, "Rhythm & Blues Notes," *Billboard*, January 1, 1955, 32.

4. *Billboard*, March 3, 1956, 22. The magazine's reporter Bob Rolontz was headhunted by RCA's Groove label as A&R man in 1955 before he returned to *Billboard* in 1958. His biggest production success was Mickey & Sylvia's "Love Is Strange" (No. 11 pop, No. 1 R&B, early 1957).

5. "Syd Nathan Addresses an A&R Meeting, December 11, 1954," released on *The King R&B Box Set*.

6. The "Hound Dog" royalty saga was related by Mike Stoller in the booklet notes by Randy Poe for *Leiber & Stoller Present the Spark Records Story* (Ace CDCHD 801).

7. Decca was involved in aborted "lease agreement" discussions with Don Pierce for masters from his Hollywood label in January 1954, confirming that the major label was keen to leap onto the R&B bandwagon at an even earlier stage. "Decca, H'w'd Records Mull R.&B. Exchange," *Billboard*, February 6, 1954, 12.

8. The Great Creatore was celebrated in Meredith Willson's musical *The Music Man*.

9. Famously, LaVern Baker was incensed at Georgia Gibbs's note-for-note copy of "Tweedlee Dee," which featured the same arrangement, the same vocal group (the Cues), and mostly the same session men. Even though Baker had a No. 14 pop hit in her own right, she went as far as petitioning her congressman to outlaw the copying of arrangements without permission. There were other, forgotten, cover versions of the song by Vicki Young (Capitol), Bonnie Lou (King), and country artist Pee Wee King (RCA Victor).

10. "Twilight Time" was another No. 1 record for the Platters (April 1958). A member of the Three Suns was Al Nevins, who became a successful Brill Building–era publisher with Don Kirshner.

11. Mercury did formally announce the introduction of a uniform "black label" policy soon after the release of the Platters' "Only You" on May 6, 1955. The official explanation was that the change was made at the request of "distributors and field men" due to "the trend for discs to break out in more than one field." A different color code, green, had been used for C&W releases in contrast to purple for R&B. Here was an early acknowledgment of the blurring of the pop, R&B, and country markets. "Mercury Drops Label Colors," *Billboard*, July 2, 1955, 20.

12. *Variety*, October 23, 1957, 53.

13. Art Talmadge also signed George Jones from Mercury, first to United Artists and then to Musicor, which had been founded at the end of 1960 by publisher/songwriter Aaron Schroeder. Jones was still produced by Pappy Daily.

14. Gleason, "Big Wheel and New Disk Deals," 67. The article was based on a feature by jazz critic Gleason in the previous week's *San Francisco Chronicle* after Morris Levy outbid Norman Granz's Clef-Verve labels for Count Basie's recording contract.

15. Tommy Vastola was still being quoted as Alan Freed's manager in *Cash Box*, October 11, 1958, 43.

16. In a story headed "Levy Again Wants In on Roost Label," *Billboard* noted, inter alia, that "jazz magnate" Morris Levy was getting out of a deal with RCA Victor for "some Birdland jazz talent" after he had already failed "to consummate a pact with ABC-Paramount." Reference was also made to the "annual Birdland Stars tour." *Billboard*, March 3, 1956, 21.

17. The first anniversary advertorial on Roulette Records was published by *Billboard*, February 3, 1958.

18. *Cash Box*, February 7, 1959, 36.

19. Guralnick, *Dream Boogie*, 308.

20. "Chain Gang," written by Sam Cooke, published by ABKCO Music.

21. According to Peter Guralnick, the actual "arrow" sounds on "Cupid" were made by Kenneth and Bobbie Sims, the Sims Twins. *Dream Boogie*, 364.

22. The Tokens' No. 1 record was nearly withdrawn at the outset due to a dispute with publisher Howie Richmond. Matters were quickly settled in his favor when it was discovered that he had owned the publishing rights to this variant of a South African folk song, "Wimoweh."

23. Dannen, "Godfather of Rock 'n' Roll," 89.

24. Cohodas, *Spinning Blues into Gold*, 307.

25. Dannen, "Godfather of Rock 'n' Roll," 89.

Chapter 14: Tin Pan Alley and Beyond

1. Gene Goodman, of course, was referring to rate increases in keeping with inflation. As of January 1, 2007, the U.S. publishers' "mechanical" statutory rate had increased to 9.1 cents per song, or 1.75 cents per minute for songs over five minutes (sometimes referred to as the "long song" rate). The royalty calculations are based on each musical composition of a sound recording sold. With CDs, in many countries the song royalty rate is determined by a percentage of the album's dealer selling price (for example, 8.5 percent in the United Kingdom as of 2006). These foreign record companies, therefore, have fixed song publishing costs per CD and accordingly are able to include more tracks per CD than their U.S. counterparts.

2. Another Benny Goodman bandboy was William "PoPsie" Randolph, the freelance photographer attached to *Cash Box* magazine.

3. Performance royalties are paid to publishers and songwriters but not to the sound recording owners. There has been successful decades-long lobbying by the broadcasters against paying fees

to record companies, basing their stance on the quid pro quo argument of giving "free" airplay in exchange—plus the potentially crippling cost.

4. Broven, *Walking to New Orleans*, 45.

5. Modern Records contract with the Dixie Blues Boys, June 6, 1955, property of Ace Records, London; Imperial Records contract with Roy Hayes, May 11, 1957, photostat copies in author's possession. One wonders, as an aside, if the Imperial hit-songwriting team of Fats Domino and Dave Bartholomew was locked into similar agreements with their songs, and if so, for how long?

6. In 1963, a BMI music publisher estimated that each reported "performance" play on local radio was worth two to three cents for the publisher and two cents for the songwriter, whereas the statutory rate for mechanical royalties was two cents (that is, one cent for each party, in theory). Dachs, *Anything Goes*, 208.

7. Compared to the BMI system, ASCAP's more complicated payoff scale, based on seniority, has been viewed as being more favorable to its songwriters over the longer term. BMI began paying affiliated songwriters from 1949.

8. In 1987, Jimmy Merchant and Herman Santiago, of the Teenagers, sued Morris Levy, Roulette Records, and others for songwriters' credits of the international hit "Why Do Fools Fall in Love." In December 1992, the U.S. federal courts ruled that Santiago and Merchant were coauthors, but in 1996 the ruling was reversed by the court of appeals on the basis of the statute of limitations. Copyright cases, stated the judgment, must be brought before a court within three years of the alleged civil violation, and the Santiago-Merchant lawsuit was not filed until some thirty years later. As a result, the authorship of "Why Do Fools Fall in Love" remains in the names of Frankie Lymon and Morris Levy. *Jimmy Merchant and Herman Santiago v. Morris Levy, Big Seven Music Corp. and Roulette Records, Inc., and Windswept Pacific Entertainment Co.*, United States Court of Appeals for the Second Circuit: Nos. 1322, 1653, 1768—August Term 1995; Argued: May 2, 1996, Decided: August 7, 1996.

9. Bill Haley's early 1956 version of "See You Later Alligator" was far superior to the poorly produced original by Cajun teenager Bobby Charles for Chess. At least Charles did benefit as the writer, with the song's title becoming a hip catchphrase. While the McGuire Sisters had a No. 1 pop hit with "Sincerely" in 1955, the Moonglows' rendition still made No. 20 pop as well as No. 1 R&B. Indicating the no-holds-barred fervor of the time, Louis Armstrong covered "Sincerely" and Johnny Ace's "Pledging My Love" on the same Decca single.

10. In addition to Paul Winley and Billy Dawn Smith, a lively school of black songwriters was active in New York during the 1950s into the 1960s, including Richie Barrett, Brook Benton, Otis Blackwell, Lincoln Chase, Don Covay, Luther Dixon, Julius Dixson, Rose Marie McCoy, Billy Myles, Clyde Otis, Winfield Scott, Charlie Singleton, and Sammy Taylor (who was with Hill & Range). Among the more established black writers were Henry Glover, Jesse Stone, and Rudy Toombs.

11. "Happy, Happy Birthday Baby," written by Margo Sylvia–Gilbert Lopez, published by Arc Music Corp./Donna Music Pub. Co.

12. "Silhouettes," written by Bob Crewe–Frank Slay, published by Regent Music Corporation. In 1956, the Rays had an unsuccessful single for Chess, and quite clearly Leonard Chess had given up on them. The Cameo hit version was a slightly different take from the original XYZ release. See also chapter 22.

13. "At the Hop" was registered in the first instance to Artie Singer, John Medora, and David White. The record, conceived as "Let's All Do the Bop" and wisely changed at the suggestion of Dick Clark, was released first on Singular Records, a tiny Philadelphia label that had been formed by Artie Singer with WPEN disc jockey Larry Brown.

14. Blanche "Bea" Kaslin (known also as Casalin), a former secretary at Herald Records, had

started Hull Records with William Miller and songwriter Billy Dawn Smith in October 1955 before launching Mascot Records in late 1957. "She was a wonderful lady," said Smith. "I learned all about the business with Hull." Around the same time as "Book of Love," Kaslin also sold to the Chess brothers the Mascot master of "Been So Long" by the Pastels (No. 24, Argo). She supplied ABC-Paramount with "Little Star" by the Elegants (No. 1 in the summer of 1958 on the Apt subsidiary) and later scored with "Daddy's Home" by Shep and the Limelites (No. 2, Hull, spring 1961). Her trusted A&R man was George "Teacho" Wiltshire.

15. Southland distributors' Gwen Kessler was hyping Ray Charles's "I Can't Stop Loving You" (ABC-Paramount) at the time. *Billboard Music Week,* May 19, 1962, 1.

16. This argument, a popular one in support of the "record men" credo, ignores the fact that an artist's earnings from personal appearances on the road were not good reasons for not paying royalties from record sales (excluding any contractual deductions, i.e., session costs, etc.).

17. See also chapter 17 for more on Roquel "Billy" Davis and Chevis Music.

18. Bigtop Records did have some success. See the section on the Bienstocks later in this chapter.

19. Gene and Harry Goodman were directors on the Brunswick Records board in the 1960s along with Decca president Milton Rackmil, Decca's Martin Salkin and Leonard Schneider, and Nat Tarnopol (Douglas, *Lonely Teardrops,* 355). In 1970, Tarnopol managed to wrestle sole control of Brunswick from Decca's then-owner, MCA. His amazing acquisition of the venerable trademark was in settlement of alleged under-reported record royalties by MCA following an audit investigation, and "a public company didn't want a problem" (from Paul Tarnopol, Nat's son). Although Tarnopol secured the Jackie Wilson masters, he did not obtain other Brunswick titles such as those by Buddy Holly.

20. The *Billboard* story was titled "Pop-Pubber in Disking Field Grows in Extent and Method: Sets Own Dates with Lesser Labels and Builds Backlog of Own Masters," March 15, 1952, 16, 18. Notable publisher/record company entrants were Gene Autry with Challenge Records in Hollywood, Bill Lowery with NRC in Atlanta, and, in the 1960s, Buddy Killen with Dial in Nashville. In New York, dual players included Lowell Music with Clock, Paxton-Winneton Music with Coed Records, Schwartz Music with Laurie, Monument Music with Madison, and Kassner Music with President and Seville.

21. Elvis Presley's Sun Records contract was hawked to Columbia, Mercury, London and possibly other labels before RCA Victor settled the deal for $40,000 through Steve Sholes. According to Julian Aberbach in his personal history, *Art Donations,* the RCA contract was prepared by Hill & Range Music's lawyer Ben Starr, and the funds were raised "with great difficulty and nervousness about the outcome." Two other agreements were signed at the same time between Presley and Colonel Tom Parker, giving Parker "25 percent of all income generated by Elvis Presley," and between Elvis and the Aberbach brothers, giving Presley a 50 percent interest with the Aberbachs in Elvis Presley Music (131). Through Steve Sholes, many mundane Hill & Range country songs were released by RCA Victor.

22. Elvis Presley wanted to record the 1949 Tony Martin hit "There's No Tomorrow" until Freddy Bienstock realized that it was set to "O Sole Mio" and thus in public domain in the United States. Bienstock commissioned fresh lyrics to the song as "It's Now or Never" and secured the publishing for the Hill & Range stable. The Presley publishing vehicles were Elvis Presley Music (BMI) and Gladys Music (ASCAP).

23. Peggy Lee's new arrangement transformed "Fever" into a superior song, overshadowing the original version as recorded by Little Willie John (King).

24. "White Bucks and Saddle Shoes," written by Doc Pomus–Mort Shuman, published by Unichappell Music Inc.

25. "Lavender Blue (Dilly, Dilly)," written by Eliot Daniel–Larry Morey, published by Walt Disney Music Co.

26. As the *Billboard* charts were accepted, over time, as the "official" U.S. listings, so the *New Musical Express* charts were viewed similarly in the United Kingdom. See also chapter 23 for Morty Craft's account of Johnny and the Hurricanes' time with Warwick Records.

27. "What's Your Name," written by Claude Johnson, published by Bug Music/It's a Hit Pub. Co./ Unichappell Music. The "shoo be doo" phrase was popularized in the Five Satins' recording of "In the Still of the Nite."

28. Even with support from Johnny Bienstock in his latter years, the in-house Bigtop productions were not reissued legitimately until 2007 because, according to the Aberbachs' lawyer in a telephone conversation with me in 2000, the masters were never "high on their radar screens." The separate EmBee Productions rights (including the masters of Del Shannon and Johnny and the Hurricanes) were long lost to the Aberbach family.

Chapter 15: Hillbilly Boogie

1. "Uncle" Art Satherley, who worked for fabled Paramount Records in the 1920s, was joint head of the Columbia "hillbilly and Western catalog" from 1945 with fellow Englishman Don Law until retiring in 1953, leaving Law in command. Music historian Colin Escott observed that "Art Satherley really preferred the West Coast because he was based there; Don Law preferred Jim Beck's studio in Dallas, Texas, and only switched reluctantly to Nashville after Beck died in 1956" (e-mail correspondence with author, February 18, 2007). Beck's accidental death by inhaling cleaning fluid fumes in the studio effectively ended the role of Dallas as a regional recording center.

2. *Billboard*, January 3, 1953, 12.

3. "Cat music" was a short-lived term for early rock 'n' roll and R&B that was coined in the South and Southwest. It was given prominence in the farsighted article "The Latest Trend: R&B Disks Are Going Pop" by Jerry Wexler and Ahmet Ertegun, p. 56. In fact, Ertegun and Wexler purloined the "Cat" name for their Atlantic subsidiary label in 1954.

4. Alta Hayes, another relatively unknown industry backroom heroine, did much to push Elvis Presley's Sun singles to Big State's jukebox-operator customers and so helped to establish Presley, and Sun Records, in the important northeast Texas area. Escott and Hawkins, *Good Rockin' Tonight*, 67.

5. Daughtrey, "The Man Who Went Giddyup," 4.

6. The desperate need for record-making materials was illustrated by an advertisement, in Bill McCall's name only: "Wanted Scrap Records. Any amount—we pay freight" (*Billboard*, June 9, 1945, 66). A subsequent advertisement expanded on the requirements: "We will pay 7¢ a pound, F.O.B. Pasadena, Calif., for worn or broken Shellac Records. WE DO NOT WANT Laminated, Glass, Aluminum or Synthetic Records" (*Billboard*, February 9, 1946, 89). The latter ad showed the name as Nelson Milling Company from the same address: 295 South Fair Oaks, Pasadena, California.

The 4 Star powerbase was confirmed by *Billboard* in late 1946: "Should Four Star record sales drop, which they show no signs of doing, the company can always turn to its own milling plant for rejuvenated profits. Operating its own factory, the diskery makes 'stampers' for many other labels in addition to its own and from these combined activities entered a gross-sales mark for '45 of over $1,500,000" (*Who's Who in Music*, 747). Bill McCall gained full control of Dick Nelson's interests in November 1946.

7. T. Texas Tyler's career was derailed in the 1950s by a combination of alcohol, drugs, and rock 'n' roll music. "Deck of Cards" provided a further publishing windfall in 1959 through disc jockey and TV host Wink Martindale's Top 10 version (Dot).

8. *Billboard*, July 1, 1950, 10. The records and labels quoted as being subject to bootlegging (all in the R&B field) were "Birmingham Bounce" by Amos Milburn (Aladdin), "Pink Champagne" by Joe Liggins (Specialty), and "The Hustle Is On" by T-Bone Walker, "Shake Shake Baby" by Archibald, and "The Fat Man" by Fats Domino (all Imperial).

9. Various, *4 Star Hillbilly Sessions*, 2.

10. In the 1992 interview with Ray Topping and the author, Don Pierce explained that "with 4 Star I had put up probably $25,000 to $30,000, which was a lot of money at that time—and I borrowed some of it from my mother." However, in a 1973 interview with Mike Leadbitter (*Let It Rock* magazine), Pierce stated the ingoing sum was $12,000. It is almost certain that Pierce was referring in 1992 to the combined stock and loan outlays. He died in 2005 before it was possible to clarify the figures with him.

11. The Slim Willet 4 Star release titled "Don't Let the Stars (Get in Your Eyes)" was a No. 1 country hit in its own right in December 1952, followed closely into the top spot by Skeets McDonald's Capitol version (which, of course, added to the publishing bounty). In 2008, Texas researcher Joe Specht had identified at least eighty versions of the song (e-mail correspondence with author, March 27, 2008).

12. "Decca, H'w'd Records Mull R.&B. Exchange," *Billboard*, February 6, 1954, 44.

13. Jack Starnes, also the manager of Lefty Frizzell, was described as "a drifter and an oilman" by Daniel Cooper in *Lefty Frizzell*, 102. "A Satisfied Mind" was a huge country song with hits by Porter Wagoner (No. 1 in July 1955, RCA Victor), Red and Betty Foley (No. 3, Decca), and Jean Shepard (No. 4, Capitol). The original Starday version was by Red Hayes (co-writer with Texas studio owner Jack Rhodes). Since then, the song has been recorded by a host of artists, including Joan Baez, Johnny Cash, Bob Dylan, and George Jones.

14. Copy of Don Pierce's undated Starday marketing letter from 1956 in author's possession.

15. *Variety*, December 19, 1956, 62.

16. *Billboard Music Week*, August 11, 1962, 4.

17. Don Pierce, letter to author, August 14, 2002.

18. Refer to chapter 8 for details of the various sales of King Records.

19. Daughtrey, "The Man Who Went Giddyup," 4.

20. Huey Meaux had extensive success with artists such as Barbara Lynn, the Sir Douglas Quintet, B. J. Thomas, and Freddy Fender, but in his old age (in 1996) he was jailed in a child pornography scandal.

21. Another reason for setting up subsidiary labels was to widen the distributor net. See chapter 3.

22. *Billboard Music Week*, June 23, 1962, 6.

23. "Harper Valley P.T.A.," written by Tom T. Hall, published by Unichappell Music Inc.

24. *Billboard* was reporting that Sam Phillips was "close to Mercury tie-up deal" as early as March 9, 1963, 1.

25. On April 30, 2004, Roy Moore reported in the *Nashville Business Journal* on-line edition that King Records had reached an agreement "a year ago" to pay "$3.5 million to cover a verdict over lost royalties." King group artists named in the class action lawsuit were Hank Ballard (King), Gene Pitney (Musicor), and the Shirelles and B. J. Thomas (Scepter).

26. SSS International had ceased manufacturing new 45–rpm releases by the mid-1970s.

Chapter 16: West Coast Rockin' and Rollin'

1. "Expansion by Bihari Bros.," *Billboard*, May 15, 1954, 16. By this time, the Biharis had their own pressing facilities again following the ARA plant sale in 1950.

2. Taking the B. B. King singles as examples, the name "Taub" appeared in the songwriting credits from King's very first RPM release (304) in the summer of 1950. "Josea" did not surface until late 1954 (RPM 416), with "Ling" in the summer of 1955 (RPM 430). Since "Ling, Ting, Tong" was a pop hit by the Five Keys at the very end of 1954, this would confirm Joe Bihari's statement concerning the derivation of Saul's "Ling" name. Jules Bihari was using the "Taub" pseudonym on Modern label releases as early as 1948, on Pee Wee Crayton's "Texas Hop" (643). It appears, therefore, that Jules Bihari controlled the songwriter action for a long time before cutting in his brothers. Even when Joe Bihari was managing the Flair label, the name "Josea" was not listed until 1954.

Certain record men seemed to eschew the songwriter-credit route, like Lew Chudd, Art Rupe, and Randy Wood. There were, of course, many genuine songwriters-cum-record men, including Bernie Lowe, Kal Mann, Johnny Mercer, Jay Miller, and Ahmet Ertegun (early on).

It should be remembered that songs are copyrighted at the Library of Congress, Washington, D.C., and that registered writer(s) do differ from the record label descriptions (and other notations). As an example, the Conrad Publishing Co. songwriter contract for Jimmy Reed's "Baby, What's on Your Mind?" dated April 22, 1957, shows Vee-Jay's Ewart Abner as 50 percent co-writer with the artist. However, the record release depicts Reed as the sole composer (the "A" side "The Sun Is Shining" became Reed's first Top 100 hit at No. 65, summer 1957). Why did Abner (not a recognized songwriter) disguise his interest, and how widespread was this practice? Refer to chapter 14 for discussion on performance royalties (also excluded from Reed's contract). For contract illustration, see Romano, *Big Boss Man*, 87–88.

3. "Kent Launches R-B Singles," *Billboard*, March 24, 1958, 3. Refer to chapter 5 for the background to the Shimkin scheme.

4. The Crown budget LP label was launched in 1957 and lasted until 1963. In time, Crown was supplanted by the Custom, United-Superior, and other marques. The Biharis also had the Mother Goose and Robin Hood budget lines for children's records and Discos Coronas for the local Mexican market (mainly mariachi and ranchero music).

5. In the late 1950s, Crown LPs were retailing at $1.98 for mono albums and $2.98 for stereo.

6. Royalty statement held in the files of Ace Records Limited, London, reproduced with permission from booklet accompanying *Long Tall Daddies* (Ace CDCHD 768).

7. Various figures quoted by Joe Bihari.

8. In 1965, Harold Battiste was to arrange, imperiously, Sonny Bono's pièce de résistance, "I Got You Babe" by Sonny & Cher (Atco). See chapter 18.

9. Harold Battiste interview extracts here taken from my article "All for One," 4–15.

10. Refer to the "End of Session" section (chapter 25) for Art Rupe's staff instructions for using Cosimo Matassa's J. & M. Recording Studio.

11. Later, in 1961, Joe Banashak's Minit label had Ernie K-Doe's No. 1 novelty hit, "Mother-in-Law," distributed by Imperial. In the same year, Banashak scored again with a No. 2 national record on Instant, Chris Kenner's "I Like It Like That (Part 1)." Both hits were produced by Allen Toussaint at the Cosimo studios, New Orleans.

12. The free promos racket seems to have started around 1951, coinciding with the rise of the one-stop. "Who Likes the 'One-Stop'? 47% of Distribs Think He's OK, Some Bearish on Trend," *Billboard*, January 26, 1952, 16.

13. *Billboard*, May 30, 1960, 6.

14. Fantasy Records—with the Specialty, Ebb, Galaxy, late Stax, Prestige, and other masters—was taken over by Concord Records in December 2004 in a deal reportedly worth $83 million.

15. See appendix E.

16. Rendezvous enjoyed big instrumental hits with a rocking version of Glen Miller's "In the Mood" by the Ernie Fields Orchestra (No. 4, 1959) and the rock-classical renditions of "Bumble Boogie" and "Nut Rocker" by B. Bumble and the Stingers, both Top 30 in 1961–62.

17. Little Jimmy Dickens's recording of "Y'All Come" was a cover of Texan Arlie Duff's original, which scored the country chart hit in 1953–54 (No. 7, Starday). Bing Crosby also covered the song for Decca (No. 20 pop).

18. Flying A Productions was Gene Autry's company that scored with *The Range Rider, Annie Oakley,* and, of course, *The Gene Autry Show.* Autry wanted to call the division "Champion" for his horse, but Decca already owned that name.

19. Danny Flores's first Kent release was in the name of Danny Boy, with the next single credited to Chuck "Tequila" Rio. When he left the Champs at the end of 1958, Flores was replaced on saxophone by Jimmy Seals with new drummer Dash Crofts—future stars Seals & Crofts; guitarist Glen Campbell joined the group in 1960.

20. "Autry Sells Interest in Challenge, Jackpot," *Billboard,* October 20, 1958, 4.

21. "Gene Autry Buys 4-Star," *Billboard,* May 16, 1960, 3.

22. Patsy Cline would be signed directly by Decca in 1960, after her second contract with Bill McCall had expired. She died in a plane crash on March 5, 1963, that also claimed the lives of Cowboy Copas and Hawkshaw Hawkins.

23. Joe Johnson said he managed to retain the writer's share of "Don't Let the Stars (Get in Your Eyes)," which he purchased after being approached by Slim Willet's widow so that she could pay off her mortgage. In 2007, the Challenge–4 Star masters and publishing were controlled by Sony-Tree of Nashville.

24. *Billboard,* August 24, 1963, 12.

Chapter 17: From Motown to Manhattan: In Almost Perfect Harmony

1. *Billboard,* March 20, 1954, 20.

2. Refer to chapter 8 for more on Joe Battle's activities.

3. Try as hard as he could, Billy Davis was unable to remember the title of his song that was recorded by 4 Star or the hillbilly act. In any case, it seemed to be quite an achievement on the part of Joe Battle to squeeze a royalty check out of Bill McCall (refer to chapter 15).

4. It is worth examining the content of the debut issue of *Rhythm and Blues* to get a feel for the early 1950s R&B age. On page 3, under the heading of "Red-Hot and Blue," there were song lyrics for "Sweet Sixteen" and "Kiss Me Baby" (both by "Nugetre," aka Ahmet Ertegun), "Junco Partner" (by Bob Shad), and "5-10-15 Hours" (by Rudolph Toombs). Articles were scattered throughout the magazine, including "Mellow Ella" (about Ella Fitzgerald), "Little Boy Blues" (Wynonie Harris), "Earl of Music" (Earl Bostic), "Sax-Appeal" (Johnny Hodges), and "Royalty in Rhythm" (Count Basie). There was a feature titled "Close Harmony" devoted to ascendant vocal groups the Clovers, the Orioles, and the Dominoes, while the growing influence of the disc jockey in this black-and-white, pre–color TV era was seen in the "Spinnin' the Blues Around" column.

5. See chapter 24 for insights on the later convergence of the pop and R&B markets.

6. Coincidentally, "The Wind" by the Diablos was scored by Maurice King, mentor of Billy Davis. Another early Detroit indie label, Staff Records (1947–50), was run by record distributor Idessa Malone with King as musical director.

7. "Shake a Hand" by Faye Adams was the 1953 crossover hit that helped to establish Herald Records. For a short period in 1952–53, R&B "answer" records were rife and, even worse, were claimed as new songs until the original song publishers tackled the problem primarily through publishers' agent Harry Fox and attorney Lee Eastman. Some of the hits subjected to the answer treatment were Ruth Brown's "(Mama) He Treats Your Daughter Mean" (Atlantic), Willie Mabon's "I Don't Know" (Chess), Willie Mae Thornton's "Hound Dog" (Peacock) (see chapter 9), and Jimmy Heap's "Wild Side of Life" (Imperial) (see chapter 10). "Answer to the 'Answers': Pubbers Train Legal Guns on Trail-Riding Indie Labels," *Billboard,* April 4, 1953, 18. As for "Jim Dandy Got Married," the writer credits have reverted to the writer of "Jim Dandy," Lincoln Chase.

8. Refer also to chapter 8 for Colonel Jim Wilson's activities with King Records.

9. The Ames vocal group is often referred to, incorrectly, as the Aims.

10. "Maybellene," written by Chuck Berry, published by Arc Music Corporation. Influenced by Bob Wills's western-swing version of the old folk tune "Ida Red" and originally titled "Ida Mae," Berry's debut hit is an early example of the hot rod subgenre that is generally considered to have been spawned by Arkie Shibley's "Hod Rod Race" for Bill McCall's Gilt-Edge label in 1950 (even before Jackie Brenston's "Rocket 88").

11. "Reet Petite," written by Roquel Davis–Berry Gordy, published by Jobete Music/Third Above Music.

12. After Bob Thiele signed Jackie Wilson to Decca, Wilson was placed on the lower-profile reactivated Brunswick subsidiary label, to general surprise. In 1986, "Reet Petite" made an incredible U.K. chart return at No. 1 after being featured in a popular television beer commercial.

13. See songwriter Paul Evans's description of the "four chords" in chapter 22.

14. Shortly afterward, United Artists Records picked up another Detroit indie hit, "You're So Fine" by the Falcons (produced by Sax Kari), from tiny Flick Records for its Unart subsidiary.

15. Refer also to Gene Goodman section in chapter 14.

16. Billy Davis's production triumphs for the Chess group included "Slip-In Mules (No High Heel Sneakers)" by Sugar Pie DeSanto (No. 48, 1964), "Selfish One" by Jackie Ross (No. 11, 1964), "We're Gonna Make It" and "Who's Cheating Who?" by Little Milton (No. 25 and No. 43, 1965), and Billy Stewart's "I Do Love You" (No. 26), "Sitting in the Park" (No. 24), and "Summertime" (No. 10) in 1965–66.

17. The Legrand label was operated out of Norfolk, Virginia, by record shop owner Frank Guida, who by utilizing a trademark Caribbean-influenced, overmodulated "party" sound notched up five Top 10 hits with Gary (U.S.) Bonds during 1960–62. The friendly yet eccentric record man, who was not popular with his artists and writers in later life due to ongoing royalty disputes, scored a second left-field No.1 hit with Jimmy Soul's "If You Wanna Be Happy" (S.P.Q.R.) in 1963. This song's original copyrighted credits are worth spelling out: words by Frank J. Guida, Carmela Guida (his wife), Joseph Royster; music by Frank J. Guida and Joseph Royster. The publisher was Guida's Rock Masters, Inc. As a result, the Guida family enjoyed 80 percent of the publishing income from the hit tune with 20 percent for Royster (also co-writer of the other Legrand No. 1, "Quarter to Three," and "New Orleans," both by Bonds).

Chapter 18: Harlem Hotshots and the Black Experience

1. The daily number of performances (and times) at the Apollo did vary through the years.

2. Bobby Robinson was alluding to Ray Charles's breakthrough with the gospel-based "I've Got a Woman" (No. 1 R&B, Atlantic, 1955).

3. As the years went by, Ahmet Ertegun's stories (as opposed to answers to direct questions) tended to have an after-dinner comedic bias rather than be models of historical accuracy. However, this flavorful tale is worth retelling, with this caveat in mind.

4. "The Closer You Are" by the Channels was a regional doo-wop hit on Whirlin' Disc.

5. "Kansas City" interview extracts here are taken from my article "Bobby's Happy House of Hits," pt. 1, 9–10.

6. "Kansas City," written by Jerry Leiber and Mike Stoller, published by Jerry Leiber Music/Mike Stoller Music.

7. Bell Sound Studios, a top New York recording destination for some twenty-five years, was founded in June 1950 by Municipal Broadcasting System engineers Allen Weintraub and Daniel Cronin from a basement room on Mott Street in Chinatown. After relocating to Brooklyn's Lafayette Street (and being disrupted by vibrations from the "A" subway train), Bell Sound was moved to Manhattan's Eighty-ninth Street and settled at West Forty-sixth Street before ending up at 237 West Fifty-fourth Street from June 1959. *Cash Box*, June 11, 1960, 31.

8. *Billboard*, May 2, 1960, 2.

9. Ibid., May 25, 1959, 8; see chapter 19 for "The Happy Organ" saga. Just four months later, another small indie label, Canadian American, had a huge No. 1 hit: "Sleep Walk" by Santo & Johnny.

10. Bobby Robinson said that his artist Clarence Junior Lewis was not related to his silent partner Fats Lewis, confirmed by Marshall Sehorn, who remembered the restaurant as "Fats' Pig 'n' Pit."

11. Sehorn's generalization, while strictly true, is not entirely accurate. Black promo men such as Paul Gayten, Sax Kari, and Dave Clark were starting to make their mark in the South around this time.

12. *Cash Box*, March 4, 1961, 29.

13. This proposed deal may possibly have been along the lines of the ABC-Paramount agreement with Chancellor Records. See chapter 22.

14. Danny Robinson ran Holiday Records, Vest, and Everlast (the last two named after his wife, Vesta) and had an interest in Cee-Jay Records.

15. The roster of Sue's bigger national hits was impressive: "Itchy Twitchy Feeling" by Bobby Hendricks (No. 25, late 1958), "A Fool in Love" by Ike & Tina Turner (No. 27 pop, No. 2 R&B, late 1960), "I Know (You Don't Love Me No More)" by Barbara George (No. 3 pop, No. 1 R&B, late 1961), "Stick Shift" by the Duals (No. 25, late 1961), "It's Gonna Work Out Fine" by Ike & Tina Turner (No. 14 pop, No. 2 R&B, late 1961), "I've Got a Woman (Part 1)" by Jimmy McGriff (No. 20, late 1962), "That's How Heartaches Are Made" by Baby Washington (No. 40, spring 1963), "Mockingbird" by Inez Foxx (No. 7 pop, summer 1963, No. 2 R&B single for the year), "I Can't Stand It" by the Soul Sisters (No. 46, spring 1964), and then "Let's Work Together (Part 1)" by Wilbert Harrison (No. 32, early 1970).

16. Paul Oliver, *Blues Fell This Morning*, 149–50.

17. For Harold Battiste's days as Specialty branch manager, refer to chapter 16.

18. Harold Battiste interview extracts here are taken from my article "All for One," 4–15.

19. *Cash Box*, October 15, 1960, 28.

20. After returning home in the early 1990s, Harold Battiste reverted to teaching and became professor of music, jazz studies, at the University of New Orleans. He also administered the All For One Foundation to document modern jazz in New Orleans.

21. "Sue Gets Sued in 330G Suit," *Billboard Music Week*, November 24, 1962, 6. It is not known how this lawsuit was resolved.

Chapter 19: On and Off Broadway

1. Starting as a music publisher's representative in 1946, Jack Hooke became co-owner and general manager of Roost Records (known also as Royal Roost) in 1949 before joining Alan Freed's organization in 1957. Teddy Reig was another partner in Roost, which was fully acquired by Morris Levy at Roulette in 1958. According to *Billboard*, Hooke was appointed A&R head of Len Levy's Hanover Records in the same year. The news story noted that recent hits published by Figure Music included "Short Shorts" by the Royal Teens (ABC-Paramount), "Jo-Ann" by the Playmates (Roulette), and "Maybe" by the Chantels (End). "Hanover Signs Jack Hooke," *Billboard*, May 26, 1958, 4.

2. "'Biggest Sampler Yet': 'Flying Saucer' Takes Off; Pubbers, Diskers Do a Flip," *Billboard*, July 28, 1956, 17.

3. Although New York is seen rightly as the home of doo-wop, there was strong vocal group support on the West Coast, Chicago, and elsewhere. In fact, two vital early New York doo-wop records, "Gee" by the Crows and "Sh-Boom" by the Chords, were broken by Los Angeles disc jockey Hunter Hancock.

4. Fascinatingly, *Billboard* used the term "oldie but goody" in a news story way back on June 5, 1948, 17.

5. *Billboard*, June 3, 1950, 27.

6. "The Happy Organ" story extracts are taken from an interview by the author with Doug Moody, first published in the booklet notes by the author to the 1993 CD *Happy Organs, Wild Guitars and Piano Shuffles* by Dave "Baby" Cortez (Ace CDCHD 386).

7. The Hammond B-3 organ, a favorite instrument in jazz and blues, was introduced in 1955. Its immediate popularity was enhanced by Bill Doggett's "Honky Tonk" hit (see chapter 8).

8. Doug Moody was right on the ball in focusing on Radio WKBW, Buffalo, which was named as a key breakout station in a contemporaneous report by *Billboard*. Also lauded in the same article were the Baltimore-Washington area (Buddy Deane, WJZ-TV), the "tough town" of New York (Alan Fredericks, WHOM), and Cleveland (WERE and KYW). Atlanta, Charlotte, N.C., and Philadelphia were described as hot areas, while the fringe cities of Toledo and Milwaukee were said to be better "starting points" than neighboring Detroit and Chicago, respectively. Pittsburgh and Seattle were described as "slipping badly," Boston was "picking up" (through WMEX), and San Francisco, St. Louis, and New Orleans were stated as being "rather cool at present." Grevatt, "Disk Breakout Power Wanes," 3 and 40. No reference was made to the major market of Los Angeles, and Nashville was mentioned only in passing.

9. Gart, *First Pressings*, vol. 7, 99, 102.

10. "Get a Job," written by Earl Beal–Raymond Edwards–William Horton–Richard Lewis, published by EMI Longitude Music.

11. *Billboard*, November 23, 1959, 2.

12. On May 18, 1959, *Billboard* ran a feature by Paul Ackerman and Bob Rolontz entitled "Nothing Like Having an 'In': 'Hip' Pressing Plants Spark New Type of Disk Promotion" (3). In describing this fresh promotional tool, the authors explained: "This new terminology, the hip plant, has developed to describe those pressing plants that supposedly have an in or a direct contact with deejays or swinging distributors, or with manufacturers who are close to a few key dee-jays." Although no names were mentioned, Silver-Park Pressing certainly fitted the bill as a "hip plant."

13. Gart, *First Pressings*, vol. 9, 76.

14. *Billboard*, June 8, 1959, 30.

15. Ibid., August 10, 1959, 8.

16. Herald-Ember's Al Silver clearly became caught up in the excitement surrounding the U.K.-headquartered Top Rank label (launched on January 30, 1959) and its attempt to set up an international indie network through New York attorney Paul Marshall. Among the other labels signed up by Top Rank, several of which had been with London, were 20th Century-Fox, Time-Shad-Brent, Vanguard, Fury, Swan, Original Sound, Vista (Disney), Coed, Cameo-Parkway, Ace, Sue, Vee-Jay–Abner, and Laurie-Legrand (in release order). Top Rank collapsed within eighteen months (described as a failed "million-pound gamble" in a front-page story by *Melody Maker*, August 13, 1960) and was taken over by EMI. A few months later, attorney Marshall set up Transglobal Music Co. for EMI, and it was through this vehicle that Vee-Jay and Swan were able to license the Beatles' first U.S. singles. See also chapter 21 on the London–American Group.

17. Parlophone's main U.S. indie licensor in the 1950s was King Records, but the releases were very poorly promoted in the United Kingdom. Even King's biggest hit, "Honky Tonk" by Bill Doggett, failed to breach the *New Musical Express* Top Thirty in late 1956.

18. Interview with Al Silver in Arnold Shaw, *Honkers and Shouters*, 460.

19. Al Silver told Arnold Shaw he was hit by a corporate tax bill totaling around $150,000 after the IRS had refused to allow his deduction claims for cash payola payments as business expenses dating back to 1953. He indicated that he liquidated all his assets (including record labels, publishing, and pressing plant) "rather than go bankrupt and hurt creditors that were good to me—it wasn't my nature." Interview with Al Silver in Shaw, *Honkers and Shouters*, 459.

20. In the same interview, in 1974, Shaw reported that Silver "had just taken a sales job" with ABC-Paramount "now run by Larry Newton." *Honkers and Shouters*, 450.

21. Tosches, "Hipsters and Hoodlums," 214.

22. Muse Products was not listed among the New York or New Jersey record distributors in the annual roundup editions of *Cash Box* for 1960 and 1961.

23. Refer to chapter 4 for the background to the formation in 1988 of the Rhythm & Blues Foundation to tackle the dire financial circumstances surrounding many R&B artists, as described by Maxine Brown. She was a recipient of the foundation's pioneer award for 1990–91.

Chapter 20: Gold Coast Platters and Stock Matters

1. As disclosed in the introduction, Shelley Galehouse is my wife.

2. Clark Galehouse's first musical job was with a theater orchestra as saxophonist during the vaudeville era. It cannot be verified that the Bernie Lowe quoted is the same person who headed Cameo-Parkway Records. However, there is a possible connection between Galehouse and Lowe through Paul Whiteman; also, it seems that some Cameo 45s were pressed by Shelley Products.

3. Clark Galehouse's daughter, Shelley, recalled her father stating that he played in Chicago clubs controlled by gangster Al Capone, who was "a good employer."

4. This record description was made on a four-record 78–rpm Pilotone album by Arizona Cliff Martin and the Cactus Cowboys in 1947. Martin recorded later for Clark Galehouse's Crest Records.

5. Simon, "Injection Molding's A-Coming?" 12, 41.

6. *Billboard* noted the trend toward injection molding in an article, "Diskers Modernize: Coast Plants Go to Injection Process" by former *Cash Box* editor Joel Friedman (June 18, 1955, 17). With Columbia Records as the leader in the field, the story stated that two other West Coast plants "out of 24" were using injection equipment: "Monarch Record Manufacturing Company, with one press, and Hank Fine's National Record Company, who press Mercury Records." Plants said to be con-

sidering injection molding, with its "lower production costs," were Capitol in San Fernando and "Jules Bihari's Cadet Record Pressing Company, Superior Recording Company and Alco Research & Engineering."

7. There is hearsay evidence that Shelley Products pressed Golden discs for Arthur Shimkin as an outsource facility in busy times of need.

8. The title of the Wailers' LP led to the group being known also as the Fabulous Wailers, partly to differentiate them from reggae star Bob Marley's later set of Wailers. Likewise, Golden Crest's Mando and the Chili Peppers preceded the rock act Red Hot Chili Peppers by many years.

9. *Cash Box*, February 6, 1964, 35.

10. Ibid., May 13, 1961, 38.

11. Ibid., August 26, 1961, 27.

12. According to researcher Russ Wapensky, the usual procedure with union contracts in the 1950s and 1960s was that a W-4 form was completed once a session was over, with copies being sent to the record company, AFM local office, AFM pension fund, and session leader and session contractor (and possibly the AFM headquarters in New York). Payments from the session were sent by the record companies to the locals and then disbursed to the musicians. A session was reported to the union in the first place by the contractor. (E-mail correspondence with author, April 28, 2007.)

13. Billy Mure played guitar on other No. 1 hits that traversed the "hit parade" pop and mainstream rock 'n' roll eras: "Rag Mop" by the Ames Brothers (Coral), "Come on-a My House" by Rosemary Clooney (Columbia), "The Doggie in the Window" by Patti Page (Mercury), and "Diana" by Paul Anka (ABC-Paramount). Other hit sessions included those that yielded "A White Sport Coat (and a Pink Carnation)" by Marty Robbins (Columbia), "Corrine Corrina" by Joe Turner (Atlantic), "Empty Arms" by Ivory Joe Hunter (Atlantic), "I'm Gonna Sit Right Down and Write Myself a Letter" by Billy Williams (Coral), "White Silver Sands" by Don Rondo (Jubilee), "Splish Splash" by Bobby Darin (Atco), "Tell Laura I Love Her" by Ray Peterson (RCA Victor), "Shout! Shout! (Knock Yourself Out)" by Ernie Maresca (Seville), and "Bobby's Girl" by Marcie Blane (Seville). Mure also produced an underground rock 'n' roll favorite, "Black and White Thunderbird" by the Delicates (Unart).

14. *"Billboard" 1963–64 International Music-Record Directory and Buyer's Guide*, August 3, 1963, 120.

15. *Billboard*, May 23, 1960, 9; *Cash Box*, December 31, 1960, 28.

16. This incident could not be followed up since the research information came to light after Joe Dreyhaupt had passed away. The Harry Fox Agency, based in New York, is a continuing fixture as a publishers' agent-trustee, with duties including the issue of mechanical licenses and subsequent royalty collections, supervising audits, and lobbying activities. Arthur Shimkin, of Golden Records, mischievously described founder Harry Fox as "a scoundrel but thoroughly entertaining." Fox had tried to sign up Shimkin on the basis that he "represented all publishers," to which Shimkin retorted, "Take your 10 percent and stick it up your nose!"

17. Story told by Lee Magid on covering Brother Bones's "Sweet Georgia Brown" with a Dusty Fletcher version (National, 1949) in Shaw, *Honkers and Shouters*, 360.

18. Other Golden Crest acts were operatic singer Igor Gorin, harpsichordist Igor Kipnis, and saxophonist Paul Brodie. The comedy team of Doug Setterberg and Stan Boreson were popular within the tight-knit Scandinavian communities of the northern states with a string of LP and cassette releases. In 1973, Golden Crest released two albums by former Mercury hit artist Rusty Draper. On the jazz front, Galehouse recorded Fletcher Henderson alumnus Don Redman with his Orchestra (including Coleman Hawkins) and New Orleans music historian Dr. Edmond Souchon, who had two Dixieland albums.

19. *1981 Annual Report Golden Crest Records, Inc. and Its Wholly Owned Subsidiaries*, in author's possession. This report revealed that "record division sales" decreased from $4.2 million in 1979 to $2.9 million in 1980 and $2.1 million in 1981.

20. Simon Sheib was president of Avnet, the electronics company that owned Liberty Records for a short while in the 1962–63 period. Incidentally, Shelley Products was the East Coast presser for Liberty-Imperial in the 1960s.

21. *New York Times*, June 1, 1980, 19, 22.

22. I made a detailed study of the Golden Crest/Shelley record operations in *American Music Magazine* 81 (September 1999), published in Sweden. Included were articles by artists John Greek of the Wailers and Paul Hotchkiss of Paul and the Four-Most and a doo-wop feature by Gordon Skadberg.

Chapter 21: The London American Group: Rockin' around the World

1. London artists included Chuck Berry, Pat Boone, Johnny Cash, Ray Charles, the Coasters, Eddie Cochran, Sam Cooke, Bobby Darin, Bo Diddley, Fats Domino, the Drifters, Duane Eddy, the Everly Brothers, Jerry Lee Lewis, Little Richard, Ricky Nelson, Roy Orbison, Carl Perkins, Del Shannon, the Ventures, the Wailers, Slim Whitman, and Larry Williams. Among the represented indie labels were Atlantic-Atco, Bigtop, Cadence, Cameo, Carlton, Challenge, Chancellor, Chess-Checker-Argo, Class, Dot, End-Gone, Excello-Nasco, Hi, Imperial, Jamie-Guyden, Jubilee-Josie, Kapp, Laurie, Liberty, Monument, Old Town, Philles, Savoy, Specialty, Starday, Sue, Sun, Swan, Tamla (early), United Artists, and Warwick. As well, there were imprints such as Ace (of Jackson, Mississippi), Anna, Clock, Coed Dore, Ebb, Era, Fabor, Fargo, Fraternity, Golden Crest, and Nomar. Stalwart enterprises such as ABC-Paramount, Herald-Ember, King, Modern-RPM, and Vee-Jay saw only a few releases on London. Paul Pelletier, *London: Complete Singles Catalogue 1949–1982* (including Elvis Presley Sun reference, p. 8).

2. The first wave of British rock 'n' rollers, influenced primarily by Elvis Presley, was hampered by hackneyed studio productions that lacked the fire and spirit of American rock 'n' roll. Aside from Cliff Richard, the best of the bunch were Billy Fury, Tommy Steele, and Marty Wilde. Skiffler Lonnie Donegan was a crucial force in introducing British teenagers to American folk songs and the medium of *playing* musical instruments.

3. The Edward Lewis segment is based on his beguiling autobiography, *No C.I.C.*, published in 1956, some five years before he was knighted. The obscure title was a barbed jab at the Bank of England's restrictive currency exchange rules of the day that were administered by the Capital Issue Committee. As for the derivation of the "Decca" trademark, Edward Lewis professed he had "no idea" but loved the name all the same. A plausible theory is that it was coined by Wilfred S. Samuel of Barnett Samuel & Sons by merging the initial "D" (either the "Dulcet" logo or the "Dulcephone" trademark) with the bulk of the word "mecca."

4. In some quarters, Jack Kapp is credited with U.S. Decca's revolutionary thirty-five-cent pricing policy. Ted Lewis was quite adamant in *No C.I.C.* that the decision was his: "Jack Kapp wanted to follow the existing pattern. . . . I could see no hope of success for such a policy" (53). Refer also to chapter 2.

5. At the instigation of the AFM in 1938 and in retaliation against radio competition, U.S. record companies started printing broadcast restriction notices on their discs. Even until 1955, releases on Savoy (78 rpm and 45 rpm), for example, still bore the legend "Not Licensed for Radio Broadcast—For Home Use on Phonograph." However, the U.S. Supreme Court's refusal to review a decision in the Pennsylvania Supreme Court way back in December 1940 confirmed that "property rights

ended with the sale of a record" and that "broadcasters could no longer be constrained from using music recorded 'for home use only.'" Sanjek and Sanjek, *American Popular Music Business in the 20th Century,* 57.

6. M. Coleman, *Playback,* 56.

7. Lewis would continue the relationship with U.S. Decca at home by releasing its recordings on the U.K. Brunswick and U.K. Coral labels.

8. "London's Dollars!" *Billboard,* December 20, 1947, 20.

9. *Billboard,* January 17, 1948, 17.

10. Ibid., December 20, 1947, 20.

11. Pelletier, *Complete British Directory of Popular 78/45 rpm Singles,* 5.

12. Colin Escott (employee at PolyGram Records at the time), e-mail correspondence with author, March 2, 2007.

13. Refer also to chapter 14 regarding the important topic of performance royalties.

14. Mimi Trepel said her job interview with London Records was conducted by Paul Marshall, the noted New York music attorney.

15. Emphasis mine. Burlington Music contract dated January 20, 1961, in author's possession by way of the files of CFG Publishing Co., with Mimi Trepel and Clark Galehouse as two of the signatories.

16. Fordham University program validation letter sent to Mimi Trepel by John Nice, dated November 18, 1981.

17. Decca would secure the international rights to Elvis Presley's recordings when it wrestled away the RCA Victor catalog from EMI in 1957.

18. Apart from turning down the Beatles and losing the Rolling Stones, U.K. Decca signed and then let go artists such as David Bowie, Joe Cocker, Van Morrison (through Them), the Small Faces, Cat Stevens, and Rod Stewart.

19. Fred Foster departed from Mercury in September 1956 just before the start of the Mercury-Starday deal with Pappy Daily and Don Pierce. Actually, Dee Kilpatrick did produce a No. 1 country hit, "No Help Wanted," in 1953 and others by the Carlisles for Mercury, but Foster's general criticism of Kilpatrick is pertinent.

20. In his notes to *The Monument Story* double CD, Fred Foster stated that he contributed $600 toward the start-up capital of $1,200. The balance was split between disc jockey Buddy Deane and the owners of J. & F. distributors, Baltimore.

21. See Fred Foster's account of how Wesley Rose engineered Roy Orbison's transfer from Monument to MGM with Sir Edward Lewis's input, chapter 24.

22. The *Billboard Music Week* booklet insert (May 26, 1962) noted that the first London American Group hit was the Joe Leahy–produced Kathy Linden record of "Billy" (No. 7, Felsted, spring 1958). In all, the London division under Walt Maguire had accrued 130 producer agreements covering over 300 singles and 25 LP releases on 40 different labels. Sales to that date were stated to be in excess of $10 million. The affiliated record men were listed in this order: Fred Foster (Monument), Joe Cuoghi (Hi), Bob Crewe and Frank Slay (XYZ and Topix), Ed Kassner, Murray Sporn, and Marv Holtzman (Seville and President), Archie Levington (Felsted), Buddy Killen (Dial), Herb Breger (Shell), Noel Ball (Scarlet), Orville Campbell (Colonial), Buck Ram (Felsted, Press), Cosimo Matassa (Dover), Jack Gold (Terrace), Gary Paxton (Felsted), Huey Meaux (Eric), Sid Parnes and Mike Stewart (Felsted), Murray Kaufman (the disc jockey Murray the K) (Splash), and Bill Smith (Felsted).

Chapter 22: Teen Scene

1. Bernie Asbell, "Sam Phillips Notes: R&R Fading but Imprint Permanent," *Billboard*, May 18, 1959, 4, 21.

2. *Billboard*, January 5, 1959, 3.

3. Gross, "Indies' Hit-'N'-Run Score," 53, 57.

4. "Smaller Record Firms Spin to Success," *Business Week*, September 7, 1957, 49–50. The next year, Lew Chudd was accorded a feature in *Fortune* magazine, titled appropriately "An Ear for Money" (November 1958).

5. *Billboard*, June 22, 1963, 40.

6. Bob Rolontz, "Chuck Willis Passes—His Life a Blues Saga," *Billboard*, April 14, 1958, 4, 12.

7. "N.Y. Operators Start New Co. in Philadelphia," *Billboard*, April 21, 1945, 67; the business was called Phonograph Service Company. See also Krivine, *Juke Box Saturday Night*, 120 (New Jersey jukebox operator Dick Steinberg interview in "King of the Title Strips" chapter).

8. Jackson, *American Bandstand*, 120. Distributor Sam Hodge was stated by Jackson to be another Jamie partner. Interestingly, Allen Sussel's daughter Jamie gave rise to the label name, while another daughter, Laura, was the inspiration behind the Laurie Records accreditation.

9. In June 1962, Harry Finfer sold his Jamie-Guyden stock to Harold B. Lipsius and disposed of his share in Universal Record Distributing Corporation. At the same time, Finfer acquired Lipsius's "silent" share in Philles Records (*Billboard Music Week*, June 30, 1962, 6). In October, however, Phil Spector bought out Finfer along with other Philles (and Jamie) partner Lester Sill to obtain full control of Philles—an amalgam of the first names of Spector and Sill. Spector was embarking on his "Wall of Sound" era, highlighted by those unforgettable girl group hits from the Crystals and the Ronettes. With Jamie-Guyden remaining in family hands, Lipsius was still at his desk until a few months before he died in 2007 at the age of ninety-three.

10. Ashley Kahn, in his book *The House That Trane Built*, quoted Larry Newton on the ABC-Paramount/Chancellor deal. Newton was more specific than Bob Marcucci in his recall: "It was similar to the motion picture business: I made a deal where ABC got 20 percent off the top, we paid all the expenses, and then we made a 75/25 split on the profits. And if they were going to sell out, I'd have the first option to buy the company" (19). ABC-Paramount made similar arrangements with labels such as Colonial, Fargo, and Hunt that were less successful at a commercial level.

11. According to recording engineer expert Tom Moulton, who later handled the session tapes, out of the twenty-seven takes of Frankie Avalon's "Dede Dinah," there was only one "nasal" take.

12. *Billboard*, June 20, 1960, 12.

13. Chancellor Records was sold by Bob Marcucci, eventually, in 2006 to Digital Music Group, which was interested in the downloading aspect, not physical product.

14. Jackson, *American Bandstand*, 45.

15. Freddy Bienstock, who was at Hill & Range Music supervising the Elvis Presley interests at the time, did not remember any controversy at all over the publishing of "Butterfly." In a further twist, however, the versions of "Butterfly" by Charlie Gracie and Andy Williams were released in England with the song credited to "September" and subpublished by "Aberbach Ltd." It seems, therefore, that a mutual arrangement was made between the Aberbach brothers and Bernie Lowe and Kal Mann.

16. See also chapter 14.

17. Swan Records, with Tony Mammarella as president and Bernie Binnick as the respected secretary-treasurer, went fully independent in spring 1961. *Billboard Music Week*, March 11, 1961, 37.

18. "Dinner with Drac (Part 1)" written by Kal Mann–Dave Appell, published by Dave Appell Music.

19. Bob Horn was dismissed as the show's host following a drunk driving arrest and rumors of a sexual liaison with one of the young *Bandstand* girls. Jackson, *American Bandstand,* 32.

20. Under Joe Tarsia's direction, Reco-Art was renamed as Sigma Sound in 1968 to herald in the Gamble and Huff "Philly sweet soul" era.

21. "Bristol Stomp," written by Kal Mann–Dave Appell, published by Dave Appell Music. According to Dave Appell, the record that inspired "Bristol Stomp" was by "a group called the Students," probably "Everyday of the Week" (Checker, reissued on Argo).

22. "Cameo-Parkway Net Sales Hit All-Time High," *Billboard Music Week,* September 8, 1962, 6.

23. Under new management, Cameo had a final No. 1 hit in 1966 with a genuine bought-in indie record: "96 Tears" by ? (Question Mark) and the Mysterians.

24. *Billboard,* September 28, 1968, 4.

25. Ibid., November 30, 1959, 2.

26. In June 1962, Nevins-Kirshner Associates launched their Dimension label with Little Eva's No. 1 hit, "The Loco-Motion," followed by Carole King's "It Might as Well Rain until September" (No. 22), with national distribution by Amy-Mala. The whole Aldon enterprise was sold in 1963—prematurely, with hindsight—in a deal worth up to $3 million to Screen Gems, a division of Columbia Pictures (as was Colpix Records). See Emerson, *Always Magic in the Air,* 183. The new president of Screen Gems–Columbia Music was the perennial Lester Sill (ex-Modern, Spark, Jamie, and Philles). The dominance of the Aldon/Screen Gems songwriters was confirmed by a "Top Publishers—1963" listing: (1) Aldon, (2) Jobete, (3) Screen Gems–Columbia, (4) Acuff-Rose, (5) Kalmann, (6) Trio, (7) Witmark, (8) Arc, (9) Sea of Tunes, (10) Presley. *"Billboard" 1964 Who's Who in the World of Music,* December 28, 1963, 51.

27. Paul Evans annotated the "1950s" four-chord format as: C–A minor–F (or D minor)–G7, or F–D minor–B-flat (or G minor)–C7. For more on triplets in rock 'n' roll, see chapter 23.

Chapter 23: Corporate Takeover and Talent Makeover

1. The ABC executives were probably stung into starting ABC-Paramount Records when other labels stepped in to mop up the huge spoils from "The Ballad of Davy Crockett" after the song was featured on the Disney/ABC-TV series between December 1954 and February 1955. Indeed, the recruitment of Sam Clark may have resulted from his association at Cadence with Bill Hayes's No. 1 "Davy Crockett" success.

2. Kay Starr had the No. 1 pop hit with "Wheel of Fortune" (Capitol, spring 1952), and among the other cover versions was a No. 6 R&B hit by the Cardinals vocal group for Atlantic. The original release was by Johnny Hartman (RCA Victor).

3. "Derby Hearing Set Nov. 9; Oberstein Bids for Catalog," *Billboard,* November 6, 1954, 28. Some of the creditors were listed: "Harry Fox, publishers' agent and trustee . . . about $10,000, Economy Record Company $6,000, Long Wear Stamper Corporation $2,053, Specialty Records, a pressing plant, $3,597, and *The Cash Box,* trade magazine, about $1,600. The government has first claim to monies accruing thru the sale."

4. *Billboard,* June 20, 1960, 12.

5. Ibid., September 29, 1956, 30.

6. Colonial Records had earlier success in 1954 with comedian Andy Griffith's career-launching *What It Was, Was Football.* The master was sold to Capitol.

7. Besides *American Bandstand,* another important ABC-TV promotional outlet for ABC-Paramount was *The Mickey Mouse Club.*

8. *Billboard,* March 3, 1958, 3.

9. *Billboard Music Week,* May 29, 1961, 1, 33.

10. Rolontz, "What Price a Diskery?", 4. Interestingly, Archie Bleyer (Cadence), Jerry Blaine (Jubilee), and Lew Chudd were said in the same article to have "talked seriously" with the Studebaker-Packard car combine for buyouts. Also Bernie Lowe (Cameo) and Al Silver (Herald-Ember) were said to be in talks with Muzak Corporation. None of these deals, of course, materialized.

11. The major MGM hits in Morty Craft's reign were "The Purple People Eater" by Sheb Wooley (No. 1, summer 1958), "Stupid Cupid" by Connie Francis (No. 14, late summer 1958), "It's All in the Game" by Tommy Edwards (No. 1, fall 1958), "It's Only Make Believe" by Conway Twitty (No. 1, late 1958), and "My Happiness" by Connie Francis (No. 2, turn of 1959).

12. *Cash Box,* November 8, 1958, 37.

13. Ibid., February 14, 1959, 45.

14. The holding company of the Seven-Arts business was United Telefilms, from Toronto. As a curious aside, Seven-Arts Productions would take over Warner Bros. Films and Records. Then, in an act that was seen as almost sacrilegious at the time, Warner Bros.–Seven Arts acquired Atlantic Records in 1967 through a leveraged $17.5 million buyout. After buying out Elektra, the group became known as WEA Records.

15. Johnny Paris insisted robustly that he and his group played on every record by Johnny and the Hurricanes (conversation with author, January 1996). For the combo's spell with Bigtop Records, refer also to chapter 14.

16. Moe Gale's history in music dated back to 1926 when he cofounded Harlem's famous Savoy Ballroom. Through this connection, he formed in 1940 the Gale Inc. agency, which within three years had a "race" book including the Ink Spots, Ella Fitzgerald, Lucky Millinder, Cootie Williams, Lil Green, and Buddy Johnson. *"The Billboard" 1943 Music Year Book,* 143 (accompanying *Billboard,* September 25, 1943).

17. In a 1956 "Spotlight on Rhythm & Blues" feature, *Billboard* listed the "major agencies booking rhythm & blues talent." In terms of number of contracted artists, the leading agency was Shaw Artists Corporation, followed by Gale Agency, Universal Attractions, Buffalo Booking Agency (connected with Duke-Peacock Records), Herald Attractions (the Specialty Records division), and Associated Booking Corporation. *Billboard,* February 4, 1956, 64.

18. The club network throughout the Deep South is known as the chitlin' circuit.

19. Adams with Cohn, *Sucker for Talent,* 101.

Chapter 24: The Payola Scandal and Changing Times

1. *Billboard,* November 30, 1959, 56.

2. Refer to chapter 12.

3. Affidavit data to the U.S. Congress subcommittee supplied to me by Charlie Gillett and used with his permission. The material was intended for his book *Making Tracks* but was edited out. As for Coed Records, it survived the payola drama and enjoyed further hits with the Crests, Adam Wade, and the Duprees.

4. *Cash Box,* May 28, 1960, 38.

5. Ibid., May 27, 1961, 30.

6. Ibid., May 28, 1960, 38.

7. The formation of ARMADA was announced in *Cash Box* (October 11, 1958, 35) with the following officers: Ewart Abner (Vee-Jay), president; Sam Phillips (Sun), vice president; Nelson Verbit (Marnel distributors), secretary; and Harry Schwartz (Schwartz Bros. distributors), treasurer.

8. *Billboard*, June 8, 1959, 2.

9. Jackson, *Big Beat Heat*, 318–19.

10. The Federal Trade Commission eventually issued, with a whimper, its Trade Practice Rules with effect from 1964. Sanjek and Sanjek, *American Popular Music Business in the 20th Century*, 146.

11. *Billboard*, July 11, 1960, 3.

12. "Indie Fails: Milwaukee Distributor Throwing in the Towel" (Sherco Tapes and Records Distributing Co.), *Billboard Music Week*, March 10, 1962, 5. Among the labels distributed were Colpix, Dooto, and Riverside.

13. In 1960, distributor Joe Martin of Apex-Martin Record Sales of Newark, New Jersey, estimated that inventory had to turn over at least seven times a year for a distributor to operate profitably. "If you carry $10,000," he said, "you must do $70,000 gross business." *Billboard*, November 14, 1960, 2.

14. *Cash Box*, August 23, 1958, 35.

15. *Billboard*, June 22, 1959, 1.

16. Ibid., May 30, 1960, 4. The principle of exclusive distribution territories was always in danger of contravening the 1890 Sheridan anti-trust act, which set out to limit cartels and monopolies.

17. As an example of the rapid changes in the independent record distributors' model, Pappy Daily's long-established Houston-based firm, H. W. Daily Company, switched direction in accordance with Al Bubis's assertive assessment of those difficult times. According to *Billboard Music Week*, H. W. Daily "has quietly moved into the one-stop business here" and is "forming its own rack-jobbing company, Records of Houston" (August 18, 1962, 8).

18. The biggest hit on Tennessee Records was "Down Yonder" by female country pianist Del Wood (No. 4 pop, 1951), while Pat Boone's first three singles appeared on Republic before he signed for Dot.

19. *Billboard*, May 4, 1963, 8.

20. Ibid., June 29, 1963, 8.

21. Ibid., September 12, 1964, 8. In a preemptive strike, Cadence Records was acquired by its top artist, Andy Williams. Therefore, he assumed full control of his old masters while his new career with Columbia was flourishing and thereby forestalled a flood of cheap budget LP releases in his name.

22. In 2007, Fred Foster made a comeback as a producer with *Last of the Breed* (Lost Highway), an album with country greats Willie Nelson, Merle Haggard, and Ray Price.

23. Refer also to chapter 11.

24. *Billboard*, January 12, 1963, 6.

25. Ibid., February 23, 1963, 49. Interestingly, *Billboard* had abandoned its dedicated pop, R&B, and country jukebox charts back in June 1957. This was an early sign of the waning power of the jukebox.

26. The event was filmed for posterity by Richard Perry in the private movie *Sliced Steak*.

27. Wexler, "A Loving Look at Henry Stone," TK-10, © Jerry Wexler 1976, reproduced with permission. Wexler gave me cameo impressions on three backroom personalities who did not appear in the book text: "Wally Shuster—a song plugger (from my turf Washington Heights) and a notorious exhibitionist; Norman Rubin—promo man for Atlantic, and a bit of a scamp; Mack Emmerman— founder and original owner, Criteria Studios, Miami" (letter to author, January 17, 2008).

28. Drucker, *Classic Drucker*, 73–74.

29. The giant corporate record conglomerates as of the end of 2007 had evolved into different beasts from the major labels of the 1940s through 1960s and operated on a global scale. RCA Victor and Columbia coexisted within Sony-BMG of Japan (and Germany), but Decca was buried within Vivendi-Universal of France. In August 2007, with the majors in technological disarray, EMI-Capitol of London, England, was acquired by private equity firm Terra Firma for 3.2 billion sterling including debt (about $6.4 billion). The Warner Music Group, including Atlantic, was the only U.S.-owned major (although the other three had U.S. headquarters). See appendix D for summary of label abodes prior to publication.

Chapter 25: End of Session: Art Rupe's New Rules at Specialty Records

1. "Specialty Buys Out Champion, Opens Branch," *Billboard*, April 4, 1953, 17.

2. "What's the Matter Now" was first cut by Lloyd Price for Specialty in 1952.

3. This session was likely recorded by Johnny Vincent but was unreleased by Specialty. Joe Dyson later recorded for Vincent's Ace label in 1957.

4. Refer to chapter 3 for more on Specialty's distribution and manufacturing operations.

5. The mechanical statutory royalty rate at the time was two cents per song, normally split fifty-fifty between publisher and songwriter. There is no reference to performance royalties.

6. Within a few months, Cosimo Matassa was to relocate to Cosimo Recording Studios at 523 Governor Nicholls Street in the French Quarter of New Orleans.

7. It seems that the errant Alonzo Stewart never recorded again for Specialty, while "the band" is unknown.

8. Art Rupe could well have been referring to Dorothy La Bostrie, the co-writer of "Tutti-Frutti," although she was hardly "fat." Little Richard's "Tutti-Frutti" session was cut at Cosimo's studio on September 3, 1955. Hannusch, *I Hear You Knockin'*, 222.

9. The lines handled by A-1 Record Distributors in summer 1954 included Abbott, Apollo, Atlantic, Chess-Checker, Crown-Flair-Meteor-Modern-RPM, Duke-Peacock, Epic-OKeh, Herald, Hollywood, Specialty, Trumpet, and United-States. *Cash Box*, July 3, 1954, 80.

10. © Art Rupe 1955, with permission (the text is reproduced as typed originally, with only minor editorial refinements). The two songs listed were released by the Chimes (Specialty 555), reviewed by *Billboard* on September 10, 1955. "Tutti-Frutti" by Little Richard (Specialty 561) first broke into the R&B charts on November 26, 1955.

11. Taped responses by Art Rupe to author's questions, March 9, 2004.

Bibliography

Record Makers and Record Labels

Adams, Berle, with Gordon Cohn. *A Sucker for Talent: From Cocktail Lounges to MCA: 50 Years as Agent, Manager, and Executive.* Los Angeles: Berle Adams, 1995.

Bastin, Bruce. *Never Sell a Copyright: Joe Davis and His Role in the New York Music Scene, 1916–1978.* Chigwell, England: Storyville Publications, 1990.

Bowman, Rob. *Soulsville U.S.A.: The Story of Stax Records.* New York: Schirmer Books, 1997.

Cohen, Rich. *Machers and Rockers: Chess Records and the Business of Rock & Roll.* New York: Atlas Books, 2004.

Cohodas, Nadine. *Spinning Blues into Gold: The Chess Brothers and the Legendary Chess Records.* New York: St. Martin's Press, 2000.

Collis, John. *The Story of Chess Records.* London: Bloomsbury Publishing, 1998.

Cook, Richard. *Blue Note Records: The Biography.* Boston: Justin, Charles and Co., 2001.

Cornyn, Stanley, with Paul Scanlon. *Exploding: The Highs, Hits, Hype, Heroes, and Hustlers of the Warner Music Group.* New York: HarperCollins, 2002.

Dahl, Bill. *Motown: The Golden Years.* Iola, WI: Krause Publications, 2001.

Dannen, Fredric. *Hit Men.* New York: Times Books, 1990.

Ertegun, Ahmet, et al. *"What'd I Say": The Atlantic Story, 50 Years of Music.* New York: Welcome Rain, 2001.

Escott, Colin, with Martin Hawkins. *Good Rockin' Tonight: Sun Records and the Birth of Rock 'n' Roll.* New York: St. Martin's Press, 1991.

Finnis, Rob. *The Phil Spector Story.* London: Rob Finnis and Rockon, 1975.

Gart, Galen. *ARLD: The American Record Label Directory and Dating Guide, 1940–1959.* Milford, NH: Big Nickel Publications, 1989.

Gart, Galen, and Roy C. Ames. *Duke/Peacock Records: An Illustrated History with Discography.* Milford, NH: Big Nickel Publications, 1990.

Gillett, Charlie. *Making Tracks: The History of Atlantic Records.* St. Albans, England: Panther Books, 1975.

———. *The Sound of the City: The Rise of Rock and Roll.* Rev. ed. London: Souvenir Press, 1983.

Goldsmith, Peter D. *Making People's Music: Moe Asch and Folkways Records.* Washington, DC: Smithsonian Institution Press, 1998.

Gordy, Berry. *To Be Loved: The Music, the Magic, the Memories of Motown.* New York: Warner Books, 1994.

Grein, Paul. *Capitol Records Fiftieth Anniversary, 1942–1992.* Hollywood: Capitol Records, 1992.

Hawkins, Martin. *A Shot in the Dark: Making Records in Nashville, 1945–1955.* Nashville: Vanderbilt University Press (with the Country Music Foundation Press), 2006.

Isoardi, Steven L. *Central Avenue Sounds: Joseph Bihari.* Los Angeles: Regents of the University of California, 1997. [A series of interviews.]

Jarrett, Ted, with Ruth White. *You Can Make It If You Try: The Ted Jarrett Story of R&B in Nashville.* Franklin, TN: Country Music Foundation/Hillsboro Press, 2005.

Kahn, Ashley. *The House That Trane Built: The Story of Impulse Records.* New York: W. W. Norton, 2006.

Keane, Bob. *The Oracle of Del-Fi: My Life in Music with Ritchie Valens, Sam Cooke, Frank Zappa, Barry White and Other Legends.* Los Angeles: Del-Fi International Books, 2006.

Kelly, Michael "Doc Rock." *Liberty Records: A History of the Recording Company and Its Stars, 1955–1971.* Jefferson, NC: McFarland, 1993.

Kennedy, Rick, and Randy McNutt. *Little Labels—Big Sound.* Bloomington: Indiana University Press, 1999. [Includes studies on Ace, Duke-Peacock, King, Monument, and Sun.]

Killen, Buddy, with Tom Carter. *By the Seat of My Pants: My Life in Country Music.* New York: Simon and Schuster, 1993.

Knoedelseder, William. *Stiffed: A True Story of MCA, the Music Business and the Mafia.* New York: HarperCollins, 1993.

Kruger, Jeffrey. *My Life with the Stars (Angels and Assholes).* Hove, England: Kruger Organisation, 1999.

Leadbitter, Mike, and Eddie Shuler. *From the Bayou: The Story of Goldband Records.* Bexhill-on-Sea, England: Blues Unlimited, 1969.

Leonard, Joe, with Shaun Mather. *Rockabilly, Radio, and WWII: Memoirs of Joe M. Leonard, Jr.* Austin, TX: Nortex Press, 2002.

Lewis, E. R. (Sir Edward). *No C.I.C.* London: Universal Royalties, 1956.

Marmorstein, Gary. *The Label: The Story of Columbia Records.* New York: Thunder's Mouth Press, 2007.

Martland, Peter. *Since Records Began: EMI; The First 100 Years.* Portland, OR: Amadeus Press, 1997.

Otis, Johnny. *Upside Your Head! Rhythm and Blues on Central Avenue.* Hanover, NH: Wesleyan University Press, 1993.

Porterfield, Nolan. *Last Cavalier: The Life and Times of John A. Lomax, 1867–1948.* Urbana: University of Illinois Press, 1996.

Posner, Gerald. *Motown: Music, Money, Sex, and Power.* New York: Random House, 2002.

Randolph, Michael. *The Soul of American Popular Music: The Photographs of "PoPsie" Randolph.* New York: Hal Leonard, 2007.

Reig, Teddy, with Edward Berger. *Reminiscing in Tempo: The Life and Times of a Jazz Hustler.* Metuchen, NJ: Scarecrow Press and the Institute of Jazz Studies, Rutgers University, 1990.

Rene, Leon, ed. *Exclusive Records: Royalty of Records—Crest of Distinctive Music.* Hollywood: Exclusive Records, 1946.

Ryan, Marc W. *Trumpet Records: Diamonds on Farish Street.* Jackson: University Press of Mississippi, 2004.

Shaw, Arnold. *Honkers and Shouters: The Golden Years of Rhythm and Blues.* New York: Collier Books, 1978.

Southall, Brian. *The A–Z of Record Labels.* London: Sanctuary Publishing, 2000.

Thiele, Bob, as told to Bob Golden. *What a Wonderful World: A Lifetime of Recordings.* New York: Oxford University Press, 1995.

Wade, Dorothy, and Justine Picardie. *Music Man: Ahmet Ertegun, Atlantic Records, and the Triumph of Rock 'n' Roll.* New York: W. W. Norton, 1990.

Wexler, Jerry, and David Ritz. *Rhythm and the Blues: A Life in American Music.* New York: Alfred A. Knopf, 1993.

Discographical

Ferlingere, Robert D. *A Discography of Rhythm and Blues and Rock 'n' Roll Vocal Groups, 1945 to 1965.* 3rd ed. Jackson, CA: Effendee Trust, 1999.

Gonzalez, Fernando L. *Disco-file: The Discographical Catalog of Rock and Roll and Rhythm and Blues Vocal Harmony Groups: Race, Rhythm and Blues, Rock and Roll, Soul, 1902–1976.* 2nd ed. New York: Fernando L. Gonzalez, 1977.

Leadbitter, Mike, Leslie Fancourt, and Paul Pelletier. *Blues Records 1943 to 1970: Volume 2, L to Z.* London: Record Information Services, 1994.

Leadbitter, Mike, and Neil Slaven. *Blues Records 1943 to 1970: Volume 1, A to K.* London: Record Information Services, 1987.

McGrath, Bob. *The R&B Indies.* 2nd ed. 4 vols. West Vancouver, Canada: Eyeball Productions, 2005–07.

Pelletier, Paul. *Complete British Directory of Popular 78/45 rpm Singles 1950–1980, Volume 1: Columbia, Decca, H.M.V.* Forest Hill, London: Record Information Services, 1986.

———. *Decca: Complete Singles Catalogue 1954–1983.* Chessington, England: Record Information Services, 1984.

———. *London: Complete Singles Catalogue 1949–1982.* Chessington, England: Record Information Services, 1982.

———. *Top Rank—Stateside—Triumph—Palette Singles/E.P. Listing.* London: Record Information Services, 1976.

Riswick, Don. *Nothin' but Instrumentals: A Compendium of Rock Instrumentals.* Portsmouth, VA: Don Riswick, 1985.

Ruppli, Michel. *The Aladdin/Imperial Labels: A Discography.* Westport, CT: Greenwood Press, 1991.

———. *Atlantic Records: A Discography.* Westport, CT: Greenwood Press, 1979.

———. *The Chess Labels: A Discography.* Westport, CT: Greenwood Press, 1983.

———. *The Decca Labels: A Discography.* Westport, CT: Greenwood Press, 1996.

———. *The King Labels: A Discography.* Westport, CT: Greenwood Press, 1985.

Ruppli, Michel, and Ed Novitsky. *The Mercury Labels: A Discography.* Westport, CT: Greenwood Press, 1993.

Topping, Ray. *New Orleans Rhythm and Blues Record Label Listings.* Bexhill-on-Sea, England: Flyright Records, 1978.

Various. *4 Star Hillbilly Sessions.* Edgware, UK: Hillbilly Researcher, 2004.

General

Aberbach, Julian J. *Art Donations from the Collections of the Aberbach Brothers.* New York: Aberbach Enterprises, 2001.

Allan, Johnnie. *A Pictorial History of South Louisiana Music 1920s-1980s.* Lafayette, LA: Jadel Publishing, 1988.

Baptista, Todd R. *Group Harmony: Behind the Rhythm and the Blues.* New Bedford, MA: TRB Enterprises, 1996.

Barlow, William. *Voice Over: The Making of Black Radio.* Philadelphia: Temple University Press, 1999.

Belz, Carl. *The Story of Rock.* 2nd ed. New York: Oxford University Press, 1972.

Bernard, Shane. *Swamp Pop: Cajun and Creole Rhythm and Blues.* Jackson: University of Mississippi Press, 1996.

Berry, Chuck. *The Autobiography.* New York: Harmony Books, 1987.

Bianco, Anthony. *Ghosts of 42nd Street: A History of America's Most Infamous Block.* New York: William Morrow, 2004.

"Billboard" 1963–64 International Music-Record Directory and Buyer's Guide. Cincinnati: The Billboard Publishing Company, 1963.

Bjorn, Lars, with Jim Gallert. *Before Motown: A History of Jazz in Detroit, 1920–1960.* Ann Arbor: University of Michigan Press, 2001.

Bronson, Fred. *The Billboard Book of Number One Hits.* New York: Billboard Publications, 1992.

Broven, John. *South to Louisiana: The Music of the Cajun Bayous.* Gretna, LA: Pelican, 1983.

———. *Walking to New Orleans: The Story of New Orleans Rhythm and Blues.* Bexhill-on-Sea, England: Blues Unlimited, 1974. Republished as *Rhythm and Blues in New Orleans.* Gretna, LA: Pelican, 1978.

Brown, Ruth, with Andrew Yule. *Miss Rhythm: The Autobiography of Ruth Brown, Rhythm and Blues Legend.* New York: Penguin Books, 1996.

Carey, Dave, and Albert J. McCarthy. *Jazz Directory.* London: Cassell, 1950.

Carson, David. *Rockin' Down the Dial: The Detroit Sound of Radio from Jack the Bellboy to the Big 8.* Troy, MI: Momentum Books, 2000.

Chapple, Steve, and Reebee Garofalo. *Rock 'n' Roll Is Here to Pay: The History and Politics of the Music Industry.* Chicago: Nelson-Hall, 1977.

Chilton, John. *Let the Good Times Roll: The Story of Louis Jordan and His Music.* London: Quartet Books, 1992.

Cogan, Jim, and William Clark. *Temples of Sound: Inside the Great Recording Studios.* San Francisco: Chronicle Books, 2003.

Cohn, Nick. *Awopbopaloobop Alopbamboom: Pop from the Beginning.* London: Weidenfeld and Nicolson, 1969.

Coleman, Mark. *Playback: From the Victrola to MP3, 100 Years of Music, Machines, and Money.* Cambridge, MA: Da Capo Press, 2003.

Coleman, Rick. *Blue Monday: Fats Domino and the Lost Dawn of Rock 'n' Roll.* Cambridge, MA: Da Capo Press, 2006.

Collier, James Lincoln. *Louis Armstrong: An American Genius.* New York: Oxford University Press, 1983.

Cooper, Daniel. *Lefty Frizzell: The Honky-Tonk Life of Country Music's Greatest Singer.* Boston: Little, Brown, 1995.

Cotten, Lee. *Reelin' and Rockin': The Golden Age of American Rock 'n' Roll, Volume II, 1956–1959.* Ann Arbor: Popular Culture, Ink, 1995.

———. *Shake Rattle and Roll: The Golden Age of American Rock 'n' Roll, Volume I, 1952–1955.* Ann Arbor: Pierian Press, 1989.

———. *Twist and Shout: The Golden Age of American Rock 'n' Roll, Volume III, 1960–1963.* Sacramento: High Sierra Books, 2002.

Cox, Bette Yarborough. *Central Avenue—Its Rise and Fall (1890–c. 1955).* Los Angeles: BEEM Publications, 1993.

Dachs, David. *Anything Goes: The World of Popular Music.* Indianapolis: Bobbs-Merrill, 1964.

Dawson, Jim. *The Twist: The Story of the Song and Dance That Changed the World.* Boston: Faber and Faber, 1995.

Dawson, Jim, and Steve Propes. *45 RPM: The History, Heroes and Villains of a Pop Music Revolution*. San Francisco: Backbeat Books, 2003.

———. *What Was the First Rock 'n' Roll Record?* Boston: Faber and Faber, 1992.

Deffaa, Chip. *Blue Rhythms: Six Lives in Rhythm and Blues*. Urbana: University of Illinois Press, 1996.

Dixon, Willie, with Don Snowden. *I Am The Blues*. New York: Quartet Books, 1989.

Douglas, Tony. *Lonely Teardrops: The Jackie Wilson Story*. London: Sanctuary, 1997.

Drate, Spencer, ed. *45 RPM: A Visual History of the Seven-Inch Record*. New York: Princeton Architectural Press, 2002.

Drucker, Peter F. *Classic Drucker*. Boston: Harvard Business School Publishing, 2006.

———. *Essential Drucker*. New York: HarperCollins, 2001.

DuBois, Nadine. *The History of Times Square Records*. Newmarket, NH: Nadine DuBois, 2007.

Emerson, Ken. *Always Magic in the Air: The Bomp and Brilliance of the Brill Building Era*. New York: Viking Penguin Books, 2005.

Escott, Colin. "50 Years of Country Music from Mercury" (CD booklet). Various artists, Mercury CD 314526691.

Escott, Colin, with George Merritt and William MacEwen. *Hank Williams: The Biography*. New York: Little, Brown, 1994.

Fong-Torres, Ben. *The Hits Just Keep On Coming: The History of Top 40 Radio*. San Francisco: Miller Freeman Books, 1998.

Ford, Robert. *A Blues Bibliography: The International Literature of an Afro-American Music Genre*. Bromley, England: Paul Pelletier, 1999.

Fox, Ted. *In the Groove: The People behind the Music*. New York: St. Martin's Press, 1986.

Franks, Tillman (with Robert Gentry). *I Was There When It Happened*. Many, LA: Sweet Dreams, 2000.

Freeland, David. *Ladies of Soul*. Jackson: University Press of Mississippi, 2001.

Gart, Galen, ed. *First Pressings: The History of Rhythm and Blues*. 12 vols. Milford, NH: Big Nickel Publications, 1986–2002.

Goodman, Fred. *The Mansion on the Hill: Dylan, Young, Geffen, Springsteen, and the Head-On Collision of Rock and Commerce*. New York: Times Books, 1997.

Grissom, John. *Country Music: White Man's Blues*. New York: Coronet Communications, 1970.

Guralnick, Peter. *Dream Boogie: The Triumph of Sam Cooke*. New York: Little, Brown, 2005.

———. *Last Train to Memphis: The Rise of Elvis Presley*. Boston: Little, Brown, 1994.

Halberstadt, Alex. *Lonely Avenue: The Unlikely Life and Times of Doc Pomus*. Cambridge, MA: Da Capo Press, 2007.

Hannusch, Jeff. *I Hear You Knockin': The Sound of New Orleans Rhythm and Blues*. Ville Platte, LA: Swallow Publications, 1985.

———. *The Soul of New Orleans: A Legacy of Rhythm and Blues*. Ville Platte, LA: Swallow Publications, 2001.

Hertzberg, Arthur. *The Jews in America: Four Centuries of an Uneasy Encounter; A History*. New York: Columbia University Press, 1997.

Hoskyns, Barney. *Waiting for the Sun: Strange Days, Weird Scenes and the Sound of Los Angeles*. New York: St. Martin's Press, 1996.

Inside the Recording Industry: An Introduction to America's Music Business. New York: RIAA, 1985.

Jackson, John A. *American Bandstand: Dick Clark and the Making of a Rock 'n' Roll Empire*. New York: Oxford University Press, 1997.

———. *Big Beat Heat: Alan Freed and the Early Years of Rock and Roll.* New York: Schirmer Books, 1991.

———. *A House on Fire: The Rise and Fall of Philadelphia Soul.* New York: Oxford University Press, 2004.

Jancik, Wayne. *The Billboard Book of One-Hit Wonders.* New York: Billboard Books, 1990.

Jasen, David A. *Tin Pan Alley: The Composers, the Songs, the Performers and Their Times.* New York: Donald I. Fine, 1988.

Kelley, Norman, ed. *R&B Rhythm and Business: The Political Economy of Black Music.* New York: Akashic Books, 2005.

Kernfeld, Barry, ed. *The New Grove Dictionary of Jazz.* New York: St. Martin's Press, 1996.

Kingsbury, Paul, ed. *The Encyclopedia of Country Music.* New York: Oxford University Press, 1998.

Krasilovsky, M. William, and Sidney Shemel. *This Business of Music: The Definitive Guide to the Music Industry.* 8th ed. New York: Billboard Books, 2000.

Krivine, J. *Juke Box Saturday Night.* Secaucus NJ: Chartwell Books, 1977.

Kukla, Barbara J. *Swing City: Newark Nightlife, 1925–50.* Philadelphia: Temple University Press, 1991.

Lackmann, Ron. *The Encyclopedia of American Radio: An A–Z Guide to Radio.* New York: Checkmark Books, 1996.

Leadbitter, Mike. *Delta Blues.* Unpublished manuscript, 1974.

———, ed. *Nothing but the Blues: An Illustrated Documentary.* London: Hanover Books, 1971.

Lydon, Michael. *Ray Charles: Man and Music.* New York: Riverhead, 1998.

Lynch, Vincent, and Bill Henkin. *Jukeboxes: The Golden Age.* London: Thames and Hudson, 1981.

MacDonald, J. Fred. *Don't Touch That Dial! Radio Programming in American Life from 1920 to 1960.* Chicago: Nelson Hall, 1979.

Malone, Bill C. *Country Music U.S.A.* Austin: University of Texas Press, 1968.

Millar, Bill. *Let the Good Times Rock! A Fan's Notes on Post-War American Roots Music.* York, England: Music Mentor, 2004.

Millard, Andre. *America on Record: A History of Recorded Sound.* Cambridge: University of Cambridge Press, 1995.

Murrells, Joseph. *The Book of Golden Discs.* London: Barrie and Jenkins, 1974.

Oliver, Paul. *Blues Fell This Morning.* London: Cassell, 1960.

Olsen, Eric, Paul Verna, and Carlo Wolff. *The Encyclopedia of Record Producers.* New York: Billboard Books, 1999.

Otfinoski, Steve. *The Golden Age of Rock Instrumentals.* New York: Billboard Books, 1997.

Passman, Arnold. *The Deejays.* New York: Macmillan, 1971.

Pavlow, Big Al. *The R&B Book: A Disc-History of Rhythm and Blues.* Providence, RI: Music House Publishing, 1983.

Pollock, Bruce. *When Rock Was Young: A Nostalgic Review of the Top 40 Era.* New York: Holt, Rinehart and Winston, 1981.

Propes, Steve, and Galen Gart. *L.A. R&B Vocal Groups 1945–1965.* Milford, NH: Big Nickel Publications, 2001.

Pruter, Robert. *Chicago Soul.* Urbana: University of Illinois Press, 1991.

———. *Doowop: The Chicago Scene.* Urbana: University of Illinois Press, 1996.

Read, Oliver, and Walter L. Welch. *From Tin Foil to Stereo.* Indianapolis: Bobbs-Merrill, 1959.

Rhythm and Blues BMI 1943–1968. New York: BMI, 1969. [Song awards listing.]

Rolontz, Robert. *How to Get Your Song Recorded.* New York: Watson-Gupthill Publications, 1963.

Romano, Will. *Big Boss Man: The Life and Music of Bluesman Jimmy Reed.* San Francisco: Backbeat Books, 2006.

Rosin, James. *Rock, Rhythm and Blues: A Look at the National Recording Artists from the City of Brotherly Love.* Philadelphia: Autumn Road Company, 2004.

Rowe, Mike. *Chicago Breakdown.* London: Eddison Press, 1973.

Russell, Tony. *Country Music Records: A Discography, 1921–1942.* New York: Oxford University Press, 2004.

Salem, James M. *The Late, Great Johnny Ace and the Transition from R&B to Rock 'n' Roll.* Urbana: University of Illinois Press, 1999.

Sanjek, Russell, and David Sanjek. *American Popular Music Business in the 20th Century.* New York: Oxford University Press, 1991.

Schiffman, Jack. *Uptown: The Story of Harlem's Apollo Theatre.* New York: Cowles, 1971.

Shapiro, Nat, ed. *Popular Music: An Annotated Index of American Popular Songs.* 6 vols. New York: Adrian Press, 1964–73.

Shaw, Arnold. *52nd Street: The Street of Jazz.* New York: Da Capo Press, 1977.

———. *The Rockin' '50s: The Decade That Transformed the Pop Music Scene.* New York: Hawthorn Books, 1974.

Simons, David. *Studio Stories: How the Great New York Records Were Made.* San Francisco: Backbeat Books, 2004.

Smith, Joe. *Off the Record: An Oral History of Popular Music.* Edited by Mitchell Fink. New York: Warner Books, 1988.

Smith, Joseph C. *The Day the Music Died.* London: W. H. Allen, 1982.

Smith, R. J. *The Great Black Way: L.A. in the 1940s and the Lost African-American Renaissance.* New York: PublicAffairs, 2006.

Smith, Wes. *The Pied Pipers of Rock 'n' Roll: Radio Deejays of the '50s and '60s.* Marietta, GA: Longstreet Press, 1989.

Solomon, Clive. *Record Hits: The British Top 50 Charts 1952–1977.* London: Omnibus Press, 1979.

Spizer, Bruce. *The Beatles Records on Vee-Jay: Songs, Pictures and Stories of the Fabulous Beatles Records on Vee-Jay.* New Orleans: 498 Productions, 1998.

Sturdivant, John, producer, and Chuck Neese, ed. *Country Music Who's Who 1972.* New York: Record World, 1972.

Toop, David. *The Rap Attack: African Jive to New York Hip Hop.* London: Pluto Press, 1984.

Townley, Eric. *Tell Your Story.* Chigwell, Essex, England: Storyville Publications, 1976.

Tracy, Steven C. *Going to Cincinnati: A History of the Blues in the Queen City.* Urbana: University of Illinois Press, 1993.

Trepel Jordan, Mimi. Unpublished autobiography, 1981.

Wallis, Roger, and Krister Malm. *Big Sounds from Small Peoples: The Music Industry in Small Countries.* London: Constable, 1984.

Warner, Alan. *Who Sang What in Rock 'n' Roll.* London: Blandford, 1990.

Whitburn, Joel. *Pop Memories 1890–1954: The History of American Popular Music.* Menomonee Falls, WI: Record Research, 1986.

———. *Top Country Singles 1944–1988.* Menomonee Falls, WI: Record Research, 1989.

———. *Top Pop Singles 1955–1996.* Menomonee Falls, WI: Record Research, 1997.

———. *Top R&B Singles 1942–1988.* Menomonee Falls, WI: Record Research, 1988.

Whitcomb, Ian. *Whole Lotta Shakin': A Rock 'n' Roll Scrapbook.* London: Arrow Books, 1982.

Who's Who in Music: The Billboard Encyclopedia of Music 1946–1947. Cincinnati: The Billboard Publishing Company, 1946.

Wilder, Alec. *American Popular Song: The Great Innovators, 1900–1950.* New York: Oxford University Press, 1972.

Wolfe, Charles K. *Classic Country: Legends of Country Music.* New York: Routledge, 2001.

Wolfman, Ira. *Jewish New York: Notable Neighborhoods and Memorable Moments.* New York: Universe Publishing, 2003.

Wunderman, Lester. *Being Direct: Making Advertising Pay.* New York: Random House, 1996.

Magazines and Newspapers

Ackerman, Paul. "Mercury Records 25th Anniversary." *Billboard,* May 27, 1972.

Broven, John. "All for One: Harold Battiste." *Blues Unlimited* 146, Autumn/Winter 1984.

———. "Bobby's Happy House of Hits: The Story of Bobby Robinson and His Famous Labels." Pts. 1 and 2. *Juke Blues,* Spring 1989; Summer 1989.

———. "The Golden Crest Records Story." *American Music Magazine,* September 1999.

———. "I Knew Leonard at the Macomba . . . Paul Gayten." *Blues Unlimited* 130, Summer 1978.

———. "Larry Dale: The New York Houserocker." *Juke Blues,* Summer 1987.

———. "The Southern Record Men: Jay D. Miller." *Blues Unlimited* 1, April 1963.

Colbert, Haines. "For Deejays: Babes, Bribes and Booze." *Miami News,* May 31, 1959.

Cooper, Daniel. "Boogie-Woogie White Boy: The Redemption of 'Hossman' Allen." *Nashville Scene,* March 4, 1993.

Dannen, Fredric. "The Godfather of Rock & Roll." *Rolling Stone,* November 17, 1988.

Daughtrey, Larry. "The Man Who Went Giddyup." *Nashville Tennessean Magazine,* December 19, 1965. [About Don Pierce.]

Delaney, Joe. "New Orleans Beginning to Challenge Chicago, Nashville as Waxing Center." *Down Beat,* January 28, 1953.

Evans, Simon. "Kroonin' with the Kool Kwintets: The Story of 'Rhythm and Blues' Magazine." *Blues and Rhythm,* February 2004.

Gleason, Ralph. "Big Wheel and New Disk Deals (Morris Levy, Music Octopus)." *Variety,* October 30, 1957.

Grendysa, Peter. "Manhattan Rides the Range—Atlantic's Rarest Country Records." *Discoveries,* September 1998.

Grevatt, Ren. "Dick Clark—a Fortune Being Shy!" *Melody Maker,* May 2, 1959.

———. "Disk Breakout Power Wanes in Traditional Debut Areas." *Billboard,* December 1, 1958.

Gross, Mike. "Indies' Hit-'n'-Run Score: Heckle Majors 'At Any Cost.'" *Variety,* October 23, 1957.

Horowitz, Is. "Donut Platters Set to Put 78's into Early Total Eclipse: Col's [Columbia's] Move to Discontinue Disks Signposts Coming 78 R.P.M. Demise." *Billboard,* April 14, 1956.

———. "Juke Box Influence on Record Business." *Billboard,* May 23, 1953.

Knoedelseder, William K., Jr. "Morris Levy: Big Clout in Record Industry; His Behind-the-Scenes Influence Is Felt Throughout the Industry." *Los Angeles Times,* July 20, 1986.

Kochakian, Dan. "The Internship of Doc Pomus." *Whiskey, Women, and . . .,* July 1982.

Leadbitter, Mike. "Serving the South: Stan Lewis." *Blues Unlimited* 105, December 1973/January 1974.

———. "Sittin' In Again." *Blues Unlimited* 109, August/September 1974. [About Bob Shad.]

Leadbitter, Mike, and Ian Whitcomb. "The Specialist." *Blues Unlimited* 104, October/November 1973. [About Art Rupe.]

"Little Indie Jackpots: Brand-New Label Can Hit It—with Real Hot Disk." *Billboard*, May 25, 1959.

Mabry, Donald J. "The Rise and Fall of Ace Records [of Mississippi]: A Case Study in the Independent Record Business." *Harvard Business History Review* 64 (Autumn 1990).

Moore, Roy. "King Records Suing Dozens over Licensing." *Nashville Business Journal* (on-line ed.), April 30, 2004.

Ostrow, Marty. "ABC-Paramount: The Big 5th!" *Cash Box*, June 25, 1960.

Paulsen, Gary (with Frank Scott, Bruce Bromberg, and Pete Welding). "Jules Bihari!" *Blues Unlimited* 68, December 1969.

Poe, Delores. "Senate Report Lauds Coin Industry, but Warns of Underworld Inroads." *Billboard*, April 4, 1960.

"Praise and Scold Coin Industry in McClellan Rackets Report." *Billboard*, April 4, 1960.

Rolontz, Bob. "Mushrooming R.&B.'s: Labels Sprout New Labels; Even Subsids Have Subsids." *Billboard*, May 23, 1953.

———. "Tenth Avenue—Street of Hope." *Billboard*, September 5, 1953.

———. "What Price a Diskery? Trend to Swap Independence for $-Backed Security." *Billboard*, December 1, 1958.

Sax, Dave. "Cowboy Copas." *American Music Magazine*, December 2004.

Simon, Bill. "Injection Molding's A-Coming? Market Eyes Cheap, Fast Kidisk Method: Adoption Soon Possible." *Billboard*, May 13, 1950.

"Smaller Record Firms Spin to Success." *Business Week*, September 7, 1957, 48–58.

Spady, James G. "Black Music and Independent Labels Have a Long History." *Philadelphia New Observer*, June 12, 1996.

Streissguth, Mike. "Old Town: An Interview with Owner and Founder Hy Weiss." *Goldmine*, May 9, 1997.

Tosches, Nick. "Hipsters and Hoodlums." *Vanity Fair*, December 2000.

Turco, Art. "Bobby Robinson: The Interview." *Record Exchanger*, nos. 10–12, 1972.

Wexler, Jerry. "A Loving Look at Henry Stone." *Cash Box*, March 27, 1976.

Wexler, Jerry, and Ahmet Ertegun. "The Latest Trend: R&B Disks Are Going Pop." *Cash Box*, July 3, 1954.

Wilson, Earl. "Alan Freed Telling All about Payola House Problems: Drops TV Shows." *New York Post*, November 25, 1959.

Selected CDs

There is a raft of independent "label story" compact discs on the market, while many key tracks are now available for downloading from Apple's "jukebox in the sky" (and others). This selected list of CDs—some of which will no longer be available with the passage of time—is annotated alphabetically by label and will serve to illustrate the music produced by the original independent record makers.

That'll Flat Git It, vol. 13, Bear Family (Germany) BCD 15972. Rock 'n' roll with an independent label feel from ABC-Paramount.

Mark Lamarr's Ace Is Wild, Westside WESA 812. The rockin' side of Johnny Vincent's Ace label of Jackson, Mississippi.

Gumbo Stew: A.F.O. New Orleans R&B, vols. 1–3, Ace (UK) CDCHD 450/462/520. Harold Battiste's starry-eyed New Orleans venture.

The Aladdin Records Story (double CD), EMI E2 30883/4. The R&B and rock 'n' roll (but not jazz) output of Leo and Eddie Mesner from Los Angeles.

Atlantic Rhythm and Blues 1947–1974 (8 CDs), Atlantic 7 82305–2. The glistening "Little Tiffany" of Ahmet and Nesuhi Ertegun, Herb and Miriam Abramson, and Jerry Wexler.

Rock 'n' Roll Bell Ringers, Ace (UK) CDCHD 1042. The Bell budget label headed by Arthur Shimkin in New York.

Cameo Parkway 1957–1967 (4 CDs), ABKCO 18771. Bernie Lowe and Kal Mann's more-than-just-a-teen-dance label from Philadelphia, with A&R man Dave Appell.

The Chess Story 1947–1975 (15 CDs), MCA 3805962. Over 330 recordings from Leonard and Phil's hallowed Chess-Checker-Argo Chicago combine; includes a CD of nice interviews of Phil Chess by Mary Katherine Aldin, and of Marshall Chess by Paul Jones.

The Class and Rendezvous Story, Ace (UK) CDCHD 461. Mostly Leon Rene's successful sojourn in West Coast rock 'n' roll with Class.

The Cobra Records Story (2 CDs), Capricorn 9 42012–2. The Chicago blues and R&B label run by Eli Toscano and Howard Bedno.

Dot Records Cover to Cover, Ace (UK) CDCHD 609; *Dot Rock 'n' Roll*, Ace (UK) CDCHD 592. The Randy Wood cover version anthology, together with the raunchier side of Dot led by Sanford Clark's "The Fool" (but no "Ape Call" by Nervous Norvus or the Dell-Vikings' classics "Come Go with Me" and "Whispering Bells").

The Excello Story, vols. 1–4, Hip-O HIPD-40149/50/56/57. Ernie Young's storied Nashville blues and R&B imprint, with J. D. Miller's Louisiana swamp blues productions.

The Fire/Fury Records Story (2 CDs), Capricorn 9 42009–2. The Bobby Robinson Harlem overview.

That'll Flat Git It, vol. 26, Bear Family (Germany) BCD 16876. The rockabilly-style 4 Star masters under Bill McCall and Don Pierce.

Eddie's House of Hits: The Story of Goldband Records, Ace (UK) CDCHD 424. Eddie Shuler's raw Louisiana sounds from Lake Charles.

The Fabulous Wailers, Ace (UK) CDCHD 675, Norton (US) CNW 901; *Golden Crest Instrumentals*, Ace (UK) CDCHD 724; *Altar of Dreams: Classic East Coast Doo Wop & Girl Groups*, Early Bird EBCD 1001. The Wailers excepted, the Golden Crest acts that just could not make the charts.

The Golden Era of Doowops: The Groups of Ember Records, Relic 7060, 7100; *The Golden Era of Doowops: The Groups of Herald Records*, Relic 7059, 7099. The vocal group perspective of Al Silver's Herald-Ember Records of New York, compiled and annotated by Donn Fileti.

The Jewel/Paula Records Story (2 CDs), Capricorn 9 42014–2. From Shreveport, Louisiana, Stan Lewis's late-starting labels with the emphasis on blues, R&B, and soul.

The Early Jin Singles: Southland Rock 'n' Roll, Ace (UK) CDCHD 878; *Floyd's Early Cajun Singles*, Ace (UK) CDCHD 743. The debut swamp pop and Cajun music on Floyd Soileau's Jin-Swallow labels out of Ville Platte, Louisiana.

The King R&B Box Set (4 CDs), King KBSCD-7002. Syd Nathan's R&B highlights from Cincinnati, Ohio, including Sydney's rants to his staff.

The Mercury Blues 'n' Rhythm Story 1945–1955 (8 CDs), Mercury 314 528 292–2. This is where Berle Adams and Irving Green started out in Chicago.

The Complete Meteor Blues, R&B and Gospel Recordings (2 CDs), Ace (UK) CDCH2 1090; *The Complete Meteor Rockabilly and Hillbilly Recordings* (2 CDs), Ace (UK) CDCH2 885. Every singles release ("A" and "B" side) from Lester Bihari's Memphis-based label.

The Modern Records Story, Ace (UK) CDCHD 784. A minuscule cross-section of the pioneering West Coast label of Jules, Saul, and Joe Bihari.

The Monument Story (2 CDs), Sony Music, A2K66106. Fred Foster's key moments on his journey from Baltimore to Nashville via Hendersonville, Tennessee.

The Complete Motown Singles, Vol. 1: 1959–1961 (6 CDs and vinyl single), Hip-O Select B0003631–02. The opening offerings from Berry Gordy's Tamla-Motown production line in Detroit.

Hy Weiss Presents Old Town Records (2 CDs), Ace (UK) CDCH2 979. The tasteful New York black sounds from Hy Weiss's inimitable enterprise.

The Rama Story, Westside (UK) WESD 215; *The End Story*, Westside (UK) WESD 205; *The Gone Story* (2 CDs), Westside (UK) WESD 206; *The Red Bird Story* (2 CDs), Charly (UK) CD LAB 105. George Goldner's remarkable New York milestones from 1953 to 1966.

The Roulette Story 1957–77 (3 CDs), Westside (UK) WESX 305. Morris Levy's eclectic New York label, from pop to jazz, including the hit Hugo & Luigi productions.

Stompin' at the Savoy (4 CDs), Savoy Jazz SVY 17435. Primarily Herman Lubinsky's Savoy releases but also selections from the acquired National and Excelsior catalogs.

The Specialty Story (5 CDs), Specialty 5SPCD-4412-2; *Art Rupe: The Story of Specialty Records*, Ace (UK) CDCH2 542. The comprehensive Specialty boxed retrospective and the big Specialty hits on two CDs, interspersed with erudite Art Rupe comments (no longer available).

Southern Soul Showcase: Cryin' in the Streets, Kent (UK) CDKEND 243. Shelby Singleton's significant southern recordings from SSS International of Nashville.

Starday-Dixie Rockabilly, vols. 1 and 2, Ace (UK) CDCHD 704 and 708. Primo southern rockabilly from the Pappy Daily–Don Pierce labels.

The Sue Records Story: The Sound of Soul (4 CDs), EMI 7243 8 28093 2 6. The Juggy Murray black music gems from New York.

Sun Record Company 50 Golden Years 1952–2002: A Commemorative Collection (8 CDs and a vinyl disc), Sanctuary (UK) FBUBX002; *The Complete Sun Singles* (5 separate CD box sets), Bear Family (Germany). Sam Phillips's enduring legacy: the Sun label of Memphis, Tennessee.

Vee-Jay: The Definitive Collection (4 CDs), Shout! Factory SHFT 82666310485. Second only to Chess in the Chicago pantheon through Vivian Carter, James Bracken and Ewart Abner.

The Doo Wop Box, Rhino R2 71463. All the prime vocal group hits, including those by the Penguins, the Flamingos, the Moonglows, Frankie Lymon and the Teenagers, and the Platters.

Golden Age of American Rock 'n' Roll, vols. 1–11 and special editions, Ace (UK). Familiar and unfamiliar Top 100 hits from 1954 to 1963, mainly on indie labels (but not exclusively so). Time-Life Music has a similar "Malt Shop Memories" series.

Index

Note: Page numbers in italic refer to illustrations.

A&M Records, 19, 65, 314
Abbey Road studios (London), 68, 306
ABC (American Broadcasting Company), 19, 369, 417, 439, 443–44, 540n1
ABC-Paramount (Am-Par) Records, 55, 80, 165, 181, 213, 262, 301, 303, 321–23, 350, 369, 373–74, 376–77, 379, 390, 392, 411, 418, 422–23, 427; ABC/DunhillRecords, 445; Apt Records, 361, 411, 444, 527n15; formation of record label by ABC and Paramount Theatres, 439–40, 441–45; Impulse Records, 445; takeover of, 445, 446, 462, 509n3, 510n7, 525n16, 533n13, 535n20, 536n13, 537n1, 539n10, 540n1
Aberbach, Jean, 65, 267–71, 273–74, 276, 423, 519n11, 527n21, 528n28, 539n15
Aberbach, Julian, 65, 89, 253, 267–71, 274, 276, 423, 516n20, 519n11, 527n21, 528n28, 539n15
ABKCO Records, 350, 432, 446, 525n20
Abner, Ewart, 16, 123, 129, 265, 457, 530n2, 542n7, *P31*
Abramson, Herb, 12, 55–56, 60–66, 68, 73, 84, 266, 448, 514n14
Abramson, Miriam. *See* Miriam Bienstock
ACA studios (Houston), 179, 473
Ace, Johnny, 35, 158, 194, 524n2, 526n9
Ace Records (U.K.), 5, 208–9, 229, 303–4, 526n5, 530n6
Ace Records (U.S.), 103, 156, 164, 176, 181, 223, 349, 444, 472, 535n16, 537n1
Ackerman, Paul, 144, 188, 204, 534n12
Acuff, Roy, 157, 277–78
Acuff-Rose Music, 49, 168–69, 266–67, 278, 463, 540n26
Adams, Berle, x, xi, 23–24; start of Mercury Records, 25–28, 29–32, 452, 510n7, 510n4 (chap. 2), 511n22, *P1–2*
Adams, Faye, 193, 324, 449–50, 524n2, 532n7
Adams, Joe, 34
Adams, Johnny, 294, 521n7
Adams, Ted, 107, 111

Addey, Mickey, 101
Adelman, Ben, 282, 385, 410
Adler, Lou, 445
AFM (American Federation of Musicians), ix, 13–15, 30, 35, 58, 63, 79–80, 84, 155, 252, 400, 429, 537n5; AFM contracts, 536n12. *See also* James C. Petrillo
A.F.O. Records, 182, 306, 353–55
"Ain't It a Shame" ("Ain't That a Shame"), 194, 362, 524n2
"Ain't Nobody Here but Us Chickens," 29
"Alabam," 287
Aladdin (Philo) Records, 12, 16, 34, 44, 50, 160, 162, 218–20, 258, 297, 299; sale to Imperial Records, 308, 309, 362, 462, 512n2, 513n26, 529n8; Score Records, 50
Alaimo, Steve, 467, 469
Albert, George, 190, 197, 203–4, 207, *P18*
Aldon Music, 436–37, 540n26
Alen, Dick, 450–53
"All American Boy, The," 145, 519n13
Allan, Johnnie, 176
Allegro studios (New York), 260, 364, 374, 419
Allen, Bill "Hoss" ("The Hossman"), 95–96; as Chess promo man, 111–12; closing years at WLAC, 114–15, 120, 224–26, 294, 366, 517nn15–16, *P9–10*; Radio WLAC, Nashville, 97–104, 109
Allen, Lee, 473
"All I Could Do Was Cry," 333, 337
Allied pressing plant (Hollywood), 37, 42
"All in My Mind," 374–75
"All Shook Up," 271, 416, 426
All South Distributing Corp. (New Orleans), 177, 289, 292, 355, 521n7
Allstate Record Distributing Co. (Chicago), 50, 128, 164
Alpert, Herb, 314, 456; and the Tijuana Brass, 314
Alpha Distributing Corp. (New York), 217, 359, 456
American Bandstand, 29, 103, 113, 120, 176, 226, 272, 278, 289, 305, 361, 369, 386, 417–20, 422, 426, 428, 430, 432, 443, 540n19, 541n7. *See also* Dick Clark

American Graffiti film, 373
American Record Corporation (ARC), 75
Ames Brothers, The, 205, 325, 536n13
AMI jukeboxes, 43, 192, 511n20
Ammons, Albert, 26–27, 103
Ammons, Gene "Jug," 27, 256
Andrews, Lee and the Hearts, 121, 144, 518n6
Andrews Sisters, The, 29
Angelic Gospel Singers, The, 110
Angel Music, 368, 370–71, 373
Anka, Paul, 300, 423, 438, 443–44, 457, 536n13
Anna Records, 319, 333, 335–38, 444, 537n1
Annie Get Your Gun Broadway show, 31
answer songs, 153, 324, 337, 524n9, 532n7
A-1 Record Distributors (New Orleans), 50, 306, 478, 543n9
"Apache," 262
Apollo Records, 16, 54–55, 139, 141, 214, 359, 509n3, 543n9; directors (1948), 514n1
Apollo Theatre (Harlem), 196, 215, 221, 264, 341–44, 374, 451, 532n1 (chap. 18)
Appell, Dave, 423–24; the Applejacks, 425, 427; at Cameo-Parkway Records, 425–32, 510n7, 540n18, 540n21, *P30*
Applebaum, Stan, 67
Aquatones, The, 379
ARA Records, 25, 45, 297; ARA pressing plant, 45, 150, 213, 530n1
Arc Music, 112, 116, 119, 127, 146, 215, 255–57, 260–62, 264–67, 338, 518n14, 526n11, 532n10, 540n26
"Are You Lonesome Tonight?" 437
Arista Records, 165, 462
Aristocrat Records, 61, 117, 121, 256. *See also* Chess Records
ARMADA (American Record Manufacturers and Distributors Association), 457–58, 468, 542n7
Armstrong, Louis, 35, 62, 69, 74, 242, 259, 270, 450, 513n19, 526n9
Arnold, Eddy, 98, 198, 268, 270, 278–79
Aron, Evelyn, 61; and Charles Aron, 117
ASCAP (American Society of Composers, Authors and Publishers), 13–14, 35, 243, 254–58, 277, 402–3, 426, 436, 439, 455, 459, 526n7, 527n22
Associated Booking (ABC) agency, 242, 450, 541n16
Assunto, Joe, 181, 292; and Watch Records, 521n7
Atkins, Chet, 132, 248, 278, 287
Atlantic Records, 1, 3, 9, 11, 16, 18, 19, 35, 40, 53, 56, 59–61; Atco Records, 3, 68, 181, 233, 262, 355, 437, 536n13; Cat Records, 66, 528n3; Cotillion Records, 228, 276; early years, 62–66; jazz artists, 67, 515n19; Progressive Music, 65, 146, 271, 514n15; Quality Records, 62, 401; rock 'n' roll era, 66–70;

sale of 71, 72, 84, 89, 94–95, 109, 116–17, 119, 121, 123, 128–29, 137, 146, 148, 162, 165, 178, 189, 194, 199, 214, 220, 222, 228, 233, 236, 270–73, 276, 279, 291, 295, 299, 323, 344, 351, 355, 382, 390, 398, 406–8, 410, 419, 423, 433, 444, 448, 458, 462, 464, 467, 514n13, 515n22, 517n3, 518n6, 522n5 (chap. 12), 524n2, 532n7, 532n2 (chap. 18), 536n13, 537n1, 540n2, 541n14, 542n27, 543n29, 543n9 (chap. 25)
Atlas-Angletone Records, 352, 361
"At the Hop" ("Let's All Do the Bop"), 262, 443, 526n13
Austin, Bob, 190, 192, 198, 200, *P18*
Autry, Gene, 157, 284, 297, 309–12, 314–18, 510n7, 527n20, 531n18, 531nn20–21
Avakian, George, 22, 73–78, 89, 243, 510n2, 515n1
Avalon, Frankie, 374, *415*, 421–23, 428, 444, 539n11
Avco-Embassy Records, 252
Axton, Estelle, 61, 71
Azoff, Irving, 89

Baby Grand club (Harlem), 54, 215, 343
"Baby Let's Play House," 110, 153
"Baby Oh Baby," 363
"Baby Scratch My Back," 109–11, 169
"Baby Workout," 107, 342
Bacharach, Burt, 275, 376
Bachman, William, 75
Backer, Bill, 340
Bailey, Mildred, 35, 383
Bailey, Pearl, 244, 259
Baker, Chet, 385, 451
Baker, LaVern, 68, 95, 144, 236, 324, 330, 434, 450, 452, 524n9
Baker, Mickey, 67, 225. *See also* Mickey & Sylvia
Balk, Harry, 273–74, 449
Ball, Noel, 111, 538n22
"Ballad of Davy Crockett, The," 85, 540n1
Ballard, Hank, 136, 138, 146, 251, 299–300, 429–30, 529n25; and the Midnighters, 131, 134, 298, 347, 452
Ballen, Ivin, 55, 142, 514n37
Bamberger, Frank, and Jack Sobel: J. & F. distributors (Baltimore), 411
Banashak, Joe, xii, 4, 50, 306, 530n11
Barclay, Eddie, 67; Barclays Records (France), 67, 401, 407
Bard, Julius, 43, 513n23
Bare, Bobby, 145, 519n13
Barge, Gene "Daddy G.," 339–40, 419
Barnett Samuel & Sons, 398; and Wilfred S. Samuel, 537n3
Barrett, Richard "Richie," 216, 398, 523n11, 526n10

Barry, Jeff, 436
Barry, Joe, 176, 291
Barry, Len, 430–31
Bart, Ben, 57, 89, 450, 469
Bartholomew, Dave, xii, 182, 299, 306, 416, 478, 526n5
Bartlett, Ray "Groovy Boy," 162
Barton, Eileen, 57
Basie, Count, 34, 103, 161, 232, 239, 243–44, 246, 344, 458, 511n17, 525n14, 531n4
Bass, Fontella, 338, 340
Bass, Ralph, 59, 121, 132, 136, 139, 146, 225, 238–39, 324, 339–40
Baton Records, 359
Battiste, Harold, 182, 306–7, 353–56, 530nn8–9, 533nn17–18, 533n20, *P22*
Battle, Joe (Von), 135, 319, 321–26, 340, 519n6, 531nn2–3, *P24–25*; Joe's Record Shop, 135, 321–23, *P24–25*; J-V-B Records, 321, 324
Baxter, Les: "De Rain," 313
BBC (British Broadcasting Corporation), 102, 263, 368
B. Bumble and the Stingers, 531n16
Beach Boys, The, 22, 89, 260, 318
"Bear Cat," 152–53
Beard, Jimmy, 37
Beasley, Bill, 461
Beatles, The, 22, 89, 122, 129, 180, 199, 207, 228, 265, 276, 305, 308, 324, 336, 372, 386, 398, 400, 408, 432, 438, 464–66, 518n16, 535n16, 538n18
Beck, Jim: and studio (Dallas), 528n1
Bedno, Howard, x; promo man, 128–30; start of Cobra Records, 123–24, 125–27
Bee Gees, The, 276, 467
Belafonte, Harry, 433
Bell, Al, 228
Bell, Benny, 86
Bell Records, 79, 86, 350, 373, 432, 516n15; Amy-Mala Records, 350, 540n26
Bell Sound studios (New York), 221, 296, 334, 346, 533n7
Beltone Records, 134, 444, 519n10
Beltone studios (New York), 139, 387, 423
Belvin, Jesse, 40, 224, 249, 299–300
Benjamin, Louis, 121
Bennett, Al, 101, 317–18, 347, 390, 510n7, 517n8, *P31*
Bennett, Jean(ie), 238–43, *P21*; and the *Personality Plugger*, 241
Bennett, Pete, 447
Bennett, Tony, 89, 143, 249, 361
Benson, Al "The Ole Swingmaster," 117, 123, 126, 129, 516n1
Benton, Brook, 31, 276, 289, 293, 419, 526n10
Berle, Milton, 59
Berlin, Irving, 56, 437, 451
Berman, Bess, 16, 54–55, 61, 214, 359, 509n3, *P6*

Berman, Ike, 16, 55, 214, 359
Berman, Irving, 58
Bernard, Rod, 176, 521n6
Berns, Bert, 406, 451–52, 470, 532n8; and Shout-Bang Records, 452
Berry, Chuck, 9, 18, 30, 116, 118, 122, 126–28, 176, 260, 263–64, 266, 326–29, 362, 406, 451–52, 470, 524n2, 532n8, 532n10, 537n1
Berry, Richard, 299, 386
Besman, Bernie, 46, 137, 518n5 (chap. 8); and Sensation Records, 135
Bestway Products pressing plant (Rahway, N.J.), 83, 275, 383–84, 516n13
"Betty and Dupree," 339
Bienstock, Freddy, 60, 65, 68, 148, 199, 267–71, 276, 296, 407, 438, 519n11, 527n22, 539n15; Carlin America Music, 269
Bienstock, Johnny, 148, 267–69, 528n28; at Big-top Records, 270–76, 406–7, 438, *P31*
Bienstock, Miriam (Abramson), 12, 59–61; Atlantic rock 'n' roll era, 66–71; 73, 217, 271, 406, 444, *P7*; early years at Atlantic Records, 62–66
"Big Bad John," 282
Big Bopper, The (J. P. Richardson), 286, 291
Biggs, Howard, 67
Big Maceo, 161, 510n6
Big Maybelle, 59
Big State Distributing Co. (Dallas), 128, 164, 279, 283, 289, 513n30, 528n4
Big Three Music (Robbins, Feist, and Miller), 66, 446
Bigtop Records, 233, 266–67, 269–76, 366, 406, 411, 449, 528n1, 537n1, 541n15; Dunes Records, 274
Bihari, Joe, ix, 2, 12, 39–42; with Chief Justice Earl Warren and Nina Warren, 157; as Joe Josea, 300, 530n2; with Meteor Records, 157–59, 160, 163, 212–14, 279, 298–303, 313, 356, 452, 462, 512n10, 520n12, 520n18, 530n7, *P3*, *P21*; start of Modern (Music) Records, 43, 44–47, 115, 151, 154–57
Bihari, Jules, 12, 40–41, 43, 46, 49, 51–52, 150–52, 154, 160, 300–301, 303, 356, 445, 452, 530n2, 536n6, *P3*; as Jules Taub, 300, 530n2
Bihari, Lester, 40–41, 157–60, 303, 520n18, *P13*
Bihari, Saul, 12, 40, 42–44, 46, 51–52, 150–52, 154, 212, 300, 303, 452, 513n16, *P3*; as Sam Ling, 300, 530n2
Bihari brothers (Joe, Jules, Saul), 34, 39, 78, 102, 119; rivalries with Sam Phillips, Leonard Chess, Lillian McMurry, 154–57, 194, 211, 220, 279, 298–302; sale of Modern Records, 303, 355, 462, 469, 516n17, 519n3, 530n1
Bihari sisters (Florette, Maxine, Rosalind), 40, 307; Serene 40
Billboard, The (*Billboard, Billboard Music Week*), x, 1, 4, 10, 25, 32, 43–44, 49, 74, 79,

89, 97, 139, 143–44,155, 160, 172, 179; *Cash Box*, 190–96, 199, 201–5, 207, 219, 221, 223, 227, 231–32, 240, 242, 248, 254, 264, 278, 286, 293, 298, 344, 359, 361, 364, 386, 389, 405, 413, 433, 435, 442, 444, 472, 510n4 (chap. 2), 521n3 (chap. 11), 521n4 (chap. 11), 522n12; 524n4, 528n26, 542n25; competing with news stories, 14–15, 17–19, 23, 28, 31, 39, 46–47, 50, 55, 59–60, 62, 71, 124–25, 147–48, 153–54, 222, 245, 267, 279, 282, 308, 321, 348, 370, 383, 390, 400, 415–16, 419, 431, 457, 459, 461, 463–64, 466, 540n3; founding of, 187–88, 521n1; new R&B and C&W terms, 188–89; Paul Ackerman (editor), Jerry Wexler at, 188

Billie & Lillie, 421, 427
Binnick, Bernie, 421, 539n17
Biondi, Dick, 366
Birdland club (New York), 243–44, 525n16
Black & White Records, 136, 141, 297, 440, 513n23
Blackboard Jungle, The, 511n18
"Blackland Farmer," 287
Blackman, E. G. "Blackie," 99, 101
Black's Combo, Bill, 366, 413
Blackwell, Chris, 401
Blackwell, Otis, 271, 390, 526n10
Blackwell, Robert "Bumps," 307
Blaine, Elliot, 227, 466; and Ben Blaine, 57, 214
Blaine, Jerry, 56–57, 59, 62, 64, 78, 210, 214–15, 217, 227, 252, 261, 344–45, 379, 388, 456, 461, 466, 468, 509n3, 514n10, 515n24, 523n9, 541n10
Bland, Billy, 210, 220, 222–23, 437
Bland, Bobby "Blue," 126, 154, 158–59, 176, 520n24
Blavat, Jerry (The Geator with the Heater), 422
Bleyer, Archie, 216, 379, 388, 426, 435, 440, 448, 463, 466, 510n7, 541n10
Block, Martin, and *Make Believe Ballroom*, 143, 195, 512n4
"Bloodshot Eyes," 137
"Blueberry Hill," 3, 136
Bluebird Records, 75, 513n19, 520n9; and Bluebird Beat, 510n6
"Blue Moon," 437
"Blue Moon of Kentucky," 198
Blue Note Records, 12, 55, 462
"Blues after Hours," 45, 213
"Blues for the Red Boy" ("Blues for the Moondog"), 518n5 (chap. 8)
"Blues in Hoss' Flat" ("Blues in Frankie's Flat"), 103
Blues Interactions (Japan), 303–4; P-Vine Records, 304
"Blues in the Night," 21
"Blues Stay Away from Me," 136
"Blue Suede Shoes," 153

Blues Unlimited, xiii, 4, 156
BMI (Broadcast Music Inc.), ix, 13–14, 188, 222, 254–55, 257–59, 277, 286, 305, 315, 368–69, 375, 402–3, 426, 436, 439, 441, 459, 511n16, 514n15, 526nn6–7, 527n22
Bogart, Neil, 432
Boggs, Professor Harold, 108
Bonds, Gary "U. S.," 205, 339, 532n17
Bono, Sonny, 304–6, 354–55, 530n8; Sonny Bono Copyright Term Extension Act (1998), 306. *See also* Sonny & Cher
"Bony Moronie," 304
"Boogie Chillen," 46, 518n5 (chap. 8)
"Boogie Woogie Santa Claus," 39
Booker T. & the MGs, 108, 366, 464
"Book of Love," 262, 264, 527n14
"Boom Boom," 266
Boone, Pat, 101–2, 142, 163, 194, 199, 227, 236, 260, 374, 537n1, 542n18
"Booted," 154
bootleg issues, 39, 124–25, 158, 179, 214, 262, 275, 281–82, 366, 390–91, 529n8
Boskent, Bill, 442
Bostic, Earl, 131, 134, 136, 531n4
Bourne, Saul "Sol," 85; Bourne Music, 85, 254
Bowen, Jimmy, 245
Bowen, Ruth, 450
Bracken, Jimmy, 16, 125, 129, *P31*
Bradley, Owen, 112, 278, 287, 425
Brand, Oscar, 222, 402
Brantley, Johnny, 221, 455–56, 523n20
Braun, David and Jules, 142, 519n12
Brave, Charlie, 364–65
Braverman, Jack, 370
"Breaking Up Is Hard to Do" (Jivin' Gene), 176, 291
Brenston, Jackie, 121, 151, 154, 532n10
Brewer, Teresa, 360, 406
Brill Building (New York) songwriting scene, 225, 227, 265, 269, 436–37, 524n10, 540n26
"Bristol Stomp," 429–30, 540n21
Bronstein, Don, 118
Bronze Records, 38, 42
Brooks, Hadda, 40, 42–44, 213
Broonzy, Big Bill, 157, 510n6
Brown, Charles, 34, 37, 40, 161, 343–44, 512n2, 512n5
Brown, Clarence "Gatemouth," 95
Brown, Devora, 61; and Jack Brown, 323
Brown, Gilbert, 101, 517n8
Brown, James, 9, 103, 109, 121, 131, 134, 139–40, 143–44, 146–48, 337, 390, 513n30
Brown, Joe, 124; JOB Records, 124, 164, 520n22
Brown, Maxine, 93, 373–78, 524n31, 535n23
Brown, Nappy, 59, 398
Brown, Roy, 97, 142, 180, 245
Brown, Ruth, 65–66, 68, 70, 144, 271, 293, 354, 532n7, *P7*

Browns, The, 198, 250, 375; Jim Ed and Maxine Brown, 164, 375
Brubeck, Dave, 74
Bruce, Monte, 446; Bruce Records, 216, 446
Bruno, Tony, 373–76
Brunswick-Balke-Collender Company, 75
Brunswick Records, 75, 107, 125, 232, 331, 339, 361, 375, 398, 515n2, 527n19, 532n12
Brunswick Records (U.K.), 3, 538n7
Bryant, Anita, 428, 434
Bryant, Willie, 225; and Ray Carroll (Willie & Ray), 213, 361
Bubis, Al(an), 542n17; and Hit Records, 461
Buchanan, Bill, 312; Buchanan & Goodman (Dickie), 203, 362; Luniverse Records, 362
Buckinghams, The, 129
Buckley, Louis, 99–100, 170; Buckley's Record Shop, 96, 99, 162
budget recordings, 85–88, 302–3, 516n17
Buffalo Booking Agency, 30, 450, 541n17
Bulleit, Jim, 101, 152, 278, 519n1
Bullett Records, 97, 101, 141, 152, 278, 281, 519n1
"Bumming Around," 282
Bundy, June, 459
Burgess, Dave, 19, 309; start of Challenge Records, 310–11; The Champs and "Tequila," 312–14, 315–18, 510n7, PC23
Burke, Solomon, 71
Burlington Music, 263, 403, 405, 538n15
Burton, Bob (of BMI), 315, P26
Burton, James, 132, 417
Burton, John Henry "Lawyer," 123, 256
Butler, Billy, 138, 351, P12
Butler, Jerry, 129, 337
"Butterfly," 426, 539n15
"Buzz-Buzz-Buzz," 307
Byrds, The, 89

C. & C. Distributing Co. (Seattle), 279, 283, 385
Cadena, Ozzie, 59
Cadence Records, 9, 85, 125, 216, 388, 410, 418, 426, 435, 440, 448, 463, 510n7, 537n1, 540n1, 541n10, 542n21
Cadets (Jacks), The, 40, 298
Cahan, Les, 139, 423
Cahn, Sammy, 266
"Caldonia," 29
Calico Records, 206
Calloway, Cab, 36, 211, 321
Camarata, Salvatore "Tutti," 31
Cameo-Parkway Records, 125, 262, 271, 314, 387, 392, 421; early years, 424–28; twist era, 429–31; sale of, 432; 444, 510n7, 526n12, 535n16, 535n2 (chap. 20), 537n1, 540nn22–23, 541n10
Campbell, Glen, 340, 531n19
Campbell, Jo Ann, 430

Campbell, Orville, 442, 538n22
Canadian American Records, 366, 533n9
Cane, Marvin, 456
Canned Heat, 356
Cannon, Freddy, 421
"Can't Help Falling in Love," 251
Cantor, Eddie, 257
Cantrell, Bill, 159, 520n17
Capitol Records, 9, 15–16, 19; Capitol Tower and studios, 298; 299, 351, 354, 360, 382, 400–401, 408, 416, 456, 462, 510n7, 516n10, 520n1, 521n2 (chap. 11), 524n9, 529n11, 529n13, 540n2, 540n6, 543n29; overview and EMI takeover, 21–23; 28–29, 35, 38, 42, 77, 80, 84, 88, 96, 98, 129, 168, 203, 206, 232, 235, 260–61, 263, 278, 281, 293; pressing plants, 22, 244, 389, 491–92, 536n6
Capris, The, 210, 227, 362
Carey, Mariah, 352
Carlisles, The, 146, 538n19
Carlson, Harry, 145, P31
Carlton, Joe, 19, 188, 235, 379, 432, 434–35, 448
Carlton-Guaranteed Records, 188, 432, 434, 448, 537n1
Carmichael, Hoagy, 25
Caronna, Joe, 181, 472
Carroll, David, 137
Carter, Calvin, 129, P31
Carter, Vivian, 16, 61, 129
Carter Family, The, 157, 168, 284
Casablanca Records, 432, 467
Case, Paul, 267, 274, 276, 438
Casey, Al, 420
Cash, Johnny, 149–50, 153, 268, 278, 295–96, 462, 529n13, 537n1
Cash Box, The, 1, 4, 10, 43, 55, 61, 66, 68, 108, 159, 187, 189–90; Bob Austin, 200; chart strategy, 201–2; competing with Billboard, 190–96, 201–5, 207; country section 197–99; launch, market, 191–94; news stories, 78, 133, 217, 247, 387–88, 390, 448; reviews policy, 205–7, 218–19, 224, 240, 248, 254, 277, 285, 344, 359, 386, 405, 409, 435, 442, 444, 460, 463–65, 467–69, 518n3 (chap. 8), 521n1, 522nn6–8, 522n12, 525n2, 535n22, 540n3; Top 100 charts and bullets, 194–96
CBS (Columbia Broadcasting System), 13, 19, 75–76, 94, 97, 388, 439, 517n2. See also Columbia Records
CBS Records (U.K.), 408
"C.C. Rider," 339, 419
"Chain Gang," 250, 525n20
"Chains of Love," 66
Challenge Records, 19, 279, 297; end of, 317, 318, 366, 398, 444, 510n7, 527n20, 531n20, 531n23, 537n1; Jat Music, 313–14; start of Challenge Records, 310–11; The Champs and "Tequila," 312–14, 315–16

Champs, The, 297, 309, 312–15, 318, 366, 531n19, *P23*. *See also* Dave Burgess

Chance, Larry, 228, 230, 524n33. *See also* the Earls

Chancellor Records, 125, 421–24, 444, 462, 533n13, 537n1, 539n10, 539n13

Chance-Sabre Records, 123

Chandler, Gene, 129

Channel, Bruce, 293

Chantels, The, 216, 534n1

"Chantilly Lace," 291

Chappell Music, 254, 263, 266, 268–69

Charles, Bobby, 260, 526n9

Charles, Ray, 9, 34, 68, 70, 72, 137, 141–42, 193–94, 248, 304, 340, 343, 354, 376, 407, 422–23, 444–45, 451, 462, 515n19, 524n2, 526n9, 527n15, 532n2 (chap. 18), 537n1

"Charlie Brown," 233

Charlton magazines, 323

Charms, The (with Otis Williams), 137, 141–42, 162, 232, 469

chart computations, 194–96, 201–2, 516n14, 522n12

Chase, Lincoln, 526n10, 532n7

Checker, Chubby, 289, 314, 429–32

Chedwick, Porky, 120

Chenier, Clifton, 174

"Cherry Pie," 298, 300

Chess, Leonard, 11, 67, 109, 111–12, 115–23, 125–30, 152, 154, 156–57, 160, 162–63, 165, 176, 209–10, 215, 222, 255–57, 261, 263–66, 319, 326–30, 336–37, 340, 343, 346, 352, 406, 457, 509n3, 520n22, 526n12, *P10–11, P31*

Chess, Marshall, 116–23, 255, 517n15, *P11*

Chess, Phil, 115, 116–19, 122, 125, 127–28, 152, 176, 222, 256–57, 259, 263, 265, 326–27, 330, 336, 343, *P11*

Chess brothers (Leonard, Phil), 12, 16, 102, 146, 150, 154, 219–20, 260–63, 338, 355, 465, 469, 527n14

Chess-Checker-Argo Records, 4, 9, 12, 16, 40, 67–68, 95, 107–9, 111–12, 116–21; sale of, 122; 123, 125, 127–29, 151–52, 154–55, 161–63, 165, 176, 194, 214–15, 220, 222–23, 252, 255; South Cottage Grove offices and studio, 326–27; 328–30, 332–33, 335–36, 338–40, 346–47, 349–51, 380, 384–85, 398, 401, 406, 410, 418, 444, 457–58, 463–64, 509n3, 517n16, 518n3, 518n6, 520n22, 523n8, 524n2, 526n9, 526n12, 527n14, 532n7, 532n16, 537n1, 540n21, 543n9; start of, 256; 257, 259–62, 279, 319, 322, 324; Ter-Mar studios, 2120, South Michigan, Chicago, 120, 518n4. *See also* Aristocrat Records

"Chicken Shack Boogie," 218

Chief Records, 126–27, 164, 375, 518n13

Chipetz, Harry, 419, 426, 431; Chips Distributing Co. (Philadelphia), 426

Chipmunks, The, 318

Chisholm, Malcolm, 120, 128

chitlin' circuit: 376, 451, 520n24, 541n18

Choates, Harry, 45, 167

"Choo Choo Ch' Boogie," 29

Chordettes, The, 216–17, 234, 299, 418, 435

Chords, The, 35, 66, 222, 236, 534n1

Chudd, Lew, 12, 16, 34, 44, 67, 162–63, 170–71, 194, 199, 308, 317, 416–17, 445, 462, 530n2, 539n4, 541n10

"Church Bells May Ring," 462

Churchill, Savannah, 58

Claiborne, Lillian (DC Records), 61, 279, 385

Clanton, Jimmy, 176, 179, 181, 472, *P14*

Clapton, Eric, 276, 523n8

Clark Five, Dave, 309

Clark, Dick, 29, 103, 113, 120, 176, 241–42, 262, 272–73, 278, 289, 314, 332, 361, 369, 386, 417–22, 426, 428–30, 432, 444, 447, 526n13; *The Dick Clark Caravan*, 428; *The Dick Clark Show*, 241, 314; payola inquiries, 455, 459, 469. See also *American Bandstand*

Clark, Sam, 213, 418, 422, 439–43, 445, 466, 509n3, 510n7, 540n1

Clark, Sanford, 102

Class Records, 35, 37, 39, 297, 308–9, 318, 537n1; Recordo Music, 309

Claunch, Quinton, 159; and Goldwax Records, 520n17

Cleveland, Reverend James, 57

Cline, Patsy, 198, 315, 385, 531n22

Clock Records, 347, 363–64, 367, 370, 373, 444, 527n20, 537n1; Lowell Music, 363–64, 370, 527n20

Clooney, Rosemary, 89, 536n13

Clovers, The, 66, 196–97, 451, 531n4, *P7*

Coasters, The, 3, 68, 206, 233–34, 434, 509n5, 537n1

Cobain, Kurt; and Nirvana, 385

Cobb, Arnett, 89

Cobra Records, 123–24, 126, 164; ABCO Records, 124

Cochran, Eddie, 317, 452, 537n1

Coed Records, 223, 456, 527n20, 535n16, 537n1, 541n3

Cogbill, Tommy, 293

Cohen, Abraham "Pop": Irv Cohen and Joe Cohen, 218–20, 358, 360, 462; "Mom" Cohen, 218

Cohen, Pat, 365

Cohen, Paul, 15, 278, 425; and Todd Records, 448

Cohn, Ed, 369–70, 419

"Cold, Cold Heart," 89

Cole, Cozy, 366

Cole, Nat "King," 22, 36, 86, 98, 188, 195, 235, 249, 321, 331, 511n17, 512n5, 521n2 (chap. 11)

Colonial Records, 46, 214, 442, 538n22, 539n10, 540n6

Colony Record Shop (New York), 193, 213, 259, 521n5 (chap. 11)

Colpix Records, 437, 445, 540n26, 542n12

Coltrane, John, 515n19

Columbia Record Club, 77–78

Columbia Records, 13, 15, 19–20, 22, 25, 28, 37, 42, 64, 72; battle of the speeds with RCA Victor, 74–78; formation of, 75, 80, 84, 86, 88–90, 94, 122, 140, 157, 203, 215, 232, 243, 252, 259, 278–79, 282, 287, 292–93, 302–3, 310–12, 374, 381–85, 390, 401–3, 408, 416, 433, 439–40, 447–48, 462–63, 510n6, 511n15, 516n10, 527n21, 528n1, 535n6, 536n13, 542n21, 543n29; Harmony Records, 88, 302; pressing plants, 25, 76, 244, 389, 392, 491. *See also* CBS

Columbia Records (U.K.), 23, 67, 372, 401, 444

"Come Go with Me," 102, 437

"Come Rain or Come Shine," 21

"Come Softly to Me," 385

"Come to Me," 335

Commodore Records, 15, 55; and Commodore Music Shop (New York), 73

Como, Perry, 143, 193–94, 255, 283, 388

"Congo Mombo," 169

Conkling, Jim (James), 22, 77, 515n1, 515n4, 516n10

Consolers, The (Iola and Sullivan Pugh), 110

Cook, Hal, 75, 515n1, 515n4

Cook, Roger, and Greenaway, Roger, 340

Cooke, Edna Gallmon (Madame), 106, 110

Cooke, Sam, 9, 143, 248–50, 306–7, 342, 355, 423, 452, 462, 525n20, 537n1

Cooley, Eddie, 271

Cooley, Spade, 268

Cooperstein, Max, 120, 128, 406

Copacabana club (New York), 250, 452–53

Copas, Cowboy, 131, 138, 145, 287, 531n22

Copyright Act, 305; Sonny Bono extension act (1998), 306

Coral Records, 9, 232, 300, 312, 536n13

Coral Records (U.K.), 538n7

"Corn Bread," 58

Cornell, Don, 361

"Corrina Corrina," 274, 536n13

Cortez, Dave "Baby," 260, 347, 364–67

Cosimo Recording Studios (New Orleans), 4, 181–82, 473, 530n11, 543n6

Cosmo Records, 56

Cosnat Distributing Corp. (New York), 56, 62, 64, 210, 214–15, 217, 226–27, 261, 303, 344–45, 387, 456, 461, 466, 509n3, 514n10

Costa, Don, 440, 443

Cotton, James, 152

Country Music Association (CMA), 198

Covay, Don, 526n10

Craft, Morty, 224, 274, 359, 369, 445–50, 468, 528n26, 541n11; Melba Records, 359

Craig, Francis, 141, 278, 281, 468

Cramer, Floyd, 164

Crayton, Pee Wee, 45–46, 213, 530n2

Creatore, Luigi, 234; at Mercury, 235–38; at RCA Victor, 248–51, 252–53, 308, *P20*; at Roulette, 243–47, 251. *See also* Hugo & Luigi

Creedence Clearwater Revival, 520n23

Crescendos, The, 109, 111

Crests, The, 144, 434, 456, 541n3

Crew-Cuts, The, 236–37, 299

Crewe, Bob, 129; and Frank Slay, 261, 265, 427, 526n12, 538n22

Crochet, Cleveland, 175

Crook, Maximillian, 273

Crosby, Bing, 16, 29, 85, 203, 239, 277, 430, 531n17

Crown Records, 298, 301–2, 516n17, 530nn4–5, 543n9. *See also* Modern Records

Crowns (Five), The, 53, 215, 220

Crows, The, 35, 534n1, *P19*

Crudup, Arthur "Big Boy," 161, 198, 510n6

"Cry," 89

"Crying in the Chapel," 215

Crystals, The, 539n9

Culley, Frank "Floor Show," 63

Cuoghi, Joe, 406, 444, 520n17, 538n22, *P29*

"Cupid," 250, 525n21

Curtis, King (Curtis Ousley), 350–51, 388

custom recordings, 285–86, 384, 389–90

"Daddy Cool," 261

"Daddy's Home," 527n14

Daily, Harold "Pappy," 164, 282, 284–86, 288, 291–92, 525n13, 538n19, 542n17; D Records, 286

Daily Co., H.W., distributors, 164, 224; and Records of Houston, 542n12

Dale, Dick, 361

Dale & Grace, 178–79, 182

Dale, Larry, 226, 523n28

Dalhart, Vernon, 15

Damone, Vic, 27, 32, *P2*

"Dance With Me Henry" ("The Wallflower"), 237, 298–99

Danny and the Juniors, 262, 443–44

Darin, Bobby, 68, 70, 72, 272, 374, 423, 434, 437, 462, 536n13, 537n1

"Darling, Listen to the Words of This Song," 220, 523n20

David, Hal, 436

Davis, Billy. *See under* Roquel "Billy" Davis

Davis, Clive, 86, 89, 196, 229

Davis, Jimmie (Governor), 170, 277

Davis, Joe, 465; and Beacon Records, 54; Celebrity Records, 440; Davis Records, 359

Davis, Maxwell, 299, 302

Davis, Miles, 74, 126, 376

Davis, Roquel "Billy," xi, 138, 224, 265, 319–20; Anna Records, 335–38; with Berry Gordy, 330–38; Billy Davis Enterprises, 320, 340; Check-Mate Records, 338; Chess Records A&R man, 338–40, 527n17, 531n3, 532n11, 532n16, *P24*; Chess Records songwriter, 326–30; Chevis Music, 265, 338–39, 527n17; early Detroit career, 321–26; exit from Detroit, 338–39; Tyran Carlo, 320, 332

Davis, Sammy Jr., 321, 452

Day, Bobby, 308–9, *FC, P22*

Day, Doris, 89, 142, 194

"Daydreamin'," 159

"Deacon's Hop, The," 58

Dean, Jimmy, 282

Deane, Buddy, 441, 516n1, 534n8, 538n20; *The Buddy Deane Show*, 441

DeAngelis, Peter, 421–23, 462

"Dear One," 227

Decca Records (U.K.), 22, 67, 263, 316, 371, 397–401, 403–5, 407–8, 410, 414, 463, 537n3, 538n17; U.K. artists lost, 538n18

Decca Records (U.S.), 9, 13, 15–16, 19, 24–25; formation of, 398–99; 400, 416, 425, 432–33, 437, 448, 462, 479, 510n6, 511n15, 512n3, 513n19, 514n13, 516n10, 524n7, 526n9, 527n19, 529n12, 531nn17–18, n22, 532n12, 537n4, 538n7, 543n29; Jack Kapp and, 28–29, 30–31, 35, 37, 42, 59, 75, 81–82, 84, 86, 94, 133,161, 163, 168, 171, 203, 207, 232–33, 260, 277–80, 282, 287, 315–16, 323, 332, 344, 360, 381; MCA purchase of Decca Records-Universal Pictures, 31, 511nn23–24; Pythian Temple studios (New York), 332

Deckelman, Bud, 159

"Deck of Cards," 281, 529n7

"Dede Dinah," 421–23, 539n11

Dee, Joey and the Starliters, 251

"Deep in the Heart of Texas," 367

Del-Fi Records, 307

Dell-Vikings, The, 102

Dells, The, 129, 339

Delmore Brothers (Alton and Rabon), The, 131–32, 136

Delta Rhythm Boys, The, 36

De Luxe Records, 17, 134, 137, 141–42, 324, 460, 518n12

DeMann, Freddy, 303

Denson, Lee, 302

Derby Records, 55, 59, 440, 540n3

DeSylva, Buddy, 21, 510n7

Deutsche Grammophon Records (Germany), 401

Dexter, Al, 277

Diablos, The, 144, 323, 531n6

Diamonds, The, 109–10, 222, 289, 418–19, 427, 437, 452

"Diana," 443, 536n13

Dickens, Little Jimmy, 310

Diddley, Bo, 35, 116, 122, 144, 260, 264, 328–29, 537n1

Dillard, Varetta, 59, 221

Dimension Records, 390, 540n26

"Dinner with Drac (Part 1)," 427, 540n18

Dion and the Belmonts, 144, 199, 225, 423, 456; Dion, 462

"Dirty Robber," 386

disco music, 228, 467

Disney, Walt, 85, 440; Disney Records, 85; (Buena) Vista Records, 445, 535n16

distributor lists (see Appendix B), 487–90

Dixiebelles, The, 113

Dixon, Luther, 526n10

Dixon, Willie, 124, 127, 264–66, 328, 518n8, 518n14

Dixson (Dixon), Julius, 146–47, 221, 418, 519n14, 523n20, 526n10; and Deb-Alton Records, 418

Dobard, Ray (Music City Records), 362

Doggett, Bill, 134, 138, 366, 418, 534n7, 535n17, *P12, P24*

Dolphin, John, 120, 284, 297, 321; Dolphin's record store, 120

Dolton (Dolphin) Records, 385, 444

Domino, Fats, 3, 4, 9, 18, 20, 95, 136, 143, 166, 178, 180, 182, 193–94, 199, 205–6, 236, 292, 304, 306, 342, 361, 385, 411, 416–17, 430, 437, 445, 451–52, 462, 470, 478, 524n2, 526n5, 529n8, 537n1

Dominoes, The, 131, 136, 193, 321, 323, 331–32, 531n4, *P17*

Don & Dewey, 179

Don & Juan, 275

Donaldson, William, 187

Donegan, Lonnie, 400, 537n2

"Don't Be Cruel," 138, 271, 416

"Don't Hang Up," 431

"Don't Let the Stars (Get in Your Eyes)," 283, 315, 388, 529n11, 531n23

"Don't You Just Know It," 444

Dootone (Dooto) Records, 297, 362, 524n2, 542n12

Dore Records, 274, 537n1

Dorsey, Jimmy, 145, 239, 511n17, 516n15, *P7*

Dorsey, Lee, 350

Dorsey, Tommy, 161, 239, 258, 516n15, *P7*

Dot Records, 19, 95; sale of, 101, 102, 111, 125, 137, 152–53, 159, 163, 170, 194, 199, 227, 236, 241, 297, 318, 347, 366, 408, 422, 426, 445, 460–61, 510n7, 513n15, 517n6, 529n7, 537n1, 542n18; start of, 101, 517n6, 517n8

Dovells, The, 430–32

Dowd, Tom, 55–56, 67, 69, 228, 273

"(Down at) Papa Joe's," 113

Down Beat magazine, 180, 521n10

Downbeat Records, 50

"Down Yonder," 274, 542n18

"Do You Want to Dance," 388

Draper, Rusty, 237, 289–90, 536n18

"Dream Lover," 437

Dreyfus, Max, 268–69, 271

Dreyhaupt, Joe, 382–84, 388, 390–91, 393, 536n16

Drifters, The, 20, 53, 66, 68, 205, 215, 423, 450, 452, 537n1, *P7*

"Drifting Blues," 34, 343, 512n2

"Drinkin' Wine, Spo-Dee-O-Dee," 63–64, 514nn13–14

Dr. John (Mac Rebennack), 182, 355

"Drown in My Own Tears," 137

Drucker, Peter, 2, 470

Duberstein, Bob, 212

"Duke of Earl," 129

Duke-Peacock Records, 16, 29, 35, 95, 110, 152; formation of, 158; 176, 194, 219, 233, 298, 304; sale of, 445; 457, 509n3, 520n14, 520n16, 524n2, 532n7, 541n17, 543n9

Duncan, Finley, 292, 294

Dupree, Champion Jack, 226

Durham, Ernie "Frantic," 456, 518n4 (chap. 8)

"Dust My Broom," 155

Dylan, Bob, 89, 355, 529n13

Earls, The, 210, 227–28, 230, 524n33

"Earth Angel (Will You Be Mine)," 239–40, 362, 437, 524n2

"Easier Said Than Done," 251

"Easter Parade," 55

Eastman, Lee, 31, 532n7

Ebb Records, 61, 307, 537n1

Eckstine, Billy, 56–57, 61

"Eddie My Love," 299

Eddy, Duane, 233, 302, 366, 420, 462, 537n1

Edison, Thomas, 393

Edsels, The, 227, 362

Edwards, Tommy, 447, 541n11

Egalnick, Lee, 137, 162

Elegants, The, 361, 411, 444, 527n14

Ellington, Duke, 34, 36, 232, 299, 511n17

Elliott, Ken "Jack the Cat," 521n7

Ellis, Ray, 67, 448

"El Rancho Rock," 314

EmBee Productions, 273–74, 528n28

Ember International Records (U.K.), 371, 401

Ember Records. *See* Herald-Ember Records

Emerson, Bill, 164, 513n30, *P29*

Emerson, Billy "The Kid," 152

EMI Records, 22–23, 129, 228, 293, 324, 363, 371–72, 399, 401, 535n16, 538n17, 543n29; EMI Music, 262, 375

Emmerman, Mack, 469

End-Gone Records, 216, 223, 244, 251, 333, 347, 368, 509n3, 534n1, 537n1

Enjoy Records, 350–52

Epic Records, 75, 176, 292, 385–86, 447, 543n9

Era Records, 297, 444, 537n1

Ernie's Record Mart (Nashville), 99, 104–11, 162

Ertegun, Ahmet, 11–12, 16–18, 56, 59–61; Atlantic rock 'n' roll era, 66–71; 72–73, 84, 94, 109, 119, 121, 137, 163, 178, 196–97, 217, 222, 233, 266, 271, 276, 294, 344–45, 366, 379, 407, 409, 433, 444, 457, 465, 515n22, 528n3, 532n3 (chap. 18), *P7*; early years at Atlantic Records, 62–66; as songwriter "Nugetre," 530n2, 531n4

Ertegun, Nesuhi, 12, 62, 67–68, 71, 73, 109, 119, 121, 366, 465

Escott, Colin, 511n6, 516n20, 528n1, 538n12

Essex, The, 251

Essex Record Distributors (Newark), 60, 217–20, 358, 360, 462, 523n14; Essex Record Shop, 217–19, 360

Essex Records, 30, 420–21

Evans, Paul; as teen star, 432–36; as songwriter, 436–38, 532n13, 540n27

Evans, Sam (*Jam with Sam*), 126

Everett, Betty, 127

Everly Brothers, The, 9, 398, 434–35, 437, 463, 537n1

"Every Beat of My Heart," 112, 517n16

Excello-Nashboro Records: Excellorec Music, 110–11, 169; Nasco Records, 109, 111; start of 105, 106–8; the hits, 109–11; sale of, 168–71, 176, 206, 373, 509n3, 537n1

Excelsior Records, 33–37, 39, 43, 52, 57, 160, 297

excise tax, 85, 301, 308, 516n13

Exclusive Records, 16, *33*, 34; collapse of, 39, 43, 46, 52, 160, 211–12, 297, 309, 512n3, 512n11, 513n14; *P4*; start of, 35–38

"Eyesight to the Blind," 214, 523n7

Fabian, 374, *415*, 422–23, 444

Fach, Charlie, 292

Fairfield Four, The, 226

Falcons, The, 532n14

"Fannie Mae," 349

Fantasy Records, 308, 520n23, 531n14

Fargo, Lou, 379; Fargo Records, 379, 537n1, 539n10

"Fat Man, The," 529n8

Feathers, Charlie, 159, *P13*

Federal Communications Commission (FCC), 94, 126, 148, 445

Federal Radio Commission, 58

Federal Records. *See* King-Federal Records

Federal Trade Commission (FTC), 139, 308, 457, 460, 542n10

Feld, Irvin and Israel, 428, 443; Irvin Feld, 452; and Super Disc Records, 278

Feller, Sid, 440

Fendermen, The, 290
Festival Records (Australia), 401
"Fever," 139, 147–48, 206, 271, 527n23
field recording trips, 59, 128, 155–57
Fields, Ernie, 531n16
Fiestas, The, 103, 210, 224–25, 523n27
Figure Music, 223, 361, 363, 375, 534n1
Fileti, Donn, 352, 358–63, 373, 465–66, 519n10
Fine, Bob, 83; Fine Sound studio (New York),
    516n9
Finfer, Harry, 141, 419–20, 458, 539n9
"Finger Poppin' Time," 138, 430
Finnegan, Larry, 227
Finnis, Rob, 102
Fire-Fury Records, 12, 109; collapse of labels,
    350, 351–52, 356, 373, 375, 462, 517n16,
    535n16; Fire-Fast Music, 348–50; "Kansas
    City" hit, 345–49
Fisher, Eddie, 143, 361
Fitzgerald, Bill, 158, 520n15, 541n16
Fitzgerald, Ella, 29, 161, 402, 531n4
Five Blind Boys of Mississippi, The, 36, 164
"Five Guys Named Moe" (and Broadway show),
    29
Five Jets, The, 324–25, 335
"5" Royales, The, 55, P6
Five Satins, The, 144, 362–63, 368, 423–24,
    528n27
"5-10-15 Hours," 65, 531n4
Flairs, The, 239; The Flares, 242
Flame Show Bar (Detroit), 273, 321, 326–27, 330
Flamingos, The, 144, 199, 221, 260, 326, 328,
    334, P24
Flash Records, 298
Fleetwoods, The, 385
Fletcher, Dusty, 56, 61, 536n17
"Flip Flop and Fly," 68
Flores, Danny (Chuck Rio), 312–13, 531n19, P23
"Flying Home," 259
"Flying Saucer, The (Part 1 & 2)," 203, 362,
    534n2
Foley, Red, 268; and Betty Foley, 529n13
Fontane Sisters, The, 101, 137, 142, 299
"Fool, The," 102
"Fools Rush In," 21
"Foot Stomping," 242
Ford, Frankie, 103, 472
Fort Knox/Trio Music, 148, 272, 540n26
Fortune magazine, 160, 416, 520n21, 539n4
Fortune Records, 323
Foster, Fred, 112–14, 282, 293, 406; start of
    Monument Records, 410–12, 413, 441–44,
    463, 465, 510n7, 538nn19–22, 542n22, P30
Four Buddies, The, 59, 321
Four Freshmen, The, 325
4 Seasons, The, 129, 444, 462
4 Star Records, 42, 134, 150, 211; 4 Star Sales
    Co., 315–16, 531n21; sale of, 315, 322, 324,

385, 388, 509n3, 528n6, 529nn9–11, 531n3,
    531n23; start of, 279–80, 281–85
Four Tops, The, 319–20, 325–27; The Ames, 325
Fox, Harry, 532n7, 536n16, 540n3; Harry Fox
    Agency, 391, 536n16
Foxx, Inez, 352, 533n15
Francis, Connie, 205, 447, 541n11
Francis, Panama, 67, 364, 388
Franklin, Aretha, 72, 322, 332, 340, 450, 470
Franklin, Erma, 332–33
Franklin, The Rev. C. L., 121, 322, 332
Franks, Tillman, 163
Fraternity Records, 145, 537n1
Fratto, Russ, 125–26, 260
Freberg, Stan, 456
Fred, John, and his Playboy Band/the Playboys,
    164, 179
Fredericks, Alan, 362, 534n8
Freed, Alan, 93, 126, 143, 195, 199, 216–17,
    220–21, 224–25, 240–43, 257, 260, 299, 311,
    359–63, 375, 418, 425, 444, 447; *Alan Freed's
    Easter Jubilee of Stars*, 221–22, 361; *Big Beat*
    TV show, 455; *Don't Knock the Rock*, 425;
    Jackie Freed, 361, P27; Jackie Music, 361; as
    "Moondog," 93; payola inquisition, 455–56,
    458–59, 518n5 (chap. 8), 523n12, 523n20,
    525n15, 534n1, P27; radio shows, 299,
    359–60, 362, 444; rock 'n' roll movies, 242,
    rock 'n' roll stage shows, 143–44, 199
Freeman, Bobby, 388
Freeman, Ernie, 153, 238, 366
Friedman, Gloria, 212
Friedman, Jake, 44, 47, 112, 263, 468, 479,
    513n30
Friedman, Joel, 192, 535n6, P21
Friedman, Mike, 381, 392
Frilot, Bert, 182
Frizzell, Lefty, 268, 529n13
Fuller, Blind Boy, 342
Fuller, Jerry, 316–17
Fulson, Lowell, 40, 45, 163–64, 303
Fuqua, Harvey (of the Moonglows), 338

Gabler, Milt, 15, 30, 55, 73, 259–60, 433, 511n18
GAC agency, 24, 314, 386, 434, 450–51, 510n4
    (chap. 2)
Gaddy, Bob, 226
Gale, Moe, 450, 541n16
Gale agency, 323, 450, 541n16, 541n17
Galehouse, Clark, 5, 209, 379; later years, 387–
    93, 535nn2–3, 538n15, P25; start of Golden
    Crest Records, Shelley Products pressing
    plant, 380–84; the Wailers, 385–87
Galehouse, Shelley, 5, 208–9, 390, 392, 522nn2–
    3, 535n1
Gamble and Huff (Kenny Gamble and Leon
    Huff), 432; and Sigma Sound studios (Phila-
    delphia), 540n20

Gant, Pte. Cecil, 34, 38, 42, 97, 278–79, 513n19
Gardner, Don, 369; and Dee Dee Ford, 350
Garner, Erroll, 57, 63, 74, 451
Garrett, Snuffy, 318
Gaudio, Bob, 444
Gavin Report, 459
Gaye, Marvin, 335, 464
Gayles, Juggy, 210, 256, 434
Gaylords, The, 236–37
Gayten, Paul, 109, 120, 125, 129, 142, 182, 335–36, 343, 518n12, 533n11; Pzazz Records, 518n12
Geddins, Bob (Down Town Records), 45
"Gee," 35, 534n3
Gee Records. *See* Tico-Rama-Gee Records
Geffen, David, 89
Gene & Eunice, 362
Gennett Records, 510n6
George, Barbara, 353–55, 533n15
"Georgia on My Mind," 445
Gersh, Bill, 191–92, 200, 203, 522n6
Gershwin, George, 266, 391
"Get a Job," 333, 363, 368–70, 372–73, 534n10
Gibbs, Georgia, 236–37, 298, 524n9
"G.I. Jive," 29
Gilbert, Jimmy, 226–27
Gillespie, Dizzy, 55
Gillette, Lee, 278
Gilt-Edge Records, 34, 38, 42, 160, 279–80, 532n10
Girl Can't Help It, The (film), 86
Gladiolas, The, 109, 373. *See also* Maurice Williams and the Zodiacs
Glaser, Joe, 240, 242, 270, 450
Glass, Paul, 50, 128–29, 164, 283, 468
Glover, Henry, 132, 136–39, 146, 148, 225, 251, 299, 324, 526n10; Glover Records, 225–26
Godfrey, Arthur, 215; *Arthur Godfrey Show*, 388
Goffin, Gerry, 377, 436
Goldband Records, 171–75, 182, 286, 521nn4–5, *P15*
Goldberg, Manny, 50
Goldberg, Phil, 50
Golden Crest Records, 5, 208–9, 379–80; Bell Records subsidiary, 85–86; 87–88, 301, 384, 516n12, 516n16, 536n7; CFG Publishing Co., 393, 538n15; Crest Records, 382, 384; Golden (Little Golden) Records, 14; formative years, 79–85; later years, 387–93, 537n19, 537n22, 537n1 (chap. 21); other artists, 536n18; Shelley Records, 380, 387; start of labels, 382, 384; the Wailers, 385–87
Goldenson, Leonard, 439
Goldmark, Aaron "Goldie," 435
Goldmark, Peter G. "Godfrey," 75
Goldner, George, 16, 69, 119, 121, 143, 216, 218–20, 233, 244, 246, 251–52, 287, 295, 330, 332–35, 340, 347, 362–63, 368, 390, 421, *P19*

gold record certification, 84
Gold Star studios (Hollywood), 298, 309–10, 312
Gone Records. *See* End-Gone Records
"Good Golly, Miss Molly," 304
Goodman, Benny, 24, 51, 161, 255, 257–59, 267, 302, 521n5 (chap. 11), 525n2
Goodman, Gene, 116, 119,172, 215, 255; Chess hits, 260–63, 264–67, 338, 427, 519n8, 521n5 (chap. 11), 525n1, 527n19, *P23*; start of Arc Music, 256, 257–59
Goodman, Harry, 255–59, 261–62, 266–67, 519n8, 527n19, *P23*
"Goodnight Irene," 157
"Goodnight My Love," 299–300
"Goodnite Sweetheart, Goodnite," 260
"Good Rockin'[Rocking] Tonight," 142, 397
Goody, Sam, 55, 370
"Goody Goody," 21, 245
Gordon, Dexter, 58
Gordon, Rosco(e), 149–51, 154–55, 158, 228, 519n8 (chap. 9)
Gordy, Anna, 335
Gordy, Berry, 138, 140, 165, 319, 324; with Billy Davis and start of Tamla-Motown Records, 330–40, 390, 431, 464, 467, 512n24, *P19*, *P24*
Gordy, Gwen, 319, 330, 335, 337–38
Gortikov, Stanley, 88
Gotham Records, 55, 110, 420, 520n22
"Gotta Travel On," 410–12
Gracie, Charlie, 425, 539n15
Graham, Michael Angelo, 385
Grammer, Billy, 410–12
Grand Ole Opry show, 94, 146, 198, 277, 279, 288, 294, 425
Granz, Norman, 28, 297, 416, 450, 525n14
"Great Balls of Fire," 153
"Great Pretender, The," 238, 262
Greek, John, 385–86, 537n22
Green, Al (*Flame Show Bar*), 273, 330–31
Green, Al (*National Records*), 23, 25, 56–57, 61, 514n5
Green, Al (*singer*), 413
Green, Irving, 23–24; start of Mercury Records, 25–26, 27–28, 30, 32, 57, 78, 82, 84, 235, 238, 240, 242, 289, 291, 293, 383, 510n7, 511nn5–6, 512n24, *P2*
Greenberg, Florence, 61, 260, 350, 376, 466, 509n3
Greenberg, Ray, 23, 25, 27, 511n5
Greenfield, Howie, 436
"Green Onions," 108
Greenwich, Ellie, 435
Gribble, Jim, 224–25
Gries, Eddie, 358
Griffin Brothers, The, 102
Grimes, Tiny, 63
Grizzard, Herman "The Old Colonel," 96, *P10*
Groove Records, 221, 232, 292, 433, 521n3 (chap. 11), 524n4

GRT, 122, 252
Guida, Frank, 532n17
"Guitar Boogie [Shuffle]," 278, 366
Guitar Gable, 169
Guitar Slim, 47, 181, 304, 307, 472, 478
Gunter, Arthur, 110
Gutshall, Jack, 35–36, 43, 56, 479, 512n11, 513n23, *P3*; Ammor Records, 36, 513n23
Guy, Buddy, 127, 339

Haddy, Arthur, 399
Haggard, Merle, 178, 542n22
Haley, Bill, 238, 260, 511n18, 526n9; and his Comets, 3, 30, 323, 420; and his Saddlemen, 279
Hall, Bill, 291
Hall, Rene, 250, 309
Hall, Rick, 164, 464
Hall, Tom T., 294, 413, 529n23
Hall, Tony, 398, 405
Hamilton, Roy, 450
Hamilton IV, George, 442
Hammond, John, 28, 62, 73
Hammond, Nathaniel "Stick-Horse," 163, 520n22
Hampton, Lionel, 63, 161, 225, 321, 511n18
Hampton, Riley, 339
Hancock, Hunter, 34, 120, 516n1, 534n3, *P21*
Handleman Co., rack jobbers, 140, 165, 519n11
"Hang Up My Rock and Roll Shoes," 419
Hanover-Signature Records, 448
Happy Fats (LeRoy LeBlanc), 167, 521n3
"Happy, Happy Birthday, Baby," 261, 526n11
"Happy Organ, The," 260, 347, 364–66, 370, 533n9, 534n6
"Harlem Nocturne," 33–34
"Harper Valley P.T.A.," 294–96, 529n23
Harpo, Slim, 109–11, 168–71, *P16*
Harptones, The (with Willie Winfield), 144, 216–17, 446
Harris, Thurston, and the Sharps, 309
Harris, Wynonie, 54, 97, 99, 131, 134, 137, 142, 531n4
Harrison, George, 398
Harrison, Wilbert, 344–49, 356, 364, 533n15
Hartstone, Leon "Lee," 409, 412
Harvey, Bill, 159
Hawkins, Coleman, 54, 58, 536n18
Hawkins, Dale, 121, 128, 163, 520n23
Hawkins, Erskine, 450
Hawkins, Hawkshaw, 131, 146, 531n22
Hayes, Alta, 279, 513n30, 528n4
Hayes, Bill, 85, 540n1
Hazlewood, Lee, 233, 302, 420
Heartbeats, The, 144, 350
"Heartbreak Hotel," 416
"Hearts of Stone," 137, 141–42, 162, 232, 469, 519n8

Heilicher, Amos and Dan, 28, 88, 511n10
Heller, Bob, 419
Heller, Eddie, 55, 215, 440
Henderson, Douglas "Jocko," 94, 225–26, 272, 359–61, 374, 419
Henderson, Fletcher, 62, 101, 299, 536n18
Hendrix, Jimi, 305
Henry, Macy, 44; and Macy's Records, 61, 513n25
Herald-Ember Records, 16, 125, 214, 223, 362–64, 368–73, 380, 524n2, 526n14, 532n7, 535n16, 537n1, 541n10, 543n9; Ember Distributors Inc., 364
Herman, Woody, 244, 302, 429
Hess, Bennie (Opera Records), 173
"Hey! Baby," 293
"Hey Paula," 178, 293
Hibbler, Al, 59
Hickory Records, 168, 198, 266–67, 463
"Higher and Higher (Your Love Keeps Lifting Me)," 339–40
"High School Hop," 302
"Hi-Heel Sneakers," 68
Hildebrand, Henry, 177, 292, 355; and Watch Records, 521n7
Hill, Big Bill, 126
Hill, Tommy, 168, 280
Hill & Range Music, 65, 153, 217, 253, 266–67; Big Top Records, 270–76, 278, 423, 425–26, 438, 449, 526n10, 527nn21–22, 539n15; country music strategy, 268; Elvis Presley, 268–71
Hilliard, Jimmy, 28
Hilltoppers, The, 3, 101–2, 241
Hi-Los, The, 325
Hi Records, 159, 366, 406, 413, 444, 520n17, 537n1, 538n22
"Hit the Road Jack," 445
HMV (His Master's Voice) Records (U.K.), 23, 372, 401
Hodge, Sam, 419, 514n37, 539n8
Hogg, Smokey, 40, 45
Holiday, Billie, 54, 126
Holford, Bill, 179
Holland, Eddie: Dozier, Lamont; Holland, Brian, 332; Lamont Dozier, 336
Holly, Buddy, 9, 449, 527n19; the Crickets, 452
Hollywood Flames, The, 307
Hollywood Records, 112, 284, 519n19, 524n7, 529n12, 543n9
"Honey Bee," 161
"Honeycomb," 246
"Honeydripper, The," 34, 36, 38
"Honey Hush," 66
"Honey Love," 66
"Honky Tonk (Part 1 & 2)," 138, 312, 318, 351, 366, 418, 534n7, 535n17
Hooke, Jack, 210, 361, 375, 455, 534n1

Hooker, John Lee, 40, 45, 129, 135, 154, 161, 265–66, 322, 518n5 (chap. 8)
Hopkins, Lightnin', 45, 126, 352, 370
Horn, Bob, 428, 540n19
Horne, Lena, 321
Horton, Walter, 154
Hotchkiss, Paul, 537n22; Paul and the Four-Most, 391
"Hot Rod Lincoln," 315
"Hound Dog," 35, 153, 233, 524n2, 524n6, 532n7
Howard, Ira, 190, 197–99, 201, 204–7, 277–78, *P18*
Howard Theater (Washington, DC), 62, 385, 451
Howlin' Wolf, 116, 121, 125, 127, 149, 151, 154–55, 162, 266, 326
"Huckle-Buck, The," 58
Huckman, Fred (R n B Records), 53
Hugg, Dick "Huggy Boy," 120
Hugo & Luigi, 234, 238, 248, 250, 274, 388, 447–48. *See also* Luigi Creatore, Hugo Peretti
"Hula Love," 245
Hull-Mascot Records, 61, 360, 527n14
Humperdinck, Engelbert, 400, 408
"Hunch, The," 335–36
Hunter, Ivory Joe, 35–36, 68, 193, 199, 513n15, 536n13
Hunter, Tab, 426
Hunter, Ty, 337
Hurte, Leroy, 38, 42
"Hustle, The," 252

"I Almost Lost My Mind," 199
"I Am Thinking Tonight of My Blue Eyes," 168
"I Can't Quit You Baby," 124, 518n8
"I Can't Stop Loving You," 376, 445, 527n15
"I'd Like to Teach the World to Sing" ("I'd Like to Buy the World a Coke"), 340
"I Don't Know," 215, 326, 532n7
"If I Knew You Were Comin' I'd've Baked a Cake," 57
"If You Wanna Be Happy," 532n17
"I Gotta Know," 437–38
"I Got You Babe," 355, 530n8
"I Heard It through the Grapevine," 337
"I Hear You Knocking," 362
"I Know (You Don't Love Me No More)," 182, 353–55, 533n15
"I Like It Like That (Part 1)," 530n11
"I'll Be Home," 163, 165, 199
"I'm a Fool to Care," 176, 291
"I'm a King Bee," 170
"I'm Available," 317–18
"I'm Gonna Move to the Outskirts of Town," 29
"I'm Leavin' It Up to You," 178–80
"I'm So Lonesome I Could Cry," 136
"I'm Stickin' with You," 245

"I'm Walkin'," 416
"I Only Have Eyes for You," 334
"I Saw Mommy Kissing Santa Claus," 259
"I've Got a Woman" ("I Got a Woman"), 68, 524n2, 532n2 (chap. 18), 533n15
"I Walk the Line," 153
"I Will Follow You," 250
"I Wonder," 36, 38, 42, 278–80, 513n19
"I Wonder Why," 456
Imperial Records, 4, 9, 12, 16, 34, 40, 44, 66, 128, 146, 153, 170–71, 179, 194, 219, 245, 258, 278, 297–99, 304; sale of, 308, 317; 316, 355, 366, 390, 416–17, 444–45, 462, 478, 513n26, 520n1, 524n2, 526n5, 529n8, 530n11, 532n7, 537n20, 537n1 (chap. 21), 541n10
Impressions, The, 445, 462
"Indian Love Call," 163
Ink Spots, The, 35, 238, 541n16
Instant Records, 530n11
"In the Still of the Nite," 362–63, 368, 373, 437, 528n27
Island Records, 352, 401
Isley Brothers, The, 248
"Is You Is or Is You Ain't (Ma' Baby)," 29
"It Might as Well Rain until September," 540n26
"It's All in the Game," 447, 541n11
"It's Just a Matter of Time," 419
"It's Now or Never" ("O Sole Mio"), 271, 437, 527n22
"It's Only Make Believe," 447, 541n11
"It Wasn't God Who Made Honky Tonk Angels" ("Did God Make Honky Tonk Angels?"), 168, 520n1

J. & M. Recording Studio (New Orleans), 180, 478, 521n10, 530n10, 543n8
Jackson, Billy, 431, *P30*
Jackson, Bull Moose, 97, 449
Jackson, Chuck, 377
Jackson, Hal, 216, 225, 361
Jackson, Mahalia, 54–55
Jackson, Michael, 303; the Jackson 5, 309
Jackson, The Rev. Jesse, 122
Jackson, Roddy, 304–5
Jacobs, Dick, 332, 433, *P23*
Jacquet, Illinois, 259
"Jailhouse Rock," 233
Jamal, Ahmed, 116, 118, 128, 518n3
Jamboree film, 245
James, Elmore, 40, 126, 155, 158–59, 352
James, Etta, 40, 116, 118, 237, 298, 329, 333, 337, 339
Jamie-Guyden Records, 179, 182, 291, 302, 366, 418; start of, 420–21; 432, 458, 462, 537n1, 539nn8–9, 540n26; Universal Record Distributing Corp., 420–21, 458, 539n9
Jan & Dean, 317

Jarrett, "Big Hugh Baby," 111
Jarvis, Al, 34–36, 512n4
Jayhawks, The, 298
Jeffries, Herb, 36
"Jenny, Jenny," 304
Jesters, The, 144
Jewell-Paula-Ronn Records, 51, 129, 164–65, 520n24
Jewel Records (Los Angeles), 51, 57
Jewels, The, 142
"Jim Dandy": "Jim Dandy Got Married," 324, 532n7
"Jim Wilson Boogie," 133
Jin-Swallow Records, 175–76, 291
Jive Five, The, 139
Jive Records, 229
Jivin' Gene, 176, 178, 291
"Jo-Ann," 246, 534n1
Johannesen, Grant, 391
John, Little Willie, 131, 134, 139, 146, 527n23
Johnnie & Joe, 261
Johnny and the Hurricanes, 274, 366, 448, 528n26, 528n28; Johnny Paris, 541n15
Johnson, Betty, 516n15
Johnson, Buddy, 225, 307, 363, 511n18, 513n19, 541n16; and Ella Johnson, 54, 451
Johnson, Hiram (Johnson Records), 363
Johnson, Joe, 279; at Challenge Records, 309–18; 510n7, 531n23
Johnson, Johnnie, 328
Johnson, Marv, 333, 335
Johnson, Pete, 26
Johnson, Plas, 3, 309; and the Johnson Brothers (with Ray), 353
Johnson, Robert, 155, 172
Jolson, Al, 204
Jones, George, 18, 164, 198, 285–86, 288, 292, 525n13, 529n13; as Thumper Jones, 285
Jones, Grandpa, 132, 146
Jones, Joe, 353–54
Jones, Quincy, 418
Jones, Rodney, 126
Jones, Tom, 400, 408, 451
Joplin, Janis, 305; and Big Brother and the Holding Company, 418
Jordan, Louis, 17, 24, 28–31, 35, 138, 161, 299, 321, 449, 511n18, 511n20, 511n22, 518n12, P2
Jordan, Murray, 403, P29
Jordanaires, The, 111
Joyce, Bobby, 365
Joyce, Jolly, 368
Jubilee-Josie Records, 59, 62, 78, 215, 252, 261, 345, 350–51, 385, 388–89, 466, 509n3, 514n10, 514n15, 515n24, 523n9, 536n13, 537n1, 541n10
"Judy in Disguise (With Glasses)," 164, 179
jukebox industry, importance of, 16–18, 41–44,

104, 136, 152, 161, 190–92, 292, 325, 479; decline of, 466, 480
"Just a Dream," 181
"Just Because," 442
Justis, Bill, 113, 153, 318, 366
"Just Walking in the Rain," 310

Kahl, Phil, 222, 353
Kalin Twins, The, 437
"Kansas City," 344–49, 364–65, 374, 533nn5–6; "K.C. Loving," 346–47
Kaplan, John, 46, 135, 137, 140
Kapp, Dave, 15, 29, 84, 448, 512n24
Kapp, Jack, 15; importance to Decca Records, 29–30, 75, 81, 398, 511n15, 537n4
Kapp Records, 448, 512n24, 537n1
Kari, Sax, 532n14, 533n11
Karsch, George "Cohort," 97
Kaslin (Casalin), Blanche "Bea," 61, 262, 526n14
Kassner, Ed, 538n22; Kassner Music, 368, 527n20; Seville-President Records, 527n20, 536n13, 538n22
Kaye, Danny, 85
KC and the Sunshine Band, 264, 467, 469
K-Doe, Ernie, 182, 530n11
Keane, Bob, 307
Keaton, Dorothy, 106, 111
Keen Records, 9, 125, 249, 307, 462
"Keep a Knockin'," 304
Keepnews, Orrin, 73
Keller, Jack, 436
Kelley, Jack, 145, 283
Kennedy, Gene, 112
Kennedy, Jerry, 293–94, 413
Kenner, Chris, 182, 530n11
Kent, Herb, 126
Kenton, Stan, 96, 302
Kent Records, 223, 301–3, 313, 530n3. See also Modern-RPM-Flair Records
Kern, Jerome, 391
Kershaw, Rusty & Doug, 168
Kessler, Danny, 75
Kessler, Gwen, 264, 513n30, 527n15
Khoury, George, 174; Khoury's Records, 174, 290
Killen, Buddy (Dial Records), 293, 408, 527n20, 538n22; Tree Music, 408
Kilpatrick, Walter "Dee," 286, 288, 411, 538n19
"Kind of a Drag," 129
King, B.B., 40, 126; with Blues Boys Kingdom Records, 300, 303, 445, 462, 519nn2–3, 530n2, P21; with Sam Phillips, 149–51, 154–55, 158, 162, 298–99
King, Ben E., 53
King, Carole, 265, 377, 436, 540n26
King, Claude, 163, 431
King, Earl, 59, 176, 182, 478, 521n7
King, Earl "Connelly," 138
King, Freddy, 131, 137, 145

King, Maurice, 321, 327, 531n6

King, Saunders, 40, 45

King-Federal Records, 9, 15, 17, 40, 66, 109, 112, 121, 128, 131; Armo Music, 137, 368, 370–71, 373; Detroit branch office, 133–37, 519n6; Henry Stone at De Luxe Records, 141–42, 143–47; hit acts, 138–40; Jay & Cee Music, 146–47; launch of King, 132–33; Lois Music, 112, 146–48, 299, 519n11; Nashville branch office, P11; Queen Records, 132; Royal Plastics pressing plant, 132, 147, P1; sale of, 147–48, 162, 194, 220, 224–25, 232, 238–39, 269, 271, 278, 281–82, 284, 287, 290, 296, 299, 322, 324–25, 330, 346–48, 380, 390, 429–30, 444, 464, 509n3, 518n5 (chap. 8), 519n11, 519n19, 524n5, 524n9, 527n23, 529n18, 529n25, 532n8, 535n17, 537n1, P9; Starday-King Records, 140, 147–48, 287

Kingsmen, The, 385–86

Kirkland, Leroy, 375, P27

Kirkpatrick, William, 98–99

Kirshner, Don, 254, 265, 436–37, 524n10, 540n26

Kissack, Ed, 409

"Kisses Sweeter Than Wine," 246

"Kiss from Your Lips, A," 327–28, 334

"Kissin' Time," 428

"Kiss Me Baby," 327

Klein, Allen, 250, 350, 432, 446

Knickerbockers, The, 317

Knight, Gladys, and the Pips, 112, 350, 517n16

Knox, Buddy, and the Rhythm Orchids, 245

Koester, Bob (Delmark Records), 4

Kolsky, Joe, 244, 247

Kornheiser, Bob, 109, P31

Korsen, Emil, 428

Krasnow, Bob, 145

Krefetz, Lou, 66, 451, P20

Kriegsmann, James, 364, 368

Kruger, Jeffrey, 371–72, 401

Krupa, Gene, 257

Ku Klux Klan, 164, 320

Laboe, Art, 362

Ladell, Harold "Mr. Blues," x, 60, 62; *Mr. Blues Show*, 217–20, 225, 360, 462, 516n1, 523n14, 523n17

Laine, Frankie, 27, 32, 89, 143, 311, 323, P2

Lamb, Charlie, 197

LaMonte, John, 251

LaPidus, Harry, 235; Peter Pan Records, 85, 235

Larks, The, 214

LaRocca, Connie (Frisco Records), 4, 61

"Last Night I Dreamed," 224, 523n25

Latin Quarter club (New York), 54, 204, 227

Lauderdale, Jack, 34, 297, 451

Laurie Records, 225, 390, 420, 423, 444, 456, 462, 527n20, 535n16, 537n1, 539n8

"Lavender Blue (Dilly Dilly)," 267, 272–73, 411, 528n25

Lavergne, Lee, 4; and Lanor Records, 169

Law, Don, 278–79, 287, 310, 528n1

"Lawdy Miss Clawdy," 304, 478, 524n2

Lazy Lester, 107, 168

Leadbelly (Huddie Ledbetter), 157, 400, 433

Leadbitter, Mike, xiii, 4, 156, 513n25, 529n10

Leaner, Ernie and George (Mar-V-Lus Records group), 128

Lee, Brenda, 199

Lee, Dickie, 293

Lee, Jack, 418–19; daughter Nancy Lee, 419

Lee, Peggy, 22, 88, 143, 206, 271, 527n23

Leedon Records (Australia), 401

Legrand Records, 339, 390, 444, 532n17, 535n16

Leiber, Jerry, and Mike Stoller, 3, 69, 89, 148, 233–34, 248, 253, 266, 269, 272, 296, 347, 388, 524n6, 533n6, P20; Spark Records, 233

LeJeune (LeJune), Iry, 171–74

Lennon, John, 265, 398

Lenoir, J. B., 124

Leslie, Cy, 87–88, 211, 466, 516n17

"Let's Stick Together" ("Let's Work Together"), 356

"Let's Twist Again," 429–30, 432

"Let the Good Times Roll," 449

"Let the Little Girl Dance," 210, 225–26, 437

"Letter Full of Tears," 350

Levine, Al, 38; and Alco pressing plant (Los Angeles), 514n37, 536n6

Levine, Harry, 440

Levitan, Cy, 388–89

Levy, George, 363, 368

Levy, Lou, 250; and Leeds Music, 512n24

Levy, Morris, 103, 119, 129, 210–11, 222, 229; early years, Roulette Records, 243–47, 251–52, 266, 269, 345, 350–51, 354, 361, 375, 448, 456, 458, 466, 510n7, 525n14, 525n16, 534n1; lawsuit, *Jimmy Merchant and Herman Santiago v. Morris Levy et al*, 526n8

Lewis, Bobby, 139

Lewis, Clarence "Fats," 348, 350, 533n10; Falew! Records, 350

Lewis, Edward "E.R."/"Ted" (Sir), 15, 29, 68, 263, 316, 372; formation of Decca Records (U.K., U.S.), 398–99; London (U.S.)-London American Records, 400–401, 403, 405–10, 412, 414, 463, 537nn3–4, 538n21, P28

Lewis, Jerry Lee, 9, 149–50, 153, 205, 293, 296, 387, 398, 462, 537n1

Lewis, Margaret, 294

Lewis, Monty, 88

Lewis, Ramsey, 116

Lewis, Smiley, 362, 478

Lewis, Stan, 51, 109, 115, 121, 129, 161–66, 176, 179, 263, 321, 462, 518n5, 520n23, P14

Liberace, 311

Liberty Records, 19, 146, 297, 317–18, 347, 385, 387, 390, 444, 462, 510n7, 537n20, 537n1 (chap. 21)

Lichtman, Irv, 10, 13, 190; editor at *Cash Box*, 199–207, 409, 465, *P18*

Lieberson, Goddard, 77, 84, 86

"Life Is But a Dream," 216–17, 523n10

Liggins, Joe, 34–36, 38–39, 49, 513n15, 529n8, *P3*

Lightnin' Slim, 108, 168

"Ling, Ting, Tong," 300

Lion, Alfred, 12, 55, 73

"Lion Sleeps Tonight, The (Wimoweh)," 250–51, 525n22

Lipsius, Harold B., 179, 418, 420–21, 458, 539n9

Lit, Hy, 419, 422

Little Anthony and the Imperials, 216

"Little Bitty Pretty One," 308–9

"Little Darlin'," 109–10, 418, 437

Little Esther, 57, 137

Little Eva, 540n26

Littlefield, Little Willie, 40, 133, 346

Little Milton, 152, 159, 339–40, 520n24, 532n16

Little Richard, 9, 35, 40, 47, 59, 102, 206, 303–4, 307, 347, 385–86, 409, 411, 451, 463, 470, 473, 513n30, 524n2, 537n1, 543n8, 543n10

"Little Shoemaker, The," 236

"Little Star," 361, 411, 444, 527n14

Little Walter, 117, 125, 127, 162, 266, 326

"Livery Stable Blues," 12

Livingston, Alan, 88

Locklin, Hank, 282, 290

Loco-Motion, The," 540n26

Logan, Don "Dandy," 164

Logan, Harold, 390, 442

"Lollipop," 146, 418

Lomax, Alan and John, 157

London, Mel, 126–27, 518n13; and Profile-Age Records, 518n13

London (London American) Records (U.K.), 3, 67, 121, 371, 386, 397; Sir Edward Lewis, 398–99, 400; foreign distribution, 401–9; 410–14, 535n16; labels/artists, 537n1

London American Group (U.S.), 80, 410–14, 444; labels/record men, 538n22

London Records (U.S.), 31, 61, 84, 242, 382, 390, 398, 400, 402–3, 527n21, 538n8, 538n14; Felsted Records, 242, 412, 432, 538n22; function of foreign distrib. dept., 404, 405–6, 408–14, 456

"Lonely Boy," 444

"Lonely Teardrops," 332, 361

Lonesome Sundown, 168

"Long Gone," 137, 162

"Long Lonely Nights," 121, 518n6

"Long Tall Sally," 304

Lorenz, George "Hound Dog," 517n1

Lormar Distributing Company (Chicago), 124–25

"Louie Louie," 299, 386

Louis, Joe Hill, 150, 154

Louisiana Hayride show, 162–63, 279, 288, 294

Lounsberry, Jim, 120

Love, Milton, 216, 222–24, 523n23

"Love Doctor Blues," 55

"Love Is Strange," 524n4

"Love Me Tender," 416

Love Records, 366

"Lover's Question, A" 419

Lowe, Bernie, 262, 269, 271, 392, 424; start of Cameo Records, 425–26, 428–29, 431–32, 510n7, 530n2, 535n2, 539n15, 541n10, *P30*; Teen-Sound Records, 425

Lowe, Jim, 101

Lowe, Sammy, 333

Lowery, Bill (NRC Records), 527n20

Lubinsky, Herman, 12, 16; start of Savoy Records, 57–58; 59–60, 78, 132, 134, 137, 213, 345, 347, 358, 407, 465, 509n3, 518n3 (chap. 8), *P6*

Lucas, Buddy, 225, 364, 516n15

"Lullaby of Birdland," 243

Lunceford, Jimmie, 36, 299

Lymon, Frankie, 220, 245, 452, 526n8; lawsuit, *Jimmy Merchant and Herman Santiago v. Morris Levy et al*, 526n8; and the Teenagers, 216, 221–23, 226, 244, 523n19

Lynn, Vera, 400, 411

Lytle, Moe, 148, 519n19

Mabley, Moms, 107, 121

Mabon, Willie, 215, 326, 532n7

Mack, Lonnie, 145

"Mack the Knife," 72

Maddox Brothers and Rose, 281

Madison Records, 86, 527n20

Madonna, 61, 143, 303

Magic Sam, 127

Magid, Lee, 54, 56–59, 213, 440, 536n17; and Central Records, 59, 440

Magnificent Montague, 120

Maguire, Walt, 242, 406, 408–9, 411–12, 538n22, *P29*

Majestic Records, 28, 32

"Make Yourself Comfortable," 237

Malaco Records, 520n24

Malone, Idessa (Staff Records), 61, 531n6

"(Mama) He Treats Your Daughter Mean," 65, 532n7

"Mambo Baby," 66, 68, 271

Mammarella, Tony (Anthony September), 289, 369, 417, 421, 426, 539n15, 539n17

Mancini, Henry, 385–86

Mando and the Chili Peppers, 384–85, 536n8

Mann, Barry, 436

Mann, Kal, 262, 269, 271, 424; start of Cameo

Records, 425–26; 427–30, 432, 510n7, 530n2, 539n15, 540n21, *P30*

Manor Records, 55, 58

Mansfield, Jayne, 73, 86

Mantovani, 400, 404, 411

Marcels, The, 437

March, Little Peggy, 248, 250

Marchan, Bobby, 349, 375

Marcucci, Bob, 421–24, 462, 539n10, 539n13

Marcus, Irving, 158

Marek, George, 246, 248

Markham, Pigmeat, 107

Marks (E.B.) Music, 254, 276

Marley, Bob, and the Wailers, 536n8

Marshall, Paul, 295, 350, 535n16, 538n14

Martin, Dean, 452

Martin, George, 372

Martin, Joe; Apex-Martin distributors (Newark), 542n13

Martin, Tony, 27, 206, 527n22

Marvelettes, The, 107, 338, 431

Marvin & Johnny, 298

"Mashed Potato Time," 431

Massler, Al, 83, 86–87, 275, 384; A.A. Records, 85, 516n13

Matassa, Cosimo, 16–18, 166–67, 179–82, 304, 306, 351, 473, 478, 521n11, 538n22, 543n6, *P14*; Dover Records, 521n11, 538n22; Rex Records, 181

Mathis, Johnny, 74, 89

Mattis, David James, 158

Maxin, Arnold, 447–48

"Maybe," 216, 534n1

"Maybellene," 126, 260, 362, 524n2, 532n8, 532n10

Mayfield, Curtis, 462

Mayfield, Percy, 49, 449

MCA agency, 314, 323, 450

MCA (Music Corporation of America), 31, 511n13, 511nn23–24, 527n19

MCA Records, 31, 350–51, 445; distribution, 317

McCain, Jerry, 164, 182

McCall, Bill, 211; start of 4 Star Records, 279–80, 281–83, 285, 287, 315, 322, 324, 385, 509n3, 528n6, 531n22, 531n3 (chap. 17), 532n10

McCarthy, Jim, 363

McCartney, Paul, 265, 305, 398

McCoy, Austin, 45

McCoy, Rose Marie, 146, 271, 526n10, *P27*

McCoy, Van, 252

McCracklin, Jimmy, 40, 45, 418

McCrae, George, 467

McCuen, Brad, 433

McDonald, Cliff, 42, 280–81

McFadden, Ruth, 220–22, 523n19

McGhee, Brownie, 58, 64; and Sonny Terry, 63, 226, 342

McGhee, Stick(s), 63–64, 514nn13–14

McGill, Rollee, 368

McGriff, Jimmy, 352, 533n15

McGuire Sisters, The, 195, 300, 526n9

McKenzie, Ed "Jack the Bellboy," 135, 517n1

McLaughlin, Ollie, 273–74

McLollie, Oscar, 39

McMurry, Lillian, 4, 61, 155–56, 158, 164, 214, 264, 520n11, 523n8

McNeely, Big Jay, 35, 37, 58

McPhatter, Clyde, 66, 68, 71, 121, 293, 419, 444, 452, 518n6, 524n2, *P7*, *P17*. *See also* the Dominoes, the Drifters

MCPS (Mechanical Copyright Protection Society, U.K.), 3

McVea, Jack, 141

Meaux, Huey, 169, 177, 179, 291, 529n20, 538n22

Melody Maker, 405, 469, 535n16

"Memphis," 145

Mendelsohn, Fred, 57, 59, 115, 218

Mercer, Johnny, 21, 36, 98, 510n7, 530n2

Mercury Records, 23–24; cover version era, 236–37; label launch, 25–28; 30–32, 35, 45, 78, 80, 82, 84, 88–89, 103, 109, 141, 150, 159–60, 160, 165, 173–74, 176, 178, 188, 222, 234–35; Mercury-Starday Records, 286, 288, 538n19; The Platters, 238–42, 245–46, 252, 286; pressing plants, 25–26, 28, 45, 491; sale of, 293, 295, 351, 367, 373, 380, 382–84, 390, 401, 408, 410–11, 413, 427, 433, 441, 444, 446–48, 452, 462, 510n7, 511n13, 512n24, 519n11, 524n2, 525n11, 525n13, 527n21, 529n24, 535n6, 536n13, 536n18, 538n19; Shelby Singleton era, 287–93; Wing Records, 232

"Merry Christmas Baby," 37

Mesner brothers (Eddie, Leo), 12, 34, 44, 162, 308–9, 469, 512n2

"Messing with the Kid," 126

Meteor Records, 40, 157–60, 303, 520n18

Meters, The, 350

MGM (Metro-Goldwyn-Mayer) Records, 22, 49, 71, 84, 128, 159, 181, 228, 278–79, 369, 388, 390, 410, 446–48, 462–63, 516n10, 538n21; big hits (1958–59), 541n11; pressing plants, 275, 389

Miami disc jockey convention (1959), 69, 443, 454–55, 458

Miami News, 444–45

Micahnik, Irving, 273, 449

Mickey & Sylvia, 353, 524n4. *See also* Sylvia Robinson

Middleman, Al, 48–49

MIDEM festival (France), 420, 469

Midwestern Hayride show, 132, 146

Milburn, Amos, 218, 299, 344, 529n8

Miller, Dave, 30, 217, 420, 446, 468, 516n17

Miller, Glenn, 24, 35, 56, 161, 172, 531n16

Miller, J. D. "Jay," 4, 109, 166–71, 176, 520n1, 521n2, 530n2, *P16*; Fais-Do-Do, Feature Records, 167; Rebel Records, 170, 521n3; Rocko-Zynn Records, 169; as songwriters J. D. Miller, Jerry West, 169
Miller, Johnny, 145, 148
Miller, Mitch, 28, 75, 78, 82–83, 86; as Columbia A&R man, 88–90; 215, 235, 259, 310, 388, 391, 446–47, 516n20, *P8*
Miller, Roger, 293, 413
Millinder, Lucky, 136, 197, 449, 541n16
Mills Brothers, The, 238
Mills Music, 381, 385; Richard Mills, 385–86
Milne, Geoff(rey), 405, 409
Milton, Roy, 35, 47–49, 232, 449
Minaret Records, 292, 294, 522n11
Mineo, Art, 385–86
Mingus, Charles (Charlie), 36, 515n19
Minit Records, 444, 530n11
Miracle Records, 50, 123, 137, 162
Miracles, The, 333, 336, 338
Mitchell, Freddie, 55
Mitchell, Guy, 143
Mitchell, Willie, 413
Mitnick, Jack, 31, 213, 511n20, 522n6 (chap. 12)
MOA (Music Operators of America), 510n11
Modern Jazz Quartet (MJQ), 67; Jackson, Milt, 54
Modern-RPM-Flair Records, 12, 16, 34, 39–40; early years, Modern (Music) Records, 43–47, 49, 51, 66, 78, 102, 141, 150, 152, 154, 159–60, 162, 194, 211–14, 219, 233, 258, 279, 297–301; Modern Music Publishing, 47, 299–300, 302, 304, 313; pressing plants, 45, 150, 213, 298, 530n1, 536n6; sale of, 303, 304, 318, 347, 356, 380, 462, 512n11, 513n24, 513n26, 513n28, 518n5 (chap. 8), 526n5, 530n2, 537n1, 540n26, 543n9. *See also* Crown, Kent, and Meteor Records
"Money (That's What I Want)," 165, 336, 524n2
"Money Honey," 66, 524n2
Monotones, The, 262
Monroe, Bill, 198, 268
Monroe, Marilyn, 3
Montalbano, Sam "S. J.," 166; and Montel Records, 178–80
Montgomery, Al, 167
Monument Records, 112–13, 282, 293, 406, 408; start of, 410–12, 413, 442–44, 463, 510n7, 537n1, 538n20, 538n22
Moody, Doug, 223, 363; "The Happy Organ" hit, 364–67; at Herald-Ember Records, 368–70, 372–73, 534n6, 534n8; Mystic Records, 373
Moody, Walter "Wally," 363–65, 370–71
Moonglows, The, 116, 144, 195, 260, 326, 328, 338, 398, 524n2, 526n9
"Moon River," 21

Moore, Clarence "Gatemouth," 95
Moore, Scotty, 132
Moore's Three Blazers, Johnny, 37, 44, 343, 512n2, 512n5
Morrill, Kent, 386
Morris, Doug, 89, 130
Morris, E. H. "Buddy," 283
Morris (E. H.) Music, 283, 418
Morrison, Jim, 305
Morros, Boris, 25
Morrow, Bruce, 362
Moss, Jerry, 314, 456, 464
"Mother-in-Law," 530n11
Motown Records. *See* Tamla-Motown Records
Moulton, Tom, 539n11
"Move On Up a Little Higher," 55
"Mr. Blue," 385
MTV, 29
"Mule Skinner Blues," 290
Mullican, Moon, 146
Mure, Billy, 249; hits accompanied, 536n2; and Valentine Records, 388–89
Murray, Henry "Juggy," 352–57
Murray the K. (Kaufman), 199, 538n22
Music City store (Hollywood), 21–22, 38
music publishers, activities of. *See* Freddy Bienstock, Johnny Bienstock, Gene Goodman sections (chapter 14)
"Music! Music! Music!" 400
Musicor Records, 242–43, 390, 511n13, 519n19, 525n13, 529n25
Musicraft Records, 28
Music Sales Co. distributors (Memphis), 44, 158, 198, 306
Mutual Broadcasting System (MBS, Mutual Radio), 19
Muzak Corporation, 541n10
"My Babe," 125
"My Foolish Heart," 256
"My Happiness," 541n11
Myles, Billy, 372, 526n10
"My Prayer," 241
"My Song," 158
"Mystery Train," 397
Mystics, The, 225
"My Toot Toot," 176, 178
"My True Story," 139

NAB (National Association of Broadcasters), 152, 519n4
NAMM (National Association of Music Merchants), 38
Nashboro Records. *See* Excello-Nashboro Records
Nashville "A" Team, 412
Nathan, Syd, 16, 60, 109, 112; branch office network, 133–37; De Luxe Records, 141–42, 143–47; death of, and King sale, 147–48, 162,

194, 225, 232, 239, 278, 283–84, 287, 290, 296, 299, 319, 324, 340, 347, 429–30, 464, 469, 509n3, 518n1 (chap. 8), 518n3 (chap. 8), 519n12, 519n16, 524n5, *P9*, *P12*; King hit acts, 138–40; King Records launch, 132–33; as songwriter Lois Mann, 146; Syd's Record Shop, 132–33

National Barn Dance show, 146

National Records, 23, 25, 55–57, 61, 66, 160, 513n19, 536n17; pressing plant, 57, 491, 514n9

"Nature Boy," 235

Navarro, Fats, 61

NBC (National Broadcasting Company), 13, 19, 24, 38, 75, 94, 168, 270, 391, 440, 517n2. *See also* RCA, RCA Victor

"Near You," 141, 278, 281, 468

Neely, Hal, 140, 147–48, 287, 296, 519n18

Nelson, Ken, 278

Nelson, Richard "Dick," 38, 42, 279–80, 528n6

Nelson, Ricky, 316–17, 416–17, 423, 462, 537n1

Nelson, Sandy, 366

Nelson, Willie, 542n22

Neville, Aaron, 263

Neville, Art, 306, *P22*

Nevins, Al, 254, 436, 540n26; and the Three Suns, 239, 524n10

Newman, Herb, 297

Newman, Jimmy, 159, 163

New Musical Express, 405, 528n26, 535n17

"New Orleans," 532n17

Newton, Larry, 55, 59, 217, 369, 392, 422–23, 440–43, 445, 510n7, 535n20, 539n10, *P31*

New York Post, 455–56

Niagara, Joe, 422

Nice, John, 405, 538n16

"96 Tears," 540n23

Noble, Ray, 34

Nobles, Gene, 46; disc jockey at Radio WLAC, Nashville, 95–103, 111, 114–15, 120, 517n8, 520n23, *P10*

Nolen, Jimmy, 131

Nomar Records, 373–74, 537n1

"No More Doggin'," 155

Noonan, Tom, 189, 521n4 (chap. 11)

Norvo, Red, 380, 383

"Now Is the Hour," 400

"Number 9 Train," 345

Nutmegs, The, 144, 373

Oberstein, Eli, 24, 27, 48, 58, 87, 368, 440, 516n17, 518n1 (chap. 8)

O'Day, Anita, 126

O'Day, Pat, 384

"Oh! Carol," 437

"Oh Happy Day," 420

"Oh Julie," 109, 111

"Oh No Not My Baby," 377

"Oh Pretty Woman," 413

OKeh Records, 35, 66, 75, 232, 268, 277, 293, 311, 364, 381–82, 447, 543n9

"Okey Dokey Stomp," 95

Oklahoma! Broadway show, 29

"Old Payola Roll Blues, The," 456

Old Town Records, 1, 16, 87, 103, 112, 118, 123, 210, 215–17, 219–22; Barry Records, 524n31; the hits, 223–28, 229–30, 361, 437, 523n11, 524nn32–33, 537n1; Maureen Music, 217, 222, 224; Paradise Records, 215–16, 222; Parody Records, 216; Twin Records, 227

Olson, Rocky, 346–47

one-stops, activities of, 124, 134, 161, 165, 177, 191, 292, 530n12

"Only the Lonely," 412

"Only You (And You Alone)," 3, 238–41, 441, 524n2, 525n11

"Oop Shoop," 298–99

"Open the Door, Richard!" 61, 141

Orbison, Roy, 149, 296, 406, 410, 412–13, 463, 537n1, 538n21, 540n3, *P30*

Original Dixieland Jazz Band, 4, 12

Original Sound Records, 362, 366, 535n16

Oriole Records (U.K.), 371

Orioles, The (with Sonny Til), 215, 323, 451, 531n4

Orleck, Joe, 190–91, 197, 200, 203–4

Orleck, Norman, 190, 203, 206, *P18*

Orloff, Ben, 24–26

Orlons, The, 431

Ostin, Mo, 89

Ostrow, Marty, 190; *Cash Box* launch and market, 191–94; *Cash Box* Top 100 charts and bullets, 194–96, 197, 200–1, 204, 207, 464, *P18*

Otis, Clyde, 58, 293, 418, 526n10

Otis, Johnny, 33–35, 57, 103, 137, 224, 232, 298, 303, 512n1, *P8*; Dig-Eldo Records, 35

"Over and Over," 309

"Over the Mountain, Across the Sea," 261

Owens, Buck, 178

Page, Frank "Gatemouth," "The Mouth of the South," 162

Page, Patti, 32, 39, 143, 194, 237, 289, 323, 536n13

Painia, Frank: Dew Drop Inn (New Orleans), 478

Paley, William "Bill," 13, 75–77

Palitz, Morty, 516n15, *P7*

Palmer, Earl, 250, 309, 472, 478

Pan American Record Distributors (Detroit), 46, 135, 140, 519n6

"Papa's Got a Brand New Bag," 140

Paragons, The, 144

Paramor, Norrie, 372

Paramount Pictures, 101, 439, 517n8

Paramount Records, 510n6, 528n1
Paramount Theater (Brooklyn), 143, 221, 428;
    (New York), 361
Pare, Gladys, 274
Parker, Charlie, 55, 57–58, 213
Parker, Fess, 85
Parker, (Little) Junior, 152, 176, 351
Parker, Tom (Colonel), 268–70, 527n21
Parkway Records. See Cameo-Parkway Records
Parlophone Records (U.K.), 23, 372, 401, 535n17
Parlo Records, 263
Parnes, Sid, 192–93, 196, 200, 538n22, P27
Parrot-Blue Lake Records, 123
Parton, Dolly, 175
"Party Doll," 245
Passions, The, 225
"Patches," 293
Pate, Johnny, 339
"Patricia," 366
Paul, Frank (Casa Grande Records), 261
Paul, Les, 20, 388, 511n17; and Mary Ford, 143
Paul & Paula, 178, 293
Paxton, Gary, 538n22
payola scandal (1959–60), 204, 454–60
Payton, Lawrence, 320, 325
Peacock Records. See Duke-Peacock Records
Pearl, Jack, 132, 136, 139, 142, 347
Pearls, The, 359, 364
Pedrick, Bobby Jr. (Robert John), 272, 411
Peer, Ralph, 157, 168, 241, 284, 511n16
Penguins, The, 239, 362, 437, 524n2
Penny, Hank, 131, 137
"Peppermint Twist (Part 1)," 251
Peretti, Hugo, 234; at Mercury, 235–38; at RCA
    Victor, 248–51, 252–53, 308, P20; at Roulette,
    243–47, 251. See also Hugo & Luigi
Perkins, Carl, 149, 205, 278, 296, 462, 537n1
"Personality," 442
Peterson, Ray, 248, 250, 274, 536n13
Peterson Quintet, Bobby, 335–36
Petit, Buddy, 37, 512n8
Petrillo, James C., 14–15, 63, 79–80, 84, 468,
    510n5; Petrillo bans on recording, (1942–44),
    14–15, 30, 35–36, 58, 277; (1948), 45, 56,
    62–63, 79–80, 400. See also AFM
Petty, Norman, 9, 449
Philadelphia International Records, 432
Philips Records (Holland and U.K.), 22–23, 178,
    252, 293, 371, 401, 462
Philles Records, 233, 537n1, 539n9, 540n26
Phillips, Dewey "Daddy-O," 150, 517n1
Phillips, Harvey, 391
Phillips, Phil, 171, 174, 290–91
Phillips, Sam, 121; [It's The] Phillips Records,
    150; at Memphis Recording and Sound Ser-
    vice, 149–52, 153–55, 157–60, 188, 270, 287,
    294, sale of Sun Records, 295–96, 355, 406,

416, 462, 473, 518n5, 519n3, 521n2, 529n24,
    539n1, 542n7, P12, P32
Phillips International Records, 113, 295, 318,
    366
Pickett, Wilson, 339, 464
Pickwick Records, 87–88, 511, 516n17; Cricket
    Records, 85, 88; group companies, 88
Pierce, Don, 2, 42, 140; at 4 Star Records,
    279–84; as songwriter William York, 287; at
    Starday Records, 284–87, 288–89, 302, 308,
    322, 324, 407, 465, 519n16, 524n7, 529n10,
    529n14, 529n16, 538n19, P32; takeover of
    King Records, 147–48, 150, 174
Pierce, Rod, 309
Pierce, Webb, 164, 282
Pilgrim Travelers, The, 49
Pilotone Records, 382, 535n4
"Pin Ball Machine," 287
Pine Top Slim, 46
"Pink Champagne," 39, 529n8
Pitney, Gene, 243, 529n25
Planet Records, 227
Plastic Products pressing plant (Memphis), 150,
    156, 159, 275, 285, 514n37, 520n21
Platt, Eddie, 312–13
Platters, The, 221–22, 238–43, 289, 299, 362,
    441, 524n2, 524n10, 525n11
Playmates, The, 246, 534n1
"Please Help Me, I'm Falling," 290
"Please Mr. Postman," 431
"Please Please Me," 129
"Please, Please, Please," 103, 139, 144
"Pledging My Love," 35, 524n2, 526n9
Pleis, Jack, 433, 437
"Poinciana," 128
Pollack, Ben, 51–52, 57
Polydor Records, 148, 390, 409; PolyGram Re-
    cords, 401, 538n12
Pomus, Jerome "Doc," 53–56, 233–34, 423, 459;
    and Mort Shuman, 53, 269, 272, 423, 527n24
Poncio, Steve, 44; and United Record Distribu-
    tors (Houston), 50, 164, 513n25
"Pony Time," 430
Porter, Cole, 56, 82, 266
Porter, Jake (Combo Records), 297
Prado, Perez, 366
Prescott, Parker, 39
Presley, Elvis, 9, 88–89, 110, 115, 138, 149–51,
    153, 159, 178, 198, 215, 233, 238, 246, 248,
    250–51, 255, 268–72, 279, 285, 296, 302, 360,
    367, 372, 387, 392, 397–98, 406, 411, 416–17,
    423, 425–26, 433, 437–38, 444, 462, 470,
    516n20, 520n18, 524n2, 527n21–22, 528n4,
    536n2, 537nn1–2, 538n17, 539n15
Prestige Records, 55, 382, 531n14
Preston, Johnny, 291
Price, Lloyd, 180, 206, 225, 304, 306–7, 390,

423, 442–45, 478, 524n2, 543n2; Double L Records, 390; KRC Records, 442
Price, Morrie, 26
Prisonaires, The, 310
"Prisoner's Song, The," 15
Professor Longhair, 180–81, 521n7
promo men, activities of, 464. See also Hoss Allen, Howard Bedno
"Promised Land, The," 176
Prysock, Arthur, 54, 228, 451, *P18*
Puente, Tito, 219–20
"Purple People Eater, The," 447, 541n11
Putnam, Bill, 127, 180–81, 298, 327, 473
Pye (International) Records (U.K.), 121, 371, 401

Quality Records (Canada), 386
"Quarter to Three," 339, 532n17
Queen booking agency, 450
"Queen of the Hop," 272
Querzergue, Wardell, 182, 521n7
Quinn, Bill (Gold Star Records), 45

Rabinowitz, Sol, 359
Rachou, Carol; and La Louisianne studio (Lafayette), 179
rack jobbing, 81, 85, 87–88, 165, 201, 371, 461, 516n17, 542n17
Rackmil, Milton, 29, 516n10, 527n19
radio breakout stations and territories, 534n8
Radio Recorders studios (Hollywood), 45, 297, 311
Raeburn, Boyd, 51, 63
Rainbow Music Shop, 55; Rainbow Record Shop, 215; Rainbow Records, 440
"Rainin' In My Heart," 109, 169
"Rainy Night in Georgia," 276
Ralke, Don, 298–99; Don, Dick & Jimmy, 298
Ram, Buck, 11, 58; Antler Records, 238, 242; Personality Productions, 238, 241; the Platters management, 238–43, 299, 381, 538n22, *P21*
"Rama Lama Ding Dong," 227, 362
Ramones, The, 143
R and B Records, 142
Randle, Bill, 103, 240, 313, 346, 517n1
Randolph, William "PoPsie," 190, 521n5 (chap. 11), 525n2
Randy's Record Shop (Gallatin, TN), 4, *93*, 94–96, 99–104, 108–9, 162, 177; Kirk and Randy's, 98
Raney, Wayne, 136, 146
rap and hip-hop, 130, 210, 263, 266, 351; sampling, 263, 352
"Raunchy," 113, 153, 366
Raven, Mike, 122
Ravens, The, 56–57, 89, 321
Rawls, Lou, 59, 250

Ray, Johnnie, 89, 143, 310, 323, 330, 361
Rayburn, Margie, 317
Rays, The, 254, 261–62, 427, 526n12
RCA (Radio Corporation of America), 74–78, 515n5. See also NBC
RCA Victor-Victor Records, 13, 15, 19–20, 22–25, 27–28, 31, 35, 37, 42, 48, 66; battle of the speeds with Columbia, 74–78, 81–82, 84, 87–88, 94, 153–54, 161, 165, 188, 193, 203, 221, 232–35, 246–52, 260, 270, 274, 278–79, 284, 287, 290, 293, 304, 308, 344, 354–55, 366–67, 372, 381–82, 384, 388, 390, 392, 397, 406, 408, 416, 421, 433, 437–40, 447, 462, 479, 510n6, 511n15, 511n16, 515n1, 515n5, 515n6, 516n10, 520n9, 521n3 (chap. 11), 524n4, 524n9, 525n16, 527n21, 529n13, 536n13, 540n2; Camden Records, 302; Nipper (dog trademark), 23, 248; pressing plants, 25, 76, 244, 389, 491; Red Seal classical, 75, 77. See also NBC, RCA
"Rebel-Rouser," 366, 420
Reco-Art studios (Philadelphia), 428–29, 540n20
"Reconsider Baby," 163
"Reconsider Me," 294
record hops, sock hops, dances, 261–62, 275, 325
record pressing process, 37, 512n10; injection molding, 383–84; milling plant, 280–81
Record World, 87, 193
Red Bird Records, 143, 233, 266, 287, 295–96, 390, 462
Red Hot Chili Peppers, 536n8
Redding, Otis, 103, 109, 180, 294, 349, 513n30
Redman, Don, 536n18
"Red River Rock," 449
Red Robin-Robin Records, 344, 352
"Red Sails in the Sunset," 367
Reed, Jerry, 293
Reed, Jimmy, 129, 176, 265, 530n2
Reed, Lou, 88
Reed, Lula, 137
Reese, Della, 59, 248, 250, 330
"Reet Petite," 320, 331–32, 340, 532nn11–12
Reeves, Jim, 164, 198, 278, 287, 360
Regent Music, 255, 257–59, 261, 427, 519n8, 532n12
Reig, Teddy, 58, 103, 219–21, 534n1
Reiner, Paul, 43, 136, 440, 513n23
Reinhardt, Django, 262, 424
Reissdorff, Bob, 385
"Release Me," 315
Relic Records, 352, 356, 373, 465
"Remember Then," 210
Rendezvous Records, 309, 531n16
Rene, Leon, 34–39, 49, 52, 211–12, 297, 308–9, 512n3, *FC, P3, P22*
Rene, Otis, 34–37, 39, 57, 512n3

Rene, Rafael "Googie," 37–38, 309, 512n10, *FC*, *P22*

Reno & Smiley, 146

Republic Records (Hollywood), 311, 315

"Rescue Me," 338–40

"Respect," 72, 470

Rey, Alvino, 96, 98

Rhodes, Jack, 529n13

Rhodes, Todd, 135, 518n5 (chap. 8)

Rhythm & Blues Foundation, 70, 515n22, 535n23

Rhythm and Blues magazine, 323, 531n4, *P17*

RIAA (Recording Industry Association of America), 84–85, 152, 484, 516nn10–11, 519n4

Rich, Charlie, 293

Richard, Cliff (Sir) [Harry Webb], 398, 444, 537n2

Richbourg, John (John R.), 95–96, 99–101, 103–4, 106–8, 111–15, 294, 337, 366, 517n4, 517nn17–18, *P10*; Rich Records, Seventy 7–Sound Plus Records, 517n17

Richmond, Howie, 94, 525n22

Ric-Ron Records, 292, 353

Ridgley, Tommy, 368

Ridley, Walter, 372

Riley, Jeannie C., 294

"Riot in Cell Block #9," 233

Rippa, Herb (Blue Bonnet Records), 45

Ritter, Tex, 261

Rivers, Johnny, 179

"R.M. Blues," 48–49

Robbins, Marty, 287, 536n13

Robert & Johnny, 210, 223, 227

Robey, Don, 16, 29, 152, 158, 298, 445, 451, 457, 478, 509n3, 520n16

Robinson, Bobby, 2, 12, 321, 341–44; Bobby's Happy House record shop (Bobby Robinson's), 215, 341–43, *P26*; "Kansas City" hit, 345–49, 350–52, 354–55, 357, 462, 517n16, 533n10, *P26*, *P32*

Robinson, Danny, 344, 350, 533n14

Robinson, Fenton, 159

Robinson, Joe, 252, 262, 350–51, 353; All-Platinum Records, Sugar Hill Records, 262, 351; Sylvia Robinson, 262. *See also* Mickey & Sylvia

Robinson, Tommy, 352, 361

Robinson, William "Smokey," 336. *See also* the Miracles

Robison, Fabor, 295; Abbott Records, 360, 543n9; Fabor-Radio Records, 295, 537n1

Robyn, Bunny, 298

Rocco and his Saints, 421, 428

Rock and Roll Hall of Fame Foundation, 9–10, 117, 138, 189, 509n1 (chap. 1)

"Rock and Roll is Here to Stay," 444

"Rock Around the Clock," 3, 30, 420, 511n18

"Rocket 88," 121, 151, 154, 518n5, 532n10

"Rockin' Robin," 308–9

Rockin' Sidney, 176, 178

"Rock Island Line," 400

"Rock Me Baby," 303

Rock-Ola jukeboxes, 17, 192, 510n9

Rockwell, Thomas "Tom," 29, 510n4 (chap. 2)

"Rock Your Baby," 467

Rodgers, Jimmie (*Roulette Records*), 245–46

Rodgers, Jimmie (*The Singing Brakeman*), 157, 188, 245, 284, 309

Rodgers and Hammerstein, 82

Rodgers and Hart, 82

Rogers, Lelan (Silver Fox Records), 294

Rogers, Leo, 216, 444, 446

Rogers, Roy, 85

Roker, Wally, 350

Rolling Stones, The, 11, 122, 169, 180, 305, 308, 400, 408, 438, 465, 538n18

Rolontz, Bob, 59–60, 189, 231–32, 416, 464, 521n3 (chap. 11), 522n5 (chap. 12), 524n1, 524nn3–4, 534n12, 539n6, 541n10

Ronettes, The, 539n9

Roost-Royal Roost Records, 525n16, 534n1

Rose, Fred, 49, 89, 168, 267, 278

Rose, Slim, 362

Rose, Wesley, 168, 198, 267, 413, 463, 538n21

"Rose and a Baby Ruth, A," 442

Rosen, David, 419

Rosenbaum, David (Rhythm Records), 45

"Roses Are Red (My Love)," 433

Ross, Stan, 298, 309–10

Ross, Steve, 89

Roulette Records, 19, 103, 125, 129, 222, 234, 243–47, 251; Planetary-Kahl Music, 435–36; sale of, 252, 353–54, 435, 448, 456, 468, 510n7, 525n17, 526n8, 534n1

Royal Teens, The, 444, 534n1

royalties, mechanical, 110, 258, 519n14, 525n1, 543n5; performance, 13, 258–59, 525n3, 543n5

royalty statement (Kent Records), 302

Royster, Joseph, 532n17

RPM Records. *See* Modern-RPM Records

Ruffin, Calvin "Houn' Dog," 385

Ruffin, David, 337

Ruffino, Joe, 181, 292, 353–54

"Runaway," 267, 273, 406, 449

"Running Bear," 291

"Running Scared," 412–13

Runyon Sales Co. distributors (New York, Newark), 31, 211–13, 217, 479, 511n20, 522n6 (chap. 12), 523n14

Rupe, Art, ix, xi, 2, 16, 20, 34, 39, 47; label launches, 48–49; 50–52, 115, 128, 162–63, 179, 194, 275; later years with Specialty Records, 304–8, 309, 407, 456, 462; new staff rules, 472–80, 509n3, 530n2, 543n8, 543nn10–11; *P4*

Rupe, Beverly, 115, 308
Rupe, Lee, 61, 307
Rush, Otis, 124, 127
Rushing, Jimmy, 34
Rydell, Bobby, 374, 423, 425, 428, 431, 444

Sabit, Vahdi, Dr., 62, 71
Sacks, Emanuel "Manie," 84
Salstone, Milt, 217, 468, *P31*; and M.S. Distrib-
    uting Co. (Chicago), 44, 128, 275
Sanders, Zell (J & S Records), 61, 261
Sandpipers, The, 85
Sands, Jodie, 422
Santo & Johnny, 366, 434, 533n9
Sarnoff, David (General), 13, 75, 81, 84
Satherley, Art (Uncle), 157, 278, 528n1
"Satisfied Mind, A," 284, 529n13
Saturday Night Fever LP, 467
Saunders, Red, 339
"Save the Last Dance for Me," 53, 423
Savoy Ballroom (Harlem), 54, 228, 342, 541n16
Savoy Records, 12, 36, 54; King Solomon Re-
    cords, 58; Regent Records, 57; start of, 57–58,
    59, 78, 110, 132, 136–37, 139, 192, 213, 218,
    322, 345, 358, 398, 407, 509n3, 537n1
Scepter-Wand Records, 61, 260, 350, 373, 376–
    77, 386, 462, 509n3, 519n19, 529n25
Scherman, Robert (Atlas-Premier Records), 48
"School Day," 260
Schroeder, Aaron, 525n13
Schuller, Gunther, 209; and NEC Records, 391
Schwartz, Bob, 390, *P31*
Schwartz, Gene, 225
Schwartz Brothers distributors (Washington,
    DC), 365, 410; Harry Schwartz, 457, 542n7;
    Schwartz, Jimmy, 365–66, 468
Scott, Clifford, 138, *P12*
Scott, Jack, 434
Scott, Joe, 159
Scott, Little Jimmy, 57, 59
Scott, Peggy, and Jo Jo Benson, 294
Scott, Winfield, 271, 526n10
"Sea Cruise," 103
Seals, Jimmy, and Dash Crofts, 531n19
"Sea of Love," 171, 174, 286, 290–91
"Searchin'," 3, 233
Sears, Zenas "Daddy," 120, 263, 517n1
Sedaka, Neil, 250, 436–37
Seeburg jukeboxes, 17, 41, 78, 192, 466, 510n9,
    519n5
"See Saw," 327–28
"See You Later Alligator," 260, 526n9
Sehorn, Marshall, 345, 348–51, 533nn10–11
SESAC (Society of European Stage Authors and
    Composers), 509n3 (chap. 1)
"Seven Little Girls Sitting in the Back Seat,"
    432, 434
Seville, David, 318

Seymour, Robin, 135
Shad, Bob, 46, 142, 159, 237, 240, 300, 379, 418,
    448, 531n4
"Shake a Hand," 324, 424, 524n2, 532n7
"Shake, Rattle and Roll," 66, 72, 524n2
"Shame on You," 268
Shannon, Del, 267, 273–74, 406, 449, 528n28,
    537n1
Sharp, Dee Dee, 431
Shaw, Arnold, 24, 373, 512n3, 535nn18–20,
    536n17
Shaw, Artie, 258, 299, 516n15
Shaw Artists agency, 57, 323, 354, 376, 428,
    450–51, 541n17; Billy Shaw, 450–51
"Sh-Boom," 35, 66, 222, 271, 534n1
Shearing, George, 243, 451
sheet music, decline of, 266–67, 269, 273, 434
Sheib, Simon, 392–93, 537n20; Sheib, Jamie, 393
Shelley Products pressing plant (Huntington
    Station, N.Y.), 380–84, 387, 389–93, 535n2,
    536n7, 537n20, 537n22
Shells, The, 363
Shelton, Roscoe, 105, 113
Shep and the Limelites, 527n14
Sheppard, Bunky, 129
Sheppard, Shep, *P12*
Sheridan, Art, 123
Sherman, Al, 281, 283, *P9*
"She Said Yeah," 305
"She's Dynamite," 154
Shimkin, Arthur, 14; A.A. Records, 85, 516n13;
    Bell Records, 85–86, 87, 301, 379, 384, 391,
    516n13, 516nn15–16, 530n3, 536n16, *P7–8*;
    Golden Records, 79–85
Shirelles, The, 376, 529n25
Shirley & Lee, 144, 162, 449
Sholes, Steve, 233, 248, 278, 367, 433, 527n21
"Short Fat Fannie," 304
"Short Shorts," 444, 534n1
"Shout (Part 1 & 2)," 248
"Shout Bamalama," 294
Shucher, Herb, 198–99, 522n11
Shuler, Eddie, 166–67, 171–75, 182, 286,
    521nn4–5, *P15*
Siegert, Ben, 48–49
"Silhouettes," 261–62, 265, 427, 526n12
Silhouettes, The, 333, 363, 368–69, 372
Sill, Lester, 44, 212–13, 233, 302, 420, 539n9,
    540n26, *P20*
Silver, Al, 16, 359, 363, 368, 370–73, 379,
    535n16, 535nn18–20, 541n10
Silverman, Max "Waxie Maxie," 62–63, 69,
    366
Silver-Park pressing plant (River Edge, N.J.),
    223, 364, 369–70, 534n12
Simon, Joe, 113–14
Simon & Garfunkel, 89; as Tom & Jerry, 516n15
Simon and Schuster, 80–83, 85–86, 516n13

Sinatra, Frank, 22, 88, 142, 203, 255, 321, 323, 331, 361, 384, 423, 452

"Since I Don't Have You," 206

"Since I Fell for You," 307

"Sincerely," 195, 260, 524n2, 526n9

Singer, Artie (Singular Records), 526n13

Singer, Hal, 58

Singleton, Charlie, 271, 526n10, *P27*

Singleton, John, 293

Singleton, Margie, 113, 288

Singleton, Shelby, 10, 19, 115, 133, 166–67, 174–76, 198–99, 251; Mercury years, 287–93; SSS Int. Records soul era, "Harper Valley P.T.A.," 294–95; Sun Records purchase, 295–96, 464–65, 522n11, *P26*, *P32*

Siracuse, Joe; and United Sound studios (Detroit), 333

Sire Records, 15, 140, 143, 145

"Sit Down Baby," 124

Sittin' In With Records, 46, 142, 448

"16 Candles," 456

"Sixty-Minute Man," 136

Skyliners, The (with Jimmy Beaumont), 144, 206

"Sleep Walk," 366, 533n9

"Slow Twistin'," 430–31

"Slow Walk," 418

Smalls, Tommy "Dr. Jive," 225, 352, 359, 361, 456

Smash Records, 176, 292, 367, 373

Smith, Arthur "Guitar Boogie," 278, 366

Smith, Bessie, 62

Smith, Bill (Major) [Le Cam Records], 293

Smith, Billy Dawn, 261, 390, 526n10, 527n14

Smith, Huey "Piano," 59, 472; and the Clowns, 349, 444

Smith, James "Okey Dokey," 95

Smith, Jimmy, 462

Smith, Joe, 204, 261, 456, 466

Smith, Mira (Ram Records), 61, 294

Smith, Steve (H.R.S. Records), 73

"Smoke Gets in Your Eyes," 242, 289

Snow, Hank, 268, 270

"So Fine," 103, 210, 224–25, 523n25

"So Much in Love," 431

Soileau, Floyd, 4, 166–67, 169; Jin-Swallow Records, Flat Town Music, Floyd's Record Shop, 175–78, 182–83, 285–86, 291, 521n8, *P15*

Solitaires, The, 216–17, 220, 222, 451, 523n23. *See also* Milton Love

Solomon, Bernie, 314; and Everest Records, 310

Soma Records, 290, 511n10

Sonet Records (Sweden), 47

song pluggers, 56, 239, 254–55, 257–58, 272

Sonny & Cher, 305, 355, 530n8. *See also* Sonny Bono

Sony-BMG Records, 229, 543n29

"So Rare," 145

Soul Sisters, The, 352, 533n15

Soul Stirrers, The, 47, 49, 164, 339

"Soul Twist," 350–51

Soundies, 29, 511n17

Sound Stage 7 Records, 100, 112–14, 293, 517nn17–18

Southern Music, 157, 284; Peer-Southern Music 367

Southland Distributing Co. (Atlanta), 44, 112, 513n30, 527n15

"South of the Border," 385

Spaniels, The (with Pookie Hudson), 129, 260, 450

Spann, Otis, 328

Sparton Records (Canada), 401

Spears, Britney, 229

Specialty Records, 4, 9, 16, 20, 34, 39–40, 47; Fidelity Records, 479; Herald Attractions agency, 307, 541n17; Juke Box Records, 48–49, 160; later years, 304–7; New Orleans branch office, 306–7, 533n17; new staff rules, 472–80; pressing plants, 514n37, 540n3; sale of, 308, 309, 318, 347–48, 353–55, 380, 456, 462–63, 524n2, 529n8, 531n14, 537n1, 541n17, 543nn1–11; start of, 49–51, 128, 146, 162–63, 179, 182, 194, 219–20, 279, 297–98; Venice Music, 146, 179, 305, 308, 477

Spector, Phil, 89, 233, 269, 274, 539n9, 540n26

"Splish Splash," 536n13

Sporn, Murray, 373, 538n22

Springfield, Dusty, 340

Spruill, Wild Jimmy, 346, 364–65, 374

SSS International Records, 287, 293, 296, 522n11, 529n26; Plantation Records, 294

Stafford, Jo, 96, 98

"Stagger Lee," 442, 444

Stanley Brothers, The, 138, 146

Stan's Record Shop (Shreveport), 161–62, 289, *P14*

Staple Singers, The, 129

Starday Records, 140, 147, 279–80; custom recordings, 285–86; Dixie Records, 286; sale of, 287, 288, 308, 407, 519n19, 521n8, 529nn13–14, 531n17, 537n1; Starrite Music, 285–86; start of, 284–85; Starday-King Records, *see* King Records

Starnes, Jack, 284, 529n13

Starr, Ben, 372, 527n21

Starr, Kay, 51, 143, 511n17, 540n2

Stateside Records (U.K.), 401

Stax Records, 61, 71, 159, 165, 228, 366, 444, 462, 464, 531n14; Volt Records, 109, 464

"Stay," 373

Stein, Seymour, 9–10, 15–16, 140; at *Billboard* and King Records, 143–46, 189, 446, 509n1 (chap. 1)

Steinberg, Irwin H., 28, 289

Stellman, Marcel, 405

Stepney, Charles, 339–40
Sterling, Louis (Sir), 399
Sterling Records, 48–49, 160
Stewart, Alonzo, 478
Stewart, Billy, 385, 532n16
Stewart, Jim, 71, 464
Stitt, Sonny, 244, 515n19
Stokes III, Jordan, 109, 517n14
Stoller, Mike, 379, 524n6. *See also* Jerry Leiber and Mike Stoller
Stone, Henry, ix; *Cash Box* feature, 467–69, 542n27, *P5*; at De Luxe Records, 141–42, 146, 162, 164, 198, 210, 252, 264, 274, 457–58; disco years, 467; early distributor, 50–52; Muriel Stone, 162, 460, 468; transshipping, 460–61; Tru-Tone and Tone distributors, 460, 467
Stone, Jesse, 67, 299, 526n10
Storm, Gale, 101
"Story Untold," 373
Storz, Todd, 454
Strachwitz, Chris (Arhoolie Records), 174–75
"Stranded in the Jungle," 298
String-A-Longs, The, 449
"Stroll, The," 289, 418–19; stroll dance, 419
Strong, Barrett, 165, 336
"Stupid Cupid," 447, 541n11
Sturgell, Dick, 50, 306, 478
Stylistics, The, 252
subsidiary labels, strategy with, 47, 292–93, 479, 490, 529n21
Sue Records, 109, 352–57; the hits, 533n15; 533n21, 535n16, 537n1
Sue Records (U.K.), 401
"Sugar Bee," 175
Sugarman, Bernard "Shugy," 522n6 (chap. 12), *P3*
Sullivan, Ed (*Ed Sullivan Show*), 314, 416, 451
Sun Entertainment Corporation, 133, 287, 295–96
Sun Records, 4, 9, 89, 113, 116–17, 149–50; Hi-Lo Music, 153, 270; sale of, 295–96, 310, 348, 360, 398, 415–16, 462, 520n15, 527n21, 528n4, 537n1, 542n7; start of, 152–53, 159–60, 198, 270, 278, 287
Superior Record Sales Co. distributors (New York), 119, 223–24, 227, 456
Supremes, The (*Motown group*), 107, 464
"Surfin' U.S.A.," 260
"Susie-Q," 121, 163, 165, 520n23
Sussel, Allan, 225, 420, 539n8
"Swanee," 204
Swanee Quintet, The, 106, 109
"Swanee River Boogie," 27, 103
Swan Records, 125, 418, 427, 432, 535n16, 539n17
"Sweet Georgia Brown," 536n17
"Sweet Little Sixteen," 260

"Swingin' the Boogie," 42
Swing Time Records, 9, 16, 34, 298, 451

"Tallahassee Lassie," 421
"Tall Cool One" ("Scotch on the Rocks"), 206, 380, 385–87
Talmadge, Art, 26, 28, 232, 236, 240, 242–43, 286, 288–89, 466, 510n7, 511n13, 525n13
Talmadge, Sid, 240, 468
Tamla-Motown Records, 107, 109–10, 140, 165, 319, 321; early years, 334–38; 340, 354, 356, 408, 424, 431, 434, 464, 467, 512n24, 537n1; Jobete Music, 429, 431, 540n26
Tampa Red, 154, 510n6
Taran, Sam, 44; and Taran Distributing Co. (Jacksonville FL), 44, 141, 479, *P5*
Tarheel Slim, 345; and Little Ann, 228, 347
Tarnopol, Nat, 266, 330–32, 334, 435–36, 527n19, *P23–24*
Tarsia, Joe, 430, 540n20, *P30*
Tatum, Art, 54
Taylor, Creed, 445
Taylor, Sammy, 376, 526n10
Taylor, Sam "The Man," 67
Taylor, Zola, 239, 241, 243
"Teardrops on My Pillow," 216
"Teddy Bear (Let Me Be Your)," 272, 425–26
Teddy Bears, The, 274
"Teen Beat," 366
"Teenager in Love, A," 423
Teen Queens, The, 242, 299
"Tell It Like It Is," 263
"Tell Laura I Love Her," 250, 274, 536n13
"Telstar," 400
Temptations, The, 337, 464
Tennessee Recording and Publishing Company, 148
Tennessee-Republic Records, 461, 542n18
"Tennessee Waltz, The" 32, 39
"Tequila," 309, 312–18, 366
Terry, Al, 167–68
Tex, Joe, 294, 337, 408
"Thank You Girl," 265
"That Lucky Old Sun," 32
"That Old Black Magic," 21
"That's All Right," 198
"That's My Desire," 27, 44
"There's a Moon Out Tonight," 210, 227, 362, 524n30
"There's Something on Your Mind (Part 2)," 349
Thiele, Bob, 73, 332, 400, 445, 448, 532n12
"Things That I Used to Do, The," 304, 472
"This Is My Story," 362
"This Should Go On Forever," 176, 521n6
Thomas, Rufus, 152, 159
Thompson, Hank, 167, 520n1
Thompson, Johnny, 310, 312
Thompson, Sonny, 137, 145, 162

Thornton, Willie Mae "Big Mama," 35, 153, 233, 524n2, 532n7
"3 O'clock Blues," 155
Thrillers, The (Thriller Records), 324–25, 335
Tico-Rama-Gee Records, 16, 216, 219, 222, 244
Tillotson, Johnny, 435, 463
Timberlake, Justin, 229
Time-Shad-Brent Records, 448, 535n16
Times Square Records (New York), 227, 362–63, 524n30
Tin Pan Alley (New York), 189, 255, 259–60, 403, 480; (London), 405
TK Records, 51, 252, 367
"To Be Loved," 332
"To Each His Own," 27
Tokens, The, 248, 251, 432, 525n22
"To Know Him Is to Love Him," 274
Toller-Bond, Dudley "D.H.," 368, 400, 408–9, 412, P29
"Tonite, Tonite," 368, 373
Toombs, Rudy, 146, 526n10, 531n4; R-T Music, 146
"Too Much Tequila," 314
"Too Pooped To Pop," 328
Topping, Ray, 229, 280, 529n10
Top Rank Records, 371–73, 401, 434, 445; Top Rank Co-op, 535n16
"Topsy (Part 2)," 366
Toscano, Eli, 123–24, 126–27, 518n15; A.B.'s One-Stop, 124; Archie Toscano, 124, 127
"Tossin' and Turnin'," 139
"Touch Me Lord Jesus," 110
Toussaint, Allen, xii, 182, 350–51, 354, 530n11
"Train to Nowhere," 312, 314
transshipping, 165, 264, 460–66, 468
"Travelin' Man," 316
Travis, Merle, 132
Treadwell, George, 66
Trenier, Claude, 36
Trepel, Miriam "Mimi" (Jordan), x, 2, 61, 401–2; at London Records, 403–9, 538nn14–16, P29
Tripp, Peter, 360, 456
Trumpet Records, 61, 155–56, 182, 214, 264, 520n9, 523n8, 543n9
"Trying," 102
"Try Me," 144
Tubb, Ernest, 268, 277, 279
Tucker, Sophie, 452
Tune Weavers, The, 261
Tunis, Jack "One Spot," 192–93, 195, 522n8
Turner, Ike, 40, 149, 151, 154; Modern Records scout, 155–56, 352, 356, 520n12
Turner, Ike & Tina, 303, 349, 352, 354, 356, 533n15
Turner, Joe (Big), 35, 54, 56, 66, 68, 72, 524n2, 536n13, P7
Turner, Sammy, 267, 272–73, 411
Turner, Tina, 355, 520n12, 523n8

Turner, Titus, 225–26
"Tutti-Frutti," 102, 473, 524n2, 543n8, 543n10
"Tweedle(e) Dee," 68, 236, 524n9
20th Century-Fox Records, 165, 367, 373, 445, 535n16
"Twilight Time," 239, 524n10
"Twist, The," 251, 429, 461
"Twist and Shout," 248
"Twistin' the Night Away," 250
Twitty, Conway, 447, 541n11
Tyler, Alvin "Red," 354, 473
Tyler, T. Texas, 281–82, 529n7
Tymes, The, 431–32

"Unchained Melody," 59
United Artists Records, 112, 165, 233, 242, 318, 333, 335, 356, 390, 444–45, 462, 511n13, 525n13, 532n14, 537n1; Boyd Records, 112, 444; Unart Records, 532n14, 536n13
United-States Records, 123, 543n9
Universal Attractions agency, 89, 323, 450–51, 541n17
Universal studios (Chicago), 127, 298, 327, 473
USA Records, 129, 164, 518n13
Utall, Larry, 86, P31

Valens, Ritchie, 307
Valentines, The, 216, 220, 364
Valley Records, 215
Variety, 242–43, 416
Varsity Records, 24, 36, 87, 382
Vastola, Tommy, 221, 243–44, 251, 458, 523n18, 525n15
Vaughan, Sarah, 237, 244, 289, 323, 458
Vaughn, Billy, 101, 153, 366
V-Disks, 15
Vee-Jay Records, 16, 61, 109, 116, 125, 127, 129, 176, 223, 265, 444–45, 457, 462, 517n16, 530n2, 535n16, 537n1, 542n7; Conrad Music, 116, 255, 265, 267, 530n2
Ventures, The, 385, 537n1
"Venus," 423, 444
Venuti, Joe, 380–81, 383, 391
Verbit, Nelson, 419, 542n7
Verve Records, 297, 416, 462; and Clef Records, 525n14
Vik Records, 293
Vincent, Gene, 9, 22
Vincent, Johnny, xii, 4, 156, 164, 176, 179, 181–82, 349, 444, 472, 543n3; Champion Records, 472
Vinson, Eddie "Cleanhead," 27
Violinaires, The, 164, 339
Virgin Records, 303
Vivendi-Universal, 23, 116, 129, 130, 543n29
Vocalion Records, 75, 381
V-Tone Records, 335

Wailers (Fabulous Wailers), The, 208, 379, 380, 385–87, 393, 536n8, 537n1, *P28*
"Walk, The," 418
Walker, Frank, 49, 84, 278, 516n10
Walker, Jack "The Pear-Shaped Talker," 225, 361
Walker, T-Bone, 30, 97, 529n8
"Walking Along," 222–23, 523n23
Wallace, Jerry, 311, 317
Waller, Fats, 511n17
Wallerstein, Edward "Ted," 64, 74–75
Wallichs, Glenn, 21–22, 36, 84, 510n7, 516n10
Ward, Billy, 193, 331, *P17*. *See also* the Dominoes
Ward, Clara, and the Ward Singers, 57
Ward, Truman, 99
Warner Bros. Distributors, 316, 444
Warner Bros. Pictures, 398, 515n2
Warner Bros. Records, 445, 463, 515n1, 515n4, 541n14; Warner Bros.-Reprise Records, 466
Warner Brothers Music, 56, 254, 266; Warner-Chappell Music, 405
Warner Music Group, 60, 446, 543n29; WEA Records, 71, 145, 541n14
Warner-Seven Arts, 448, 541n14
Waronker, Si, 297, 317, 510n7, *P31*
Warren, Jim, 50
Warwick, Dionne, 376
Warwick Records, 274, 366, 448–49, 528n26, 537n1
Washington, Baby, 352, 357, 533n15
Washington, Dinah, 27, 89, 289
Wasserman, Lew, 31
Waters, Ethel, 402
Waters, Muddy, 11, 116, 118–19, 122, 126–27, 161–62, 256, 265–66, 327–29, 339–40
Wax, Morty, 387
Waxie Maxie's [Quality] record store (Washington, DC), 62–64, 348, 366
WDIA radio (Memphis), 151–52, 158–59
Weavers, The, 157
"We Belong Together," 210, 223, 227, 437
Webster, Ben, 58
Webster, Katie, 171
"Wedding, The," 216–17, 220
Weill, Cynthia, 436
Weinberg, Eli, 451
Weiner, Jack, 120
Weinstock, Bob, 55
Weintrob, Al(len), 222, 533n7
Weiss, Barry, 229, 524n31
Weiss, George, 211, 223
Weiss, George David, 237, 251
Weiss, Hy (Hyman, Hymie), 1–2, 16, 87, 103, 115, 119, 121, 129, 162, 208–10; the hits, 223–28, 229–30, 301, 359, 361–62, 368, 379, 393, 440, 446, 451–52, 456–57, 465–66, 522n5 (chap. 12), 523nn10–12, 524n31, 524n33,

P18–19; salesman for Exclusive, Modern, Cosnat, 210–15; start of Old Town Records, 215–22; wife Rosalyn (Roz), 209, 217, 229
Weiss, Sam, 119, 162, 210–14; launch of Superior distributors, 223–24, 228–29, 522n4; start of Old Town Records, 215–17, 220–22
Welk, Lawrence, 311, 517n8
Wells, Junior, 126
Wells, Kitty 168
Wells, Mary, 107
WERE radio (Cleveland), 240, 313, 534n8
Weston, Paul, 96
Wexler, Jerry, xi, 1–2, 11–12, 16, 19–20, 23, 32, 56, 59–60, 64; at Atlantic Records, 66–73; 89, 94–95, 109, 119, 129, 137, 163, 181; at *Billboard*, coins R&B term, 188–89, 196–97, 199, 209–10, 222, 228, 266, 271, 276, 379, 409, 433, 444, 450, 452, 464, 466; Henry Stone *Cash Box* article, 467–69, 509n1, 509n2 (chap. 1), 515n24, 516n15, 521n2 (chap. 11), 522n3, 522n5 (chap. 12), 528n4, 542n27, *P7*
"What Am I Living For," 419
"What'd I Say," 72, 248
"What's Your Name," 275, 528n27
"Wheel of Fortune," 51, 440, 540n2
"Wheels," 449
"When," 437
"When It's Sleep Time Down South," 35, 309
"When the Swallows Come Back to Capistrano," 35, 309
"When You Dance," 373
Whirlin' Disc Records, 345, 533n4
"Whispering Bells," 102
White, Maurice (of Earth, Wind and Fire), 339
"White Bucks and Saddle Shoes," 272, 411, 527n24
"White Christmas," 430
Whiteman, Paul, 35, 380, 425, 535n2; *TV-Teen Club*, 425
Whitman, Slim, 163, 278, 537n1
"Whole Lot of Shakin' Going On," 153
WHOM radio (New York), 213, 361–62, 534n8
"Who's Sorry Now," 447
"Who Threw the Whiskey in the Well?" 99
"Why," 423, 444
"Why Do Fools Fall in Love," 216, 221–22, 226, 244, 526n8
Wilder, Alec, 82, 90, 391
"Wild One," 428
WILD radio (Boston), 120, 261
"Wild Side of Life, The," 167–68, 520n1, 532n7
Willet, Slim, 283, 285, 388, 529n11, 531n23
William Morris agency, 249, 450, 512n24
Williams, Andy, 426, 435, 463, 539n15, 542n21
Williams, Buster (Robert), 44, 121, 150, 156, 160, 275, 284, 306, 416, 514n37, 518n5, 520n21
Williams, Dootsie, 297

Williams, Hank, 49, 89, 136, 166, 172, 198, 278–79, 410, 446

Williams, Hank Jr., 317

Williams, J. Mayo, 29, 511n16; and Harlem-Ebony Records, 514n13

Williams, Jerry "Swamp Dogg," 389

Williams, Kae "Loudmouth," 368–69, 419; and Junior-Kaiser Records, 368

Williams, Larry, 47, 304–5, 307, 537n1

Williams, Mal, 374–77

Williams, Maurice, and the Zodiacs, 373. *See also* The Gladiolas

Williams, Paul, 57–58, 452

Williams, Shannon, 104–5; at Ernie's Record Mart, 106–8, 109–11, 171, *P16*

Williams, Tony, 239–41

Williamson, Sonny Boy (#1), 510n6, 520n9

Williamson, Sonny Boy (#2), 122, 125, 152, 156, 162, 214, 264, 266, 326, 520n9, 523n8

"Willie and the Hand Jive," 35

Willis, Chuck, 68, 339, 419

Wills, Bob, 30, 157, 172, 268, 532n10

Wilson, Jackie, 107, 143, 266, 319–20, 330–32, 337–38, 342, 361, 423, 435, 527n19, 532n12, *P23*

Wilson, Jim (Colonel), x; King Records branch manager, 132–37, 138–41, 147–48, 325, 330, 518n4 (chap. 8), 532n8, *P24*

Wiltshire, George "Teacho," 67, 527n14

"Wind, The," 323, 531n6

Winley, Paul, 260, 344, 348, 351–52, 526n10; Winley Records, 351–52

Winslow, Vern "Doctor Daddy-O," 517n1

Winston, Jerry (Onyx Records), 359

Wisner, Jimmy, 431–32; as Kokomo, 432

"Witch Doctor," 318

"With All My Heart," 421

Witherspoon, Jimmy, 40

WJLB radio (Detroit), 322, 518n4 (chap. 8)

WKBW radio (Buffalo), 366, 534n8

WLAC radio (Nashville), 46, 94–112, 114–15, 120, 124, 161, 176, 224, 260, 263, 294, 366, 520n23; programs: *After Hours*, 96; *The Dance Hour*, 97, 99, 102; *Early Morning Gospel Time*, 114; *Ernie's Record Parade*, 100; *Randy's Record Hi-Lights*, 102; Royal Crown sponsored shows, 103, 114

WLIB radio (New York), 143, 361, 402–3

WNJR radio (Newark), 60, 143, 217–18

Wolff, Francis, 55

Wolfson, Mack, 209, 389, 391, 393

Wonder, Stevie (Little), 165, 464

"Wonderful World," 249

Wood, Len "L.G.," 371–72, 517n1

Wood, Randy: early years, 97–103, 109, 115, 137, 142, 152, 163, 170, 177, 217, 297, 318, 321, 347, 422, 460–61, 510n7, 513n15, 517nn7–8, 530n2; Ranwood Records, 517n8

"Wooden Heart," 293

Woods, Georgie, 272, 419, 456

Woodstock LP, 276

Wooley, Sheb, 447, 541n11

"Work with Me Annie," 136, 298

WOV radio (New York), 143

Wright, Billy, 59

Wright, Jimmy, 226

WSM radio (Nashville), 94, 277

Wunderman, Lester, 77

Wurlitzer jukeboxes, 17, 41, 192, 466, 510n9, 519n5, 523n7

WVON radio (Chicago), 121, 126, 340

"X" Records, 293, 421

"Y'all Come" ("You All Come"), 310, 531n17

"Ya Ya," 350, 355

"Yakety Yak," 233

Yetnikoff, Walter, 89

"You Are My Sunshine," 277

"You Can't Sit Down," 112

"You Could Be My Love," 215, 220

"You Got What It Takes," 333

Young, Ernie, 99–100, 103; at Ernie's Record Mart, 106–8, 109–11, 169–71, 177, 321, 509n3, 517n11; in the Excello-Nashboro studio, 105–6; jukebox operator, 104–5

Young, Faron, 164

Young, Lester, 57

Young, Reggie, 132, 294

"Young Blood," 234

Your Hit Parade, 86, 202, 516n14

"You're Mine," 223

"You're So Fine," 532n14

"You Send Me," 249, 307

"You Talk Too Much," 353

Zacherle, John, 427

Music in American Life

Only a Miner: Studies in Recorded Coal-Mining Songs   *Archie Green*

Great Day Coming: Folk Music and the American Left   *R. Serge Denisoff*

John Philip Sousa: A Descriptive Catalog of His Works   *Paul E. Bierley*

The Hell-Bound Train: A Cowboy Songbook   *Glenn Ohrlin*

Oh, Didn't He Ramble: The Life Story of Lee Collins, as Told to
  Mary Collins   *Edited by Frank J. Gillis and John W. Miner*

American Labor Songs of the Nineteenth Century   *Philip S. Foner*

Stars of Country Music: Uncle Dave Macon to Johnny Rodriguez   *Edited by Bill C. Malone
  and Judith McCulloh*

Git Along, Little Dogies: Songs and Songmakers of the American West   *John I. White*

A Texas-Mexican *Cancionero:* Folksongs of the Lower Border   *Américo Paredes*

San Antonio Rose: The Life and Music of Bob Wills   *Charles R. Townsend*

Early Downhome Blues: A Musical and Cultural Analysis   *Jeff Todd Titon*

An Ives Celebration: Papers and Panels of the Charles Ives Centennial Festival-
  Conference   *Edited by H. Wiley Hitchcock and Vivian Perlis*

Sinful Tunes and Spirituals: Black Folk Music to the Civil War   *Dena J. Epstein*

Joe Scott, the Woodsman-Songmaker   *Edward D. Ives*

Jimmie Rodgers: The Life and Times of America's Blue Yodeler   *Nolan Porterfield*

Early American Music Engraving and Printing: A History of Music Publishing in America
  from 1787 to 1825, with Commentary on Earlier and Later Practices   *Richard J. Wolfe*

Sing a Sad Song: The Life of Hank Williams   *Roger M. Williams*

Long Steel Rail: The Railroad in American Folksong   *Norm Cohen*

Resources of American Music History: A Directory of Source Materials from Colonial Times
  to World War II   *D. W. Krummel, Jean Geil, Doris J. Dyen, and Deane L. Root*

Tenement Songs: The Popular Music of the Jewish Immigrants   *Mark Slobin*

Ozark Folksongs   *Vance Randolph; edited and abridged by Norm Cohen*

Oscar Sonneck and American Music   *Edited by William Lichtenwanger*

Bluegrass Breakdown: The Making of the Old Southern Sound   *Robert Cantwell*

Bluegrass: A History   *Neil V. Rosenberg*

Music at the White House: A History of the American Spirit   *Elise K. Kirk*

Red River Blues: The Blues Tradition in the Southeast   *Bruce Bastin*

Good Friends and Bad Enemies: Robert Winslow Gordon and the Study of American Folksong
  Debora Kodish

Fiddlin' Georgia Crazy: Fiddlin' John Carson, His Real World, and the World of His Songs
  Gene Wiggins

America's Music: From the Pilgrims to the Present (rev. 3d ed.)   *Gilbert Chase*

Secular Music in Colonial Annapolis: The Tuesday Club, 1745–56   *John Barry Talley*

Bibliographical Handbook of American Music   *D. W. Krummel*

Goin' to Kansas City   *Nathan W. Pearson, Jr.*

"Susanna," "Jeanie," and "The Old Folks at Home": The Songs of Stephen C. Foster
   from His Time to Ours (2d ed.)   *William W. Austin*

Songprints: The Musical Experience of Five Shoshone Women   *Judith Vander*

"Happy in the Service of the Lord": Afro-American Gospel Quartets in Memphis   *Kip Lornell*

Paul Hindemith in the United States   *Luther Noss*

"My Song Is My Weapon": People's Songs, American Communism, and the Politics of
   Culture, 1930–50   *Robbie Lieberman*

Chosen Voices: The Story of the American Cantorate   *Mark Slobin*

Theodore Thomas: America's Conductor and Builder of Orchestras, 1835–190   *Ezra Schabas*

"The Whorehouse Bells Were Ringing" and Other Songs Cowboys Sing   *Guy Logsdon*

Crazeology: The Autobiography of a Chicago Jazzman   *Bud Freeman, as told to Robert Wolf*

Discoursing Sweet Music: Brass Bands and Community Life in Turn-of-the-Century
   Pennsylvania   *Kenneth Kreitner*

Mormonism and Music: A History   *Michael Hicks*

Voices of the Jazz Age: Profiles of Eight Vintage Jazzmen   *Chip Deffaa*

Pickin' on Peachtree: A History of Country Music in Atlanta, Georgia   *Wayne W. Daniel*

Bitter Music: Collected Journals, Essays, Introductions, and Librettos   *Harry Partch;
   edited by Thomas McGeary*

Ethnic Music on Records: A Discography of Ethnic Recordings Produced in the United States,
   1893 to 1942   *Richard K. Spottswood*

Downhome Blues Lyrics: An Anthology from the Post–World War II Era   *Jeff Todd Titon*

Ellington: The Early Years   *Mark Tucker*

Chicago Soul   *Robert Pruter*

That Half-Barbaric Twang: The Banjo in American Popular Culture   *Karen Linn*

Hot Man: The Life of Art Hodes   *Art Hodes and Chadwick Hansen*

The Erotic Muse: American Bawdy Songs (2d ed.)   *Ed Cray*

Barrio Rhythm: Mexican American Music in Los Angeles   *Steven Loza*

The Creation of Jazz: Music, Race, and Culture in Urban America   *Burton W. Peretti*

Charles Martin Loeffler: A Life Apart in Music   *Ellen Knight*

Club Date Musicians: Playing the New York Party Circuit   *Bruce A. MacLeod*

Opera on the Road: Traveling Opera Troupes in the United States, 1825–60
   Katherine K. Preston

The Stonemans: An Appalachian Family and the Music That Shaped Their Lives
   Ivan M. Tribe

Transforming Tradition: Folk Music Revivals Examined   *Edited by Neil V. Rosenberg*

The Crooked Stovepipe: Athapaskan Fiddle Music and Square Dancing in Northeast Alaska
   and Northwest Canada   *Craig Mishler*

Traveling the High Way Home: Ralph Stanley and the World of Traditional Bluegrass Music
  John Wright

Carl Ruggles: Composer, Painter, and Storyteller   *Marilyn Ziffrin*

Never without a Song: The Years and Songs of Jennie Devlin, 1865–1952
  Katharine D. Newman

The Hank Snow Story   *Hank Snow, with Jack Ownbey and Bob Burris*

Milton Brown and the Founding of Western Swing   *Cary Ginell, with special assistance
  from Roy Lee Brown*

Santiago de Murcia's "Códice Saldívar No. 4": A Treasury of Secular Guitar Music from
  Baroque Mexico   *Craig H. Russell*

The Sound of the Dove: Singing in Appalachian Primitive Baptist Churches
  Beverly Bush Patterson

Heartland Excursions: Ethnomusicological Reflections on Schools of Music   *Bruno Nettl*

Doowop: The Chicago Scene   *Robert Pruter*

Blue Rhythms: Six Lives in Rhythm and Blues   *Chip Deffaa*

Shoshone Ghost Dance Religion: Poetry Songs and Great Basin Context   *Judith Vander*

Go Cat Go! Rockabilly Music and Its Makers   *Craig Morrison*

'Twas Only an Irishman's Dream: The Image of Ireland and the Irish in American Popular
  Song Lyrics, 1800–1920   *William H. A. Williams*

Democracy at the Opera: Music, Theater, and Culture in New York City, 1815–60
  Karen Ahlquist

Fred Waring and the Pennsylvanians   *Virginia Waring*

Woody, Cisco, and Me: Seamen Three in the Merchant Marine   *Jim Longhi*

Behind the Burnt Cork Mask: Early Blackface Minstrelsy and Antebellum American
  Popular Culture   *William J. Mahar*

Going to Cincinnati: A History of the Blues in the Queen City   *Steven C. Tracy*

Pistol Packin' Mama: Aunt Molly Jackson and the Politics of Folksong   *Shelly Romalis*

Sixties Rock: Garage, Psychedelic, and Other Satisfactions   *Michael Hicks*

The Late Great Johnny Ace and the Transition from R&B to Rock 'n' Roll   *James M. Salem*

Tito Puente and the Making of Latin Music   *Steven Loza*

Juilliard: A History   *Andrea Olmstead*

Understanding Charles Seeger, Pioneer in American Musicology   *Edited by Bell Yung
  and Helen Rees*

Mountains of Music: West Virginia Traditional Music from *Goldenseal*   *Edited by John Lilly*

Alice Tully: An Intimate Portrait   *Albert Fuller*

A Blues Life   *Henry Townsend, as told to Bill Greensmith*

Long Steel Rail: The Railroad in American Folksong (2d ed.)   *Norm Cohen*

The Golden Age of Gospel   *Text by Horace Clarence Boyer; photography by Lloyd Yearwood*

Aaron Copland: The Life and Work of an Uncommon Man   *Howard Pollack*

Louis Moreau Gottschalk   *S. Frederick Starr*

Race, Rock, and Elvis   *Michael T. Bertrand*

Theremin: Ether Music and Espionage   *Albert Glinsky*

Poetry and Violence: The Ballad Tradition of Mexico's Costa Chica   *John H. McDowell*

The Bill Monroe Reader   *Edited by Tom Ewing*

Music in Lubavitcher Life   *Ellen Koskoff*

Zarzuela: Spanish Operetta, American Stage   *Janet L. Sturman*

Bluegrass Odyssey: A Documentary in Pictures and Words, 1966–86   *Carl Fleischhauer
and Neil V. Rosenberg*

That Old-Time Rock & Roll: A Chronicle of an Era, 1954–63   *Richard Aquila*

Labor's Troubadour   *Joe Glazer*

American Opera   *Elise K. Kirk*

Don't Get above Your Raisin': Country Music and the Southern Working Class
Bill C. Malone

John Alden Carpenter: A Chicago Composer   *Howard Pollack*

Heartbeat of the People: Music and Dance of the Northern Pow-wow   *Tara Browner*

My Lord, What a Morning: An Autobiography   *Marian Anderson*

Marian Anderson: A Singer's Journey   *Allan Keiler*

Charles Ives Remembered: An Oral History   *Vivian Perlis*

Henry Cowell, Bohemian   *Michael Hicks*

Rap Music and Street Consciousness   *Cheryl L. Keyes*

Louis Prima   *Garry Boulard*

Marian McPartland's Jazz World: All in Good Time   *Marian McPartland*

Robert Johnson: Lost and Found   *Barry Lee Pearson and Bill McCulloch*

Bound for America: Three British Composers   *Nicholas Temperley*

Lost Sounds: Blacks and the Birth of the Recording Industry, 1890–1919   *Tim Brooks*

Burn, Baby! BURN! The Autobiography of Magnificent Montague   *Magnificent Montague
with Bob Baker*

Way Up North in Dixie: A Black Family's Claim to the Confederate Anthem
Howard L. Sacks and Judith Rose Sacks

The Bluegrass Reader   *Edited by Thomas Goldsmith*

Colin McPhee: Composer in Two Worlds   *Carol J. Oja*

Robert Johnson, Mythmaking, and Contemporary American Culture   *Patricia R. Schroeder*

Composing a World: Lou Harrison, Musical Wayfarer   *Leta E. Miller and Fredric Lieberman*

Fritz Reiner, Maestro and Martinet   *Kenneth Morgan*

That Toddlin' Town: Chicago's White Dance Bands and Orchestras, 1900–1950
Charles A. Sengstock Jr.

Dewey and Elvis: The Life and Times of a Rock 'n' Roll Deejay   *Louis Cantor*

Come Hither to Go Yonder: Playing Bluegrass with Bill Monroe   *Bob Black*

Chicago Blues: Portraits and Stories   *David Whiteis*

The Incredible Band of John Philip Sousa   *Paul E. Bierley*

"Maximum Clarity" and Other Writings on Music   *Ben Johnston, edited by Bob Gilmore*

Staging Tradition: John Lair and Sarah Gertrude Knott   *Michael Ann Williams*

Homegrown Music: Discovering Bluegrass   *Stephanie P. Ledgin*

Tales of a Theatrical Guru   *Danny Newman*

The Music of Bill Monroe   *Neil V. Rosenberg and Charles K. Wolfe*

Pressing On: The Roni Stoneman Story   *Roni Stoneman, as told to Ellen Wright*

Together Let Us Sweetly Live   *Jonathan C. David, with photographs by
    Richard Holloway*

Live Fast, Love Hard: The Faron Young Story   *Diane Diekman*

Air Castle of the South: WSM Radio and the Making of Music City   *Craig P. Havighurst*

Traveling Home: Sacred Harp Singing and American Pluralism   *Kiri Miller*

Where Did Our Love Go? The Rise and Fall of the Motown Sound   *Nelson George*

Lonesome Cowgirls and Honky-Tonk Angels: The Women of Barn Dance Radio
    Kristine M. McCusker

California Polyphony: Ethnic Voices, Musical Crossroads   *Mina Yang*

The Never-Ending Revival: Rounder Records and the Folk Alliance   *Michael F. Scully*

Sing It Pretty: A Memoir   *Bess Lomax Hawes*

Working Girl Blues: The Life and Music of Hazel Dickens   *Hazel Dickens
    and Bill C. Malone*

Charles Ives Reconsidered   *Gayle Sherwood Magee*

The Hayloft Gang: The Story of the National Barn Dance   *Edited by Chad Berry*

Country Music Humorists and Comedians   *Loyal Jones*

Record Makers and Breakers: Voices of the Independent Rock 'n' Roll Pioneers   *John Broven*

The University of Illinois Press
is a founding member of the
Association of American University Presses.

Composed in 9.5/14 Trump Mediaeval
with Folio display
by Jim Proefrock
at the University of Illinois Press
Designed by Dennis Roberts
Manufactured by Cushing-Malloy, Inc.

University of Illinois Press
1325 South Oak Street
Champaign, IL 61820-6903
www.press.uillinois.edu